CONCEPTUAL STRUCTURES
Current Research and Practice

ELLIS HORWOOD SERIES IN WORKSHOPS

CONCEPTUAL STRUCTURES
Current Research and Practice

Editors: TIMOTHY E. NAGLE, JANICE A. NAGLE AND
LAURIE L. GERHOLZ
Unisys Corporation, St Paul, The University of Minnesota, Minneapolis,
and Minnesota, USA
PETER W. EKLUND
Department of Computer Science
University of Adelaide, Australia

ELLIS HORWOOD
NEW YORK   LONDON   TORONTO   SYDNEY   TOKYO   SINGAPORE

First published in 1992 by
ELLIS HORWOOD LIMITED
Market Cross House, Cooper Street,
Chichester, West Sussex, PO19 1EB, England

A division of
Simon & Schuster International Group
A Paramount Communications Company

Printed and bound in Great Britain
by Redwood Press, Melksham

British Library Cataloguing in Publication Data

A catalogue record for this book is available from the British Library

ISBN 0–13–175878–0

Library of Congress Cataloging-in-Publication Data

Available from the publisher

Contents

Dedicated to
S. I. Hayahawa

Foreword

This book presents a diverse collection of contributions to research in conceptual structures and is the first such collection of its kind. It remedies the lack of source material in conceptual structure research, being a comprehensive survey of applications and theoretical work in the field.

When John Sowa's *Conceptual Structures: Information Processing in Mind and Machine* (1984) was first published it created significant interest. Inspired by the elegance and simplicity of conceptual structures, researchers in computer science and artificial intelligence began to use them in knowledge-base, text retrieval and natural language processing systems. More often than not conceptual structures were a means to an end, a vehicle by which researchers could develop systems and represent knowledge. For this reason there has been an enormous dispersal of conceptual structures research: from neural networks to database systems, data modeling to natural language processing, from knowledge representation to database query languages. This volume unifies those efforts whose common representational theme is conceptual structures.

Annual workshops on conceptual structures have been held since 1985, but proceedings have proved difficult to obtain. This has meant that aspiring researchers have had little more than Sowa's original source on which to base their work. Attending workshops is difficult for globally dispersed researchers and, in an effort to address the problem, the Fifth Annual Workshop on Conceptual Structures was held over two locations. The first half at AAAI in Boston and the second in Stockholm at ECAI. Once the workshop papers had been assessed and presented, the authors were asked to extend and elaborate their submissions. This book catalogues their efforts.

The volume is divided into five parts, appendices and a bibliography. Part I begins with a summary of conceptual graph theory by John Sowa, followed by chapters which extend the formal and theoretical aspects of conceptual structures.

In chapter 2, Bosco Tjan *et al.* explore a simple extension to conceptual structure theory which enables quantification over set referents. An explicit scope, restrictor, and quantifier are introduced into the set referent notation. This extension allows us to represent information like, "There are at least ten large towns in New Jersey". Tjan shows that a variant of first-order predicate calculus which handles numerical quantifiers, finite set referents and set coreferences in conceptual graphs is conservative and thus sound and complete. In chapter 3, further work within the same research group by David Gardiner *et al.* demonstrates the viability of an uninstantiated concept as a specification of constraints on the set of referents. Their use of a "situation model" methodology (and model building operations as set constraints) suggests the development a more concise modeling representation.

In chapter 4, Heather Pfeiffer and Roger Hartley observe that part of the definition of conceptual structures includes concepts organized in a type lattice. When structures built out of these concepts are operated upon by graph operations, it often happens that the same concept can be instantiated with different individuals. In many cases it is preferable to keep such individuals separated although there are situations where further processing should assemble the individuals into a set. Pfeiffer and Hartley's representation and implementation reflect an extension of Sowa's theory which defines and processes sets.

In chapter 5, Pavel Kocura offers an alternative solution to the problems of set referents in conceptual structures. His treatment uses a token for a set concept referent instead of the set itself. These tokens are subsequently subordinated to a set specific type lattice. Finally, in Part I, supplementing the conceptual structure display form to achieve full expressiveness is the theme of John Esch's first paper in this volume.

In Part II, chapters explore semantic metric and alternative representational and architectural paradigms. Norman Foo *et al.* give a modification of Sowa's metric on conceptual graphs. "Semantic distance", as they call it, is computed by locating the least subtype which subsumes two given types, and adding the distance from each given type to the subsuming type.

Another chapter on the issue of expressiveness is presented by Peter Creasy and Bernard Moulin. In chapter 9, the authors examine an integrated conceptual schema (Peckham and Maryanski, 1988) and suggest extensions to conceptual structure theory through which this goal can be achieved.

In chapter 10, Andrew Feller and Rob Rucker present a set of conceptual structure principles for meta-modeling a class of structured systems analysis primitives using conceptual graphs and type hierarchies. These primitives are constructed into the structured analysis language IDEF0 (Ross, 1977).

Sowa's theory of conceptual structures has been adopted in chapter 11 as the common knowledge representation formalism for a number of knowledge engineering projects. In chapter 11, an extendable graph processor which forms the nucleus of various conceptual processors is described by Brian J. Garner *et al*.

Since the introduction of a "Situation Data model"(based on Barwise and Perry (1983)), at an early conceptual structures workshop, William M. Tepfenhart has developed a conceptual basis set for several problem domains by applying the model to assist in identifying concepts and conceptual relations that comprise the conceptual basis set for various problem domains. Chapter 12 discusses the results.

Much of conceptual structure theory concerns itself with traversing a generalization hierarchy (or lattice). Part III contains chapters addressing this area.

Since the conceptual graph operations of projection and maximal join involve the corresponding actions of classification and subsumption in inheritance, Gerard Ellis examines these operations in term of their efficiency. He suggests a compiled intermediate form of conceptual graphs which encapsulates taxonomic subsumption. Ellis's compilation means that the subsumption test is implemented by a theorem prover rather than a subgraph isomorphism algorithm. But where does the generalization lattice come from in the first place?

In conceptual structures we often talk of type hierarchies and avoid the issue of their creation. In chapter 14, Guy Mineau shows how induction can be used to build a generalization lattice from first-order conceptual graphs. Automatically inducing the generalization lattice means that we need only define our knowledge base in terms of conceptual structures. Further in this vein is the following chapter, where the issues of consistency and ambiguity in the generalization hierarchy are addressed. How can we guarantee the monotonic nature of the generalization hierarchy in nonmonotonic domains? The integrity of the generalization hierarchy must be ensured. This is an issue which I take up in chapter 15.

Another important issue in conceptual structure research is that of normalization. Different graphs which encode similar meanings are bound to arise in much the same way that different people will use different language to express the same meaning. In chapter 16, Guy Mineau looks at normalized conceptual graphs, a reduced intermediate form of conceptual graph, in which the transparency of the representations expressiveness is maintained but internal normalization can in part be achieved.

In chapter 17, Debbie Leishman describes an analogical tool based on the evaluation of partial correspondences over conceptual graphs. The tool forms analogies and performs analogical inferencing. Having tested the implementation against several well-known examples of analogy, she shows that it compares favourably with existing systems (Gentner and Seziorski, 1986) (Indurkhya, 1985) (Russell, 1987) (Gick and Holyoak, 1983).

Temporal reasoning is the theme of Part IV. In chapter 18, John Esch examines the representation of temporal intervals (Allen, 1983) in conceptual graphs. The chapter deals with a number of fully ordered relations for constraining tense in temporal processing. In chapter 19, Bernard Moulin and Daniel Côté explore ways of interpreting natural language sentences (in French) to Allen-based (Allen, 1983) ordered relations for constraining tense. In chapter 20, a new conceptual graph node called a *demon* is introduced to express temporal knowledge. The demon's syntax and semantics are similar to an actor's with the addition that a demon actually creates its output concepts.

Conceptual graphs are intended to capture the meaning of all types of sentences including those modal sentences that are to be found at the heart of everyday discourse. However, the status of modal sentences in conceptual structures is not clear. In chapter 20, Jerrold L. Aronson takes up the cudgel on temporal modalities in conceptual structures.

In Part V of this volume concentrates on conceptual structures in natural language and text retrieval. In chapter 21, Jean-Francois Nogier and Michael Zock operate from the principle that the the core meaning of words and texts (sentences) can be expressed by the same formalism, namely conceptual graphs. This allows them to model the process of lexical choice by matching definition graphs on an utterance graph. In so doing, a natural mechanism for paraphrasing and explaining the conceptual differences between a set of words results.

In chapter 22, F. Antonacci *et al.* describe a system called DANTE for analyizing press agency releases in the domain of finance and economics. These texts are reduced to conceptual graph form which provides the basis of a knowledge-base from which queries may be answered. In chapter 23, Maria Teresa Pazienza and Paola Velardi describe the knowledge representation used for the DANTE system. The representation provides a means to solve syntactic ambiguity even for very complex sentences.

Natural language processing essentially consists of encoding and decoding the meaning of sentences. The encoding is used to carry out the generation of sentences. In the reverse process, the decoding is used to understand a sentence. In chapter 24, Stéphane Bornerand and Gérard Sabah present a decoding method based on a syntactic parsing to guide the coding from sentence to conceptual structure.

In chapter 25, Jonni Harrius uses Rhetorical Structure Theory (Mann, 1988) as the basis for an implementation of a system for text generation in an expert critiquing paradigm (Miller, 1986). The chapter demonstrates that conceptual structures and rhetorical structure theory are complementary in this domain.

Afke van Rijn's chapter discusses the generation of text from a conceptual dependency graph (Schank, 1975) using a method that integrates the syntactic and semantic processing of an utterance. In the integration, a syntactic context free grammar is augmented with information on the coupling between conceptual roles of concepts and syntactic roles of constituents. The input graph is scanned in such a way that every concept node and conceptual relation is traversed at least once. The words forming an utterance are found by matching the input conceptual dependency graph with lexical items that also contain graphs. A prototype of a language generator in Prolog illustrates these ideas.

Eileen Way explores conceptual graph isomorphism using the literary metaphor as a vehicle for her study. Way argues that through conceptual structures and dynamic type theory we can avoid "literal" interpretations of metaphorical language and instead appreciate more fully the true meaning of natural language utterances. In chapter 28, Sung Myaeng describes ongoing work for a framework for conceptual structure theory in information retrieval.

In chapter 29 the deductive capacities of a pure logic resolution on conceptual graphs give the query-language user a pertinent final answer, even when the question cannot be strictly established as a logical consequence of the conceptual graphs knowledge base. If a query deduction fails, Jean Fargues suggests a mechanism to explain why a sentence has been found incompatible with a rule clause or why a rule clause is too specific to be applied to the database.

In the appendix two short papers are presented. In the first, Tim Nagle *et al.* offers a notation for describing various types of graph matchers for conceptual structures is given as a ten-position vector whose values describe the features such matchers might include. In the second, John Esch presents the syntax for the linear form of conceptual graphs. Finally, the volume includes a comprehensive bibliography of published material in conceptual structures.

The prospects, both intermediate and long term, for conceptual structures are bright. There is substantial research interaction taking place, and an international collaborative project (called PEIRCE) is about to get underway with the goal of developing a suite of conceptual graph-based tools. August 1993 will see the First International Conference on Conceptual Structures in Quebec-City, Canada. In addition, discussion continues on international standards for knowledge interchange, and conceptual structures may yet play a pivotal role in that debate.

Finally, on behalf of all the editors, I acknowledge the Departments of Computer Science at the Universities of Linköping and Adelaide for providing the necessary computing facilities to prepare this volume, and thank the contributors for their patience and support.

Peter W. Eklund
Adelaide, 1992

BIBLIOGRAPHY

Allen J. F. (1983), "Maintaining Knowledge about Temporal Intervals", Communications of the ACM, Vol 26, no. 11.

Barwise, J. and J. Perry (1983) *Situations and Attitudes*, MIT Press.

Gentner, D. and M. Seziorski. (1986) "Historical Shifts in the Use of Analogy in Science", To appear in (eds) B. Gholson, W.R. Shadish, and A Graesser, *Psychology of Science*.

Gick, M. and K. Holyoak. (1983) "Schema Induction and Analogical Transfer". Cognitive Psychology 15, pp. 1-38.

Indurkhya, B. (1985) "A Computational Theory of Metaphor Comprehension and Analogical Reasoning", PhD thesis, University of Massachusetts.

Mann, W. (1988) "Language Generation and explanation", in *Advances in Natural Language Generation*, (eds) M. Zock and A. Sabah, Pinter.

Miller, P. (1986) *Expert Critiquing Systems*, Springer-Verlag.

Peckham, J. and Maryanski, F. (1988) "Semantic Data Models," ACM Comp. Surveys, 20, 3.

Ross, D.T. (1977). "Structured Analysis (SA): A Language for Communication Ideas," IEEE Transactions on Software Engineering, SE3(1):16-34.

Russell, J.S. (1987) "Analogical and Inductive Reasoning", PhD thesis. Stanford University.

Schank, R.C. (ed) (1975) *Conceptual Information Processing*, North-Holland.

Sowa, J. F. (1984) *Conceptual Structures: Information in Mind and Machine*, Addison-Wesley, Reading, MA.

Preface

The process of conceptual analysis and manipulation is much like attempting to carve gelatin. The concepts we seek to crystallize out of the world normally do not stand still; they are so amphorous that at what ever level of detail we attempt to define them, we usually need a level of definition yet another level deeper. In the end, what we end up with often doesn't look much like what we had in mind when we started.

In his landmark work *Science and Sanity* (1933), Alfred Korzybski describes his notion of General Semantics as the principles that humans use (or fail to use) in mapping the external world and symbols into internal representations and beliefs. His primary focus was on our tendency to treat labels and abstractions of objects as though they were the objects themselves resulting in non-rational interactions with the world around us.

The late S. I. Hayakawa brought Korzybski's ideas out of the shadow of obscurity into public light. It was through Hayakawa's writings, such as *Language and Action* (1939) that Korzybski's idea, "the map is not the territory", has become part of our culture. It was Hayakawa who modeled and showed us how to put into practice Korzybski's suggestions on analyzing and decomposing the symbols used in the world around us into their component parts.

In investigating problems in data modeling, William Kent begins his *Data and Reality* (1978) with his tribute to Hayakawa: "A message to map-makers: highways are not painted red, rivers don't have county lines running down the middle, and you can't see contour lines on a mountain". In what has become a classic work in database literature, he succeeds in applying the principles of General Semantics to data representation in order to tease apart the world we live in from our machine representations of it. He makes explicit our common assumptions and reveals the contradictions that arise from attempting to crystallize and segment a dynamic, interconnected and view dependent world.

It was John Sowa in his *Conceptual Structures: Information processing in mind and machine* (1984) that brings us to our current volume. It is in these machine processable structures that these authors use to map the gelatinous semantics of thought into the crystalline syntax of hardware.

Tim Nagle,
Eagan, Minnesota, 1992

BIBLIOGRAPHY

Hayakawa, S.I., (1939) *Language and Thought for Action*, Hardcourt, Brace and Co., New York.

Kent, W. (1978) *Data and Reality*, North-Holland Publishing Co., Amsterdam.

Korzybski, A. (1933) *Science and Sanity*, The Science Printing Co., Lancaster, Pennsylvannia.

Sowa, J.F. (1984) *Conceptual Structures: Information Processing in Mind and Machine*, Addison Wesley, Reading, MA.

Part I

Notation

1

Conceptual Graphs Summary

John F. Sowa
IBM-SREC,
500 Columbus Ave,
Thornwood, NY 10594 USA

ABSTRACT

Conceptual graphs are a system of logic based on the existential graphs of Charles Sanders Peirce and the semantic networks of artificial intelligence. The purpose of the system is to express meaning in a form that is logically precise, humanly readable, and computationally tractable. With their direct mapping to language, conceptual graphs can serve as an intermediate language for translating computer-oriented formalisms to and from natural languages. With their graphic representation, they can serve as a readable, but formal design and specification language.

1.1 CONCEPTUAL GRAPHS

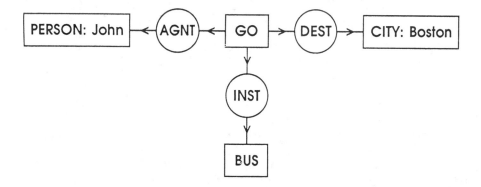

Fig. 1.1 A conceptual graph.

A conceptual graph is a diagram that represents the literal meaning of a sentence. It shows the concepts (represented by boxes) and the relations between them (represented by circles). As an example, the conceptual graph in Fig. 1.1 represents the sentence *John is going to Boston by bus*. Fig. 1.1 has four concepts: [PERSON: John] and [CITY:Boston] refer to specific instances of a person and a city; [GO] refers to some unspecified instance of going; and [BUS] refers to an unspecified bus. The AGNT relation shows that John is the agent of going, DEST shows that Boston is the destination, and INST shows that a bus is the instrument.

The concept and relation types are based on language-independent semantic principles. Besides English, conceptual graphs have been used to represent French, Italian, German, and Japanese. For English, the AGNT relation normally maps to the subject, INST to the preposition *by*, and DEST to the preposition *to*. For Japanese, AGNT, INST, and DEST would typically map to the postpositions *ga*, *de*, and *e*, which follow, rather than precede the nouns they govern. With that mapping, the graph in Fig. 1.1 could be translated to the following sentence in Japanese:

> *John ga basu de Boston e iku.*

> John (AGNT) bus (INST) Boston (DEST) go (present-tense).

This is the kind of sentence that could be generated by a language processor that used only local clues to do the mapping. A more sophisticated processor might take into account the emphasis and level of formality to generate a sentence like the following:

> *John wa basu de Boston e ikimasu.*

> John (topic) bus (INST) Boston (DEST) go (present, polite-form).

The first version would be intelligible to a Japanese speaker, but a version that uses additional background information would sound more natural.

Since conceptual graphs are a system of logic, they can also be translated to other versions of logic, such as predicate calculus. The formula operator ϕ, described in Section 12, does the translation. In Fig. 1.1, the four concepts have the *type labels* PERSON, GO, CITY, and BUS; ϕ translates each of them into monadic predicates $person(x)$, $go(x)$, $city(x)$, and $bus(x)$. Conceptual relations are translated into predicates with one argument for each arc. The relation labels AGNT, DEST, and INST become the dyadic predicates $agnt(x, y)$, $dest(x, y)$, and $inst(x, y)$. The arrow pointing towards the circle is argument 1, and the arrow pointing away is argument 2. The entire graph in Fig. 1.1 maps to the following formula in predicate calculus:

$$(\exists x)(\exists y)(person(John) \wedge go(x) \wedge city(Boston) \wedge bus(y)$$
$$\wedge agnt(x, John) \wedge inst(x, y) \wedge dest(x, Boston)).$$

This formula may be read, "There exists an x and a y where John is a person, x is an instance of going, Boston is a city, y is a bus, the agent of x is John, the instrument of x is y, and the destination of x is Boston". The operator ϕ maps the names John and Boston to constants in logic, and it assigns a variable x for [GO] and a variable y for [BUS]. The proliferation of variables in a predicate calculus formula tends to make it less readable than the equivalent conceptual graph.

Although the box and circle notation is readable, it is hard to type, and it takes up a lot of space on the printed page. For convenience, there is a *linear notation*. that uses square brackets for the boxes and rounded parentheses for the circles. For the simple sentence *John is going to Boston*, the graph can be written on a single line:

> [PERSON: John]←(AGNT)←[GO]→(DEST)→[CITY: Boston].

When a graph has complex branches, it cannot be drawn in a straight line. In Fig. 1.1, the three relations attached to the concept [GO] make the graph nonlinear. For such branches, a hyphen is used to show that the relations are continued on subsequent lines:

```
[GO]-
    (AGNT) → [PERSON: John]
    (DEST) → [CITY: Boston]
    (INST) → [BUS].
```

In this form, a conceptual graph resembles a frame: the conceptual relations correspond to the slot names; the type labels correspond to constraints on the slot fillers; and the names John and Boston correspond to slot fillers. Conceptual graphs, however, are more general than frames, since they can represent all of logic, but frames can only represent a limited subset of logic.

1.2 REFERENTS

Concepts represent the meanings of words. Like words, they may refer to entities, actions, properties, or events in the world. To distinguish the type of the referent from the specific individual, the concept box is divided in two parts: *a type field.* on the left and a *referent field.* on the right. The concept [PERSON: John] is an *individual concept.* with *type.* PERSON and *referent.* John. The concepts [BUS] and [GO] are called *generic concepts.* because they do not identify a particular individual; they specify only the type, not the individual.

Besides names, the referent field may contain symbols to represent the definite article *the.*, a quantifier like *every*, or plural nouns and sets. To illustrate various kinds of referents, following are some sample sentences in English and their semantic representations in conceptual graphs:

- *Every dog eats meat.*

    [DOG: ∀] ← (AGNT) ← [EAT] → (PTNT) → [MEAT].

    The universal quantifier "∀" in the referent field represents the English word *every*. The AGNT relation indicates that every dog is an agent of eating; the PTNT relation indicates that meat is the patient or thing eaten.

- *Lucky and Macula are eating..*

    [DOG: Lucky,Macula] ← (AGNT) ← [EAT].

    The referent {Lucky, Macula} represents a set of two named individuals, whose type is specified by the label in the type field. This graph specifies both Lucky and Macula as agents of eating, but omits the thing eaten.

- *Which dog is eating the meatball?.*

    [DOG: ?] ← (AGNT) ← [EAT] → (PTNT) → [MEATBALL: #].

    The question mark ? triggers a search for the instances that satisfy some query - in this case, *Which dog?*. The symbol # is called an *indexical referent*; it indicates some context-bound referent, usually indicated by a pronoun or the English article *the.*

- *Macula is eating some bones..*

    ```
    [DOG: Macula]←(AGNT)←[EAT]→(PTNT)→[BONE: {*}].
    ```

    The symbol {*} is called the *generic plural*; it indicates a set of unnamed instances of type specified by the type label BONE.

- *She is eating four bones..*

    ```
    [FEMALE: #]←(AGNT)←[EAT]→(PTNT)→[BONE: {*}@4].
    ```

    The pronoun *she.* is represented by the concept [FEMALE: #], which indicates a context-bound referent of type FEMALE. The referent {*}@4 indicates a set of four unnamed instances of type BONE.

A generic concept like [BUS] is actually an abbreviation for the full notation [BUS: *], where the asterisk indicates an unspecified referent of type BUS. In the *basic notation* for conceptual graphs, only three kinds of referents are permitted:

- *Existential*: The symbol * indicates the existence of some individual of the appropriate type. It corresponds to an existential quantifier ∃ in logic.

- *Individual marker*: The symbol # followed by an integer, such as #538693, identifies a unique individual. It corresponds to a constant in logic or a serial number in a database.

- *Literal*: A quoted string like "abc" or a number like 3.14159 identifies an individual by its form. It corresponds to a constant in logic or a literal in a programming language.

Names, quantifiers, and sets are called *extended referents*. They are defined by the way they expand into the basic notation. The simplest example of an extended referent is a name like *John..* The concept [PERSON: John] is a *name contraction.* of a graph with only basic referents:

```
[PERSON: #42109]→(NAME)→[WORD: "John"].
```

Note the use of quotes: John is a person, but "John" is a literal of type WORD. This graph may be read "The person #42109 named John". The individual marker #42109 is a unique identifier within the system. If there is only person named John in the current context, the short form [PERSON: John] is acceptable. If there are several people named John in the context, the individual marker may be appended to the name: [PERSON: John#42109].

Plural referents such as {*} are only used with countable things like cats, trees, and events. Mass nouns like *water.* and *money.* are not normally used in the plural. They refer to stuff that is measured rather than counted. The concepts that express mass nouns may therefore have a measure specification, such as [WATER: @5 liters] read "five liters of water", [MONEY: @ $5] read "five dollars", or [TIME-PERIOD: @ 5 seconds] read "a period of five seconds". Measure specifications are outside the basic notation; the concept [WATER: @ 5 liters] is a *measure contraction* of the following graph:

```
[WATER]→(MEAS)→[AMOUNT: 5 liters].
```

This graph may be read "Some water in the amount of five liters". The phrase *5 liters* is a name of the amount of water. The mass of water itself does not have a name. If it is necessary to identify the water for future references, it may be assigned an individual marker:

[WATER: #867489] → (MEAS) → [AMOUNT: 5 liters].

In the sentence *I poured 5 liters of water into the pot and boiled it for 15 minutes*, the pronoun *it* does not refer to the amount 5 liters, but to the instance of water #867489.

The symbols ?, !, and # are called *control marks*. Although they occur in the referent field of a concept, they do not identify the individual referent directly. Instead, they trigger processes of search and inference:

- *Question*: The question mark ? asks the listener to search for a referent whose identity is unknown to the speaker. In the concept [DOG: ?], it triggers a search for a specific dog that meets the conditions specified by the graph. The name of the dog or some other identifier is the answer returned to the person who asked.

- *Assertion*: The assertion mark, represented by the ! symbol, is the opposite of the question mark. It indicates new information that the speaker wants to bring to the listener's attention. In response to the question *Which dog is eating the meatball?* the answer might be *Lucky* is the culprit, with emphasis on *Lucky*. That emphasis is shown by the mark ! after the referent: [DOG: Lucky !].

- *Indexical*: The symbol # triggers a search through the nest of contexts for something that is known to both speaker and listener. In [MEATBALL: #], the marker # indicates a specific meatball whose identity is presumably known to both parties. When the search is complete, the # mark is replaced by a coreference link to a previous concept or by a unique identifier such as #538693. Other examples of indexical referents include #I and #you for the pronouns *I* and *you*; #this and #that for the deictic pronouns *this* and *that*; and #now for the time in the current context. All these referents can be defined in terms of a single *essential indexical* (Perry, 1979), which corresponds to the definite article *the*. The indexical #I, for example, may be defined as *the speaker in the current context*, which uses two occurrences of *the*.

The ? mark triggers a *goal directed* or *backward chaining* search for an answer. It appears on a generic concept whose referent is to be determined. The ! mark, however, triggers a *data driven* or *forward chaining* update to the listener's knowledge. It normally appears on an individual concept that conveys some new piece of information. For database systems, the ? mark is used in queries, and the ! mark is used in updates.

1.3   TYPE HIERARCHY

Concept types are organized in a hierarchy according to levels of generality. Fig. 1.2 shows a sample type hierarchy with the *universal type* ⊤ at the top. Under ⊤ are two very general types ENTITY and SITUATION. Under ENTITY are physical objects, abstractions, and datatypes. Under SITUATION are processes, states, events, and actions. Below them, the types become progressively more specialized down to PET-BEAGLE, TRAILER-TRUCK, and SAUNTER. The hierarchy of all the types and subtypes together with their definitions is also called a *taxonomy*.

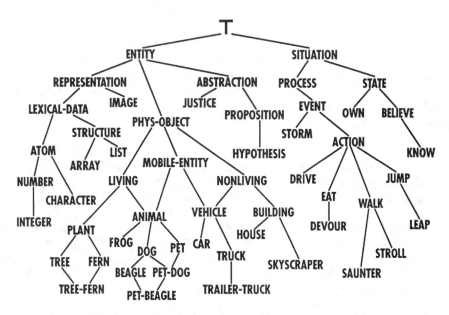

Fig. 1.2 - A type hierarchy.

On the left of Fig. 1.2, the branch headed by DATA includes all the types and subtypes of data. Under ATOM are the simple data types, such as numbers and characters; under STRUCTURE are the complex data types, such as lists, arrays, and records. In the NIAM system (Wintraecken, 1990), the types and subtypes of data are called *lexical object types* (LOTs) because they can be exactly represented by symbols on a piece of paper or in computer storage. All other types, including physical objects, abstractions, and situations, are called *nonlexical object types* (NOLOTs). There is a basic test for distinguishing LOTs from NOLOTs: if something can be stored in a computer and retrieved in exactly the same form, it is a LOT; anything that cannot be stored and retrieved by computer is a NOLOT. This distinction is important for databases, which can only represent LOTs directly. To represent a NOLOT, a database system must assign it a unique identifier called a *surrogate*. The distinction is also important for knowledge bases. In the Cyc system (Lenat and Guha 1990), the type LOT is called RepresentedThing. In conceptual graphs, LOTs are represented by literals in the referent field of a concept; the surrogates for NOLOTs are represented by individual markers consisting of the symbol # followed by a unique integer for every individual known to the system.

Types of entities can be further classified as *role types* or *natural types*. An individual can be recognized as an instance of a natural type by its own attributes or characteristics. DOG, for example, is a natural type: one can tell that an animal is a dog by looking at it. A role type, however, depends on relationships with external entities. PET is a role type: any animal can be a pet if it is in a certain relationship with a person; no attribute of the animal itself can distinguish a pet from a nonpet. MAN and WOMAN are natural types, but UNCLE, MOTHER, PEDESTRIAN, STUDENT, EMPLOYEE, MANAGER, and LAWYER are role types. In Fig. 1.2, HYPOTHESIS is a role type: a hypothesis is a proposition that is assumed as the basis for a proof. ASSERTION is another role type: it is a proposition that is being asserted.

For man-made objects, the distinction between natural types and role types still applies. A nail, for example, has a characteristic shape that is always distinguishable. Therefore, NAIL is a natural type. When a nail is being used for its common purpose of fastening two things together, its role type is FASTENER. Even when it is being used for other purposes, such as conducting electricity, it still conforms to its natural type NAIL. Its role type, however, may become

1.4   ELECTRICAL–CONDUIT.

The hierarchy in Fig. 1.2 is not a tree, since some types have more than one immediate supertype. The concept type, PET-DOG, for example, is a subtype of both DOG and PET. But since BEAGLE is a subtype of DOG, there is also a type PET-BEAGLE as a subtype of both PET-DOG and BEAGLE. Such types cause the hierarchy to become a more general *acyclic graph*. To preserve some order in the hierarchy, the theory of conceptual graphs defines it as a *lattice*. An acyclic graph can be converted into a lattice by adding extra nodes like PET-BEAGLE and one specialized node at the bottom $\perp$, called the *absurd type*. Nothing that exists can be an instance of $\perp$, but it is used for completeness: every type is a subtype of $\top$ and a supertype of $\perp$. The following operators apply to type labels in the lattice:

- *Proper subtype*: $s < t$ means that type s is a more specialized type than t; DOG $<$ ANIMAL.

- *Subtype*: $s \leq t$ means that either $s < t$ or $s = t$; DOG$\leq$ANIMAL and DOG$\leq$DOG.

- *Supertype*: $s \geq t$ means $t \leq s$, and $s > t$ means $t < s$.

- *Minimal common supertype*: $s \cup t$ is a type label that is a supertype of both s and t and it is a subtype of any other common supertype; MOBILE-ENTITY = ANIMAL $\cup$ VEHICLE.

- *Maximal common subtype*: $s \cap t$ is a type label that is a subtype of both s and t and it is a supertype of any other common subtype; PET-DOG = PET $\cap$ DOG.

- *Conformity*: $t :: i$. means that the type t is an appropriate type label for the individual i; CAT::Yojo. Everything conforms to type $\top$, and nothing conforms to type $\perp$.

- *Denotation*: δt is the set of all individuals that conform to type t. The denotation of $\top$ is everything that exists, and the denotation of $\perp$ is the empty set.

Types are categories of thought, not sets of things. Sets and subsets of all existing things also form a lattice, and the denotation operator δ maps the type lattice into the set lattice. Fig. 1.3 shows δ mapping type labels into sets: FROG is a type in the conceptual system, and δFROG is the set of all frogs in the world. But δ is not a one-to-one mapping. There are many more things in the world than people may happen to think about, and some types that people think about do not exist. Some types like UNICORN map into the empty set, other types like HUMAN and FEATHERLESS-BIPED map into the same set, and a randomly selected set of things may not correspond to any type.

Fig. 1.3 - Types and denotations.

The universal type ⊤ imposes no constraints on its referents. Its denotation δ⊤ is everything that exists; and the concept [⊤: *] means "Something exists". The universal type ⊤ is also called the *undefined type*, since one of its most common uses is to leave the type of a concept unspecified when it can be inferred from other constraints. For convenience, a concept with no type label is assumed to have the type ⊤. Therefore, [⊤: *] may be abbreviated as [⊤] by omitting the referent or [*] by omitting the type. When a named concept has the type omitted, the colon should be written to avoid ambiguity: [JACK] is a concept of a jack, but [:Jack] is a concept of something named Jack.

1.5   CONCEPTUAL RELATIONS

When a conceptual relation connects two concepts, it shows that some relationship holds between their referents. There are three kinds of conceptual relations:

- *Primitive*: The dyadic relation LINK is the only primitive in the formal theory. All other conceptual relations may be defined in terms of it.

- *Starter set*: As a starter set for representing logic, natural language semantics, and common applications, there is a set of basic conceptual relations that are widely used. Each relation in the starter set has a recommended mapping to and from English, but any of these relations and their mapping rules may be replaced or revised as linguistic theory develops.

- *Defined*: Any relation used in logic, relational databases, or entity-relationship diagrams may be used as a defined conceptual relation. Defined relations would not have an automatic mapping to and from natural languages. A database designer might specify an English phrase for the relation or define it in terms of the basic relations in the starter set.

Fig. 1.4 shows three different ways of representing the sentence *A cat is chasing a mouse.* The top graph uses the defined relation CHASING, which is neither a primitive nor one of the relations in the starter set. The middle graph uses the relations AGNT and PTNT, which are two of the basic linguistic relations in the starter set. The bottom graph uses only the primitive relation LINK and two special concepts [AGENT] and [PATIENT], which represent the equivalent information in concept form rather than relational form.

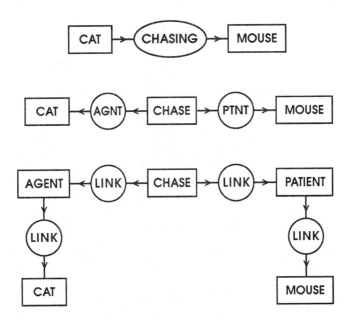

Fig. 1.4 - Three conceptual graphs for a cat chasing a mouse.

When a relational database or an entity-relationship diagram is mapped to conceptual graphs, most of the relations would be defined relations similar to CHASING in Fig. 1.4. The arrows on the arcs indicate the expected direction for reading the graph - in this case, *a cat chasing a mouse.* For conceptual relations whose names are nouns or abbreviations of nouns, the following conventions are commonly used:

- When a graph is read in the direction of the arrows, the arc pointing towards the circle is read *has a,* and the one pointing away from the circle is read *which is.*

- When a graph is read against the flow of the arrows, the arc pointing away from the circle is read *is a,* and the one pointing towards the circle is read *of.*

As an example, the following graph represents the sentence "A man is at the door":

    [MAN] → (LOC) → [DOOR: #].

For this graph, the reading in the direction of the arrows is *A man has a location which is the door.* The reading against the flow of the arrows is *The door is a location of a man.*

For conceptual relations derived from prepositions and conjunctions, the arrows point in the direction of normal English word order. The next graph, for example, may be read "A cat on a mat":

```
[CAT] → (ON) → [MAT].
```

These rules are simplified examples of the way conceptual graphs are translated into English. More sophisticated rules would take advantage of the richness of English syntax and vocabulary in order to generate more elegant prose. Since conceptual graphs are language independent, analogous rules could be stated for French, Japanese, or any other natural language.

A sample starter set of conceptual relations was presented in Appendix B3 of *Conceptual Structures* (Sowa, 1984). Further work on this topic is being done by many research groups in linguistics and artificial intelligence. Following are examples of relations in the starter set:

- *Case relations*, also called *thematic roles*, show how the action or state expressed by a verb is related to the entities expressed by the subject, object, and other complements. They include agent (AGNT), patient (PTNT), state (STAT), experiencer (EXPR), recipient (RCPT), instrument (INST), destination (DEST), and result (RSLT).

- *Spatial relations* include the simple location (LOC) as well as more specific ones that correspond to spatial prepositions such as (IN), (ON), and (ABOV).

- *Attributes* include the general (ATTR) as well as more specific ones, such as (CHRC) for characteristic or (PART) for having as part.

- *Intersentential relations* relate contexts that include one or more conceptual graphs as referents. They include relations like before (BFOR), after (AFTR), cause (CAUS), purpose (PURP), method (METH), and logical operators like (AND) and (OR).

- *Mathematical relations* include measure (MEAS), greater-than (>), less-than (<), equal (=), not-equal (≠), average (AVG), count (CNT), and functional arguments (ARG1) or (ARG2).

- *Metarelations* describe the way concept types and relations relate to one another and to conceptual graphs. They include kind (KIND), subtype (SUBT), description (DSCR), statement (STMT), and representation (REPR).

These are some basic relations that are common to many different domains. The starter set need not be fixed for all time, since new relations can always be defined. In fact, different starter sets may be standardized for different industries and application areas. But a good starter set can reduce the effort for new application development and can provide a common vocabulary to facilitate communication.

Although the primitive relation LINK and most of the basic relations in the starter set are dyadic (having two arcs), other relations defined in terms of them can have any number of arcs. The relation BETW, for example, has three arcs: its first two arcs are linked to the things on either side of a third. The graph in Fig. 1.5 may be read "a person between a rock and a hard place".

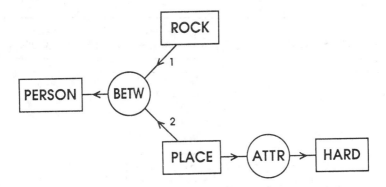

Fig. 1.5 - A conceptual relation with three arcs.

The first two arcs of the BETW relation are numbered to distinguish them. For any conceptual relation, the last arc is always the one with the arrow pointing away from the circle. Fig. 1.5 may be represented by the following graph in the linear form:

```
[PERSON] ← (BETW) –
     1 ← [ROCK]
     2 ← [PLACE] → (ATTR) → [HARD] .
```

1.6 SITUATIONS AND CONTEXTS

Situation semantics (Barwise and Perry, 1983) has been widely adopted as one of the most flexible ways of defining the semantics of language. Each *situation* is a finite configuration of some aspect of the world in a limited region of space and time. A situation may be a static configuration that remains unchanged for a period of time, or it may include processes and events that are causing changes. It may include people and things with their actions and attributes; it may be real or imaginary; and its time may be present, past, or future. A situation may be as large as the solar system or as small as an atom, and it may contain nested situations that describe smaller and more detailed aspects of the world.

In conceptual graphs, a situation is represented by a *context*, which is a concept that contains one or more propositions that describe the situation. The propositions in a context could be expressed by a paragraph of English sentences or by a collection of conceptual graphs. In Fig. 1.6, the graph for a cat chasing a mouse is nested inside a concept of type SITUATION. The inner context with the nested graph describes the situation; and the outer context contains concepts and relations that say how the situation relates to external times, places, and things. The relation DUR for *duration* shows that the situation lasted for a time period of 13 seconds. The relations FROM and TO show that the time period started at the time 19:29:32 Greenwich Mean Time and ended at 19:29:45.

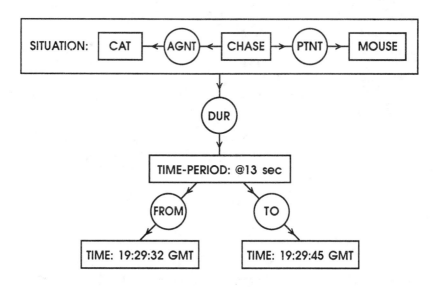

Fig. 1.6 - Showing the duration of a cat chasing a mouse.

The relation between a situation and the propositions that describe it is *description* (DSCR); the relation between a proposition and the graph that states it is *statement* (STMT). The next graph describes a situation of a cat on a mat:

$$[\texttt{SITUATION}] \rightarrow (\texttt{DSCR}) \rightarrow [\texttt{PROPOSITION}] \rightarrow (\texttt{STMT}) \rightarrow$$
$$[\texttt{GRAPH}: \ [\texttt{CAT}] \rightarrow (\texttt{ON}) \rightarrow [\texttt{MAT}]].$$

This graph shows a situation that has a description that is a proposition that has a statement that is expressed by the conceptual graph for *A cat is on a mat*. Since that is a rather long-winded explanation, two simplifications are convenient: *statement contraction* and *description contraction*. By statement contraction, the graph that states a proposition is moved into the referent field of the concept of type PROPOSITION:

$$[\texttt{SITUATION}] \rightarrow (\texttt{DSCR}) \rightarrow [\texttt{PROPOSITION}: \ [\texttt{CAT}] \rightarrow (\texttt{ON}) \rightarrow [\texttt{MAT}]].$$

By description contraction, the conceptual graph that states the proposition that describes the situation is moved into the referent field of the concept of type SITUATION:

$$[\texttt{SITUATION}: \ [\texttt{CAT}] \rightarrow (\texttt{ON}) \rightarrow [\texttt{MAT}]].$$

This graph may be read "A situation of a cat on a mat". When a conceptual graph occurs in a referent field of type GRAPH, it is used as a literal; when of type PROPOSITION, it is used to state a proposition; when of type SITUATION, it is used to describe a situation. The operations of description and statement contraction are analogous to name contraction, which was described in Section 2.

If a graph appears in a referent field of type PROPOSITION or SITUATION, the conceptual processor can recognize the type discrepancy and do an appropriate expansion as needed. This expansion is like a *type coercion* in programming languages. Since sentences in ordinary language can state propositions and describe situations, they can also appear in a referent field of type PROPOSITION or SITUATION. The following graph represents the sentence *There exists a situation described by a proposition stated by a sentence represented by the string "A cat is on a mat"*:

```
[SITUATION]→(DSCR)→[PROPOSITION]→(STMT)→
          [SENTENCE]→(REPR)→[STRING: "A cat is on a mat"].
```

There are three possible contractions for simplifying this graph to just a single concept:

```
[SITUATION]→(DSCR)→[PROPOSITION]→(STMT)→
          [SENTENCE: "A cat is on a mat"].

[SITUATION]→(DSCR)→[PROPOSITION: "A cat is on a mat"].

[SITUATION: "A cat is on a mat"].
```

As with conceptual graphs, a quoted character string represents a literal when it occurs in the referent field of a concept of type STRING. By representation contraction, the literal could be moved to the referent field of a concept of type SENTENCE; by statement contraction, to the referent of a concept of type PROPOSITION; and by description contraction, to the referent of a concept of type SITUATION. The ability to include quoted text in the referent field allows conceptual graphs to represent hypertext networks. For each hypertext card, the text could be represented by a quoted string in the referent field of a concept. Links to other cards would then be represented by conceptual relations linked to the concepts for those other cards. An entire hypertext network could then be represented by a giant conceptual graph, where the referent of each concept could contain text, nested conceptual graphs, or any other type of lexical object (LOT).

Since contexts are represented as concepts, conceptual relations may be linked to them. Fig. 1.6, for example, shows a situation linked by the relation DUR to a time period. Fig. 1.7 shows a graph for the sentence "Tom believes that Mary wants to marry a sailor". The patient relation (PTNT) links the concepts BELIEVE and WANT to contexts that contain the belief or the desire. Following are some other conceptual relations typically linked to contexts:

- *Negation*: (NEG) is a monadic relation that denies the proposition it is linked to. Since it occurs frequently in logic, it may be abbreviated with the symbol ¬.

- *Modality*: (MODE) is a dyadic relation that links a proposition to a concept that expresses its modality or likelihood.

- *Point in time*: (PTIM) is a dyadic relation that links a situation to the point in time at which it occurs.

- *Tense and aspect*: Various relations for tenses and aspects can be defined in terms of the more primitive relations for point in time (PTIM), successor (SUCC), and duration (DUR).

- *Intersentential relations*: Complex connections may be expressed by adverbs and conjunctions that relate clauses, sentences, paragraphs, and even entire chapters.

Those connections could be represented by relations like before (BFOR), after (AFTR), cause (CAUS), method (METH), and consequence (CNSQ). Most of these relations can be defined in terms of more primitive ones.

Relations that link contexts are especially important for handling connected discourse. Each sentence in a dialog or a story could be represented by a conceptual graph. The entire story could itself be represented by a giant conceptual graph with many nested contexts linked by relations that express time and causality.

In Fig. 1.7, BELIEVE and WANT are states that have experiencers (EXPR) rather than agents. What Tom believes is a proposition, but what Mary wants is a situation. In general, negation, modalities, and the patients of verbs like *think* and *know* are linked to contexts of type PROPOSITION; times, locations, and the patients of verbs like *want* and *fear* are linked to contexts of type SITUATION. When a person occurs as the subject of some verb, the underlying relation is agent (AGNT) if the person is actively doing something; experiencer (EXPR) if the person is experiencing a mental state; and state (STAT) if the person is in a more passive state that is neither an action nor an experience. For each concept type, the lexicon would indicate which relation types are expected. The rules for mapping conceptual graphs to and from natural languages take account of the proper concept and relation types.

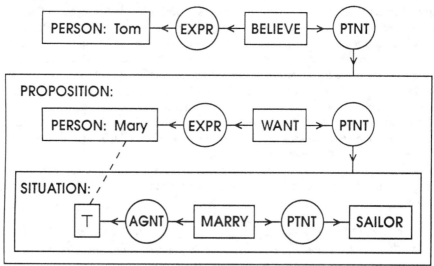

Fig. 1.7 - A nested proposition containing a nested situation.

The dotted line in Fig. 1.7 is called a *coreference link*. It shows that the concept [T] in the innermost context refers to the same individual as the concept [PERSON: Mary] in the containing context. Following is the linear form for that graph:

```
[PERSON:  Tom] ← (EXPR) ← [BELIEVE] → (PTNT) → [PROPOSITION:
    [PERSON:  Mary*x] ← (EXPR) ← [WANT] → (PTNT) → [SITUATION:
        [*x] ← (AGNT) ← [MARRY] → (PTNT) → [SAILOR] ]].
```

In the linear form, variables are used to show coreference links. The variable *x shows that the concept [*x] is coreferent with [PERSON: Mary*x]. The concept [*x] is an abbreviation for [⊤: *x], which uses the type ⊤, since the type PERSON has already been specified on the coreferent concept. As this example illustrates, the box and circle diagrams tend to be more readable than the linear form when there are multiple levels of nested contexts.

Whatever the types of the contexts, the way they are nested determines the scope of quantifiers. In Fig. 1.7, the existential quantifier on SAILOR is inside the situation of Mary's desire, which is existentially quantified inside Tom's belief. If Tom is mistaken, the desire to marry a sailor, which Tom imputes to Mary, might not exist - she might have very different intentions. Even if Tom's belief is correct, Mary's desire may remain unfulfilled. In fact, her ideal sailor might not exist in the real world, since the quantifier occurs only within the scope of her desire. In general, the scope of a quantifier is the context in which it occurs, including any other contexts nested within that context. The formula operator ϕ preserves the scoping when it maps a conceptual graph into predicate calculus. For Fig. 1.7, the equivalent formula would be

$$(\exists x)(person(Tom) \wedge believe(x) \wedge expr(x, Tom) \wedge ptnt(x,$$
$$(\exists y)(\exists z)(person(Mary) \wedge want(y) \wedge situation(z) \wedge$$
$$expr(y, Mary) \wedge ptnt(y, z) \wedge descr(z,$$
$$(\exists u)(\exists v)(marry(u) \wedge sailor(v) \wedge agnt(u, Mary) \wedge ptnt(u, v)))))).$$

This formula may be read "There exists an x where Tom is a person, x is an instance of believing, the experiencer of x is Tom, and the patient of x is the proposition that there exists a y and a z where Mary is a person, y is an instance of wanting, z is a situation, the experiencer of y is Mary, the patient of y is z, and the description of z is the proposition that there exists a u and a v where u is an instance of marrying, v is a sailor, the agent of u is Mary, and the patient of u is v". All the detail in this formula is expressed by the graph of Fig. 1.7, but in a much more readable form.

Negation (NEG) is one of the most common relations attached to contexts. The following graph uses negation to express the sentence *Sam does not own a car*:

```
(NEG) → [PROPOSITION:
            [PERSON: Sam] → (STAT) → [OWN] → (PTNT) → [CAR]].
```

The relation STAT indicates that Sam is in the state of owning. Since negations occur frequently, this graph may be simplified to the following:

```
¬[ [PERSON: Sam] → (STAT) → [OWN] → (PTNT) → [CAR]].
```

The first simplification is to replace the relation NEG with the symbol ¬. The second is to omit the type label PROPOSITION, since the relation NEG or ¬ implies that the type must be PROPOSITION (or some subtype, such as HYPOTHESIS).

All Boolean operators can be defined by combining negations with conjunctions: implication $(p \supset q)$ is equivalent to $\neg(p \wedge \neg q)$; disjunction $(p \vee q)$ is equivalent to $\neg(\neg p \wedge \neg q)$. In conceptual graphs, no relation is needed for conjunction, since two or more graphs in the same context have an implicit AND relation between them. Negation is represented by NEG or ¬ attached to the context. If $*p$ and $*q$ represent arbitrary conceptual graphs, an XOR relation for exclusive OR may be defined by the following equivalence:

[*p](XOR)[*q] is equivalent to ¬[¬[*p] ¬[*q]] ¬[[*p] [*q]].

For a symmetric relation like XOR, the direction of the arrows is irrelevant, and they may be replaced with simple lines. Instead of an implication relation (IMPL) as the equivalent of ⊃, it is more readable to use the notation "IF *p THEN *q" to represent ¬ [*p ¬ [*q]]. The following graph uses the IF-THEN notation to represent the sentence *If Sam owns a car, then Sam drives to school*:

```
IF  [PERSON: Sam] → (STAT) → [OWN] → (PTNT) → [CAR]
THEN [PERSON: Sam] ← (AGNT) ← [DRIVE] → (DEST) → [SCHOOL].
```

In the more basic notation with ¬, this graph expands to

```
¬[ [PERSON: Sam] → (STAT) → [OWN] → (PTNT) → [CAR]
  ¬[[PERSON: Sam] ← (AGNT) ← [DRIVE] → (DEST) → [SCHOOL]]].
```

For readability, the IF-THEN notation is convenient. For theoretical analysis, the basic ¬[*p ¬[*q]] notation is preferable, since it shows the logical structure more clearly. But either form can be converted to the other by substituting "IF" for the outer "¬ [" and "THEN" for the nested "¬ [" In the IF-THEN form, the closing brackets "]]" before the final period are dropped.

The concept types STATE, PROCESS, and EVENT are subtypes of SITUATION, and they may be nested inside one another to any depth. Fig. 1.8 shows a concept of type PROCESS, which contains a nested state $s1$, followed by an event e, followed by another state $s2$. The successor relation (SUCC) shows the sequence of states and events. The state $s1$ has a duration of 15 seconds, the event e occurs at a *point in time* (PTIM) of 20:23:19 GMT, and the state $s2$ has a duration of 5 seconds.

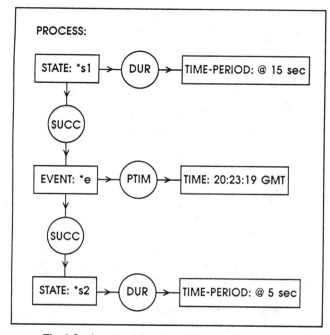

Fig. 1.8 - A process described by a conceptual graph.

A state is a static situation that does not change noticeably over a long time, a process is a situation that makes a change during some period of time, and an event is a situation that causes a change in a very short time. The distinction between a long time and a short time depends on the amount of significant detail. In process descriptions, there is usually a characteristic time interval, called a *clock tick*, which distinguishes states, processes, and events: A state is a situation that does not change appreciably during one or more clock ticks; an event is a situation that causes a significant change in less than a clock tick; and a process is a situation that causes a change over a period of several clock ticks. In human activities, a clock tick of one second is adequate for describing most processes; but in sports competitions, one hundredth of a second is common. In computer simulations, a clock tick of one nanosecond may be necessary. And in describing geological processes, a clock tick of one century may be used.

The contexts that describe states, events, and processes may be nested inside one another to any depth. Fig. 1.8, for example, might represent the process of blowing out the candles on a birthday cake. The state s1 would represent the candles burning for 15 seconds while the guests sing Happy Birthday. Then event e is the act of blowing out the candles, and state $s2$ represents the candles smoking for 5 seconds. Fig. 1.9 is an expansion of state $s1$ to show the nested graphs that describe the candles burning and the guests singing.

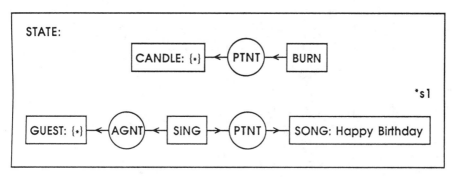

Fig. 1.9 - Expanded description of state $s1$ in Fig. 1.8

In Fig. 1.9, the details of the singing are not described. Even though singing is a process with sound and movement, those details are unimportant at this level of description, and the entire process may be considered a single, unchanging state. With more detail and a finer clock tick, the singing might be considered a process with each note as a separate event. But with a clock tick of one minute, the entire process in Fig. 1.8 could be considered as just one event. With no detail and a clock tick of one day, even the birthday party itself could be treated as a single event. The type SITUATION includes all the entities and happenings in some region of space and time. Depending on the point of view, the same situation may be described at many different levels of detail. When change is not significant, a situation might be called a state; with a long clock tick, it might be called an event; and with a short clock tick, it might be considered a process consisting of multiple events.

Fig. 1.10 shows the process box for Fig. 1.8 nested inside a larger box that describes a birthday party as a situation. Inside the box for the birthday party, the top graph says that 40 guests x are giving presents to a person named Marvin. There are also 50 candles on a cake. Inside the nested process box, the first state is described by graphs for the candles y

burning and the guests singing Happy Birthday. The next event is described by a graph for
Marvin blowing out the candles y. And the last state is described by a graph for the candles
generating smoke.

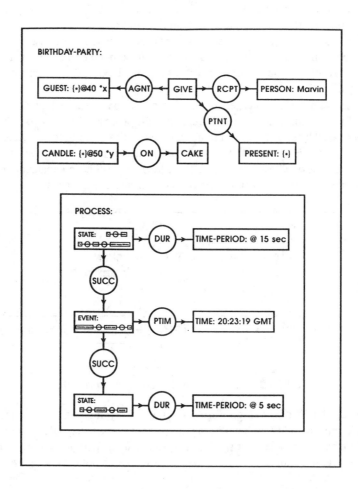

Fig. 1.10 - Nested contexts for describing Marvin's birthday party.

The example of a birthday party illustrates the conceptual graph notation with a familiar
situation. But exactly the same techniques could be used to describe a manufacturing
process, a courtroom trial, or the steps in the execution of a computer program. For all
of these purposes, the subtypes of SITUATION can be described by nests of contexts
containing conceptual graphs. Other notations for describing processes and events - flow
charts, state-transition diagrams, dataflow diagrams, or Petri nets - can be translated to
similar nests of conceptual graphs.

1.7 COREFERENCE LINKS

Two concepts that refer to the same individual are *coreferent*. For the sentence *Mary is a teacher*, the conceptual graph would contain the two concepts [PERSON: Mary] and [TEACHER]. To show that they are coreferent, they are connected with a dotted line, called a *coreference link*:

      [PERSON: Mary]- - -[TEACHER].

When the operator ϕ maps this graph into a formula, the dotted line becomes an equation $Mary = x$, where x is the variable that corresponds to the teacher:

$$(\exists x)(person(Mary) \wedge teacher(x) \wedge Mary = x).$$

In effect, this formula says that there exists a teacher x who is the same as the person Mary. When a graph contains many dotted lines that cross each other in complex ways, they can become hard to follow. As an alternate notation, variables preceded with an asterisk, such as $*x$ or $*y$, can be used to show coreference links. The following graph is exactly equivalent to the one above:

      [PERSON: Mary *x] [TEACHER: *x].

In the linear form, variables are necessary to show complex cross references. In the pure graph form, they are not needed, but they may be used when there are many crossing lines. Two coreferent concepts in the same context may be joined to form a single concept. Since TEACHER is a common subtype of PERSON and TEACHER, both concepts in the graph may be joined to form a single concept [TEACHER: Mary].

If coreferent concepts are in different contexts, no joins are possible. Negation is the most common relation that requires separate contexts to prevent coreferent concepts from being joined. As examples, consider the next two sentences:

Some dog is not a pet.

It is false that some dog is a pet.

These two sentences are not synonymous: the first one is true, since many dogs are strays; and the second is false, since many dogs are pets. In the first one, the negation includes the phrase *a pet* within its scope, but not the subject *some dog*. In the second sentence, however, the negation includes both parts in its scope. The negative contexts in Fig. 1.11 show the scopes explicitly.

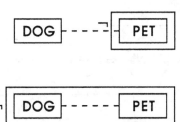

Fig. 1.11 - Negations with different scopes.

The first graph in Fig. 1.11 states that there exists a dog and that it is false that the same individual is also a pet. The second one states that it is false that there exist a dog and a pet that are the same individual. The formula operator ϕ would map these two graphs to the following formulas in predicate calculus:

$(\exists x)(dog(x) \wedge \neg pet(x)).$

$\neg(\exists y)(dog(y) \wedge pet(y)).$

In the linear notation, the two graphs in Fig. 1.11 would be written in the following form:

```
[DOG: *x]  ¬[  [PET:  *x]].
```

```
¬[  [DOG: *y]  [PET:  *y]].
```

In the second of these two graphs, both coreferent concepts are in the same context. Therefore, they could be joined to form a single concept of the common subtype PET-DOG:

```
¬  [  [PET-DOG]].
```

This graph may be read "It is false that there exists a pet dog."

The arcs that link concepts and relations may not cross context boundaries; only coreference links may cross those boundaries. Therefore, extra coreference links may be needed when parts of a sentence are inside and other parts are outside the scope of a negation. In the sentence *Some dog doesn't eat meat*, the subject *some dog* is outside the the the negation, but everything else in the sentence is within the negation. The following graph shows that scope:

```
[DOG:  *x]  ¬[[*x]←(AGNT)←[EAT]→(PTNT)→[MEAT]].
```

Literally, this graph may be read "There exists a dog x, and it is false that x eats meat". Within the negation, the extra concept [*x] serves as a point to which the AGNT relation is attached.

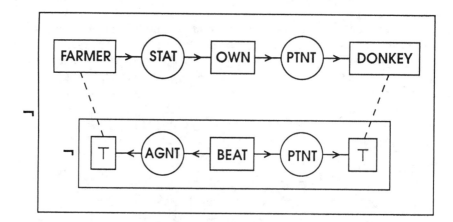

Fig. 1.12 - Conceptual graph for "If a farmer owns a donkey, then he beats it."

Since the IF-THEN construction is defined in terms of two negations, coreference links are often required to link concepts in the IF-context to concepts in the THEN-context. As an example, Fig. 1.12 represents the sentence *If a farmer owns a donkey, then he beats it.* The pronouns *he* and *it* in the sentence correspond to concepts of type $\top$ in the graph. In the linear form, Fig. 1.12 becomes

```
¬[[FARMER: *x]→(STAT)→[OWN]→(PTNT)→[DONKEY: *y]
    ¬[[*x]←(AGNT)←[BEAT]→(PTNT)→[*y]]].
```

With the symbols IF and THEN, the result is the following graph:

```
IF  [FARMER: *x]→(STAT)→[OWN]→(PTNT)→[DONKEY: *y]
THEN [*x]←(AGNT)←[BEAT]→(PTNT)→[*y].
```

This linear form can be read directly as an English sentence: "If a farmer x owns a donkey y, then x beats y."

Although variables in logic serve the same purpose as pronouns in English, the referent of a pronoun may be ambiguous. In the first stage of translating English to conceptual graphs, pronouns and nouns marked with the definite article *the* are normally represented with concepts containing the indexical referent #. In the second stage of analysis, the marker # is replaced by a coreference link to some other concept. The correct link is determined by searching for an appropriate concept of the same type or a compatible type. For the sentence, *If a farmer owns a donkey, then he beats it*, the initial stage of the analysis would generate a graph of the following form:

```
IF  [FARMER]→(STAT)→[OWN]→(PTNT)→[DONKEY]
THEN [MALE: #]←(AGNT)←[BEAT]→(PTNT)→[¬HUMAN: #].
```

To resolve # references, the rules for searching the nest of contexts are based on the discourse representation theory by Kamp (1981a,b). For the concept [MALE: #], there is no explicitly marked male in the THEN-context or the surrounding IF-context. It is possible that either the farmer or the donkey could be male, but only the donkey is nonhuman. As in this example, the resolution of contextual references may depend on probabilities rather than certainties. In a natural language system, a menu could be presented on the screen, and the user could select which option was intended. After the references have been resolved, either by algorithm, guessing, or menus, the # markers are replaced by coreference links.

A concept may be coreferent with another concept that represents an entire proposition. Consider the sentence *I told Bob that classes were canceled, and he mentioned it to Mary.* In the first stage of analysis, the pronoun *he* may be represented by [MALE: #], and *it* may be represented by [¬HUMAN: #]. When the # markers have been resolved, the agent of [MENTION] is coreferent with Bob, and the patient is coreferent with the proposition that classes were canceled:

```
[TELL]-
    (AGNT)→[PERSON: #I]
    (RCPT)→[PERSON: Bob *x]
    (PTNT)→[PROPOSITION: [CLASS: {*}∀]←(PTNT)←[CANCEL]
*y],
```

```
[MENTION]-
   (AGNT) → [*x]
   (RCPT) → [PERSON: Mary]
   (PTNT) → [*y].
```

The hyphen after [TELL]- is terminated by the comma; then the hyphen after [MENTION]-links to the remaining relations. When complex graphs are written in the linear form, the hyphen-comma pairs may be nested to any depth; indentation emphasizes the nesting for the human reader, but even without indentation, the commas and hyphens are unambiguous. Variables are written at the end of the referent field in a concept box, but they are associated with the entire referent. In this example, *x shows a coreference link to a concept with the referent *Bob*, and *y shows a coreference link to a context containing a nested graph. The past tenses of the verbs *told, were,* and *mentioned* are not shown in this example; but they could be shown by a context box with an attached relation (PAST) surrounding the entire graph.

Things that are mentioned separately in one statement may be grouped together in another statement. If the things have names, the names may be grouped in a plural referent like Lucky,Macula If they are not named, their coreference variables may be grouped inside the braces of a plural referent. The following graph represents the sentence *I see three animals - a lion, a tiger, and a bear*:

```
[PERSON:#I] ← (AGNT) ← [SEE] → (PTNT) → [ANIMAL:{*x, *y, *z}@3]
[LION: *x] [TIGER: *y] [BEAR: *z].
```

1.8   DEFINING CONCEPT AND RELATION TYPES

New types of concepts and relations can be defined in terms of simpler ones. The basic mechanism for all definitions is λ-abstraction: some conceptual graph forms the body of the definition, and the Greek letter λ specifies one or more generic concepts in the graph as formal parameters. The following λ-expression defines a type of CAT that is owned by some person:

```
(λx)  [CAT: *x] ← (PTNT) ← [OWN] ← (STAT) ← [PERSON].
```

The header $(\lambda\ x)$ specifies x as the variable that identifies the concept [CAT: *x] as the formal parameter. The body of the definition adds the information "is owned by some person." The next equation associates the type label PET-CAT with that λ-expression:

```
PET-CAT = (λx)  [CAT: *x] ← (PTNT) ← [OWN] ← (STAT) ← [PERSON].
```

This equation defines PET-CAT as a special type of CAT. The type label on the formal parameter (in this case, CAT) is a supertype of the newly defined type PET-CAT. The supertype is called the *genus*, and the defining graph is called the *differentia*.

As this example shows, a type label is a name of a λ-expression. In any concept, the type label can be replaced by the λ-expression that defines it. Since the symbol λ is not available on most typewriters, that definition could also be specified in an extended notation with the keyword *type*:

```
type PET-CAT(x) is
     [CAT: *x]←(PTNT)←[OWN]←(STAT)←[PERSON].
```

In the pure graphic notation, the variable *x may be eliminated by placing the symbol λ in the referent field of the concept that represents the formal parameter:

```
[CAT: λ]←(PTNT)←[OWN]←(STAT)←[PERSON].
```

The symbol λ allows new types to be defined that have no labels. That feature is especially important for representing some of the complexities of natural languages, including scope of quantifiers, relative clauses, and anaphoric references.

Negated type labels, such as ¬HUMAN for nonhuman, can be defined in terms of the corresponding type enclosed inside a negation. Following is a definition of ¬HUMAN:

```
type ¬HUMAN(x) is
     [T: *x] ¬[ [HUMAN: *x]].
```

This definition says that x is of type ¬HUMAN if it is of any type ($\top$) and it is not HUMAN. All other negated type labels can be defined by a similar pattern: For any type t, the type ¬t can be defined by replacing HUMAN in these examples with the type label t. Once concept types such as FLAMMABLE and PLEASANT have been introduced, the negated types ¬FLAMMABLE and ¬PLEASANT could be used without explicit definitions.

In the definition of PET-CAT, the property of being owned by a person is added to the property of being a cat. Such a definition uses conjunction as the only Boolean operator. In general, any logical operator may be needed in a definition. The definition of PENNILESS, for example, requires a negation:

```
type PENNILESS(x) is
     [STATE: *x]←(STAT)←[PERSON: *y]
     ¬[ [*y]→(POSS)→[PENNY]].
```

This definition says that PENNILESS is a state x of a person y, where it is false that y has possession (POSS) of a penny.

New types of conceptual relations can also be defined by λ-abstraction. The relation CHASING in Fig. 1.4 may be defined in terms of the concept [CHASE] and the more basic relations AGNT and PTNT:

```
CHASING = (λ x,y)
     [ANIMATE: *x]←(AGNT)←[CHASE]→(PTNT)→[ENTITY:*y].
```

This definition says that CHASING has two formal parameters x and y, where x is an animate being that is the agent of chasing, and y is an entity that is being chased. In the notation without the symbol λ, this definition could be written with the keyword *relation*:

```
relation CHASING(x,y) is
     [ANIMATE: *x]←(AGNT)←[CHASE]→(PTNT)→[ENTITY:*y].
```

In the pure graph notation, the variables x and y could be avoided by marking the formal parameters with the symbols λ_1 and *lambda*$_2$:

```
CHASING=[ANIMATE:λ₁]←(AGNT)←[CHASE]→(PTNT)→[ENTITY:λ₂].
```

Just as type labels in concepts can be replaced by λ-expressions, the label CHASING in the first graph of Fig. 1.4 may be replaced by its defining λ-expression:

```
[CAT]→
  ([ANIMATE:λ₁]←(AGNT)←[CHASE]→(PTNT)→[ENTITY:λ₂])
                     →[MOUSE].
```

Relations containing λ-expressions instead of labels are used for representing elliptical expressions in natural language. Consider the sentence *Yojo chased a mouse; Lucky, a squirrel; and Macula, a rabbit.* In the first stage of analyzing the sentence, a parser would have undefined relations linking Lucky to the squirrel and Macula to the rabbit. In the next stage, it could construct a λ-expression from the first clause and copy that expression to the undefined relations for the second and third clauses.

For simplicity in the theoretical foundations, negation and conjunction are the only primitives used in conceptual graphs. But for convenience, all other Boolean operators may be defined. As an example, the exclusive-OR relation (XOR) mentioned in Section 5 may be defined by the following form:

```
relation XOR(p,q) is
    [PROPOSITION: *p] [PROPOSITION: *q]
    ¬[ ¬[*p] ¬[*q]] ¬[[*p] [*q]].
```

Some of the relations in the starter set can also be defined in terms of others. The relation BFOR, for example, could be used to show that the events in one context occurred before those in another context. BFOR can be defined in terms of the PTIM (point in time) and SUCC (successor) relations:

```
relation BFOR(x,y) is
    [SITUATION:*x]→(PTIM)→[TIME]→(SUCC)→
                        [TIME]←(PTIM)←[SITUATION:*y].
```

This definition says that BFOR links a situation x to a situation y where x has a point in time, which has a successor, which is the point in time of the situation y. Whenever the relation BFOR occurs in a graph, it could be replaced by the sequence of concepts and relations from x to y. That replacement is called *relational expansion*.

The past tense marker PAST is a monadic relation defined in terms of point of time (PTIM), successor (SUCC), and the contextually defined time #now. Following is its definition:

```
relation PAST(x) is
        [SITUATION:*x]→(PTIM)→[TIME]→(SUCC)→[TIME:#now].
```

This definition says that the situation x is past if its point in time is a time that has as successor the contextual time #now. More complex tenses, such as past perfect, refer to multiple reference times, including the time #now of the utterance and the time of some other event that serves as a comparison.

Frame systems allow hyphenated attributes like COUNTRY-OF-RESIDENCE. Such attributes could be defined as two-place relations in conceptual graphs:

```
relation COUNTRY-OF-RESIDENCE(x,y) is
        [PERSON: *x]→(STAT)→[LIVE]→(IN)→[COUNTRY: *y].
```

This definition has two formal parameters x and y, where the person x is in the state of live in a country y. With this definition, the relation (COUNTRY-OF-RESIDENCE) could be used in conceptual graphs in the same way as the attribute in a frame system. But whenever the details are relevant, the definition could be expanded to recover the implicit concepts and relations.

Recursive definitions of types and relations are also permitted. In database systems, recursive relations are necessary for certain kinds of queries. The relation REPORT-TO, for example, might be defined recursively in terms of the relation MANAGER-OF:

```
relation REPORT-TO(x,y) is
    [EMPLOYEE:*x] [EMPLOYEE:*y]
    [[*y]→(MANAGER-OF)→[*x]]-
        (OR)-
    [[*y]→(MANAGER-OF)→[EMPLOYEE]←(REPORT-TO)←[*x]].
```

This definition says that employee x reports to employee y if either y is the manager of x or y is the manager of an employee that x reports to. With this relation, the question *Who are the employees who report to Tom?* could be translated to the following query graph:

```
[EMPLOYEE: {*}?]→(REPORT-TO)→[EMPLOYEE: Tom].
```

To answer this question, the system would have to translate the query graph to a language like Prolog that supports recursion. But in doing the translation, the compiler would have to generate code that avoids getting the system into a recursive loop: it would have to test MANAGER-OF before invoking the recursive relation REPORTS-TO. Like predicate calculus, conceptual graphs are a purely declarative form of logic. Prolog, however, is a logic-like language that depends on an interpreter with a fixed order of execution. In translating a declarative language into Prolog, the compiler may have to reorder the code to avoid getting the Prolog interpreter into a loop.

1.9   QUANTIFICATION

In natural languages, quantification has three parts: a *quantifier*, a *restrictor*, and a *scope*. The quantifier may be a word like *every* or phrase like *almost all*. The restrictor determines the domain over which quantification ranges. It can be a single word like *elephant* in the sentence "Every elephant has a long nose", or it can be a phrase like "shiny new penny" in the sentence "Place every shiny new penny in the box". The scope is the context over which the quantification extends; it may be a phrase, a sentence, or even an entire paragraph. The quantifier, the restrictor, and the scope make up the *tripartite structure* of quantification.

In conceptual graphs, the three parts are shown explicitly. The quantifier itself goes into the referent field of a concept, the restrictor goes into the type field, and the scope is the entire context in which the quantifier occurs. For a simple quantifying phrase like *every elephant*, the restrictor is just the type label in the concept [ELEPHANT: ∀]. With restrictive modifiers, however, a graph for the entire phrase or clause goes in a λ-expression in the type field. As an example, consider the sentence "Every elephant that performs in a circus earns money". The following graph is not a correct representation:

```
[ELEPHANT: ∀]-
     (AGNT) ← [PERFORM] → (IN) → [CIRCUS]
     (AGNT) ← [EARN] → (PTNT) → [MONEY].
```

In this graph, the quantifier ∀ ranges over all elephants. This graph represents a very different sentence, *Every elephant performs in a circus and earns money.*

The restrictor in the original sentence is the entire phrase *elephant that performs in a circus*, which defines a subtype of elephant from which the quantifier ∀ selects. To restrict the scope of ∀, one could define the type CIRCUS-ELEPHANT as a subtype of ELEPHANT that performs in a circus:

```
type CIRCUS-ELEPHANT(x) is
     [ELEPHANT: *x] ← (AGNT) ← [PERFORM] → (IN) → [CIRCUS].
```

Then the next graph represents the sentence *Every circus elephant earns money*:

```
[CIRCUS-ELEPHANT: ∀] ← (AGNT) ← [EARN] → (PTNT) → [MONEY].
```

If the type CIRCUS-ELEPHANT occurs frequently, it is reasonable to define a special type label for it. But it is unreasonable to define a new type label for every restrictive relative clause. Instead, the defining λ-expression can be placed directly in the type field of the concept:

```
[[ELEPHANT: λ] ← (AGNT) ← [PERFORM] → (IN) → [CIRCUS]: ∀]-
     (AGNT) ← [EARN] → (PTNT) → [MONEY].
```

Since the symbol λ marks [ELEPHANT] as the formal parameter, the graph is read with the noun *elephant* as the head of the noun phrase and the remainder of the defining graph in the relative clause: *Every elephant that performs in a circus earns money.* But if λ were placed in the concept [CIRCUS], the noun *circus* would become the head:

```
[[ELEPHANT] ← (AGNT) ← [PERFORM] → (IN) → [CIRCUS: λ]: ∀]-
     (AGNT) ← [EARN] → (PTNT) → [MONEY].
```

This graph may be read "Every circus in which elephants perform earns money".

In English, the scope of quantifiers is determined partly by the syntax of the sentence and partly by the *precedence level* of the quantifier itself. Consider the next two sentences:

Every man in Department 99 married a woman from Boston.

A woman from Boston married every man in Department 99.

In the first sentence, the universal quantifier on *man* includes the existential quantifier on *woman* within its scope: for every man in that department, there exists a woman from Boston, and most likely a different woman for each man. In the second sentence, the existential is outside the scope of the universal, and that same woman must have married every one of the men. In these two examples, the scope of the quantifiers is determined by the syntax of the sentences. But sometimes, the effect of syntax can be overruled by a quantifier that has higher precedence, as in the following sentence:

Every man in Department 99 married a certain woman from Boston.

Words like *certain* or *particular* have a strange status in English: They do not refer to any type of thing or event in the world, and they do not map into a quantifier or other operator in logic. In this example, the effect is to increase the precedence of the existential quantifier in order to give it wider scope. The effect of such words on the scope of quantifiers has been studied in detail by Hornstein (1985).

Since conceptual graphs are intended as an intermediate language between language and logic, some of their features are designed for a direct mapping to language, and others are designed for a direct mapping to predicate calculus. For the scope of quantifiers, the nesting of contexts has an exact correspondence to the order of quantifiers in a formula. But to simplify the mapping to and from natural languages, different quantifiers also have precedence levels that correspond to the different levels in natural language. The implicit existential quantifier, which corresponds to the indefinite article *a*, normally has the lowest precedence. Whenever a concept with a universal quantifier ∀ occurs in the same context as the implicit existential, ∀ includes the existential in its scope. As an example, consider the sentence *Every man married a woman*, which has the following graph:

```
[MAN: ∀]←(AGNT)←[MARRY]→(PTNT)→[WOMAN].
```

The ∀ quantifier takes precedence over the implicit existentials on [MARRY] and [WOMAN], and the corresponding formula in predicate calculus puts ∀ first:

$$(\forall x)(\exists y)(\exists z)(man(x) \supset (marry(y) \wedge woman(z) \wedge (agnt(y,x) \wedge ptnt(y,z)))).$$

This formula says that for every man x, there exists an instance of marrying y and a woman z, where y has agent x and patient z. But if there is only one woman whom every man married, the existential quantifier on [WOMAN] could be placed in a context outside the context in which [MAN: ∀] occurs:

```
[WOMAN: *x]
[  [MAN: ∀]←(EXPR)←[MARRY]→(PTNT)→[*x]  ].
```

The variable $*x$ shows that [*x] in the nested context is coreferent with the concept [WOMAN: *x] in the outer context. This graph represents the sentence *There exists a woman, and every man married her*.

Although nesting is a general way of showing scope of quantifiers, it can sometimes obscure the underlying sentence structure. Consider the sentence *Every man married a certain woman*, where the word *certain* causes the existential quantifier to have wide scope. Instead of showing the scope by means of nesting, the notation @certain may be used to represent an existential quantifier with high precedence:

```
[MAN: ∀]←(AGNT)←[MARRY]→(PTNT)→[WOMAN: @certain].
```

The quantifiers on the three concepts in this graph each have a different precedence: [MARRY] has the default existential quantifier with low precedence; [MAN: ∀] has a universal quantifier with medium precedence; and [WOMAN: @certain] has an existential quantifier with high precedence. When the graph is translated to predicate calculus by ϕ, the effect of the precedence level is to move the quantifier for [WOMAN] to the front of the formula:

$$(\exists z)(\forall x)(\exists y)(woman(z) \wedge (man(x) \supset (marry(y) \wedge agnt(y,x) \wedge ptnt(y,z)))).$$

The quantifier @certain is not a primitive in the conceptual graph theory, since it can always be replaced by an implicit existential quantifier in a containing context. When the graph containing @certain is expanded, the previous graph with [WOMAN: *x] in the outer context is derived. The replacement of precedence levels with nests of contexts is the first step in the definition of ϕ in Section 12.

The universal quantifier ∀ can also be expanded into a nest of contexts with only the implicit existential. As an example, consider the sentence *Every farmer who owns a donkey beats it*, which may be represented by the following graph:

```
[[FARMER: λ]→(STAT)→[OWN]→(PTNT)→[DONKEY]: ∀]-
     (AGNT)←[BEAT]→(PTNT)→[¬HUMAN: #].
```

The universal quantifier ∀ is defined by its expansion into an existential quantifier and two negations. That expansion is done in three steps: first, draw two negative contexts around the whole graph; then move the universally quantified concept into the space between the inner and outer negations, leaving the concept [⊤] in its original place; finally, replace the quantifier ∀ with a coreference link to the concept [⊤]. Following is the result of expanding the above graph:

```
¬[ [[FARMER: λ]→(STAT)→[OWN]→(PTNT)→[DONKEY]: *x]
   ¬[ [*x]←(AGNT)←[BEAT]→(PTNT)→[¬HUMAN:#] ]].
```

Now the λ-expression can be expanded because the referent field contains only a simple existential quantifier:

```
¬[ [FARMER: *x]→(STAT)→[OWN]→(PTNT)→[DONKEY]
   ¬[ [*x]←(AGNT)←[BEAT]→(PTNT)→[¬HUMAN:#] ]].
```

The next step is to resolve the # marker to [DONKEY] in order to derive the equivalent of Fig. 1.12. Finally, the two negations can be replaced by the IF-THEN form. The result is the following graph, which may be read "If a farmer x owns a donkey y, then x beats y":

```
IF  [FARMER: *x]→(STAT)→[OWN]→(PTNT)→[DONKEY: *y]
THEN  [*x]←(AGNT)←[BEAT]→(PTNT)→[*y].
```

Plurals in natural languages are generalized quantifiers, and conceptual graphs represent them in the same way as other quantifiers. As examples, consider the next three sentences:

Every elephant that performs in a circus earns money.
Some elephants that perform in a circus earn money.
Many elephants that perform in a circus earn money.

These sentences have similar syntax, and the corresponding conceptual graphs represent them in parallel ways. Following is the graph for *every elephant*:

```
[[ELEPHANT: λ]←(AGNT)←[PERFORM]→(IN)→[CIRCUS]: ∀]-
     (AGNT)←[EARN]→(PTNT)→[MONEY].
```

When this graph is translated to the predicate calculus, the restrictor becomes the antecedent of an implication:

$$(\forall x)(\forall y)(\forall z)((elephant(x) \land perform(y) \land circus(z) \land agnt(y, x) \land in(y, z)) \supset$$
$$(\exists u)(\exists v)(earn(u) \land money(v) \land agnt(u, x) \land ptnt(u, v)).$$

The plural referent {*} is a kind of generalized quantifier that goes in the same field as ∀. Following is the graph for *some elephants*:

```
[[ELEPHANT: λ#]←(AGNT)←[PERFORM]→(IN)→[CIRCUS]: {*}]-
   (AGNT)←[EARN]→(PTNT)→[MONEY].
```

This graph is structurally similar to the previous one, but the formula in predicate calculus is quite different:

$$(\exists S)(set(S) \land (\forall x \in S)(\exists y)(\exists z)(\exists u)(\exists v)$$
$$(elephant(x) \land perform(y) \land circus(z) \land agnt(y, x) \land in(y, z) \land$$
$$\land earn(u) \land money(v) \land agnt(u, x) \land ptnt(u, v))).$$

The quantifying word *many* behaves syntactically like *some*, but it has no counterpart in the standard predicate calculus. In conceptual graphs, it is represented by the symbol @many:

```
[[ELEPHANT: λ]←(AGNT)←[PERFORM]→(IN)→
   [CIRCUS]:{*}@many]→(AGNT)←[EARN]→(PTNT)→[MONEY].
```

Semantically, a graph with the quantifier @many has denotation *true* if a large number of entities that satisfy the λ-expression (elephants that perform in a circus) also satisfy the conditions of the attached subgraph (earn money). But what is considered a large number depends on the type: a group of many ants is likely to have more members than a group of many elephants.

1.10 HIGHER ORDER TYPES

Natural languages have *higher-order words*, whose instances are types rather individuals. Examples from biology include *kingdom, phylum, class, order, family, genus*, and *species*; from automobile registration, *make* and *model*; and for characteristics, *color, shape, quality*, and *condition*. A failure to notice the difference between first-order and second-order words leads to fallacious syllogisms like the following:

> *Clyde is an elephant.*
> *Elephant is a species.*   *Therefore,*
> *Clyde is a species.*

The fallacy results from a *nondistributed middle term*: the phrase *an elephant* in the first premise does not refer to the same thing as the noun *elephant* in the second premise. With the article, *an elephant* refers to an individual of type ELEPHANT. Without the article, *elephant* behaves like a proper name for the entire elephant kind or type. Following are three more sentences that illustrate the same phenomenon, where a count noun with an indefinite article refers to the individual, but without the article refers to the type:

> *Fred's car is a Camaro.*
> *Camaro is a type of Chevrolet.*
> *Every Camaro is a Chevrolet.*

The first sentence refers to an individual car. The second sentence relates the type CAMARO to the type CHEVROLET. The third sentence again refers to instances: it means that every instance of a Camaro is also an instance of a Chevrolet. The second sentence implies the third, but it does so by making a statement about types that would require a higher-order logic. The third statement requires only first-order logic about individuals.

In conceptual graphs, the concept [ELEPHANT] represents the phrase *an elephant*, and the concept [TYPE: elephant] represents *elephant* without the article. The following graph represents *Clyde is an elephant*:

```
[T: Clyde]- - -[ELEPHANT].
```

The concept [T: Clyde] has the type T, which is the top of the type hierarchy, and the proper name *Clyde* as its referent. It implies that there exists something named Clyde of some undefined type. The concept [ELEPHANT] says that there exists an elephant. Then the coreference link that connects the two concepts says that they both refer to the same individual. The ϕ operator maps this graph to the following formula:

$$(\exists x)(elephant(x) \land x = Clyde).$$

When two coreferent concepts occur in the same context, they may be joined. In this case, the result would be [ELEPHANT: Clyde], which corresponds to the simplified formula elephant(Clyde). The second premise, *Elephant is a species*, maps to a conceptual graph in the same way:

```
[TYPE: elephant]- - -[SPECIES].
```

This is a higher-order statement about types. Words like *type* and *species* do not refer to individuals, but to types of individuals. Instead of proper names in their referent fields, concepts of those types take other type labels, written in lower case to show that they are not being used as ordinary names. This graph corresponds to the following formula:

$$(\exists x)(species(x) \land type(elephant) \land x = elephant).$$

Since SPECIES is a subtype of TYPE, the two concepts can be joined to form [SPECIES: elephant], which corresponds to the formula species(elephant). These graphs and the formulas derived from them correctly capture the meaning of the English sentences while avoiding the fallacies. Another important relation is KIND, which relates a type label in the type field of a concept to the type in the referent field of another concept:

```
[ELEPHANT] → (KIND) → [TYPE: elephant].
```

This graph may be read "An elephant is of type elephant". The KIND relation links any concept *c* to a concept of type TYPE whose referent is the type label of *c* or some supertype of *c*. In effect, the KIND relation allows a type to be written in the referent field where it is possible to quantify over it: it allows conceptual graphs to represent higher-order logic.

A common issue that comes up in both database design and knowledge engineering is the proper way to represent colors, shapes, and other characteristics. Should the English word *red* be represented by a monadic predicate, a type whose instances are various patches of redness, or an individual entity that can occur as the value of a COLOR slot in a frame? Fig. 1.13 has three conceptual graphs, each of which shows one possible way of representing the English phrase *a red ball*.

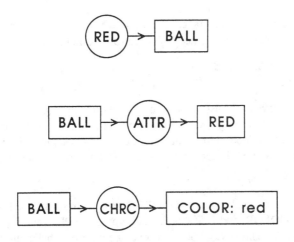

Fig. 1.13 - Three possible ways of representing a red ball.

The first graph has a monadic relation for the adjective *red* attached to a concept for *a ball*. The formula operator ϕ would map this graph into the kind of formula that is usually given in a textbook on logic:

$$(\exists x)(red(x) \wedge ball(x)).$$

This formula says that there exists an x that is red and is also a ball. Linguists with an inclination towards logic tend to adopt a similar representation. Those with an inclination towards case grammar tend to represent adjectives and verbs as concepts linked by case relations to the concepts expressed by nouns. That representation corresponds to the second graph in Fig. 1.13, which says that a ball has attribute (ATTR) red. When translated into predicate calculus by the ϕ operator, both concept nodes are assigned existential quantifiers and the relation (ATTR) becomes a dyadic predicate:

$$(\exists x)(\exists y)(ball(x) \wedge red(y) \wedge attr(x, y)).$$

This formula says that there exist two entities x and y, where x is a ball, y is an instance of redness, and the attr predicate relates x to y. In databases and frame systems, the most common approach is to define a COLOR domain with values such as red, blue, or green. That approach corresponds to the third graph in Fig. 1.13, which treats *red* as the name of an instance of type COLOR. In predicate calculus, that graph corresponds to the following formula:

$$(\exists x)(ball(x) \wedge color(red) \wedge chrc(x, red)).$$

This formula says that there exists a ball x, red is a color, and x has characteristic red.

With conceptual graphs, the primary design guideline is to take the simplest linguistic form as basic (what linguists call the *unmarked form*). The second guideline is to map content words (most nouns, verbs, adjectives, and adverbs) into concept nodes, and to map function words (prepositions, conjunctions, and inflectional endings) into conceptual relations. According to these guidelines, the basic representation for the phrase *a red ball* would be the second graph in Fig. 1.13:

```
[BALL]→(ATTR)→[RED].
```

This is the form that has an instance of ball linked to an instance of redness. The relation RED in the first graph may be defined by the following definition:

```
relation RED(x) is
    [ENTITY: *x]→(ATTR)→[RED].
```

This definition says that RED is a monadic relation that applies to entities that have attribute RED. The third graph, which corresponds to the usual database representation, treats red not as a type label, but as an individual of the second-order type COLOR. The conceptual relation (KIND) is needed to relate type labels to the names of types:

```
[RED]→(KIND)→[TYPE: red].
```

The type label RED is a subtype of COLORED: everything that is red is colored. But red is an instance of COLOR, and COLOR is a subtype of TYPE. Therefore, red must also be an instance of TYPE. The next graph represents the phrase "a ball colored the color red":

```
[BALL]→(ATTR)→[COLORED]→(KIND)→[COLOR: red].
```

This combination of the ATTR relation and the KIND relation frequently occurs in knowledge representations. The characteristic relation (CHRC) may be defined as an abbreviation for that combination:

```
relation CHRC(x,y) is
    [T: *x]→(ATTR)→[T]→(KIND)→[TYPE: *y].
```

The universal type T is used in this definition to avoid placing restrictions on the types of concepts that can have attributes or that may be used as attributes. The definition says that CHRC relates an x of any type, which has an attribute of any type to the type y of the attribute. With the CHRC relation, the relationship between the ball and the color red may be represented by the third graph in Fig. 1.13:

```
[BALL]→(CHRC)→[COLOR: red].
```

This graph may be read "A ball of color red". The ATTR relation links the ball to concepts of type RED and COLORED, which are derived from the adjective *red* and the participle *colored*. The CHRC relation links the ball to a concept of type COLOR, which is derived from a noun. That is a common distinction between attributes and characteristics: attributes typically represent adjectives, and characteristics represent second-order nouns, whose referents are derived from the corresponding adjectives.

All the biological ranks, from kingdom to species, are types whose instances are other types: [KINGDOM: animal], [GENUS: felis], and [SPECIES: felis-catus]. Each rank represents a subtype of TYPE, but they are not subtypes of one another: FELIS-CATUS is a subtype of FELIS, but SPECIES is not a subtype of GENUS. The *every*-test can be used to check subtypes:

Every felis catus is a felis.
Every felis is a carnivore.
Every carnivore is an animal.

But a species is not a genus. The same pattern holds for make and model: Chevrolet is an instance of make, and Camaro is an instance of model; every Camaro is a Chevrolet; but a model is not a make. Besides second-order words like *species* and *model*, English also has third-order words like *rank* and *characteristic*:

First order:	A box is a rectangle.	A felis is a carnivore.
Second order:	Rectangle is a shape.	Felis is a genus.
Third order:	Shape is a characteristic.	Genus is a rank.

All first-order types are instances of the second-order type TYPE. All second-order types, such as KINGDOM and SHAPE, are subtypes of TYPE. The second-order types are instances of third-order types: [RANK: kingdom] and [CHARACTERISTIC: shape]. Those third-order types may be subtypes of a more general third-order type, say TYPE'. But the higher-order types cannot be subtypes of $\top$, the top of the first-order hierarchy; otherwise, a contradiction would arise. If TYPE and TYPE' were in the same hierarchy as $\top$, it would be possible to define the paradoxical type of all types that are not instances of themselves. To avoid that paradox, types of different orders should be kept in disjoint hierarchies.

1.11 PLURALS

In predicate calculus, every plural noun phrase requires two quantified variables: one that represents a set, and one that ranges over the elements of the set. Those quantifiers may interact with other quantifiers in complex ways. As an example, consider the sentence *Every trailer truck has 18 wheels*. The universal quantifier for *every trailer truck* has precedence over the existential quantifier for the set of wheels. Following is the conceptual graph:

[TRAILERTRUCK: $\forall$]→(PART)→[WHEEL: {*}@18].

As before, the symbol {*} represents some unspecified entities of type WHEEL, and the operator @18 says that there are 18 of them. The operator ϕ maps this graph to the following formula:

$$(\forall x)(trailertruck(x) \supset (\exists S)(set(S) \land count(S, 18) \land$$
$$(\forall y \in S)(wheel(y) \land part(x, y))).$$

This formula has three quantifiers: a universal quantifier $(\forall x)$ that ranges over trailer trucks, an existential quantifier $(\exists S)$ for a set of wheels for each x, and a universal quantifier $(\forall y)$ that ranges over wheels in S. In this case, the universal quantifier over trailer trucks includes the other two quantifiers in its scope.

For the trailertruck example, the quantifiers for the set of wheels had narrower scope than the quantifier over trailer trucks. But sometimes the quantifiers associated with a plural noun have wider scope than the quantifiers for other things in the sentence. In such cases, they are said to *distribute* over the other things. To show the scope of quantifiers, the plural referent {*} may have a prefix that shows a distributive, a collective, or a cumulative interpretation:

- *Distributive*: Dist{*} is the distributive symbol that implies the widest scope for the quantifiers associated with the set. Each element of the set participates separately in the pattern of relationships expressed by the sentence.

- *Collective*: Col{*} is the collective symbol that implies the narrowest scope for the quantifiers associated with the set. All the elements of the set participate together in the relationships expressed in the sentence.

- *Default*: {*} makes the least commitment; it is consistent with either the collective or the distributive interpretations and other states intermediate between them.

- *Cumulative*: Cum{*} is the cumulative symbol. It indicates that the entire collection participates in the attached relations as a single unit.

The symbol {*} is called a *generic plural* because it gives no indication of which individuals it contains. A specific plural like *Bill and Mary* would be represented {*Bill, Mary*}, and a partially specified plural like *Bill, Mary, and others* would be represented {*Bill, Mary*}. All of these forms may occur in the referent field of a concept with a prefix like Dist and a numeric count, as in [PERSON: Dist{*Bill, Mary*}@5], which would represent five persons distributively including Bill, Mary, and others.

For the sentence *Nine ladies are dancing*, the default representation gives no indication of whether the ladies are dancing the same dance or separate dances. But the sentence *Nine ladies are each dancing* suggests that they are dancing separately. Therefore, the prefix Dist with the plural referent indicates that interpretation:

```
[LADY: Dist{*}@9]←(AGNT)←[DANCE].
```

This graph indicates that the ladies distribute over the dances: for each lady there is an instance of dancing that is different from the dances by all the other ladies. That condition is difficult to state with only the quantifiers $\exists$ and $\forall$. To represent such relationships succinctly, the quantifiers $\exists!$ for exactly one and $\exists!!$ for uniqueness must be introduced. The quantifier $\exists!$ is defined by the following formula:

$$(\exists!x)P(x) \equiv (\exists x)(P(x) \wedge (\forall y)(P(y) \supset x = y)).$$

The quantifier $\exists!$ indicates that there exists one and only one object that satisfies the condition. But for the distributive interpretation of plurals, the $\exists!!$ quantifier is needed to show that for each lady x, there is a unique dance y that is different from the dance for any other lady. That quantifier is defined by the following formula:

$$(\forall x)(\exists!!y)P(x,y) \equiv$$
$$(\forall x)(\exists y)(P(x,y) \wedge (\forall z)(P(x,z) \supset y = z) \wedge (\forall w)(P(w,y) \supset x = w)).$$

This definition takes into account the dependency of y on x. If y depends on several variables $x_1, x_2, \ldots$ the definition can be generalized by treating x and w as vectors of variables.

Using the $\exists!!$ quantifier, the ϕ operator can generate the following formula for the ladies dancing distributively:

$$(\exists S)(set(S) \wedge count(S,9) \wedge$$
$$(\forall x \in S)(\exists!!y)(lady(x) \wedge dance(y) \wedge agnt(y,x))).$$

In this formula, $(\exists y)$ is replaced by $(\exists!!y)$ to indicate that for each lady x, there is a separate dance y. For *Nine ladies are dancing together*, the prefix Col indicates a collective interpretation:

[LADY: Col{*}@9]←(AGNT)←[DANCE].

Col causes the quantifiers for the set to have narrower scope than the quantifier for the dance:

$$(\exists y)(dance(y) \land (\exists S)(set(S) \land count(S,9) \land$$
$$(\forall x \in S)(lady(x) \land agnt(y,x)))).$$

In these examples, the different interpretations are represented by local changes to the graph, but the ϕ operator causes those local changes to propagate throughout the formula. The default reading that there may or may not be a separate instance of dancing for each lady is consistent with either the distributive or the collective reading. But the distributive and collective readings are inconsistent with one another.

The cumulative prefix may be used to expand the count modifier to a concept of its own. In the previous graphs for the nine ladies, the count @9 is used in the referent field of a concept of type LADY. But in order to say that there are more lords than ladies, the count must be in the referent field of a separate concept. The following graph says that the set of ladies cumulatively has a characteristic cardinality of 9:

[LADY: Cum{*}]→(CHRC)→[CARDINALITY: 9].

This graph is the expanded form of the concept [LADY: {*}@9]. It implies that the set of ladies taken together has a cardinality 9, but not that each lady has a cardinality 9. The concept type CARDINALITY is a subtype of INTEGER: it is a role type In the mapping by ϕ, this graph becomes

$$(\exists S)(set(S) \land (\forall x \in S)lady(x) \land cardinality(9) \land chrc(S,9)).$$

The predicate $count(S,n)$, which was used in the previous examples, is an abbreviation for $(chrc(S,n) \land cardinality(n))$. The following graph says that the cardinality of the lords is greater than the cardinality of the ladies:

[LORD: Cum{*}]→(CHRC)→[CARDINALITY]→(>)→
           [CARDINALITY]←(CHRC)←[LADY: Cum{*}].

The subgraph between the lords and the ladies could be used to define a MORETHAN relation:

relation MORETHAN(x,y) is
    [T:Cum{*}*x]→(CHRC)→[CARDINALITY]→(>)→
           [CARDINALITY]←(CHRC)←[T: Cum{*}*y].

Then the sentence *There are more lords leaping than ladies dancing* could be represented by the following graph:

[LORD: {*}*x]←(AGNT)←[LEAP]

[LADY: {*}*y]←(AGNT)←[DANCE]

[*x]→(MORETHAN)→[*y].

This graph may be read "Some lords x are leaping, some ladies y are dancing, and there are more x than y". This example uses the default form of $\{*\}$ in the first two lines, but the definition of MORETHAN implies the cumulative form of the plural. Coreference links like x or y show that both coreferent concepts refer to the same individual or collection of individuals, but each concept may have a different prefix for the plural marker $\{*\}$.

With two plural nouns in the same sentence, the number of interactions between quantifiers increases further. Consider the sentence *Five blocks are supported by three pyramids*. Since pyramids have pointed tops, a person could assume that the pyramids must be used collectively to support the blocks. Nothing is implied, however, about the number of blocks supported by each group of three pyramids. Following is the conceptual graph for that sentence:

```
[BLOCK: {*}@5]←(PTNT)←[SUPPORT]→
       (INST)→[PYRAMID: Col{*}@3].
```

This graph says that five blocks are the patient of support and three blocks collectively are the instrument of support. The operator ϕ maps this graph to a formula that shows the scope of quantifiers explicitly:

$$(\exists S)(set(S) \wedge count(S,5) \wedge (\forall x \in S)(block(x)\wedge$$
$$(\exists T)(set(T) \wedge count(T,3) \wedge (\exists z)(support(z)\wedge$$
$$(\forall y \in T)(pyramid(y) \wedge ptnt(z,x) \wedge inst(z,y)))))).$$

This formula says that there exists a set S of 5 blocks, and for each x in S, there is a set of 3 pyramids and an instance z of support, where the block is the patient of support and each of the three pyramids is the instrument of support. The universal quantifier on blocks ($\forall x$) has wide scope, including the existential quantifier on the instances of support and the quantifiers on the pyramids. The universal quantifier on pyramids ($\forall y$) has the narrowest scope. This formula permits, but does not require the instance of supporting and the set of pyramids to be different for each block.

The distributive interpretation requires a unique instance of supporting and set of pyramids for each block. In English, it may be represented by the word *each* in the sentence *Five blocks are each supported by three pyramids*. That word is represented by the prefix Dist in the conceptual graph:

```
[BLOCK:Dist{*}@5]←(PTNT)←[SUPPORT]→
       (INST)→[PYRAMID:Col{*}@3].
```

The formula for the distributive interpretation has two slight changes from the default; it uses the quantifiers $\exists!!T$ and $\exists!!z$ instead of the simple existentials:

$$(\exists S)(set(S) \wedge count(S,5) \wedge (\forall x \in S)(block(x)\wedge$$
$$(\exists!!T)(set(T) \wedge count(T,3) \wedge (\exists!!z)(support(z)\wedge$$
$$(\forall y \in T)(pyramid(y) \wedge ptnt(z,x) \wedge inst(z,y)))))).$$

Whereas the default formula allows multiple blocks to share the same set of pyramids and instance of support, the quantifiers $\exists!!T$ and $\exists!!z$ require each block to have its own set of pyramids T and instance of support z. This formula implies that there are exactly 5×3 or 15 pyramids.

The collective interpretation implies that all the blocks collectively are supported by one set of three pyramids, also acting collectively. In English, it is suggested by the word *all* in the sentence *Five blocks are all supported by three pyramids*. The conceptual graph has the prefix Col for both the blocks and the pyramids:

```
[BLOCK: Col{*}@5]←(PTNT)←[SUPPORT]→
         (INST)→[PYRAMID: Col{*}@3].
```

In the corresponding formula, the quantifier $\forall x$ over blocks and the quantifier $\forall y$ over pyramids both have the narrowest scope:

$$(\exists z)(support(z) \wedge (\exists S)(set(S) \wedge count(S, 5)\wedge$$
$$(\exists T)(set(T) \wedge count(T, 3) \wedge (\forall x \in S)(block(x)\wedge$$
$$(\forall y \in T)(pyramid(y) \wedge ptnt(z, x) \wedge inst(z, y)))))).$$

This formula shows a single instance of support z, where all the blocks are the patient of z and all the pyramids are the instrument of z. It implies that there are exactly 3 pyramids.

The distributive interpretation, which implies 15 pyramids, is inconsistent with the collective interpretation, which implies 3 pyramids. Both of them, however, are consistent with the default, which allows 3, 6, 9, 12, or 15 pyramids. In general, the default makes the weakest assumption: it is implied by either the distributive or the collective assumptions. When English sentences are mapped to conceptual graphs, the default symbol may be inserted in the referent field for any plural noun. As the representation is refined, the prefixes Col or Dist may be added. Sometimes the prefixes are determined by explicit words like *each, all,* or *together*. But sometimes background knowledge must be used, such as the knowledge that the pointed top of a pyramid cannot support a block by itself and three of them must be used collectively.

The cumulative prefix is used when the entire collection participates as a single unit. As an example, consider the sentence *Four tires cost $75 each*. The Dist prefix would be used to show that each tire costs $75 by itself:

```
[TIRE: Dist{*}@4]→(STAT)→[COST]→(PTNT)→[MONEY:@ $75].
```

The corresponding formula in predicate calculus would have unique existential quantifiers for the cost y and the money z within the scope of the quantifier x over the tires:

$$(\exists S)(set(S) \wedge count(S, 4) \wedge (\forall x \in S)(tire(x)\wedge$$
$$(\exists!! y)(\exists!! z)(cost(y) \wedge money(z) \wedge stat(x, y) \wedge ptnt(y, z) \wedge measure(z, 75)))).$$

This graph indicates that for each tire x, there is a unique instance of costing y and a unique instance of money z; but each instance of money z has the same measure, $75. In a cumulative interpretation, the sentence *Four tires cost $300* would be represented by the following graph:

```
[TIRE: Cum{*}@4]→(STAT)→[COST]→(PTNT)→[MONEY: @$300].
```

In this graph, the Cum prefix causes the set of tires as a group to cost $300. In the corresponding formula, the cost y and money z are not within the scope of the quantifier x over the tires:

$$(\exists S)(set(S) \wedge count(S,4) \wedge (\forall x \in S)tire(x)\wedge$$
$$(\exists y)(\exists z)(cost(y)\wedge money(z)\wedge stat(S,y)\wedge ptnt(y,z)\wedge measure(z,\$300))).$$

The Cum prefix is used in operations like count, average, or total, which are performed on an entire set. Operations that apply to individual elements use the Dist or Col prefixes. The default {*} is normally used when there is insufficient information to indicate the exact scope. A natural language analyzer (or a person) might either use background knowledge or ask the speaker to clarify the statement.

As these examples illustrate, getting the quantifiers correct in predicate calculus is a tedious, error-prone task. In conceptual graphs, quantification is specified by concept nodes rather than operators placed in front of a formula or subformula. This difference makes it possible for an entire noun phrase together with all of its implicit or explicit quantifiers to be mapped into a single concept node. Consequently, the mapping from English to the graphs is more direct; then the formula operator ϕ can take care of the details of sorting out the quantifiers and their scope.

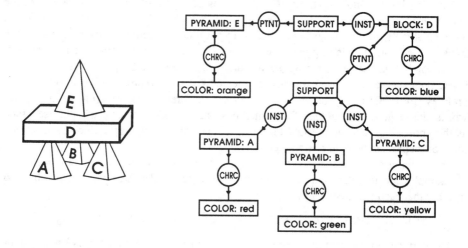

Fig. 1.14 - A structure described by a conceptual graph.

1.12   ACTORS

When everything is represented in conceptual graphs, all computations and inferences can be performed by copying, matching, and modifying graphs. But to interact with programs in other languages, to access an external database, or to perform any kind of input and output, conceptual graphs must be linked to something outside the conceptual processor. Those links are supported by diamond-shaped nodes called *actors*. The diamond shape emphasizes the similarity to the relation nodes in entity-relationship diagrams. But actors are more general than database relations: it is irrelevant to the conceptual graph whether an actor produces a value by computation, by table lookup, or by receiving a message from an external source.

Without actor nodes, a question mark in a concept node can only be answered by matching that concept to some other concept that has a known referent. As an example, consider the next two questions and their corresponding conceptual graphs:

1. *What pyramid is supported by a block?*

    [PYRAMID: ?] ← (PTNT) ← [SUPPORT] → (INST) → [BLOCK].

2. *What color object is supported by something green?*

    [COLOR: ?] ← (CHRC) ← [OBJECT] ← (PTNT) ← [SUPPORT] →
                 (INST) → [ENTITY] → (CHRC) → [COLOR: green].

Each of these questions is mapped to a *query graph* - a conceptual graph that contains a question mark in the referent field of one or more concepts. For the first query graph, the concept types, relations, and directions of arcs exactly match the top part of Fig. 1.14. The answer is the referent E in the concept [PYRAMID: E], which matches [PYRAMID: ?] in the query graph. Sometimes, however, the types do not match exactly. For the second query graph, there is an approximate match extending from Block D of color blue to Pyramid B of color green. The fact that the query graph is perfectly straight, but the path through Fig. 1.14 bends around corners is not significant, since the placement of the nodes in a diagram is irrelevant. What is significant is that the match cannot be completed until the type OBJECT is restricted to the subtype BLOCK and the type ENTITY is restricted to PYRAMID. The operation of changing the graphs in order to complete the pattern match is called *maximal join*. It is the graph analog to the unification algorithm used in theorem provers (see Section 3.5 of *Conceptual Structures*). Since graph matching or unification is used in a great many applications, special algorithms have been developed to make it efficient (Levinson and Ellis 1992).

OBJECT-LIST   SUPPORTED-BY

OBJECT	SHAPE	COLOR	SUPPORTEE	SUPPORT-OBJ
A	pyramid	red	D	A
B	pyramid	green	D	B
C	pyramid	yellow	D	C
D	block	blue	E	D
E	pyramid	orange		

Fig. 1.15 - A relational database for the structure in Fig. 1.14.

With a relational database, the information in Fig. 1.14 may be stored in tables whose shape is very different from a graph. Fig. 1.15 shows a database with two relations: OBJECT-LIST is a table with domains OBJECT, SHAPE, and COLOR; SUPPORTED-BY is a table with domains SUPPORTEE and SUPPORT-OBJ. The relations OBJECT-LIST and SUPPORTED-BY do not correspond to any of the circles in Fig. 1.14, and the domain

COLOR is the only one that corresponds to any of the concept types in Fig. 1.14. Yet the data in the two tables of Fig. 1.15 can still be represented by a conceptual graph: the two tables OBJECT-LIST and SUPPORTED-BY become conceptual relations; and the three domains OBJECT, SHAPE, and COLOR become concept types. Fig. 1.16 shows a conceptual graph that represents the data in the two tables of Fig. 1.15.

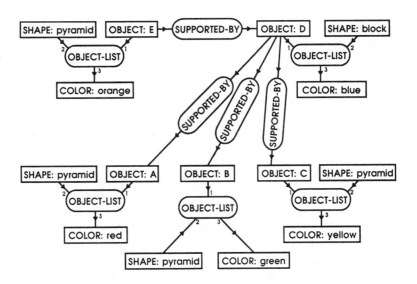

Fig. 1.16 - A conceptual graph that represents the relational database.

Fig. 1.16 shows how the tables of a relational database can be mapped to one or more conceptual graphs. The relations in such graphs, however, are usually complex ones like (OBJECT-LIST) and (SUPPORTED-BY) instead of the more primitive relations that are used to represent sentences in English. Since the primitive relations have a direct mapping to language, Fig. 1.14 can be read as a single sentence: "The pyramid E of color orange is supported by the block D of color blue, which is supported by the pyramid A of color red, the pyramid B of color green, and the pyramid C of color yellow." In order to map Fig. 1.16 into English, a short phrase must be assigned to the two relation types. The relation SUPPORTED-BY maps to "is supported by" when read in the direction of the arrows, or to "supports" when read in the opposite direction. The relation OBJECT-LIST has three arcs, which may be mapped to the pattern "Arc-1 with Arc-2 and Arc-3" With that mapping, Fig. 1.16 may be read "The object E with shape pyramid and color orange is supported by the object D with shape block and color blue, which is supported by the object A with shape pyramid and color red, is supported by the object B with shape pyramid and color green, and is supported by the object C with shape pyramid and color yellow". This example illustrates a general principle:

- Conceptual graphs that use only the primitive relation types in the starter set have a standard mapping to natural languages.

- Conceptual graphs with other relation types can also be mapped to natural languages, but only if each relation type is assigned a suitable phrase pattern for each target language.

Diagrams in the NIAM language usually include two phrases for each binary relation: one for each way of reading the relation (Wintraecken, 1990). With conceptual graphs, it is possible to include the English readings in *syntactic annotations* inside the boxes and circles. Although such annotations are sometimes useful, the graphs are more general when the syntax rules are kept separate. That separation makes them language independent: with different mapping rules, the same graphs can be mapped into any natural language.

To relate the graphs in Figs. 14 and 16 to one another, the more complex types must be defined in terms of the more primitive ones. The following definitions introduce four subtypes of OBJECT: BLOCK is an object with a block shape; PYRAMID is an object with a pyramid shape; SUPPORTEE is an object that is a patient of support; and SUPPORT-OBJ is an object that is an instrument of support.

```
type BLOCK(x) is [OBJECT: *x]→(CHRC)→[SHAPE: block].
type PYRAMID(x) is [OBJECT: *x]→(CHRC)→[SHAPE: pyramid].
type SUPPORTEE(x) is [OBJECT: *x]←(PTNT)←[SUPPORT].
type SUPPORT-OBJ(x) is [OBJECT: *x]←(INST)←[SUPPORT].
```

The next two definitions introduce a triadic relation of type OBJECT-LIST and a dyadic relation of type SUPPORTED-BY:

```
relation OBJECT-LIST(x,y,z) is
    [SHAPE: *y]←(CHRC)←[OBJECT: *x]→(CHRC)→[COLOR: *z].

relation SUPPORTED-BY(x,y) is
    [OBJECT: *x]←(PTNT)←[SUPPORT]→(INST)→[OBJECT: *y].
```

By exanding or contracting these definitions, Fig. 1.14 could be converted to Fig. 1.16 or vice versa. The definitional mechanisms provide a systematic way of restructuring a database or knowledge base from one format to another (Sowa, 1990).

Restructuring a large database is a lengthy process that is sometimes necessary. But to answer a single question, it is usually much faster to restructure the query graph than to restructure the entire database. To access a relational database such as Fig. 1.14, the definitions can be used to translate the concept types in the query graph to concept types that match the domains of the database. Instead of translating the relations, however, it is more convenient to provide a descriptor for every database relation that shows how it maps to the concepts and relations in a conceptual graph. The OBJECT-LIST relation in Fig. 1.15, for example, may be described by the English sentence *Every object has exactly one shape and exactly one color*. That sentence maps to the following conceptual graph:

```
[SHAPE: @1]←(CHRC)←[OBJECT: ∀]→(CHRC)→[COLOR: @1].
```

The CHRC relation says that shape and color are characteristics of an object; the universal quantifier on [OBJECT: ∀] includes the other two concepts in its scope; and the @1 symbol represents the quantifier for *exactly one*.

Although the conceptual graph describes the relationship, it doesn't show how the color and shape of an object could be determined. To show how the concepts in the graph are related to the domains of a database, the descriptor must include an attached *actor node* that specifies a database relation and its links to the concepts. Fig. 1.17 shows an actor, represented by a diamond node, with dotted lines linking it to the three concepts of the conceptual graph. The graph describes how an object is related to its shape and color, and the actor node names the database relation OBJECT-LIST, which stores the shapes and colors for each object. The actor and the graph together represent a descriptor for the database relation. In database terminology, OBJECT is the *key domain* of the OBJECT-LIST relation, and the domains SHAPE and COLOR are dependent on that key.

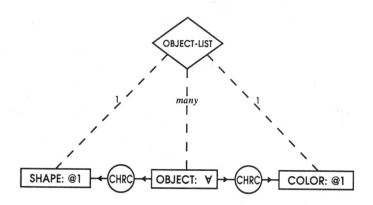

Fig. 1.17 - Descriptor for the OBJECT-LIST relation.

The diamond shape for actors is used to emphasize their similarity to the diamond nodes in an entity-relationship diagram. In fact, every diamond in an E-R diagram can be attached to a conceptual graph that provides additional information about the relation. In Fig. 1.17, the conceptual graph doesn't say anything new, since the quantifiers ∀ and @1 specify the same information as the words *many* and *1* on the dotted lines. Fig. 1.18, however, shows the descriptor for the SUPPORTED-BY relation, where the conceptual graph adds more information. The diamond with its dotted lines simply says that SUPPORTED-BY is a many-to-many relation from SUPPORTEE to its supporting object, SUPPORT-OBJ. The quantifiers in the referent fields of the concepts say that for every instance of support, there is exactly one supportee, and a set of one or more objects that serve collectively as instruments of the support. If there is only one supporting object, as in Block D supporting Pyramid E, the prefix Col and the braces can be dropped. But for the three pyramids that support Block D, the Col prefix would indicate that they serve collectively in a single instance of support.

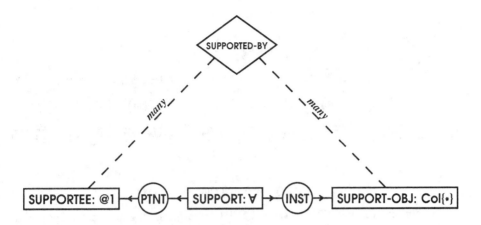

Fig. 1.18 - Descriptor for the SUPPORTED-BY relation.

To illustrate the use of actors for accessing a relational database, consider the same question used with the database in Fig. 1.14. The question *What pyramid is supported by a block?* would be translated to the following query graph:

```
[PYRAMID:  ?]←(PTNT)←[SUPPORT]→(INST)→[BLOCK].
```

None of the three concepts in this graph match any of the domain names in either the OBJECT-LIST or SUPPORTED-BY relations. The type labels PYRAMID and BLOCK happen to have the same spelling as some of the data in the SHAPE domain, but a database is normally considered to have information about instances, not types (see the discussion about higher-order types in Section 9).

In order to relate the concept types in the query graph to the domains in the database, the system must use the definitions of BLOCK, PYRAMID, SUPPORTEE, and SUPPORT-OBJ as subtypes of OBJECT. When the types BLOCK and PYRAMID in the query graph are expanded, the result is the graph for the question *What object of shape pyramid is supported by an object of shape block?*

```
[SHAPE:  pyramid]←(CHRC)←[OBJECT:  ?]←(PTNT)←[SUPPORT]-
                 (INST)→[OBJECT]→(CHRC)→[SHAPE:  block].
```

The next step is to perform *joins* of this query graph to the two descriptors in Figs. 1.17 and 1.18. The result is the graph in Fig. 1.19. For further discussion of the methods of using conceptual graphs in database query, see Sections 6.4 and 6.5 of *Conceptual Structures* (Sowa, 1984).

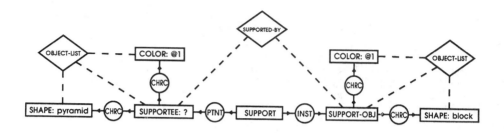

Fig. 1.19 - Query graph with attached actor nodes.

In the concept [SUPPORTEE: ?] in Fig. 1.19, the question mark corresponds to the SELECT verb in SQL. It marks the concept whose referent is to be found; the concept type corresponds to the domain name. The three diamond nodes indicate three database accesses to answer the question: the SUPPORTED-BY relation must be accessed once; and the OBJECT-LIST relation must be accessed twice. The concepts [SUPPORTEE: ?] and [SUPPORT-OBJ] each have a pair of dotted lines connecting them to diamond nodes. Each pair indicates that the corresponding database relations must be joined on the corresponding domains. Each of these correspondences may be translated to part of an SQL query: The concept [SUPPORTEE: ?] maps to the SELECT-clause that begins a new query; the names of the three relations are listed in the FROM-clause; and the combination of conditions becomes the WHERE-clause. Following is the complete SQL query that may be generated from Fig. 1.19:

```
SELECT SUPPORTEE
    FROM SUPPORTED-BY, OBJECT-LIST A, OBJECT-LIST B
        WHERE SUPPORTEE = A.OBJECT
        AND    A.SHAPE = 'pyramid'
        AND    SUPPORT-OBJ = B.OBJECT
        AND    B.SHAPE = 'block'
```

The two conditions "SUPPORTEE = A.OBJECT" and "SUPPORT-OBJ = B.OBJECT" correspond to the two joins of descriptors represented by conceptual graphs as well as the two joins of their corresponding relations. In general, the join of two conceptual graphs that describe two database relations produces a larger graph that describes the joined relation. The two conditions "A.SHAPE = 'pyramid'" and "SHAPE = 'block'" test the values in the referent fields of the corresponding concepts. The two concepts of type COLOR in Fig. 1.19 were carried along by the joins, but they are not needed to answer the question.

Block D by itself is sufficient to support Pyramid E, but three pyramids are needed to support Block D. Following is the conceptual graph for the question *Which block is supported by three pyramids?*

[BLOCK: ?] ← (PTNT) ← [SUPPORT] → (INST) → [PYRAMID: {*}@3].

The symbol {*}@3 uses the default plural, since the question did not specify whether the pyramids were supporting the block collectively or distributively. The descriptor in

Fig. 1.18, however, contains the necessary background information: the symbol Col{*} indicates that the supporting objects act collectively. To answer this question, the concept types BLOCK and PYRAMID would be expanded according to their definitions, and the graphs in Figs. 1.17 and 1.18 would be joined to the query graph to derive the following conceptual graph:

```
[SHAPE: block]←(CHRC)←[OBJECT: ?]←(PTNT)←[SUPPORT]-
     (INST)→[[SUPPORT-OBJ: λ]→(CHRC)→[SHAPE: pyramid]:
Col{*}@3].
```

The λ-expression that defines BLOCK may be expanded as before, but the λ-expression for PYRAMID must remain in the type field, since the process of λ-expansion may not be applied when the referent contains a universal quantifier or a plural referent such as Col{*}@3. The concept marked with λ has the type label SUPPORT-OBJ, which is the common subtype of OBJECT and SUPPORT-OBJ. When the graphs are joined, the actor nodes are carried along to generate a conceptual graph with attached actors similar to Fig. 1.19; following is the corresponding SQL query:

```
SELECT SUPPORTEE
     FROM SUPPORTED-BY, OBJECT-LIST A, OBJECT-LIST B
         WHERE SUPPORTEE = A.OBJECT
         AND    A.SHAPE = 'block'
         AND    SUPPORT-OBJ = B.OBJECT
         AND    B.SHAPE = 'pyramid'
         GROUP BY SUPPORTEE HAVING COUNT(SUPPORT-OBJ) = 3
```

The last line of this query is derived from the plural referent Col{*}@3. The Col prefix becomes "GROUP BY" in SQL, and the count @3 translates to "HAVING COUNT(SUPPORT-OBJ) = 3."

As these examples illustrate, the original queries expressed as conceptual graphs are much simpler than the corresponding queries in SQL. Both graphs are almost one-for-one translations of the original English questions:

What pyramid is supported by a block?

```
[PYRAMID:?]←(PTNT)←[SUPPORT]→(INST)→[BLOCK].
```

What block is supported by three pyramids?

```
[BLOCK:?]←(PTNT)←[SUPPORT]→(INST)→[PYRAMID:{*}@3].
```

There are two reasons why the SQL queries are so much more complex than either the English or the conceptual graph: first, SQL requires the concept types BLOCK and PYRAMID to be expanded to their definitions; second, SQL requires the database relations and their domains to be named explicitly. Background information from type definitions and database descriptors such as Figs. 1.17 and 1.18 must be used to derive an expanded query graph like Fig. 1.19. That expanded graph contains all the detail necessary to derive the SQL query.

The graph in Fig. 1.14 is similar to the storage representations used in object-oriented databases. This similarity is not accidental, since conceptual graphs support the kinds of features needed for an object-oriented system: the hierarchy of concept types corresponds to the class hierarchy in an O-O system; and the direct connectivity of concepts and relations in the graphs corresponds to the connected storage structures in an O-O database. Conceptual graphs can be used to describe or access any kind of database system. With appropriate descriptors, such as Figs. 1.17 and 1.18, they can support relational databases. The mapping from conceptual graphs to O-O databases is even more direct, and the graphs could serve as an intermediate language for mapping between the different kinds of database systems.

Database actors compute the requested values by table lookup, but other actors might represent procedures. Even the process of parsing and interpreting English sentences and mapping them into conceptual graphs could be represented by an actor. The following graph shows an actor for mapping a sentence to a conceptual graph:

```
[SENTENCE: "A cat is on a mat"]→<Interpreter>→
          [GRAPH: [CAT]→(ON)→[MAT]].
```

The actor <Interpreter> takes a sentence as input and generates a conceptual graph as output. The procedure that implements that actor is symbolized by the actor node.

Actors can have any number of arcs. The actor in Fig. 1.17 had three arcs, and the one in Fig. 1.18 had two arcs. Actors with only one arc could also be used for input and output. Another use for actors with one output and no input is to represent default values. The following graph, for example, represents the sentence *Every dog has four legs*:

```
[DOG: ∀]→(PART)→[LEG: {*}@4].
```

The count @4 may be expanded with the CHRC relation linked to a concept [CARDINAL-ITY: 4]. Following is the full form:

```
[DOG: ∀]→(PART)→[LEG: {*}*x]
```

```
[Cum{*}*x]→(CHRC)→[CARDINALITY: 4].
```

This graph may be read "Every dog has as part some legs x, and the set x has cardinality 4". Two separate concept nodes are required for the set of legs, since the plural marker {*} has different prefixes in each node. If the exact number of legs may change, the next graph says that every dog has a set of legs of some unspecified cardinality. To provide the default value, the actor <Const 4> can be invoked to produce the constant 4 upon request.

```
[DOG: ∀]→(PART)→[LEG: {*}*x]
```

```
[Cum{*}*x]→(CHRC)→[CARDINALITY]←<Const 4>.
```

From the information that Lucky and Macula are dogs, the following graphs may be inferred:

```
[DOG: Lucky]→(PART)→[LEG: {*}*x]
```

```
[Cum{*}*x]→(CHRC)→[CARDINALITY]←<Const 4>.
```

```
[DOG: Macula]→(PART)→[LEG: {*}*y]

[Cum{*}*y]→(CHRC)→[CARDINALITY]←<Const 4>.
```

In neither of these graphs has the actor <Const 4> been invoked to produce the value 4. Now suppose that someone says "Lucky has three legs. How many legs does Macula have?" The first sentence causes the cardinality for Lucky's legs to become 3, and the question triggers the actor on Macula's graph to produce the value 4:

```
[DOG: Lucky]→(PART)→[LEG: {*}*x]

[Cum{*}*x]→(CHRC)→[CARDINALITY: 3]←<Const 4>.

[DOG: Macula]→(PART)→[LEG: {*}*y]

[Cum{*}*y]→(CHRC)→[CARDINALITY: 4]←<Const 4>.
```

Note that the actor is not invoked until its value is requested. Therefore, the value 3 for Lucky does not conflict with the default value 4 that the actor would have produced if requested. In Macula's case, there was no explicit information, and the actor was triggered by the question. For handling defaults, actors provide a localized method that is similar to the default slots on frames. More global methods would use nonmonotonic logic and belief revision.

1.13   MAPPING TO PREDICATE CALCULUS

Since conceptual graphs form a complete system of logic with their own rules of inference and model-theoretic semantics (Sowa, 1984), there is no need to map them to any other version of logic. Yet the definition of the ϕ operator that maps conceptual graphs to predicate calculus is interesting for several reasons: it explicitly shows the structural differences between the two systems, it enables theoretical advances made with one system to be adapted to the other, and it allows programs that use one system to interact with programs based on the other. The mapping by ϕ, however, is only defined for features that can be represented directly in predicate calculus. Since the control marks ?, !, and # do not have counterparts in predicate calculus, they cannot be translated.

To simplify the definition of ϕ, it is convenient to break it down into several stages. The first stage partitions the conceptual graph into multiple contexts, in each of which there is only one kind of quantifier. The second stage starts from the outermost context and works inward, translating the graphs in each context to formulas in a sorted predicate calculus, using λ-expressions for defining new sorts whenever a λ-expression occurs in the type field of a context. Finally, the third stage translates the sorted predicate calculus to an unsorted form. As an example, consider the graph for *Every trailer truck has 18 wheels*:

```
[TRAILER-TRUCK: ∀]→(PART)→[WHEEL: {*}@18].
```

The first step is to note that the ∀ quantifier has precedence over {*}. Therefore, the concept with that quantifier is placed in the outer context, and another context box is drawn around the rest of the graph:

```
[TRAILER-TRUCK: ∀*x]

[ [*x]→(PART)→[WHEEL: {*}@18]].
```

When the graph is split in this way, a coreference link must be drawn between the concept in the outer context and the node [*x] that serves as a place holder in the inner context. This partitioned graph may be read "For every trailer truck x, x has 18 wheels". The next step is to translate this graph to a sorted predicate calculus, working from the outermost context inward. A separate variable must be assigned to each quantifier. All the relations in each context are mapped to predicates with the same number of arguments, and they are linked by conjunctions.

$$(\forall x : trailer\text{-}truck)(\forall y \in \{*\}@18 : wheel)part(x, y).$$

The third step is to expand the sort expressions according to appropriate rules for each type of quantifier (except for generalized quantifiers like @many, which cannot be translated further):

$$(\forall x)(trailer\text{-}truck(x) \supset (\exists S)(set(S) \land count(S, 18) \land$$
$$(\forall y \in S)(wheel(y) \land part(x, y)))).$$

Following are some observations about the translation process:

1. Ellipses, anaphora, and other phenomena that depend on syntactic annotations should be resolved before the ϕ operator is applied. Any annotations that change the quantifier precedence should be replaced by contexts that explicitly delimit the quantifier scope.

2. After all surface-related features have been resolved, the syntactic annotations may be erased: in concept and relation nodes, everything from the semicolon to the closing bracket or parenthesis is treated as a comment.

3. There is a precedence ranking for quantifiers: universals take precedence over existentials, and plural existentials take precedence over simple existentials.

4. A plural referent always results in two quantifiers: the outer one (which could be existential or universal) governs the set as a whole, and the inner one is a universal quantifier that ranges over the elements of the set.

5. The prefixes Dist and Col on plural referents affect the precedence of the two quantifiers for the set and its elements: Col lowers the precedence relative to other quantifiers in the context; Dist raises the precedence, and it forces lower precedence existentials to switch from $\exists$ to $\exists!!$ quantifiers.

6. Nested contexts limit the scope of quantifiers in the same way as parentheses in predicate calculus. But within a single context, all of the quantifiers can be ordered according to their precedence.

7. If the type field of a concept is a λ-expression $(\lambda x)g(x)$ where g is a conceptual graph, then the sort expression in the sorted predicate calculus is $(\lambda x)\phi g(x)$.

8. When the sorted predicate calculus is translated to the unsorted formula, a universal quantifier of the form $(\forall x : t)p(x)$ expands to the form $(\forall x)(t(x) \supset p(x))$, and an existential quantifier $(\exists x : t)p(x)$ expands to $(\exists x)(t(x) \land p(x))$.

9. After the translation to the unsorted predicate calculus, an application of a λ-expression $(\lambda y)t(y)(x)$ may be converted to $t(x)$.

As this discussion shows, the mapping from conceptual graphs to predicate calculus is nontrivial. Conceptual graphs have been designed to simplify the mapping to and from natural languages; but since natural languages do not map smoothly to predicate calculus, much of the complexity appears in the definition of ϕ. This complexity is one more illustration of the unnaturalness of the predicate calculus as a semantic representation for natural language.

BIBLIOGRAPHY

Barwise, Jon, and John Perry (1983) *Situations and Attitudes*, MIT Press, Cambridge, MA.

Hornstein, Norman (1985) *Logic as Grammar*, MIT Press, Cambridge, MA.

Kamp, Hans (1981a) "Events, discourse representations, and temporal references," *Langages* 64, 39-64.

Kamp, Hans (1981b) "A theory of truth and semantic representation," in *Formal Methods in the Study of Language*, ed. by J. A. G. Groenendijk, T. M. V. Janssen, & M. B. J. Stokhof, Mathematical Centre Tracts, Amsterdam, 277-322.

Lenat, Douglas B., and R. V. Guha (1990) *Building Large Knowledge-Based Systems*, Addison-Wesley, Reading, MA.

Levinson, Robert, and Gerard Ellis (1992) "Multi-level hierarchical retrieval," *Knowledge Based Systems*, in press.

Peirce, Charles Sanders (1897-1906) Manuscripts on existential graphs. Some are reprinted in *Collected Papers of Charles Sanders Peirce*, edited by Arthur W. Burks, Harvard University Press, Cambridge, MA, vol. 4, pp. 320-410; others are summarized by Roberts (1973).

Perry, John (1979) "The proble of the essential indexical," *Nous*, vol. 13, pp. 3-21.

Roberts, Don D. (1973) *The Existential Graphs of Charles S. Peirce*, Mouton, The Hague.

Sowa, John F. (1984) *Conceptual Structures: Information Processing in Mind and Machine*, Addison-Wesley, Reading, MA.

Sowa, John F. (1990) "Definitional mechanisms for restructuring knowledge bases," in Z. W. Ras, M. Zemankova, & M. L. Emrich, eds., *Methodologies for Intelligent Systems*, 5, North-Holland Publishing Co., New York, pp. 194-211.

Sowa, John F. (1991) "Towards the expressive power of natural languages," in J. F. Sowa, ed., *Principles of Semantic Networks*, Morgan Kaufmann Publishers, San Mateo, CA, pp. 157-189.

Wintraecken, J. J. (1990) *The NIAM Information Analysis Method: Theory & Practice*, Kluwer Academic Publishers, Dordrecht.

2

Representing and Reasoning with Set Referents and Numerical Quantifiers

Bosco S. Tjan, David A. Gardiner and James R. Slagle
University of Minnesota,
Computer Science Department,
200 Union Street S.E., Minneapolis, MN 55455, USA

ABSTRACT

We give a simple and uniform extension to conceptual graph notation. This extension easily represents, among other things, collective and distributive set referents. A distributive set referent is a partial instantiation, which is a restriction on how a concept variable can be instantiated. A collective set referent is a concept type of some collection of individuals, whose contents can be expressed by a distributive set. A quantification over a set referent has three components, a scope, a restrictor and a quantifier. We extend the referent field of a concept node to explicitly represent these components.

To develop a reasoning system for conceptual graphs with set referents, we need a logical framework. We add numerical quantifiers to first-order predicate calculus with equality (PCE). We show that the resulting system (PCEN) is a conservative extension of PCE, and therefore, is sound and complete. PCEN can handle the notions of numerical quantifiers, finite set referents and set coreferences in conceptual graphs. These are three sources of difficulties in conceptual graph theory. The power of PCEN shows that a general set theory is not needed for defining the semantics of conceptual graphs with set referents. A brief look at the inference mechanism for PCEN suggests that resolution with paramodulation is not practical for PCEN, but natural deduction with direct inference rules operating on numerical quantifiers can be viable. Because of the similarities between PCEN and conceptual graphs with set referents and numerical quantifiers, the same conclusion also applies to reasoning with conceptual structures.

2.1 INTRODUCTION

Conceptual structures, as developed by Sowa (1984), is a rich knowledge representation language intended to incorporate many concepts in natural and formal languages. Like any other formalisms, when it was first introduced, several important concepts and their rules of inference were left undefined. Among them are set referents and the related concepts such as numerical quantifiers and set coreferences.

Several years ago we began to approach this lack of formalism with the introduction of a formal syntax to represent set referents, coreferences, and numerical quantifiers. We called our representation the extended notation for conceptual graphs (Gardiner *et al.*, 1989) (refer to Slagle *et al.* (1990) for a summary of our research.) The semantics of the extended notation was first given in game-theoretic semantics (Tjan and Slagle, 1988) and later with a translation to predicate calculus amended with set theory (Tjan *et al.*, 90). (Readers can also refer to Gardiner *et al.* (1992) in this volume the translation.) A set of direct inference rules for the extended notation was also proposed in Tjan *et al.* (1990).

We are not interested in handling a set as a mathematical object in conceptual structures, but would like to use the *RsetS* mechanism to represent a group of individuals and to make reference to a portion of the group or its members. In other words, we are interested in representing and reasoning with what are the conceptual structures analogies to plural terms and their quantifiers in a natural language. Perhaps judging from the complexity, some consider our extension unnecessary. This chapter will argue otherwise. In particular, we point out that any formalism that attempts to handle plural terms and numerical quantifiers will have to provide mechanisms functionally similar to the *scope list, domain,* and *cardinality* of our extended notation.

We encountered a major difficulty when trying to formulate the inference mechanism for the extended notation. The proposal in Tjan *et al.* (1990) was not satisfactory. Other researchers who are trying to formalize inference with sets in conceptual graphs seem to meet with similar obstacles. So far we are not aware of any satisfactory approach in the area.

In this chapter we shall develop a predicate calculus with numerical quantifiers, and use it as a tool to study the inference mechanisms needed for reasoning with set referent and numerical quantifiers. Our studies conclude that:

(a) under certain reasonable limitations, our notation can be expressed in first-order predicate calculus with equality, and thus has a sound and complete proof theory;

(b) some sound and complete inference mechanisms similar to resolution with paramodulation are impracticable for numerical quantifiers;

(c) natural deduction with direct inference rules that operate on numerical quantifiers may be a desirable approach.

2.2   MEANING OF A SET REFERENT

To represent a plural term in natural language, a formalism will have to provide a way that allows individuals to be grouped into a set. Furthermore, the formalism should be able to quantify the set and to simultaneously refer to all or a portion of those individuals in the set. In conceptual structures a set referent is introduced to be such a representation (Sowa, 1984). With this application of set referents in mind, we need to address two important issues: first, how to quantify over a set referent, and second, how to coreference a set referent. Both received considerable treatment on the syntax and semantics sides, in Tjan & Slagle (1988) and later in Gardiner *et al.* (1989). In this chapter we intend to focus on only the first question, namely, on the quantification of set referents. But prior to the discussion of quantification, we need to address a fundamental question.

What is a set referent in conceptual structures? A short answer is that a set referent is not a set. To justify this and to say what it *is*, we need to look at some generally agreed usages of set referents.

The most obvious usage of a set referent is to represent plural nouns. A sentence such as

"*Some dogs are black.*"   (2.1)

is represented in a conceptual graph as

[DOG: *] → (COLR) → [BLACK]   (2.2)

where the * is called a generic set referent. It is clear that what (2.1) concerns are dogs, not those mathematical objects that we called sets. "Being black" is a property of the dogs in a set, not of the set containing dogs. Therefore, the implicit existential quantified variable of [DOG: *] ranges over some individual dogs, rather than over some sets containing dogs.

Also notice that the generic set referent used in (2.2) has a *distributive* sense, rather than a *collective* sense as suggested in Sowa (1984). The plural use of "dog" in (1) does not suggest that the dogs are black together. The sentence concerns individual dogs separately. Common use of plural nouns does not by default suggest a collective sense; on the contrary, it suggests a distributive sense. Hence when used to represent plural nouns, a set referent is distributive and should be prefixed by *Dist* in Sowa's original notation. These comments on [DOG: *] also apply to distributive set referents in general.

Another usage of a set referent is to provide the sense of collectiveness. The sentence

"*John and Mary own a house together.*"   (2.3)

can be represented in a conceptual graph as;

[PERSON:*Coll* {John, Mary}] ← (AGNT) ← [OWN]
                          → (PTNT) → [HOUSE]   (2.4)

The collective set referent *Coll* {John, Mary} suggests that John and Mary are agents of a single act of owning. This usage seems to favor the interpretation of *Coll* {John, Mary} as a mathematical set. One is then tempted to consider [PERSON: *Coll* {John, Mary}] as a set and that the act "owning" is performed by a set rather than by persons. The fallacy of this can be revealed by considering the sentence

"*John and Mary dance together.*"   (2.5)

which can be represented as

[PERSON: *Coll* {John, Mary}] ← (AGNT) ← [DANCE].   (2.6)

A set cannot dance. It is clear that the act of dancing refers to the persons even though the collective usage of {John, Mary} stresses the point that there is only one act of dancing shared by two persons.

If set referents are not sets, then what are they? They are *partial instantiations* of the concept variables. An *instantiation* is a step in a semantic interpretation that substitutes an *individual* (i.e. a constant) for a concept variable. We used this step within a partial-information game-theoretic semantics framework to provide a formal semantics for conceptual graphs (Tjan & Slagle, 1988), following the approach of (Hintikka, 1977). Speaking loosely, we define the truth value of a conceptual graph by a game between two players, *Myself*, who tries to show that a subgraph of the world model is an instance of the graph in question, and *Nature*, who tries to show otherwise. If *Myself* has a winning strategy, then the semantic value of the graph is truth. For example, if the statement "there is some animal", or equivalently the graph;

$$[ANIMAL: \ *x] \ (or \ simply \ [ANIMAL]) \tag{2.7}$$

is true, then *Myself* should be able to instantiate the variable x to some individual that is an animal. If the statement "Everything is animal", or equivalently

$$[ANIMAL: \ *y \ \forall] \ (or \ simply \ [ANIMAL: \ \forall]) \tag{2.8}$$

is true, *Nature* must instantiate the variable y with some individual that is not an animal in order to win. Notice that for these cases, namely that of existential and universal quantifiers, there is no restriction on how the players would pick the individuals for an instantiation.

A partial instantiation limits the individuals that may be used to instantiate the variables and the ways the instantiation should be carried out. For example, the distributive set referent in the conceptual graph

$$[DOG: \ Dist \ \{Rover, \ Ranger\}] \rightarrow (COLR) \rightarrow [BLACK] \tag{2.9}$$

restricts the possible instantiations of the implicit existential quantified variable of the concept DOG to only Rover and Ranger. By being distributive, the set referent also indicates that each instantiation results in a separate graph, and all these graphs are in a conjunction. This is to say that (2.9) is to be interpreted as

$$[DOG: \ Rover] \rightarrow (COLR) \rightarrow [BLACK]$$
$$[DOG: \ Ranger] \rightarrow (COLR) \rightarrow [BLACK] \tag{2.10}$$

Consider another case. The collective set referent in the graph

$$[PERSON: \ Coll \ \{John, \ Mary\}] \leftarrow (AGNT) \leftarrow [OWN]$$
$$\leftarrow (PTNT) \rightarrow [HOUSE] \tag{2.11}$$

says that

"John and Mary together own a house." (2.12)

The collective set referent suggests that the instantiations of the implicit variable of concept PERSON be John and Mary, but the instantiations should result in a single graph with a *composite* (or *collective*) concept:

$$[2\_PERSON\_COLL] \ -$$
$$\leftarrow (IN\_COLL) \leftarrow [PERSON:John]$$
$$\leftarrow (IN\_COLL) \leftarrow [PERSON:Mary]$$
$$\leftarrow (AGNT) \leftarrow [OWN] \rightarrow (PTNT) \rightarrow [HOUSE] \tag{2.13}$$

where 2_PERSON_COLL is the concept type of "a collection of two persons", and IN_COLL is the relation type of "being in a collection".

According to Sowa (1984, page 116), (2.11) was understood as equivalent to

```
[OWN]  -
    → (AGNT) → [PERSON:John]
    → (AGNT) → [PERSON:Mary]
    → (PTNT) → [HOUSE],                                      (2.14)
```

which in our opinion is incorrect. Observe that (2.13) implies that John owns the house since the statement is a subgraph of (2.13), but (2.12) does not. The ownership belongs to John and Mary as a whole, but not to either one of them (and thus comes the collective set referents in (2.11)). Further notice that (2.13) can be expressed as

```
[2_PERSON_COLL]  -
    ← (IN_COLL) ← [PERSON: Dist {John, Mary}]
    ← (AGNT) ← [OWN] ← (PTNT) ← [HOUSE].¹                   (2.15)
```

With this understanding, every collective set referent can be expressed in terms of a distributive set referent. Therefore, it suffices to develop a theory of representation and reasoning on only the distributive set referents. From now on, we shall drop the *Dist* or *Coll* prefix.

To summarize our view, a distributive set referent is a restriction on how a concept variable can be instantiated. A collective set referent is a concept type representing some collection, whose members can be expressed with a distributive set. With this understanding, we propose a uniform representation of set referents in the next section, and argue for its necessity.

2.3   SET REFERENTS AND NUMERICAL QUANTIFIERS

Now we have an understanding of what a set referent means. The next step is to develop a representation for it. Two uses for a set referent distinguish it from an individual referent. It can be quantified, and a subset of its members can be referenced. We shall focus our attention on the quantification aspect. We discuss elsewhere (Tjan & Slagle, 1988) that the same notation can also house a generalized coreference link for a subset reference.

As pointed out in Sowa (1989), quantification has three parts in natural languages: a *quantifier*, a *restrictor*, and a *scope*. The quantifier may be a word like "every", "some", a phase like "almost all", a number, or a range of numbers. The restrictor determines the domain over which quantification ranges. It is the "things" that are being quantified over, typically a noun or a noun phase. The scope is the context over which the quantification extends. For example, in the sentence,

"Every house in Edina has at least two bedrooms."   (2.16)

there are two quantifiers: "every" and "at least two". The restrictor for "every" is "house in Edina", and that for "at least two" is "bedrooms". The scope of the first quantifier is over the entire sentence, where that of the second is only over the word "bedrooms".

---

[1] Strictly speaking this is incorrect. A scoping mechanism will be introduced in the next section so that when expanded, the graph with John and that with Mary will both refer to the same 2_PERSON_COLL, the same action OWN, and the same HOUSE.

In conceptual graph notation, as specified in Sowa (1989), the quantifier goes into the referent field, the restrictor is the concept in the type field, and the scope is the entire context. In Tjan and Slagle (1988), and later in Gardiner *et al.* (1989), we took a different approach by explicitly representing all three components in the referent field. In our opinion, while Sowa's notation works well for simple quantifiers such as "every" or "some", it becomes inconvenient, if not inadequate, when it comes to representing numerical quantifiers such as "at least two". However, it is important to point out at this time that the semantics of a set referent that we proposed, and the issues on inference that we shall discuss are general in nature and do not depend on the notation.

In Sowa's notation, the scope of a quantifier is over the entire context. If there are two or more kinds of quantifiers, their relative scopes are determined by precedence rules. This works fine if all quantifiers of the same kind *commute* in scopes. This is the case for the simplest kind of quantifiers such as "every" and "some". For example, a sentence such as

"Some man loves some woman."   (2.17)

will have the same meaning regardless of whether the first quantifier is over the entire sentence and the second is just over the noun "woman", or the other way around. This is not the case for numerical quantifiers as made evident by the different meanings of the following two sentences:

"There are at least two professors teaching at least two courses."   (2.18)

"There are at least two courses taught by at least two professors."   (2.19)

Numerical quantifiers do not commute. In a sense, a numerical quantifier is a composition of an existential quantifier followed by a universal quantifier. The former asserts the existence of a set of a certain size. The latter states the property of each member. Sowa's solution is to use nested contexts, but we prefer an explicit quantification scope designator, which we called a *scope list*.

A scope list is a list of concept variables enclosed in parentheses. For a quantifier, a scope list designates those quantifiers whose scope the quantifier in question is under. For instance, if a concept has a scope list (x, y), the scope of its quantifier will be under the scopes of the quantifier with concept variable x and that with concept variable y. Another way of looking at a scope list is to see it as specifying the functional dependency among concepts. A concept having a scope list (x, y) means that the instantiation of its concept variable depends on the instantiations of the concept with variable x and that with variable y. The two understandings are essentially the same. With scope lists, we represent (2.18) and (2.19) as (2.20) and (2.21) respectively.

```
[TEACH:  (x,  y) z  *  @1]  -
   → (AGNT) → [PROFESSOR:  ( ) x  *  @2−∞]
   → (PTNT) → [COURSE:  (x) y  *  @2−∞]
```
                                                                                 (2.20)

```
[TEACH:  (x,  y) z  *  @1]  -
   → (AGNT) → [PROFESSOR:  (y) x  *  @2−∞]
   → (PTNT) → [COURSE:  ( ) y  *  @2−∞]
```
                                                                                 (2.21)

In this notation, a referent field begins after the colon. The first item in a referent field is the scope list, which is a list of variables enclosed in a pair of parentheses. The concept variable is to the left of a scope list. There are two more items following the concept variable, *domain* and *cardinality*, which we shall discuss shortly. A domain is designated by a pair of braces, while a cardinality is the part that begins with an "@" sign.

The next issue is on the restrictors of a quantification. Sowa (1989) considers the the type field to be the restrictor. Thus for each quantification, either a defined type or a lambda abstraction will be used as a restrictor. But for a numerical quantification, a restrictor can also be a set of individuals, as in the sentence:

> "At least two of John, Mary, and Tom own a house."   (2.22)

In general, whenever a quantifier is applied over a set referent, the individuals in the set referents become at least part of the restrictor. Having to express every set referent as a concept type is unnatural and technically tedious, and we think that this is unnecessary.

We add a component, called a *domain*, into the referent field of a concept. A domain is a list of individuals enclosed in braces {}. It is understood as the set of individuals over which the quantification ranges. Using the notion of instantiation, a domain defines, and thus restricts, the set of individuals with which the concept variable can be instantiated. Except for *proportional quantifiers*, such as "all", "half" or "most of", a concept type does not need to be part of the restrictor. It can be considered as a predicate separated from the quantification. For example, the following two sentences say the same thing:

> "<u>Two cats</u> are sitting on a mat."   (2.23)

> "<u>Two things</u> are sitting on a mat, and they are cats."   (2.24)

In general we shall consider the domain component to be the restrictor of a quantification. Only for a proportional quantifier will we include the concept type as part of the restrictor. In our notation, (2.22) is represented as;

```
[OWN: (x, y)z * @1] –
    →(AGNT)→[PERSON: ()x {John, Mary, Tom} @2-∞]
    →(PTNT)→[HOUSE: (x)y * @1-∞].                          (2.25)
```

For concept PERSON, the domain John, Mary, Tom is the restrictor of the numerical quantification. It is not by coincidence that the notation of a domain is the same as a set referent in Sowa's notation. Yet strictly speaking, it is the entire referent field that specifies a partial instantiation, that we consider as a set referent. Furthermore, we take the domain * to mean the universe of discourse.

The third issue concerns quantifiers. Although in Sowa (1989) quantifiers are placed into the referent field, they are considered as an abbreviation. For example, the concept node [MAN: * @2] is considered as an abbreviation for

```
[MAN: *]→(QTY)→[NUMBER: 2].                                (2.26)
```

In our notation however, we do not consider a quantifier to be such an abbreviation. We call the quantifier *cardinality*. We take this stand to avoid some theoretical complications. If we follow Sowa (1984, 1989) to allow a quantifier to be an abbreviation of some combination of concepts and relations, it will be hard to prevent a quantifier from becoming a variable, being coreferenced or further quantified. In case of numerical quantifiers, if we cannot impose such restrictions, the quantification theory will be at least as strong as number theory, which does not have a complete proof theory.

In summary, we have proposed a notation that extends the referent field of a concept node to explicitly state all three components of a quantification. This notation can represent a generic referent and a set referent with identical formats and uniform semantics. Except for an individual referent, the referent field of a concept always has four components in our extended notation. From left to right, they are the scope list, the concept variable, the domain and the cardinality. The cardinality "$@1-\infty$" is used for the existential quantifier, "$@$all-all" for the universal quantifier, and "$@a - b$", where a, b are some non-negative integers, for a numerical quantifier.

2.4   REASONING WITH SET REFERENTS AND NUMERICAL QUANTIFIERS

In Gardiner *et al.* (1989) and Tjan *et al.* (1990), we give a translation between our notation and PCS (predicate calculus with set theory) to define the semantics of conceptual graphs. There, the cardinality (numerical quantifier) in a concept node was understood as a constraint on the size of the *instantiation set* of the concept node. The instantiation set of a concept node is the set of those individuals that can individually satisfy the entire graph when instantiated in the node. This understanding was an attempt to unify the interpretations of the existential, universal and numerical quantifiers. It also provided a natural means to handle the notions of set referents and set coreferences. Because of this uniformity, PCS became a good tool to understand the semantics of conceptual graphs with extended notation.

From this translation, one may suggest an inference system for conceptual structures by first converting conceptual graphs to formulas in set theory, and then relying on a general theorem prover to determine the validity of the resulting formulas. This approach, however, is undesirable in practice and in theory. In practice, mechanical theorem proving for general set theory is inefficient. In theory, for any consistent formulation of the axioms, there are true formulas that are not provable. This is because general set theory is incomplete. We shall show that under certain reasonable restrictions, conceptual graphs with set referent and numerical quantifiers can be made less powerful than general set theory and can be expressed in predicate calculus with equality. Since predicate calculus with equality is complete, so is the theory of conceptual graphs with extended notation.

Resolution with a technique called paramodulation is efficient in determining the unsatisfiability of a formula in predicate calculus with equality. Therefore, one might expect that a similar mechanism should also be feasible for conceptual graphs with set referents and numerical quantifiers. We shall soon demonstrate that this is not the case. We add numerical quantifiers to predicate calculus with equality (PCE), and show that the resulting calculus (PCEN) is a conservative extension of predicate calculus with equality. PCEN highly parallels the form of a restricted version of our extended notation. We show that the complexity of expressing a PCEN formula in PCE with conjunctive normal form is extremely high and thus it is impractical to use resolution with paramodulation to perform inference on PCEN formulas.

Failing to use resolution with paramodulation as an inference mechanism for conceptual graphs with extended notation, we study an alternative inference mechanism for PCEN.

This study results in an argument in favor of natural deduction and direct inference, which was attempted in Tjan *et al.* (1990), and provides a pointer on how a set of direct inference rules can be formulated for PCEN.

2.5 PREDICATE CALCULUS WITH NUMERICAL QUANTIFIERS

We add a quantifier $(@_n x)$, to be read as "there exist at least n x", to first-order predicate calculus with equality (PCE), and call the resulting calculus first-order predicate calculus with equality and numerical quantifiers (PCEN).

PCEN includes all the formula formation rules in PCE. Furthermore, if β is a formula in PCEN and x is a free variable in β, then $(@_n x)\beta$, where n is a non-negative integer, is also a formula in PCEN. We intend the intuitive meaning of $(@_n x)\beta$ to be "there exist at least n x's, such that β". Moreover, as a convention, we shall use $(@_n^m x)\beta$, to be read as "there exist n to m x's such that β", to stand for the formula $(@_n x)\beta \wedge \neg(@_{m+1} x)\beta$. We call this convention $(C@)$.

We give the formal semantics of PCEN in the usual model-theoretical way. We define interpretations of a PCEN formula and its constituents with respect to an assignment function. Let U, called the *universe of discourse*, be a set of individuals. Let f, called an *assignment function*, be a function from the set of variables in PCEN to U. Let $\mathcal{I}^f$, called an *interpretation* over U relative to f, be an assignment of the "semantic values" to constants, variables, function symbols, predicates and formulas in PCEN in the following ways:

1. If α is a constant in PCEN, then $\mathcal{I}^f(\alpha)$ is an element in U.

2. If α is a variable in PCEN, then $\mathcal{I}^f(\alpha)$ equals $f(\alpha)$.

3. If α is an n-place function symbol in PCEN, then $\mathcal{I}^f(\alpha)$ is an n-place function from U^n to U.

4. If α is an n-place predicate in PCEN, then $\mathcal{I}^f(\alpha)$ is an n-place function from U^n to the set $\{T, F\}$. Moreover, if d_1, d_2 are elements in U, then $\mathcal{I}^f(=)(d1, d2)$ is F if and only if d_1 is distinct from d_2.

5. If α is an n-place function symbol in PCEN and if $t_1, \ldots, t_n$ are terms, then $\mathcal{I}^f(\alpha(t_1, \ldots, t_n))$ equals $\mathcal{I}^f(\alpha)(\mathcal{I}^f(t_1), \ldots, \mathcal{I}^f(t_n))$, which is an element in U.

6. If α is an n-place predicate in PCEN and $t_1, \ldots, t_n$ are terms, then $\mathcal{I}^f(\alpha(t_1, \ldots, t_n))$ equals $\mathcal{I}^f(\alpha)(\mathcal{I}^f(t_1), \ldots, \mathcal{I}^f(t_n))$, which is either T or F.

7. If α and β are formulas in PCEN, then $\mathcal{I}^f(\neg\alpha)$, $\mathcal{I}^f(\alpha \wedge \beta)$, $\mathcal{I}^f(\alpha \vee \beta)$, $\mathcal{I}^f(\alpha \rightarrow \beta)$ and $\mathcal{I}^f(\alpha \leftrightarrow \beta)$ are the respective truth-table values of $\neg, \wedge, \vee, \rightarrow$, and $\leftrightarrow$, evaluated at $(\mathcal{I}^f(\alpha), \mathcal{I}^f(\beta))$.

8. If β is a formula in PCEN, then

    (a) $\mathcal{I}^f((\forall x)\beta)$ is T if and only if for every assignment function g that is identical to f everywhere except possibly in the assignment at x, $\mathcal{I}^g(\beta)$ is T.

    (b) $\mathcal{I}^f((\exists x)\beta)$ is T if and only if there is some assignment function g that is identical to f everywhere except possibly in the assignment at x, such that $\mathcal{I}^g(\beta)$ is T.

(c) $\mathcal{I}^f((@_n x)\beta)$ is T, where n is a non-negative integer, if and only if there are at least n distinct assignment functions $g_1, \ldots, g_n$ that are identical to f everywhere except possibly in their assignments at x and such that $\mathcal{I}^{g_i}(\beta)$ is T for all i, where $i = 1, \ldots, n$.

Furthermore, a PCEN formula α is said to be *satisfiable* if there is an interpretation $\mathcal{I}$, and an assignment function f, such that $\mathcal{I}^f(\alpha)$ is T; otherwise, it is said to be unsatisfiable. A formula a is valid if $\mathcal{I}^f(\alpha)$ is T for every interpretation $\mathcal{I}$ and every assignment function f.

We define a two-place predicate $\neq$, such that $x \neq y$ denotes $\neg(x = y)$. Also, let P be a two-place predicate in PCEN. We define $P[x_1, \ldots, x_n]$ to be the conjunction of P applied to each distinct pair among $x_1, \ldots, x_n$. For example, $\neq [x_1, x_2, x_3]$ stands for the conjunction $(x_1 \neq x_2) \wedge (x_2 \neq x_3) \wedge (x_1 \neq x_3)$. For $n < 2$, we define $P[x_1, \ldots, x_n]$ to be a tautology. Furthermore, if Q is a quantifier and β is a formula, we shall write $(Qx_1, \ldots x_n)\beta$ to denote $(Qx_1) \ldots (Qx_n)\beta$. We write β_s^t to represent the term or the formula identical to β except with all occurrences of the term s replaced by the term t. Finally, we write $\beta(x_1, \ldots x_n)$ to indicate that $x_1, \ldots x_n$ are the only free variables in a term or formula β.

PCEN is a conservative extension of PCE, in the sense that a formula in PCEN is valid if and only if an equivalent formula in PCE is valid. The equivalence between a PCEN formula and a PCE formula can be seen easily when (8c) is compared to (4). If β is a PCE formula with free variable x, then a PCEN formula $(@_n x)\beta$ has the same value under all interpretations and assignment functions as the PCE formula

$$(\exists x_1, \ldots, x_n)(\beta_x^{x_1} \wedge \ldots \beta_x^{x_n} \wedge \neq [x_1, \ldots, x_n]) \tag{2.27}$$

Since PCE is sound and complete and since PCEN is a conservative extension of PCE, PCEN is also sound and complete. We can easily obtain a proof theory for PCEN by appending to a proof theory for PCE the axiom schema:

$$(@_n x)\beta \leftrightarrow (\exists x_1, \ldots, x_n)(\beta_x^{x_1} \wedge \ldots \wedge \beta_x^{x_n} \wedge \neq [x_1, \ldots, x_n]) \tag{A@}$$

2.6 INFERENCE IN PCEN

We shall discuss two ways of doing inference in PCEN, using resolution with paramodulation, and using natural deduction. We shall see that the first approach is impracticable for PCEN. An understanding of the latter may aid us in finding an efficient inference mechanism.

Resolution with paramodulation is commonly used to determine the unsatisfiability of a PCE formula expressed in clausal form, and hence to determine the validity of its negation. Roughly speaking, paramodulation allows one to infer the clause $P(b) \vee Q(c) \vee R(d)$ from the clauses $P(a) \vee Q(c)$ and $a = b \vee R(d)$. Essentially, it is the inference rule of replacing equal with equal. We shall not define paramodulation in this paper. Interested readers are referred to Chang and Lee (1973).

A formula in PCEN may consist of numerical quantifiers of the form $(@_n x)$ or $(@_n^m x)$. The latter can be expressed in the former by the convention $(C@)$. Then by repeatedly applying the axiom $(A@)$, we can obtain an equivalent formula in PCE. The equivalent formula can then be expressed as a set of clauses, to which resolution with paramodulation can be applied.

Though plausible in theory, the approach is impracticable if applied as suggested. Too many clauses will be so generated from a PCEN formula. For example, a simple formula such as

$$(@_3^8x)(@_1^5y)(Person(x) \land House(y) \land Own(x,y)), \qquad (2.28)$$

which intends to say that "there are 3 to 8 persons, and each of them owns 1 to 5 houses", will require as many as 4.64×10^{13} clauses in PCE to represent it. In general, the number K_n of clauses resulted from expressing a formula of the form

$$(@_{a_n}^{b_n} x_n) \ldots (@_{a_1}^{b_1} x_1)\beta \qquad (2.29)$$

is given by the following pair of recursive relations,

$$K_n = a_n K_{n-1} + \frac{1}{2}a_n(a_n - 1) + (D_{n-1})^{(b_n+1)} \qquad (2.30)$$

$$D_n = (D_{n-1})^{a_n}((b_n + 1)K_{n-1} + \frac{1}{2}b_n(b_n + 1))^{(D_{n-1})^{(b_n+1)}}$$

K_0 = *the number of clauses needed to express* β
D_0 = *the product of the numbers of atoms in all the clauses.*

We have not yet found any efficient scheme in using resolution with paramodulation on PCEN formulas, though we think that such a scheme may exist. One approach may be to avoid expanding the atom $\neq [x_1, \ldots, x_n]$, and rely on a special mechanism to reason about it. This will replace the $a_n(a_n - 1)/2$ term in K_n and the $b_n(b_n + 1)/2$ term in D_n by the constant 1. In this case, formula (2.26) will be expanded into 3.23×10^{11} clauses.

Often, an inference system should not be required to expand a PCEN formula into clausal form in order to make an inference. For example, formula (28) can be inferred directly from

$$(@_3^3x)(@_1^5y)(Person(x) \land House(y) \land Owns(x,y)). \qquad (2.31)$$

To help us construct a direct inference system on PCEN, we shall formulate a natural deduction system for PCEN. In a natural deduction system, an introduction (I) rule and an elimination (E) rule are specified for each logical entity, such as a connective or a quantifier. For a typical natural deduction system of first-order predicate calculus (PC), readers are referred to Prawitz (1965). Following Skidmore (1987), we add the rules ($= E$) and ($= I$) to a natural deduction system of PC to obtain a natural deduction system of PCE.

($= E$) From $s = t$ and β, where s and t are terms and β is a formula, we may infer either β_s^t or β_t^s.

($= I$) We may infer $t = t$, where t is a term.

This system is sound and complete. We proceed in the same manner to form a natural deduction system for PCEN.

(@$E1$) From $(@_nx)\beta$, where β is a formula and $n > 0$, we may infer $(\exists x_1, \ldots, x_n)$ $(\beta_x^{x_1} \land \beta_x^{x_n} \land \neq [x_1, \ldots x_n])$, where $x_1, \ldots, x_n$ do not occur in β.

($@I1$) From $(\exists x_1, \ldots, x_n)\,(\beta_x^{x_1} \wedge \ldots \wedge \beta_x^{x_n} \wedge \neq [x_1, \ldots x_n])$, we may infer $(@_n x)\beta$.

This pair of rules yield a sound and complete system for PCEN. The soundness can be seen by justifying the rules from the definition of $\mathcal{I}^f$. The completeness is obtained by observing that $(A@)$ is provable from $(@E1)$ and $(@I1)$. Three more rules are also added to the system.

($@E2$) From $(@_n x)\beta$, where β is a formula and $n > 1$, we may infer
$(\exists x_1, \ldots, x_k)\,(@_{n-k} x)\,(\beta \wedge \beta_x^{x_1} \wedge \ldots \wedge \beta_x^{x_k} \wedge \neq [x, x_1, \ldots x_k])$, where $k < n$ and $x_1, \ldots, x_k$ do not occur in β.

($@I2$) From $(\exists x_1, \ldots, x_k)\,(@_n x)\,(\beta \wedge \beta_x^{x_1} \wedge \ldots \wedge \beta_x^{x_k} \wedge \neq [x, x_1, \ldots x_k])$ where $x_1, \ldots, x_k$ do not occur in β, we may infer $(@_{n+k} x)\beta$.

($@\Sigma$) From $(\forall v)(\forall w)(\forall y)((\alpha(v, y) \wedge \alpha(w, y)) \rightarrow v = w)$ and
$(\exists x_1, \ldots, x_n)\,((@_{a_1} y)(\alpha(x_1, y) \wedge \beta(y)) \wedge \ldots \wedge (@_{a_n} y)(a(x_n, y) \wedge \beta(y)) \wedge \neq [x, x_1, \ldots x_k])$, we may infer $(@a_1 + \ldots + a_n y)\beta(y)$.

Rule ($@E2$) extracts existential quantifies from a numerical quantifier, while rule ($@I2$) integrates existential quantifiers into a numerical quantifier. Rule ($@\Sigma$) combines multiple numerical quantifiers into a single quantifier by addition, when the sets of individuals they quantified over are disjointed. These three rules do not add anything new to PCEN, since all of them are derivable from ($@E1$), ($@I1$) and other rules in the system. Their presence, however, will provide more direct means of inference with formulas containing numerical quantifiers. This is especially true for ($@\Sigma$), which allows "addition", and in case of $a_1 = \ldots = a_n$, "multiplication" of numerical quantifiers. We call all these rules *direct inference rules*.

We end this section with an example showing an inference applied directly to PCEN formulas as a demonstration of the use of a direct inference rule ($@\Sigma$). Given "there are at least five blocks, each of which is supported by at least three pyramids" and "no pyramid supports more than one block", we want to infer that "there are at least fifteen pyramids".

1. *[Premise]* $(@_{5x})(@_{3y})(Block(x) \wedge Pyramid(y) \wedge Support(y, x))$

2. *[Premise]* $(\forall x)(\forall y)(\forall z)((Block(x) \wedge Block(y) \wedge Pyramid(z)$
$\wedge Support(z, x) \wedge Support(z, y)) \rightarrow x = y)$

3. $[1 : @E1]$ $(\exists x_1, \ldots, x_5)$
$((@_{3y})(Block(x_1) \wedge Pyramid(y) \wedge Support(y, x_1)) \wedge \ldots$
$(@_{3y})(Block(x_5) \wedge Pyramid(y) \wedge Support(y, x_5))\wedge$
$\neq [x_1, \ldots x_5])$

4. $[2, 3 : @\Sigma, \alpha(x, y) \equiv$ $[Block(x) \wedge Pyramid(y) \wedge Support(y, x), \beta(y) \equiv$
$Pyramid(y)]\ (@_{15y})Pyramid(y)$

Q.E.D.

Note that although a natural deduction system for PCEN are generate shorter proofs, it does not necessarily lead to an efficient implementation of a mechanical theorem prover. This is because there is no good way to decide which inference rule to use. Further studies are needed in this area.

2.7   PCEN AND CONCEPTUAL GRAPHS

PCEN provides a theoretical framework for developing and verifying inference systems for conceptual graphs with numerical quantifiers. The meaning of a numerical quantifier in PCEN is compatible with that in our extended notation of conceptual structures. Instead of stating the cardinality of an instantiation set, a numerical quantifier in PCEN asserts the existence of a minimum number of distinct individuals. If we restrict the domain to a finite list of individuals or to the universe of discourse, and require that functional dependencies represented by the scope list have a linear structure (i.e. if x and y are in the scope list of z, then either x is in the scope list of y or y is in the scope list of x), then every conceptual graph with extended notation can be translated into PCEN. For example, the conceptual graph in (2.25) can be translated to PCEN as:

$$(@_2^\infty x)(@_1^\infty y)(Person(x) \wedge House(y) \wedge Own(x,y)$$
$$\wedge(x = John \vee x = Mary \vee x = Tom)). \tag{2.32}$$

Since PCEN is sound and complete, there is a sound and complete proof theory for conceptual graphs with extended notation. If we can construct an efficient theorem prover for PCEN, we may also be able to construct one for conceptual graphs.

A natural deduction system for PCEN provides us with hints on how to formulate a set of direct inference rules for conceptual structures with extended notation. Observe that a slight modification of $(@E2)$ and $(@I2)$ will make $(@E1)$ and $(@I1)$ unnecessary. Therefore, if we have a set of inference rules for conceptual graphs that handles first-order predicate calculus, the equality rules $(= E)$ and $(= I)$, and the modified versions of $(@E2)$ and $(@I2)$, then we know that this set of rules is complete. To improve efficiency, we also shall add rules that correspond to $(@\Sigma)$.

There is a desire in the conceptual graph community to reason with sets. Yet a major motivation for doing so is to handle cardinality, which correspond to numerical quantifiers in PCEN, and finite sets of individuals. Although the notion of sets is inherent in the notion of numerical quantifiers, we have shown with PCEN that to do reasoning with these quantifiers, a system does not need to mention sets at all. By the same token, we argue that it is unnecessary to include set theory in conceptual structures just in order to handle cardinality. Set-coreference can also be expressed in PCEN without an explicit reference to a set. A statement with set-coreference, unlike numerical quantifiers, does not translate into a concise formula in PCEN. For example, a statement such as "there are five persons, each of them owns at least two donkeys, and at least two of the persons beat their donkeys" will have to be expressed in terms of $\exists$ and $\neq$ rather than just "@". This may mean that inference with set-coreference could be inefficient.

In Tjan *et al.* (1990), we proposed a set of direct inference rules for conceptual structures with extended notation. The set of rules is divided into Rule 1 and Rule 2. Rule 2, which consists of fives sub-rules, has some of the advantages of the natural deduction and direct inference that we have discussed. In particular, Rule 2c resembles (@Σ). Gardiner *et al.* (1991) defines a set of graph operations for conceptual graphs. These operators are implemented as the building blocks for our conceptual structures reasoning system. These operations are constructed from intuition. One way to determine their completeness and soundness is to express them in PCEN.

BIBLIOGRAPHY

Chang, Chin Liang, and Richard Char Tung Lee. (1973) *Symbolic Logic and Mechanical Theorem Proving*, Academic Press, New York.

Gardiner, D. A., B. S. Tjan, and J. R. Slagle. (1989) "Extended Conceptual Structure Notation", in Proceedings of the Fourth Annual Workshop on Conceptual Structures. Edited by J. A. Nagle and T. E. Nagle. pp 3.05.1-3.05.11. Available from AAAI. Also available as TR89-88 from the Computer Science Department, University of Minnesota, Minneapolis.

Gardiner, D. A., B. S. Tjan, and J. R. Slagle. (1992) "Extending Conceptual Structures: Representation Issues and Reasoning Operations", in (eds) T. Nagle, J. Nagle L. Gerholz and P. Eklund, *Conceptual Structures: Research and Practice*, Ellis Horwood.

Hintikka, J. (1977) "Quantifiers in Natural Languages: some Logical Problems", in *Game Theoretical Semantics*, edited by E. Saarinen. D. Reidel Publishing Company, London, England.

Prawitz, D. (1965) *Natural Deduction: a Proof- Theoretical Study*, Almqvist & Wiksell, Stockholm.

Skidmore, A. (1987) "Summary of the Inference Rules of Elementary Logic". University of Kansas, Department of Philosophy.

Slagle, J. R., D. Gardiner, and B. S. Tjan. (1990) "Reasoning with Conceptual Structures: Year Two Final Report". Department of Computer Science, University of Minnesota, Minneapolis. NTIS, TR 90-22.

Sowa, J.F. (1984) *Conceptual Structures: Information Processing in Mind and Machine*, Addison Wesley, Reading.

Sowa, J.F. (1989) "Conceptual Graph Notation", in *Proceedings of the Fourth Annual Workshop on Conceptual Structures*. Edited by J. A. Nagle and T. E. Nagle. pp 7.01.1-7.01.22. Available from AAAI.

Tjan, B. S., and J. R. Slagle. (1988) "A Conceptual Structure Semantic Theory Based on a Semantic Game with Partial Information", in *Proceedings of the Third Annual Workshop on Conceptual Graphs*. pp 3.2.8.1-3.2.8.11. Available from the AAAI.

Tjan, Bosco S., David A. Gardiner, and James R. Slagle. (1990) "Direct Inference Rules for Conceptual Graphs with Extended Notation", in *Proceedings of the Fifth Annual workshop on Conceptual Structures*, (eds) P. Eklund, and L. Gerholz, Linköping University, ISBN 91-7870-718-8.

3

Extending Conceptual Structures: Representation Issues and Reasoning Operations

David A. Gardiner, Bosco S. Tjan and James R. Slagle
University of Minnesota,
Computer Science Department,
200 Union Street S.E., Minneapolis, MN 55455, USA

ABSTRACT

Symbolic knowledge representations have historically been based on first order predicate calculus (FOPC) due to the known soundness, completeness, decidability, and tractability of FOPC and, often pragmatically, the availability of FOPC inference engines. The expressive power of FOPC is insufficient to represent much of the knowledge that people use. FOPC integrated with a constrained set capability provides greatly increased expressive power. We have developed a semantic network representation, based on Sowa's conceptual structures, that uses sets as an integral part of the representation. We view an uninstantiated concept as a specification of constraints on the set of referents that may instantiated the concept. We have found that a combination of four constraint-type, functional dependency, domain, and cardinality-provides far greater representational capability than standard FOPC-based languages while maintaining a precisely defined semantics. In this chapter we discuss this representation and the reasoning operations we have developed for it.

3.1 INTRODUCTION

The overall objective of our research has been to develop a computer system that clearly and concisely represents the knowledge that is used in diagnostic reasoning and can reason with that knowledge. We are oriented toward highly-interactive systems that assist a human user in solving a problem rather than on autonomous systems. Thus, one of the goals of our reasoning system is to take a minimal specification of a problem and expand it into a model sufficient for determining a solution to the problem. We call this kind of model a *situation model*.

Researchers in knowledge representation tend to take two divergent approaches. The most popular is to have a representation that has limited expressive power but is tractable. The KL-ONE family of representations has tended to be of this type. The other approach is to focus on representational power, usually aiming for the expressive power of natural language.

Advocates of this position, by necessity, avoid focusing on computational complexity. The first approach is generally more pragmatic, the second is more ambitious. Our work clearly fits in the second category. While we consider computational complexity issues and are concerned with them, our approach is to make a representation work before we worry about making it work efficiently.

3.2   REPRESENTATION ISSUES

We chose Sowa's conceptual structures as a base for our work for several reasons. Conceptual structures are a generalization of other semantic network knowledge representations. Sowa did an excellent job of integrating many kinds of semantic network (and other) structures into his theory. These structures include declarative graphs, dataflow graphs, a type hierarchy, type definitions, and schemata. In addition, Sowa provides a rigorous definition of the representation, reasoning operations, and semantics in his theory. This allows modification and extension of the theory.

Our extended version of conceptual structures is based on treating an uninstantiated concept as a specification of instantiation constraints, that is, constraints on the set of referents that may instantiate a concept. We have found that a set of four constraints, used together, provides great expressive power. Those four constraints are concept type, functional dependency, domain, and cardinality.

Concept type is used in virtually all semantic network representations. Anything that might instantiate the concept must conform to the concept type. Cardinality, particularly interval cardinality, is also relatively common in knowledge representations. Thus, these two alone are not exceptional but they are essential.

Functional dependency is implied in any representation that has the full power of FOPC. Few, if any, of those representations express functional dependency explicitly. For example, Sowa's notation assumes that each concept is existentially quantified. To achieve universal quantification, nested negated contexts must be used. any complex quantification, such as $\exists x \forall y$, requires even greater nesting. We have found that explicit specification of functional dependency is critical to minimizing the complexity of graphs. This is equivalent to specification of the skolem function parameters for each skolemized concept.

Specification of the domain of instantiation for a concept is something that other representations have attempted, but none that we have encountered deal with it in a general fashion. The conventional handling of domain is in disjunction, for example, *Mary loves John or Bob*. In our representation, conjunction and disjunction are isomorphic, as are all relations between them. Standard disjunction indicates that one or more members of the domain may instantiate the concept. Conjunction indicates that all members of the domain instantiate the concept. By using domain and cardinality, we can represent conjunction, disjunction, and a relation such as *Mary loves two of John, Bob, Harry, and Martin*, all with the same notation. We also allow a domain to be a function, which allows us to represent a sentence such as *There are five computers in the accounting department and one of them has a laser printer attached.*

The combination of these four constraints appears to be unique to our representation and also appears to provide sufficient expressive power for most complex reasoning systems.

3.3 NOTATION

In this section we describe our extended conceptual structures notation. We want to emphasize that the expressive power of our representation is independent of the notation. We have simply found conceptual structures to be a suitable framework in which to embed these representational capabilities.

3.3.1 Referents

To use an analogy with physical systems, the stable state for a concept is to have a referent. That is, rather than discussing some unknown man in *There is a man who loves Mary*, we want to be able to say *John Jones loves Mary*. Similarly, the objective of any discussion of a set is to identify the members of the set. Therefore, we need a definition of a *referent*.

Definition A *referent* is an individual marker, a text string enclosed in double quotes, a number, a conceptual graph, or a set.

Strings are straightforward. A number may be an integer, real, or complex number. A conceptual graph is preceded by a #[1]. A set is enclosed in braces and also preceded by a #. A set referent is different than the concept domain, as is spell discussed below in the section "Instantiation Constraints". Note that, with the exception of a constant (string or number), every referent begins with a #.

In representing knowledge we must distinguish between an individual and that individual's name. Every individual must be uniquely identified, yet names are not necessarily unique and not all concepts have names. For example, the person John Smith is a unique individual but his name is not unique. The individual act of dressing that John did this morning is unique but does not have a name.

Sowa's notation provides a set of *individual markers* that provide a unique identifier for each individual. Individual markers in the original notation are a # followed by an integer. Since these tend to be meaningless by themselves, we replace the integer with a string. Thus, the individual marker for John Smith may be `#John_Smith_from_Milwaukee`. This notation is for convenience only-there are no more semantics associated with the string than with the integer. The same approach has been used in the CYC project. Lenat and Guha discuss the advantages and dangers of using meaningful names for concept types and individual markers:

> . . . *the names are scaffolding that helps us now, in the early stages, as we build up the Cyc KB. Eventually, the names can all go away (for example, they could be replaced by randomly generated symbols). . . Although we see this as possible (circa the end of this century), we likewise see little reason for going out of our way to give the units meaningless names, especially during the initial stages of the project. It makes life easier if we can recognize the printed forms of these units . . . However, this decision is fraught with hidden danger: new knowledge enterers tend to recognize and understand "too much"*

---

[1] This simplifies parsing. Otherwise, a parser encountering an "(" would have difficulty determining whether this was a scope list or a conceptual graph beginning with a relation.

from these expressive English names-more than is there in the rest of the unit!
(Lenat and Guha, 1990, page 342)

A name with semantic connotations is expressed using an attached concept. For example,
if we want to express that John Smith's first name is "John" and his last name is "Smith",
we would do so with the following graph:

```
[PERSON: #John_Smith_from_Milwaukee] -
    → (FIRST-NAME) → [STRING: "John"]
    → (LAST-NAME) → [STRING: "Smith"]
```

Assumption There is a set I of *individual markers*. Each individual marker is unique and
is of the form *#string*.

3.3.2   Instantiation

Our discussion of instantiation up to this point has been informal. Before continuing we
must define instantiation.

Assumption There are three forms of the referent field that correspond to three kinds of
concepts. The referent field of

- an *instantiated* concept is a referent.
- a *constrained* concept is *instantiation* constraints.
- a *pronoun* concept is the variable corresponding to a constrained concept.

A pronoun concept is a shorthand way to indicate that two concepts have the same
instantiation constraints. Thus, if several constrained concepts have the same instantiation
constraints, the constraints can be specified in one concept with the other concepts being
pronouns. This saves space and prevents inconsistency. For reasoning purposes, pronoun
concepts are expanded to include the full constraint specification.

Definition Concepts with the same concept variable are members of the same *coreference
class* and therefore have identical instantiation constraints.

Assumption A pronoun concept is converted to a constrained concept by replacing the
referent field of the pronoun concept with the referent field of the constrained concept
in its coreference class.

3.3.3   Instantiation Constraints

The instantiation constraints of a constrained concept are specified using the following
format:

scope-list variable domain @cardinality control-mark

For example, the concept *There exist five or more computers* is represented as

```
[COMPUTER: ()c * @5-∞°].
```

The *scope list* is a list of zero or more concept variables enclosed in parentheses and indicates that the concept is functionally dependent on the members of the coreference classes specified in the scope list[2]. The default scope list is (), that is, null.

The *variable* identifies the coreference class of the concept. The default variable is unique.

The *domain* is a set of referents that are candidates for instantiation. There are four forms for the domain:

- Explicit specification of the set, such as {#Tom, #Dick, #Harry}

- Specification of a range, such as {3−6}. This can be used for sequenced types (such as numbers) only.

- The generic domain {*}, which contains all possible referents

- A function that returns a set of referents.

In the original notation, a generic set referent {*} is provided. It is interpreted as *zero or more elements*, with the kind of element assumed to be an individual. In our notation, the set {*} is interpreted as the set of all referents but is not itself a referent. It is the default domain.

Definition {*} is the set of all referents.

Elements in the domain may be separated by either a comma or a semicolon. The domain is different than a set referent. A set referent is valid only for a concept that is a subtype of the type SET. Thus, the concept of the set of people Tom, Dick, and Harry would be represented with a concept of type PERSON-SET. It could not be of type PERSON as a set referent would not conform to that type. The first graph below is instantiated with a set referent. The second graph is constrained.

```
[PERSON-SET: # {#Tom, #Dick, #Harry}].
[PERSON:  p {#Tom, #Dick, #Harry}@1−∞].
```

The *cardinality* specifies the number of referents that exist for each value of the scope list variables. The cardinality may be a range of (non-negative) integers in the form *min-max*, which refers to the number of individuals conforming to the concept type[3]. For a concept in a query, the cardinality field may instead contain a directive indicating how the cardinality should be determined (see the section on Queries below). The default cardinality is 1-∞, which means that there exists at least one. A cardinality containing a single number indicates an exact cardinality (minimum and maximum are the same).

The *control mark* directs the reasoning process in instantiation of the concept. The default control mark "∘" means that the current state of instantiation is acceptable[4]. Control marks are discussed below in the section on Queries.

---

[2] An easier way to think of this is to assume that there is only one concept in each coreference class. Then the scope list specifies the concepts that the current concept is dependent on.

[3] We have also experimented with allowing a selection of integers in the form $opt_1, \ldots, opt_n$ and a fuzzy count such as "many" or "few", or "all", For the purposes of our current work in reasoning, we allow only the interval cardinality and the "all" cardinality.

[4] For the balance of this paper, we shall assume the default control mark for each concept without actually writing them.

Assumption The following functions may be applied to any concept c. If the field does not exist in the concept, NIL is returned.

- $referent(c)$ returns the referent of c (fully instantiated concepts only).

- $scope\text{-}list(c)$ returns the scope list of c (constrained concepts only).

- $variable(c)$ returns the variable of c (constrained and pronoun concepts only).

- $domain(c)$ returns the domain of c (constrained concepts only).

- $cardinality(c)$ returns the cardinality of c (constrained concepts only).

- $control\text{-}mark(c)$ returns the control mark of c (constrained concepts only).

3.3.4   Instantiation Function

The original denotation operator δ maps a type label to the set of instances of that type in a model. Instead, we define a δ *function* for mapping a type label or lambda abstraction to the set of all referents of that type. This function is necessary for defining the instantiation set.

Definition The *denotation* function δ may be applied to any type label or lambda abstraction t. $\delta(t)$ returns the set containing all referents conforming to type t.

Assumption Each constrained concept c has an associated *instantiation set*, denoted as $IS(c)$, such that $IS(c) \subseteq \delta(type(c)) \cap domain(c)$.

Our approach to the representation and interpretation of constrained concepts is to assume the existence of an *instantiation function*. The input variables of the function are specified in the scope list. For each distinct list of values for the input variables, the instantiation function returns an instantiation set. This instantiation set is a subset of the domain and has a cardinality meeting the constraints specified by the concept cardinality. For example, consider the graph representing the sentence *Two or more of the computers #1, #2, #3, and #4 run exactly three programs each.*

```
[COMPUTER: ()c{#1,#2,#3,#4}@2−∞] ← (AGNT) ← [RUN: (c,p)r@1−∞]
        → (PTNT) → [PROGRAM: (c)p @3].
```

To interpret this graph, we start with the COMPUTER concept because it has a null scope list. The concept indicates that there are two or more individuals of type COMPUTER that will make the graph true. Furthermore, these individuals are a subset of the set $\{\#1,\#2,\#3,\#4\}$[5]. For each one of these individuals, the instantiation function for the concept PROGRAM returns exactly three individuals of type PROGRAM. For each computer-program pair, the instantiation function for the concept RUN returns at least one instance of running.

The domain of the COMPUTER concept in the graph above is a four element set that only loosely constrains the instantiation of the concept. The domains of the PROGRAM and RUN concepts are the default $\{*\}$, which is no constraint at all. Both cases are called *loose* constraints. An example of a tight constraint is the COMPUTER concept in;

---

[5] Since there are only four referents in the domain, the cardinality of the concept could just as well be 2-4.

```
[COMPUTER: () c{#1,#2}@2] ← (AGNT) ← [RUN: (c,p) r@1-∞]
        → (PTNT) → [PROGRAM:  (c)p @3].
```

There are exactly two individuals in the concept's instantiation set, and those individuals are specified in the domain. A graph containing a concept with a tight constraint can be expanded into a conjunction of graphs. For the graph above, the expansion would be the conjunction of the graphs;

```
[COMPUTER:  #1] ← (AGNT) ← [RUN:  (p1) r1  @1-∞] → (PTNT) →
                    [PROGRAM:  () p1 @3]

[COMPUTER:  #2] ← (AGNT) ← [RUN:  (p2) r2  @1-∞] → (PTNT) →
                    [PROGRAM:  () p2 @3].
```

Definition If the cardinality of a concept c is a single number i, and if $|domain(c)| = i$, the instantiation constraint of c is called *tight*. If $|domain(c)| < i$, the constraint of c is *inconsistent*. Any instantiation constraint that is not tight or inconsistent is called *loose*.

Assumption Let u be the conceptual graph containing a tightly constrained concept c with a null () scope list, and let the $domain(c) = \{r_1, \ldots, r_n\}$. u may be replaced by a conjunction of graphs $u_1, \ldots, u_n$ where each u_i is a copy of u with the referent field of c replaced by r_i, the concept variables of concepts containing $variable(c)$ in their scope lists standardized apart, and with $variable(c)$ removed from all scope lists in u_i.

3.3.5 Comparison to Sowa's Sets

Since our representation is based on Sowa's, and Sowa does provide a set capability, in this section we compare our set capability to his.

The original notation included four kinds of sets: collective, distributive, disjunctive, and respective (Sowa, 1984, page 117-119). The basic ideas behind these sets are good but the actual capabilities of the notation are limited.

A tightly constrained concept in our notation is identical to a concept with a distributive set in the original notation. The collective set, which Sowa used as the default, is defined in the original notation as having all elements participating in the same relationship together. We found the semantics of this kind of set elusive. The definition implies that a referent can be a set, which is problematic in that a set is a mathematical entity. For example, the graph (using the original notation) for the sentence *John and Mary are dancing* (using our individual marker notation) is;

```
[PERSON:  {#John, #Mary}] ← (AGNT) ← [DANCE].
```

means that a set containing John and Mary is dancing. Sets don't dance, people do. Rather than attempting to represent a collective set, we use a concept of type COLLECTION to represent the set of referents participating in the relationship and a relation IN-COLL to specify the members of the collection. For the example above, we would say that *There is a couple consisting of John and Mary that is the agent of dancing.* Our representation of the sentence is;

```
[COUPLE: ()c {*} @1] -
    → (IN-COLL) → [PERSON: (c)p {#John, #Mary}@2]
    ← (AGNT) ← [DANCE: (c)d @1].
```

3.3.6 Queries

Until now, discussion of our notation has been oriented toward declarative assertions. The notation must also be used for representing queries. The primary difference between a query and an assertion is that the query graph may be modified by the reasoning process and the query may place constraints on how it may be answered.

As noted above, the referent field of a constrained concept always contains a control mark and may contain a cardinality directive rather than a normal cardinality. The cardinality directive "?" indicates that the cardinality is not known and directs the reasoning process to determine the cardinality using either deduction or enumeration. A cardinality of "!" indicates that the cardinality is not known and directs the reasoning process to determine it through enumeration. For example, assume that we want to determine how many IBM System/38 computers exist. The query graph for this is;

```
[SYSTEM/38: ()s {*}@?].
```

If our knowledge base contained the assertion;

```
[SYSTEM/38: ()t {*}@3],
```

by deduction we could answer that there are three System/38s. To determine this by enumeration, the knowledge base would have to contain three (and only three) concepts such as;

```
[SYSTEM/38 #3141]   [SYSTEM/38 #5926]   [SYSTEM/38 #5358]
```

Control marks act as instantiation directives. The control mark "°" means that the reasoning process should reason about the concept with its current instantiation. The control mark "?" means that the reasoning process should attempt to make the concept tightly constrained. The mark "!" means that the concept should be fully instantiated[6]. For example, the query *Are there exactly three System/38s?* would be represented as;

```
[SYSTEM/38: ()s {*}@3 °].
```

In contrast, the query *What are the (exactly) three System/38s?* would be represented as;

```
[SYSTEM/38: ()s {*}@3 ?].
```

The former can simply be proved (or fail to be proved) true. No referents are required. To accomplish the latter, the reasoning process replaces the generic domain with all suitable referents, such as in;

---

[6]A partially instantiated concept in an assertion always has a control mark of "°". The control mark of a concept in any other structure, such as a schema or type definition, may be any of the three marks.

```
[SYSTEM/38:  ()s {#3141,#5926,#5358} @3].
```

Note that the reasoning process must confirm that the actual cardinality of the domain is within the constraints of the concept cardinality and modify the reasoning mark accordingly.

Use of the "!" control mark would direct the reasoning process to fully instantiate the concept, producing the three fully instantiated concepts shown above.

3.3.7   Coreference

A knowledge representation requires a way to indicate that two values are the same or related. For example, consider the sentence *There is a man who thinks that Mary loves him.* The man doing the thinking is the same as the man who, in the context of the thought, is loved by Mary. The coreference in this example can be expressed with variables. We extend the idea of coreference to functions to allow more complex relationships.

Definition There are two forms of coreference between concepts:

Simple coreference, in which the coreferent concepts have the same instantiation set or referent (for fully instantiated concepts). For constrained concepts, this is specified using identical concept variables.

Domain coreference, in which there is a functional relationship between the instantiation set of one concept and the domain of another.

Simple coreference is the coreference provided by the original notation. Domain coreference allows us to represent such sentences as *Each of five computers has three terminals attached to it, and two of those computers have a laser printer attached:*

```
[COMPUTER:  ()c {*} @5]←(ATTACHED)←[TERMINAL:  (c)t {*} @3]

[COMPUTER:  ()d IS(c) @2]←(ATTACHED)←[LASER-PRINTER:  (d)p
                                     {*} @1]
```

Where the function IS returns the instantiation set of the parameter concept, as described previously.

3.3.8   Contexts

The example sentence above, *There is a man who thinks that Mary loves him,* requires a grouping referred to as a *context.* That is, the sentence does not assert that Mary loves anyone, it asserts that there is something that some man is thinking. That thought happens to be about Mary loving him.

In Sowa's original theory, contexts are provided as a mechanism for grouping conceptual graphs. They are intended to be isomorphic to concepts but the isomorphism is limited. Propositions are also given two conflicting interpretations. By definition (Sowa, 1984, page 139), a graph within a proposition is defined to be *asserted* by that proposition. For example, the proposition (original notation);

```
[PROPOSITION:  {u}]
```

is interpreted as u. The truth of the proposition is dependent on the truth of the graphs contained in the proposition. This is appropriate for logical nesting, which is one of the primary uses of propositions. It is <u>not</u> appropriate for expressing modality. Sowa gets around this by inserting modal symbols in the interpretation of modal graphs, but no formal definition of the ϕ operator for modal graphs is provided. The problem with the original notation is in having a proposition assert a graph rather than just using the proposition as a grouping mechanism. We have solved this problem by treating a proposition the same as any other concept.

Definition A *graph set* is a set referent containing one or more conceptual graphs. Each graph set conforms to the concept type PROPOSITION.

Definition Let p be a concept of type PROPOSITION whose domain is either the generic domain or contains only graph sets. A graph g in a graph set of the domain of p is said to occur in the *context* of p (Sowa, 1984, page 139).

Thus, [PROPOSITION: #{u,v}] asserts only that {u,v} is a proposition. The truth of the contents of a proposition is determined by attached relations. For example, consider the following four graphs:

(1) [PROPOSITION:
    #{[PERSON: #Mary]→(LOVES)→[PERSON: #John]}]

(2) (TRU)→[PROPOSITION:
    #{[PERSON:#Mary]→(LOVES)→[PERSON:#John]}]

(3) (NEG)→[PROPOSITION:
    #{[PERSON:#Mary]→(LOVES)→[PERSON:#John]}]

(4) [PERSON: #John]→(BELIEVES)→[PROPOSITION:
    #{[PERSON: #Mary]→(LOVES)→[PERSON: #John]}]

The first graph states only that *"Mary loves John"* is a proposition. The second graph states that *Mary loves John* is a true statement, while the third graph states that it is a false statement. The last graph states that *"John believes that Mary loves him"*, but does not assert whether she really does.

3.3.9 BNF for Notation

The following is our notation for concepts in our extended conceptual structure notation. For an excellent BNF description of the remainder of the conceptual structure notation, see Esch (1988).

Our syntax for concepts is presented here using Backus-Naur Form. Bold-face is used for literal strings. All punctuation and math symbols, except those described below, are literal strings. The following special symbols are used:

::=   "Defined as"
| "Or"
*   "Zero or more of the preceding" (note that this is superscript)
+   "One or more of the following"
       concept ::= [type-field: referent-field]
       referent-field ::= instantiation-constraints | referent | variable
       cardinality ::= min-max | all | cardinality-options | fuzzy-count | ? | !
       cardinality-options ::= non-negative-integer option-element
       conceptual-graph-element ::= ,conceptual-graph
       control-mark ::= ° | ? | !
       domain ::= {referent referent-list-element*} | {*} | function
       function ::= function-name(variable-list)
       function-name ::= string
       fuzzy-count ::= **many** | **few**
       graph-set ::= null | #{conceptual-graph conceptual-graph-element*}
       individual-marker ::= #string
       instantiation-constraints ::= scope-list variable domain @cardinality control-mark
       max ::= non-negative-integer | ∞
       min ::= non-negative-integer
       number ::= integer | real | complex
       option-element ::= ,non-negative-integer
       referent ::= individual-marker | text-string | number | graph-group
       referent-list-element ::= ,referent
       scope-list ::= (variable-list)
       string ::= letter*
       text-string ::= "string"
       type ::= type-label | lambda-abstraction
       variable ::= string
       variable-list ::= nil | variable variable-list-element*
       variable-list-element ::= ,variable

3.4   TRANSLATION TO LOGIC

We have developed a ϕ operator to translate graphs in our representation into first order logic with naive set theory and functions. The basic idea of the operator is that each variable associated with an uninstantiated concept specifies the existence of an instantiation set. The instantiation set is a subset of the domain of the concept, and the size of the instantiation set is constrained by the cardinality. Each element of the domain is a member of the instantiation set if and only if it conforms to the type of the concept and if the graph, with the concept instantiated by that element, is true. The ϕ operator requires a slightly more general type function than Sowa provides (Sowa, 1984, page 79).

Assumption For a concept or relation c, the function *type* returns the type label or lambda abstraction in the type field of c.

Assumption The operator ϕ maps conceptual graphs into formulas in the predicate calculus with (naive) set theory. If u is a group of conceptual graphs then

- If the outermost context[7] of u has fully instantiated concepts $c_1, \ldots, c_n$ with null scope lists and are not of type $\top$, then let T_i be the predicate with the same name as $type(c_i)$, $1 \leq i \leq n$. The translation of u is

$$\bigwedge_{i=1,\ldots,n} \left(T_i\left(referent(c_i)\right) \wedge \phi u'\right.$$

where u' is u with each c_i replaced by a fully instantiated concept with $referent(c_i)$ as the referent and $\top$ as the type.

- If the outermost context of u has n constrained concepts $c_1, \ldots, c_n$ with null scope lists, and there is no fully instantiated concept with null scope list in the outermost context that is not of type $\top$, then let T_i be the predicate with the same name as $type(c_i)$, and let $\mathcal{V}_1, \ldots, \mathcal{V}_n$ and $v_1, \ldots, v_n$ be new variables. The translation of u is

$$\exists \mathcal{V}_1, \ldots, \mathcal{V}_n \wedge_{i=1,\ldots,n} \left(\mathcal{V}_i \subseteq domain(c_i) \wedge cardinality - expression_i\right)$$

such that;

$$\forall v_1 \in domain(c_1), \ldots, \forall v_n \in domain(c_n), \left(\wedge_{i=1,\ldots,n} (v_i \in \mathcal{V}_i)\right) \leftrightarrow$$

$$\left(\wedge_{i=1,\ldots,n} (T_i(v_i))\right)$$

where u' is u with three modifications: c_i is replaced by a fully instantiated concept with v_i as the referent and $\top$ as the type; the pronoun concepts corresponding to c_i are fully instantiated with v_i ; and u' has $variable(c_i)$ removed from all scope lists in u. The $cardinality\text{-}expression_i$ is

  - $min_i \leq |\mathcal{V}_i| \leq max_i$ if $cardinality(c_i)$ is of the form $min_i\text{-}max_i$
  - $(|\mathcal{V}_i| = option_{i,1} \vee \ldots \vee |\mathcal{V}_i| = option_{i,n})$ if $cardinality(c_i)$ is of the form $option_{i,1} \ldots, option_{i,n}$
  - $|\mathcal{V}_i| = |\delta(type(c_i)) \cap domain(c_i)|$ if $cardinality(c_i) = \text{"all"}$

- If all of the top level concepts in u are fully instantiated and of type $\top$, let $r_1, \ldots, r_n$ be the relations in u and for each r_i, let $c_{i1}, \ldots, c_{ik}$ be the concepts attached to r_i. Let R_i be the subgraph of u consisting of r_i and $c_{i1}, \ldots, c_{ik}$. u is represented as the conjunction of all ϕR_i where
$R_i = (\phi r_i)(referent(c_{i1}), \ldots, referent(c_{ik}))$. ϕr_i is defined as follows:

  - If $type(r_i)$ is a non-logical relation of arity n, $\phi r_i = \lambda x_1, \ldots, x_n T_i(x_1, \ldots, x_n)$, where T_i is the predicate with the same name as the type of r_i.
  - If $type(r_i) = \text{NEG}$, $\phi r_i = \lambda x \left(\neg \left(\wedge \left(\bigcup_{a \in x} \{\phi a\}\right)\right)\right)$

---

[7]See (Sowa, 1984, page 141)

- If $type(r_i) = \text{TRU}$, $_{\phi}r_i = \lambda x \left(\wedge \left(\bigcup_{a \in x} \{\phi a\} \right) \right)$
- If $type(r_i) = \text{PSBL}$, $_{\phi}r_i = \lambda x \left(\Diamond \left(\wedge \left(\bigcup_{a \in x} \{\phi a\} \right) \right) \right)$
- If $type(r_i) = \text{NECS}$, $_{\phi}r_i = \lambda x \left([] \left(\wedge \left(\bigcup_{a \in x} \{\phi a\} \right) \right) \right)$

Other logical relations can be translated in a similar fashion[8].

3.5   REASONING METHODS

A problem with a powerful notation such as we have described is that reasoning is difficult. A common approach to implementing a non-standard knowledge representation reasoning system is to translate the representation into a standard representation (such as first order logic) and then use an existing inference engine. One problem with this approach is that the new representation can then be no more powerful than the standard representation, although it may be much more concise. There can also be problems of efficiency, since a complex representation will generally translate to large formulas in the base representation.

The logic formulas produced by our ϕ operator are complex, even for relatively small graphs. In (Tjan *et al.*, 1990) we show that a simple expression that can be expressed with two concepts and a relation in our representation required 1.35×10^{15} clauses in predicate calculus with equality. While the translation used in that paper is somewhat different than the ϕ operator described in this paper, it indicates that traditional theorem provers are inadequate to deal with a translation of our representation. Therefore, we are developing reasoning mechanisms to reason directly with our representation.

In our work on reasoning we are focusing on what we call *situation model creation*. Solving almost any real-world problem involves traversing an enormous search space. Human experts are able to solve such problems and give explanations that make the "path" through this search space seem simple and obvious. They create mental models that capture the most important aspects of a situation. We refer to these models as *situation models*. In this section we present a mechanism for creation of situation models using our extended conceptual structure representation. This mechanism is intended to make automated reasoning more efficient, to make user questioning more efficient (which is essential to make an expert system accepted in a real-world environment), and to use experience to improve reasoning and questioning.

In solving a problem, an expert has an almost infinite amount of information available but little of that information is relevant to the problem. An expert will usually begin solving a problem with a general survey of the situation and then focus on specific aspects. The process involved has been described as being *hypothetico-deductive*. That is, the expert develops a set of hypotheses based on initial observations, makes observations to confirm or refute those hypotheses, and then creates a revised set of hypotheses based on the new information available (Patil, 1987). Eventually, the expert has developed a mental model of the situation that allows the problem to be solved. Note that this approach produces true situation models. Using a technique such as abduction produces models that are likely to be true, but are not necessarily true[9].

---

[8]Note that the logical relations apply to concepts of type PROPOSITION only.

[9]Coombs and Hartley at the New Mexico State University have done work partly related to ours, but using an abductive approach (Coombs and Hartley, 1987).

Situation models are applicable to many kinds of reasoning, including diagnosis and robot planning (Chatila and Laumond, 1985)[10]. For the purposes of our work, we are focusing on diagnostic reasoning. Diagnosis can be described as an iterative process of situation model creation (or enhancement) and inference.

3.5.1   Schemata and Schematic Expansion

The hypothesis generation part of our reasoning is done with *schematic expansion*. In his theory, Sowa describes a conceptual structure called a *schema*, which can be treated as a hypothesis. Sowa describes a schema as follows:

> The basic structure for representing background knowledge for human-like inference is called the *schema*. It is a pattern derived from past experience that is used for interpreting, planning, and imagining other experiences. . . schemata correspond to Ceccato's *constellations*, Minsky's *frames*, and Schank and Abelson's *scripts* . . . Each schema presents a *perspective* on one way a concept type may be used. . . Unlike type definitions, which represent necessary conditions, a schema may not be true for every use of the type. . . schemata improve understanding by setting up expectations and preparing slots for future inputs. (Sowa, 1984, page 128-130)

An example of a schema, in English, would be *A System/38 may have a model number.* The following is Sowa's formal definition of a schema (Sowa 1984, page 104, 129):

Definition A *schematic cluster* for a type t is a set of monadic abstractions $\{\lambda a_1 u_1, \ldots, \lambda a_n u_n\}$ where each formal parameter a_i is a concept of type t and each u_i is a conceptual graph called the *body*. Each abstraction $\lambda a_i u_i$ in the set is called a *schema* for the type t.

Our reasoning mechanisms, like those that Sowa developed, are based on a set of fundamental operations. Sowa's *canonical formation rules* - copy, restrict, join, and simplify - were intended to preserve selectional constraints and falsity[11]. Our fundamental operations are simply a base set of operations for reasoning with conceptual structures. Three of our operations (copy, join, and simplify) are identical to three of Sowa's formation rules. Our specialize operation [12] is more general than Sowa's *restrict* rule.

Assumption There are five *fundamental operations* on conceptual graphs:

- *Copy*. Make an exact copy of a conceptual graph.

---

[10]In robot planning, the models are called *world models*.

[11]As is shown in Slagle, *et al.* (1988), the original formation rules d o not preserve selectional constraints. The problem with the Sowa's approach is that it makes an implicit assumption that only canonical graphs for concepts will be restricted. Because the canonical graph for a relation tends to be very general, restriction of a relation canonical graph often allows derivation of a graph that would violate the constraints specified by a corresponding concept canonical graph. Therefore, we check selectional constraints using the projection operator.

[12]By definition, a specialization may involve adding more concept and relation nodes to the original graph. For our purposes, we assume that specialization involves modifications only to the existing concept and relation nodes.

- *Specialize.* If g is a conceptual graph, produce a graph that logically implies g.

- *Generalize.* If g is a conceptual graph, produce a graph that g logically implies.

- *Join.* Given two identical concepts c and d, either in the same graph or different graphs, erase d and attach all arcs of conceptual relations that had been linked to d to c.

- *Simplify.* If two conceptual relations r and s are identical, have exactly the same number of arcs, and every arc of r is linked to exactly the same concept as the corresponding arc of s, then erase s and all of its arcs.

Specializing includes specializing individual nodes in a graph and adding nodes to a graph. To distinguish between these two kinds of specialization, we define *node-wise specialization.*

Definition Specialization of a conceptual graph that does not involve addition or deletion of nodes to the graph is called *node-wise specialization.*

A *situation model* is a set of conceptual graphs. A situation model may be expanded either by adding an assertion to the set or by schematic expansion. Schematic expansion adds a schema graph to an existing model graph. Sowa defines a *schematic join* based on his *maximal join* operation for expanding schemata. We define a *schematic expansion* algorithm that is similar to Sowa's schematic join but more general. Our schematic expansion uses a *schematic match.*

Definition Let $s = \lambda a\, u$ be a schema for type t and let m be a conceptual graph with a concept c such that $c :: t$[13]. If there is a subgraph u' of a node-wise specialization of u, and if there is a subgraph m' of a node-wise specialization of m such that, with the possible exception of truth values, $u' = m'$, then there is a schematic match between s and m. A *schematic match* is identified by the ordered pair (u', m').

By this definition, the only schemata that will match a graph are schemata for the concept types contained in the graph. Therefore, a schema must be defined for each concept type to which it may apply. For example, consider the schema for the sentence *A System/38 runs [the programming language] RPGIII.* If we want this schema to be considered any time a situation model contains a concept of type "RPGIII" or "SYSTEM/38", the same schema body would be used in definitions for both concept types.

Definition A set of conceptual graphs for which no joins may be performed is called *join-free.* A set of conceptual graphs for which no simplifications may be performed is called *simplified.* A set of conceptual graphs for which no joins or simplifications can be performed is called *minimal.*

Assumption *Schematic expansion* is performed as follows. Let M be a minimal set of conceptual graphs and let m be a conceptual graph in M. Let $s = \lambda a\, u$ be a conceptual schema where there is a schematic match (u', m') between u and m.

---

[13] "::" is the symbol for the conformity relation. $c :: t$ means that concept c conforms to the type t.

1. To M add a graph w that is a copy of u.

2. Specialize w to produce a subgraph w' corresponding to u'.

3. Join and simplify to minimize M.

This schematic expansion algorithm is notation independent and will produce a graph that has the minimum number of nodes possible. The complex part of the algorithm, as with Sowa's maximal and schematic joins, is in identifying the corresponding subgraphs (w' and u' in the algorithm above).

3.5.2   Schematic Matching

While the algorithms related to schematic matching have so far been notation independent, implementation of the schematic match requires identification of corresponding subgraphs, which is notation dependent. The fundamental principle of the schematic join is that the result of the join logically implies the original two graphs. For example, if m is the model graph, s is the schema graph, and m' and s' are the matching subgraphs, then the minimization of m' and s' logically implies m and s. In the algorithms we discuss in this section, we allow specialization of the schema graph only. This simplifies the matching algorithms, which are complex even for this simpler case.

Our schematic matching algorithm, which is under development, has three phases: relation-based matching, dependency matching, and elimination of conflicts.

The first phase, relation-based matching, uses a non-deterministic graph matching algorithm with modifications for our representation. The modifications occur in the node matching portion. Matching relations is easy, especially if a relation type lattice is excluded: the relations must be identical to match. Fully instantiated concepts are also simple and essentially identical to matching in Sowa's original notation. The difficulties come in dealing with constrained concepts. The basic technique is to match on each of the fields: scope list, variable, domain, and cardinality. The scope list, domain, and cardinality all interact, so the process becomes complex.

The basic relation-based matching algorithm builds an AND/OR tree of node matches using a recursive algorithm. The tree is converted into a Boolean expression in prefix form. Disjunctions are moved out using conjunctive distribution, with the result being a linear disjunction of *matchings*. A matching is a permissible combination of matches. Each matching is maximally extended.

While the node matching algorithm requires a matching between scope lists, nodes that match individually may require substitutions that conflict with other node matches. In essence, we must match two overlapping graphs. In one graph, concepts are connected by relations. In the other graph, concepts are connected by dependencies. Consider matching the following two graphs:

```
G1
[T:  ()a] -
    → (R) → [T:  ()b]
    → (R) → [T:  (a)c]
    → (R) → [T:  (b)d]
```

G2

```
[T:  ()a']  -
   →(R)→[T:  ()b']→(R)→[T:  ()b"]
   →(R)→[T:  (a')c']
   →(R)→[T:  (b")d']
```

Note that the concept and relation types are irrelevant in this example. The concept matches from relation-based matching are $\{a \to a', b \to b', c \to c', d \to d'\}$, where a-a' means that "a" is matched with "a'". The dependency-based concept matches are $\{a \to a'(c \to c'), b \to b''(d \to d')\}$, where the first match, $a \to a'$, comes from the relation-based match $c \to c'$ and the second match comes from matching $d \to d'$. There is a conflict between the relation-based and dependency-based matchings: we have $b \to b'$ in one and $b \to b''$ in the other. This conflict is eliminated by removing the match $d \to d'$. Therefore, the resulting match is $\{a \to a', b \to b', c \to c'\}$.

3.5.3 Deduction

We are taking two approaches to developing a deduction algorithm for extended conceptual structures. The first is called *v-resolution validation*, which is the dual of resolution refutation. The other approach is *natural deduction*. Both approaches make use of the reasoning matching algorithms discussed in this paper. The deduction algorithms are discussed in detail in the preceding chapter in this volume (Tjan *et al.*, 1992).

3.5.4 Control Mechanisms

Efficient control mechanisms are needed for the reasoning mechanisms that we have discussed. In Gardiner and Slagle (1989) a control mechanism for schematic expansion is described. A brief overview of that mechanism is described in this section.

Since hypotheses are represented by schemata, the key to efficient situation model creation is selection of schemata to expand. Our approach to schema selection incorporates both context and history. There are five factors that are used to determine the expected usefulness of a schema: type overlap, referent overlap, historical usefulness, line of reasoning, and stochastic factor. Type and referent overlaps are used in determining the relevance of a schema in the current situation model. The system keeps track of which schemata are usually associated with success. It also "learns" lines of reasoning in the form of schemata that are usually expanded together and the order in which they tend to be expanded. Last, the system incorporates a stochastic factor to improve performance.

Type overlap provides an indication of whether a schema has any conceptual relationship to the current situation model and therefore whether expansion should take place at all. There are two conditions under which no expansion should take place. The first case is where there is no overlap between the schema and the situation model. This type of expansion is prohibited by the definition of schematic expansion. The second case in which expansion should not take place is if *all* of the information in the schema is already contained in the situation model.

Actors provide a procedural method for instantiating concepts and are therefore efficient. If the situation model contains all of the declarative but not all of the procedural knowledge in the schema, the schema offers a possible inexpensive instantiation and therefore the expansion is very desirable. The remaining cases, where the schema adds declarative knowledge or both declarative and procedural knowledge are both desirable.

Consider the following rule: *This schema is particularly applicable if disk utilization is high.* This rule, like many heuristics used in expert reasoning, is difficult to represent symbolically. A common method used is to pick some threshold value and make a rule. For example, *If disk utilization is greater than 90%, apply this schema.* But the schema may be relevant at less than 90% in some situations and not until 99% in others. An expert diagnosing performance problems might be slightly interested in a disk utilization of 85%, a little more interested in one of 90%, and very interested in one of 98%. Thus, a schema involving disk utilization is more likely to be useful for higher disk utilizations than for lower ones. To represent an expert's interest in certain referent values, a *referent interest function* may be defined for any concept in a schema. The function may have any definition. It may be continuous, such as would be appropriate in the situation described above, or it may have discrete values. A discrete value function would be used to represent *This schema is particularly applicable to System/38s #31415, #92653, and #58979.* The default referent interest function for a concept is the constant zero. Referent interest functions can be pre-defined or they can be learned using statistical information from previous reasoning sessions.

Historical usefulness is the simplest of the factors. It is simply the fraction of the times the schema has been expanded that has lead to success.

For our purposes, we consider a line of reasoning to be a sequence of hypotheses that has a history of leading to a successful situation model. There are two parts of a line of reasoning. First, a set of hypotheses that tend to be used together. Second, the order in which those hypotheses tend to be applied. For some lines of reasoning the order is critical and for others the order is less important. A hypothesis may be in several lines of reasoning and the order that hypotheses in a line of reasoning are applied may vary. Over time, one line of reasoning may split into several or several lines of reasoning may converge into one. Because lines of reasoning are dynamic, do not have clear boundaries, and interact with one another, a connection-based approach is well suited to representing them.

With the learning system described, certain hypotheses are going to become favorites and others will hardly ever be used. Assuming that the same kinds of problems are presented to the system regularly, lines of reasoning will become clearly defined. The lines of reasoning that become defined may not be the best possible. Schemata that have not been used for awhile but are now relevant will be overpowered by those that are in established lines of reasoning. Randomly "boosting" the expected usefulness of a hypothesis provides an opportunity for these kinds of hypotheses to surface.

All of these factors are defined as functions, and a general *expected usefulness function* is computed.

3.6 CONCLUSIONS

We believe that handling uninstantiated concepts as specifying instantiation constraints provides a much clearer approach to the issues of knowledge representation than alternative approaches. The combination of constraints specified in our representation-type, functional dependency, domain, and cardinality-provide expressive power exceeding that of first order predicate calculus in a concise representation.

Situation model creation is critical to many kinds of problem solving, but the situation model language must be sufficiently powerful to represent the necessary characteristics of the model. The combination of extended conceptual structures with the model building operations presented is an effort to address this problem.

BIBLIOGRAPHY

Chatila, Raja And Laumond, Jean-Paul (1985). "Position referencing and consistent world modeling for mobile robots", Proc. IEEE Int. Conf. On Robotics And Automation, St. Louis, MO, pp. 249-265.

Coombs, Michael J. And Hartley, Roger T. (1987). "The MGR algorithm and its application to the generation of explanations for novel events", International Journal Of Man-Machine Studies 27: 679-708.

Esch, John W. (1988). "Toward an interchangeable linear form for conceptual graphs". Proc. Of The Third Annual Workshop On Conceptual Graphs.

Hintikka, Jaakko (1974). "Quantifiers Vs. Quantification Theory". In Esa Saarinen, Editor, *Game Theoretical Semantics*, D. Reidel Publishing Company, London.

Lenat, Douglas B. And Guha, R.V. (1990). *Building Large Knowledge-Based Systems: Representation And Inference In The Cyc Project*. Addison-Wesley.

Michalski, Ryszard S., Carbonell, Jaime G., And Mitchell, Tom M. (1983). *Machine Learning*. Morgan Kaufmann, Los Altos, Ca.

Patil, Ramesh S. (1987). "A Case Study On Evolution Of System Building Expertise: Medical Diagnosis". *AI in the 1980's And Beyond*, edited By W. Eric L. Grinson And Ramesh S. Patil. Mit Press, Cambridge, MA.

Rumelhart, David E., McClelland, James L., And The PDP Research Group (1986). *Parallel Distributed Processing: Explorations In The Microstructure Of Cognition*. MIT Press, Cambridge, MA.

Slagle, James R., Gardiner, David A., Esch, John W., and Nagle, Timothy E. (1988). "Selectional constraints in knowledge representation". Unpublished Report. University Of Minnesota, Minneapolis.

Sowa, J.F. (1984) *Conceptual Structures: Information Processing in Mind and Machine*, Addison Wesley, Reading.

Tjan, Bosco S., Gardiner, David A. And Slagle, James R. (1992). "Representation and reasoning with set referents and numerical quantifiers". in (eds) T Nagle, J Nagle, L Gerholz and P Eklund *Conceptual Structures: Research and Practice*, Ellis-Horwood.

4

The Conceptual Programming Environment, CP

Heather D. Pfeiffer and Roger T. Hartley
New Mexico State University,
Las Cruces, USA

ABSTRACT

The Conceptual Programming environmental, CP, being developed at the Computing Research Laboratory (CRL) is a representational framework for use with dynamic, open-world, problem solving applications. In this paper we present the formal basis for the CP representation system, a definition of elements of the environment, and a discussion of the basic operations in the system. The CP system currently is a "working" representation system, and the foundation for several applications.

4.1 INTRODUCTION

The Conceptual Programming environment, CP, is an ongoing project at CRL, and is based on developing a knowledge representation environment with a graphical foundation (Hartley, 1986) (Pfeiffer, 1986) (Hartley and Coombs, 1991). These graphs are based on Sowa's conceptual structures (Sowa, 1984, 1990) with operations defined for the graphs. However, CP has extended features in both syntactic and semantic aspects of the representation (Eshner and Hartley, 1988) (Pfeiffer and Hartley, 1989, 1990).

Part of the definition of conceptual structures includes concepts organized in a type lattice (Sowa, 1984). When structures built out of these concepts are operated upon by graph operations, it often arises that the same concept can be instantiated with different individuals. In many situations it is preferable to keep such individuals separated, but there are cases where further processing should be done by assembling the individuals into a set. This operational need is in addition to the more obvious one of representing propositions about sets of objects in the conceptual structure language (Gardiner *et. al*, 1989). The CP representation has been extended to be able to define and process sets, going one step beyond Sowa's original ideas.

Concepts that have been instantiated with individuals are called *individualized concepts* as opposed to *basic concepts* (Pfeiffer and Hartley, 1988). Individualized concepts require special processing to be incorporated into the graph operations. Through the use of *feasibility heuristics*, limits can be placed on the functionality of the operators so that only semantically viable graphs can be generated.

Another extension to Sowa's conceptual graph theory is the addition of support for a spatio-temporal domain. An ontology for objects, events, states and processes is provided within the conceptual structures framework. However, this requires a syntactic extension that provides functional relation support, *actors*, rather than relying on purely logical inference techniques.

One example application that uses the CP environment is a problem solving system also developed at CRL. In this system, the process of solving a problem is one of constructing a graph, called a *model*, out of graphs that can be thought of as data, definitions and previously created models. Thus, at all times a partially completed model holds relevant data. The graph operations, *join* and *project* (Sowa, 1984, 1990), are used to create and update the actual models. Because solutions are found by generating models during the reasoning process, the general approach has been termed "Model Generative Reasoning, MGR".

4.2   BASIS OF THE REPRESENTATION SYSTEM

4.2.1   Graph Definition

CP is a knowledge representation environment based on graphs. These graphs are implementations of Sowa's conceptual structures and retain many of the features of conceptual graph theory. Although there exists a mapping from conceptual graphs to formulae in first-order predicate calculus, FOPC, the operations used in the CP system take advantage of the graphical representation. We therefore study the graphs and the graph operations using graph theory instead of FOPC.

A big advantage in using logic as the foundation for a representation system is that it is a well-defined and a familiar formalism. The semantics are also well understood. However, since graphs are the basis of the CP system, graph theory can provide an equally well-defined formalism in which to study and evaluate the graphs and graph operations.

In order to formalize the definition of the graph structures and operations, we first present some definitions from graph theory. A *digraph* D is an irreflexive binary relation on a finite set V of elements called *nodes*. It is customary to draw the nodes as prominent points and to draw each ordered pair (u, v) in the relation as a directed edge from u to v, called an *arc*. In a *bipartite graph* there are nodes of two different kinds, called *colors*, and every arc joins two nodes of different colors. In our description of conceptual structures, the two colors in representing bipartite digraphs will be concepts and relations.

In a *labeled digraph* the nodes are designated by a set of labels l_1, l_2, $\cdots$, l_p where $p = |V|$, the number of nodes. In order to define precisely a conceptual structure, a more general formulation is required. A *multilabeled digraph* allows for labels to occur more than once, i.e., the mapping from the node set V onto the set of labels may be many-to-one. An *asymmetric digraph* does not contain a symmetric pair of arcs, such as both (u, v) and (v, u). Such digraphs are also called *oriented graphs*.

A *conceptual structure* CS is a connected multilabeled bipartite oriented graph. The two colors of nodes in a conceptual structure are called *concepts* and *relations*. Each label in a concept node consists of two fields, the *type* field and the *referent* field. The type field is an element of the set of concepts defined in a type lattice[1] The referent field contains

---

[1] see section 4.2.2.

the individual specialization (if any) relation node consist of the single *relation* field. This relation field depicts the relationship (predicate) between the adjoining concept nodes within the conceptual structure. Fig. 4.1 shows a conceptual structure with nine (9) nodes. Following Sowa, the concept nodes are presented as squares (or rectangles) and relation nodes as circles (or ovals).

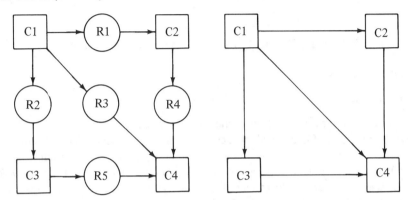

Fig. 4.1 A conceptual structure, with four concepts, five relations, and nine labels.

Fig. 4.2 The concept digraph CD(CS) of a given conceptual structure CS, obtained by suppressing the relational nodes.

The relation nodes in a conceptual structure provide a semantically interpreted relationship between the concept nodes they connect. In logic terms the relation nodes are analogous to predicates while the concept nodes represent the terms. The graph operations on these conceptual structures, however, are purely syntactic structural operations, and do not directly use these semantic relations. Therefore, a new class of graphs, without these relations, is equally interpretable by the graph operations. This class of graphs, called *concept digraphs*, are conceptual structures with the relation nodes and their incident arcs removed and replaced by a single arc. More generally, a conceptual structure may have relation nodes with several arcs entering and leaving. Thus, the concept digraph **CD** of a conceptual structure CS written **CD**(CS), is derived by replacing each relational node and all its incident arcs by a complete bipartite digraph, whose arc set replaces directed paths of length two in the original conceptual structure. This is the identical construction to that in which the line digraph (Harary and Norman, 1961) of a given digraph is formed. The direction of the new arc is the same as that of the original arcs. Thus, two nodes in the concept graph are adjacent if and only if they are connected by a directed path through a relational node. Fig. 4.2 displays the concept digraph of the conceptual structure shown in Fig. 4.1.

4.2.2 Type Hierarchy

All the concept objects in the representation system are defined to be a member of a *type*. We then define a *type hierarchy* as a partial ordering on the set of concept types, with the symbol $\leq$ designating the ordering. Given a set of labels $\{a, b, c\}$, if $a \leq b$ then a is called a *subtype* of b and b is called a *supertype* of a, written $b \geq a$. If $c \leq a$ and $c \leq b$ then c is called a *common subtype* of a and b. If $c \geq a$ and $c \geq b$ then c is called a *common supertype* of a and b. We can then define the *type lattice* as the the type hierarchy plus the operators $\cup$ and $\cap$. The *minimal common supertype* of a and b, written $a \cup b$, has the property that for any type t, if $t \geq a$ and $t \geq b$, then $t \geq a \cup b$. The *maximal common subtype* of a and b, written $a \cap b$, has the property that for any type t, if $t \leq a$ and $t \leq b$, then $t \leq a \cap b$. In order to make the lattice complete, we introduce the labels $\bot$ and $\top$ such that for any type t, $\bot \leq t \leq \top$.

4.3   EXTENSIONS TO BASIC CONCEPTUAL STRUCTURES

4.3.1   Formalizing Sets

Set Distinctions

The first distinction to make between the CP formalization of sets and Sowa's theory is between a collection of individuals that can be considered as separable, and collection that cannot be taken apart. We call the first a *set* and the second a *group*. A group is considered indivisible and acts semantically just like one individual (the phrase *compound individual* could be used)[2]. A set is said to have the property *open*, whereas a group is *closed (or atomic)*. As a result, a set can be added to, but a group cannot.

The second distinction is between sets of conjoined individuals, and sets of alternative individuals. These properties can be added to either sets or groups, leading to four types of set:

> conjunctive set, e.g. a and b and possibly others
> disjunctive set, e.g. a or b or possibly others
> conjunctive group, e.g. a and b only
> disjunctive group, e.g. a or b, but no others

There are two special cases that need attention. One is where a set or group only contains one member. This is easier to understand when a set, which can be extended, has only one known member. A group, which is of fixed size, is really a collection of more than one member; the group of one is an anomaly. However, it is certainly the case, that if we allow a set of one member, then it would appear to be neither conjunctive, nor disjunctive unless we apply the property of conjunctiveness to the set and not to its members. If we do apply the property to the set then we can take care of the other special case, the empty set, as well.

The next distinction to make is that of *order*. Adding the property of order to a set makes a *list*. Adding the same property to a group makes a *tuple*. Adding the disjoint/conjoint property can produce a total of eight distinct set types *via*

> a disjunctive set (open, unordered, disjunctive)
> a conjunctive set (open, unordered, conjunctive)
> a disjunctive group (closed, unordered, disjunctive)
> a conjunctive group (closed, unordered, conjunctive)
> a disjunctive tuple (closed, ordered, disjunctive)

---

[2]The word *set* will hereafter refer to a collection of unknown, and therefore extensible size; *collection* will refer to a generic assemblage of items.

a disjunctive list (open, ordered, disjunctive)
a conjunctive list (open, ordered, conjunctive)
a conjunctive tuple (closed, ordered, conjunctive)

Set Types

The types of sets that have been formulated within the CP system are as follows:

Basic sets:

- Open Sets - sets delimited by using "{}" (for 'Unordered' sets) or "()" (for 'Ordered' sets); these sets are potentially infinite and possibly have a variable length. Internal to CP, they are referred to as "?SET"[3].

- Closed Sets - sets delimited by "[]" (for 'Unordered' sets) or "⟨⟩" (for 'Ordered' sets) as a notation; these sets operate as a 'unit' and have a fixed length. They are operated on as if they are a single, atomic individual that specializes a concept, i.e. the set cannot be broken up or added to. Internal to CP , they are referred to as "?GROUP".

As mentioned above, within these basic sets, there are two sub-types of set:

- Ordered - members are separated by ','; they display an ordering of elements. Internal to the systems, they are referred to as "O*".

- Unordered - members are separated by ',' or ';'; they will have no particular order of elements.

Within 'Unordered' sets, there are three possibilities:

- Conjunctive ("and") – Sowa's 'collective' set, where members are separated by ','; each member of the set is "anded" with the other members of the set. Internal to the systems, they are referred to as "C*".

- Disjunctive ("or") – Sowa's 'distributive' set, where members are separated by ';'; each member is 'ored' with the other members of the set. Internal to the systems, they will be referred to as "D*".

- Single Item – the set only has one member. This only applies to "Open" Sets represented in "Open" form; they are assumed to be conjunctive in nature when ambiguities arise. Internal to the systems, they will be referred to as "S*".

These types of sets have a number of possible interrelationships to each other. In fact, a generalization lattice can be formed, and is displayed in Fig. 4.3. The idea is that each of the attribute pairs have a generalization relation. Thus, an ordered set (a *tuple*) is less general than an unordered one, as long as the other attributes remaining the same, i.e. $T < U$. Similarly, closed sets with fixed size are less general than open sets which are potentially infinite, i.e. $A < O$. Finally a conjunctive set is less general than a disjunctive

---

[3] In this and subsequent notations, the '?' is a place holder for a single letter, and '*' for any number of letters.

set, i.e. $C < D$. The empty set, denoted by the property E is more general than any, and the singleton set, denoted by the attribute S is more general than a multi-element set (adding members specializes a set). We have also included the simple individual as I in the lattice, and a further manifestation of the simple individual as I' for reasons that will become clear when we discuss how sets are processed within the CP system. The top node of the lattice is the absence of an individual.

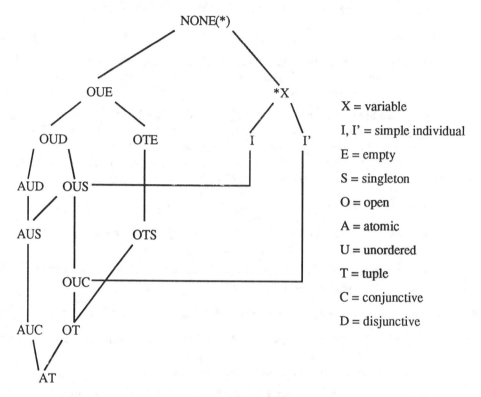

X = variable

I, I' = simple individual

E = empty

S = singleton

O = open

A = atomic

U = unordered

T = tuple

C = conjunctive

D = disjunctive

Fig. 4.3 Set Lattice.

Sets as Data Structures

It may be useful to identify the various set types as data structures whose names and operational properties are more familiar. Starting with an unordered open set, we have the usual 'mathematical' *set*, that is often not a basic data structure, but is implemented as an abstract data type, ADT. If the size of the set is fixed (making it atomic), but kepted unordered, the idea of a *group* is generated. However, as a data structure this would be a *record* or a *structure*. An ordered open set is a *list*, and adding the property of atomicity turns the list into a *tuple*. Finally there is no easy correspondence to the conjunctive/disjunctive property, but the notion of an *enumeration* captures some of the disjunctive flavor as does the *union* in C.

This range of set types, i.e *set, group, list* and *tuple* allow the operational side of conceptual structures to be expanded enormously by giving them the flavor of data structure (more than in most programming languages) while retaining the basic conceptual structures philosophy.

4.3.2 Defining the Overlay Level

Sowa has shown how unknown objects (nodes with no individual field) can be computed by an *actor* node that corresponds to a function in standard logics. Actor nodes of this kind are diamond-shaped boxes connected to concept nodes with dashed lines. In our extensions to conceptual graph theory, these actors are given the capability of computing *quantitative* constraints in a Prolog fashion, i.e. of doing constraint propagation through a system of values and variables. This is the overlay level of CP .

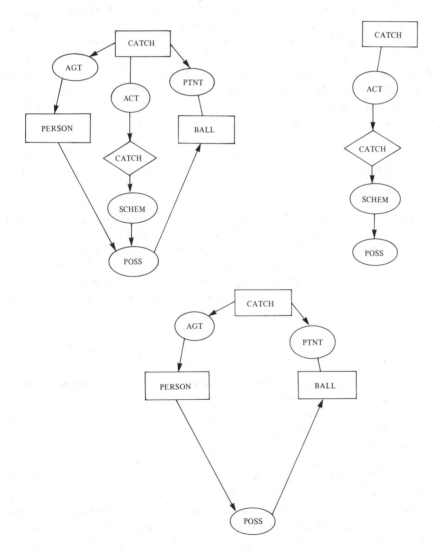

Fig. 4.4 A conceptual graph, an actor overlay and the overlaid graph.

An actor can best be thought of as an implicit relation between semantic objects represented in graphical form. The relation can be made explicit by interpreting the constraints expressed by the actor and its connections (inputs and outputs, roughly speaking) just as a rule in a rule-based system can be thought of as an implicit relation between its left and right-hand sides. 'Firing' the rule computes the relation. The CP actors however, can be run forwards or backwards, or operate as constraint checkers, just as a Prolog rule can. In this manner an actor can compute a missing relation. Temporal actors compute missing temporal relations, and spatial actors compute missing spatial relations.

Within the overlay level, there are actually three sublevels, *feasibility heuristics*, *runtime constraints*, and *spatio-temporal constraints*. The feasibility and runtime constraint levels use quantitative actors as described above. The spatio-temporal level uses *qualitative actors* that propagate constraints among moments in time when acts occur and locations of objects in space. This level requires a syntactic extension to conceptual graphs in order that the diagrams not become too confused and thus lose their force. The inputs and outputs of a spatio-temporal actor are things like acts, events, objects, regions, etc. i.e. the language of the ontology of space and time. In conceptual graphs many of these ontological entities are represented by two or more objects related through a single relation node. Some way of connecting an actor to one of these partial graphs is thus required. We have chosen to extend the syntax of conceptual graphs for these actor connections by allowing arcs to come out of a relation node, and be connected to an actor through a special spatio-temporal relation node. In the basic theory relation nodes can only connect to concept nodes. Our extension presents no ambiguity, however, since a relation node connected to another relation node must be an actor input or output.

Since the actor and its relations are additions to an already existing graph, we can think of the addition as an *overlay* graph. The analogy here is of overhead slides being laid on top of one another to produce a complete diagram. Fig. 4.4 shows a graph, a simple one-actor overlay and the graph that results from laying the overlay on the first graph. These overlays are based on the definitional conceptual graphs within the system. The type hierarchy relates either the subgraph or supergraph relationships of the definitional graphs. This gives *context* to the definitional conceptual graphs of a knowledge base and allows specification and generalization during evaluation of graphs.

Feasibility Heuristics

During analysis of the CP system, it was discovered that the *feasibility* (the ability for a graph to complete the model generation process) of a graph could be checked. By adding a *type checking* mechanism, defined to be a methodology for the structural analysis of the graphs (Sethi, 1989), to the operations available in the CP system, the feasibility of a graph could be specified by the analyst and the complexity of the system could be reduced.

The feasibility heuristics work at a 'compile time' level of computation as opposed to a 'runtime' level. The graphs are created as overlays to a particular definitional graph. Each overlay contains at least one or more actors. These actors have a functional procedure associated with them and this function is executed when the actor is evaluated during the join operation. Unlike the runtime constraints or spatio-temporal levels, these actors are evaluated during the join operation in order to do semantic checks or to act as a type checking mechanism. This mechanism checks the inputs to the feasibility actors for specified values, and if these values do not pass the associated test(s) then the constraint function has failed. This failure to join can be viewed as an incompatibility between structured types during the generation of the new graph. The feasibility heuristics have been introduced into the CP system in order to speed up and make the join operator more efficient.

Runtime Constraints

Runtime constraints implement Sowa's original actors in conceptual graphs with two additions: 1) each actor may behave like a formal constraint on a state or concept referent as well as a function, and 2) constraint actors may take as input a state as well as a single concept referent. Like feasibility heuristics, runtime constraints focus on the quantitative functional relations. They give the CP system the flexibility to reject *models* that are in some way incorrect, just as a program will abort on an error such as when the user divides by zero.

Time and Space Constraints

In this section we summarize an ontology for space/time that will prove suitable for representation in the extended conceptual graph theory outlined above. It is mainly aimed at determining what things can be inputs or outputs to spatio-temporal actors. All of Sowa's base theory is incorporated, including the primitive relations, and the simple breakdown of concept types into objects, acts and properties. The simple existence of objects and acts (and perhaps relations between them) is not sufficient alone to form a model of space/time. In particular we need to talk about *properties* of objects and acts. This not only serves to differentiate different types and instances of these types, but also will serve as the basis of the integration of space and time. Objects can have two sorts of property. One sort is an intrinsic property, which we shall call (after Sowa) a *characteristic*. This is a member of that set of features without which the object would not be an object, such as its size, shape and mass. They are basically spatial in nature, with a less important temporal component. For instance, an object has a shape and size and mass, the persistence of which ensures the object's continued existence. On the other hand, objects can have accidental features, that are more temporal (i.e. changeable) in nature. These include, color, temperature, speed, etc. These are *attributes*. The object with its collection of properties makes a *state*. One relation and its associated object and property (or properties in the case of multi-way relations) is a *partial state*.

Acts also have attributes and characteristics. These properties are either temporal or spatial in nature. Characteristics include rate, acceleration (or qualitative counterparts like quickness) and start and end times (both moments). Attributes, which are more spatial in nature, include direction, range, and orientation. The act and its properties makes a *process*. One relation, with its act and property is a *partial process*.

Objects participate with a single act to form an *event*. The relationships here are the standard case relations well-known in knowledge representation. Thus, agent, patient, experiencer, instrument etc. relate an act to its participants. The spatial cases, such as location, path, direction etc. are considered here as properties of an act, as are the temporal cases such as duration and rate. The case relations cannot form partial processes or states, whereas the spatial and temporal ones can. In fact, it is probably better to think of the *event* as the atomic unit (albeit with structure) corresponding to an act, and the *experience* as atomic in the spatial sense. An experience is a single object and all its associated acts. Events are time-independent since their acts carry with them a time interval, one of the distinguished characteristics mentioned above. Experiences are location-independent, since their objects carry an intrinsic region with them.

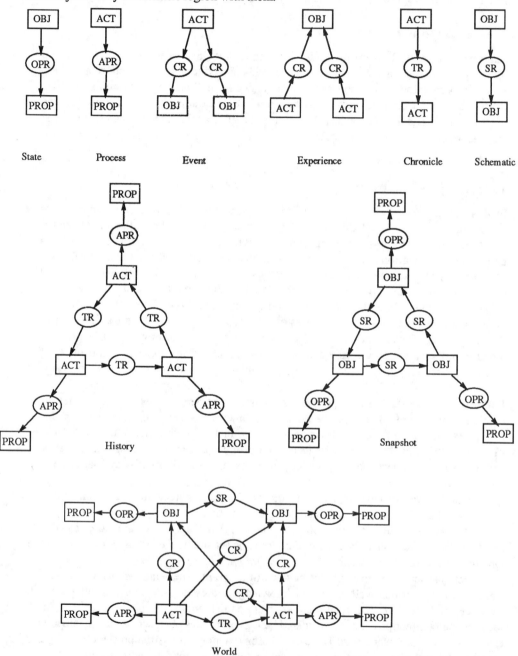

Fig. 4.5 Canonical graphs for each of the spatio-temporal entities.

Fig. 4.5 shows canonical graphs for each of the ontological entities introduced above. In the diagram, three concept types are used: PROP, ACT and OBJ. There are five kinds of relation label, each of which stands for a set of relations disjoint from any other set.

They are:

- SR: a Spatial Relation, between two objects,

- TR: a Temporal Relation, between two acts,

- CR: a Case Relation, between an act and an object,

- APR: an Act Property Relation between an act and one of its properties,

- OPR: an Object Property Relation between and object and object and one of its properties

Rules in CP are represented as spatio-temporal actors, whose sole job is to act as confluence points for the knowledge structures that have to be related. All of the actors are constraint-like in that they can operate forwards or backwards. However, temporal actors are often regarded as operating forwards, in the direction of time. Thus, inputs to an actor are pre-conditions for the actor's firing, and outputs are post-conditions. In the temporal domain, inputs are partial states and schematics, since these are exactly what is expected to change in time. For instance, the possession of a ball by a person is a partial schematic; the possession of the same ball by another person is another one. Each temporal actor also has an act (really a process) as input, at least one partial state or schematic as input and one as output. The crucial part of the whole idea of the overlay comes, however, with the temporal relationships that the act bears to the inputs and outputs. We have appealed to simple ideas of causality to analyze the possible relationships. Firstly, let us call partial states and schematics collectively *situations*. Causally speaking, a situation can enable or trigger an act, and the act can terminate that situation (or not). If, in addition, we allow the *absence* of a situation to have the same causal status i.e. enabling or triggering, then we arrive at a total of eight combinations of a single input situation and an act. These are displayed in Fig. 4.6 in time chart form (time increases to the right) with each one having the situation on top and the act below. A vertical line on an end-point indicates a change start to stop (or vice versa), and an arrow head indicates an unknown end-point. These time charts are similar in use and meaning to the time maps of Dean and McDermott (1987).

Notice that each of the interval pairs (except 6 and 7) have correspondence to Allen's relations (Allen, 1985).

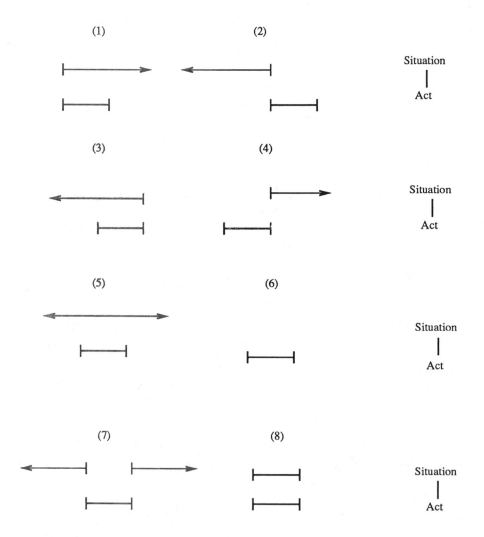

Fig. 4.6 Time charts for the input temporal relations. (1) is a triggering enablement where the situation triggers the act and persists after the act finishes. (2) is the inverse where the absence of the situation is the trigger. (3) is a temporary enabling condition where the situation that enables the act disappears at the end of the act. (4) is again the inverse. (5) and (6) are permanent enabling conditions where the situation (or its absence) persists even though the act terminates. (7) shows an interrupt enablement where the situation is interrupted by the act, but resumes after the act finishes. (8) is the inverse of this, but can also be seen as the situation and act coinciding in their start and end points.

The same ideas can be applied to output situations, changes in which are caused by an act. An output situation can be started by an act's starting, started by the event's ending or coincide exactly with the event[4]. Again the inverses involving the situation's absence complete the picture. Now we get six possibilities (Fig. 4.7).

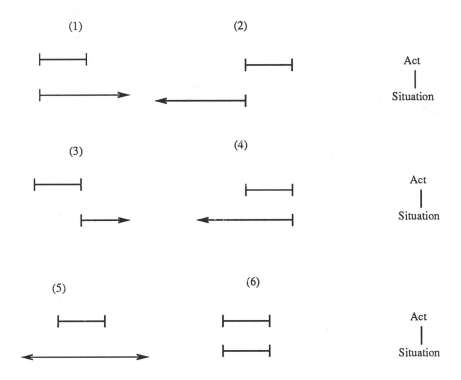

Fig. 4.7 Time charts for the output temporal relations.

We can now apply the same notions to create spatial actors corresponding to the temporal actors just discussed. Where the temporal overlay placed partial states or schematics in temporal relationship, the spatial one places partial processes or chronicles in spatial relationships. Clearly we need at least two partial processes or chronicles to do this, together with an object (properly an experience) so we will need at least two acts. Notice that in both the single act cases, the only spatial inference is that all objects occupy the same region as the act. Only when two acts occur can entities be spatially differentiated. Similarly, when only one object participates in several events, no temporal differentiation can be made, since there can be no change of state.

Each spatial rule will be represented by an actor corresponding to an object. Whereas the temporal actors are directional, according to the forward flow of time, there is no such constraint on spatial actors. They execute, therefore, very much like Prolog rules, i.e. they can operate forwards or backwards. Since there is no distinction between inputs and outputs, no relation to a spatial actor has an arrow-head. There are two partial chronicles - the succession of temporal relations between the three acts. Objects can partially or totally

---

[4]Moreover, the effect can be delayed, as in the delay between a ball being thrown and it breaking a window.

constrain a partial chronicle, or not at all. These factors give rise to seven possible classes of spatial relations (Fig. 4.8).

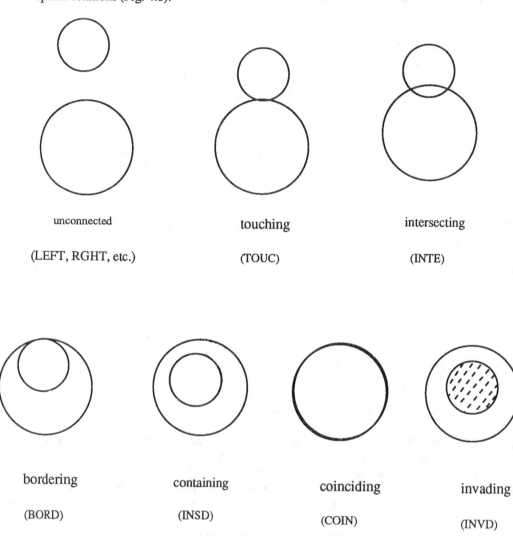

unconnected	touching	intersecting
(LEFT, RGHT, etc.)	(TOUC)	(INTE)

bordering	containing	coinciding	invading
(BORD)	(INSD)	(COIN)	(INVD)

Fig. 4.8 The dyadic spatial relations which can appear in a spatial map.

Through the use of spacial and temporal actors, CP is able to operate over space and time.

4.4 CP GRAPH OPERATORS

Using the basic representation given above, CP has two operators, *join* and *project*, that can manipulate the graphs and overlays by following the rules laid out by the type hierarchy (Hartley and Coombs, 1989). These operators are duals (i.e., union and intersection), therefore, the description of join is, in some sense, the dual of the description of project. Let us start by describing the join operator.

4.4.1   Join

Sowa's join operation is defined on concept types only. The job of the binary operation join is to merge two graphs at a single point where both graphs contain the same concept label, or a subtype. CP join, (M_b), is always *maximal*, i.e., labels *may* be restricted by replacement with a label of any subtype, and graphs *will* be merged on the maximum number of nodes. An example is given in Fig. 4.9. The functionality of join over a set of graphs G is:

$$\text{maximal join: } G \times G \rightarrow 2^G$$

There can be more than one maximal join, hence the powerset notation on the set of all graphs G. Join is a binary operation but multiple graphs can be joined by composing it with itself. Unfortunately, there is good reason to believe that join is not commutative when semantic considerations come into play (Pfeiffer and Hartley, 1989), but for now we will assume there is no problem.

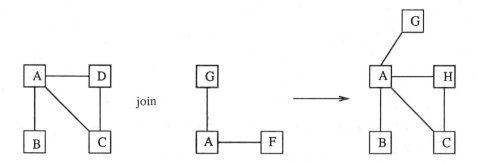

Fig. 4.9 An example of maximal join (M_b $(D, F) = H$).

Since restrictions are allowed, it is clear that two nodes are joinable as part of a maximal join operation if they contain types that have a maximal common subtype. So NARCOTIC can be restricted to OPIUM, and so can POISON. Thus nodes containing NARCOTIC and POISON join to produce OPIUM. If two concepts have only $\perp$ (bottom) as their common subtype, then the maximal common subtype is not considered to exist. The logical inference corresponding to join can be displayed as:

$$\frac{\begin{array}{c} \text{NARCOTIC(a)} \\ \text{POISON(a)} \\ \forall x \; OPIUM(x) \rightarrow NARCOTIC(x) \\ \forall x \; OPIUM(x) \rightarrow POISON(x) \end{array}}{\text{OPIUM (a)}}$$

4.4.2 Project

Project is the inverse of the operation join. It is based on the same idea of merging two graphs, but this time taking the minimal common supertype of the concepts, (M_p). Just as join is maximal, so project is as well. Another similarity is that, just as bottom was not allowed with join, so top is not allowed with project. If join is likened to set union, in that all nodes not joinable are just left alone, and come along for the ride, then project is like set intersection. All nodes that are not projectable are simply dropped from the resultant graph, along with their associated relation nodes.

Project's functionality is the same as join:

The example in Fig. 4.10 shows projection with the reduced form of graphs. These operand graphs are the same as in Fig. 4.9.

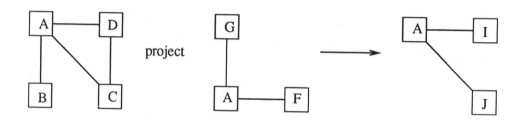

Fig. 4.10 An example of projection (M_p (D, F) = I and M_p (G, C) = J).

Since join and project are duals, we will not waste space by repeating the same arguments that we presented for join.

The following set of correspondences are sufficient to indicate how project works:

Join		Project
Join	$\longleftrightarrow$	Project
Max. Common Subtype	$\longleftrightarrow$	Min. Common Supertype
Union	$\longleftrightarrow$	Intersection

4.5 EXTENSIONS TO THE GRAPH OPERATORS

4.5.1 Sets

Set Processing

The maximal join operation can be extended to cover individuals if the set/individual lattice is treated in the same way as the concept type lattice. Thus, for example, an atomic, unordered disjunctive (AUD) set such as [A;B;C] will join to an open, unordered conjunctive (OUC) set such as {B,C,D} to give an atomic, unordered conjunctive (AUC) set [A,B,C,D].

This works because of two things. Firstly, AUC is the maximum common subtype of AUD and OUC, according to the lattice. Secondly, the membership of the resultant set is the union of the memberships of the original two sets. This latter constraint follows the nature of join as an *abductive* operation (Hartley, 1990). For concept types A, B and C, where C is a subtype of A and B, the join of A and B produces C because

$$(C \rightarrow A) \wedge (C \rightarrow B)$$

from the type lattice. Similarly from the set lattice,

$$(AUC \rightarrow AUD) \wedge (AUC \rightarrow OUC)$$

hence the join of AUD and OUC produces AUC.

We can now explain the presence of two simple individuals I and I' in the lattice. The join of two unequal, simple individuals is now a conjunctive set of both of them[5]. Thus the join of (names) A and B is {A,B}. Again the logical implications work correctly:

$$(\{A, B\} \rightarrow A) \wedge (\{A, B\} \rightarrow B)$$

When making inferences about sets of individuals, we will be concerned largely with inheritance of properties between an individual and a set containing it. This may be characterized for a set of individuals I and any type t by the following form:

$$P(I) \rightarrow \bigwedge_{i \in I} P(i) \wedge \bigwedge_{i \in I} Conform(i) = t$$

where Conform is a map between individuals and the lowest (in terms of subtype) type to which it conforms [6].

The above rule can be used either abductively or deductively. Abduction will produce inferences involving a set of individuals from propositions about the individuals separately, whereas deduction will produce inferences about individuals from propositions about a set of them.

Examples of abductive inferences are:

Example 1:
John likes ice-cream
Mary likes ice-cream
_____
(Possibly) John and Mary like ice-cream

This is abductive, hence the prefix *possibly* because their is uncertainty about the time periods involved (John could like ice-cream at a different time period from Mary).

Example 2:
John kicked the ball
Mary kicked the ball
_____
(Possibly) John and Mary kicked the ball

It is unlikely (but possible) that they kicked the ball at the same time, but likely that there is a (short) time period during which they both kicked the ball.

_____

[5] We realize that some practitioners will not like this, but it is not hard to think of examples from reasoning where it is essential.

[6] We assume a standard lattice of types in which the arcs mean subtype when they point downwards, and supertype going upwards.

Examples of deduction are:

Example 1:
John and Mary have red hair
_____
John has red hair, and
Mary has red hair

This inference is correct, whereas it is possible to use the rule incorrectly as in:

Example 2:
John and Mary won the game
_____
John won the game, and
Mary won the game

Here the group consisting of John and Mary is indivisible, so the rule cannot be used.

An Example of Set Usage in CP

As an example of complex processing involving sets, we present a portion of a military intelligence demonstration program[7]. The demonstration involves the generation of enemy intentions based on simple physical intelligence about the position and movement of ground troops. At a particular point in the processing, the reasoning engine, MGR, has generated possible avenues of approach and the estimated time of arrival at each avenue for each of a number of divisions. Since each is an alternative route for the division to take, there is a need for a disjunctive set. Two such sets are as follows (these are extracts from larger graphs – here we use the linear form):

```
[UNIT:D39] → (POS) →
        [AAETA:{⟨C,@77⟩;⟨[C,B],@96⟩;⟨ B,@96⟩;⟨[B,A],@115⟩}
[UNIT:D4] → (POS) →
        [AAETA:{⟨B,@46⟩;⟨[B,A],@85⟩;⟨C,@131⟩;⟨[C,B],@131⟩}
```

Note that each triple four alternatives each one of which is an Avenue-ETA pair (a tuple). In some tuples the avenue is a simple name (A, B or C) whereas in some it is a fixed size group of two avenues e.g. [C,B].

The next stage is to break the disjuncts and produce separate graphs from the possible alternatives. The control structure of MGR produces eight graphs of which the following are two: [UNIT:D4] → (POS) → [AAETA:⟨B,@46⟩] and [UNIT:D39] → (POS) → [AA-ETA:⟨C,@77⟩] Since these alternatives only consider the movements of individual divisions, and the plan presumably involves several divisions (including D4 and D39) MGR then joins these alternatives to a schema containing empty lists for both UNIT and AA-ETA i.e. [UNIT:(*)] → (POS) → [AAETA:(*)] Each division is joined separately, which is possible because of the open nature of (*). Proper order is maintained by the list property of the resultant graph. Thus the join of the two graphs for D4

---

[7]This work is sponsored by the USAICS, Fort Huachuca under a contract with TRADOC.

and D39 separately with the schema produces: `[UNIT:(D39,D4)]`→`(POS)`→`[AA-ETA:((C,@77),(B,@46))]`. The semantics of the () notation for ordered sets ensures the correspondence between a division name and its AA-ETA.

4.5.2 Spatio-Temporal Level

The symmetries alluded to in the introduction can be seen by considering a canonical graph with two acts and two objects (actually objects or properties) and their possible relations. A fully connected version is shown in Fig. 4.11. The CR labels denote case relations, TR is a temporal relation and SR is a spatial relation, as in the diagram of the canonical forms (Fig. 4.5). Since both TR and SR are present, there is no reason to specify an act actor, whether spatial or temporal, since their job is to compute missing relations. Whether the actor is temporal or spatial it can only fire if all of its inputs and/or outputs are satisfied. Currently CP 'executes' such a network (a CP *program*) with a breadth-first traversal of the network, passing tokens to partial states, schematics, chronicles or processes when actors do fire. When an actor fires, its time chart (or spatial map) is merged with its global form in such a manner that the constraints between moments and intervals or locations and regions are obeyed. It is possible for the merge to prove impossible. In this case, the simulation fails, and no final inference may be drawn. This is very like a Prolog program that says 'no' to a query, or to an over-constrained system of equations that has no solution.

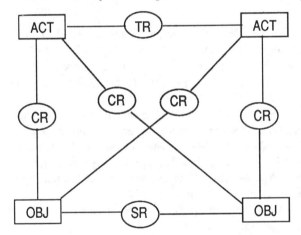

Fig. 4.11 The canonical space/time square, where ACT denotes any act, OBJ any object, and CR, SR and TR denote any case, temporal or spatial relation respectively. No relations are missing, so no actors are needed. The directionality of the relations is left unspecified.

The end result is a global time chart and a spatial map showing the relationships of the various regions and time intervals. The two can be correlated through the objects and acts involved. The execution of the program is best considered as a simulation of the behavior of that part of the world being represented. The success of the simulation (i.e. the successful computation of all temporal and spatial constraints) is evidence for the accuracy of the model. If the program fails to run, i.e. there are actors left unfired, then the model is inaccurate. This technique forms the basis of MGR's problem-solving technique where the schemata are pieced together with the aim of producing a successful simulation (Coombs and Hartley, 1987).

4.6   CONCLUSION AND FUTURE ENHANCEMENTS

In this paper we have presented a representation system based on graph structures along with the graph operations that are defined over these graphs. The representation system, the Conceptual Programming environment (CP), has been used in decision support (Coombs and Hartley, 1987), situation analysis (Coombs and Hartley, 1989), robot task planning (Coombs *et. al*, 1986) qualitative physics (Eshner and Hartley, 1988), and genetic sequence mapping (Fields *et. al*, 1989). Systems built using this representation framework are intended to be used in real time, dynamic situations, therefore integrating the representation with the basic graph operations.

Acknowledgements

Some of the research discussed in this paper is due to the on going work of Daniel P. Eshner. We wish to acknowledge the important research he has done.

BIBLIOGRAPHY

Allen, J. (1985) "Maintaining knowledge about temporal intervals" Communications of the Association of Computing Machinery, vol. 26, no. 11, pp. 832-843.

Coombs, M.J., R.T. Hartley and H.D. Pfeiffer (1986) "Conceptual reasoning in mobile intelligent robots" Report 1. to Sandia Mobile Robot Project, CRL, New Mexico State University, Las Cruces.

Coombs, M.J. and Hartley, R.T. (1987) "The MGR algorithm and its application to the generation of explanations for novel events", Memorandum in Computer and Cognitive Science, MCCS-87-97, CRL, New Mexico State University, Las Cruces.

Coombs, M.J. and R.T. Hartley (1989) "Design of a software environment for tactical situation development" Proc. of the US Army Symposium on Artificial Intelligence Research for Exploitation of the Battlefield Environment, El Paso.

Dean, T.L and D.V. McDermott (1987) "Temporal data base management" Artificial Intelligence, vol. 32, pp. 1-55.

Eshner, D.P. and Hartley, R.T. (1988) "Conceptual programming with constraints" Proc. of the Third Annual Workshop on Conceptual Structures, Minneapolis, pp. 3.1.2-1 - 3.1.2-6.

Fields, C.A., H.D. Pfeiffer, and T.C. Eskridge (1991) "Knowledge representation and control in **gm1**, and automated DNA sequence analysis system based on the MGR architecture" *International Journal of Man-Machine Studies*, vol. 34, pp. 549-573.

Gardiner, D.A., Tjan, B., and Slagle, J.R. (1989) "Extended conceptual structures notation" Proc. of the Fourth Annual Workshop on Conceptual Structures, Detroit, pp. 3.05-1 - 3.05-11.

Harary, F. and R. Z. Norman (1961) "Some properties of line digraphs" Rendicouti del Circolo Mat. di Palermo, vol. 9, pp. 161-168.

Hartley, R. T. (1986) "The foundations of conceptual programming" Proc. of the First Rocky Mountain Conference on AI, Boulder, pp. 3-15.

Hartley, R.T. and Coombs, M.J. (1991) "Reasoning with graph operations", In (ed) J.F. Sowa, *Principles of Semantic Networks*, New York, NY: Addison-Wesley.

Hartley, R. T. and Coombs, M. J. (1990) "Conceptual programming: foundations of problem solving" Memorandum in Computer and Cognitive Science, MCCS-88-129, CRL, New Mexico State University, Las Cruces.

Pfeiffer, H. D. (1986) "Graph definition system" Proc. of the Second New Mexico Computer Science Conference, Las Cruces, pp. 97-103.

Pfeiffer, H.D. and Hartley, R.T. (1989) "Semantic additions to conceptual programming" Proc. of the Fourth Annual Workshop on Conceptual Structures, Detroit, pp. 6.07-1 - 6.07-8, (eds) by J. Nagle and T. Nagle, Available from AAAI.

Pfeiffer, H.D. and Hartley, R.T. (1990) *"Additions for SET representation and processing to conceptual programming"* Proc. of the Fifth Annual Workshop on Conceptual Structures, pp. 131-140, (eds) P. Eklund and L. Gerholz, Linköping University pp. 131-140., ISBN 91-7870-718-8.

Sethi, R. (1989) *Programming Languages Concepts and Constructs*, Reading, MA: Addison Wesley.

Sowa, J.F. (1984) *Conceptual Structures*, Reading, MA: Addison Wesley.

5

Towards a Deep-Knowledge Semantics for Conceptual Graphs

Pavel Kocura
Department of Computer Studies,
Loughborough University of Technology,
Loughborough, LE11 3TU, United Kingdom

5.1 INTRODUCTION

Sowa's conceptual graphs could be likened to a conceptual LEGO set in that they make it possible to construct, in a principled way, complex concept structures from individual building blocks. As long as certain criteria on how the building blocks should be put together are met, any imaginable model can be constructed. The criteria are essentially determined by the coupling interfaces of the building blocks. Their design, and the matching mechanism, should ensure that the blocks could be combined together only in permissible ways. This requires a high degree of standardization - all blocks, i.e. all concepts, should be used by standard operations in the same way. This is what generally happens in Sowa's theory.

However, there is one major exception - the treatment of sets. Other researchers have commented on some of the gaps in the representation of sets in the theory of conceptual graphs. Tjan *et. al* (1989b) have suggested a solution, but their approach, although very sophisticated, went further in the same direction, putting more information into the referent field, and thus even further departing from a uniform representation and treatment of concepts.

The proposed approach deals with sets in the same way as with any other concepts. Normally, with non-set concepts, a referent, generic or individual, stands for an object. Departing from this rule, the original conceptual graphs representation of sets puts into the referent field not just a symbol standing for a set, but the set itself. In this notation, one has to refer to a set always by quoting it fully, instead of referring to a it by its identifier. Apart from theoretical fragility, this also has practical implications: displaying a graph including hundreds of elements, which is a realistic situation, would not result in a user-friendly interface.

Sowa's type lattice does not have the natural type label SET. This is a major departure from the otherwise uniquely principled architecture. As a result, only sets of objects that comply with a single type label can be represented, and thus a lot of information about the elements is lost. It is not possible to specify arbitrary sets, i.e. sets containing elements of different types, by extension.

Also, the original set representation does not include a comprehensive definition of the standard set relations and operations (inclusion, subtraction, union, intersection and symmetrical difference). It should be possible, by definition, to express these relations in terms of conceptual graphs, using the standard graph operations of projection and/or maximal join.

The reason for the anomalous representation of sets, compared to the rest of the theory, is Sowa's goal of representing natural language statements in conceptual graphs as directly as possible. Obviously, it is very important to be able to refer to complex concepts and situations in a very parsimonious, succinct way, but it is even more important to be able to reason about them. Without a detailed underlying semantics, translation of natural language statements into conceptual graphs inevitably results in representing intrinsically very complex conceptual structures by a semantic "shorthand". However, for inferences about the natural language statements it is imperative that any surface expression be decomposable into its elementary, ontologically determined constituents. The motivation of the new approach to the representation of sets in conceptual graphs is the processing of deep knowledge. We will show that the deep-knowledge-based approach to the representation of sets satisfies both objectives - direct translation from natural language and reasoning.

5.2   A NEW NOTATION FOR SET CONCEPTS

First let us show the difference between the new notation and Sowa's. The following example is in Sowa's notation.

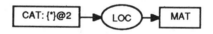

"Two cats are on a mat."

To translate this into the new set representation, let us assume a high-level, natural type label SET, which represents an ontological category similar to those of ENTITY, STATE, EVENT, ACT, etc. The type SET is the least common supertype of all types of sets. We use this type label as the genus of the definitions of more specialized set type labels by specializing it with the type labels of the set members, e.g.

```
type CAT_SET(x) is
```

This definition specifies any set with at least one [CAT] member. To exclude any non-cat elements, the definition can be tightened, as shown in the following graph, which gives the definition of a set equivalent to Sowa's [CAT: {*}]:

type CAT_SET(x) is

5.2.1 Set Cardinality

Sowa represents set cardinality by putting numerical information into the referent field of the set concept., e.g. [CAT: {*}@2]. This notation does not conform to the general principle of abstraction, namely, that any specialization should be reflected in the type label. Following this principle, we define the type label of an n-member set, n-SET, using λ-abstraction, in the following way:

type 2_CAT_SET(x) is

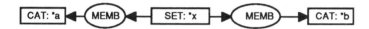

This general definition of the type 2_MEMBER_SET may be tightened by explicitly excluding any other elements, as shown in the following graph.

type 2_MEMBER_SET(x) is

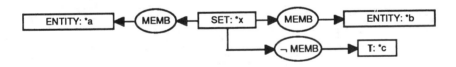

Alternatively, we may get the same result by defining or assuming as a primitive the relation (CARD), which links a set to a number corresponding to its cardinality, e.g.

type 2_CAT_SET(x) is

As conceptual graphs are finite by definition, it is not feasible to have a general n-member set model for every imaginable n in the definition catalogue. An individual model of an n-member set will be constructed recursively for any particular n if and when needed.

Thus, the new notation gives a full equivalent of Sowa's set [CAT {*}@2], namely, 2_CAT_SET, where 2_CAT_SET < 2_SET, and 2_CAT_SET < CAT_SET. However, the notation is not limited to sets with members of the same type.

5.2.2   Representing Surface Semantics

Relying on the proposed set representation, the Thematic Relations Hypothesis, which will be discussed in the second half of this paper, we can represent the situation as

```
type ONE_APPLE_ONE_PEAR_ONE_DOG_ONE_CAT_SET(x) is
```

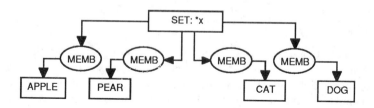

where LOC_spc < STATE.

The following graph enables us to reason about the cats and their doings individually, and still keep the set-oriented view:

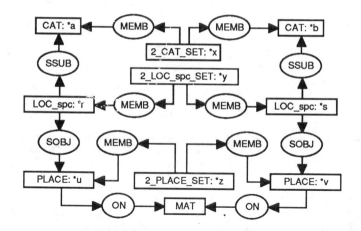

We may still want to use a shorthand notation to map the surface semantics of natural language sentences in the same way that Sowa's notation does. For this we have to define a layer of set-oriented relations, each of which represents a set of identical relations between non-set concepts. In the case above, we may bundle all the individual relations (SSUB) into the set relation (SSSUB) or Set of States SUBject:

```
relation SSSUB(x,y) is
```

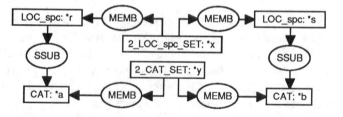

The relation (SSSUB) says that each element of the set 2_CAT_SET is in the relation (SSUB) to one of the elements of the set 2_LOC_spc_SET.

Then $[2\_CAT\_SET:*y] \leftarrow (SSSUB) \leftarrow [2\_LOC\_spc\_SET:*x]$.

Now we have to "bundle" the individual relations (SOBJ) into the set relation (SSOBJ), Set of States OBJect:

```
relation SSOBJ(x,y) is
```

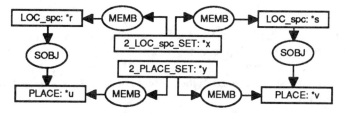

The relation (SSOBJ) states that each element of the set $[2\_LOC\_spc\_SET: *x]$ is in relation (SOBJ) to a unique member of the set $[2\_PLACE\_SET: *y]$.

Then $[2\_LOC\_spc\_SET:*y] \rightarrow (SSOBJ) \rightarrow [2\_PLACE\_SET:*z]$.

The following graph uses the high-level set relations to map the original sentence more directly:

where the type $ON\_MAT\_PLACE = (\lambda x) [PLACE: *x] \rightarrow (ON) \rightarrow [MAT]$. We may not want to, or be able to, specify the set concept LOC_spc_SET any further. Then we may define, from the full, expanded graph, the relation label SET_LOC. This will give us a direct, "surface" equivalent of the original sentence.

"There are two cats on a mat."

This graph says that there is a set of two cats, and both of these cats are to be found on a single mat. It has the form of the original graph in Sowa's notation, but its individual concepts can be decomposed into the individual, deep-level building blocks.

It needs to be stressed here that the relation (SET_LOC) does not say that it is *the set* 2_CAT_SET that can be found on the mat. The relation refers just to its members. A set is an abstract concept defining a grouping and, as such, it can be located only in one's mind.

5.2.3   Further Examples

To illustrate the new set representation, let us translate some of the sentences used by Tjan *et al.* (1989b).

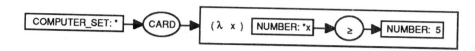

"There exist five or more computers."

The graph above says that there exists a set of computers whose cardinality is equal to or greater than five. The following sentence, *"Two or more of the computers #1, #2, #3 and #4 run exactly three programs each"*, was used by Tjan to illustrate his set formalism. Let us see how it could be represented in the new set notation. First, we need to define the following individual set:

```
individual 4_COMPUTER_SET(#2939) is
```

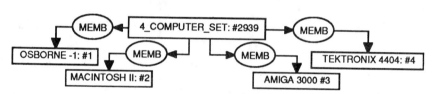

Next we define the type label for a computer set with a cardinality equal to or more than two:

```
CARD ≥ 4_COMPUTER_SET(x) is
```

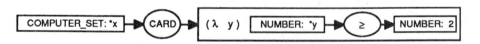

Then a set conforming to the type CARD ≥ CARD2_COMPUTER_SET can be a subset of our [SET: #2939]:

```
type CARD≥4_COMPUTER_SUBSET_OF_4_COMPUTER_SET_#2939(x) is
```

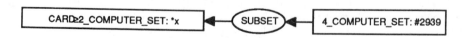

This type label describes a set with 2 or more elements which is also a subset of the set [4_COMPUTER_SET: #2939].

Next let us represent the phrase *"a computer runs exactly three programs:"*

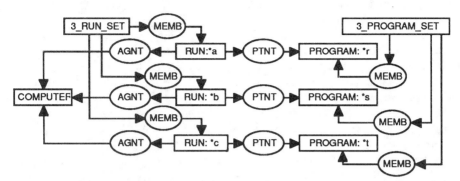

We can define "set relations" in the same way as in the cats-on-mat example and use them to contract the above graph:

The following graph represents the original sentence in a contracted form of the new notation:

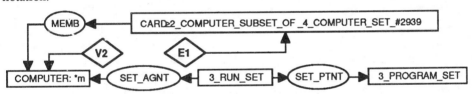

The graph literally says: *"There exists a subset of the set* [4_COMPUTER_SET: #2939] *such that it has at least two elements, and all members of this subset run exactly three programs each".* Which is the same as the sentence, *"Two or more of the computers #1, #2, #3 and #4 run exactly three programs each".*

Because conceptual graphs are not a linear notation, the order of quantifier application has to be indicated explicitly by the ordinal number in the actors. The interpretation of the actors will depend on the interpretation of the graph. If we use the logical interpretation, the operator ϕ translating the graph into a first-order predicate logic formula will factor out the quantifiers in the right order. In a model-oriented interpretation, e.g. in a query, the actors will search the knowledge base to establish whether there really are two or more computers in [4_COMPUTER_SET: #2939] that run three programs each. For the model-oriented interpretation of the graph, the quantifier actors will contain procedures for the automatic checking of the validity of quantified statements against the knowledge base of the system.

5.3   SET RELATIONS AND OPERATIONS

Using the new set formalism, we can express conventional set relations and operations. Moreover, we can define operations which do not necessarily apply to identical elements, like the conventional set operations, but elements which are only compatible. This compatibility is determined by the type and relation lattices, conformities, and by other, domain-specific constraints defined by λ-abstractions and by the conceptual and relational catalogues. It would be desirable, both theoretically and practically, if the concept-set operations could utilize standard conceptual graphs operations, namely, projection and maximal join. The proposed set representation meets this requirement.

The operational definitions of most set operations will use variants of a maximal join. These will operate only on set elements. The specialized "head" concept of a set, the node [.....SET], will be effectively eliminated from the operation by replacing its type with the general type SET. The reason for this is to avoid inevitable type clashes between the heads of the sets involved. We may surmise, however, that such clashes would be largely avoided if the set type and set inclusion hierarchies were developed in greater detail. For this we need to develop a "calculus" generating the type label of each set from the type labels of the set's members. Then, if there is a set relation between any two explicitly represented sets, this relation will be reflected in the relative position of the type labels of their heads in the type lattice.

5.3.1 The Empty Set

The type label SET gives the unspecified generic set [SET], which corresponds to Sowa's generic set *. The empty set is defined as an individual set which has no members whatsoever:

```
individual EMPTY_SET(#) is
```

5.3.2 Subset Relation (SUBS)

The elementary interpretation of the subset relation is based on projection. If [SET: *x]→(SUBS)→[SET: *y], then there exists a projection of a subgraph of the expanded [SET: *x] onto the body of the expanded [SET: *y]. In this case the head of [SET: *y] is omitted from the operation. Provided the system can generate automatically set type labels from the labels of their elements, a new head will be generated for any subgraph of [SET: *x]. The type label of this head will be a supertype of the type label of [SET: *y] and will be included in the projection.

[SET: *y] may include concepts whose type labels can be restricted to make the projection possible. Whether such a restriction is possible will depend on domain specific knowledge.

With the above definition of the relation (SUBS), [SET: *y] may represent several distinct subsets of [SET: *x]. It may be necessary to specify preference rules which determine the order in which individual projections will be considered. For example, do we first project a generic concept on a compatible individual concept, or is it better to first match generic concepts in one set with compatible generic concepts in the other set. These questions will require more research into the semantics of operations on concept sets.

The following graph shows [SET: *a]→(SUBS)→[SET: *b] in expanded form.

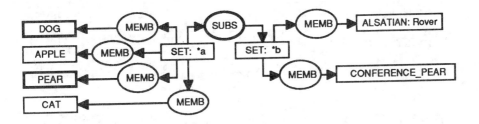

5.3.3 Set Union <SUNI>

The operation of set union is defined as an actor which asserts a new graph equal to the maximal join(s) of the graphs of the input sets. The following graph shows an example of a set union.

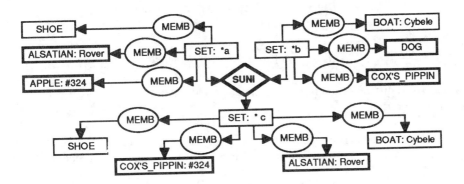

5.3.4 Set Intersection <SINT>

The operation of set intersection is defined operationally by an actor. To generate an intersection of sets a and b, the actor de-restricts the type labels of the heads of the sets to the generic concept with the minimal common supertype in the type field. Then it performs a maximal join on the graphs representing the sets. If there is a maximal join, the actor identifies the nodes taking part in the maximal join and generates a new type label, and a new generic referent or, if required, a new individual identifier for the head of the sub-graph, as shown in the following example.

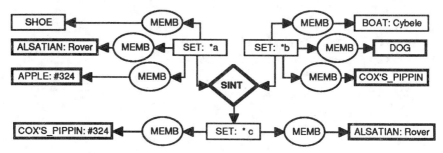

5.4 JACKENDOFF'S SEMANTIC SYSTEM

Drawing from Gruber (1965), Miller & Johnson-Laird (1976) and others, and on the basis of extensive empirical linguistic study, Jackendoff has suggested a semi-formal system which, although at first sight quite dissimilar to Sowa's, maps directly into it.

Let us illustrate this correspondence by translating the following formula in Jackendoff's notation into conceptual graphs .

$$
\begin{array}{ccccc}
\text{TYPE} & \text{TOKEN} & \text{TYPE} & \text{TOKEN} & \text{TOKEN} \\
GO_{Posit} & ([\text{DOG}], & [\text{FROM}([& \text{DOOR}]) & \text{TO}([\text{TABLE}])]) \\
\text{Event} & \text{Object} & \text{Path} & \text{Object} & \text{Object}
\end{array}
$$

"The dog went from the door to the table."

Three basic differences between this notation and Sowa's conceptual graphs can be immediately noticed:

1. The type structure is indicated by "supertypes" attached, as subscripts, directly to the individual objects. This type structure is not developed into a comprehensive type lattice.

2. The distinction between individual concepts and generic concepts is indicated by the attached markers (superscripts) TYPE and TOKEN. There is no provision for individual identifiers or named variables.

3. Jackendoff's is a functional notation. Its objects are created by nested functions which have other nested objects as their arguments. Although his semantics is compositional, this linear, nested syntax is "closed", i.e. intrinsically unable to express this compositionality. For example, we might want to add more information about the dog's progress, about the characteristics of the dog itself, or the door or the table. This information would have to be added inside the nested structures, which would become quickly unreadable. Alternatively, separate statements would have to be constructed for each new piece of knowledge.

5.4.1 Translating Jackendoff's notation into conceptual graphs

The following informal algorithm describes the procedure of translating Jackendoffs notation into conceptual graphs:

1. Identify the individual objects of the formula and separate the type information in the
   subscripts. Using the subscripts and the names of the objects, create a comprehensive
   type lattice. From our example, we get the following:

   GO_spc $<$ ... $<$ EVENT $<$ ... $<$ ENTITY $<$ T; [1]
   DOG $<$ ... $<$ ANIMAL $<$ ... $<$ PHYSICAL_OBJECT $<$ ... $<$ ENTITY $<$ T;
   PATH $<$ ... $<$ ENTITY $<$ T; [2]
   TABLE $<$ ... $<$ FURNITURE_OBJECT $<$ ... $<$ PHYSICAL_OBJECT $<$ ENTITY $<$ T.

2. Create a concept box for each identified object. Place the object type label into the
   type field of the concept.

3. Substitute a generic referent or a named variable for every occurrence of the supertype
   marker TYPE, and a unique individual identifier for every object marked with the
   marker TOKEN, producing:

        [GO].   [PATH].   [DOG: #].   [TABLE: #].

4. Identify any explicit conceptual relations that appear in the formula. Identify any
   relational links between objects that are given implicitly by the position of the
   parameters inside the brackets of the function representing an object. The present
   formula contains two explicit relational links, TO and FROM. Two implicit relation
   links will be associated with the concept [GO].

5. "Unbundle" the individual objects by turning the functions inside out. Substitute
   suitable relation types for explicit or implicit relational links, using infix notation.
   "Rebundle" the objects, using lambda expressions. Thus, the object [... GO ...
   ], which is a function of the objects [... DOG] and [... PATH ...], gives
   us the following graph:

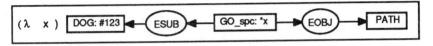

where ESUB stands for Event SUBject, and EOBJ stands for Event OBJect.

---

[1] The type label GO is the least common supertype of all types representing EVENTS and ACTS of change
in any domain. The subscript spc indicates the spatial domain.
[2] Adapted from Jackendoff (1983, p188.)

However, the object [... PATH ...] is a function of the objects [...
DOOR] and [...TABLE]. After opening [... PATH ...] and attaching
the explicit relational links TO and FROM to it, we get:

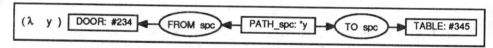

By substituting the complex concept PATH_spc into the first graph (and opening the
λ-abstraction for convenience), the translation is complete:

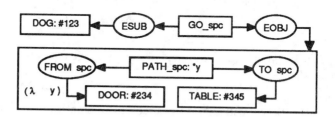

"The dog went from the door to the table."

Jackendoff's system does not include any structure processing or inference, although it
does assume simple implication. Property inheritance is only sketched, without a formally
defined type lattice.

On the other hand, it provides a theoretically principled, cognitively sound and empirically supported compositional system of deep-knowledge semantics.

The main contribution of Jackendoff's system to the semantics of conceptual graphs
is the of development the Thematic Relations Hypothesis, which is originally based on a
hypothesis stated by Gruber (1965).

The thematic relation hypothesis develops the observation that meanings of concepts in
most semantic fields are "analogs" of spatial concepts and relations. In his book *Semantics
and Cognition*, (Jackendoff, 1983), Jackendoff shows how the thematic relations hypothesis
paradigm applies to various semantic categories. We have shown that Jackendoff's syntax
maps directly into the syntax of Sowa's conceptual graphs. Therefore, any system based on
conceptual graphs can use the thematic relations hypothesis as theoretically and empirically
sound semantic foundations.

5.4.2   The Thematic Relations Hypothesis (TRH)

TRH In any semantic field including [EVENTs], [STATEs] and equivalents of the ontological primitives of [PLACE], [PATH], [GO], and [ENTITIES] serving as theme, the
principal conceptual relations associated with [EVENTs], [STATEs], [PATHs], and
[PLACEs] are a subset of those used for the analysis of spatial location and motion.

Theme the [ENTITY] whose analogs of spatial location or motion in a given semantic
field are asserted.

Semantic fields mainly differ, from the point of view of the thematic relations hypothesis, in the following criteria:

- What [ENTITIES] appear as theme.
- What [ENTITIES] appear as reference points, i.e. analogs of [PLACEs].
- What [STATE] replaces the concept of location in the spatial field.
- What [EVENT] replaces the concept representing movement in space.[3]

5.4.3 Semantics of Space

Let us introduce a simplified semantics of space. A [PLACE] in a spatial system can be identified either by its individual referent, namely, by its coordinates, or by its relations to other [PLACES]:

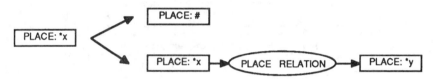

The names of place relations are the prepositions of spatial prepositional phrases, e.g. AT, IN, ON, ABOVE, UNDER, OVER, BETWEEN, etc. Because in a specific coordinate system the position of a [PLACE] will never change, there is no need to express the spatial relations between different [PLACES] as time-dependent states.

5.4.4 Location of Entities in Space

A [PHYS_OBJ] has to occupy a [PLACE]. In an open, dynamic spatial system, a [PHYS_OBJ] may occupy a [PLACE] only temporarily. For example, it could be moving through the space and the [PLACE] would be part of its trajectory. Alternatively, a [PHYS_OBJ] could first enter the system by being generated in one [PLACE], then move on and leave the system by being destroyed. In an open system, the occupation of a [PLACE] by a [PHYS_OBJ] will usually have a temporal dimension, i.e. it will be expressed as a temporary [STATE]. We may represent this as

where LOC_spc < STATE, SSUB stands for State SUBject, SOBJ for State OBJect'[4].
Where [LOC_spc] need not be further specified, e.g. where the objects described are immovable in the given coordinate system, the whole group (SSUB) ← [LOC_spc] → (SSOB) may be contracted into the relation (LOC). In a dynamic system, the stative concept [LOC_spc] will be further specialized with temporal information. The following are elementary rules for a simple spatial system:

---

[3] Adapted from Jackendoff (1983 p. 188).
[4] These relations do not correspond to case relations.

5.4.5   The Spatial Field

- Each object has to occupy precisely one [PLACE];

- No [PLACE] can be occupied by more than one object (unless objects are nested);

- Not every [PLACE] in our system is necessarily occupied by an object.

- Objects can move from [PLACE] to [PLACE].

In the following graph, the ['PLACE_ON_THE_MAT'] is a function of the concept [MAT], which in turn will be related, directly or indirectly, to a set of coordinates in a coordinate system.

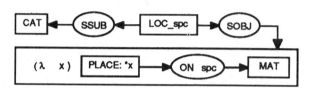

"A cat is on a mat."

In semantic categories other than of space, the analogs of [PLACE] will be [PER-SON] in the *possessive* and responsibility fields, [POINT-IN-TIME] or [PERIOD] in the *temporal field*, or various *characteristics*, e.g. [COLOUR], [OCCUPATION], [REPRO-DUCTIVE_STATUS], or existence, non-existence, or any of its degrees, in the *existential* field. Illustrating the application of the thematic relations hypothesis to these fields is beyond the scope of this paper.

5.4.6   Connecting Places - [PATH_spc]

The type PATH_spc represents a major ontological category, namely, explicit or implicit connections between [PLACEs]. The concept [PATH_spc] is essential for all [EVENTs] of movement, [STATEs] expressing orientation, and [STATEs] of a physical realization of a path.

A [ROUTE_spc] is a [PATH_spc] linked explicitly by the PATH relation (VIA) to one or more [PLACEs] through which it passes. These [PLACEs] may be defined extensionally by listing them, or intensionally by providing a function which specifies conditions under which a [PLACE] lies on a [ROUTE_spc]. A [ROUTE_spc] can be composed from an ordered set of adjoining subpaths.

Compositionality of [PATH_spc] and [ROUTE_spc]

The concept of [PATH_spc] does not determine a unique [ROUTE_spc] between its ends. Two end-points define a [PATH_spc], but a single [PATH_spc] may include an infinity of physical [ROUTE_spc] instantiations.

A [ROUTE_spc] may be recursively decomposed into an implicitly ordered aggregation of subroutes between individual [PLACEs], e.g.

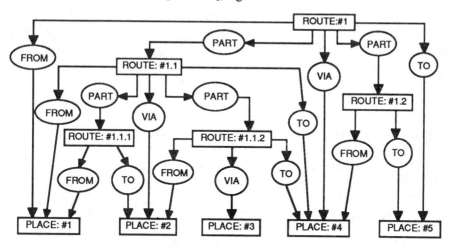

The above are representations of a [PATH_spc] or [ROUTE_spc] by extension. It is possible to define a [ROUTE_spc] by intension, by defining a coordinate system and a function which describes the given [ROUTE_spc]. In this case the coordinates of the individual [PLACEs] on the [ROUTE_spc] are interrelated by an actor:

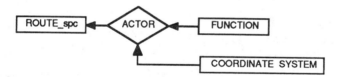

A [PATH_spc] is specified by at least one reference [PLACE], and at least one of a number of natural relations. Generally:

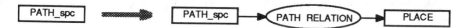

PATH_RELATION labels include FROM, TO, AWAY_FROM, TOWARD, and VIA. Path relations (AWAY_FROM_spc) and (TOWARD_spc) refer to a [PATH_spc] without one of its end-points. Conceptual relations (DIRECTION_spc) and (ORIENTATION_spc) may be derived from the relations (AWAY_FROM_spc) and (TOWARD_spc).

The relation label BETWEEN is defined by means of a [PATH_spc] and the natural relation ON_spc:

```
relation BETWEEN(x, y, z) is
```

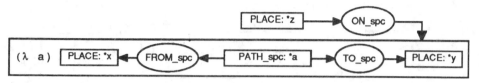

The above definition is incomplete in that it has to include certain assumptions about the shape of [PATH_spc: *a], namely, that it is straight.

In other semantic fields, according to the TRH, the analogs of a [PATH_spc] will be the time continuum in the temporal field, a chain of responsibility, i.e. an ordered set of people, a space of characteristics, e.g. the sequence of colours of a ripening apple, or the gradual stages of, for example, the transformation of a ball of wool into a new sweater.

5.4.7   Movement in Space - [GO_spc]

The traversal of a physical object along a [PATH] is represented as

"A physical object moved along a path."

where ESUB = Event SUBject, EOBJ = Event OBJect and GO_spc < EVENT[5].

The basic [EVENT] of motion is [GO_spc]. The [PHYS_OBJ] that does the moving, *Theme*, is linked to it by the relation (ESUB). The reference point, linked by the relation (EOBJ), is always a [PATH_spc] or a more specific [ROUTE_spc]. The assertion of a [GO_spc] activates a rule which cancels the original position of Theme and asserts its new position at the end of the [PATH_spc]. Thus the concept [GO_spc] is an elementary source of inferences about the dynamic behaviour and spatial position of objects. The following example represents the lowest common denominator of all situations where John changed his spatial location along a [PATH_spc] ending in Boston:

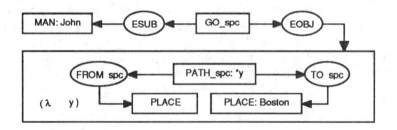

"John went to Boston."

---

[5]The terms object and subject do not have their usual linguistic meaning here. They are just convenience labels to identify specific types of links between concepts.

John is not necessarily the agent - he might have been abducted and transported to Boston against his will, or without even knowing it. The following graph illustrates such a situation:

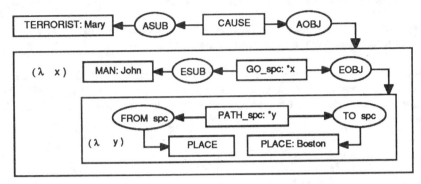

"*A terrorist, Mary, kidnapped John and took him to Boston.*"

where ASUB = (intentional) Act SUBject, and AOBJ = (intentional) Act OBJect. In the default interpretation of the sentence John went to Boston, John is the intentional agent of his own travel.

Compositionality of [GO_spc]

Like a [ROUTE_spc], a [GO_spc] can be composed from its sub-events. The composition of a [GO_spc] is partly determined by the composition of the [ROUTE_spc] to which it is linked, namely, there is a separate sub-event [GO_spc] for every individual subroute. Additional information describing the behaviour of the physical object, and the characteristics of the individual sub-events and subroutes, as well as any other relevant information, can be attached to the individual nodes.

The open and flexible formalism of conceptual graphs and the deep-knowledge semantics make it possible to give a "blow-by-blow" description of complex processes taking place not only in the spatial domain, but in any other domain that maps into the TRH. The description of a process can be compared to a series of snap-shots. Each of the "film frames" describes a grouping of concepts that is meaningful or valid at that particular time. The individual groupings are connected by standard PATH relations, across the "frames", into an analog of a [PATH] or [ROUTE].

5.5   CONCLUSION

The paper has proposed a new schema for the representation of sets which offers the following advantages:

- It is isomorphic with the representation and handling of ordinary conceptual graphs. This makes the resulting system more homogeneous and and the operations on graphs more coherent.

- It is object-oriented in that it uses encapsulation, namely, it uses a token for a set concept referent instead of the set itself.

- It introduces a specific set type lattice.

- It outlines set operations based on the standard conceptual graphs operations.

- It provides a direct definition path from a deep-knowledge representation to a shorthand representation of natural language statements.

Also, we have introduced a deep-knowledge motivated semantics for conceptual graphs based on a Jackendoff's developments of the Thematic Relations Hypothesis. This new semantics forms the basis of a consistent methodology for the modelling of different semantic fields.

BIBLIOGRAPHY

Gruber, Jeffrey S. (1965) "Studies in Lexical Relations", Doctoral dissertation MIT, Cambridge; Indiana University Linguistics Club, Bloomington, Ind. Reprinted as part of *Lexical Structures in Syntax and Semantics*, North-Holland, Amsterdam 1976.

Herskovits, Annette (1986) *Language and Spatial Cognition - An interdisciplinary study of the prepositions in English*, Cambridge University Press 1986.

Jackendoff, Ray (1983) *Semantics and Cognition*, The MIT Press.

Jackendoff, Ray (1985) "Multiple Subcategorization and the t-Criterion: The Case of Climb Natural Language and Linguistic Theory 3", pp.271-295.

Jackendoff, Ray (1987) *Consciousness and the Computational Mind*, The MIT Press.

Jackendoff, Ray (1990) *Semantic Structures*, The MIT Press.

Rucker, Rob (1989) "Conceptual Structure in the Curriculum: Graduate Level Course-work Experience", Proc. of the Fourth Annual Workshop on Conceptual Structures, Detroit, August 20 -21.

Sowa, John, F. (1984) *Conceptual Structures: Information Processing in Mind and Machine* , Addison-Wesley.

6

Graphical Displays and Polymophism

John W. Esch
Unisys Corp
PO Box 64663, MS F2L09,
St. Paul, Mn, 55164-0525 USA

ABSTRACT

Sowa has specified a mathematically well-defined, integrated set of conceptual structures (Sowa, 1984). They include concepts, relations, actors, their types, contexts, and canons. He also defines a graphical symbology for displaying contexts and conceptual graphs with concept, relation, and actor nodes. But he does not give a display form for the rest of the conceptual structures. This chapter extends the display form to cover all of the conceptual structures. It also extends "concepts" in the theory of conceptual graphs to be polymorphic with respect to their referents. This leads to using different display symbols for concepts depending on what kind of referent they have.

6.1 BACKGROUND

After ten years of research on knowledge representations, Brachman (1989) concludes that three types of objects are essential to represent knowledge. They are concepts, roles, and individuals. Concepts "are descriptions with potentially complex structure, ...; concepts correspond to one place predicates, and thus are applied to one individual at a time." Roles "are simple formal terms for attributes; they correspond to two place predicates, and are used to relate two individuals at a time." And individuals "are simple formal constructs intended to directly represent objects in the domain of interest; individuals are given properties by asserting that they are described by concepts (e.g. "chardonnay is a grape") and that their roles are filled by other individuals (e.g. "Ron's vice-president is a penzias"). Brachman utilizes the CLASSIC language, similar to the examples in the quotes above, as a notation for representing knowledge.

One of the few other knowledge representations that has been studied for a similar length of time is conceptual graphs as described by Sowa (1984). Where Brachman uses a language notation, Sowa uses a graph notation. "In the graphs, concept nodes represent entities, attributes, states, and events, and relation nodes show how the concepts are interconnected." "Conceptual relations specify the role that each concept plays."

Brachman and Sowa use "concept" the same way. Brachman's "roles" are almost the same as Sowa's "relations". The difference is that Sowa's relation's are n-adic (being able to relate any number of concepts together) while Brachman's roles are only diadic (being able to relate to just two concepts to each other). Their use of individual is the same.

While the use of concepts, relations/roles, and individuals is basically the same, the two representation schemes are quite different in scope. In CLASSIC the focus is on concepts while in conceptual graphs the focus is on graphs, a collection of concepts and their relationships to each other.

Sowa (Sowa, 1984) provides a graphical notation for drawing conceptual graphs. However, he also describes some other conceptual structures, including type lattices, contexts and canons, for which he does not give adequate, and in some cases any, graphical notations.

For types (sometimes also called classes) the problem of a corresponding graphical notation was addressed by Harel (1988) in an elegant application of Euler circles, which later evolved into Vern diagrams. Harel calls his notation for representing types "blobs". While Harel provides an excellent foundation, a few refinements are needed. Those refinements cover the cases of: a type as a collective set of its extension, untangling complex cases of common super types, and indicating a type's individuals. Also, graphical representations distinguishing relations from their types and actors from there types are needed.

Sowa (1984) gives a graphical notation for contexts. Each conceptual graph makes an assertion. A context is a box around a collection of graphs that denotes their conjunction, the logical AND of the assertions made by the contained graphs. However, when a context is shrunk to the size of a concept, it is impossible to distinguish them from concepts.

Sowa (1984) does not give any graphical notation for canons, which correspond to formally defined knowledge base, nor for collections of individuals of the same type (the type's extension or a subset of them).

Lastly, with all these new display symbols, rules are needed for which can and can't be connected by arcs. Along with the rules, a consistent interpretation for the arcs that are allowed is also needed.

In summary, the following problems for graphical representation of conceptual structures exist:

1. Untangling complex supertypes

2. Representing a type's extension as a collection

3. Distinguishing concepts and contexts

4. Representing a type's extension

5. Representing a canon

6. Representing sets

7. Rules for arcs and their interpretation

6.2 GRAPHICAL DISPLAY EXTENSIONS

The overall solution is to represent entities (concepts, contexts, individuals, and canons) by rectangles, their types by roundtangles, sets of entities by dashed roundtangles, and relationships among them by ovoids or circles. In addition, things that have content are open while those that do not are closed (solid). Details of this solution, as it relates to the above identified seven graphical notation problems, are described in this section. The basic ideas were first described in a paper presented at the Fifth Annual Workshop on Conceptual Structures (Esch, 1990).

As described by Harel (1988), each type is represented by a "blob" or roundtangle that may overlap to indicate commonality or subtype as in Fig. 6.1.

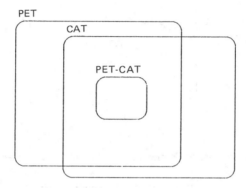

Fig. 6.1 Overlapping Types with Common Subtype[1].

In this example, the two large roundtangles represent the type PET and CAT and the smaller one, which is contained in the intersection of the two large ones, represents the type PET-CAT. This denotes that PET-CAT is a subtype of both PET and CAT. Thus, a PET-CAT concept or individual is also a PET and a CAT.

For complex common supertypes the drawing of the many possible intersections on a planar surface many become impossibly difficult. To simplify the problem an alterative graphical notation called a type coreference link is used as shown in Fig. 6.2.

In Fig. 6.2, the dashed line indicates coreference, i.e. that the things connected denote the same thing. In this case, since types are being connected, it is a type coreferent link.

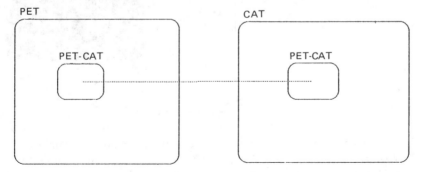

Fig. 6.2 Using Type Coreferent Links to avoid Overlapping.

---

[1] Examples are copyrighted screen dumps of CONSTRUCT.

For complex type lattices it may not be possible to draw all of the types on the page or screen at the same time. To cover this case, a coreferent stub is used as shown in Fig. 6.3.

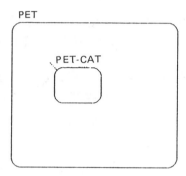

Fig. 6.3 Use of Coreferent Stubs for Off-Screen Supertypes.

This example indicates that there is an off-page or off-screen coreferent type. A label can be used to give a page number or numbers, identifiers, or number of other coreferent types.

The second problem is representing a type's extension as a collection. The extension of a type consists of all individuals of that type. The extension of the type PET is the set of all things (individuals) that are PETs. In some situations one needs to depict the extension of a type as a collection or whole. For example, the shareholders of a corporation own it collectively, not individually. For easy visual recognition the same shape is used but it is made solid as is shown in Fig. 6.4.

Fig. 6.4. Open Type Roundtangle & Closed Collective Extent

In this example the solid roundtangle denotes the collection of all individuals of type PET. Note that it is distinct from the type PET but, of course, closely related.

The third problem is distinguishing concepts and contexts. The technique used to solve the second problem can be generalized and re-applied. The generalization is that open and solid versions of the same shape are not the same, but have different meaning. A general interpretation is that a solid shape denotes some specific thing, while an open one denotes some class or collection of things.

Contexts represent the conjunction of a collection of graphs and concepts represent a single object or entity. So concepts, with the above rule, should be solid rectangles and contexts should be open rectangles as shown in Fig. 6.5.

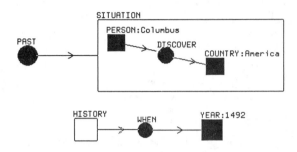

Fig. 6.5. Distinguishing Concepts from Contexts.

Interpreting the PAST relation as a monadic predicate for past tense leads to "Columbus discovered America." In this case there is only one graph in the context whose assertion, "Columbus discovers America," is in the past.

Contexts can, as shown above, participate in conceptual graphs in the same way as concepts. In some cases, because of the complexity of the context, it is desirable to shrink it to the same size as a concept. In other cases, it is desirable to expand it, as above, so that its contents can be seen. Context can also have type labels. For example, consider the type HISTORY which is defined as a SITUATION context that occurred in the past. An unexpanded or contracted graph using HISTORY is also shown in Fig. 6.5.

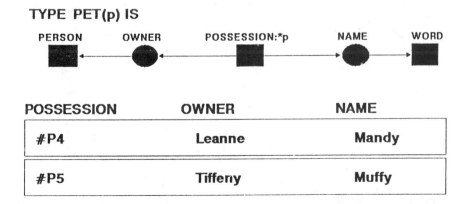

Fig. 6.6. Representing Individuals of a Type.

It is clear, based on the open/solid distinction, that HISTORY is a context with content and that YEAR is a concept with 1492 as its referent.

The fourth problem is representing a type's extension. All knowledge representations provide a way to represent a single individual's characteristics or properties. This may be a set of statements in a language, a form-like listing, or a graph. The problem is graphically representing all the individuals.

All individuals of a type share the definition of that type. That definition will normally define attributes and the ranges of values for those attributes to which each individual conforms. Each individual is, in effect, a copy of the type definition with specific values of the attributes filled in. Thus, if the type PET is defined as a specialization of type POSSESSION having attributes NAME and OWNER, then each PET will have values for these attributes. They can be presented graphically as a table with headings of POSSESSION, NAME and OWNER as shown in Fig. 6.6.

Any type may have either or both subtypes and individuals. The next step, involving the fourth problem, is to determine a graphical notation for types that covers all combinations of subtypes and individuals.

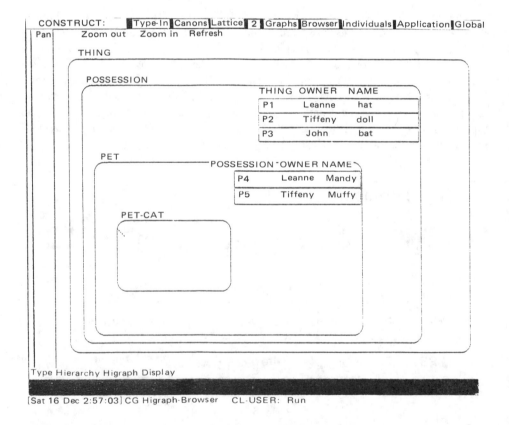

Fig. 6.7. Combined Representation of Types & Individuals [4]

The solution is to divide, conceptually, the roundtangle into halves, the left being for subtypes and the right for individuals as shown in Fig. 6.7. (Other partitionings are equally as valid but not as intuitive.)

In this made-up example, the type THING has a subtype but no individuals, the type POSSESSION has both a subtype and individuals, and the type PET also has both. In real knowledge bases, there would probably be multiple subtypes and many more individuals. The accuracy of this particular type structure is not important here. What is important is the graphical composition of both the subtype and individual information inside the roundtangle representing the type. A wide range of possibilities exist for laying out the sizes, shapes and positions of the subtypes and individuals. What's important is the joint display of both kinds of information.

The fifth problem is representing canons. A canon is specified by Sowa (1984) as a formal, mathematically well-defined knowledge base. It consists of a type lattice, individuals conforming to types in the lattices, and a conceptual basis. A conceptual base is just a set of assumptions or assertions expressed as a set of graphs. A canon can be thought of as a composition of a context and a type lattice. Any graphical notation for it must include possible subtypes, individuals, and conceptual graphs.

With this in mind, the solution is to use the context symbol (an open rectangle) and extend its contents to include both types and graphs. Its layout is: types toward the upper left, individuals toward the upper right, and graphs toward the lower half. Other arrangements are possible. What's important is the composition of the three kind of information inside one symbol for the canon as shown in Fig. 6.8.

The sixth problem is the graphical representation of sets. Sowa (1984) provides a way in the linear form to express a concept whose referent is a set. In it, each member of the set conforms to the type of the concept. The set is expressed in a linguistic list form. The graphical notation used by Sowa to form concepts of an individual and concepts of a set does not distinguish these two cases.

The notation adopted to make the distinction clear needs to be consistent with the notation for types and incorporate the idea of the set as a collection. The solution is to choose an easily distinguished variant of the roundtangle. Since the roundtangle denotes the extension of a type, it represents all individuals of that type. A set may be, and normally is, a proper subset of the type's extension. Thus, the variation selected needs to suggest, intuitively, something less than the full extension of the type. For this purpose, a broken roundtangle was chosen. (Dashed or dotted or something similar will do.) It denotes a set of elements all of whom conform to the type label on the set. To denote the collective set; that is, the set as a collection, a solid roundtangle with a variable or name to denote the particular set is appropriate.

Fig. 6.8 also illustrates a set and its collection. The open, dashed roundtangle denotes a set of OSTRICHes. Which particular set, since there could be many sets of the same individuals, is distinguished by the variable *set1. The solid roundtangle denotes the same set as a collection.

It is important to note that the graphical notation for representing individuals of a type (from the solution to the fourth problem) can also be applied to representing elements of sets as is also shown in Fig. 6.8.

The seventh problem is rules for arcs among the new display symbols and a consistent interpretation for them. Sowa (1984) defined conceptual graphs as bipartite with the two kinds of nodes being concepts and relations. This is the reason that concepts must be polymorphic with respect to their meaning in a conceptual graph. However, it doesn't mean that in the display form we can't use a variety of symbols for concepts. The choice of display symbols is based on the kind of referent.

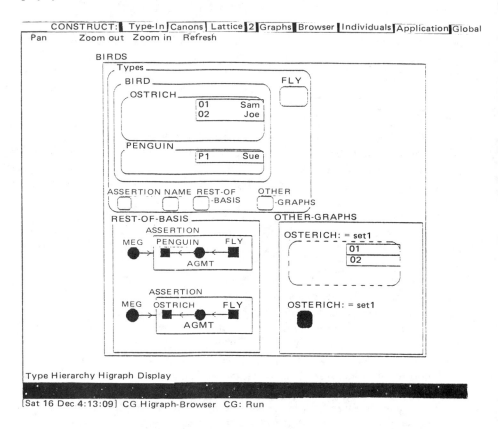

Fig. 6.8. Combining Representations and Representing Canons.

The problem is to insure that there is a consistent rule for interpreting graphs which have other display symbols. Sowa defined the ϕ operator to give one such interpretation, in this case in terms of predicate logic statements. The key is to have the intuitive mapping, that one would give a graph based on the display symbols, match the mapping for phi. In most cases Sowa has defined the mapping for ϕ to cover different kinds of referents. He states (Sowa, 1984) that a for-all quantifier can be placed in the referent field and that the interpretation is universal quantification over the rest of the graph which is existentially quantified by default.

This only solves half of the problem. One must be able to express both for-all there-exists and there-exists for-all scoping because they are different. The solution ties in with the interpretation of distributive sets. When a set is distributive, e.g. [CAT: DISTFelix, Rolf], the interpretation is that the rest of the graph applies to each member of the set. This is a there-exists for-all interpretation, e.g. there-exists a MAT on which were all CATs.

If one extends the set to all CATs, e.g. [CAT: for-all], then one has a consistent interpretation for sets (dashed roundtangles) and types (solid roundtangles).

The question immediately arises, how does one represent the complementary case, for-all there-exists? This is where the beauty of using symbols for types and sets that have insides and outsides becomes evident again. In the solution to the untangling types problem, having an inside allowed the containment principal to be used to define where subtypes could be drawn. The there-exists for-all case has the type or set symbol connected on its outside to the rest of the graph. The complementary case is to allow it to also be connected on the inside. The natural interpretation is: for-all members of the containing symbol, there-exists the rest of the graph connected on the inside.

There are many different cases. To cover a representative sample of them, a short story was written called The Apartment Story. It consists of a sequence of sentences about a set of renters and a type consisting of the persons which own the apartment. Fig. 6.9 gives the story and corresponding conceptual graphs in both display and linear forms.

A roundtangle was chosen for both types and sets because the extension of a type is a set. Adopting the distributive rule for graphs containing concepts with set or for-all referents makes the interpretation by ϕ of such graphs to be almost the same. The roundtangle was also chosen because it has an inside and outside which naturally distinguishes the there-exists for-all case (graph connected on the outside) from the for-all there-exists case (graph connected on the inside).

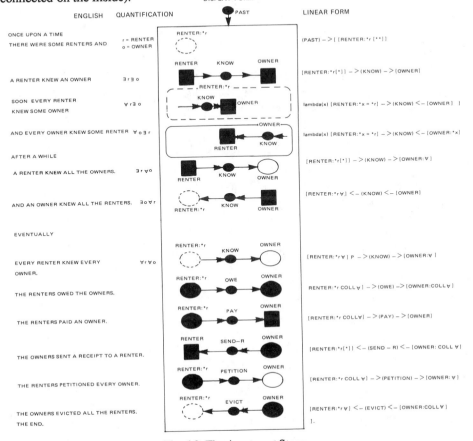

Fig. 6.9. The Apartment Story.

One loose end to wrap up is the distinction between outside and inside of open rectangle symbols that denote contexts or canons. Their normal use in a graph is to have arcs for a graph connected to its outside as a concept node. But, since they are open symbols, they can contain graphs. A rule is needed for when they connect to the inside of the rectangle.

The solution to arcs which connect to the inside of a rectangle is to remember that they are just a specialized display symbol for a concept. Consequently, any such inside arc should be interpreted as a connection to the concept represented by the rectangle. A simpler way to think about it is that it is a graphical shorthand for connection to a rectangle which is coreferent with its container as shown in Fig. 6.10.

In effect, the contained rectangle is a reference to itself, the containing rectangle; it is a form of recursive reference. If any inside connections are first expanded, then the normal rules used by ϕ for mapping graphs to predicate logic statements apply. (See the chapter on temporal intervals for an example which uses this technique.)

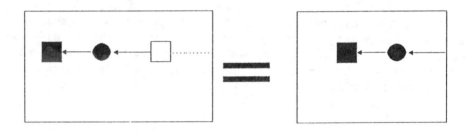

Fig. 6.10. Graphical Shorthand for Self Reference.

6.3 POLYMORPHIC CONCEPTS EXTENSION

The idea that concepts should be polymorphic with respect to their referent has been fully developed in (Esch, 1989). To be polymorphic a concept's definition, semantics, and operations should be independent of its referent. An application may choose to make a dependence, but the theory of conceptual graphs should not.

A context is supposed to contain a set of graphs. So, is a context with just one graph in it the same as just the graph? Can a context concept be generic, have just a variable, name, or even an individual as the referent? The converse of this question is, can any concept potentially become a context? Consider the following examples:

```
[STATE]-                                                     [1 p413]
    (DUR) → [TIME-PERIOD]
    (LOC) → [PLACE].
[STATE: *x]                                                  [1 p415]
[STATE: Cold]
[STATE: [RAIN]]                                              [1 p416]
[STATE: [PERSON:You] ← (EXPR) ← [WET]]                       [1 p416]
[GRAPH: [CAT] → (ON) → [MAT]]                                [7 p2-7]
[SITUATION: [CAT] → (ON) → [MAT]]                            [7 p2-7]
[SITUATION: 'A cat is sitting on a mat']                     [7 p2-8]
```

Again, is there a difference between having a graph or a context as a referent; that is, are the following the same?

```
[GRAPH:  [CAT]→(ON)→[MAT]].
[GRAPH:[[CAT]→(ON)→[MAT]]].
```

The critical issue is deciding for an arbitrary concept what referents it can have. More specifically, for arbitrary type label TL, do referents of nothing, variable, string, name, individual, concept, graph, and context make sense and, if so, what is their interpretation? The following table gives a consistent set of interpretations.

[concept:referent]	Interpretation
[TL:] = [TL]	Something exists that conforms to type TL.
[TL:variable]	The individual corresponding to the variable conforms to type TL.
[TL:name]	The individual corresponding to the name conforms to type TL.
[TL:individual]	The individual conforms to type TL.
[TL:set]	Each member conforms to the type TL.
[TL:concept]	The concept is about some individual and that individual conforms to type TL.
[TL:graph]	The graph conforms to a pattern defined by type TL.
[TL:context]	The context conforms to a pattern defined by type TL.
[TL:string]	An interpretation of the literal conforms to type TL.

The concept as referent case can also be interpreted as the concept being a degenerate case of a graph.

These do not all conform to Sowa's theory and those differences must be resolved. In particular, [TL:graph] and [TL:context] are potentially different and need to be examined more thoroughly. The goal is to reach some degree of polymorphism; that is, the idea that a concept and the basic operations on it are independent of what kind of referent the concept has.

Type labels are really shorthand for a graph which defines a pattern. Based on the principal of substitution, this means that the type label field can also have graphs and contexts. Allowing them in both the type label field and the referent field provides a great deal of uniformity, both simplifying and generalizing the theory at the same time. The general form for a concept becomes:

[type-field:referent-field]

where the type-field can be a type label or a λ abstraction and the referent-field has the following form:

[names][variables][referent].

The names part has the form name[=name=...=name] and the variables part has the form *variable[=*variable=...=*variable]. The referent part has the form:

string | graph | context | individual | set | for-all.[2]

The process of putting a concept in some "standard" form is called normalization. Here it involves 1) creating a type for any λ abstraction in a type field and replacing the lambda abstraction with its corresponding type label, 2) individualizing any referent that is not already an individual, and 3) replacing lines of identity (coreferent links) with an appropriate sequence of variables. The individualization process converts all strings, graphs, and contexts to individuals with the strings, graphs or context forming the basis of the definition graphs for the individual.

A consistent interpretation can then be given to normalized graphs. One such interpretation is given by the ϕ function which was extended in Esch (1989), based on the above table, to cover the situation of having graphs and contexts as referents. The simplest way to think about it is that ϕ must always apply the monadic predicate for the type to the referent. To do so the referent must first be individualize if it isn't already.

With polymoriphic concepts the theory of conceptual graphs is independent of what kind of referent a concept has. Polymorphic concepts fit naturally with the display forms presented in the first part of this chapter because the display forms can be thought of as just defining different display symbols for different referents. However, the symbols were deliberately chosen to emphasize the interpretation that those referents have in the theory.

6.4 SUMMARY

This chapter has presented solutions to eight graphical display form problems. These solutions are based on general design principals for selecting appropriate graphical notations.

The first general principal is to have common features for things denoting collections that are easily distinguished from things denoting single objects or entities. The novel feature here is selecting roundtangles and variations of them to denote collections and rectangles to denote objects or entities. Note that the rounded corners are easily distinguished from square corners. Thus, types and sets fall in the first category and concepts, individuals, contexts, and canons fall in the second category.

The second general principal is to utilize the difference between open and solid graphical symbols. For types and sets, an open roundtangle denotes all individuals or members of the type or set and the solid or shaded roundtangle denotes the collective type or set. For rectangles the interpretation is that there exists an object or entity. The solid rectangle denotes a concept while an open one denotes a context or canon. The later two are easily distinguished by the layout of the graphical symbols contained within them. Utilizing both open and solid symbols requires the label and other information to go on the outside which is different from how they are defined in Sowa (1984) and Harel (1988).

The last general design principal is called the museum room metaphor. For graphical symbols that are open (implying they can have content) the arrangement of graphical symbols within them is as uniform as possible. The rule adopted was subtypes toward the top and left, individuals toward the top and right, and graphs toward the left and bottom.

---

[2](See Gardiner (1989) for more advanced possibilities.)

Based on these general design principals, graphic symbols were presented to solve the problems described previously. Those problems and solutions are:

PROBLEM	SOLUTION
Untangling complex subtypes	type coreferent link
Representing a type's extension	solid roundtangles as a collection
Distinguishing concepts and contexts	Solid rectangle for concepts. Open rectangle for contexts.
Representing a type's extension	tables of individuals
Representing a canon	open rectangle
Representing a set	dashed or shaded roundtangle
Rules for arcs and their interpretation, roundtangles	outside: there-exists for-all inside: for-all there-exists
Rules for arcs and their interpretation, rectangles	outside: polymorphic concepts inside: self-reference

And, for open symbols, the display of their contents follows the museum room metaphor principal for the placement of the contents inside the symbols. Fig. 6.11 summarizes the display notation.

Lastly, this chapter has also applied the idea of polymorphism to concepts in a way consistent with both the linear and display forms of conceptual graphs.

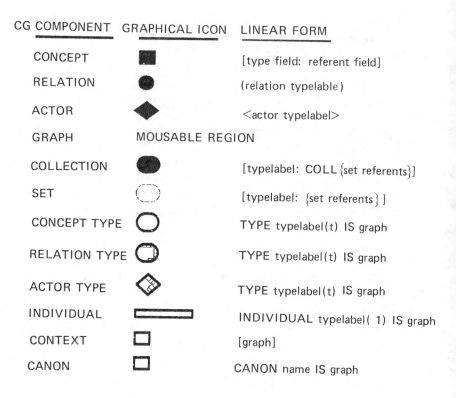

CG COMPONENT	GRAPHICAL ICON	LINEAR FORM
CONCEPT	◼	[type field: referent field]
RELATION	●	(relation typelable)
ACTOR	◆	<actor typelabel>
GRAPH	MOUSABLE REGION	
COLLECTION	◉	[typelabel: COLL {set referents}]
SET	⬭	[typelabel: {set referents}]
CONCEPT TYPE	◯	TYPE typelabel(t) IS graph
RELATION TYPE	◯	TYPE typelabel(t) IS graph
ACTOR TYPE	◇	TYPE typelabel(t) IS graph
INDIVIDUAL	▭	INDIVIDUAL typelabel(1) IS graph
CONTEXT	▢	[graph]
CANON	▢	CANON name IS graph

Fig. 6.11. Graphical Display Notation Summary.

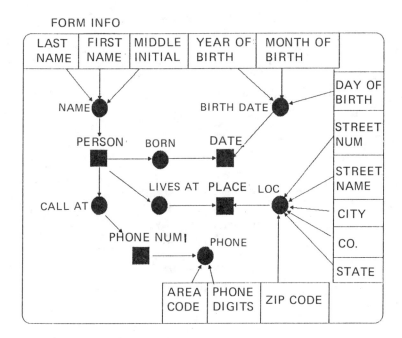

Fig. 6.12. Graphical Displays for Relation Types.

6.5 FUTURE WORK

Roundtangles were used to graphically represent concept types based on Harel's "blobs" (Harel, 1988). He also used them to represent relations types. An n-adic relation over n types is a relation over the n-wise cross product of the n types. Harel denoted this graphically by partitioning the interior of the blob into n distinct regions, each representing one of the n types. What is needed is a good way to combine this highly intuitive graphical display for the domain of the relation with the graph which defines the relation over that domain. An initial idea is to allow the partitioning to ring the inside boundary and leave the very middle open for the defining graph. An example is shown in Fig. 6.12. Note that the λ abstraction to define the FORMq INFO relation would require 14 variables.

Another problem to be addressed is a graphical display for actor types. Here there is a natural choice, an open diamond. However, how defining graphs are drawn inside it is not clear. In particular, how is the domain of input and output concept types specified. One approach would be to allow partitionings as for relation types with the defining graph toward the interior as shown in Fig. 6.13.

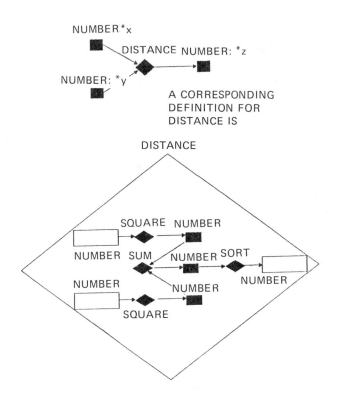

Fig. 6.13. Graphical Displays for Actor Types.

Providing graphical displays for relation types and actor types expands the possible kinds of symbols that can be connected by arcs to form graphs. A significant future challenge is to define which cases make sense and provide a well-defined interpretation for each; e.g. by extending the ϕ function.

BIBLIOGRAPHY

Brachman, R., (1989) "The CLASSIC Knowledge Representation System, or, KL-ONE: The Next Generation," Workshop on Formal Aspects of Semantic Networks, Catalina Island, CA.

Brachman, R., (1989) "CLASSIC: A Structural Data Model for Objects," J. Clifford, B. Lindsay & D. Maier Eds., Proc. of 1989 ACM SIGMOD International Conference on the Management of Data, pp. 58-67, ACM Press, New York, 1989.

Esch, John, W. (1990) "Graphical Displays for Conceptual Structures", in Proc. of the Fifth Annual workshop on Conceptual Structures, (eds) P. Eklund, and L. Gerholz, Linköping University, ISBN 91-7870-718-8.

Esch, J. and T. Nagle Morgan L. Yim & L. Gerholz, (1989) "Resolving Polymorphism in the Theory of Conceptual Graphs," Proc. Fourth Annual Workshop on Conceptual Structures, (eds) J. Nagle & T. Nagle, Detroit, Mich.

Harel, D., (1988) "On Visual Formalisms,", Comm. of ACM, Vol. 31, No 5. p. 514.

Gardiner, D., B. Tjan, and J. Slagle (1989) "Extended Conceptual Structures Notation", Proc. Fourth Annual Workshop on Conceptual Structures, (eds) J. Nagle & T. Nagle, Detroit, Mich., Aug. 20-21, 1989.

Sowa, J.F. (1984) *Conceptual Structures: Information Processing in Mind and Machine*, Addison Wesley, Reading.

Sowa, J.F. (1988) "Conceptual Graph Notation,", in Proc. Third Annual Workshop on Conceptual Graphs, (ed) J. Esch.

Part II

Semantics and Representation

7

Semantic Distance in Conceptual Graphs

Norman Foo
Computer Science Department,
University of Sydney,
Sydney 2006, Australia

Brian J. Garner
Department of Computing and Mathematics,
Deakin University,
Geelong 3217, Australia

Anand Rao
Australian Artificial Intelligence Institute,
1 Grattan Street,
Carlton 3053, Australia

Eric Tsui
Expert Systems Group,
Continuum Australia
100 Mount Street,
North Sydney 2060, Australia

ABSTRACT

A modification of Sowa's metric on conceptual graphs is proposed and defended. The metric is computed by locating the least subtype which subsumes the two given types, and adding the distance from each given type to the subsuming type. Implementations using this metric are described, the relevance of it to fuzzy problems is explained.

7.1   PROPOSED METRIC

Given two concepts $C1$ and $C2$ with types $T1$ and $T2$, Garner and Tsui (1987) have proposed a modification of Sowa's semantic distance between $C1$ and $C2$ as follows. Find the concept $C3$ which generalizes $C1$ and C2 with type $T3$ such that $T3$ is the most specific type which subsumes $T1$ and $T2$; the semantic distance between $C1$ and $C2$ is the sum of the distances from $C1$ to C3 and $C2$ to $C3$. It should be clear that this is indeed a metric, satisfying reflexivity, symmetry and the triangle inequality.

In this paper we explain this definition in several ways, describe its use in an extensive implementation, and suggest how it may help solve problems in fuzzy concepts.

7.2   IMPLEMENTATION AND EXPLANATIONS

Garner and Tsui (1987) first used this metric in an important component of the conceptual graph systems that were designed in Deakin University. They have applied this semantic distance to study a memory model that can

- store graphs without predefining a fixed set of attributes (ie. labels);

- index the incoming structures in multiple locations of the memory (knowledge base), if necessary;

- generalise between incoming structure and existing (indexed) structures;

- identify graph-subgraph relationships;

- handle exact and partial matching of stored structures based on an input pattern;

- store all structures economically; and

- propose new structures (ie. rules, graphs, concepts) by integrating (joining) a generalised pattern with another pattern.

The success of the metric led naturally to an investigation of its philosophical plausibility and this yielded a number of explanations. The explanations come from a variety of disciplines.

The first is anti-unification, which has been investigated by many workers in computational logic. In this, we are given two terms and it is desired to find a most specific term which specializes to the two terms. In the notation above, replacing "term" by "concept", the concept $C3$ is in fact the anti-unifier of $C1$ and $C2$ when the appropriate conventions are established for what is meant by unification in the framework of types.

The conventions needed are precisely those given in Rao and Foo (1987) where a substitution is a finite set of the form $\{v_1/t_1, ..., v_n/t_n\}$ with each t_i is a specialisation of the concept v_i.

In explanation-based learning (Mitchell et al., 1986) we have the notion of abduction and generalization. Given instances of objects it is desired to find the best generalization or explanation for them. Denoting the objects by $O1$ and $O2$ (more objects follow the same reasoning) a good generalization is an object $O3$ such that $O3$ subsumes $O1$ and $O2$, and it does so in the most economical way. We will argue that the proposed distance measure satisfies this criterion.

If O and O' are both generalizers of $O1$ and $O2$, and O is a subtype of O' then the logical formula $\forall X(O(X) \rightarrow O'(X))$ holds. Hence the hypothesis O is stronger then O', or equivalently O is more economical since a stronger hypothesis admits fewer models. Thus, among the generalizers of $O1$ and $O2$, we should pick their least member if one exists.

In arguing thereafter that the distance between $O1$ and $O2$ should then be measured by going through such an $O3$ we rely on the taxonomic inspiration which follows.

Thirdly, in taxonomic classifications there are metrics which indicate the closeness of relationships between species which resemble the one suggested.

There is no classification scheme which is satisfactory for all purposes. Sowa (personal communication) has drawn attention to the relevance of *salience* in determining distance between concepts. He cites a hypothetical discussion on some dog, and notes that in ordinary discourse the super-type likely to be the generalizer is "animal" rather than "vertebrate" even though the latter is a sub-type of the former. Context and salience can be viewed in our framework as *sub-lattice selectors* - they suppress some types and shrink the type lattice. Within any one context, however, the taxonomic precedents in biology are instructive.

Perhaps the simplest demonstration of the metric suggested above is in the discipline of genetics. Amino acid sequences of different species are compared. "A direct measure of genetic distance is given by the number of amino acid replacements that have occurred since the taxa from which the proteins are obtained *shared a common ancestor* (Purves and Orians, 1983 - our italics). This technique has the merit of being objective in that it is not dependent on behavioral traits.

Finally, we explain why the $C3$ above is the solution to some minimal extension for the analogs of the logical constraints $C1\ ra\ C$ and $C2\ ra\ C$.

In fact this is closely related to the abduction discussion above. Suppose we have the two logical expressions $C1(X) \rightarrow C(X)$ and $C2(X) \rightarrow C(X)$ and we want the smallest models of these for the predicate (type) C. The answer is given by McCarthy's *circumscription* (Lifschitz, 1985). In the established notation the solution for such a C is $A(C) \wedge \forall c \neg (A(c) \wedge c < C)$ where the $<$ sign is a comparison of predicate extension. If the generalizers of $C1$ and $C2$ have a least element, that is the unique solution to this circumscription.

7.3 FUZZY PROBLEMS AND AN EXAMPLE

An interesting application of semantic distance is the following. Wittgenstein's problem about games is often cited as an impediment to rule-based systems. The problem was intended to show that no fixed set of intensional descriptions of "game" will suffice. The concept "game", like most everyday concepts, seems to have flexibility in usage. There are two ways to handle this. In the first way we invoke belief revision to extend the denotation of terms when old denotations prove inadequate. The other is to build schemas for concepts which admit other concepts which resemble them. Woods (1986) has argued strongly that it is this ability to talk about resemblance which empowers KR beyond mere logic. We will add to his argument the distance measure proposed above by exhibiting an example of how the measure can be biased in different directions to yield several templates "like" the original. A combination of both belief revision and distance measures is probably necessary.

Consider the following partial hierarchy of schemas;

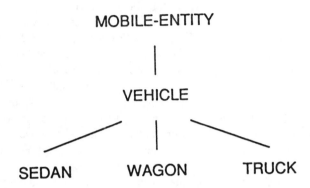

These may be used to provide background information for language understanding programs. The system could, either as a result of its accumulated information (evidence) or be told explicitly, determine that a new class has to be introduced to differentiate the roles of a SEDAN/WAGON and a TRUCK. As a result, the above hierarchy would need to be revised/refined, the CAR schema introduced into the hierarchy.

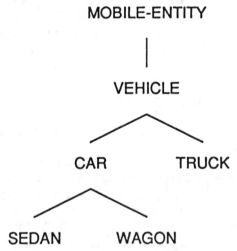

Since the subsumer-subsumee relationship and the semantic distance between all pairs of adjacent entities must be strictly enforced at all times, the following properties must hold:

(a) CAR < VEHICLE, CAR > SEDAN and CAR > WAGON; and

(b) SD between SEDAN (WAGON) and VEHICLE = SD between CAR and VEHICLE + SD between CAR and SEDAN (WAGON)

The above two restrictions enforce constraint on the definition of CAR.

7.4   KNOWLEDGE CORRELATION

Finally, we describe how semantic distance can be applied to correlate three types of knowledge in a Canonical Graph Model (Tsui, 1988). These three types of knowledge are, in an increasing order of sophistication, concepts, graphs and rules.

For concepts, adjacent types in the type hierarchy are assigned a semantic distance of 1. The semantic distance between two types is defined as the sum of the semantic distance from each of the two types to their minimal common supertype (MCS). If UNIVERSAL is the MCS, then the semantic distance between these two types is assigned to infinity. In the Canonical Graph Model (CGM), semantic distance is applied to the following properties must hold:

(a) determine the relevancy between concepts in a default (pre-defined) graph with certain words captured from the input sentence (Garner, Lukose and Tsui, 1987) so as to adapt the default graphs to build an initial set of intermediate graph(s); and

(b) restrict the level (degree) of generalisation of a concept label so that over-generalisation of concepts (therefore graphs) does not occur.

The semantic distance between two graphs is defined as the sum of the semantic distance between corresponding pairs of concepts in the two graphs. If there is no matching pair of corresponding concepts, then the semantic distance for the graphs is undefined. Semantic distances between graphs serve to determine pairs of relevant graphs to be maximally joined and assist the semantic interpreter (SI) (loc. cit.) in the formation of intermediate graph(s) at each level of the parse tree. These intermediate graphs are propagated to the next level of the parse tree and semantic distances are again evaluated to determine which pairs of graphs should be (maximally) joined.

For rules, the notion of a semantic distance is much more difficult and abstract to be defined. At this stage, we define rule subsumption as rule A subsumes rule B iff all the assertions (represented as graphs) in A subsumes corresponding assertions in B. There are at least three good reasons why a correlation measure between rules is useful:

1. During knowledge acquisition, rules captured by the system, whether from the same session or not, may subsume each other thereby leading to redundancy in the knowledge base.

2. An intelligent knowledge acquisition program should be able to generalise on input rules based on commonalities found in these rules. In other words, structural knowledge among rules are automatically discovered and made explicit.

3. Both the generalised rule(s) and the actual rules can be applied during reasoning (deduction) leading to a wider applicability of the rule set and better explanations.

Multi-valued logics are being studied (Garner, 1989) for the formalisation of a correlation measure between abstractions.

BIBLIOGRAPHY

Garner, B.J., (1989); unpublished notes.

Garner, B.J., Lukose, D. and Tsui, E. (1987); "Parsing Natural Language through Pattern Correlation and Modification", Proc. of the 7th International Workshop on Expert Systems & Their Applications, Avignon '87, France, pp. 1285-1299.

Lifschitz, V.; "Computing Circumscription": Proc. 9th IJCAI, 1985.

Purves and Orians; (1983) *Life - the Science of Biology*, Willard Grant Press, Boston, MA.

Mitchell, T.M., Keller, R. M. and Kedar-Cabelli, S.T. (1986); "Explanation-based Generalisation: A Unifying View", ML-TR-2, Computer Science Department, Rutgers University, New Jersey.

Rao, A. and Foo, N. (1987); "CONGRES - Conceptual Graph Reasoning System", Third Conference on Artificial Intelligence and Applications, (IEEE), Florida.

Tsui, E. (1988); "Canonical Graph Models", Ph.D. thesis, Department of Computing and Mathematics, Deakin University, Australia, 1988.

Woods, W.A. (1986); "Important Issues in Knowledge Representation": Proc. IEEE, October 1986.

8

A Neural-Network Approach to Implementing Conceptual Graphs

George G. Lendaris
Systems Science Program,
Portland State University
Portland, OR 97207-0751, USA

ABSTRACT

In this chapter we explore the possibility of using neural networks to implement some important manipulations on conceptual graphs. A major benefit of implementing conceptual-graph manipulations on neural networks (NNs) would be a significant reduction in computation time as well as some other benefits that accrue from the distributed representation properties of NNs.

8.1 INTRODUCTION

Conceptual structures are a representation in symbolic form of the intellectual constructs called concepts and concept-relations. There has been no intrinsic difficulty with the symbolic nature of conceptual graphs regarding their implementation on our usual symbol-processing computers. Neural networks, however, are not symbol processors *per se*. Therefore, a necessary first step in the present endeavor is to develop a representation for conceptual graphs that functions as a non-symbolic representation when used as input to a neural network. In this chapter, we look at some aspects of how neural networks operate, to better understand the needs of a representation schema for input to such networks.

A number of books on neural networks have recently been published, many of them offering a good introduction to the subject. A readable general overview (no equations) is given in Caudill and Butler (1990). A list of 10 other recent books is included at the end of this chapter. We will describe here those aspects of neural networks needed as background for the present problem context.

A neural network can be thought of as a device that has n input terminals and m output terminals (re Fig. 8.10). The input and output signals may be either continuous or binary valued. The internal architecture of the device is generally parallel. At a given point in time, the input signals are set to some combination of values; the device processes all these inputs simultaneously; and at the end of the processing cycle (a fixed amount of time), presents appropriate values on all the output terminals.

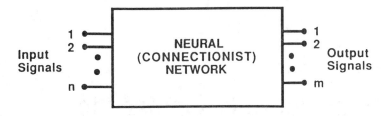

Fig. 8.1 Neural Network: device with n input terminals and m output terminals, continuous or binary-valued signals.

Moving inside the device, a neural network is typically made up of a collection of simple (neuron-like) processing elements whose interconnection parameters are adjusted during training (re Fig. 8.2). For any particular setting of the adjustments, the network performs one of the mappings possible for that network, where the set of possible mappings is determined by the type and number of elements and the pattern of their interconnections (Lendaris and Stanley, 1963, 1965a, 1965b). The set of mappings achievable by a NN as its internal parameters are adjusted is significantly smaller than the set of all possible ones (for a usefully large number of inputs, that is), and because of this, there is no guarantee that a given neural network device can be adjusted to perform a mapping that a user happens to desire. But, since any problem can be represented to a neural network in various ways, and since the desired mapping depends explicitly on the representation, it behooves the researcher to take care in selecting the representation, so that the mapping to be performed on the associated "signals" has a chance for successful implementation by the neural network. At the present time, there is no formal theoretical basis to guide such selections, so *ad hoc* methods still have to be used.

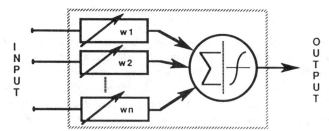

Fig. 8.2 Graphical representation of typical neuron-like processing element in a connectionis network. Each element has a value on its output, usually ranging from 0 to 1. The amount fed into an element is determined by the adjustable parameter called a connection weight (w_j); the weight can take on positive or negative values. The element adds up the weighted inputs, and applies the transformation (on the right side of the dashed line) to the sum to yield the element's output. The output of an element feeds one or more other elements. The term "layers" refers to the organization of the elements in the network. If each element receives input only from the environment, then there is only 1 layer. If outputs from the units in the first layer feed into another set of units, that set constitutes a 2nd layer. If outputs from the units in the second layer feed into another set of units, the latter set of units constitutes a 3rd layer, and the 2nd layer is said to be "hidden" (from the environment).

There are many tasks that human beings know how to do, but don't know how they do these tasks well enough to directly design a machine to do them (e.g., reading human handwriting, recognizing human faces, making good wine, etc.). We refer to the human performance ability in these cases as a skill. A person is able to pass a skill on to another person by entering into a teacher-pupil relationship with that person. A key aspect of what neural network researchers do is to develop methods that will allow a machine to emulate a "pupil" role, and learn certain tasks by interaction with its environment, with or without a teacher role (supervised or non-supervised learning). The algorithmic procedure for accomplishing this task is generally called a "training (or, learning) algorithm." neural networks!training

The supervised training process typically proceeds as follows: (i) a network of neuron-like processors with a starting set of connections and connection weights is given an input pattern; (ii) the network computes an output; (iii) the output is inspected and compared with the desired output for that input; (iv) if not correct, then changes in the connection parameters within the network are made in such a way that it is less likely the same output would be calculated for the given input pattern; (v) if correct, then usually nothing is done, but, in principle, a change in the weights could be made in such a way that it will be more likely the same output would be calculated for the given input pattern; (vi) steps (i)-(v) are repeated for all the input patterns in the "training set"; (vii) the training algorithm determines how many times to repeat step (vi). A key difficulty during training is that of losing "good" information already accumulated when adjustments are made for a current training input.

Coupled with the above considerations is the important notion of generalization. When applied to human processing, this term normally means that after one is exposed to a certain set of inputs and associated correct outputs, a pattern is perceived that allows one to generate correct outputs for inputs not previously seen. In the context of training a neural network, (correct) generalization again means that only a portion of the data from the problem environment is used during training, and the network gives correct answers to the rest of the available data. A crucial issue: how is correct generalization from a training set achieved? A key notion here is the underlying pattern in the data. Associated with any pattern are regularities, and with regularities, constraints. Much can be said about this topic, but the key idea is that regularities/constraints must be present within and among the training data for (good) generalization to be possible. This condition is satisfied in normal real-world applications. The "rule(s)" developed by the NN to determine an output for a given input must in some sense embody the constraints implicit in the data.

The remainder of this chapter is organized as follows. In section 8.2, a representation schema is developed for conceptual graphs that will allow them to be input to neural networks; section 8.3 takes the reader on a walk through a candidate implementation of an important conceptual-graph manipulation called PROJECTION: section 8.3.1 defines the PROJECTION operation, and develops two PROPERTIES that must hold for the PROJECTION, section 8.3.2 describes a method to test for one of these properties via a neural network, and section 8.3.3 cites some experimental results; section 8.4 discusses an extension of the representation schema for multiple copies of relations and concept types; section 5 sketches a possible extension of the methods given in section 8.3 for PROJECTION to another important conceptual-graph manipulation called MAXIMAL JOIN; section 8.6 suggests the possibility of using neural networks as memory for conceptual-graph knowledge bases; and finally, section 8.7 provides a summary of the chapter.

8.2   REPRESENTING CONCEPTUAL GRAPHS FOR PARALLEL PROCESSING

As indicated in the previous section, neural networks are not symbol processors, so we are obliged to develop a non-symbolic means of representing conceptual graphs in order to use neural networks to implement operations on them. In the vocabulary of Fig. 8.1, whatever representation schema we develop, its components will be the "signals" presented at the input terminals of the neural network device.

8.2.1   Basics of Sowa's Conceptual Graph Formalism

Conceptual graphs are defined in detail in this book in Sowa's chapter on notation. Of specific interest here is the fact that a conceptual graph consists of two different kinds of nodes (concept nodes and relation nodes) and directed arcs. An arc connects a concept node to a relation node, or a relation node to a concept node; connections are not allowed between nodes of the same type. An example of a generic conceptual graph is given in Fig. 8.3a.

Circles with relation labels, squares with concept labels, and lines with arrows on them are used to depict a conceptual graph in a graphical format– called the "display form," usually the form preferred by human observers. An alternative "linear form" with parentheses around relation labels, brackets around concept labels, and arrow indicators is used to represent a conceptual graph for easier input to computers via keyboard, and output via conventional printers. This latter form has been useful for the serial-type, symbolic processing typical in implementations to date. See Fig. 8.3b for a linear-form representation of the conceptual graph shown via the display form in Fig. 8.3a.

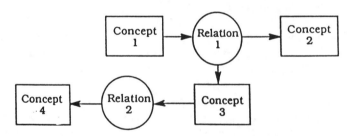

Fig. 8.3a - Generic example of a conceptual graph (Display form).

```
(RELATION 1)-
            -> [CONCEPT 3] -> (RELATION 2) -> [CONCEPT 4]
            <- [CONCEPT 1]
            -> [CONCEPT 2]
```

Fig. 8.3b Linear Form representation for the conceptual graph shown via Display Form in Fig. 8.3a.

8.2.2   Components of Knowledge Systems using Sowa's Formalism

The problem environment to be used in the remainder of this chapter will be knowledge systems that use conceptual graphs, and the tasks we will want the neural network to perform are manipulations related to conceptual graphs. Knowledge systems using Sowa's formalism typically comprise the following components:

1. First, a knowledge engineer gathers together data which are coalesced into (true) assertions, and these in turn are represented via conceptual graphs[1].

2. A catalog of all the concept types is created and maintained (let $numC$ be the number of entries).

3. A hierarchy tree is created and maintained which encodes the sub- and super- type relationships among the concept types. This hierarchy is used for checking validity of restrictions and generalizations of conceptual graphs.

4. A catalog of all the relation types is created and maintained (let $numR$ be the number of enries).

5. A relation definition dictionary is created and maintained. For each type in the relation catalog, there is listed a set of rules (constraints) which dictate the number of arcs leaving and entering the node, and the maximal type of the concept to which each arc may be attached (maximal here means the highest concept type in the hierarchy to which it is allowed to connect the given arc).

6. A catalog of names for individuals (also called markers) appearing in the knowledge base is created and maintained. Each marker in this list carries an indication of its associated concept sub-type; the latter is used for making conformity checks.

7. A restriction operates on a concept to yield either a concept which is a sub-type of the original, e.g., [person] to [man], or, a concept which has been specialized to an individual in the context, e.g., [person] to [person:Gregory] - also called an instantiation.

8. A generalization operates on a concept to yield a concept which is a super- type of the original, e.g., [man] to [person].

9. The conformity operation checks to determine whether the concept type associated with the name of the individual assigned during a restriction is appropriate to the concept to which it was assigned–e.g., [man:Gregory] vs. [woman:Gregory][2].

8.2.3   Hints from nature

As mentioned earlier, the task before us is to devise a non-symbolic way to represent conceptual graphs. A natural question is, if we don't use symbols, then what do we use? We need only look to biological systems for an answer: values. That is, biological systems obtain data from their environment via their sensors. The sensors provide the brain with a variety of signals, and these signals have values and time-of-occurrence relationships. The signals coming from each of the sensors no doubt have their own definite meaning, and this meaning does not (normally) change with time. We use these observations to guide us

---

[1]The entire problem context (typically represented via a semantic network, which may or may not use the Sowa conceptual-graph formalism) is taken into account when defining and choosing the concept and relation labels to be used in the conceptual graphs.

[2]The reader may wish to look ahead to Fig. 8.10.

in developing a representation for conceptual graphs. It is important to keep in mind that the "sensors" and "signals" can be defined in an abstract and/or arbitrary way, but a key requirement is that the resulting encoding must contain the information about the problem environment that is needed to perform the desired operations. As examples, the signals may be voltage values from an array of light sensors upon which photographic images are projected; the signals may be numbers representing a set of dynamic characteristics–position, velocity, acceleration, etc.–of a problem environment where physical objects are in motion; the signals may correspond to names of individuals in an extended family and the various relationships that can exist between pairs of the individuals (e.g., brother, husband, wife, sister, etc.) What can we use as the equivalent to sensors and signals to represent conceptual graphs?

The answer suggested here is to use a matrix form (and certain associated vector form) representation of conceptual graphs.

8.2.4   Full Matrix Representation

It is well known in graph theory (Roberts, 1976) that a unique connection matrix (CM) representation exists for certain types of graphs (including those of interest here). The connection matrix contains as many rows (and columns) as there are nodes in the graph. A distinct row and column of the matrix is assigned to each node in the graph. In conceptual graphs, the arcs have arrows on them (i.e., are directed); direction is normally from Row node to Column node in connection matrixes, but this choice is arbitrary. Using this convention, an entry of 1 is placed in the (Row i, Column j) slot of the matrix if there exists a directed arc connecting node i to node j in the graph. No entry (or equivalently, a 0 entry) is made where there is no corresponding connection.

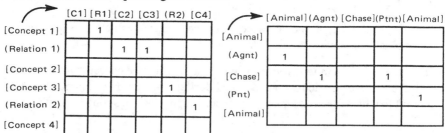

Fig. 8.4a. Connection Matrix for conceptual graphs in Figs. 3a & 6, with arbitrary row and column assignment.

Any conceptual graph can be represented via a connection matrix (CM) of the type described above. We let the CM play the role of "sensor", with each slot providing a "signal" whose value is 1 or 0. The CM may be constructed by assigning to each node in the conceptual graph a different row and column in the matrix, and by entering a 1 in those slots where a (directed) connection exists from the row to column nodes. See Fig. 8.4a. However, if done in this way, each conceptual graph with different concept and relation nodes would have a connection matrix of different size, and with different row (and column) labels. But, the meaning of each signal coming into the neural network is supposed to stay the same over time–i.e., a requirement that the structure of the matrix be the same for all conceptual graphs, with only the matrix entries changing. One possibility is to create a template matrix with $(numR + numC)$ rows and columns, and assign to each row/column one of the concepts in the concept- type catalog or one of the relations in the relation catalog. A connection matrix for a given conceptual graph would then be created simply by entering 1's in the appropriate slots of the template matrix. In this way, each concept type and each relation corresponds to a particular position in the row sequence and a particular position in the column sequence of the CM. This position encoding of concept types and relations is the key attribute of the proposed encoding schema for our intended application.

8.2.5   Reduced Matrix Representation

Since there are no connections among nodes of the same type in a conceptual graph, if the concept nodes are assigned to rows (and columns) adjacent to one another, and the relation nodes assigned to the remaining rows (and columns), then there are no entries in the upper left and lower right quadrants of the matrix (see Fig. 8.4b). This observation suggests another form. Choose a (reduced size) matrix having only as many rows as there are relation types in the knowledge base catalog $(numR)$, and only as many columns as there are concept types $(numC)^3$. Let the entries in the matrix be 3-valued, so that, for example, if a connection goes from the relation to a concept (row to column), use a +1; if the connection is in the other direction, use a -1; if there is no connection, use a 0. Let us call this matrix a Relation-Concept connection matrix, or, R-C connection matrix. See Fig. 8.4c (left side).

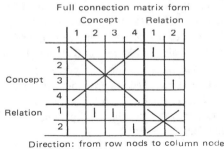

Full connection matrix form

Direction: from row nods to column node

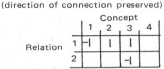

Modified Connection Matrix
(direction of connection preserved)

Connection Matrix Form used here
(direction information NOT preserved)

1 = from row to columns nodes
−1 = from columns to row nodes
blank = no connection

1 = connection between nodes
blank = no connection

R−C CONNECTION MATRIX

Figs. 8.4b & 8.4c. Connection Matrix forms for conceptual graph shown in Fig. 8.3a, with organized row and column assignments.

It turns out that direction information can be relaxed in some cases and still allow for significant conceptual graph operations to be performed. For these cases, the requirement

---

[3] This row/column assignment is chosen to take advantage of the obvious mnemonic: the R for relation is assigned to rows, and the C for concepts to columns.

for ternary valued entries in the (reduced size) R-C connection matrix can be relaxed to 2-values: 1 for connection, 0 for none. For ease of discussion, binary-valued entries will be used for remainder of this paper. See Fig. 8.4c (right side).

The rules listed in the relation definition dictionary (item 5 in the list given earlier in this section) entail corresponding constraints in what appears in a connection matrix. For each relation row, there is a specified number of 1's that should appear in the row (the number of arcs coming to and going from the node), and there is only a certain subset of concept columns in which each 1 may be placed (the specified maximal concept type or any of its subtypes)[4]. The reader may look ahead to Fig. 8.5 for examples.

As described so far, the connection matrix (full and reduced) only allows representation of conceptual graphs containing at most one copy of any specified relation or concept type. There are cases where more than one copy of a relation or concept type is needed in a conceptual graph; the connection matrix template method can be expanded to accommodate these, and will be described in section 8.4, but this simpler version is sufficient for development of the basic concepts.

8.2.6   Vector Representation

For database query type operations, a further reduction in representation is possible. The reduction here is based on the fact that for any given conceptual graph, the R-C connection matrix will be very sparse; only a small fraction of all possible rows will have non-zero entries. Therefore, the suggestion is to store only those rows of the R-C connection matrix that have non-zero entries. We call these RC-vectors (their length is $numC$). With this method, another vector is required so the position information for each of the RC-vectors may be retrieved; this vector is called an R-vector. Its length is $numR$, and is constructed for the conceptual graph by placing a 1 in the slots corresponding to the relation nodes in the given conceptual graph. The RC- vectors are stored in an order corresponding to the sequence of 1's in the R- vector. Further, a C-vector is constructed; its length is $numC$, and 1's are placed in slots corresponding to all the concept type nodes in the given conceptual graph (the reader may look ahead to Fig. 8.11).

8.2.7   CG Canonical Operations via Matrix Representations

We have thus succeeded in designing a representation schema for conceptual graphs that is non symbolic vis-a-vis its role as input device to neural networks. A key question remains: Is the information content of this schema sufficient to allow the manipulations required for conceptual graphs in knowledge systems? One way to answer this question is to demonstrate that the four conceptual graph canonical operations for conceptual graphs can be carried out using the representations.

In the following, each of the four canonical operations is described, and then shown to be implementable with the CM representation schema.

JOIN: If two conceptual graphs both contain a concept node of the same type, then the graphs may be JOINed at that (common) concept node. The resulting conceptual

---

[4] For the ternary case, +1's correspond to arcs leaving the relation node, and 1's to the arcs entering the relation node. Constraints apply accordingly.

graph contains one copy of that concept node, and, appended to this node are all the (directed) arcs [and associated graph components] that were previously appended to the two (similar) nodes in the conceptual graphs being joined. See Fig. 8.5.

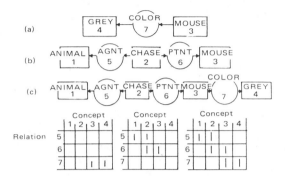

Fig. 8.5 Example of JOIN via R-C Connection Matrix representations.

It is easy to see in principle, that the connection matrix (CM) of the JOINed graph is obtainable simply by doing a logical-or operation on the connection matrices for the two graphs to be joined. That is, create the CM of the JOIN by entering a 1 in a slot if there is a 1 in the corresponding slot in the CM of either of the two graphs being joined. See Fig. 8.5 for an example. A slight complication arises if the CMs of the two graphs being joined have a 1 in the same slot–more about this in section 8.4 and in the discussion about SIMPLIFY below.

We have the opportunity to observe here how easy it would be, in principle, to perform the entire JOIN operation in the time it takes to inspect one pair of corresponding slots in the two CMs–no matter how many nodes the given conceptual graph contains. This could be accomplished by having in hardware the equivalent of three CM template matrixes, and separate hardware included to do the logical-or operation for each slot in the templates–i.e., to look at each of the corresponding slots in two of the filled in matrixes, and enter the result in the corresponding slot of the third matrix. All of these operations would be done in parallel, so the whole matrix is done in the time it takes to do an operation on one slot.

SIMPLIFY: When two conceptual graphs are JOINed, some relations in the resulting graph may become redundant. Remember that all relation nodes appended to both of the original concept nodes that were JOINed are appended to the one copy of the concept node in the JOINed graph. It is possible that the same type of relation node had been appended to both concept nodes in their respective graphs before the JOIN. If so, the JOINed graph will have two copies of this relation node type (we are talking about the definition of JOIN here, not the present implementation). Every relation node has a number of arcs specified by its definition, and each arc has a specified maximal concept type associated with it. If the corresponding arcs for both of the duplicated relation nodes go to the same concept types, respectively, then one of these relation nodes is considered redundant. The SIMPLIFY operation consists of deleting one of each pair of redundant relation nodes.

For a JOIN operation to result in a redundant Relation (call it rR), certain constraints exist on the relative positions of the 1s in the connection matrices of the conceptual graphs prior to the JOIN. The corresponding 1s would have to be in concept locations which are either (i) the same type, or (ii) one is a subtype of the other. In case (i), one need only check whether the concept in either (or both) of the conceptual graphs being JOINed has been individualized (assigned a marker). If so, those concept nodes will have to be treated separately (e.g., via a CONFORMITY check). If neither has been specialized, then the logical-or operation is allowed to proceed, and the SIMPLIFY would be automatically performed. In case (ii), it is possible (after the JOIN) to do a RESTRICTION (see section 8.3.2) which would render the two concept nodes the same, and hence, a SIMPLIFY would then be in order.

COPY: In principle, there is no difficulty in making a copy of the connection matrix. It is possible that in some implementation it would be desirable to use the same hardware as for the JOIN to do the COPY, rather than to provide a means for making a direct transfer to the location where the copy is to be stored. This could be accomplished by moving the connection matrix of the conceptual graph to be COPIED into the (hardware) matrix template described in the JOIN discussion, and a logical union performed with a matrix template containing all 0 entries. The (hardware) result matrix would contain a COPY of the original CM.

RESTRICT: This operation (defined in item 7 of the list at the beginning of this section) requires access to the concept-type hierarchy (item 3). The process is different in nature from the above three, and will be discussed later (in section 8.3.2).

Sowa (1984) demonstrates that most operations on conceptual graphs can be accomplished using the above four canonical operations. A particular operation, PROJECTION, is discussed in the next section.

8.2.8 Comments

First comment: the above matrix-form representation was developed to serve as input to neural networks. Once accomplished, this same representation could be used to explore more conventional parallel implementations. The presentation strategy for the remainder of this chapter is to develop design ideas for such implementations. The reason for this is that in the process of developing a conventional means of implementing the desired conceptual graph manipulations, we also develop better insights for the intended neural network implementation(s).

Second comment: it would be possible to create and store a full connection matrix representation for each of the conceptual graphs in the given knowledge base. It is clear, however, that explicit use of such a representation would be wasteful of space in a computer, since only a small fraction of the possible nodes are ever used in an individual conceptual graph. There are methods for efficiently encoding and manipulating such sparse matrixes in serial machines, but these considerations will not be pursued here. For parallel implementations, each slot in the matrix would require a slot in a register, or a separate input to a neural network. Therefore, it behooves us to develop a more frugal way of representation. The reduced matrix and vector representations described earlier offer such a mechanism. These will require fewer input terminals for the neural networks, and of course, less memory for storing the information.

8.3 PROJECTION

8.3.1 Projection Operation for Database Query

In Sowa's chapter on notation in this book, he discusses the PROJECTION operation for conceptual graphs, and suggests that this operation could be used to answer database queries. We here pick up on that suggestion, and use it as a candidate application upon which to begin the analysis required to check out some implementation details. We will walk through the process that would be required to accomplish PROJECTION using the connection matrix representation developed in the previous section–with the specific goal of parallel implementation of the operations. In the analysis given in this section, it will become clear that the operations on conceptual graphs we consider can be implemented using parallel architectures of a standard variety. Our position for the remainder of the chapter, however, is that these operations could alternatively be implemented using neural networks, and that this is a good objective to strive for.

For the purposes of this section's analysis, we assume the problem context to be a database which contains a large number of "fact" conceptual graphs (we here call these FactCGs). A query is to be made via a properly formulated query conceptual graph (QueryCG). The query process brings up each FactCG and determines if it contains a candidate answer for the query, i.e., a specialization of the QueryCG. The PROJECTION operation maps general conceptual graphs into more specialized ones, therefore, Sowa's suggestion is equivalent to testing if the QueryCG PROJECTS into the FactCG.

We borrow an example given in Sowa's chapter: "The sentence Yojo is chasing a grey mouse is more specialized than the sentence Some animal is chasing an animal." Conceptual graphs for these two sentences are given in Fig. 8.6. The PROJECTION operation is said to map the upper (more general) graph of Fig. 8.6 into the lower (more specialized) one. For each concept or relation in the upper graph, there corresponds one of the concepts or relations in the lower graph. In particular,

```
[ANIMAL]  ⟶  [CAT:Yojo]
[ANIMAL] ⟶  [MOUSE]
[CHASE]  ⟶  [CHASE]
(AGNT)   ⟶  (AGNT)
(PTNT)   ⟶  (PTNT)
```

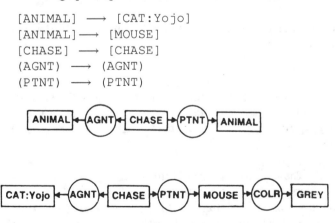

Fig. 8.6 Example of a more general vs. a more specialized conceptual graph.

We note that the lower (more specialized) graph contains the concept [GREY] and the relation (COLR) is not contained in the upper graph. It is typical for PROJECTION to map a general graph into a proper subgraph of a specialized one.

We state a modified version of the definition of PROJECTION given in (Sowa, 1984, page 99), using the letters Q (for QueryCG) and F (for FactCG) in place of his v and u. The reader may find it convenient to refer to Fig. 8.6, and relate Q (Query) to the upper conceptual graph, and F (Fact) to the lower conceptual graph.

In following the data-base query discussion using PROJECTION, the reader may consider the upper graph to be a QueryCG, and the lower one a FactCG.

> *DEFINITION: For any conceptual graphs Q and F where F is a specialization of Q ($F < Q$), there exists a mapping $\pi: Q \rightarrow F$, where $\pi(Q)$ is a subgraph of F called a projection of Q in F. The "projection operator" π has the following properties:*

> > *For each relation R in Q, $\pi(R)$ is a relation of the same type in $\pi(Q)$.*
> > *If relation R in Q has n arcs, then $\pi(R)$ in $\pi(Q)$ also has n arcs.*
> > *If an arc of R is linked to a concept C in Q, then the corresponding arc of $\pi(R)$ must be linked to $\pi(C)$ in $\pi(Q)$.*
> > *For each concept C in Q, $\pi(C)$ is a concept in $\pi(Q)$ where*
> > *type($\pi(C)$) is a SUBtype of type(C)*
> > *(i.e., $\pi(C)$ is either identical to C, or,*
> > *it is a restriction of C)*
> > *If C is individual, then*
> > *referent($\pi(C)$) = referent(C).*
> > *If C is generic, then*
> > *$\pi(C)$ may be either generic or individual.*

We can deduce from this definition that for a given FactCG to be an answer to (i.e., a specialization of) the QueryCG, the following properties must be true:

PROPERTY 1: For each relation node in QueryCG, at least one relation node of the same type must exist in the FactCG.

> **Comment 1:** For each relation node in QueryCG, there must be an identical relation node in the FactCG; however, since the projection of QueryCG is allowed to be a SUBgraph of the FactCG, the FactCG could have more than one relation node of the type being checked–hence the "at least one" quantifier in the Property 1 statement.

> **Comment 2:** The projection mapping is not necessarily 1:1 (Sowa, 1984, page 99). This means, for example, that two relation nodes of the same type in QueryCG could map onto one relation node (of the same type) in the FactCG. Therefore, even if there is more than one relation node of a given type in QueryCG, it is possible for there to be fewer relation nodes of that type in the FactCG[5].

---

[5] For this possibility, however, each relation type involved must have all of its corresponding arcs present (refer to item 5 in the earlier list), and each of these arcs must be connected to a concept node of an appropriate sub-type.

PROPERTY 2: (i) For each concept type in QueryCG, at least one concept node which is a subtype (i.e., is identical to or is a specialization) of that type must exist in the FactCG; (ii) each concept node in the FactCG must be linked to the same relation type(s) as is its corresponding concept node in QueryCG.

   Comments 1 & 2: regarding relation nodes apply also to concept nodes, *vis-a-vis* part (i) of PROPERTY 2.

   Comment 3: Regarding part (ii) of PROPERTY 2, it is possible that a concept node in one graph is linked to a relation node of one type, while in the other graph a concept node of the same type is linked to a relation node of another type. Therefore, even if the requirement that each concept type in QueryCG be found in the FactCG is met, a further test may be needed to check if in the FactCG the concept node of each specified type is linked to a corresponding relation node of the appropriate type, and perhaps, to check if the link has the correct direction.

We recall that the arcs used in conceptual graphs have arrows on them to indicate a direction, and further, we showed in the previous section how the connection matrix method represents this direction. Though this direction information is needed for manipulations of conceptual graphs in some contexts (e.g., in language processing applications), it appears we can accomplish the PROPERTY 1 and PROPERTY 2 tests without the direction information. Accordingly, in the method developed below, we temporarily relax the directionality requirements associated with the links attached to each relation node in order to effect a first level search; direction tests would be applied as a further sift, if and as needed. Preliminary analysis of this approach indicates that there is no loss related to the PROPERTY 1 test. For the PROPERTY 2 test, no correct FactCG would be missed, but it will be possible for a FactCG that does not satisfy the query to be selected (e.g., where Comment 3 applies). The latter FactCGs would have to be eliminated via a 2nd level operation.

This observation about direction information is an important one. Under the assumption that direction information is not needed, the reduced matrix representation introduced in the previous section may be used, with only +1 connection entries. Recall, this R-C connection matrix is significantly smaller than the full matrix representation.

We assume that all the conceptual graphs created by the knowledge engineers (FactCGs) are stored, perhaps in linear form, and that they are accessible to the data-base query program (the problem context for this presentation). The tack taken here is to encode each of the FactCGs with the vector representation (smaller still from the R-C connection matrix) introduced in the previous section. The operations for the PROJECTION test are to be performed using the vector representations. A certain amount of discrimination power in the tests is lost in these reductions. Although this could result in FactCGs being selected which do not satisfy the query, more importantly, all correct FactCGs should be selected. Thus, the operations based on the vector representation will select a (presumably) small subset of the FactCGs as candidate answers to the query, and a refinement kind of check will then be done on these candidates, perhaps using the complete conceptual graph (linear form?), as is currently done in other implementations. The payoff for allocating the extra memory required for storing the vector (partial) representations is increased speed of processing.

We begin by creating two vector templates: an R-vector template and a C-vector template. Each position of the R-vector template corresponds to one of the relations in the knowledge base catalog, and each position of the C-vector template corresponds to one of the concept types in the knowledge base catalog. Thus, the dimension of each of these vector templates will be $numR$ and $numC$, respectively.

An R-vector is constructed for each FactCG as follows: a 1 is entered into the R-vector template at the positions corresponding to each relation type appearing in the FactCG. Similarly, a C-vector is constructed for each FactCG: a 1 is entered into the C-vector template at the positions corresponding to each concept type appearing in the FactCG. In addition, an R-vector and a C-vector are constructed for the QueryCG.

In a sense, the operations to be proposed with these vectors are akin to a "key word search," where the key words used in the search are the relations and concept types included in the QueryCG. The search begins with a PROPERTY-1 test to find those FactCGs that have the same relation types as does the QueryCG (this test simultaneously uses all the relations in QueryCG as "key words"). Next, the PROPERTY-2 test is used on the FactCGs which passed the PROPERTY-1 test, and finds those that have the same concept types, or sub-types thereof, as does the QueryCG (this test simultaneously uses all the concept types in QueryCG as "key words"). Following this, a CONFORMITY check is performed (discussed in the next section) as appropriate on the FactCGs that pass the PROPERTY-2 test. Finally, fetch the full representation of the FactCGs that pass the CONFORMITY check, and do more refined checks and manipulations as needed for the given query, and as appropriate to the specific implementation[6].

The test for PROPERTY 1 is particularly simple:
Have three hardware registers whose length is at least $numR$. Create an R-vector for the QueryCG (call it Query-R-Vector), and store it in one of the registers. Then, sequentially bring into one of the other registers the R-vector for each of the FactCGs (call them Fact-R-vectors). For each one, perform the following test: Fact-R-vector $\geq$ Query-R-Vector, on a bit by bit basis. Enter a 1 in the third register for each bit that fails the test. If at least one bit is set to 1 in the third register (this can be checked in hardware via a large OR gate), the FactCG fails the test, so go on to the next FactCG. See Fig. 8.7. If no bits in the third register are set to 1, then the current FactCG may be tested for PROPERTY 2. Depending on the implementation, the FactCGs that pass the PROPERTY 1 test may be stockpiled in an appropriate place in memory for the next test (PROPERTY 2), or, the next test could be performed immediately.

The reader may imagine that the upper graph of Fig. 8.6 is represented via 1's entered in the slots corresponding to (AGNT) and (PTNT) in the 2nd register from the left in Fig. 8.7, and the lower graph of Fig. 8.6 is represented via 1's entered in the slots corresponding to (AGNT), (PTNT) and (COLR) in the leftmost register. The > test will be passed for each slot, since for each 1 in the 2nd register there is a 1 in the corresponding slot of the 1st register. Thus the

---

[6]In practice, an implementation could be designed to do the concept "key word" check on a FactCG as soon as it passes the relation "key word" test. Hardware and time considerations would be the deciding factors. For applications where the first fact matching with the query is acceptable output, this approach would be preferable.

answer register will contain all zeros, and the FactCG will be shown to posses
PROPERTY 1.

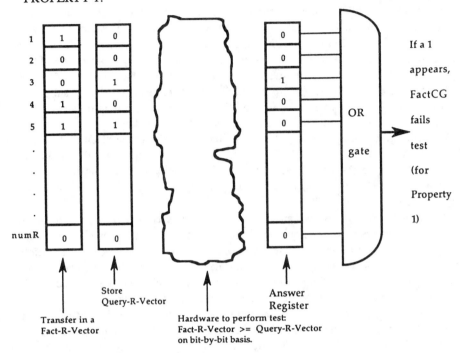

Fig. 8.7 Parallel implementation schema for PROPERTY-1 test.

The above is all that is needed to check for PROPERTY 1. The R-vector indicates which
of the relations are used at least once in the corresponding conceptual graph. Thus, the
simple$\geq$ test suggested above accomplishes the "at least one" criterion of PROPERTY 1.
Because of Comments 1 & 2, it is not needed to check the specific number of times the
relation appears in the compared conceptual graphs.

The test for PROPERTY 2 is a bit more complicated than the one shown above for
PROPERTY 1. This is occasioned by the fact that a SUBtype of the concepts is allowed
(this is where the restriction comes in) in contrast to the equality of relations required for
PROPERTY 1. To check for the existence of a subtype relationship between a pair of concept
types, the concept-type hierarchy will have to be accessed. A possible implementation for
this test using standard parallel registers (similar to the configuration shown in Fig. 8.7)
is described in the next paragraph. This method would be straightforward, but entails a
huge memory requirement. Circumventing the memory requirement, as well as additional
speed enhancement, are direct motivations for pursuing the neural network possibility
instead. This will be the topic in section 8.3.2, wherein we take advantage of the C-vector
representation schema we have developed, and use these as inputs to neural networks.

For completeness, we mention a possibility using conventional parallel registers to
effect a PROPERTY-2 test. This method consists of creating a sub- hierarchy vector whose
template vector is the same as that for the C-vector (i.e., is length $numC$). One of these
vectors would be created for each concept. A 1 would be entered in the slot for the given
concept, and, additional 1's would be placed in the slots for all the concepts which are sub-

types of the given concept–i.e., all those concept types in the sub-hierarchy whose root is the given concept type. Then, to determine whether concept A is a sub-type of concept B, simply look in the sub-hierarchy vector for concept B at the slot corresponding to concept A and see if there is a 1 there. If so, then concept A is a sub-type of concept B; if not, then the sub-type relation is not satisfied. This test could be performed with a hardware configuration similar to that shown in Fig. 8.7. For this test, the registers would have to have $numC$ slots, and the test hardware would only need to perform the AND function, bit by bit. Nevertheless, this method would require that there be stored $numC$ sub-hierarchy vectors, each of which is $numC$ long, and this entails a storage requirement of $numC^2$ bits. If $numC$ is on the order of 10,000, the numbers get quite large.

We have demonstrated so far that it is possible to implement the PROPERTY-1 and the PROPERTY-2 tests for the PROJECTION operation using standard parallel architectures. The suggestions so far are implementable with current VLSI technology. However, as indicated earlier, our objective in this chapter is to explore the possibility for implementing these operations via a neural network.

We went through the above analysis to give a concrete demonstration to ourselves that: (i) the desired operations on conceptual graphs are in fact doable using the chosen representation schema, and; (ii) the operations are implementable in a straightforward way, so our confidence in setting out to train neural networks to do the same operations is enhanced. One might ask why use a neural network at all, since the implementation is already so straightforward? Researchers in neural networks are demonstrating that a number of attributes accrue to connectionist networks that make them appealing. Fault tolerance is a key one of these attributes, and this accrues from the distributed representation nature of connectionist networks. Because the information is stored in a distributed way throughout the electronic (or other) implementation, even if a few percent of the internal devices fail, the impact on the overall operation can be negligible. In local representation devices, failure of internal components means total absence of the pieces of data that were stored therein. Also, for accesses to the concept hierarchy (re. the PROPERTY-2 test), there will be significant speed and memory size advantages on the side of the neural networks vs. parallel hardware added to serial machines.

8.3.2   Neural Network for test of Projection - Property-2

In the previous section, we explored using conventional parallel registers to implement the PROPERTY-1 and PROPERTY-2 tests for the PROJECTION operation. In this section, we proceed to explore implementing the PROPERTY-2 test using connectionist (neural) networks. The best situation would be if a neural network could perform the entire PROPERTY-2 test in one step. A procedure is described for using a neural network with this capability assumed. In addition, however, two other procedures are given, each using a neural network of successively less capability. For even the lowest assumed capability, it is argued that use of neural networks to perform the suggested operations on conceptual graphs can still effect a significant reduction of processing time (due to the potentially large number of accesses to the type/subtype checking operation to be discussed later, and, whereas the time for this operation in serial machines will depend upon the depth of the concept tree, in neural networks the operation will always be done in one "chunk" of processing time).

For the remainder of our discussion, we may assume a kind of neural network "black box." Referring to Fig. 8.8, the connectionist network box is to have 2 groups of $numC$ (the number of concept types in the knowledge base catalog) input terminals. Each of the terminals in the first group will be assigned to one of the concept types, and a similar assignment given to the terminals in the second group. The assignment of concept types to these terminals is made to correspond in a useful way to the assignment of concept types to the slots in the C-vector template. Having two groups of input terminals allows presenting concepts from two conceptual graphs as ordered pairs, and asking about their relative level on the hierarchy. The output of the network may be as simple as four wires; one each for the answers: lower, same, higher, not comparable (i.e., on a different branch of the tree).

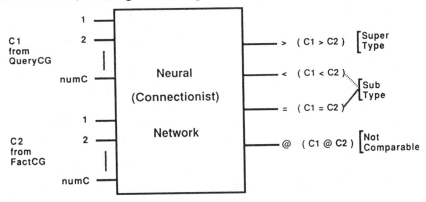

Fig. 8.8 Neural network is trained to accept two C-vectors (or, RC-vectors), and to compare the two via the concept-type hierarchy.

What specific neural network configuration should be inside the box is a research issue of its own. Further, what training algorithm should be used is also a topic for research. The larger the number of concepts in the knowledge base catalog, the more input nodes will be required. The number of input nodes has direct impact on the amount of time it takes to train a network, and an important research topic will be to develop methods of modularizing the present problem so the train time scales reasonably.

For the application here contemplated, once the catalog of concept types and the associated concept-type hierarchy for a knowledge base is developed, the neural network could be trained and used without subsequent modification. A practical issue, however, is what happens when one more concept is added to the catalog? Does the training algorithm allow for simple addition of one more piece of data with its relationships to the other data, or does the training process have to start over from scratch? Difficulties of this nature have been experienced by others (Rumelhart et al.., 1986), as well as in the experiments to be described below. The author's experiments to date, however, have suggested ways to recast the problem definition in a way that will (hopefully) allow training (sub) neural networks to learn portions of the concept-type hierarchy lattice, and put these together as modules in a composite neural network. The implications of this refined method to reducing training time are potentially significant.

From the point of view of the present development, the training problem, per se, is not the focus; rather, the focus is to argue the plausibility that a neural network can implement the desired operations on conceptual graphs. For this purpose, we assume that a neural network "black box" can be developed, and proceed to consider if and how it could be used to effect the PROPERTY 2 test for the PROJECTION operation in the data-base context.

We assume that information about which FactCGs passed the PROPERTY 1 test is available, and that only these FactCGs will be dealt with in this pass. From the overall process point of view, it would be easiest if we were able to present the C-vector of the QueryCG (call it Query-C-vector) to the first group of input nodes (re Fig. 8.8), and the C-vector of the current FactCG (Fact-C-vector) to the second group of input nodes, and then have the network (trained to) answer the following question: for each concept type with a 1 input in the first group, does there correspond at least one subtype of it with a 1 input in the second group? If the network could be trained to accomplish this procedure, then it would only need two outputs: one for yes, and one for no. This would solve the PROPERTY 2 test directly. But the likelihood of developing a connectionist network to solve as complex a problem as this is no doubt low at the present time. Even if the training-algorithm difficulties were to be solved for this kind of application, designing the set of inputs to be used for training the network so it is possible for the network to infer the task we want it to perform remains as an important problem. These are all subjects for research.

Since it is presently unknown whether a neural network could learn to do the entire PROPERTY-2 test directly, we explore below a more modest function for the network to learn. To accommodate this more modest function, however, a number of supporting sub-procedures need to be designed by us for the rest of the system to perform.

The more modest task we propose for the neural network is as follows (re Fig. 8.8): present to the first group of input nodes one of the concept types which appears in the QueryCG (i.e., one of the active slots in the Query-C- vector), and to the second group of input nodes, present one of the concept types which appears in the current FactCG (i.e., one of the active slots in the Fact-C-vector). Then, for this pair of activated terminals, have the neural network answer the (simpler) question regarding the location of the second concept type on the hierarchy relative to the first (e.g., lower, same, higher, not comparable). The author has obtained positive results on this (sub)task. There are a number of degrees of complexity in testing for PROPERTY 2 between the simple test suggested in this paragraph, and the much more complex one of testing for PROPERTY 2 directly. An example of a test between the two extremes so far suggested is to present to the first group of input nodes one of the concept types which appears in the QueryCG (as in the simplest test), and to the second group of input nodes, present the entire C-vector of the current FactCG (as in the most complex test), and then have the neural network answer the question whether there is at least one instance of the query concept type, or one of its subtypes, in the FactCG. After the "simplest" test has been shown to be doable by neural networks, a progression of tests leading to the direct test could be researched. So far, though it now has been demonstrated that the simplest task can be performed by a neural network, a lot of collateral design experiments are required before proceeding with the progression of experiments suggested in the previous sentence.

Returning to the simplest test, one possibility for implementation is as follows:

Assume we have a neural network box which has two groups of input terminals equivalent to two C-vector templates, C_1 and C_2, i.e., has $2 \times$ (numC) inputs. The rules for input are that one slot in each of the C-vectors is to be active at any one time, and the output will have four terminals to represent the following (re Fig. 8.8):

The active slot of C_2 is a restriction of the active slot of C_1 ($<$)
The active slot of C_2 is the same type as the active slot of C_1 ($=$)
The active slot of C_2 is a generalization of the active slot of C_1
($>$) The active slot of C_2 is not comparable to the active slot of
C_1 (@)

Recall our definition of the R-C connection matrix, and refer again to Fig. 8.11: each of the rows corresponds to one of the relations in the knowledge base catalog, and each of the columns corresponds to one of the concept types. A 1 is entered in those slots where there exists a relation node and concept node in the network, and there is a connection between them. This will be a very sparse matrix, because each row will typically have only 2-3 entries, and based on reported experience, with a maximum of some 5 entries (even when the number of columns is very large). Also, the number of relations used in a given FactCG is typically a small subset of $numR$.

Recall also, that the R-vector is derived by "projecting" the rows of the R-C connection matrix into a column vector whose length is the same as that of the matrix ($numR$). A 1 is entered into a slot of the R-vector when the corresponding relation exists in the graph (and therefore there is at least one 1 entry in the corresponding row of the matrix). Thus, the "active" slots (those with a 1 in them) of the R-vector indicate which relations are included in the graph, and simultaneously, which rows in the R-C connection matrix are non-zero. There are a number of ways to efficiently encode sparse matrixes; however, to keep the graphical presentation of the present development a little more obvious, the active slots in the R-vector will be our indicator for the rows being stored, and we will keep the rows stored in their entirety. Thus, we will say that associated with each active slot in the R-vector for a conceptual graph, is an RC-vector which shows the connections of the associated relation node to the concept nodes of the graph. This RC-vector is simply the corresponding row of the R-C connection matrix. The length of the RC-vector is thus $numC$.

By storing the R-vector and associated RC-vectors for a conceptual graph, we store only those rows of the R-C connection matrix that have at least one 1 in them, plus the R-vector. The rows are stored as an ordered set, and the R-vector plays the role of key for the RC-vectors, and in addition, the important role of facilitating a fast test for PROPERTY 1 in a data base query process using the PROJECTION operation.

Recall also, that the C-vector is derived by "projecting" the columns of the R-C connection matrix into a row vector whose length is the same as the width of the matrix–i.e., $numC$. The difference between the C-vector and the RC-vectors is that the C-vector has active slots for all the concept types used in the associated graph, whereas the RC-vectors each have active slots only for those concept types connected to the specified relation node of the graph. The C-vector is the union of all the RC-vectors for a graph, i.e., the union of all rows in the R-C connection matrix for the graph.

At the present stage of the author's research it is not clear whether the proposed procedure for simply comparing the C-vector of the QueryCG with the C-vectors of the FactCGs to test for PROPERTY 2 will be efficient in actual practice. It was pointed out earlier that it is possible for FactCGs that do not satisfy the query QueryCG to pass the PROPERTY-2 test. Determination of the quantity of such false responses can only be made empirically, as they will depend upon the characteristics of the particular knowledge base. For the purpose of exploring the various possibilities, assume that the method would not be acceptable, and consider the implementation consequences. First of all, recourse would have to be made to the RC-vectors, and this entails a requirement for considerably more memory. On the other hand, the subtype (restriction) checking needed for PROPERTY 2 will no doubt be faster for the RC-vectors (since fewer possibilities need to be cycled through) than it would be for the C-vector, so it could in fact turn out being worth the extra allocation of memory to gain the speed advantage. Let us assume for the rest of the development that the RC-vectors will be required, and determine the associated process.

Since the FactCGs we will be testing for PROPERTY 2 have already passed the test for PROPERTY 1, we are guaranteed that for every active slot in the Query- R-vector, the same slot in the Fact-R-vector will also be active–i.e., if a relation node of a given type exists in QueryCG, then one also exists in the FactCG. We fetch the pair of RC-vectors corresponding, respectively, to a selected active slot in the Query-R-vector and to the same slot in the current Fact-R-vector being tested for PROPERTY-2. The entries in these two RC-vectors indicate, respectively, the concept nodes connected to the specified relation node in the QueryCG and to those connected to the specified relation node in the FactCG. In practice, each of these RC-vectors will typically have 2-3 non- zero entries, and at most 5. For each of these entries in the RC-vector for the QueryCG, we are to determine if there is an entry in the FactCG RC-vector which is a subtype. The neural network box previously shown in Fig. 8.8 will be used to make this test.

Since we assume there will normally be only 2-3 entries in each RC-vector, it may be possible for a neural network to perform a direct test on the RC- vectors for PROPERTY 2 (in contrast to our earlier speculation that this is unlikely for the C-vectors, which potentially have many more entries). If so, then a procedure such as the following would accomplish the PROPERTY 2 test for the candidate FactCG.

> Sequentially apply to the neural network (NN) one of the RC-vectors for the QueryCG and the corresponding RC-vector for the FactCG; if the NN indicates a lower- or equal- type relation, go to the next pair of RC-vectors; continue until all RC-vectors of the QueryCG are considered. If a higher or not- comparable response is given for any pair of RC-vectors, then because of part b) of PROPERTY-2, discard the present candidate FactCG and go on to the next one in the stockpile which passed part a) of the PROPERTY-2 test. Those FactCGs which pass this test are stockpiled in memory for the next part of the processing.

In serial machines, the subtype checks required for the PROPERTY 2 test would likely have to be done pairwise–i.e., separately testing each (active) concept in the QueryCG with each (active) concept in the FactCG. The number of steps for this process will depend on $numC$, and where in the hierarchy the particular concepts being tested lie. For the purpose of exploring the least- capability situation, let us assume that we assign only this bare-bones task to the neural network. Even in this case, the neural network approach will no doubt still be faster than serial searching of the hierarchy–especially for large values of $numC$. This is because, if a neural network can perform this check (preliminary experiments indicate that one could), it should do so in a constant increment of time, no matter where the concepts lie in the hierarchy tree.

The (bare-bones) task of making the subtype test on only one pair of entries at at a time could be accomplished with a connectionist network as follows:

Start with the query Query-R-vector. Go to its first active slot and fetch the associated RC-vector. Fetch the corresponding RC-vector for the current FactCG (via the Fact-R-vector). The assumption here is that only one of the entries in each of the RC-vectors can be tested at a time. Going from left to right in the Query-RC-vector, find the first active slot. Pick the same corresponding slot in the candidate Fact-RC-Vector. (Remember, there are typically 2-3, with max 5, active slots in the RC-Vectors.) If both slots have a 1 in them, then there is a type match. If they do not, then, keeping the same slot in the Query-RC-vector, find another[7] active slot in the Fact-RC-vector. Present this pair of slot positions to the neural net (NN) and determine if they pass the test. If not, repeat the process. Continue until find a pair that passes the subtype check, or, until the end of the Fact-RC-vector is reached (if this happens, then this FactCG fails the test, so go on to next FactCG to be checked.) When the subtype check is passed for a given slot in the Query-RC-vector, then find its next active slot, and repeat the process. Continue through all the active slots in the Query-RC-vector (at most 5 of these). If successful for each of these, then go to the next active slot in the Query-RC-vector, fetch the associated RC- vector, and repeat the process above. Continue this process until cover all active slots in the query Query-R-vector. If successful for each of these, then the current FactCG is a candidate answer to the query. If fail test at any point in the process, then discard the current FactCG and go to the next one.

There are many details that will have to be tended to when developing an actual implementation of the above. The purpose here was to demonstrate how a neural network could be used to perform some of the conceptual graph processing in constant time, and hence speed up the process by a potentially significant factor. The more of the tasks the connectionist network could be trained to do, the greater the potential speed up. An important topic of research is to determine which level of tasks a neural network can be trained to do in practical contexts within a reasonable amount of time. With the rapid advancements occurring in the hardware arena, the limitations are not likely to come from this aspect. Rather, as indicated earlier, the development which will make the largest step toward practical application of the connectionist approach will be creation of training strategies that will converge in a reasonable amount of time–and just as important, will require short update times, for adding new data after the initial training is done.

One aspect that has not been given attention yet here is the case where a concept node has an individual marker assigned to it–i.e., the concept has been restricted to an individual. An example might be [person:Irene] or [man:Gregory]. This becomes important, for example,

---

[7]The strategy will be determined by how the concepts are ordered in the RC- vector. E.g., if we always have subtypes of a given concept type assigned to slots to the right of the slot for that given type, then the word "another" could be replaced by "next". Generally, this implies building a kind of meta-knowledge into the hardware rather than having to incorporate it into the software control (thus, the "work" has only to be done once).

when in the process of testing PROPERTY 2 it is determined that a concept node of the FactCG is lower on the hierarchy tree than the corresponding concept node of the QueryCG. If this FactCG concept node has an individual marker assigned to it, a CONFORMITY test is required before performing the RESTRICTION.

As stated before, we assume a table is available which contains a list of all markers (names) used for individuals, and with each marker there is listed the concept subtype to which the marker normally applies.

Let us go through an example (re Fig. 8.9). Suppose we are comparing concept node [girl] with the restric... concept node [person:Irene] during the PROPERTY-2 test, and want to know if the RESTRICTION to [girl:Irene] is legitimate. A restriction is "legitimate" if the referent of the token CONFORMS to the concept being restricted; with respect to the hierarchy tree, this means that the token's referent concept type is on a common branch of the tree with the concept to be restricted. We assume that when the FactCG containing the [person:Irene] concept node was originally created for the knowledge base, a check was made that it was legitimate to restrict [person] via the Irene marker (whose referent is [female-person]). With this assumption, it is only necessary to check that [girl] CONFORMS to [female-person]. If we have a neural network such as the one in Fig. 8.8, this test if very simple: checking [girl] and [female-person], the network yields the "<" output signal (i.e., "lower, in the same branch of the tree"). On the other hand, if we had been comparing [boy] with [person:Irene], and wanted to know if the RESTRICTION [boy:Irene] is legitimate, when we check [boy] with [female-person], the neural network yields the "not comparable" output signal– i.e., [boy] is on a different branch of the tree. In this case, CONFORMITY fails, and we cannot make the RESTRICTION [boy:Irene].

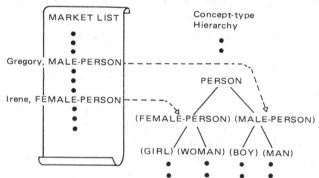

Fig. 8.9 Names in the marker list include the concept-type referent for each marker. These are used to accomplish the CONFORMITY check. A marker can only be assigned to its referent concept type or to a concept type above or below it in the hierarchy. With the drawing as a visual aid, it is easy to see that the name Irene should not be assigned to the concept type boy[8]. A suggested process for determining presence or absence of conformity via a neural network is given in the text.

In the above example, if we were not willing to make the assumption that the FactCG restriction was properly checked, then the test here must include this test as well. The procedure would be as follows. We check [girl] with [person] via the neural network of Fig.

---

[8]The referent concept type for Irene is said to not conform to the concept type boy

8.8, and find that [person] > [girl]. Now take into account that [person] is restricted to Irene; look up Irene in the marker list, and note that this marker has [female-person] as its referent. Check [female-person] with [girl] via the neural network to find that [female-person] > [girl]. Therefore, CONFORMITY holds, and [girl:Irene] is ok. On the other hand, suppose we are comparing [boy] with [person:Irene] and want to know if [boy:Irene] is legitimate. When we check [boy] with [person] via the neural network, we find that [person] > [boy]. As before, we now take into account that [person] is restricted to Irene; we look up Irene in the marker list, and again note that this marker has [female-person] as its referent. This time, when we check [female-person] with [boy] via the neural network, we find that [female-person] is not comparable to [boy]. i.e., [boy] is on a different branch of the tree. Therefore, CONFORMITY check fails, and we cannot make the RESTRICTION [boy:Irene].

This example demonstrates the potentially large number of accesses to the type/ subtype checking operation that could be needed to perform the RESTRICTION & CONFORMITY check operations. As indicated before, the neural network makes the type/subtype operation possible in constant time, no matter where in the hierarchy the pair being checked falls. Given such a potential time savings for each type/subtype check, the cumulative reduction of throughput time could be truly significant.

8.3.3   Early experiments to train neural networks on concept sub-type tests

In the previous section, we assumed that a neural network "black box" could be developed to perform the concept sub-type test, and then proceeded to demonstrate that such a NN black box could be used to effect the PROPERTY-2 test for the PROJECTION operation in the data-base context. In this section, we mention some early experiments which do indeed demonstrate that the concept sub-type test can be done by a neural network.

From a theoretical point of view, a concept-type hierarchy is a lattice. Accordingly, the experimental procedure was to define an abstract lattice, and use this as a proxy for a concept-type hierarchy. The lattice used is shown in Fig. 8.10. This lattice has 16 nodes, and was designed to provide paths of different length and complexity. The graphical representation of the data structure shown in Fig. 8.10 contains within it the answers to all possible questions "What relation is concept C_i to concept C_j?"[9]. This is obvious to each of us human observers. The key experimental question is how do we get this information inside the neural network, and such that the NN can provide correct answers for every possible $[C_i \; ?R \; C_j]$ question?

---

[9]Notation: $[C_i \; ?R \; C_j]$.

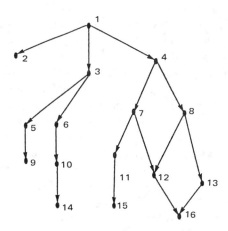

Fig. 8.10 Sample lattice for concept-type hierarchy experiments.

An important sub-problem here turns out being how to design the set of data to be used in training the NN. To answer questions of the type $[C_i$?R $C_j]$, we need to have more information than that represented directly in the Connection Matrix. Consider Fig. 8.10 again. By visual inspection, it is possible to state that $C3 > C14$, but we must also note that the path from node 3 to node 14 contains three links (path length = 3). It is not immediately obvious how (in general) to determine that $C3 > C14$ directly from the Connection Matrix. Fortunately, there exists a technique for creating a Reachability Matrix of a graph (Warfield, 1976), where the Reachability Matrix contains a 1 in the (i, j) position if a directed path of any length exists between node i and node j. The Reachability Matrix is calculated from the Connection Matrix via an algorithm that involves raising a modified version of the Connection Matrix to increasing powers until some stopping condition is met. In the experiments carried out to date, the Reachability Matrix has been found to be useful for an organized development of the training data sets.

For these experiments, a neural network of the "backpropagation" paradigm was used. With reference to Fig. 8.8, the NN was provided with 2 groups of 16 inputs. Each group of 16 inputs is fully interconnected (feedforward only) to a separate group of 4 neurodes, these two groups of 4 constituting a layer of 8 neurodes. The outputs of these 8 neurodes are fully connected to a next layer of 8 neurodes, and finally, these 8 are fully connected to an output layer of 4 neurodes. This configuration has what is known as two "hidden" layers.

There are $16 \times 16 = 256$ possible $[C1$?R $C2]$ questions of the type described earlier for the given lattice. A training set consisting of 1 each of these questions was created, but it was decided not to use the $[C_i$?= $C_j]$ question, because this is trivial to answer prior to applying the NN to the task. The NN learned to answer all the remaining 240 questions perfectly. Thus, the inprinciple question of whether a NN can be trained to answer the concept sub-type question is answered in the affirmative.

As a knowledge base is being developed, it could happen that the underlying lattice of concept types expands over time. It is important to determine if the NN can be made to learn this knowledge in a piecemeal fashion, i.e., to train the NN to incorporate the new concept types as they evolve in the lattice (i.e., an updating procedure). An experiment was fashioned that trained the top 4 nodes first, then nodes (5,6,9,10,14), and then the remaining nodes. As one might expect, one cannot simply train the net with only the new nodes at each stage; the net "forgets" what it learned in the first stage if it is not "reminded" once in a while what it learned before. Empirically, it was found that a reminder rate of about 1 in 4 served to maintain the old knowledge while the new was being trained. The negative result of this part of the experiment was that it took about 100,000 presentations to learn each stage of training– therefore, it took approximately 300,000 presentations to learn the lattice via staged training whereas, it only took about 100,000 to learn the whole lattice from scratch.

A more circumscribing set of experiments is getting underway to explore the above and related phenomena further. In particular, ideas are emerging for training sub-NNs to learn sub-lattices of the larger lattice, including special sub-lattices which represent the linkages between the other sub-lattices, and joining the sub-NNs together appropriately into a composite NN. These ideas are in their developmental stages, and nothing is ready to be reported yet.

8.4   MULTIPLE COPIES OF RELATIONS AND CONCEPT TYPES

An aspect that was mentioned earlier, but not yet addressed, is the case where a conceptual graph contains more than one copy of a relation or of a concept type. To accommodate these, the R-C connection matrix, the R-vector, the C-vector, and the RC-vectors need to be augmented.

The main requirement we must take into account in augmenting the representation schema, is that it remain standardized. For use in neural networks, it is important that the R-vector, C-vector, and RC-vectors (non-zero rows of the R-C connection matrix), have a fixed assignment of relation/concept types to the slot positions. If it weren't for this latter constraint, we could simply add extra rows for the additional relation nodes, and extra columns for the extra concept nodes. Each of the extra rows and columns would be labeled, and in symbol processing machines, the labels can be used to keep track of everything. BUT, for the neural network application, the position is the label, and once the network is trained, the terminals each represent a specific role in the problem context.

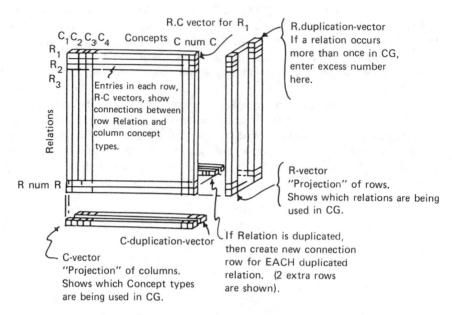

Fig. 8.11 Relation-Concept Connection Matrix (R-C connection matrix). Rows in matrix are called RC-vectors.

Consider first the case where there are multiple copies of relations, but not of concept types. We define an R-duplication-vector template. This template has the same number of slots and the same relation assignments to the slots as does the R-vector template. The R-duplication-vector for a conceptual graph is made as follows: if a relation occurs more than once in the conceptual graph, the excess number is entered in the corresponding slot of the R-duplication-vector template. Refer to Fig. 8.11. From an implementation point of view, use of 2-bit subregisters for the duplication vectors allows up to 4 occurrences of a given relation; with a 3-bit subregister, 8 occurrences of a relation are allowed (anecdotal reports based on research implementations indicate that this is probably an extreme upper limit for typical uses). In practice, there will likely be very few entries in the duplication vectors, so it will probably be more efficient to carry this data in a list rather than via a full vector representation. But for graphic purposes in the present development, and for potential use with neural networks, we will continue to use the vector representation.

For each extra copy of a relation in the conceptual graph, create a new RC-vector (this represents connections of the given duplicate relation node to concept nodes). In Fig. 8.11, these new RC-vectors are shown stock-piled in the 3rd dimension so the number of rows in the R-C connection matrix is not changed. Whatever scheme is created in an implementation to store/fetch RC-vectors pertaining to the active slots in the R-vector can be used to store/fetch the RC-vectors created for the duplicate nodes, only using the R-duplication-vector as the key.

Thus, what we have is an additional set of RC-vectors (corresponding to the duplicated relations), and these can be handled in the same way as the other RC-vectors for operations discussed to this point. It is important to keep in mind that the dimensions of the R-vector template or RC-vector template did not change in this part of the augmentation.

Duplication of concept types in a conceptual graph presents a greater difficulty. It seems we are stuck with having to add columns to the connection matrix to allow for representing the duplicated concept types. The classical AI example of an arch (Sowa, 1984, page 71) provides a case in point. One portion of the conceptual graph for an arch is [brick]→(right)→[brick]. Here we have the relation (right) connected to two distinct nodes of type [brick]. The RC-vector for the relation (right) must be able to show two connections, and to do this, there need to be two slots in the RC-vector template, both of which correspond to separate instances of the concept [brick]. Our augmentation will thus have to provide a means for adding a new slot to the RC-vector template (and therefore, a new column to the R-C connection matrix and, of course, a new entry for all the RC-vectors–this latter is important because other relations could connect, separately, to these two instances of [brick] as well.)

If we were doing this by hand, we would probably insert a second column for the concept [brick] next to the original one in the R-C connection matrix. Then, in doing the PROJECTION tests by hand, we would have visual access to the labels for the columns to help us keep track of the operations. However, since we need to have position invariance for the concept types, we explore another alternative.

Create a C-duplication-vector in the same way as the R-duplication-vector was described above. This entails placing a number in a slot of a C-vector-like template to indicate the extra number of copies of the associated concept type which appear in the graph. Do this with the original definition of the C-vector template. We will add extra slots to the RC-vector template (and therefore extra columns to the R-C connection matrix) according to information contained in the C-duplication-vector. The additions are, therefore, tailored to each conceptual graph. Even though there will be slots added to the RC-vector template, the C-vector template will stay fixed.

To accomplish position invariance, we propose the following schema. Moving from left to right in the C-duplication-vector, as we encounter a non-zero entry, read the number in the slot, and add that many slots on the right end of the RC-vector template. These slots will thereafter represent (for the given conceptual graph) the concept type associated with the active slot in the C-duplication-vector. Repeat this addition process for each non-zero entry in the C-duplication-vector, as we traverse it from left to right. The concept type represented by each of the new slots in the RC-vector template has a position referent in the C-duplication-vector, and the position referent for different graphs is made unique by using a fixed procedure (left-to-right, in this case) in assigning the new slots according to the entries in the C-duplication-vector.

There are a number of intricacies that will have to be attended to for implementing the above, but it should be conceptually clear that the PROPERTY 2 tests can be performed with this representation schema. A simple modification in the next-to-last sentence in the procedure given earlier: viz., "If a higher or not-comparable response is given for any pair of RC-vectors, then bring in the connection row for each duplicated relation and perform the same test. If all of these give higher or not-comparable responses, then, because of part b) of PROPERTY 2, discard the present candidate FactCG and go on...." In the context of implementing this in a serial machine augmented with parallel registers as suggested earlier, the main consideration will be how many additional slots to make available in the registers that are to accommodate the augmented RC-vectors. There is no apparent theoretical basis for making this determination–rather, the number will have to be determined empirically. The knowledge base to be implemented will have to be studied to determine a typical maximum number of duplications of concept types that occur in the FactCGs– perhaps forfeiting certain extreme cases. This portion of the register will be used only when there are duplications occurring in the conceptual graph. Perhaps this portion of the register can be dubbed "duplication reservoir".

The next important question for us to consider is, can this means of representation be used with connectionist machines?

Let us provide the connectionist network with two additional sets of $numC$ input terminals (see Fig. 8.12) to accommodate the C-duplication-vector templates (for the QueryCG and the FactCG) plus enough extra terminals in the two sets of terminals associated with the RC-vector templates to accommodate the size of the duplication reservoir. Up to this point in our discussions, we have used only binary inputs for the connectionist networks. The C-duplication-vectors will be allowed to give input values appropriate for indicating the number of duplications. With this kind of hardware configuration, the network still learns what it did before with respect to the first $numC$ slots of the RC-vector templates. The meaning of the remaining terminals in the (augmented) RC-vector groups is defined by entries in the C-duplication-vectors. As before, we have two sets of all the terminals, so the network can be given the QueryCG and a FactCG upon which to perform the PROPERTY-2 test (row at a time from their respective R-C connection matrixes.) This means of accommodating multiple copies of concept types is expensive–in the sense that there is more than a doubling of input terminals. A more efficient encoding of the duplications is another item for research. Another possible approach to this issue, however, is implicit in research reported by Touretsky & Hinton (1985) wherein they show that connectionist networks are capable of dealing with linked lists. This is one way of looking at what we have here–and represents another item for research.

This concludes a first pass at considering the usability of the proposed matrix-form representation and its associated vector-form representations to carry out a database query task via the PROJECTION operation. All the major functions that need to be done are seen to be doable in principle. Further, suggestions for implementing these in serial machines augmented with parallel registers for the key operations have been provided. And most pertinent to the purpose of this chapter, subtasks of the database query task have been defined which appear to be plausible candidates for implementation with neural networks.

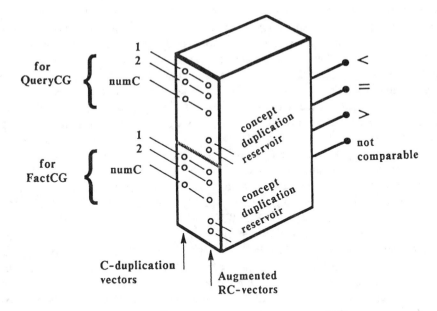

Fig. 8.12 Input terminals added to network shown in Fig. 8.8 to accommodate multiple copies of concept-type node. So far, all inputs to the neural networks have been binary valued. The C-duplication vectors are here allowed to have values > 1, to indicate number of duplications.

8.5   PERFORMING MAXIMAL JOIN OPERATIONS

In Sowa's notation chapter in this book, and in section 3.5 of his 1984 book, Sowa stresses the importance of the operation called MAXIMAL JOIN. Its importance lies in its being analogous to similar operations in a variety of other AI systems, as well as being the basis for the applications presented in sections 3.6, 4.1, 4.7, 5.6, and 6.5 in Sowa (1984).

The one diminishing attribute of MAXIMAL JOIN cited by Sowa in section 2.4, is that "..maximal join requires a nondeterministic search for nuclei before the process can begin.." This issue has not yet been researched for the representation schema proposed here, but it appears that the methods presented in the previous section for performing a data base query via the PROJECTION operation would be applicable to the MAXIMAL JOIN o peration with little modification. If this turns out to be true, then the difficulty mentioned by Sowa is largely overcome.

The definition for MAXIMAL JOIN given by Sowa is as follows: "The join rule allows two concepts to be joined at a time. By repeated joins, restricts, and simplifies, a simple join of two concepts may be extended to a much larger join of two subgraphs. If the join is extended as far as possible, it is called a maximal join."

In section 8.3 (of this chapter), it was shown that the JOIN operation is accomplished via a logical-or operation on the cells of the connection matrixes of the two graphs being operated on. It was not emphasized there, but via this operation, all concepts which appear in both conceptual graphs being joined are automatically merged in the one step. Thus, if we are given two conceptual graphs CG1 and CG2 to be (maximally) JOINed, then via the logical-or operation on the connection matrixes of CG1 and CG2, the connection matrix for the resultant graph CG3 contains simple joins of all the concept nodes that appeared in both CG1 and CG2. This is a major step in the process of accomplishing a MAXIMAL JOIN[10]. Regarding a potential SIMPLIFY operation in CG3, by definition, there must have existed common relations in CG1 and CG2. Existence of such common relation nodes can be checked easily via the R-vectors for the two conceptual graphs. The test would be similar to the PROPERTY 1 test for the PROJECTION operation, except that an AND of the two R-vectors would be performed instead of the < test. Via such a (modified) test, the only candidate relations for a SIMPLIFY in CG3 would be those slots in the answer R-vector register containing a 1 (re Fig. 8.7). A SIMPLIFY can be done only if the two RC-vectors associated with each pair of common relations identified are identical. To make them identical, it could require a process of RESTRICTION and CONFORMITY checks, etc., but this process is similar to the PROPERTY-2 test for the PROJECTION operation.

Clearly, a more detailed analysis of the above will be needed before definite conclusions can be drawn. However, if the PROPERTY 1 and PROPERTY 2 tests can be adapted to the MAXIMAL JOIN process, then–as is true for the PROJECTION operation–the process could be speeded up significantly over those methods indicated in Sowa's earlier statements. Such a speed up could be effected primarily via application of connectionist type devices, as the PROPERTY-2 test is the more significant time consumer. But even if the connectionist technology is slow in developing, VLSI technology is here, and special purpose parallel equipment could be appended to serial machines for performing the PROPERTY-1 tests (and the PROPERTY-2 tests if the associated large memory requirement is acceptable) for a still-significant improvement in speed.

8.6   NEURAL NETWORKS AS MEMORY FOR CONCEPTUAL GRAPHS

In the preceding discussions, the R-, R-duplication-, RC-, C-, and C-duplication vectors were created as a means for representing conceptual graphs. All of these, except the C-vector, are to be stored in memory, and to be available for the PROPERTY-1 and PROPERTY-2 tests as indicated. It has been assumed that these vectors will be available for parallel transfer into either the registers of Fig. 8.7 or the neural network device of Fig. 8.8. The actual physical type of memory system to be used has not yet been discussed.

Except for the type/subtype portion of the PROPERTY-2 test, all of the procedures discussed so far could be implemented via a serial machine with access to certain special-purpose hardware (parallel registers, per Fig. 8.7). The purpose of this section is to mention the possibility of using connectionist networks as memory for conceptual graphs.

Discussion of this topic could occupy a chapter of its own; indeed, others have spent the better part of entire books dealing with this issue, e.g., (Kohonen, 1980) (Kohonen, 1984) (Hinton & Anderson, 1981). We simply mention that parallel distributed memory systems have a potential for manifesting properties of a "higher level" than properties normally associated with simple memorizing devices. Descriptors that give hint of such properties

---

[10]Caution: A check for restriction to individuals will have to be made on each of the concept node pairs before they are merged. Also, details remain to be worked out regarding duplicate relations.

are: associative, content addressable, inductive generalization, implicit knowledge, graceful degradation, fault tolerance, etc.

The methods discussed in the preceding sections actually implement some of these attributes. For example, as described, the query process via PROJECTION can legitimately be considered an associative retrieval or content addressing method, depending on how one chooses to view the various procedures introduced. But these have more to do with the properties of conceptual graphs, the operations defined on them, and the representation schema suggested herein, rather than on the neural network implementation.

There is ample evidence in the connectionist literature to indicate that vector patterns of the type defined above can be stored in connectionist networks. Further, there is evidence that associative and/or content addressing can be performed in such memories. Conceptual graph applications would serve a useful problem context for guiding research in using neural networks for memory. This is because the operations to be performed on conceptual graphs are becoming well defined for various types of applications (the application chapters in this book attest to this), so researchers will have definite processing requirements to shoot for in developing connectionist memories. It could turn out, for example, that some of the PROPERTY-1 and PROPERTY-2 tests could be done implicitly in such memories. If so, then, for example, a QueryCG could be specified for a query, represented appropriately, and presented to the input terminals of the connectionist memory. The output of this memory device could be, say, those FactCGs that have PROPERTY 1, and these are passed to the neural-network device that performs PROPERTY-2 tests. As the capabilities of these devices are improved, perhaps it is not too far fetched to expect that one day, the connectionist memory can be trained to do the entire process.

8.7 CONCLUSION

Connectionism is a term that refers to massively parallel networks (of neural-type elements) in which information is stored mainly in parameters associated with connections of the elements rather than explicitly in the elements themselves. The connection parameters in such networks are determined during a process of "training" (or "learning") rather than by traditional design methods. There are a number of desirable properties that accrue to connectionist (neural) networks by virtue of their distributed nature, (e.g., fault tolerance, associative properties, etc.), and these provide good reasons for pursuing research to bring such networks to reality. As researchers in the field are aware, significant issues remain to be resolved before neural networks can be used to implement large knowledge bases.

An objective of this chapter has been to demonstrate that connectionist devices could meaningfully be used in implementing conceptual graphs, and indeed offer significant speed up of the two most important of the operations for conceptual graphs, namely, PROJECTION and MAXIMAL JOIN. These two operations extend into a wide range of AI and database type applications, so speeding them up by, potentially, several orders of magnitude can have important ramifications. In addition, it was suggested that a neural-network type memory system could prove important to conceptual-graph knowledge bases. To accomplish these glowing potentialities, however, substantive progress must be made in the realization of connectionist machines with large numbers of elements and interconnections, and specifically, in the development of training algorithms whose convergence time scales polynomially rather than exponentially. Whether this latter is a realistic hope or not, only time will tell–there are, however, tantalizing insights being offered that fuel the hope.

The state of the art in building knowledge bases with conceptual graphs is also in its early stages. Numbers currently associated with research knowledge bases are 70-100 relations, and 100-200 concept types. As we learn more about how to do it, more substantive contexts will be implemented, and for these, the numbers will change. Though the number of relations will likely stay on the order of 100-200, the number of concept types will more likely go over 1,000– perhaps to 10,000. Numbers of this magnitude will pose serious challenges for any kind of implementation, including neural networks.

It is known that successful development of neural network applications requires that careful attention will have to be given to analyzing and understanding the structure and constraints of the problem context as well as to those of the network. To improve the likelihood that the task to be performed is contained within the repertoire of functions achievable by the network (quite aside from the training issue), the researcher will have to undertake the specific activity of matching constraints implicit in the problem environment with those involved in the network structure.

For this reason, the author feels that research in conceptual graph applications and in connectionist machine development will both benefit by a strong interaction of the two. Requirements from each field can be used jointly as motivation for design of experiments and for the insightful thinking that will be required. The latter is a very necessary ingredient because, as progress is made in building solid state and/or optical hardware for implementing "simulated neurons," the biggest issue will continue to be: what do we do with them? We know a lot more know than we did in the 1960's, but there are still some quantum leaps for us to make.

BIBLIOGRAPHY

Abu-Mostafa, Y.S. & D. Psaltis (1987), "Optical Neural Computers," Scientific American, Mar, pp. 88-95.

Ackely, D.H., G.E. Hinton, & T.J. Sejnowski (1985), "A Learning Algorithm for Boltzman Machines," Cognitive Science, vol. 9, pp. 147-169.

Barto, A.G. & P. Anandan (1985), "Pattern-Recognizing Stochastic Learning Automata," IEEE Transactions on Systems, Man, and Cybernetics, vol. SMC-15, no. 3, May/June, pp. 360-375.

Fahlman, S.E. & G.S. Hinton (1987), "Connectionist Architectures for Artificial Intelligence," IEEE Computer Magazine, Jan, pp. 100-109.

Feldman, J.A. & D.H. Ballard (1982), "Connectionist Models and Their Properties," Cognitive Science, vol. 6, pp. 205-254.

Hinton, G.E. (1986), "Learning Distributed Representations of Concepts," Proc. Eighth Annual Conference of the Cognitive Science Society, Amherst, MA.

Hinton, G.E. & J.A. Anderson, (eds) (1981), Parallel Models of Associative Memory, Lawrence Erlbaum Assoc., Hillsdale, NJ.

Hinton, G.E. & T.J. Sejnowsky (1986), "Learning and Relearning in Boltzmann Machines," Ch. 7 in Parallel Distributed Processing: Explorations in the Microstructure of Cognition, Vol. 1, (ed) Rumelhart, McClelland, et. al, The MIT Press, Cambridge, MA.

Hopfield, J.J. (1982), "Neural Networks and Physical Systems with Emergent Collective Computational Abilities," Proc. National Academy of Sciences USA, vol. 79, no. 8, pp. 2554-2558, National Academy of Sciences, Wash., D.C., Apr.

Kohonen, T.K. (1980), *Content-Addressable Memories*, Springer-Verlag, Berlin.

Kohonen, T.K. (1984), *Self-Organization and Associative Memory*, Springer-Verlag, Berlin.

Lendaris, G.G. & G.L. Stanley (1963), "On the Structure-Dependent Properties of Adaptive Logic Networks," GM Defense Research Laboratories Report TR63-219, Jul, 117 pp.

Lendaris, G.G. & G.L. Stanley (1965a), "Self Organization: Meaning and Means," Information System Sciences; Proc. of the 2nd Congress, Spiegel J. & D. Walker, eds., Spartan Books, Baltimore, pp. 459-476.

Lendaris, G.G. & G.L. Stanley (1965b), "Structure and Constraint in Discrete Adaptive Networks," Proc. of the National Electronics Conference, vol. XXI, pp. 500-505.

Lendaris, G.G. (1988a), "Conceptual Graph Knowledge Systems as Problem Context for Neural Networks," Proc. of the International Conference on Neural Networks (ICNN-88), IEEE, July.

Lendaris, G.G. (1988b), "Representing Conceptual Graphs for Parallel Processing," Proc. of AAAI Third Annual Workshop On Conceptual Graphs (AAAI-88), AAAI, Menlo Park, CA 94015, Aug.

Lendaris, G.G. (1988c), "Neural Networks, Potential Assistants To Knowledge Engineers," HEURISTICS, Journal of the International Association of Knowledge Engineers, Kensington, MD 20895, vol 1, no 2, Dec 1988.

Lendaris, G.G. (1989a), "Experiment on Implementing the Concept-Type Lattice in a Neural Network," Proc. of Fourth Annual Workshop on Conceptual Graphs, IJCAI-89, Detroit, MN

Lendaris, G.G. (1989b), "Testing the Use of a Neural Network to Implement a Basic Data-base Function," Proc. of NORTHCON-89, IEEE, Oct.

Lendaris, G.G. (1990b), "Conceptual Graphs as Vehicle for Improved Generalization in a Neural Network Pattern Recognition Task," in Proc. of the Fifth Annual workshop on Conceptual Structures, (eds) P. Eklund, and L. Gerholz, Linköping University, ISBN 91-7870-718-8.

McCulloch, W.S. & W.A. Pitts (1943), "Logical Calculus of the Ideas Immanent in Nervous Activity," Bulletin of Mathematical Biophysics, vol. 5, pp. 115-133.

Minskey, M.L. & S. Papert (1969),*Perceptrons: An Introduction to Computational Geometry*, The MIT Press, Cambridge, MA.

Parker, D.B. (1986), "Second Order Backpropagation: An Optimal Adaptive Algorithm for Any Adaptive Network," Proc. of the International Congress on Neural Networks (ICNN), San Diego, CA, June.

Roberts, F.E. (1976), *Discrete Mathematical Models*, Prentice-Hall, Englewood Cliffs, NJ.

Rosenblatt, F. (1962), *Principles of Neurodynamics*, Spartan Books, Wash. D.C.

Rumelhart, D.E., J.L. McClelland & the PDP Research Group (1986), *Parallel Distributed Processing: Explorations in the Microstructure of Cognitions*, Volumes 1 & 2, The MIT Press, Cambridge, MA.

Sowa, J.F. (1984), *Conceptual Structures: Information Processing in Mind and Machine*, Addison-Wesley, Reading, MA.

Touretsky, D.S. & G.E. Hinton (1985), "Symbols Among the Neurons: Details of a Connectionist Inference Architecture," Proc. of the 9th International Joint Conference on Artificial Intelligence (IJCAI, vol 9), Morgan Kauffman, Los Altos, CA, pp. 238-243.

Widrow, B. (1962), "Generalization and Information Storage in Networks of Adaline Neurons," Self Organizing Systems - 1962, M.C. Yovits, et al, eds., Spartan Books, Wash. D.C., pp. 435-461.

Recent books on neural networks

Caudill, M. & C. Butler (1990), *Naturally intelligent systems*, MIT Press.

Dayhoff, J. (1990), *Neural network architectures*, Van Nostrand Reinhold.

Freeman, A.F. & Skapura, D.M. (1991), *Neural networks*, Addison-Wesley.

Hecht-Nielsen, R. (1990), *Neurocomputing*, Addison-Wesley.

Hertz, J., A. Krogh & R.G. Palmer (1991), *Introduction to the theory of neural computation*, Addison-Wesley.

Khanna, T. (1990), *Foundations of neural networks*, Addison-Wesley.

Maren, A., C. Harston & R. Pap (1990), *Handbook of neural computing applications*, Academic Press.

Pao, Y-H. (1989), *Adaptive pattern recognition and neural networks*, Addison Wesley.

Simpson, P.K. (1990), *Artificial neural systems*, Pergamon.

Wasserman, P.D. (1989), *Neural computing*, Van Nostrand Reinhold.

9

Adding Semantics to Semantic Data Models

Peter Creasy
Department of Computer Science,
University of Queensland,
St. Lucia 4067, Australia

Bernard Moulin
Département d'informatique,
Universite Laval,
Ste Foy, Quebec G1K 7P4, Canada

ABSTRACT

Information Systems design methodologies include a phase called data conceptual modeling. During this phase relevant objects, their properties and propositions involving these objects are identified and described in a data conceptual schema. Semantics are generally specified by constraints on possible database populations and no meaning is associated with the proposition names, apart from intuitive meaning. Using conceptual graphs as a conceptual schema language provides semantics at the proposition level. However conceptual graphs as proposed by Sowa are not ideal as a conceptual schema language. This has led us to propose an extended conceptual graphs model. In this paper we discuss the issues of data conceptual modeling, the extended model and a comparison with two information systems models.

9.1   INTRODUCTION

Information Systems design has become an important area in recent years as the advent of cheaper computing leads to "computerisation" of enterprises. The various methodologies take the systems analyst (or designer) and user through various phases resulting in a database, procedure specification etc. One of the phases in these methodologies is a data conceptual modeling phase where a model of the data perspective is built. During this phase relevant object classes, their properties and propositions involving these classes are identified and described in a data conceptual schema. The propositions represent possible fact instances. Semantics are provided at two levels:

- an informal level through the naming of the propositions;

- a formal level using constraints that restrict the instances which the propositions would otherwise permit.

Such schemas are expressed with languages called semantic data models (SDM) (Peckham and Maryanski, 1988)[1] Semantics of such models are not a linguistic level semantics such as provided by conceptual graphs. The informal level of semantics is open to different interpretations, while the restriction of fact instances does not necessarily convey meaning to any observer.

Alternatively, Sowa's (1984) conceptual graphs, while providing a linguistic level semantics are not ideal as a conceptual schema language. We have discussed some of the points involved elsewhere (Creasy and Moulin, 1989). As a solution to the problem we propose an extension to conceptual graphs which essentially combines the best points from conceptual graphs and semantic data models.

In section 9.2 we discuss the data conceptual modeling process. Section 9.3 examines the approach of using semantic data models and conceptual graphs as conceptual schema languages. We propose an extension to conceptual graphs in section 9.4 and show the equivalence with two fact-based semantic data models in section 9.5.

9.2   DATA CONCEPTUAL MODELING

During the data conceptual modeling phase the designer interacts with users in order to identify and describe the objects of the real world which are relevant for the application(s) to be built.

The designer interviews the users and attempts to select within their discourses some propositions which s/he considers useful for describing the relevant objects along with their properties. This task involves a naming activity as well as the selection of relevant concepts and propositions.

Various methodologies, such as NIAM (Verheijen and Van Bekkum, 1982; Nijssen and (Halpin, 1989) and REMORA (Rolland and Richard, 1982), suggest that the designer describes the relevant properties of the so-called Universe of Discourse in the form of elementary propositions, which will be used as inputs for data conceptual structures design. Then the designer attempts to "translate" the propositions in the form of data conceptual structures, according to the syntactic rules provided by the chosen semantic data model.

From a cognitive point of view, we can consider that the designer plays the role of an "intuitive human natural language understanding system": s/he interprets the natural language sentence obtained from the user, and, applying syntactic rules of an SDM, s/he creates a data conceptual structure which is supposed to represent "the semantic content" of the sentence.

The designer repeats this task for the various sentences obtained from the users and merges (or joins) the various data conceptual structures together in order to build a data conceptual schema. Then s/he validates his conceptual diagrams with the user, trying to compare them with what the user has said about the properties of the real world: for that purpose the designer must find some way to explain to the user how to interpret this

---

[1]The word "semantics" in this phrase indicates that they include more semantics than Codd's (Codd, 1970) original relational model.

abstract diagrammatic language. Fig. 9.1 provides a simplified picture of the design process. Although these steps are not usually performed consciously by the human designer, it is worth studying them if we want to build intelligent design systems to help designers. Several design tools intend to provide aids in automating the part of the design process that has been included in the dotted rectangle in Fig. 9.1.

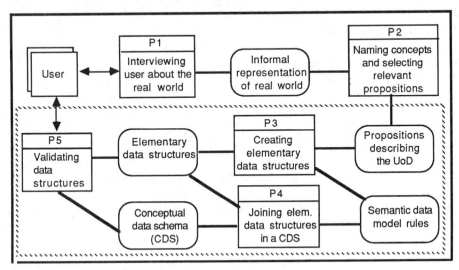

Fig. 9.1: Modeling the designer's behaviour

Process P3 is equivalent to a natural language analyzer which interprets the natural language propositions (theoretically at the lexical, syntactic and semantic levels) in order to generate data structures, which are represented in the formalism of the semantic data model. Most SDMs represent data structures in a form which is equivalent to semantic nets: they correspond to the conceptual level of the representation. In addition process P3 must provide rules (usually called constraints) which describe the set theoretic properties of the data structures: they correspond to the instance level of the representation. These constraints indicate declaratively which properties hold on the sets of instances associated with the concepts and relations of the data structure.

Process P4 applies specific rules to combine together the elementary data structures and create the conceptual data schema. In most design tools these processes are automated in very simplistic ways: only simple elementary sentences are accepted by the system; the system's behaviour is dependent on the chosen SDM; there is no normalized way of specifying relationships between concepts.

9.3   SEMANTIC DATA MODELS AND CONCEPTUAL GRAPHS

Semantic data models provide two kinds of notions:

- at the conceptual level: some semantic net representation associating concepts (or "entities" or "entity types") with conceptual relations (or "relationships" or "fact-types");

- at the instance level: the so-called constraints which enable the designer to specify the properties holding between the instance sets that correspond to the concepts and conceptual relations. When "populating the data base", only facts which verify these constraints can be recorded.

These two representation levels are important because an SDM must provide a conceptual language for interpreting semantically the users' sentences (providing the characteristics of the extension of the data base). SDMs such as NIAM can be extended to allow general constraints to be specified, using techniques similar to those used in conceptual graphs. However the semantics are always expressed as syntactic restrictions on the fact populations at the instance level. The semantics of the fact types are expressed informally by their naming and informal definitions in the data dictionary. Formal languages are not used to give any meaning to the fact types in SDMs. This has led us to the examination of the conceptual graph theory as a formal language to express data conceptual schemas.

Conceptual graphs provide a sound theory for representing knowledge structures at a conceptual level, with richer semantics based on results from cognitive psychology, natural language processing as well as logic. Conceptual graphs are also associated with a formal mapping to first order predicate logic. However conceptual graph theory does not provide means for specifying the set-theoretic properties of the database extension as SDMs do. Consequently we suggest the following guidelines for "adding more semantics to data models":

- use the conceptual graph model as a formal underlying conceptual language, providing richer semantics to SDMs: the conceptual graph model can be used as a "pivot model" to integrate conceptual data schemas developed with different SDMs;

- extend the conceptual graph model (called ECG model in this paper) in order to support constraints specification for the instance level of SDMs;

- provide a mapping between the ECG and some SDM such as E-R model or NIAM model. In the next section, we present the extended conceptual graph model ECG.

9.4 REFINING CONCEPTUAL GRAPHS FOR DATA MODELING

Basically we propose to refine some conceptual relation properties within the framework of conceptual graph theory in order to be able to describe semantic structures which are equivalent to those that are obtained with data conceptual models.

In order to use conceptual graphs to model data conceptual structures, we have to define a formal mapping between conceptual graphs and a derived relational database structure. We propose a new approach in which instead of marking concepts with quantifiers, we will mark conceptual relations with cardinalities in order to be able to map conceptual relations with functional dependencies in a derived relational structure (Moulin, 1989; Creasy and Moulin 1989).

This approach is directly compatible with data conceptual models and enables us to manipulate conceptual structures, using the operations that are applicable to conceptual graphs. We describe data conceptual structures using conceptual graphs. Hence all the definitions and techniques introduced by Sowa to specify and manipulate conceptual graphs hold in our framework.

9.4.1   The Proposed Model

In order to use conceptual graphs to design databases we must differentiate two levels of abstraction: the conceptual and instance levels.

The instance level corresponds to the extension of the database and contains the object occurrences stored in the database. Each object occurrence can be associated with an object type (or domain). We use a formalism derived from Codd's relational data model to represent data structures at the instance level.

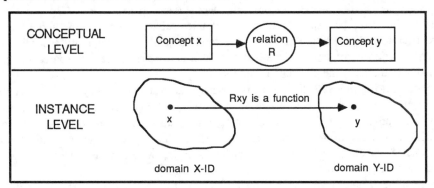

Fig. 9.2: The mapping between conceptual and instance levels

The conceptual level corresponds to the intension of the database and contains the data constructs used to structure the object occurrences stored in the database. We shall use a formalism derived from Sowa's conceptual graph theory to represent data structures at the conceptual level.

The mapping between conceptual and instance level

In this section our examples are related to the conceptual graph:

$$[PERSON] \leftarrow (BENF) \leftarrow [EARN] \rightarrow (PTNT) \rightarrow [SALARY]$$

- Each concept `[CONCEPT-TYPE:concept-referent]` is associated with a unique identifier CONCEPT-TYPE-ID which can either be chosen by the designer, or automatically generated. For instance `[PERSON]` is associated with PERSON-ID as an identifier. At the instance level the concept identifier represents a domain of objects occurrences that conforms to the type label of the associated concept.

- Each conceptual relation (which will be mapped to a database relation) is characterized by a relation type and a referent `(RELATION-TYPE:relation-referent)`: the RELATION-TYPE corresponds to the name which is currently assigned to the relation in Sowa's theory; the relation-referent is chosen in order to identify uniquely various conceptual relations with the same RELATION-TYPE.

- Each conceptual relation `(RELATION-TYPE:relation-referent)` is associated with a unique identifier CONCEPTUAL-RELATION-ID which can either be chosen by the designer, or automatically generated. For instance, the conceptual relation `(BENF:EAR-PER)` is associated with BENF-EAR-PER-ID as an identifier.

- Each binary conceptual relation R, such as $[X] \rightarrow (R) \rightarrow [Y]$, can be mapped to a database relation $R\text{-}ID$ (according to Codd's relation data model), where $X\text{-}ID$, the identifier of the input concept X, is the key or independent domain, and $Y\text{-}ID$, the identifier of the output concept Y, is an attribute dependent on the key.

At the instance level the relation $R\text{-}ID$ corresponds to a function from the domain of values of $X\text{-}ID$ to the domain of values of $Y\text{-}ID$: it is usually called a ("strong") functional dependency in the relational model. We have the following property: For each value x of $X\text{-}ID$ we can associate one and only one value y of $Y\text{-}ID$, such as $y = R - ID(x)$.

Fig. 9.2 illustrates the mapping that we have defined between the conceptual and instance levels. Therefore the direction of conceptual relation arrows is meaningful according to the set theoretic interpretation at the instance level and characterizes the source and the destination domains of the associated function.

In Moulin (Moulin, 1982) the notion of "weak functional dependency" was introduced to deal with some of the issues related to the problem of so-called "null values" (Codd, 1979). A function F defines a weak functional dependency between domains $X\text{-}ID$ and $Y\text{-}ID$, if there exists a domain $Z\text{-}ID$ subset of $Y\text{-}ID$, such as F defines a strong functional dependency between $X\text{-}ID$ and $Z\text{-}ID$. According to F we can associate to each value x of $X\text{-}ID$ at most one value y of $Y\text{-}ID$, such as $y = R - ID(x)$.

Hence at the instance level, the relation $R\text{-}ID$ may correspond to a function which defines either a weak or a strong functional dependency between the associated domains.

- Each n-ary conceptual relation R, such as $[X_1], \ldots, [X_n] \rightarrow (R) \rightarrow [Y]$, can be mapped to a database relation $R\text{-}ID$ (according to Codd's relational data model), where the concatenation of input concept identifiers $\{X_1\text{-}ID \mid \ldots \mid X_n\text{-}ID\}$ is the key of the relation, and $Y\text{-}ID$, the identifier of the output concept, as an attribute dependent on the key.

At the instance level the n input concepts $\{[X1], \ldots, [Xn]\}$ are mapped to the Cartesian product of domains $X_1\text{-}ID, \ldots, X_n\text{-}ID$ and $R\text{-}ID$ is a function from $X_1\text{-}ID \times \ldots \times X_n\text{-}ID$ to the domain of values $Y\text{-}ID$.

Specifying relationship constraint

The specification of integrity constraints is an important issue in data conceptual modeling (Brodie, 1984). Relationship constraints are those of mappings in mathematics (e.g. $1:1$, $1:N$, $N:M$ etc.), as well as constraints concerning the existence of object occurrences and the dependency of one object on other objects. The referential integrity, for instance, requires that if object A is referred to by object B, then B can exist only if A exists.In data conceptual models relationship constraints have been often specified by associating cardinalities with the relationships that relate entities.

Given two domains $E1$ and $E2$, a binary relationship R existing between $E1$ and $E2$ defines two mappings $R : E1 \rightarrow E2$ and $R^{-1} : E2 \rightarrow E1$, one the inverse of the other. Cardinality of the mapping refers to the number of occurrences of $E1$ that can be related to occurrences of $E2$, and vice versa. For each mapping of a binary relationship we can specify a minimum and a maximum cardinality (Tsichritzis and Lochovski, 1982). Cardinalities can take the values 0, 1 or n.

On the branch relating entity $E1$ and relationship R we associate a couple of integers *(min-card1, max-card1)* which represent the minimal and maximal cardinalities of the mapping $R : E1 \rightarrow E2$. Conversely on the branch relating entity $E2$ and relationship R we associate a couple of integers *(min-card2, max-card2)* which represent the minimal and maximal cardinalities of the mapping $R^{-1} : E2 \rightarrow E1$.

Consider the example of Fig. 9.3 where using the formalism of the E-R model, we represent the relationship EARNS linking entities EMPLOYEE and SALARY, and the cardinalities corresponding to the constraint every employee earns a unique salary.

In our framework each conceptual relation can be mapped either with a weak or a strong functional dependency at the instance level. We propose to mention that characteristic at the conceptual level by associating cardinalities with conceptual relations.

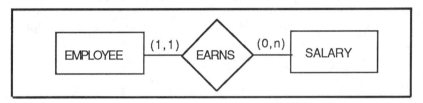

Fig. 9.3: Cardinalities in the ER model

Given the binary conceptual relation [Conc.i]→(Rel.k)→[Conc.j], we can associate with it the following minimal (n_i) and maximal (x_j) cardinalities

$$
\begin{array}{ccccc}
 & n_i, x_i & & n_j, x_j & \\
\texttt{[Conc.i]} & \longrightarrow & \texttt{(Rel.k)} & \longrightarrow & \texttt{[Conc.j]}
\end{array}
$$

Since in our framework conceptual relations are mapped to functional dependencies, $x_i = 1$ and $x_j = n$. If $n_i = 1$ we have the mapping to a strong functional dependency; if $n_i = 0$ we have the mapping to a weak functional dependency. The participation of each occurrence of concept j in the relation may be mandatory $(n_j = 1)$ or optional $(n_j = 0)$. The cardinality x_j equals 1 in the only case where the relation, which will be labelled (EQVL), indicates an equivalence between the two concepts.

Refining the definition of conceptual relations

As a rule we can state that according to the properties of conceptual relations in our framework, it is sufficient to indicate minimal cardinalities on the arrows of the relation, since maximal cardinalities are always 1 on the source concept side, and generally n on the sink concept side. We propose the following notation :

$$[\texttt{Conc.i}] - n_i \rightarrow (\texttt{Rel.k}) - n_j \rightarrow [\texttt{Conc.j}]$$

If $n_i = 1$ this notation is equivalent to the logical formula :

$$(\forall x) \ (\exists 1 \ y) \ (\texttt{Conc.i(x)} \supset \texttt{Conc.j(y)} \land \texttt{Rel.k(x,y)}).$$

If $n_i = 0$ this notation is equivalent to the logical formula :

```
(∀x)  (∃0 y)  (Conc.i(x) ⊃ Conc.j(y) ∧ Rel.k(x,y))
```

with the convention that (∃0) represents an "outmost" existential quantifier.

If $n_j = 1$ every occurrence of Conc.j must be related at least with one occurrence of Conc.i. If $n_j = 0$ some occurrence of Conc.j may not be related with an occurrence of Conc.i.

For instance the conceptual graph:

```
[PERSON]← 0−(BENF)← 1−[EARN]−1 →(PTNT)−1 →[SALARY].
```

bears the properties : "for every occurrence of earning we associate a unique occurrence of person and a unique occurrence of salary";"it can exit some occurrences of persons without any earning"; "every occurrence of salary must be at least related to one occurrence of earning".

These definitions can be extended to n-ary conceptual relations. Consider the example of a map composed of areas separated by frontiers. The graph:

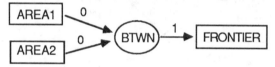

is equivalent to the logical formula:

$$(∀x) (∃y) (∃0\ z) (AREA1(x) ∧ AREA2(y) ⊃ FRONTIER(z) ∧ BTWN(x,y,z));$$

but every FRONTIER must be associated with two AREAs.

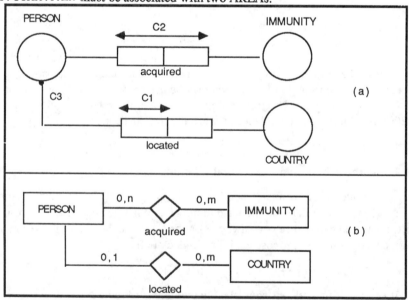

Fig. 9.4: The NIAM and ER models

Our interpretation of conceptual relations enables us to provide a richer semantics in order to use conceptual graphs for database conceptual modeling. Furthermore we do not need to introduce quantifiers in concept referents, neither actors in conceptual graphs to specify functional dependencies. Consequently using our framework for specifying data conceptual structures, we are able to apply the operations that Sowa defined on conceptual graphs in order to manipulate data conceptual schematas.

In our framework actors are used to specify procedural information which must be associated with conceptual graphs: procedures to determine the value of some attributes according to derivation rules, logical mapping with specialized procedures etc.

9.5   THE EQUIVALENCE OF ECG, E-R AND NIAM Models

Two widely used conceptual schema languages are NIAM and E-R (Chen 1976). Examples of conceptual (sub)schemas are shown in Figs. 4(a) (NIAM) and 4(b) (E-R). The fact types express that people may acquire immunity (Acquire) and may be located in a country (Located).

There is an implied predicate on the entity types (sets) PERSON, IMMUNITY and COUNTRY which specify the entity population. In Fig. 9.4(a) the constraint $C1$ (arrow) is a functional dependency which expresses person $\rightarrow$ country, while $C2$ expresses person, immunity $\rightarrow$ $\oslash$. The constraint C3 is a mandatory role constraint (viz. every person is located in a country). These structures may be mapped to relational structures using what are essentially synthesis algorithms.

We have shown elsewhere (Creasy, 1988) the awkwardness of mapping between NIAM and conceptual graphs. To demonstrate the mapping between ECG, NIAM and E-R we restrict the examples to binary relationships. Examples of the equivalences between the ECG, NIAM and E-R models is shown in Fig. 9.5. In Figs. 9.5(a) and 9.5(c) the conceptual relation EQVL indicates the one to one mapping. All three models permit subtyping, with E-R and NIAM explicitly represent subtyping.

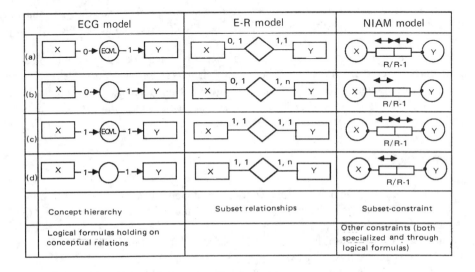

Fig. 9.5: A comparison of the ECG, NIAM and ER models

The constraints can be expressed in conceptual graphs using existential graphs. A similar technique has been used to extend NIAM (Creasy, 1989) beyond the specialised constraints. This enables expressions of the power of first order logic to be expressed. E-R, however, has few constructs to enable constraints to be specified beyond the cardinality constraints.

With the ECG model we have a language as powerful as NIAM and E-R. We can use conceptual relations which correspond to the relationship sets of E-R and fact types of NIAM. However, we also can use the well-understood conceptual relations to provide the additional semantics missing from SDMs. This can be done by defining each relationship set or fact type with conceptual graphs. For example the NIAM fact type VISIT of Fig. 9.6(a) can be defined by the ECG diagram of Fig. 9.6(b). This allows the informal naming semantics to be reinforced with linguistic level semantics.

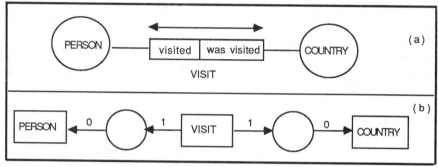

Fig. 9.6: Definition of NIAM fact type with ECG

9.6   CONCLUSION

We believe that semantic data models should be able to represent more of the Universe Of Discourse than is currently possible. An important feature of graphical conceptual schemas is that a user (who is the universe of discourse expert) and the designer/analyst, who communicate through the conceptual schema, should have as much of the semantics unambiguously presented to them as possible.

We have argued that this is not currently sufficiently done. Conceptual graphs offer an opportunity to represent more meaning from the Universe Of Discourse. The extension we have made to conceptual graphs takes advantage of this feature of conceptual graphs while permitting the functional dependencies, so important to mapping data structures, to be represented in an integrated conceptual schema.

BIBLIOGRAPHY

Brodie, M.L. (1984) "On the Development of Data Models," in *On Conceptual Modelling, Perspectives from Artificial Intelligence, Databases, and Programming Languages,* (eds) Brodie *et al.*, Springer Verlag, New York.

Chen, P.P. (1976) "The Entity-Relationship Model - Toward a Unified View of Data," ACM Trans. Database Syst. 1, 1 (Mar), pp9-36.

Codd, E.F. (1970) "A Relational Model of Data for Large Shared Data Banks," Comm. ACM Vol. 13, No. 6.

Codd, E.F. (1979) "Extending the Database Relational Model to Capture More Meaning," ACM Transactions on Database Systems 4, 4.

Creasy, P.N. (1988) "Extending Graphical Conceptual Schema Languages", Internal Report, University of Queensland.

Creasy, P. N. (1989) "ENIAM: A More Complete Conceptual Schema Language" to be presented to the 15th International Conference on Very Large Data Bases, Amsterdam, August 1989.

Creasy, P.N. and Moulin B. (1989) "Refining Conceptual Graphs for Data Conceptual Modelling,in proceedings of the" in Proc. of the Fourth Annual Workshop on Conceptual Structures, (eds) J. Nagle and T. Nagle, Available from AAAI.

Moulin, B. (1982) *Une méthode pour la modélisation du systéme d'information en environnement centralisé et réparti,* in Proc. of the 1982 Canadian Information Processing Society National Conference, CIPS'82, Saskatoon, May 1982.

Moulin, B. (1989) "Refining the Conceptual Graph Theory to Model Data Conceptual Structures," Technical Report No. 106, Computer Science Department, University of Queensland, Australia, February 1989.

Moulin B., Kabbaj A. (1988) "Architecture de SMGC: un systîme de manipulation de graphes conceptuels," in *Les actes du colloque international informatique et langue naturelle,* Nantes, France, October 1988.

Nijssen, G.M. and Halpin, T.A. (1989) *Conceptual Schema and Relational Database Design: A Fact-Based Approach,* Prentice Hall.

Olle, T.W., Sol, H.G. and Verijn-Stewart, A.A. (eds) (1982) *Information Systems Design Methodologies: A Comparative Review,* North-Holland, Amsterdam.

Peckham, J. and Maryanski, F. (1988) "Semantic Data Models," ACM Comp. Surveys, 20, 3.

Rolland, C. and Richard, C. (1982) "The Remora Methodology for Information Systems Design Management" in Olle *et al.* (1982).

Sowa, J.F. (1984) *Conceptual Structures: Information Processing in Mind and Machine,* Addison-Wesley, Reading, Massachusetts.

Tsichritzis, D.C., Lochovsky, F. H. (1982) *Data Models,* Prentice Hall, Englewood Cliffs, N.J.

Verheijen, G.M.A. and Van Bekkum, J. (1982) "NIAM: An Information Analysis Method" in Olle *et al.* (1982).

10

Meta-Modeling Systems Analysis Primitives

Andrew Feller
Boeing Commercial Aircraft Group,
Seattle, Washington, USA

Rob Rucker
Arizona State University,
Industrial and Management Systems Engineering Research Center,
Tempe, Arizona, USA

ABSTRACT

We present a set of conceptual structure principles for "meta-modeling" a class of structured systems analysis primitives using conceptual graphs and type hierarchies. The meta-model of these primitives is referred to as a canon. We apply this canon to the well known structured analysis "language", IDEF0. Schemata for the graphic and annotation features of IDEF0 are presented, along with derived extensions to the language useful for manufacturing communication systems analysis. The need for the canon to contain two type hierarchies, a conceptual one and a conceptual relational one, is shown and detailed. The concept type hierarchy lays out two basic categories of IDEF0 model primitives: entity and activity, while the conceptual relation hierarchy lays out the interactions (cross products) between these two types and their subtypes, i.e. (entity, entity), (entity, activity), and (activity, activity). Given the approach suggested by this paper, the IDEF0 constructs can be clearly organized and classified, and in addition, the capabilities and limits of the model can be graphically studied.

10.1   INTRODUCTION

Our presentation begins with a general discussion of the meta-modeling approach for analyzing systems analysis primitives. The approach is then applied to IDEF0 model elements, and their interactions. As an aid to the reader, the main features of IDEF0 are first presented along with several graphical examples. Once the IDEF0 model is placed in a broader perspective, general structural features emerge as well as gaps that need some attention, specifically, timing and feedback. As a result of examining the IDEF0 meta-model, the authors were led to develop several enrichments involving both the syntax of the model, and interpretative modifications including ideas from Petri Nets. The resultant enhanced IDEF0 model was implemented in object oriented software supporting a timed petri-net simulation.

10.2   THE META-MODEL ENVIRONMENT

The application of conceptual structure principles to the systems analysis domain can clarify our understanding of the structured techniques used in systems analysis. This clarity is generated by "disambiguating" the primitive constructs used by systems analysis tools and techniques, making explicit the representational adequacy (or inadequacy) of the modeled toolset. By abstracting "up" one layer, we can gain a broader perspective that allows a grasp of the basic features of a modeling technique before we get lost in the mechanics of trying to use it. We have constructed a diagram, Fig. 10.1, that captures some idea of this approach.

Our application of conceptual structure principles to a systems modeling technique yielded a model-of-a-model, or "meta-model", which allowed further work to both automate the existing toolset, and to enhance it by incorporating additional primitives which the analysis exposed as lacking for our particular purpose. The environment is considered to be very general and could be, as it was for the authors, an electronics assembly line. In this particular case, an IDEF0 model was constructed to specify the requirements for shop floor data communications associated with the electronics assembly line, and then enhanced by conceptually analyzing the available primitives using the ideas developed here. This resulted in an enhanced modeling approach tailored to the problem at hand.

The meta-modeling approach discovered through this process revolved around the development of two distinct type hierarchies, one for systems analysis primitives, and a second one for the interactions allowed between these primitives, i.e.: primitive cross-products. These two type hierarchies fit nicely within the proscribed definitions for "concept" and "conceptual relation" type hierarchies respectively. This discovery then allowed us to use conceptual graphs to diagram and explore the modeling constructs which the primitives and their allowed interactions support, and to think of some new ones. Our results are presented following an introduction to the IDEF0 modeling language given below.

10.3   THE IDEF0 LANGUAGE

Structured Analysis (SA) was developed in the mid-1970's by Douglas T. Ross and his colleagues at SofTech (Ross, 1977) as a general approach for handling complex system problems. The graphical techniques of SA are incorporated into a methodology called Structured Analysis and Design Technique SADT[1] which include personnel roles and an author reader cycle for model development and refinement. SA was adopted as one of the definition tools (IDEF0) in the Integrated Computer Aided Manufacturing (ICAM) program, and has since been used to formally model many manufacturing enterprises. The graphical language of SA provides a limited set of primitive constructs for building a structured graphical model similar to a blueprint which is based on a sequence of diagrams with concise supporting text. The notation is based on boxes and arrows. In activity modeling, the boxes represent activities, events, or "happenings", and the arrows represent entities or "things". The arrows furthermore represent connections between happenings by explicitly

---

[1] SADT is a Trademark of SofTech, Inc.

delineating the linking together of happenings by things. The diagrams are arranged into a hierarchical tree structure based on rigorous decomposition of the activities appearing in a high-level overview diagram. The decomposition strategy is directed by the model's purpose, and the depth and scope of the decomposition is constrained by the models viewpoint. This decomposition of diagrams is applied recursively until the depth exposes sufficient detail to accomplish the model's purpose.

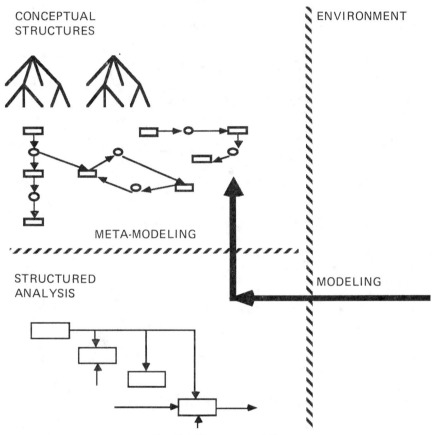

Fig. 10.1 The meta-modeling process

Ross claims that SA derives its structure from the way our minds work, and from the way we understand real-world situations and problems. In particular, SA partitions a universe of discourse into two sets: its activities or "happenings", and its entities or "things".

> "...consideration of how we view our space-time world shows that we always understand anything and everything in terms of both things and happenings. This is why all of our languages have both nouns and verbs-and this, in turn, yields the means by which SA language is universal, and can absorb any other language as a component part. SA supplies rigorous structural connections to any language whose nouns and verbs it absorbs in order to talk about things and happenings." (Ross, 1977)

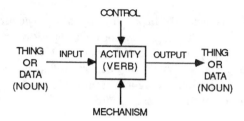

a) Structured Analysis Box

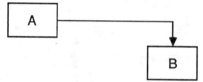

b) Output of box A is input to box B
   (Sequence)

A

B

c) Output of box A is control to box B
   (Dominance)

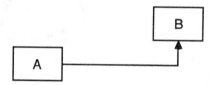

d) Output of box A is mechanism to box B
   (Support)

Fig. 10.2 SA graphical notation

SA accomplishes this bold claim by mapping the nouns in natural language to arrows, and the verbs in natural language to boxes. Additional features in the graphical language allow explicit graphical delineation and classification of some of the relationships between the things and activities in a model.

Specifically the interactions between entities and activities are classified graphically as either input, control, output, or mechanism, and given an "ICOM" code which is unique for the diagram. Certain other interactions are also represented such as entity bundling and branching, and dominance, sequence, and support interactions between activities. Fig. 10.2. provides an overview of the graphical conventions for the SA box, the fundamental construction for representing activities.

The description for the box features are as follows: Input: that which is operated on or transformed by the function represented within the box. Output: that which is created from the input by means of the function represented within the box. Control: that which directs the function represented to occur at a specific time or in a specific manner. Mechanism: that which performs the function represented (both equipment and personnel).

These primitives are however insufficient for representing system dynamics.

> "The SADT box and arrow language describes all the activities and things of a system, and thus helps to describe the functionality of a system. Sometimes, however, just the graphics of an SADT activity model is an insufficient description of how a system actually operates. Notice that we said 'insufficient' not 'inaccurate.' If properly developed, a validated SADT activity model accurately describes system functionality from a static perspective, but this may not be enough to describe the other aspects of system operation and behavior required to get a complete understanding of how a system is expected to work." (Marc, 1988)

Two SA notations which may be used to augment a diagram are property labels, and activation rules. A property label is a square note, attached to either a box or an arrow by a squiggle, that describes a single property of the connected model element. IDEF0 has provision for an activation rule structure that allows a description of the conditions under which a box may be activated. Activation rules in SA are based on a notation similar to an abstract grammar that describes a single combination of input, control, mechanism, and output for a specific activity of a particular model. Activation rules are made up of a box number, a unique activation identifier, preconditions, and postconditions, and represented with the following syntax:

> "box * activation : preconditions ⟶ postconditions."

The activation rules can further be identified to a particular model if more than one model is being considered. The preconditions and postconditions are logical expressions of ICOM codes joined by Boolean operators, and used to describe what is required for, and what results from, a given activation of the related activity box. An example activation rule from (Marc, 1988) for an activity "Setup Machining Place" is presented in Fig. 10.3. The use of property labels and activation rules is optional, governed by the modeler's discretion and desire to make explicit various details about the system under study.

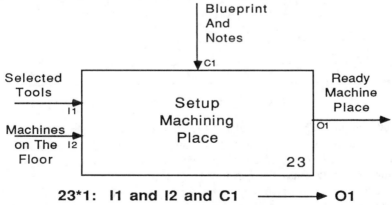

$$23*1: \quad I1 \text{ and } I2 \text{ and } C1 \quad \longrightarrow \quad O1$$

Fig. 10.3 An IDEF0 activation rule

Figs. 10.4 and 10.5 provide an example of the use of the IDEF0 language to present a high level perspective on a production environment. Together these diagrams represent the general flow of both information and material through the critical activities performed in the environment under study. The context for our implementation environment is shown in Fig. 10.5. This diagram is the explosion or "child" diagram of the middle box shown in Fig. 10.4.

10.4   META-MODELING SA USING CONCEPTUAL STRUCTURES

IDEF0 or Structured Analysis (SA) divides a system ontology into two primitive object classes: activities, and entities. The activity concept, represented as a box in SA, is a specialization of the more general concept of an "act". In SA, an activity participates in specialized relationships with entity concepts, represented as arrows. The SA entity is a specialization of the more general concept of an "entity". These primitives are specialized in that they can interact with each other in only a limited number of well defined ways.

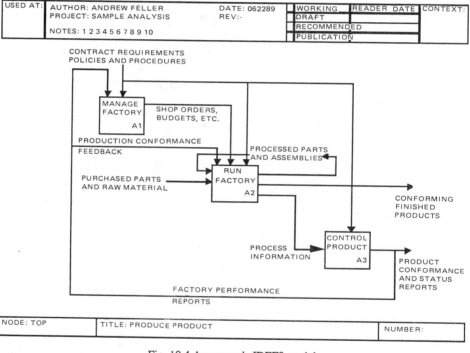

Fig. 10.4 An example IDEF0 model

SA in general, and IDEF0 in particular, is an extremely general systems analysis modeling tool. The generality comes from the fact that any kind of system related activity can be represented. The SA box can represent a manufacturing operation performed on a part, an information processing transaction performed on a database, a resource delivery performed on a fixture, or even a hiring activity performed on an employee. The common element between these examples is that the box is used to represent a transformation from a "before" to an "after" state of affairs. The arrow is a generic icon used to represent all entities which interact with, or are transformed by, the activities in the model. This general treatment of activities and entities is given rigor, however, in allowing only four roles for entities to assume with respect to a given activity: input, output, control, or mechanism. The SA graphical notation represents the limited ways in which the entity and activity modeling primitives can interact by attaching interacting arrows to a specific side of the box based upon the interaction's type. For example, in SA, an entity arrow which interacts with an activity as an input always points to the activity boxes' left side, an output points away from the right side, a control enters from the top, and a mechanism from the bottom. These role types are not assumed by the entities of themselves, but rather by the entities with respect to a given activity. For example, the same electronic assembly may be an output from one manufacturing activity, and an input to another, subsequent manufacturing activity. These relationship roles apply to the interactions or "relations" between the entities and their related activities.

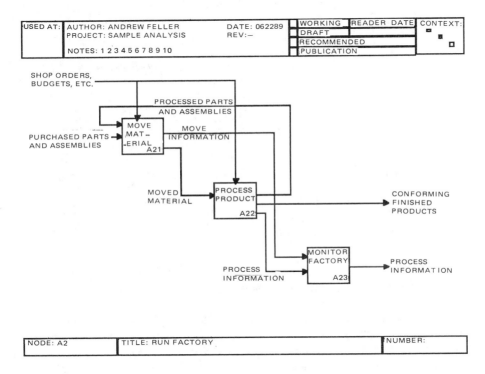

Fig. 10.5 IDEF0 Diagram of manufacturing context for this study.

These observations about the IDEF0 language provided the rationale for our meta-modeling approach. Both the activity and entity concept classes, and the limited classes of their interactions allowed in SA are represented. Based on the analysis of the IDEF0 primitives, a pair of type hierarchies have been constructed. Here we have chosen to consider three types of model element: Activation rules, activities, and entities. These are concepts that may be o rganized in a type hierarchy as shown. If we consider how these concepts may be interconnected, we are led to construct the conceptual relation hierarchy shown in the lower part of Fig. 10.6.

10.5   SA PRIMITIVES AS CONCEPTUAL GRAPHS

We apply our type hierarchy and the basics of Conceptual Graph notation in order to model the IDEF0 activity element, called the SA box. This is shown in Fig. 10.7. A Conceptual Graph representation of the SA activation rule is also shown in this figure. Of particular importance is the ability to visualize these definitions and also directly implement them in software which can be used for analysis of the resulting model.

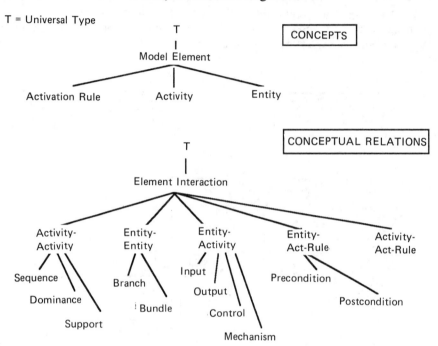

Fig. 10.6 Type hierarchies for structured analysis/IDEF0.

The type definition for a model activity indicates the four allowed entity-activity interaction types (input, control, output, mechanism) and also indicates that the activity is labeled with a node number. The activation rule's type definition is more interesting. Here, the activity's related input, control, and mechanism entity sets are related to the activation rule as "pre-conditions", and the activity's output entity set is analogously related to the activation rule as a "post-condition". The activation rule is then related to the activity (AR-ACT) whose pre- and post-conditions are being modeled. Additional type definitions for SA primitives modeled as conceptual relations are given in Fig. 10.8. These relational definitions explicitly represent the relationships created between activities by the configuration of their connecting entities. Extensions to the set of available modeling primitives will also be presented by means of conceptual graphs in the next section.

Type Model Activity (X) is:

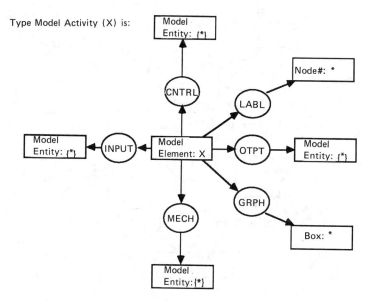

Type Activation Rule (X) is:

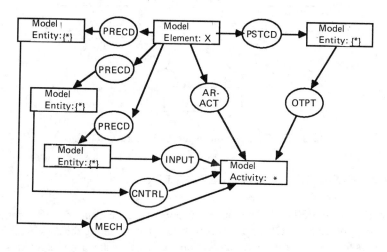

Fig. 10.7 Type definitions for IDEF0 activation rules Relations

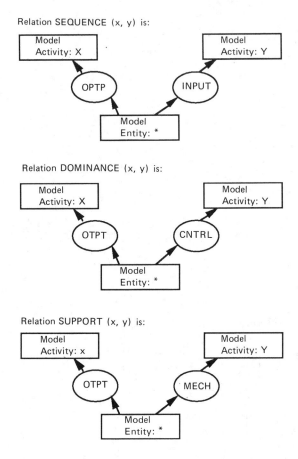

Fig. 10.8 Type definitions for IDEF0 activity relations

10.6   APPLYING THE CANON: IDEF0 EXTENSIONS

The extensions to IDEF0 were developed to support a practical application in data communications requirements specification. This task required modeling the data communication
requirements for tracking the status of electronic assemblies at various stages prior to final
assembly. In modeling the process the authors made use of the extended type hierarchies
shown in Fig. 10.9. The extensions incorporated in these hierarchies fall into two categories,
new modeling concepts, and new conceptual relations. The new modeling concepts are
developed as either specialization subtypes of the model activity and model entity concept
types, or entirely new (to IDEF0) concepts included to provide for model execution. The
new conceptual relations are developed either to relate the new concepts, or as extensions
to the set of role types allowed in the traditional IDEF0 methodology.

The original IDEF0 primitive classes of entity and activity are subclassified using an
object oriented approach. This approach is motivated by the observation that entities present
in a manufacturing system can be classified according to differences in the fundamental
nature of the entities and the mechanisms which manipulate and transform their attributes.

One fundamental breakdown suggested by the graphic classification of entities found in A-Graphs (Lundsberg, 1979) is the "real" or physical entity versus the "message" or information entity. This object oriented breakdown according to the fundamental nature of the entity and its relationships with the environment allows specialization of attribute definitions appropriate for the entities subtype. For example, information entities can be assigned a size attribute indicating the average number of bytes the entity contains, or a material entity can be assigned a handling code that specifies the type of material handling required. This classification allows the conceptual canon to represent information about the entities in the model, and supports the development of software to perform analysis based on this information. Additional extensions for information entities could include data dictionary references and a complexity index representing the amount of computing resources required to store and extract the entity.

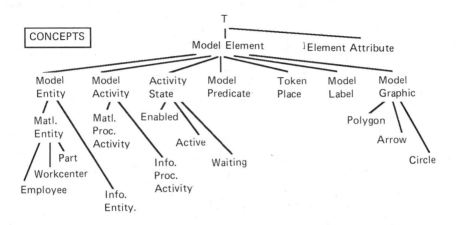

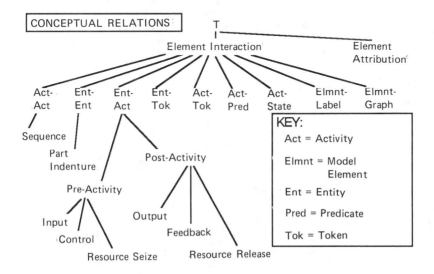

Fig. 10.9 An extended type hierarchy for IDEF0 in an application context.

The activity primitive is broken down in a similar fashion. A corresponding classification of activities in the meta-model is defined based upon the types of entities which are transformed from "input" to "output". An activity which transforms material using information only for control and feedback can be classified as a material processing activity (MPA), while an activity which processes information as its primary function (information entities as both input and output) can be classified as an information processing activity (IPA). Classifying the activities in this way corresponds roughly to several modeling approaches used in practice including the IDEF0 triple diagonal (Shunk, 86), and IBM's Integrated Manufacturing Modeling System (IMMS) (Engelke *et al.*, 1985).

The above discussion is made more explicit in Figs. 10 and 11 which present conceptual graph type definitions. These type definitions are still relatively coarse. Additional, more specialized subtypes for material entities such as classes of machine or operators could easily be added, but are left out at this point to allow flexibility for specific applications.

TYPE DEFINITIONS

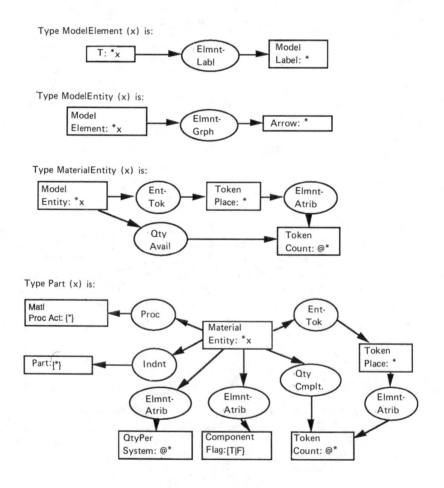

Fig. 10.10 Type definitions for IDEF0 extensions - entity specialization.

The set of interaction classes provided by IDEF0 is also extended to include additional role types and structural connections important for modeling manufacturing information and control systems.

TYPE DEFINITIONS

Type Model Activity (x) is

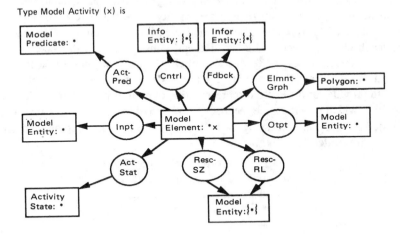

Type Material Processing Activity (x) is

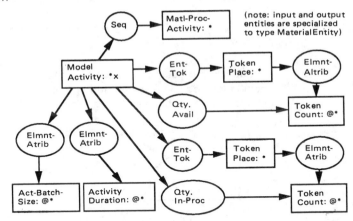

Fig. 10.11

As mentioned earlier, the role interactions provided for in IDEF0 are mapped to the canon's conceptual relations. The set of role types is expanded to include feedback interactions, and to provide domain roles which more clearly define the notion of manufacturing resources. The conceptual relations then formalize the allowed roles which manufacturing entities can assume in the knowledge representation. The expanded set of role relations

follows naturally from the initial meta-model of interactions between IDEF0 modeling elements presented earlier. The expansion proceeds by first noticing that the interactions between entities and activities can be divided into two major classes: those which must precede the commencement of an activity's activation ("pre-activity" interactions), and those which come after ("post-activity" interactions). In typical IDEF0 activities, there are three pre-activity interactions (input, control, and mechanism), and one post-activity interaction (output). The input/output pre-activity, post-activity pair suggests a similar arrangement be devised to model pre-activity, post-activity pairs for the control and mechanism relations too. This idea is incorporated into the knowledge base design as control/feedback, and mechanism_seize / mechanism_release pre-activity, post-activity relation pairs.

An example of this type of extension made to the set of explicit IDEF0 interaction classes is the feedback role which an information entity may assume with respect to an activity. IDEF0 provides for modeling feedback implicitly by directing an entity which interacts as an output from one activity, to another activity where it interacts as a control. Extending IDEF0 to provide for the explicit representation of an information feedback interaction at the activity which generates the feedback allows feedback information flow requirements predicated on material processing in the factory to be explicitly represented for analysis. Fig. 10.12 illustrates this idea.

Feedback represented implicitly based
on subsequent control relationship.

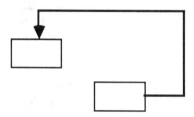

Feedback represented explicitly at the
point the fedback is generated without
relation to its subsequent use.

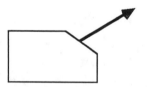

Fig. 10.12 Feedback representations

The additional classes of interaction were made explicit by examining the cross products of the basic modeling primitive classes. This technique of examining the cross products of major primitive classes to aid in classification and "disambiguation" of the interaction classes was significant in the development. The explicit representation of the interaction classes adds rigor to the basic IDEF0 language, and provides a necessary vehicle for its extension.

10.7 INCORPORATING PETRI NET PRIMITIVES IN THE IDEF0 CANON

Manufacturing data communication system requirements originate from both the dynamics and the communication needs associated with the physical process. So far, our discussion has only addressed the representation of entities linked to the processes (activities) which generate and require them. In this section, new concepts and conceptual relations are presented which provide for the necessary representation of system dynamics. These concepts center around the use of logic based triggers and tokens to indicate the local state of entities and activities in the modeled system.

A manufacturing (material processing) activity can be modeled as a Petri net. An example of such a net is shown in Fig. 10.13. This net incorporates a set of pre-activity entity/activity relations as input places t o the activity start transition, along with a new relation (input place) called a model predicate or "trigger". During processing, tokens are held in a processing place, and on completion, a second transition fires, reloading a corresponding set of related post-activity places.

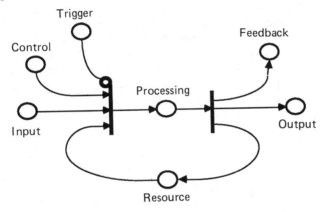

Fig. 10.13 A Petri net for a manufacturing activity

This network model of a manufacturing activity incorporates places for tokens which specifically represent the information components required to be communicated through the manufacturing information system. The Petri net model represents the timing and concurrence of the events impacting information flow and their prerequisite conditions, allowing the dynamical features of the information requirements model to be analyzed through procedures for net execution.

Activity states can be used to represent the presence of tokens in various combinations of an activity's related places. If all input places for a given activity are loaded as required by the activity's predicate or "trigger", then the activity is in the "enabled" state, and can be activated. On activation, a specified number of tokens are removed from the input places, and "combined" to form tokens in the activity's "in-process" place. The activity remains active for a duration determined from an attribute of the activity. At the end of this time, the "activity-end" transition loads the output places from the activity, and the activity enters a "waiting" state.

The "trigger" or model predicate is a key primitive required in our representation. Similar to the activation rule of SA, the trigger defines preconditions for the activation of a modeled activity, and is used to control execution and analysis of the dynamic features of the modeled system. The simplest trigger predicate checks for the presence of tokens in the input places, requiring that the typical Petri-net preconditions for transition firing be satisfied for activation. More complex predicates may check for additional conditions such as the presence of a specified number of tokens in an input place to allow processing of a "batch", or some other condition in the model.

The set of triggers in a model can be grouped together as a schematic cluster for the model predicate concept. Specific trigger instances are defined as conceptual graphs using the material implication ("if p - then q") construction: ("$\neg(p \wedge \neg q)$"). Trigger graphs assert certain conditions in the m odel which must be met for an activity to be enabled, and are associated with specific activities by another conceptual relation. An example model predicate or trigger graph is given in Fig. 10.14. This graph asserts that an activity is enabled if the token place associated with the activity's input entity contains a number of tokens equal to or greater than the activity's batch size. Trigger graphs such as this provide a formal basis for representing the dynamics of the modeled system, and organize the model execution conditions for software implementation.

Unlike SA, we recommend that each activity have only one possible type of activation. Also, the activation "rule" or trigger may include model elements which do not interact with the activity as input, control, or mechanism (e.g., a timed trigger). Restricting activity definitions to one type of activation is similar to the event partitioning basis for defining essential activities as developed by McMenamin and Palmer (1984). This partitioning of activities according to triggering events is shown by McMenamin and Palmer to be useful for exposing implementation technology independent system requirements.

Schema for Model Predicate is:

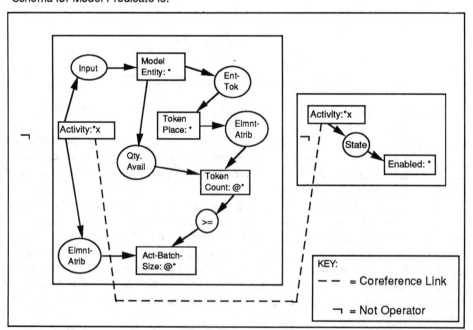

Fig. 10.14 Trigger graph

Another significant component of the conceptual canon is a set of token placement attributes or "places" used in the entity and activity classes for representing timing and concurrency. This feature allows Petri net style execution of the requirements model to develop a dynamic profile of the information flow required to support the modeled manufacturing system. This feature is similar to the approach developed by Ward (1986) for the transformation schema. The token placement attributes are used together with an activity-duration attribute and the trigger schemata to define a Timed Petri net.

10.8   EXTENDING THE SYNTAX OF IDEF0 - FROM BOXES TO POLYGONS

The increased number of roles which entities can assume with respect to a given modeled activity makes the four sided SA box icon inadequate for diagramming the model's structure. Fig. 10.15 presents an enhanced graphic for representing the additional entity-activity interaction relationships.

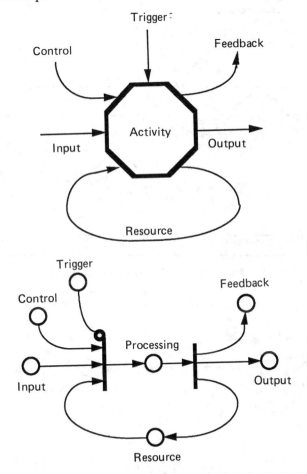

Fig. 10.15 Enhanced graphic for SA extension - modeled after the Petri-net icon.

The icon formalizes the Petri-net model of an activity presented earlier which is also reproduced here for comparison. The left- and right-hand faces of the polygon represent the pre-activity and post-activity entity-activity interaction (conceptual relation) classes, respectively. Emulating the SA approach for classifying entity/activity interactions using separate faces of a graphic activity icon has the virtue of providing an easily grasped image for human comprehension. This extended SA icon for manufacturing communication systems analysis helps differentiate between the material flow and the information flow in the modeled system. In addition to the increased number of sides to represent the added interaction classes, different line and border formats can be used to delineate the activity and entity concept classes into two major subclasses: the information/information-processing subclass, and the material/material-processing subclass. This feature is best supported by a computer graphics system, but could be manually emulated with colored or dotted lines. To demonstrate the enhanced graphic, our sample structured analysis is diagramed using the new icon and given in Figs. 16 and 17.

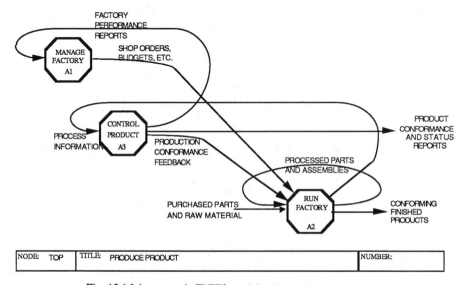

Fig. 10.16 An example IDEF0 model using extended syntax.

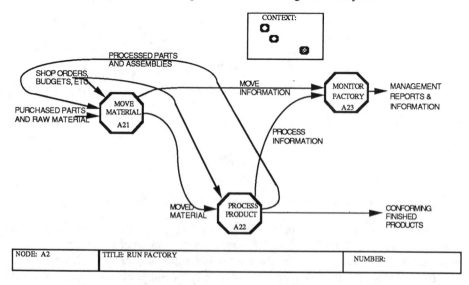

Fig. 10.17 Diagram of manufacturing context using extended syntax.

10.9 SUMMARY

We have presented an approach to 'meta-modeling' a well known systems analysis methodology, IDEF0. The intent of the meta-model is to expose the underlying structure of the IDEF0 concepts and their interconceptual linkages. We have used the formal methodology of conceptual graphs (Sowa, 1984), in order to do this. As a result of this conceptual analysis we have extended IDEF0 by incorporating some additional concepts and interconceptual linkages. Additional extensions to IDEF0 were incorporated from Petri Net ideas to support the development of an executable simulation. The syntax of the IDEF0 language was revised by suggesting a hexagonal rather than a square activity node in order to accommodate the new roles for entities and their interactions beyond that of input, output, control, and mechanism.

The meta-model approach organized the complex modeling environment which allowed structured enhancements, and further supported our implementation of object oriented software for analyzing manufacturing communication requirements using timed Petri net simulation. This software was successfully developed in the Smalltalk/V environment by directly implementing the type hierarchies as software object class hierarchies, with only minor modifications.

This work has applications to other systems analysis methodologies in addition to IDEF0. Since other systems are also constructed from primitives and rules of combination, they too may profitably be analyzed by the fundamental methods presented in this paper. Based on the principles of this Conceptual Graph approach, schemata can be developed to represent the way particular modeling methodologies use their concepts and conceptual relations. This allows straight-forward comparison between the modeling methodologies' representational adequacy for a specific task, and can lead to the development of new modeling primitives (concepts and/or relations) to augment the standard set which a modeling tool may provide. The development of a conceptual canon for systems analysis also provides a structured approach for integrating some of the developments in AI into the field of structured systems analysis.

BIBLIOGRAPHY

Borgida, A., S. Greenspan and J. Mylopoulos. (1985) "Knowledge Representation as the Basis for Requirements Specifications", IEEE Computer, April:82-91.

Engelke, H., J. Grotrian, C. Scheuing, A. Schmackpfeffer, W. Schwarz, B. Solf, and J. Tomann. (1985). "Integrated Manufacturing Modeling System," IBM Journal of Research and Development, 29(4):343-355.

Feller, A.L. and R. Rucker. (1989). "Extending Structured Analysis with AI: An Application to Data Communications Modelling," Proceedings of the International Federation for Information Processing, [Working Group 5.3.] Tempe, AZ, Nov. 8-10, 1989. p. 171-180

Kampfner, R. (1987). "A Hierarchical Model of Organizational Control for the Analysis of Information Systems Requirements," Information Systems, 12(3):243-254.

Kampfner, R. (1985). "Formal Specification of Information Systems Requirements," Information Processing & Management, 21(5):401-414.

Lundsberg, M., G. Goldkuhl, and A. Nilsson. (1979). "A Systematic Approach to Information Systems Development-II: Problem and Data Oriented Methodology," Information Systems, ?(4):93-118.

Marca, D.A. and C.L. McGowan. (1988). *SADT*. McGraw-Hill Book Company.

McMenamin, S.M. and J.F. Palmer. (1984). *Essential Systems Analysis*. Englewood Cliffs, Prentice Hall, Inc, New Jersey

Peterson, J.L. (1981). *Petri Net Theory and the Modeling of Systems*. Prentice-Hall, Inc., New Jersey

Ross, D.T. (1977). "Structured Analysis (SA): A Language for Communication Ideas," IEEE Transactions on Software Engineering, SE3(1):16-34

Ross, D.T. and Kenneth E. Schoman Jr. (1977). "Structured Analysis for Requirements Definition," IEEE Transactions on Software Engineering, SE3(1):6-15.

Ross, D.T. 1985. "Applications and Extensions of SADT," IEEE Computer, April:25-33.

Rucker, R. and A.L. Feller. 1989. "Using Conceptual Structure Principles for Meta-modeling a Structured Analysis Tool, IDEF0," Proceedings of the Fourth Annual Workshop on Conceptual Structures, American Association of Artificial Intelligence, Detroit, MI, Aug. 20-21, 1989, pp. 4.05.1 - 4.05.12.

Shunk, D. , B. Sullivan, and J. Cahill. 1986. "Making the Most of IDEF Modeling - The Triple-Diagonal Concept," CIM Review, Fall, pp. 12-17.

SofTech, Inc. 1981. "Integrated Computer-Aided Manufacturing (ICAM) Architecture Part II Volume IV - Function Modeling Manual (IDEF0)". Wright-Patterson AFB, Materials Laboratories, Ohio.

Sowa, J.F. (1984) *Conceptual Structures: Information Processing in Mind and Machine*, Addison Wesley, Reading.

Ward, P.T. 1986. "The Transformation Schema: An Extension of the Data Flow Diagram to Represent Control and Timing," IEEE Transactions on Software Engineering, SE12(2):198-210.

11

Extendible Graph Processing in Knowledge Acquisition, Planning and Reasoning

Brian J. Garner, Eric Tsui, Daniel Lui, Dickson Lukose and Jane Koh
Department of Computing and Mathematics,
Deakin University,
Geelong 3217, Victoria, Australia

ABSTRACT

This chapter provides an overview of various knowledge engineering projects conducted at Deakin University. Sowa's theory of conceptual structures has been adopted as the common knowledge representation formalism for all the projects and an Extendible Graph Processor (EGP) which forms the nucleus of various Conceptual Processors (CP), is described. The research projects summarized in this paper, including on-going research, encompass knowledge acquisition tools, knowledge-based parsing techniques, representation of planning knowledge, reasoning paradigms, automated M.I.S. design, knowledge elicitation, explanation generation and real-time knowledge base technology.

11.1 RELATED WORK IN GRAPH PROCESSING

Recent examples of conceptual graph processors have been implemented by Morton and Baldwin (1985). They have extended the theory in Sowa (1984) to cover fuzzy referents and fuzzy projections. The program SINFIN (semantic interface for fuzzy information) translates natural language queries into database queries. Adam and Fargues (1984) use conceptual graphs for automated knowledge acquisition as well as for semantic analysis and knowledge processing. Rao and Foo (1986) implemented the graph processor CONGRES (conceptual graph reasoning system) that parses linear forms of conceptual graphs into corresponding PROLOG facts. Based on simple template matching techniques, CONGRES can also generate PROLOG structures for concept type definitions (Sowa and Way, 1986) as well as type hierarchy and conformity relation tables. The data structures adopted by Rao and Foo (1986) and Garner and Tsui (1988a) are very similar and one structure can be converted to another by a simple PROLOG routine.

Sowa and Way (1986) designed and implemented a semantic interpreter using conceptual graphs to decode natural language sentences. Pazienza and Velardi (1986) applied conceptual graphs to capture pragmatic knowledge on word uses in order to disambiguate word senses in semantic parsing. Nagle (1988) applied graphs to perform discourse analysis of visual objects in object-oriented environments. Brown *et al.* (1988) are working on generating or encoding natural language sentences from conceptual graphs.

The rest of this paper addresses further domain independent knowledge acquisition components in the EGP (e.g. knowledge base editor, batch processor, interactive concept classifier and the rule acquisition system) as well as domain dependent processing modules (e.g. semantic interpreter, audit planner, internal control questionnaire generator and goal interpreter) in the EGP. We are investigating as one approach to high level reasoning the advantages of implementing an actor system into the CGP to facilitate research into conceptual programming (Hartley, 1985) (Hartley, 1987).

11.2   KNOWLEDGE ACQUISITION FOR THE EGP

Four Knowledge Acquisition sub-systems for the EGP have been developed. They are:

- the knowledge base editor (KBE);

- the batch processor for the KBE;

- the interactive concept classifier (ICC) and the

- rule acquisition system for conceptual structures (RASCS).

A brief description of each of the above system is outlined below.

11.2.1   Knowledge base editor (KBE)

The knowledge base editor is designed for encoding conceptual structures in the EGP through a simple user-machine dialog. It acts as a graph-based editor for the EGP. The current version of the KBE at Deakin University enables the user to construct knowledge in the following form.

- graphs (simple graphs as well as nested graphs)

- abstractions (schemas, prototypes and type definitions)

- simple inference nets (rule based system utilizing conceptual graphs)

After the structures are created, they can be passed to the canonical graph processor (CGP) for graph processing and subsequently stored in the graph dictionary for future use. The following is a dialog session with the KBE: (The objective of the session is to create and store the graph for *"John is driving a red car fast."*)

```
        KNOWLEDGE BASE EDITOR (KBE¹)

$INFERENCE NET EDITOR ( $INE> )
$INE> edit johng.
$$NEW GRAPH CREATED: johng
```

---

[1] User input is given in italics.

```
$$CGE(johng)  >create relation agnt.
$$CONCEPTUAL RELATION CREATED: -(AGNT)- ...(15002)
$$CGE(johng) > person is the agnt of drive.
$$CONCEPT CREATED: [DRIVE] ... (15004)
$$CONCEPT CREATED: [PERSON] ... (15005)
$$ASSERTION CREATED: agnt(15002) of drive(15004) is person(15005).
$$SOWA'S NOTATION: [DRIVE]->(AGNT)->[PERSON]
$$CGE(johng) > person is john.
$$SPECIALIZATION: [PERSON:john] (15005)
$$CGE(johng) > lf graph.
     [DRIVE] -
       ->(AGNT)->[PERSON:john].
$$CGE(johng) > create relation obj.
$$CONCEPTUAL RELATION CREATED: -(OBJ)- ...(15006)
$$CGE(johng) > the obj of drive is a car.
$$CONCEPT CREATED: [CAR] ... (15007)
$$ASSERTION CREATED: obj(15006) of drive(15004) is car(15007).
$$SOWA'S NOTATION: [DRIVE]->(OBJ)->[CAR]
$$CGE(johng) > create relation attr.
$$CONCEPTUAL RELATION CREATED: -(ATTR)- ...(15008)
$$CGE(johng) > color is the attr of a car.
$$CONCEPT CREATED: [COLOR] ... (15009)
$$ASSERTION CREATED: attr(15008) of car(15007) is color(15009).
$$SOWA'S NOTATION: [CAR]->(ATTR)->[COLOR]
$$CGE(johng) > red is the color.
$$SPECIALIZATION: [COLOR:red] (15009)
$$CGE(johng) > lf graph.
    [DRIVE] -
     ->(AGNT)->[PERSON:john]
     ->(OBJ)->[CAR]->(ATTR)->[COLOR:red].
$$CGE(johng) > create relation cont.
$$CONCEPTUAL RELATION CREATED: -(CONT)- ...(15010)
$$CGE(johng) > the cont of car is person.
$$ASSERTION CREATED: cont(15010) of car(15007) is person(15005).
$$SOWA'S NOTATION: [CAR]->(CONT)->[PERSON:john]
$$CGE(johng) > create relation manr.
$$CONCEPTUAL RELATION CREATED: -(MANR)- ...(15011)
$$CGE(johng) > the manr of drive is fast.
$$CONCEPT CREATED: [FAST] ... (15012)
$$ASSERTION CREATED: manr(15011) of drive(15004) is fast(15012).
$$SOWA'S NOTATION: [DRIVE]->(MANR)->[FAST]
$$CGE(johng) > lf graph.
     [DRIVE] -
     ->(AGNT)->[PERSON:john]<-(CONT)<-[CAR]->(ATTR)->[COLOR:red]
     ->(OBJ)->[CAR]
     ->(MANR)->[FAST].
$$CGE(johng) > lf person.
     [PERSON:john] -
     <-(AGNT)<-[DRIVE] -
->(OBJ)->[CAR]->(ATTR)->[COLOR:red]
```

```
-> (MANR) -> [FAST],
    <- (CONT) <- [CAR].
$$CGE (johng)  > write graph.
$$WRITE TO FILE johng.pl COMPLETED
$$EXIT: CGE>
```

An automatic "graph-to-data-structure" checker is also available. This routine can be invoked to verify the correctness of the generated PROLOG facts and statements (by the KBE and other programs) and is a useful tool for debugging in a program/system development environment. In short, the KBE enables the user to create his/her own conceptual structures without requiring any working knowledge of PROLOG.

11.2.2   Batch processor for the knowledge base editor

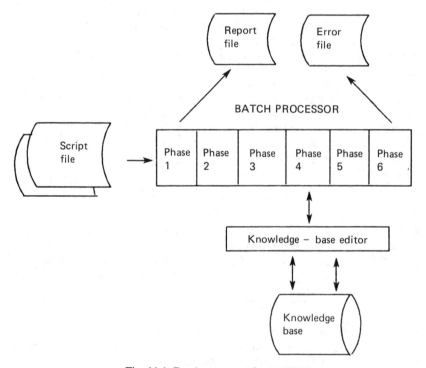

Fig. 11.1: Batch processor for the KBE.

The batch processor (BP) for the knowledge base editor (Garner *et al.*, 1987a) depicted in Fig. 11.1 relieves the knowledge engineer from interactively manipulating/modifying/creating the knowledge base. Rather than invoking the KBE, one enters a set of scripts (i.e. KBE statements) into a script file and passes the file to the BP. Firstly, the BP performs syntactic checks on the script followed by semantic and integrity checks on the conceptual structures that are modified/constructed. The BP then invokes the KBE to execute each of the script statement to execute the necessary operation(s).

Each script file contains at least one script frame. Each script frame consists of one or more script statement(s). Ideally, each script statement is a valid KBE command. The "$" is treated as a delimiter for the script frames. Each script frame must begin with "$" in the first line followed by a number of script statements and terminated by a "$" in the last line. An example of a script file is shown in Fig. 11.2.

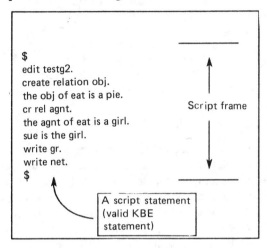

Fig. 11.2: A script file named "test5".

A sample dialogue session with the BP is presented below.

```
            BATCH PROCESSOR FOR THE KBE

BP > process.
K.B.E. BATCH PROCESSOR STARTED AT : Wed Feb 11 22:40
Enter file name(s): test5.
More (y or n): n.
Phase I :: Script file analysis
        Report written into file : errorp1
Phase II :: Script statement analysis
Phase III :: Script frame analysis
Phase IV :: Knowledge Base Modification
    [ SCRIPT FRAME 1 ]
    [edit, testg2, .]
    [create, relation, obj, .]
    [the, obj, of, eat, is, a, pie, .]
    [cr, rel, agnt, .]
    [the, agnt, of, eat, is, a, girl, .]
    [sue, is, the, girl, .]
    [write, gr, .]
    [write, net, .]
$$WRITE TO FILE testg2.pl COMPLETED
$WRITE TO INFERENCE NET DATA FILE indata3.pl
$WRITE TO GRAPH DICTIONARY graphdic.pl
*Updating Semantic Dictionary: Type Definitions:typedef.pl
*Updating Semantic Dictionary: Relational Definitions:reldef.pl
```

```
*Updating Semantic Dictionary: Composite Individuals:cidef.pl
*Updating Semantic Dictionary: Schemata Definitions:schdef.pl
*Updating Semantic Dictionary: Prototypes:protodef.pl
$EXIT FROM KNOWLEDGE BASE EDITOR
Phase V :: Integrity Checking
Phase V1 :: Collecting rejected scripts
Report from phase I is written into :: errorp1
Rejected scripts are written into :: errorp2-4
        Number of script processed :: 1
        Number of script rejected :: 1
K.B.E. BATCH PROCESSOR TERMINATED AT : Wed Feb 11 22:42
```

11.2.3 Interactive concept classifier (ICC)

The type hierarchy lattice in the extendible graph processor maintains type-subtype relationships for all the recognized type labels (both concepts and relations) in the processor. Being in a lattice, a type t can have one or multiple subtypes and supertypes. Types are further categorized into role types and natural types. The type UNIVERSAL is a supertype of all declared types and the type ABSURD is a subtype of all declared types.

The interactive concept classifier (ICC) (Garner *et al.*, 1987) allows a user to query existing type-subtype relationships, modify the lattice and classify (insert) new types into the lattice. A complete range of editing facilities (operations) is available on the ICC. A list of all the available operations and a brief description for each one of them is given in Table 1.

Operation	Description
add t_1, t	
add $t_1,t_2,...,t_n$ $<t<t_{n+1},...,t_m$	add news arc(s) to the lattice
minus $t_1,t_2,...,t_n$ $<t<t_{n+1},...,t_m$	deletes existing arc(s) from the lattice
rename t_1 t_2	renames a type label from t_1 to t_2
path t_1 t_2	displays the semantic path and distance from t_1 to t_2
list all types	lists all the recognised types in the lattice
save	save the lattice in a file
$t_1 < t_2$	checks if t_1 is a subtype of t_2
$t_1 > t_2$	checks if t_1 is a supertype of t_2
t<?	lists all supertypes of t
t>?	lists all subtypes of t
classify t	classify t into the lattice (through a user-machine dialogue)
loop/cycle	checks if there exists loops(s) or cycle(s) in the lattice
quit/end	quits the Interactive Classifier (without save)
info	prints information about commands in the ICC
info c	prints information about the command c

Table 1: List of all the operations in the ICC.

The most important operation in the ICC is the classify command. When a new type t is presented to the lattice, it has to be inserted at the appropriate location in the hierarchy with all its supertypes and subtypes properly identified. Without the classify command, the user would have to inspect the hierarchy visually and execute appropriate add and minus operations to classify/insert t. Without the ICC, the user has to apply his/her own common sense knowledge to properly classify a new type and to use a UNIX editor to update/insert the requisite PROLOG fact(s).

11.2.4   Rule acquisition system for conceptual structures (RASCS)

To encode production rules into the EGP, a rule acquisition system for conceptual structures (RASCS) has been implemented (Lui, 1986). A rule in the EGP consists of graphs on both sides of the rule plus a set of first order logic operators. In addition to the encoding of rules, RASCS also verifies the consistency and integrity of rules as well as the validity of binding variables within each rule. Fig. 11.3 gives a typical rule creation dialog with RASCS for the rule: "The use of an encryption key as the agent of transmission forces secure transmission".

```
$ rascs
 RULE ACQUISITION SYSTEM FOR CONCEPTUAL STRUCTURES
 yes
 5?- rulein.
 LHS: transmit__agent.
 RHS: transmit__secure.
 CAUSAL RELATION: cause.
 Rule constructed:
 rule(3, cause, transmit__agent, transmit__secure, [])
 [PROPOSITION: [TRANSMIT:*:14393] -
                                      ->(AGNT)->[KEY:*:14394]]
 ->(CAUSE)->
 [PROPOSITION: [TRANSMIT:*:14397] -
                                      ->(CHAR)->[FORM:secure:14398]].
 ENTER NEW BINDING GROUP:
 1 > 14393, 14397.
 2 > .
 rule(3, cause, transmit__agent, transmit__secure, [[14393, 14397]])
 [Rule stored into rule base]
 [PROPOSITION: [TRANSMIT:*x1] -
                                      ->(AGNT)->[KEY:*]]
 ->(CAUSE)->
 [PROPOSITION: [TRANSMIT:*x1] -
                                      ->(CHAR)->[FORM:secure]].
 [RULE ACQUISITION SESSION COMPLETED]
```

Fig. 11.3: Dialog session with RASCS on the creation of a rule[2].

11.3   CONCEPTUAL GRAPH FOR AUDIT PLANNING

11.3.1   Application of Artificial Intelligence in Auditing

Modern developments in digital communications, desktop publishing and decision support systems have opened a new chapter in audit automation. Of particular interest is the

---

[2](i) A binding group denotes the binding of a list of groups of coreferent concepts. (ii) Concept [A:B:C] denotes A as the type label; B as the referent and C as a unique identifier for the concept.

extension of decision support strategies through the provision of expert advisors for planning and reasoning as an important application of contemporary research in artificial intelligence. The conceptualization of the audit function needs updating. Contemporary EDP audit techniques such as Generalized Audit Software Packages (GASP) and statistical sampling packages have played significant roles in automating compliance and substantive tests. However, there is very little research on the automation of the other major steps (e.g. planning of an audit) in a typical audit assignment. In particular, the adequacy of system-based auditing (Weber, 1982) as a foundation for the audit of modern information systems has been challenged.

Knowledge-based auditing (Garner and Tsui, 1985b) (Garner and Tsui, 1986e)[3] is proposed as an extension to system-based methodology to automate the processes of designing audit plans, evaluating internal control systems and providing decision support for auditors using pragmatic (real world) knowledge and causal knowledge.

Accepting that the scope and diversity of commercial information systems are increasing, the need for more effective methodologies and greater selectivity in field work can still be met by extension of the computer-assisted audit approach to include productivity aids based on conceptual models. These meta-information systems for conceptual modeling and requirements specification have been defined by the International Standards Organization (ISO/TC97/WG3, 1982).

As Vasarhelyi (1984) noted, "The potential of automation is restricted by the human information processing limitations of the individual auditor. Consequently, the audit process is often too detailed and complex for complete assimilation by an auditor. Because improved information supply is only beneficial to the extent that auditors can collect and use it, expert systems (Hansen and Messier, 1984a) are being designed to aid the auditor as an expert judge. These systems incorporate the judgemental rules used by the "expert auditors" to help other auditors in evaluating specific audit evidence".

The majority of the published work on AI systems in EDP auditing is concerned with decision support and expert systems. Most of these systems are rule based models and are developed from expert system shells. Designers have not focussed on the knowledge maintenance aspects of these systems and the difficulty in updating expert knowledge. Most importantly, these systems may lack a unified knowledge representation framework.

Messier and Hansen (1982), Garner and Tsui (1986e), Koh (1986), Jamieson (1986) and Fogelgarn (1986) presented surveys of recent AI systems in EDP auditing. Examples of such research include Dillard and Mutchler's (1984, 1986) work on designing an expert system to assist the auditor in forming an opinion, Hansen and Messier's (1982, 1984a) work on developing methodologies for building decision support systems in EDP auditing. Dungan and Chandler's (1983) work on the development of an expert system to simulate and analyze audit judgements and through the above two processes, investigate the domain of audit judgements, is also worthy of note.

Bailey et al. (1979, 1984) developed the TICOM (the internal control model) expert system that evaluates the reliability of a client's internal control system. Braun (1983) developed an expert system that simulates and evaluates the audit decision process, and the system can also discover decision rules used by auditors by applying the method of learning from examples.

---

[3] see section 11.3.3 on page 231.

Hansen and Messier (1984a, 1985) successfully developed the EDP-XPERT system for auditing advanced computer controls. EDP-XPERT assists the auditor in audit judgements on the reliability of controls in large computer installations. Dungan and Chandler (1985) presented the microcomputer based expert system AUDITOR. AUDITOR assists the user in estimating the dollar amount of a client's uncollectable accounts receivable. More articles on the formulation and evaluation of expert systems and audit judgements can be found in Deloitte *et al.* (1986).

11.3.2 Audit Planning

Office automation in the interests of the efficiency and effectiveness of audit professionals is attracting greater interest and investment by management. Professional offices such as an audit office have been surprisingly slow to automate given the paper intensive nature of audit planning and reporting, and the time typically allocated by auditors to these activities. Mar (1983) pointed out that as the scope and complexity of audit tasks increased, the proportion of the auditor's time allocated to planning will double with major reduction in the time allocated to field work (ref Fig. 11.4).

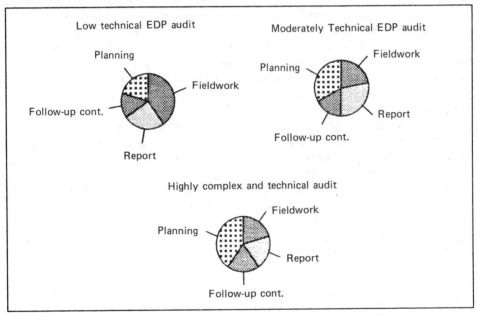

Fig. 11.4: Current audit time allocations (adapted from Mar (1983)).

As Vasarhelyi (1984) wrote about the importance of audit planning to the entire audit profession, "associated with the task of long (and short) term staff assignment is the evaluation of audit risk, analytical review, choice of audit effort assignment, timing of the audit and level of interim and year-end effort. Data processing integrates these processes into a homogeneous and court-defendable program. Once the prescribed steps are followed (and documented) through an interactive design of an audit plan, the plan follows the general firms guidelines limiting discrepancies in audit quality. In an audit practice, audit planning automation poses a different set of problems. The emphasis will be shifted from materiality subject examination of financial statements to reliance and quality of data at the diverse levels of search for evidence. Planning will be strongly associated to corporate growth and management strategy".

Noting also Boritz' (1983) views on the subject, "even though much has been written about (audit) planning from a conceptual perspective, when it comes right down to actually doing it, it seems that the implementation burden is often so overwhelming that it actually prevents formal planning activities from being adequately instituted, despite everyone's wishes to the contrary. ... It is probably impossible to survive in the corporate world without making some effort at planning (i.e. anticipating events and providing for them)".

Unfortunately, apart from the systems described below, the authors are not aware of any other automated planning systems in the audit domain. Problem solvers for planning and understanding in a commercial environment are, therefore, urgently needed to support quality planning processes (Garner et al., 1986).

In the area of planning, Davis and Strobel (1980) discussed computer programs that assist the user in implementing proper estate plans. As Davis and Strobel (1980) wrote, "estate planning involves much more than simply preparing a will and considering alternative distributions of property at death. Planning must necessarily be concerned with the minimization of estate and inheritance taxes, income taxes, and probate costs. It also involves lifetime financial planning, charitable giving, employee benefits and executive compensation, and post mortem planning."Shpilberg et al. (1986) developed the ExperTAX expert system that supports the corporate tax accrual and planning process. ExperTAX is able to guide the staff accountant through the information gathering process and directs the user to relevant issues. ExperTAX is also one of the few examples of AI systems in auditing that addresses the problem of interactive knowledge acquisition.

The comprehensive audit planning system (CAPS) (Boritz, 1983) is a desktop decision support system for the planning of internal audit. It is used to develop a microcomputer based decision support system for enhancing internal audit planning activities. CAPS is predominantly a procedural based system, as opposed to most expert systems which mainly consist of declarative knowledge coupled with procedural attachments. As Boritz (1983) wrote, "a procedural system first structures the task environment, then uses embedded procedural knowledge to accomplish relatively well-specified goals. In contrast, a declarative system gathers knowledge, in the form of condition-action rules, providing a relatively unstructured problem-solving environment."

11.3.3 Knowledge base auditing

The development of a knowledge based audit methodology involves three basic extensions of system-based audit (Garner, 1985):

1. a general knowledge base incorporating the audit methodology and generic structure of the problem domain. Parts of this structure exist as predefined internal control structures and audit processes (models);

2. automated knowledge acquisition tools, using modern formalisms for the representation of lexical, syntactic, semantic and pragmatic (real world) knowledge, are required to provide the operational knowledge necessary for financial and comprehensive audit of specific auditee environments;

3. reasoning processes are encoded as causal knowledge. For example, causal knowledge of information technology facilities and services includes knowledge of the relationships between operational outcomes in the decision process. When management control fails, causal relationships as determined from current reviews, are used to create an explanation for the failure. Techniques adopted from conventional plan and goal (objective) understanding systems can be applied to the task of generating explanations and using them as indices to management processes;

4. in a later section, a conceptual graph model for audit planning is defined as the basis for future expert advisors in decision support.

11.3.4 Audit planning and the planning process

The objective of an independent audit is an expression of opinion on the truth and fairness of the accounts issued annually by a company to its shareholders. This objective is achieved by the auditor carrying out a number of procedures which are designed either to test the integrity of the accounting system in operation (compliance tests), or to check the accuracy of individual items which form part of the accounts themselves (substantive tests). Generally, the audit planning process involves:

(a) assessment of the nature of the business which the client conducts;

(b) identification of the critical areas of the audit;

(c) response to any requests from the client for the audit service to be extended to additional areas;

(d) development of an outline of the way in which the audit will be conducted;

(e) provision of the resources necessary to carry out the audit plan; and

(f) monitoring progress on the audit to ensure that the assignment is proceeding in line with the plan, or that the plan is amended to reflect changing circumstances.

The aim of the audit planning process is to identify the critical areas which need to be addressed by the auditor in reaching an audit opinion, and to suggest the approach which may seem to be appropriate for the audit of those areas. In doing this, the auditor is making a subjective assessment of the areas of audit exposure or risk associated with the circumstances of the client. The result of the planning process is the audit plan. The audit plan is a broad document or statement of the approach which the auditor believes will enable an opinion on the truth and fairness of the financial statements to be issued at the end of the assignment. Adequate planning of the audit is vital in ensuring that the audit is carried out in the most efficient way and is also effective. The audit plan, including the planning decisions contained therein, is therefore one of the most important workpapers relating to the audit and should be reviewed and approved by the partner before detailed work commences.

The audit plan must be a dynamic document which is reviewed and amended throughout the course of the engagement to ensure its appropriateness to the circumstances of the cient. In addition to responding to changes in the nature of the client's activities or the general business environment, the audit approach will need to be reviewed in the light of interim audit results. The planning process therefore must continue throughout the course of the audit engagement. The extent of audit planning will vary from client to client depending, in part, on the size and complexity of the client's systems. On a relatively simple engagement, the audit plan may be quite short and concise.

In practice, an auditor must ensure that the service being provided is cost-effective to the client. Consequently, it is essential for the whole engagement to be carefully tailored to the client's circumstances and to be monitored at all times. This will ensure that the procedures adopted will be relevant to at taining the audit objective.

11.3.5   Knowledge representation in the audit planner

An application of the extendible graph processor is the design and implementation of a decision support system for automated audit planning, the audit planner. The principal objectives of developing the audit planner are to demonstrate that audit planning can be automated to a reasonable extent, and given that a framework for canonical graph models is already available, such a system can be rapidly prototyped. The problem of generating audit plans for a computer based system with particular reference to risk analysis was specifically chosen for investigation. Expert knowledge about audit planning was acquired from literature, researchers' experience and from communications with practising professionals. In an automated planning system such as the audit planner, the above planning process can be viewed as comprising the following generic phases and components:

Decision Analysis This corresponds to the strategic/procedural knowledge that is required to compose/synthesise a plan for a particular goal. In the audit planner, the simulation of the auditor's decision process is represented by the (Prolog) inference engine. In addition, the inference engine invokes the JOIN, MAXIMAL JOIN, TYPE EXPANSION and PROJECTION operations in the process of formulating a draft (intermediate) plan. For example, during the planning process, input specifications may have to be elaborated with various attributes of risk analysis. In the audit planner, the above is achieved by invoking the TYPE EXPANSION operation:

```
CGP  7>  typedef input_specs.
type INPUT_SPECS(*x)  is
     [INPUT_SPECS:*x]  −
```

```
                    -> (AIM) -> [RISK_ANALYSIS]
                    -> (CPY_TYPE) -> [TYPE:type]
                    -> (COST) -> [BUDGET:budget]
                    -> (TIME) -> [HOURS:hours].
CGP  8>  typedef risk_analysis.
         type RISK_ANALYSIS(*x) is
           [RISK_ANALYSIS:*x] -
                -> (RELIANCE) -> [INT_CONTROL] -> (COMPLIANCE) -> [POLICY]
                <- (AIM) <- [INPUT_SPECS] -> (CPY_TYPE) -> [TYPE:*type].
CGP  9>  expand risk_analysis input_specs.
    [... DETECTED 3 CONCEPT(S) AND 2 CONCEPTUAL RELATION(S) FOR
    MAXIMAL JOIN ...]
    * <TYPE EXPANSION>: Expanding [RISK_ANALYSIS] in input_specs
    by type(RISK_ANALYSIS) gives temp2055 [DONE]
CGP 10>  lf temp2055.
         [INPUT_SPECS] -
           -> (AIM) -> [RISK_ANALYSIS] -
                -> (RELIANCE) -> [INT_CONTROL]  -> (COMPLIANCE) -> [POLICY],
           -> (CPY_TYPE) -> [TYPE:*type]
           -> (COST) -> [BUDGET:*budget]
           -> (TIME) -> [HOURS:*hours].
```

Representation of plan structures This corresponds to how the necessary plans and actions are stored in the computer. In the Audit Planner, all the (generic) plans are
stored as canonical graphs or type definitions. The following in an example of the
type definition for input specifications:

```
     CGP  7>  typedef input_specs.
     type INPUT_SPECS(*x) is
             [INPUT_SPECS:*x] -
                 -> (AIM) -> [RISK_ANALYSIS]
                 -> (CPY_TYPE) -> [TYPE:type]
                 -> (COST) -> [BUDGET:budget]
                 -> (TIME) -> [HOURS:hours].
```

Representation of Planning Constraint For an audit plan, examples of planning constraints are risk factors, policy guidelines, auditor's skill and the total number of
hours allocated to the audit. These constraints can either be known facts or user
supplied restrictions. User supplied restrictions include:

- the type of audit to be conducted;

- total amount of time allocated for the audit;

- an estimate of the cost (in monetary terms) of the audit;

- the nature of the client's business and the size of the client's organisation; and

- the extent of the level of assurance desired by the user for a particular audit.

Planning constraints are represented as a combination of Prolog facts and rules. The following is an example of a PROLOG fact known to the system about the various attributes of a particular policy guideline in a firm's audit manual:

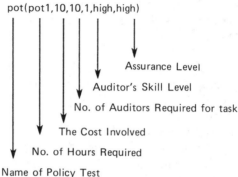

```
pot(pot1,10,10,1,high,high)
```

Assurance Level

Auditor's Skill Level

No. of Auditors Required for task

The Cost Involved

No. of Hours Required

Name of Policy Test

Performance evaluation and feedback A good plan is complete, unbiased, implementable, verifiable and leads to good results. Feedback facilities in the audit planner permit ongoing revision of the intermediate plans. Conflicting in formation is avoided and resources are appropriately shared among the plans. Sometimes it is possible to evaluate the individual aspects of plans, but it is rarely possible to evaluate a plan without actually implementing it and seeing it work. Ultimately, the measure of the quality of a plan must be based upon the results achieved in using it; but this cannot be a foolproof measure. Even the best plans may not lead to good outcomes.

11.3.6   Control knowledge in the audit planner

The flow of control in the audit planner is depicted in Fig. 11.5. Input specifications to the Audit Planner are entered via a structured question-answering dialog and the input is then converted to canonical graph for subsequent processing. For example, part of the input for a risk analysis audit is shown below:

```
     * THE AUDIT PLANNER *
Type of Audit  :  risk_analysis.
Time Available(hours)  :  50.
Budget Allocated($0)  :  4000.
Type of Company(small,med,large)  :  small.
Level of Assurance Required(low,med,high,n)  :n.
```

Once the specifications for an audit are known, the audit planner attempts to synthesise an inital set of plans that can be further evaluated (e.g. evaluated by domain dependent and independent planning constraints). There exist four global objectives in the entire planning process. These are:

- avoidance of plans that are deemed inappropriate for the current case;

- the use of plans that satisfy the specified objectives (goals);

- the minimization of the consumption of resources; and the

- avoidance of mutually exclusive entities in the same plan.

For plan selection, the audit planner relies on the use of a inference net (Garner and Tsui, 1985a) (Hansen and Messier, 1984a) to guide the composition of an initial set of plans. Each node in the inference net contains information that will aid in the selection of a particular (sub)plan. These nodes are represented as canonical graphs. The initial set of plans are formulated by extracting appropriate pre-stored planning actions in the knowledge base. The knowledge base is actually a library of plan-action templates with implicit information attached to it. Audit information such as the amount of time required, the cost involved, the required skill level of the auditors and the objective of the plans-actions are maintained in these plan-action templates. In addition to the templates, the knowledge base also contains a library of template graphs that are necessary to formulate a skeletal plan for output in the conceptual graph format. The selection mechanism is based on a nominated set of criteria (e.g. minimal cost, minimal resource utilization, maximum audit assurance).

Once a initial set of plans is generated, the process of plan evaluation begins. A user-supplied canonical graph that specifies the limitation of the resources for the current problem is cross-checked with the values (referents) in the initial set of "plan" graphs. This operation is achieved by the use of the PROJECTION routine in the CGP. The PROJECTION routine was used for similar purpose in Maruyama (1988). The projected values are cross-checked with the values in the graph for resource limitation. If the projected values exceed the specified values, then the plan is rejected and a backtracking mechanism is applied in order to formulate an alternative solution (plan). If the projected values are less than or equal to the specified values, then the plan is accepted and stored in the global database and the process of plan selection continues. When all possible solutions have been evaluated and stored, the stored plans (i.e. successful plans) are again evaluated (for global consistency*) and arranged in ascending cost and displayed to the user.

During the plan evaluation process, the system may ask the user to alter (e.g. increase the total amount of a resource) the input specification and/or to confirm certain attributes/characteristics of the audit that are not supplied in the original specifications. The above processes, plan selection, plan evaluation and feedback, are repeated until either a set of feasible plans are formulated or there is no plan for the current specifications.

The output of the audit planner is either a set of assertions or canonical graphs that describe the characteristics of the formulated audit plan(s). A sample set of assertions for an audit plan is presented below:

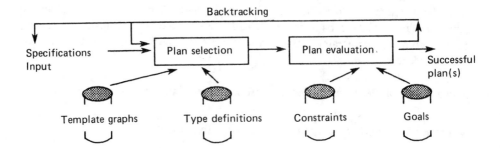

Fig. 11.5: Overall flow of control in the audit planner.

```
Audit Plan
Internal Control(s) required ...
Internal Control : ic2
Risks Handled : [r2, r3]
Time Involved : 5 hours
Cost Involved : 500 ($0)
No of Auditors Required : 2
Auditor Skill Level : med
Assurance Factor : high
  Code : r2.
  risk 2 = unauthorised access to ADP assets
Internal Control : ic1
Risks Handled : [r1]
Time Involved : 10 hours
Cost Involved : 1000 ($0)
No of Auditors Required : 1
Auditor Skill Level : med
Assurance Factor : high
Policy Test(s) to be conducted ...
Policy Test : pot2
Policies Handled : [p2, p3]
Time involved : 3 hours
Cost Involved : 300 ($0)
No of Auditors Required : 1
Auditor Skill Level : low
Compliance Factor : med
Policy Test : pot1
Policies Handled : [p1]
Time involved : 10 hours
Cost Involved : 1000 ($0)
No of Auditors Required : 1
Auditor Skill Level : low
Compliance Factor : med
```

Updating the knowledge structures in the audit planner can be done through the use of the knowledge base editor and the rule acquisition system for conceptual structures. The

KBE is used to create/modify graphs and definitions and the RASCS is used to encode the inference net.

11.4 REASONING PARADIGMS

Our research in reasoning covers the following three main areas:

- natural language processing using knowledge-based parsing;

- intelligent question generation;

- goal interpretation process.

11.4.1 Knowledge-based natural language parsing techniques

We tackle the problem of schema selection by first composing default/generic structures from natural language sentences and then modifying these structures to facilitate schema selection. Contrary to conventional knowledge-based parsing techniques, i.e. frame-based parsing, disambiguation rules and discrimination nets, only a limited set of generic/default structures is stored and these structures are modified and subsequently correlated with pre-stored schemas before actually joining them (Garner *et al.*, 1987b). Our method of parsing does not require the system to store a massive set of schemas, but rather, a highly-developed knowledge base with various types of knowledge organised hierarchically. Complementing the knowledge base is a set of pattern modification strategies and pattern correlation functions. To avoid combinatorial explosion in manipulating graphs five classes of pattern correlation function are applied. Disambiguation of lexically ambiguous words, mainly due to different prepositional and verb senses, outlined in Tait (1985) and Birnbaum (1985) is achieved by the application of the maximal join operation, while the problem of phrase attachment and structural ambiguity outlined in Hirst (1984) is resolved by using semantic clusters. Processing of linguistic information provides output in the form of conceptual graphs that constitute the input to a conceptual processor (Obermeier, 1984). The importance of this approach is that control or application-oriented knowledge can now be structured as implicit knowledge in a well-structured knowledge base and appropriate knowledge engineering tools[4] have been developed for the acquisition and elicitation of knowledge for such a knowledge base.

The parser and the semantic interpreter (SI) generate a set of semantically correct (or "canonical") graphs after an input sentence is correctly and successfully analysed. A subset of Heidorn's (1972) augmented phrase structure grammar (APSG) rules is transformed into a corresponding set of definite clause grammar (DCG) rules. These DCG rules serve as input to an APSG parser generator which then generates the basic syntactic parser. The semantic interpreter operates on the output of the syntactic parser including parse tree(s) of instantiated production rules.

The current version of the SI consists of roughly 50 grammar rules and a lexicon of approximately 300 words. The natural language processing sub-project at Deakin University is part of an expert advisor project directed towards the ultimate development of a conceptual

---

[4] see section 11.2 on page 222.

processor for reasoning. The semantic interpreter together with the parser amounts to roughly 5000 lines of PROLOG and operates in conjunction with a versatile tool CGP, approximately 12,000 lines of PROLOG, that manipulates conceptual graphs.

11.4.2   Question generation

One of the most important measures of machine intelligence is the ability for a machine to examine the knowledge base and generate necessary questions to ask the user. To enhance the productivity of auditors and to research the above issue, (Garner and Tsui, 1985) designed and implemented a knowledge-based audit questionnaire generator. Canonical graphs are stored in nodes of an inference net and a dialog session between the user and the generator is carried out based on the way the inference net is traversed as well as the knowledge atoms (graphs) in each node. Key components of the questionnaire generator include a (simple) knowledge base, a dialog maintainer, a (partial) canonical graph processor, a blackboard model and a questions generator (Fig. 11.6).

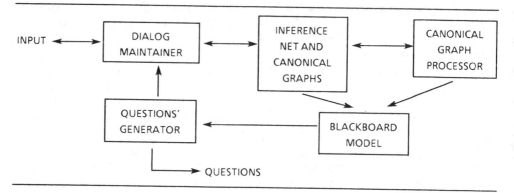

Fig. 11.6: Components fo the questionnaire generator system.

The goal of the system is to ask the user (internal or external auditor) to type in an audit proposition (e.g a statement about (the lack of) certain internal control) and the generator will assemble together a set of questions for the user to review. The output questions may appear to be very "simple-minded" to an experienced user, but nevertheless, the questions are not pre-stored. The "knowledge atoms" required to assemble the questions are kept in the knowledge base. In addition, an access mechanism to extract the "knowledge atoms" from the knowledge base is provided and the knowledge base is dynamic.

Knowledge representation for the questionnaire generator requires the use of a dynamic knowledge base, consisting of an inference net and canonical graphs. One of the most common ways of representing expert's knowledge is in the form of production rules. Such rules can typically represent an expert's line of reasoning thus accounting for the decision making process. Numerical values can be attached to each production rule so that the "degree of certainty" (i.e. the degree to which the belief or evidence supports the conclusion) of each rule can be specified.

Canonical graphs (Sowa, 1984) are used to represent information in each node of the inference net. The following shows an example of a canonical graph for the concept "expense claim":

```
[EXPENSE-CLAIM]    → (NATURE)  → [EXPENSE-TYPE]
                   → (EVIDENCE) → [DOCUMENT]
                   → (STATUS)  → [VERIFY]
                   → (AMOUNT)  → [VALUE].
```

Knowledge processing by the questionnaire generator involves two key tasks, namely:

(a) identify a "key area of interest" in the input proposition;

(b) develop methodologies for extracting "information requirements" from the knowledge base to assemble questions for output.

The concept of a "discrimination net" is used to identify a "key area of interest" from an input proposition. A discrimination net is a tree designed to differentiate various kinds of information into different branches of the tree. Naturally, each node in the net (except for the terminating node) has a test to be performed and the truth of the test will determine the selection of a branch.

Once a "key area of interest" is identified by the discrimination net, this area is taken as the goal of the reasoning process. A backward chaining mechanism is then applied to traverse all nodes in the goal node and while traversing a node, information is extracted from the canonical graph(s) in the node. Information extracted is eventually passed on to the questions' generator which composes questions from the input knowledge atoms.

A special backtracking strategy, which is neither purely depth-first nor breadth-first, had to be devised for the inference net in view of the following issues;

- related questions have to be collated together in output;

- no duplicate question is to be generated in the same run although some nodes may be traversed more than once;

- while traversing a node, attempts are made to extract from the input proposition so that unfilled "slots" in the knowledge base are filled. To some extent, processing each subsequent node relies on the information extracted (or deduced) from previous node(s);

- traversal of the inference net has to be efficient.

Run time examples of the questionnaire generator can be found in Garner and Tsui (1985b).

11.4.3   Goal interpretation

Two important functions of every discourse understanding system (e.g. natural language processing systems and story understanding systems) are to identify the goals and the plans from user input. The goal of a user has to be hypothesised and followed by a plan recognition process that should not only construct a (set of) plan(s) but can also explain all the user actions. In an automated planning system, the planner has to determine the user goal from the user input, and then a plan is constructed so that, when the plan is executed, the user goal is fulfilled.

USER $\xrightarrow{\text{aims}}$ goal-states

PLANNER $\xrightarrow{\text{goal-states}}$ plans

Automated planning systems require the capability to detect achievable goals whether predefined or not, as it is pointless to plan for an indeterminate goal, and for poorly defined aims, the prospect of success using conventional planning strategies will be unacceptably low! Since the user may attempt to communicate their aims in a number of ways, it is also essential to provide within the goal interpretation function a mapping mechanism (between user aims and achievable goals) of broad application. An extensible framework for goal interpretation in automated planning systems has now been developed (Garner *et al.*, 1986).

The objective of goal interpretation is to identify achievable goal states from user input (i.e. user aims). A user goal is said to be achievable if the goal specifications and the goal requirements can be satisfied. A goal state contains all the information required for the preparation of a plan to achieve the goal. By constructing a goal state, the chance of failure in planning is greatly reduced and the efficiency of a planning system is vastly improved. An overview of this goal interpretation process is shown in Fig. 11.7. In this framework, a goal tree represents the capability of a system to reason about user goals. A goal is decomposed into subgoals. The same decomposition process can be applied to the subgoals, and so on. The terminal goal nodes of a goal tree represent basic elements or "goal primitives".

The interpretation process thus involves the identification of goal primitives from user aims. A goal primitive is said to be identified if the image (pattern) of the goal primitive can be found from the user aims. A higher level goal node is selected as the user goal, in which all identified goal primitives are subgoals. The requirements of this user goal can be made explicit by traversing through the inference rules stored in the rule-base. If all the requirements can be satisfied, a goal state is constructed by joining the goal requirements, the selected user goal and the associated goal primitives.

Once the goal states are constructed, the goal is known to be achievable (otherwise the goal interpreter will not form a goal state). Where a planner rejects a goal state, the goal interpreter will backtrack to the user goal selection process and try to select another appropriate goal node as the user goal. The interpreter will then try to construct a goal state for this new user goal.

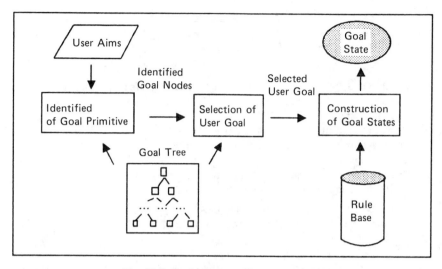

Fig. 11.7: Goal interpretation process.

The advantage of this (extended approach) is that it provides better explanations and better goal interpretation in knowledge-based systems. By adding structural knowledge (i.e. causal relations) and strategic knowledge (i.e. strategies for reasoning with causal relations) to rule-based systems, planning and reasoning with inexact matches becomes feasible and facilitates new mechanisms for indexing abstractions (conceptual structures).

The following is a dialog session for the construction of a goal state (as shown in Fig. 11.9) according to the user input graph (Fig. 11.8).

```
$ gi
GOAL INTERPRETATION

yes
11?- gpi(U).
   [Goal Interpreter Initialization]
   [Construct Goal Primitive List]
   [Search for Subgoal relation]

User Input Graph: user_graph.
   [Build Select Goal Node Process Table]

Checking Primitives ...
Interpreted User Goal(s): [eft]
Goal Node Graph: [transmit_type_eft]
Primitives identified: [transmit_obj_money, transmit_mode_medium,
transmit_init_user, transmit_rcpt_user]

TRAVERSING THROUGH RULE-BASE

SEARCHING STRATEGY: Forward Chaining using (NECS) rules
Checking rules ...
All fired rules: [201, 205, 206, 204]
Making deductions from rules ...
Goal requirement graphs are: [wg357, wg358, wg359, wg360]
Checking requirement(s) ...
```

```
Requirement - wg357 found in KB.
Requirement - wg358 found in KB.
Requirement - wg359 found in KB.

*** WARNING: Requirement - wg360 NOT found in KB.

SEARCHING STRATEGY: Backward Chaining using (CAUSE) rules
Checking rules ...
All fired rules: [203]
Making deductions from rules ...
Goal Requirement graphs are: [wg361]
Checking requirement(s) ...
Requirement - wg361 found in KB.
   [All requirements are satisfied]

JOIN USER INPUT GRAPH WITH GOAL REQUIREMENT GRAPHS
   [Goal State Constructed: temp3294]
   [TRANSMIT]-
     -> (AGENT) -> [KEY]
      -> (OBJ) -> [MONEY:n100]<-(POSS)<-[USER:username]->
           (ACCESS)->[MEDIUM:xyz]<-(ACCESS)<-[USER:daniel]
      -> (INIT) -> [USER: username]
      -> (MODE) -> [MEDIUM: xyz]
      -> (RCPT) -> [USER: daniel].

12?- ctrl D
End of Session
$
```

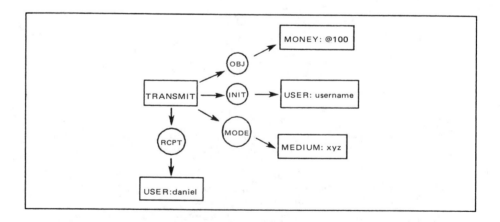

Fig. 11.8: An example of a user input graph for the transmission of $100 from a user to Dianiel via a certain network XYZ.

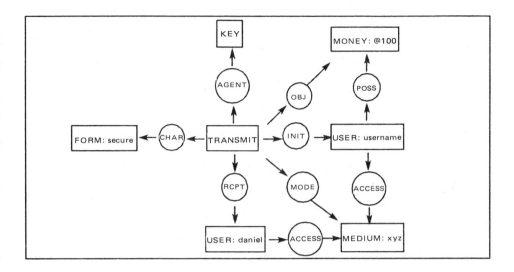

Fig. 11.9: Constructed Goal State Graph. Satisfied goal requirements include: (i) sender has $100 in his account; (ii) both users can access XYZ; (iii) XYZ must be a secure medium for such transmission and; (iv) an encryption key is required to secure the transmission.

11.5   COMPLETED RESEARCH

11.5.1   Knowledge base management system (KBMS)

On going research at Deakin University into the use of conceptual graphs for knowledge acquisition include the design and implementation of a self-organising conceptual dictionary (SOCD) (Garner and Tsui, 1988b). Such a dictionary should ultimately demonstrate the following capabilities. It should be able to:

- store graphs without predefining a fixed set of attributes (ie. labels);

- index the incoming structures in multiple locations of the memory (knowledge base), if necessary;

- generalise between incoming structure and existing (indexed) structures;

- identify graph-subgraph relationships;

- handle exact and partial matching of stored structures based on an input pattern;

- store all structures economically; and

- propose new structures (ie. rules, graphs, concepts) by integrating (joining) a generalised pattern with another pattern.

The SOCD can be treated as a knowledge base management system (KBMS) for conceptual graphs. Hence the SOCD not only provides the above capabilities but also allows high flexibility for the knowledge engineer to tailor the characteristics of a general SOCD for any expert system that requires to store a massive set of graphs. Characteristics of the SOCD that can be specified by the user include (but are not limited to) the following:

- mode of operation (Simple or Advanced);

- number of generalisations permitted each time the SOCD indexes a new structure;

- minimum and maximum level in the dictionary that generalisation is permitted;

- breadth first or depth first generalisation strategies;

- type of memory to be simulated (episodic or semantic);

- semantic Distance tolerance for avoiding over-generalisations.

11.5.2 Application of dynamic knowledge in the design of distributed operating systems

This project investigated an abstraction called SYSTEMS MAP based on conceptual graph theory for representing the knowledge requirements of distributed operating systems. This knowledge-base has been used on an interactive basis for the design of an UPPER KERNEL (higher level functions such as job management) for a distributed system (Garner and Kutti, 1987).

The SYSTEMS MAP comprises knowledge about the configuration of the distributed system, services available and users enrolled. An interface to the systems map is provided via the Knowledge-Base Editor (KBE) which makes a set of functions available for both users and the system. This facilitates the creation, modification and accumulation of graphs in maintaining the systems map dynamically, as well as to search for and schedule users' requests (Kutti, 1989).

We elected to use conceptual graphs for encoding the knowledge of the peripherals and distributed system for the following reasons:

- graphs or maps are seen to directly reflect the configuration of distributed systems in terms of the entity-relationship model;

- configuration and reconfiguration are standard graph operations;

- graphs provide a unified representation of domain knowledge objects called " SYS- TEM" along with a set of algorithms for scheduling and network management;

- conceptual graphs encode semantic information,which is useful in building a natural language interface to the outside world;

- graphs provide a flexible and dynamic data structure for accumulating knowledge as the domain size or status changes;

- graph notation in representing systems knowledge offers the capability for abstraction and better understanding of the systems design.

The tools developed for graph manipulation are directly applicable to the design of distributed systems requiring intelligent objects for their specification and for system evaluation. This approach is expected to identify the role of AI in the design of intelligent operating systems; e.g. the role of episodic memories!

11.5.3 Complex reference resolution (CRR) in M.I.S. design

CRR is one of the new approaches to the application of conceptual graphs in the business area. It has been developed to reduce the difficulty of interaction between managers and system analysts. More specifically, CRR is a complex reference interpreter where the references come from the requirement specifications given by the manager. Some references might be more complicated, and need deep knowledge about business policies and models before progress can be made (Jiramahasuwan, 1988). In order to interpret complex references, CRR needs a conversational advisor comprising domain knowledge, structural knowledge and strategic (business) knowledge. Tools are also needed to manipulate this knowledge. Conceptual graphs have been used to represent these three classes of knowledge and an extendible graph processor has been implemented to process these conceptual structures. As examples, join may be used to expand detail knowledge about the concepts. Also projection is used to focus on key concepts such as exception reports. CRR has its own automatic reorganisation capability, which is very useful for learning new concepts. Final output from CRR is in the form of QUERY GRAPHS which can be mapped directly to the SQL.

11.5.4 A canonical graph model for knowledge elicitation

The aim of this research is to extend contemporary work on canonical graph models with an active agent paradigm and control structures suitable for the acquisition of planning and strategic knowledge (Garner and Lukose, 1990a, 1990b). An actor system has been completed enabling a current value programming environment - the computation of results for some concepts and the transformation of knowledge content conveyed in conceptual graphs (Garner and Lukose, 1989).

In view of the knowledge formation procedures set out in Garner *et al.*, (1987), the representation formalism for the planning elements are considered to be essential. Studies into conventional representation techniques for the planning elements together with the design of a unifying representation of the planning elements, incorporating active agents, has enabled us to identify and store planning heuristics in a form of an executable conceptual structure called the PROBLEM MAP (Garner and Lukose, 1990b, 1991a, 1919b).

11.5.5 Continuous scene analysis

In this project, semantic and pragmatic information is used to identify and classify both individual objects and sub-scenes (concepts) in the scene analysis process. Scene analysis involves not only the process of matching individual object shapes and texture, but also involves reasoning about the spatial and contextual relationships among objects. Continuous scene analysis is seen to require temporal reasoning logic and access to real world knowledge to establish event - action relationships. Image understanding may well require, in addition, a goal-plan-understanding mechanism, where human actions require interpretation.

The proposed system for scene analysis under study at Deakin University explores the use of adaptive concept (object) classification and model-directed reasoning for image understanding (re Fig. 11.10).

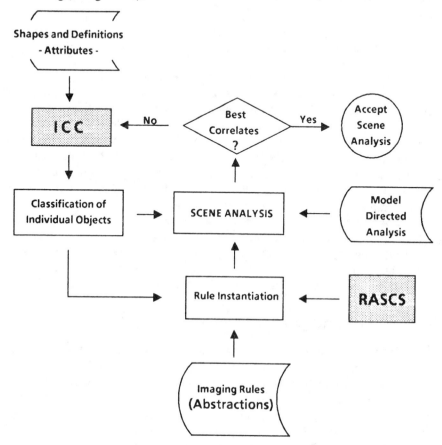

Fig. 11.10: ICC for scene analysis.

The reduction of the search space in scene analysis is achieved through two novel techniques:

(i) Intelligent selection through goal interpretation (Garner, Lui and Tsui, 1986) of the appropriate subset of objects required for scene (concept) classification; and

(ii) Use of explanation-based learning to provide an expanding definition of "normality", thereby reducing the number of "exceptions" that need to be considered.

Object definition is treated as the symbolic description of an object class which shows its essential features including its structural decomposition (ie. subparts) and the related spatial relations, physical appearance for each parts and the object as a whole. Object recognition, hence, involves the identification of these essential features in order to classify the unknown object (represented as image data) as a type/subtype/schema of an object class. The type-subtype relationship of object classes is represented in the ISA hierarchy. The relationship among subparts (ie. structural decomposition) of an object is represented in the PARTOF hierarchy. The physical appearance of the object and its subparts will be represented in the VISUAL network with spatial relation between adjacent subparts. The relationships of these three hierarchies are shown in Fig. 11.11.

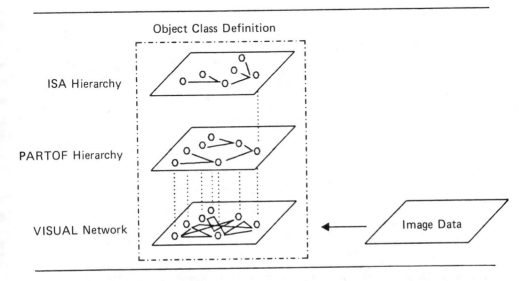

Fig. 11.11: The relationship among ISA and PARTOF hierarchies and VISUAL network.

Fig. 11.12 illustrates the interactions among the hierarchies. For example, a chair is subtype of furniture, chair is composed of a back, a seat, 4 legs, and a leg is a long thin rectangle under the seat which is a horizontal parallelogram with a rectangle above and perpendicular to it at one edge.

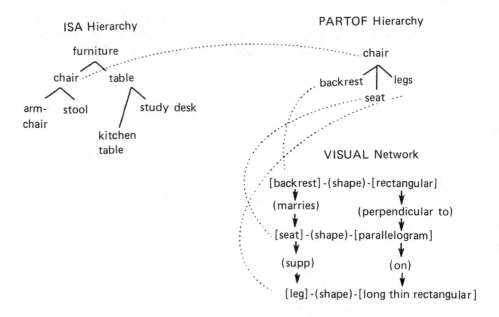

Fig. 11.12: The description of object class - chair.

11.6   ON-GOING RESEARCH

11.6.1   Case-based reasoning

Case-based reasoning is a problem solving method which relies on past experiences (cases) to provide a model for solving the current problem. Briefly, the current case is compared to known cases, and the case which is most appropriate to the current case is then selected (recalled) for further applicability/suitability tests. If the tests do not show any inconsistency in the current case, and the preconditions for applying the solution are satisfied, then the candidate solution is adopted with appropriate modifications, if any. Feedback on the proposed method and solution may be sought from the user. If the proposition is accepted, then the current case is integrated into memory for future use. If the proposition is rejected by the user, then the system would have to re-examine the basis for case selection, explain the failure and, if possible, propose another plan.

Clearly, a selection and evaluation process, which is driven by a cognitive model representing many views of the problem is more likely to provide acceptable results. Hence, we propose the use of a cognitive model (to be implemented as a meta-level structure supported by appropriate actors) to substantiate the user's initial input of the problem description with expert views on the particular problem, and using expert cues as part of the selection criteria, finding the most appropriate case to match (Garner, et al., 1989). The use of the cognitive model will enhance the selection process. After the case has been selected, the cognitive model could be used to evaluate the proposed plan (solution).

One obvious benefit derived from using a cognitive model which encompasses the views of not just one but many experts, is that the set of attributes describing the problem is more complete, than if only the user's set is used, as they are gathered from more than one expert.

This is especially useful in an advisory system where the best advice is derived from the composite view of many experts.

Application of CBR in automated design of management controls is also currently being investigated. This study not only will provide our research team with indepth knowledge on case adaptation and case base reasoning, but also will attempt to address the complex problems involved in designing management controls.

11.6.2 Knowledge indexing

In this project, we are investigating various techniques to index conceptual structures. Our preliminary case study on indexing journal articles involved performing a semantic analysis on the abstract of the journal article, followed by a process based on goal-interpretation to identify possible goal states that a reader will attain if he/she reads the journal paper (Garner and Lukose, 1991d). This goal-state information is utilised to index the journal article. This technique is consistent with the premise that a user usually wants to read a particular journal article to attain certain knowledge. Therefore, the user query indicating the knowledge he/she wants to attain is sufficient to retrieve appropriate articles indexed on goal themes.

There is growing recognition that cost-effective retrieval will only result when documents can be retrieved on the basis of their semantic content, rather than an ad-hoc collection of keywords! The prospects for the development of such systems are now excellent due to a better understanding of the modes of interaction appropriate to discourse understanding and to the development of active parsers utilising goal interpretation methods (Garner and Lukose, 1991c).

11.6.3 Theme directed reasoning in creative information processing

In this research, we investigate the scope and limitations of creative processes in the context of a goal interpretation metaphor for theme-directed reasoning (Garner and Smith, 1990). Roger Schank has demonstrated the value of scripts in generating expectations. He also demonstrated the psychological plausibility of scripts in human information processing and memory models. We are investigating the addition of a third ingredient: roles. For example, DOCTOR, PATIENT, TEACHER, STUDENT are all roles which people may take on and give clues as to clusters of goals, reasoning strategies and scripts which might be activated in a given encounter.

11.7 CONCLUSION

Conceptual graphs have been shown to provide a unifying knowledge representation scheme for complex, real world problems and to support novel executable knowledge structures suitable for both planning and reasoning, but also appropriate for real time control.

More recently, we have demonstrated the feasibility of using prototypical knowledge for automated knowledge acquisition and have developed an architecture for decision support in unstructured environments. Our current research into conceptual graph models is focussing on case-based interaction for management intelligent systems utilising recent breakthroughs in discourse understanding and theme directed reasoning. Commercial exploitation of some of our work (eg. automated document indexing) is in prospect.

Acknowledgements

We would like to thank Frank O'Carroll for writing an initial version of the APSG parser generator in PROLOG, Charlene Chong for encoding the FRAME DISPLAYER in the canonical graph processor and improvements to the KBE, and Betty Cheng for implementing the ICC. Grateful acknowledgement is made to Deakin University (Postgraduate Scholarships), Corporate Research Services' (Scholarships) and the Australian Research Grants Scheme (ARGS) under contract numbers A48615479, A48831041 and to Iris Chan for providing assistance in compiling the reference lists.

BIBLIOGRAPHY

Adam, J-P. and Fargues, J. (1984) "KALIPSOS: A Text Processor for Knowledge Acquisition," IBM Europe Institute, Natural Language Processing, Davos, Switzerland, July 30 - August 3, 1984.

Baldwin, J.F. (1985a) "Support Logic Programming for Expert Systems," Information Technology Research Center and the Department of Engineering Mathematics, University of Bristol.

Baldwin, J.F. and Crabtree, B. (1986) "C.R.I.L. - A Concept Relational Inference Language for Knowledge Engineering," presented at the IBM Workshop on Conceptual Graphs, 18-20th August, 1986, Thornwood.

Berg-Cross, G. and Hanna, J. (1986) "Database Design Using Conceptual Graphs," presented at the IBM Workshop on Conceptual Graphs, 18-20th August, 1986, Thornwood.

Foo, N.Y. and Rao, A.S. (1986) "Modality and Truth Maintenance in a Conceptual Processor," presented at the IBM Workshop on Conceptual Graphs, 18-20th August, 1986, Thornwood.

Garner, B.J. (1987) "Corporate Language Systems: Technical Issues and Their Management Implications," Proceedings of the Fourth South Pacific Area Regional Conference, 17-19th March, 1987, Brisbane.

Garner, B.J., Chong, C., Jiramahasuwan, A., Lui, D., Lukose, D. and Tsui, E. (1987) "Actor Implementations for Cybernetic Reasoning Systems," Proceedings of the 2nd Annual Conceptual Graph Workshop, IBM Paris Scientific Center, 2nd-4th September, 1987, Paris.

Garner, B.J. and Forrester, C.L. (1986) "Progress in Concepts of Decision Support for Unstructured Problem Environments," Proceedings of the First Australian AI Congress, 18-21st November, 1986, Melbourne.

Garner, B.J. and Lui, D. (1987) "A Conceptual Graph Model for Key Management in Public Network," Proceedings of the Congress of Cybernetics and Systems, 18th-20th March, 1987, New Delhi.

Garner, B.J. Lukose, D. and Tsui, E. (1987a) "A Batch Processor for the Knowledge Base Editor, Technical Report 87/4, Xerox AI Laboratory, Division of Computing and Mathematics, Deakin University, February.

Garner, B.J. Lukose, D. and Tsui, E. (1987b) "Parsing Natural Language through Pattern Correlation and Modification," Proceedings of the 7th International Workshop on Expert Systems and Their Applications, Avignon '87, 13-15 May, 1987, France, p1285-1299.

Garner, B.J. and Kutti, S. (1987) "Application of Dynamic Knowledge in Designing Distributed Operating Systems," Proceedings of Applications of AI V, John F. Gilmore, Editor, SPIE Proc. 784, 18-20 May, Orlando, 1987.

Garner B.J. and Tsui, E. (1985c) "First Report on the Design and Implementation of the Canonical Graph Processor", WPS-85-02, Division of Computing and Mathematics, Deakin University, December.

Garner B.J. and Tsui, E. (1986c) "An Extendible Graph Processor and its Applications," presented at the IBM Workshop on Conceptual Graphs, 18-20th August, 1986, Thornwood.

Garner, B.J. and Kutti, N. (1987); "Application of dynamic knowledge in the design of a distributed operating systems", Proceedings of the Applications of AI V, SPIE Proc. 786, J.F. Gilmore, Editor, 18-20 May, Orlando, Florida.

Garner, B.J., Larkin, K.E. and Tsui, E. (1989); "Prototypical Knowledge for Case-based Reasoning", DARPA Workshop on Case-based Reasoning, 31st May - 2nd June, Pensacola Beach, Florida, p258.

Garner, B.J. and Lukose, D. (1989); "Integrated Actor Paradigm For Knowledge Based Systems, Knowledge Based Computer Systems", edited by S. Ramani, R. Chandrasekar and K.S.R. Anjaneyulu, Lecture Notes in Artificial Intelligence sub-series of the Lecture Notes in Computer Science series No. 444, Springer-Verlag.

Garner, B.J. and Lukose, D. (1990a); "Goal Interpretation as a Knowledge Acquisition Mechanism" in *Expert Systems for Management and Engineering*, (eds) E. Balagurusamy and J. Howe, Ellis-Horwood Limited, p. 100-114.

Garner, B.J. and Lukose, D. (1990b); "Strategic Knowledge Elicitation Utilising Goal Interpretation Methodology", in *Computer Systems and Applications: Recent Trends,* (ed) E. Balagurusamy and B. Sushila, Tata McGraw-Hill Publishing Company Limited, p. 521-537.

Garner, B.J. and Lukose, D., (1991a); "Goal Specification Graphs for Strategic Knowledge Elicitation", Proceedings of the Workshop on Knowledge Acquisition for Knowledge Based Systems, Pokolbin, N.S.W., Australia, 20-23 August.

Garner, B.J. and Lukose, D., (1991b); "Actor Graphs: A Novel Executable Conceptual Structure", Proceedings of the IJCAI'91 Workshop on Objects and A.I., Sydney, Australia, 25th. August.

Garner, B.J. and Lukose, D., (1991c); "Progress Report on Automated Document Indexing and Retrieval", Department of Computing and Mathematics, Faculty of Science, Deakin University, Geelong, Victoria, Australia, 3217.

Garner, B.J. and Smith N. (1990); "Information Processing Models of the Creative Process", Proceedings of the First National Conference in Cognitive Science, Sydney, Australia.

Hartley, R.H. (1985) "Representation of Procedural Knowledge for Expert Systems," Proceedings of the IEEE Conference on Artificial Intelligence Applications, December 11-13, Miami Beach, Florida.

Hartley, R.H. (1987) "The Foundations of Conceptual Programming", Computing Research Laboratory and Department of Computer Science, New Mexico State University.

Hurwitz, A. and Marshall, J.B. (1986) "An Intelligent Help System for IBM VM/SP," paper presented at the IBM Workshop on Conceptual Graphs, 18-20th August, 1986, Thornwood.

Jiramahasuwan, A. (1988); "Intelligent Knowledge-Based System For Managerial Information Support", MSc Thesis, Department of Computer and Mathematics, School of Sciences, Deakin University, Geelong, Victoria, Australia, 3217, July.

Koh, J. E.K. (1986) "Expert Planners/Audit Planner, Honours thesis, Division of Computing and Mathematics, Deakin University, November, 1986.

Kutti, S. (1989); "A Knowledge-Based Kernel For Distributed Systems", Ph.D. Thesis, Department of Computing and Mathematics, School of Sciences, Deakin University, Geelong, Victoria, Australia, 3217, February.

Lui, D. (1986); "User guide to RASCS, Division of Computing and Mathematics, Deakin University.

Martin, T.P., Baldwin, J.F. and Pilsworth, B.W. (1986) "A Fuzzy Prolog Interpreter", Information Technology Research Center and the Department of Engineering Mathematics, University of Bristol.

Morton, S.K. and Baldwin, J.F. (1985) "Conceptual Graphs and Fuzzy Qualifiers in Natural Language Interfaces," presented at the Cambridge Conference on Fuzzy sets, 1985.

Morton, S.K. (1986) "The Incorporation of Uncertainty into the Theory of Conceptual Graphs," paper presented at the IBM Workshop on Conceptual Graphs, 18-20th August, 1986, Thornwood.

Pazienza, M.T. and Velardi, P. (1986) "Pragmatic Knowledge on Word Uses for Semantic Analysis of Texts," paper presented at the IBM Workshop on Conceptual Graphs, 18-20th August, 1986, Thornwood.

Plantinga, E. (1986) "Mental Models, Ambiguity and Metaphor," paper presented at the IBM Workshop on Conceptual Graphs, 18-20th August, 1986, Thornwood.

Salveter, S.C. (1979) "Inferring Conceptual Graphs," Cognitive Science 3, pp. 141-166.

Sowa, J.F. (1984) "Conceptual Structures: Information Processing in Mind and Machine, Addison Wesley, Reading, 1984.

Sowa, J.F. (1986a) "Notes on Conceptual Graphs", informal notes prepared by the author, August.

Sowa, J.F. (1986b) "Using a Lexicon of Canonical Graphs In a Semantic Interpreter, M. Evens, ed., *Relational Models of the Lexicon*, Cambridge University Press, pp. 113-137.

12

Using the Situation Data Model to Construct a Conceptual Basis Set

William M. Tepfenhart
Mary Marin Consulting,
923 Warren Way,
Richardson, Texas 75080, USA

12.1   INTRODUCTION

Previous efforts by the author have been dedicated to the development of the Situation
Data Model (SDM). The SDM was introduced to the conceptual graph community at the
Third Annual Workshop on Conceptual Graphs in a paper entitled "The Situation Data
Model" (Tepfenhart and Lazzara, 1988). At the workshop, the SDM was presented as a
model derived, in part, from the theory of Situation Semantics described in *Situations and
Attitudes* by John Barwise and John Perry (1983) and, in part, from the theory of Conceptual
Graphs described in *Conceptual Structures – Information Processing in Mind and Machine*
by J. F. Sowa (1984).

Since the introduction of the SDM, the author has developed a conceptual basis set
for several problem domains by applying the SDM to assist in identifying concepts and
conceptual relations that comprise the conceptual basis set for these problem domains.
One of the surprising results of these efforts has been the observation that at high levels
of abstractions the same concepts and conceptual relations have consistently occurred and
reoccurred from problem domain to problem domain. This observation is consistent with
expectations voiced by many attending the previous workshop.

The top-level concepts and conceptual relations that were identified in the course of
this work are presented in this paper. Considerations concerning how these concepts and
conceptual relations were identified; the computational considerations that were taken into
account; and the relationship of a conceptual basis set to a lexicon are also presented in
order to establish their value.

12.2   THE CONCEPTUAL BASIS SET

An intelligent agent possesses and employs in problem solving a set of concepts and
conceptual relations. Since the set of concepts and conceptual relations is employed in
problem solving, one must expect that concepts and conceptual relations are arranged in a
structure which not only enables problem solving, but, in fact, simplifies computation. The

set of concepts and conceptual relations possessed by an intelligent agent and the structure within which they are arranged is termed a conceptual basis set.

The importance of a conceptual basis set resides in the application of it in problem solving. The term "problem solving" is employed to refer to the activities associated with interacting with an environment and communicating perceptions and interpretations of that environment in a natural language. Since the goal of artificial intelligence is to achieve an intelligent machine, it follows that an intermediate goal is to define a conceptual basis set that can be stored within the memory of the machine and employed in problem solving.

A critical problem of artificial intelligence concerns definition of a conceptual basis set that enables problem solving. Currently, this problem has been addressed in three vastly different approaches:

1. ignoring the problem,

2. lexical analysis, and

3. conceptual modeling.

Each approach has had its successes and failures. The intent of this section is to describe these approaches and to contrast them with a fourth - percept based conceptual modeling for development of ontological models of problem domains.

Ignoring the problem is often the approach taken in development of a rule-based expert system. This approach does not require capturing the semantics in the rule-base, but does require that the semantics be maintained in an informal manner by the user and developer. While this has resulted in programs that function well for small problem domains, where the conceptual complexity is minimal, there have been difficulties in scaling expert systems to larger problem domains. The problems associated with scaling to larger problem domains all reside in semantic ambiguities encoded in the rule base.

The lexical approach is derived from linguistic studies of word meanings. The conceptual basis set is constructed by identifying the meaning associated with a word and then introducing a concept to represent that meaning in the conceptual basis set. In terms of the meaning triangle shown in Fig. 12.1, this approach concentrates on the virtual link between the symbol and the percept in an attempt to identify the concept. The difficulty of this approach is that one is attempting to solve many problems at once, namely, establishing a comprehensive vocabulary for a domain; identifying the percepts associated with the domain; defining the individual concepts; and linking them into the conceptual basis set. Beyond the problems that arise as a consequence of the indirect route taken to define the concept, an addition problem of this approach is that the resultant conceptual basis set will usually be poorly structured for use in problem solving.

Conceptual modeling attempts to identify the conceptual basis set directly by employing a model of semantic meaning. This is achieved by employing definitional relationships among conceptual elements based on necessary and sufficient conditions. The core relationship is the type-of relation. Unfortunately, the type-of relation is often ambiguous in its application. For example, Smokey the Bear can be referred to as a type of bear and a type of tame animal. Superficially, these two type-of relationships have different implications. Namely, one type-of relation is denoting membership to a class defined according to a maximal set of shared physical attributes and characteristics while the other type-of relation is denoting membership to a set defined by a shared behavior in particular circumstances. This type of modeling has been employed in the development of the concepts and conceptual relations in semantic networks with some success. However, this approach fails for extremely large networks and numerous problems have been experienced with identifying and defining primitive conceptual elements.

An alternative approach to developing an ontological model is to leverage direct observations of the problem domain. The primitive conceptual elements are established in terms of interpretations of the types of things that can be perceived, the relationships that can exist among them, and past perceptions of the domain. In terms of the meaning triangle shown in Fig. 12.1, this approach defines the conceptual basis set from a foundation based on percepts as opposed to a foundation based on a symbols. The link between the subject of the definition and the source of the definition is direct as opposed to the indirect route of the lexical approach.

The Meaning Triangle

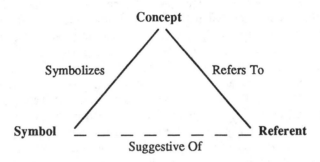

Fig. 12.1 - The Meaning Triangle illustrates the relationship between a symbol, concept and referent. It should be noted that the referent enters the system in the form of a percept for the thing through the process of observation. A symbol enters the system in exactly the same way. The only direct link between symbol and referent is through the pathway that incorporates the concept. The arc between symbol and referent is only a virtual link.

While there is a connection between primitive conceptual elements and perception, these are not the only conceptual elements that are incorporated into a conceptual basis set derived in this approach. Additional conceptual elements are incorporated into the conceptual basis set that are not directly derived from perceptions. These are derived conceptual elements. They are defined by identifying substitutions that simplify the conceptual structures in which past observations are expressed. Hence repeated observations of things sitting on top of other things can be employed to define the concepts for BASE, APEX, and STACK to name a few.

Structure is added to the conceptual basis set by enforcing constraints on the conceptualization of the model in terms of the mechanisms and techniques by which the conceptual elements are achieved. Primitive conceptual elements are organized according to the mechanism and manner in which perception is performed. Derived concepts are organized along the same lines, but also further restricted by the conceptual structure from which they were defined. It should be noted that using different assumptions concerning how perception is performed can lead to entirely different conceptual basis sets.

Developing the conceptual basis set along these lines simplifies using it in problem solving for several very good reasons. First, primitive conceptual elements are the observables within the domain and, as a result, will be the fundamental terms employed in describing both, the problem states to be solved and past experiences in problem solving. Second, derived conceptual elements enable problem solving to be performed using simplified conceptual structures. Finally, the structure of the conceptual basis set eliminates ambiguity from the forced traceability back to observations of the domain, facilitates the introduction of new conceptual elements by use of the assumptions of perception, and simplifies search since similarly related conceptual elements will be in close proximity within the conceptual basis set.

One of the principle problem solving capabilities desired in artificial intelligence is the ability to process natural language. In order to achieve this, it is necessary to derive a lexicon which provides the mapping of a word to its' meaning - namely a conceptual element. By examination of the meaning triangle it can be seen that the lexicon is a set comprised of words with their relationship to the concepts and conceptual relations of the conceptual basis set. The relationship employed in a lexicon is that the word x communicates y of the conceptual basis set. This relationship has several significant consequences with regard to development of a lexicon and testing the validity of a conceptual basis set.

Given a conceptual basis set and a vocabulary, the lexicon can be developed identifying what conceptual element is communicated by a given word. The development of a lexicon is simplified by the fact that the developer has at his disposal both the word and potential meanings of the word and is now attempting to correlate them on the basis of a very specific relationship. This development approach is to be contrasted with a lexical study. In a lexical study, identifying the meaning of the word from its grammatical category and usage in sentences to identify the percept that it indirectly refers to is much more demanding.

There are additional reasons for developing a lexicon in this manner - reason independent of attempting to achieve natural language understanding capabilities. In particular, developing a lexicon in this approach provides a means to establish the completeness of the conceptual basis set. In the case where the conceptual basis set is incomplete, there will be words which communicate a conceptual element missing in the conceptual basis set. This allows questions to be raised concerning what types of perceptions are required in the problem domain but were not addressed.

12.3   THE TOP-LEVEL OF THE CONCEPTUAL BASIS

The Situation Data Model is an ontological model that is highly dependent on direct observations of a wide variety of human centered problem domains - observations that have been described by Barwise and Perry (1983). The Situation Data Model identifies the types of things that can be perceived and organizes them in a fashion that is consistent with the manner in which humans tend to organize them. The structure of the conceptual basis set is achieved by use of constraints derived predominantly on vision.

The following subsections presents the concepts and conceptual relations which comprise the top-level of a conceptual basis set that has been constructed using the Situation Data Model. However, prior to their presentation, a few issues concerning the the discussion of the concepts and conceptual relations presented here should be addressed.

First, the majority of the text concerns the definitions of the concepts and conceptual relations without describing the structure of the conceptual basis set which they comprise. The structure of the top-level of the conceptual basis set is illustrated in Figs. 12.2 and 12.3. As can be seen in these figures, the structure of the conceptual basis set is hierarchical. The adoption of a hierarchical structure was a consequence of the constraint that the structure must simplify computation. While there are many who might question that a hierarchical structure is appropriate for a conceptual basis set, this type of structure is the simplest for computational purposes. It should also be noted that this structure has an underlying structure of conceptual graphs linked to each node which are not illustrated. The underlying structure provides the capabilities often associated with a semantic network.

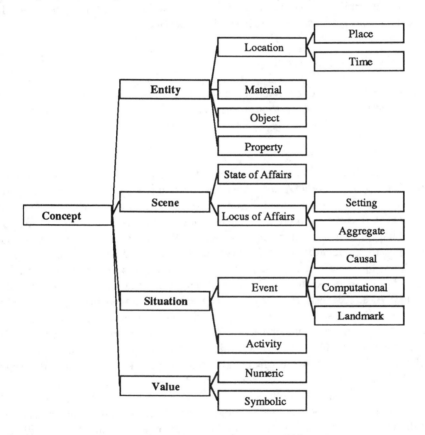

Fig. 12.2 The Top-level of the concept hierarchy.

Second, presentation of the conceptual elements is achieved through the use of labels. The labels are employed for two separate purposes. The first purpose is provide a label that allows distinguishing between conceptual elements and allows a means to refer to conceptual elements. If this were the only purpose, labels such as CONCEPT-1 would have been employed since the tendency is to view labeling as a type of lexical operation. The second purpose is to provide an intuitive interpretation of the concept such that a detailed examination of the conceptual definition is not necessary. However, the intuitive interpretation is only an approximation to the concept. The fact that the labels are approximations to the meaning illustrates one problem concerned with communicating definitions for elements of a conceptual basis set. This problem is that the only way to communicate concepts is through the use of natural language references to them, but these references are often ambiguous. As a consequent, it becomes very difficult to express a precise definition for a concept in terms of words whose meanings are subjective.

Finally, the top-level of the conceptual basis set is still in development. The concept and conceptual relations are still be refined. Some distinctions among concepts that could have been made have not been made and the consequences of these types of decisions have not been fully explored. This is reflected in the presentation where some concepts have very long detailed descriptions and others have very short descriptions. In short, the top-level of the conceptual basis set presented here is still in a state of evolution.

12.3.1   The Top-Level Concepts

The following paragraphs define the top-level concepts that have been determined to be consistent from problem domain to problem domain. The abstraction hierarchy for these top-level concepts are shown in Fig. 12.2.

Abstract Object Abstract objects are objects that have an individual conceptual manifestation in the real world. A conceptual manifestation is a label used by a cognitive agent to denote a composite of the physical manifestations of one or more concrete objects. An abstract object does not, in fact, have a corporeal reality, but can be said to exhibit the physical manifestations of concrete objects associated with it. As a result, it is possible to identify properties that must be associated with abstract objects. All abstract objects have conceptual properties, are aggregations of one or more concrete objects, and have a distributed location given by the locations of the objects which form it. As stated, abstract objects are used by a cognitive agent to denote the physical manifestations of an aggregate of one or more concrete objects. The manner in which the aggregate of the concrete objects is formed determines whether the abstract object is extended or localized. An abstract object is the former if it is a loosely bound group of entities acting in concert. An abstract object is the later if it is an arbitrary aspect of a concrete object. When abstract objects are extended, they are aggregates of loosely bound concrete objects. Abstract objects which are extended are insubstantial with difficult to define boundaries. Objects such as corporations, governments, and military services belong to this group. For example, a government is an individual entity that encompasses the individuals who rule, those individuals under that rule, and is bounded by the region of space over which that rule extends. A government, through the actions of the concrete objects that compose it can effect actions in the real world, actions which are beyond the abilities of the individual objects. When abstract objects are localized, they are labels for the properties of some portion of a concrete object which has been endowed properties not normal to that object. Objects such as property, currency, and time-zones are examples of localized abstract objects. For example, property is an entity that encompasses an arbitrary division of the earths surface with the properties that it has an owner, terrain features, and a boundary line.

Activity An activity is a fully developed situation which can consist of many scenes each of which is linked to its preceding and following scene by an action. Activities derive their importance since they are the contexts within which intelligent agents function. Examples of activities are playing a game, monitoring a system, studying a new domain, and diagnosing a disease.

Aggregation An aggregation is a type of locus of affairs used to denote a set of concepts and the relationships among them as a single concept. An aggregation is similar to a setting with the exception that the relationships of the aggregation with other concepts in a situation are expected to change while the relationships between a setting and the other concepts are expected to be static. An example of an aggregation is a flock of ducks. A flock of ducks fly in a characteristic v-shaped formation such that the same relationships hold among the ducks at all times. Of significance is that a flock of ducks may enter the location of a situation at some point in time and exit the situation at a later point in time.

Attribute An attribute is a directly measurable physical property of an object or material. An attribute has a value defined with respect to some standard object. The standard of comparison is some object with an attribute that has been accepted as a standard of comparison. Properties such as length and mass are examples of attributes. Objects such as a one meter stick and a one kilogram bar are examples of standards of comparison for the attributes of length and mass respectively.

Capability A capability is an ability of an object or material to perform actions, be used to perform an action, or effect changes in the real world. The value defined for a capability is Boolean, either the capability is present or it is not. For example, most birds and all planes have the capability of flight but to compare their capabilities is meaningless. That is, it is meaningful to compare how two things execute that capability, but not meaningful to compare the fact that both are capable of exhibiting the same ability. Properties such as the ability to fly and the ability to carry payloads are examples of capabilities.

Casual Event A causal event can be employed to denote necessary causal relations that exist between two scenes. For example, if an initial scene contains a bolt of lightening then a following scene must contain thunder. Causal events can be employed in a computational manner to identify expectations for situations and thus control computational complexity by a considerable degree.

Characteristic A characteristic is a physical aspect of an object or material. Characteristics are given values defined in terms of an object that exhibits the identical characteristic. For example, color is a characteristic of an object with a value given in terms of the color of another object (hence fire-engine red, lemon yellow, etc.). Properties such as color and pattern are examples of characteristics. Properties such as state (liquid, gaseous, solid, etc.) and form (cubic, egg-shaped, spherical, etc.) are also examples of characteristics.

Computational Event A computational event is a type of situation employed to change the structure of one expression of one form into another. Computational events include substitution of a locus of affairs for a subgraph of a scene, inversions of relations, and mathematical operations over values. Computational events are incorporated as part of the conceptual basis set since the operations they denote are learned, as opposed to an explicit processing structure in the mind.

Concrete Object Concrete objects are objects that have an individual physical manifestation in the real world. The nature and character of concrete objects can be specified since they have individual physical manifestations. All concrete objects have physical properties, occupy a volume of space, and have a location determined by the region of space occupied by the object. Objects such as airplanes, cars, people, animals, and radios belong to this group. As stated previously, physical objects occupy a volume of space. The way in which an object occupies space is important. An object can be substantial or insubstantial depending on its surface characteristics and the definiteness of the volume it occupies. When an object is substantial, the volume of space it occupies is well-defined and is given as the interior of a distinct boundary called a surface. Whatever is interior to the surface is the object and whatever is exterior to the surface is not. For example, a block of ice occupies a well defined volume of space interior to the surface of the block and hence is a substantial object. When an object is insubstantial, the volume of space it occupies is ill-defined. In this case, there exists a boundary such that whatever is interior to the boundary is clearly the object and there exists a second boundary such that whatever is exterior to that bound is not the object. The necessity of specifying two boundaries to identify the topological surface of an object is what makes that object insubstantial and the volume of space ill-defined. For example, a cloud has an indistinct boundary and hence is an insubstantial object.

Entity The common usage of the word entity is to denote something which has separate and distinct existence and objective or conceptual reality. The definition for entity that is adopted here reflects this usage, but does so by stating the types of things which have a separate and distinct reality in terms of well recognized categories of entities. The definition for an entity is: An entity is an object, property, material, or location. The terms object, property, material, and location are used in a technical sense to delimit several important and distinct categories of entities. These categories are distinct in the sense that a particular entity is a member of one and only one of them.

Event An event is a special situation which consists of only three elements: an initial scene, a final scene, and an action which links the two. Events can be used to enforce causality (such as causal events), employed as a landmark for time against which situations are measured (landmark events), or employed to represent conceptual computations (computational event).

Feature A feature is a limited surface aspect of an object. A feature has a value obtained by its similarity to a prototypical feature of another object. For example, a branch of a tree is a feature of a tree defined by its surface similarities to a prototypical branch. Properties such as noses, terrain, and other shape related characteristics of objects are examples of features.

Label A label is an alpha-numeric value which is used to denote a particular instance or class. A label may be either a numeric value or a symbolic value. A label is assigned an object through the process of labeling and is accomplished by the actions of an active agent. The values 001-23-443 and 0929959 are examples of numeric labels such as might be used in a part number or serial number. Name values, such as Sam and Spot, are symbolic labels used to denote a particular person or, in the case of spot, a dog.

Landmark Event A landmark event is a type of situation which occurred at some previous time and is employed as a landmark for determining values of comparison for temporal locations. Restated, landmark events are events whose time of occurrence is employed as a value of comparison for current situations. For example, the death of Jesus is a landmark event whose time of occurrence is defined to be 0 A.D. and is employed as a value of comparison for the time of events which have occurred since then.

Location Common usage of the word location is to denote a position or site occupied or available for occupancy or marked by some distinguishing feature. The definition for property that is adopted here reflects this usage, but incorporates temporal aspect to the definition as well. The definition for a location is: A location is a place and/or time which can be occupied by an object. A location has values determined by comparison to space and time standards. It should be noted that a location is not necessarily distinct.

Locus of Affairs A locus of affairs is a scene which serves as token for a number of concepts and the relationships which hold among them without change throughout a situation. Thus, a locus of affairs can be a setting or an aggregate of entities. The purpose for which a locus of affairs is employed in a conceptual graph is to minimize the number of concepts and the relations that hold among them that must be processed.

Material Common usage of the word material is to denote the elements, constituents, or substances of which something is composed or can be made. The definition for property that is adopted here reflects this usage without constraint. The definition for a material is: A material is a constituent substance of an object. By this definition, it is meant that a material is a substance that composes an object. A material is characterized as being massive; constructed from other materials or objects; as having properties; and as filling some location. Example materials are: water, butter, metal, concrete, and air. As stated previously, objects occupy some volume of space. Materials are the substance of an object and fill the volume of space occupied by an object. It should be noted that only concrete objects have volumes that are filled by materials since abstract objects do not actually have corporeal existence. Materials are limited in the type of properties that they can manifest and on how those properties are manifested. For example, materials can have attributes based only on a per unit of material basis. Other properties, such as characteristics and capabilities can be associated with materials as well. Materials can not have features, since features are a traits associated with the surface of an object. Hence, a material such as water can have properties such as density (an attribute), liquid state (a characteristic), and the ability to dissolve other materials (a capability), but can not have a feature. Note that a body of water can have features such as waves, but that a body of water is a concrete object composed of the material water and that the waves are associated with the body and not the material.

Object Common usage of the word object is to denote the class of material things that can be perceived by the senses. The definition for object that is adopted here reflects this usage, but does so by stating that objects must be discrete and countable. The definition for an object is: An object is a thing which has a manifestation in the real world. By this definition, it is meant that an object is something that has a physical or conceptual existence in the real world. An object is characterized as being discrete; countable; constructed from other objects or materials; as having properties; and as occupying some location.

Place A place is a region of space. A place is typically described in terms of a set of connected points in space with a name used to denote that set of points. Each point occupies an infinitesimal volume in three dimensions. Connected points are two points which share a common side. A place can be dispersed or specific. An dispersed place occupies many points while a specific place occupies a single point. In many cases, the three dimensional nature of space is suppressed since places are often related to surfaces of objects, such as the surface of the earth. A region of space is named by: (1) coordinates defined with respect to a global standard location, (2) coordinates defined with respect to a local standard location, or (3) an inexact relationship to the location of a landmark object. The locations given by (0' longitude, 10' latitude), on a table, and a sea (in the sense of the region of space occupied by a body of water) are examples of places.

Property Common usage of the word property is to denote a trait or quality belonging and especially particular to an individual or thing. The definition for property that is adopted here reflects this usage, but does so by stating that the only types of things that have traits are objects or materials. The technical definition of a property is: A property is an attribute, characteristic, feature, or capability of an object or material. By this definition it is meant that a property is a trait of an object or material. It should be noted that a property can only exist only in conjunction with an object or material, and not as an individual independent of another entity. The terms attribute, characteristic, feature, or capability are used in a technical sense and are further defined in the paragraphs below. It should be noted that the distinctions among attributes, characteristics, features, and capabilities are best conveyed by example rather than description.

Scene The common usage of the word scene is to denote a state of the world described in terms of the entities and the relationship that hold among them at a particular point in time. The definition for a scene that is adopted here reflects this usage. The definition for a scene is: A scene is a state of the world described in terms of the entities and the relationship that hold among them at a particular point in time. Scenes are means to denote with a single symbol a complex set of statements that define a state of the world. There are some necessary conditions which must be present in a description of the world in order for that description to constitute a scene. First, there must be a location of interest present, even if that location is generic (a position and a time). Second, a scene must describe the state of the world for one and only one temporal location. Third, every entity in the description must stand in relation to some other entity in the description. Finally, every relation that appears in a scene must be complete (a complete relation is one in which the number and type of entities that are required as target and subject of the relation are present).

Setting The common usage of the word setting is to denote the background in which a situation unfolds. The definition for a setting that is adopted here is consistent with this usage with the recognition that a setting is a specialized locus of affairs employed to denote the unchanging portion of the scenes which comprise a situation.

Situation The common usage of the word situation is to denote the way in which something is placed in relations to its surroundings. The definition for a situation that is adopted here extends this usage to incorporate the temporal nature of the real world. The definition for a situation is: A situation is denotation for a set of scenes and the actions which connect them. Situations are a single denotation to represent a complex set of statements that describe a series of events in the world. In many texts, a situation used in this manner is sometimes referred to as a context. There are some necessary conditions which must be present in a description of the world in order for that description to constitute a situation. First, there must be a location of interest present, even if that location is generic (a position and a time). Second, a situation must describe the world as a sequence of scenes each scene ordered such that a scene previous to it must have occurred at an earlier time. Third, every scene in the description must be connect to some other scene in the description. Finally, every action must be complete (a complete action is one in which the type of scenes required as target and subject of the relation are present).

State of Affairs A state of affairs is a description of the world at an instant in time. While it is a specialization of scene, a state of affairs is expected to change at the next instant of time. This should be compared with a locus of affairs which is expected to be static within the time frame of a situation.

Time A time is period of TIME (where TIME is used to denote the temporal dimension). A time is typically described in terms of a set of connected segments of TIME with a name used to denote that set of slices. Each slice occupies an infinitesimal segment in one dimension. Connected slices are two slices in which the end of one slice is the start of the other. A time can be dispersed or specific. An dispersed time occupies many slices while a specific time occupies a single slice. To further clarify the distinction between a dispersed time an a specific time consider a time period such as an hour as an example of a dispersed time and the time 3:00 am as a specific time. A time is a given a value established by: (1) the value of a standard clock, (2) the value of a relative clock, or (3) relationship to the time of a landmark event. The locations given by 1:30 Greenwich time, 6:30 local time, and after the explosion and examples of times.

Value Common usage of the word value is to denote a numerical quantity that is assigned or is determined by calculation or measurement. The definition for value that is adopted here reflects this usage, but includes non-numeric quantities and labels as well. The technical definition for a value is: A value is a measure of comparison or a label. A value can be numeric or symbolic. The difference between values which are measures of comparison and those which are labels is significant.

Value of Comparison A value of comparison is a ratio of a common property of two objects. A value of comparison is a ratio associated with an object as a result of the process of measurement. In the process of measurement one object is the subject of the measurement while the other object is a standard of measurement. However, a value of comparison, as an value, is independent of both the object of measurement and the standard of measurement. A numeric value of comparison is a number. The values 1.2, 2.3, and 1 million are examples of numeric values. A symbolic value of comparison is an interpretation of the ratio of a common property of two objects. It is often the case that a numeric value can be coerced into a symbolic value, but the reverse is not possible. A symbolic value of comparison is a symbol. The values faster, longer, and heavier are examples of symbolic values. Note that in the example that the standard of comparison is not included as part of the value. In many cases, a value of comparison is incorrect given in the form - 1.2 meters. This form of denoting a value is actually a shorthand notation for specifying a value and the standard of measurement, a pair of values required for meaningful comparison of values associated with two separate objects. For the comparison of the values assigned two separate objects to be meaningful requires that both values are derived from an identical standard of comparison. It is meaningful to compare a small plane with a large plane and state that the large plane is bigger since the standard of comparison is the same prototypical plane. However, it is not meaningful to compare a large mouse with a small elephant and state that the large mouse is bigger since the standards of comparison which determined the values are different.

12.3.2   The Top-Level Conceptual Relations

The following paragraphs define the three top-level conceptual relations that have been determined to be consistent from problem domain to problem domain. The conceptual relations which fall below the top-most level are briefly described in their parent. The abstraction hierarchy for these top-level conceptual relations are shown in Fig. 12.3.

Action The common usage of the word action is to denote the bringing about of an alteration by force or through a natural agency. The definition for action that is adopted here reflects this usage, but reflects that the alteration is from one scene (a description of one state of the world) to another. The definition for an action is: An action denotes the alteration from one scene to another. Actions are directed and typically have restrictions on the subject and target scenes accepted by the action. That is, the relationship among scenes is directed. Restrictions on the subject and target scenes of an action are often given in terms of the most abstract member which can be used in that aspect of the action. There are two major types of actions, concrete and computational. Concrete actions are those that describe an actual change between two scenes. Computational actions are those that describe how a scene may be re-expressed such that computational comparison between scenes is simplified.

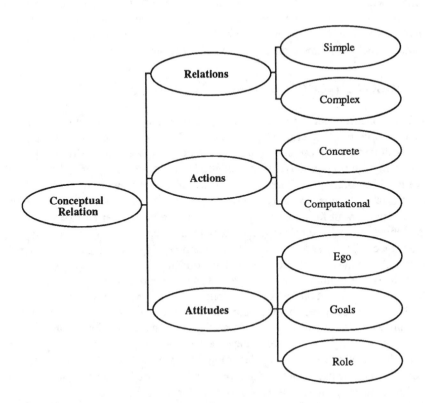

Fig. 12.3 The top-level conceptual relation hierarchy.

Attitude The common usage of the word attitude is to denote a mental position with regard to a state or fact. The definition for attitude adopted here reflects this usage, but includes the consideration that it is a relationship between a conscious entity and the situation in which that entity is an element in light of the recognition that only conscious entities can adopt mental positions and that states and facts occur within the context of a situation. Attitudes can be indicative of ego, goals, or roles. Examples of ego attitudes include likes and dislikes. Examples of goal attitudes include wants and desires. Examples of role attitudes include command, servility, ruler, and ruled.

Relation The common usage of the word relation is to denote an aspect or quality that connects two or more things or parts as being or belonging or working together or as being of the same kind. The definition for relation adopted here reflects this usage, but includes the consideration that a relation has an interpretation. The definition for a relation is: A relation is a means to conceptually connect two or more entities or values. Relations are typically directed with a subject and a target of the relationship. That is, the relationship among objects is directed with at least one entity the subject of the relation and at least one entity the target of the relationship. Usually there are restrictions on the types of subjects and targets accepted by the relation. Restrictions on the subjects and targets of a relation are often given in terms of the most abstract member which can be used in that aspect of the relation. There are two major categories of relations, simple and complex. Simple relations are those which exist between two entities and are by definition binary. Complex relations are employed to denote a network of simple relations as a computational simplification.

12.4 SUMMARY AND CONCLUSIONS

It was the intent of this paper to introduce the top-level concepts and conceptual relations, the utility of the conceptual basis set, and indicate how the conceptual basis set was developed. With respect to these intentions, these topics have been presented in as great of detail considering the limitations of article length. However, some topics relevant to this paper have not been presented. One area, in particular, was the nature of the underlying layer of structure in the conceptual basis set. Discussion of this aspect of the conceptual basis set will have to wait for another opportunity. Another area, referred to several times and not presented, concerns employing the conceptual basis set in problem solving. This topic is the subject of another paper entitled, "Problem Solving Using a Conceptual Graph Representation," which was also presented at the workshop.

It is the belief of the author that the concepts and conceptual relations presented here form the top-level of any conceptual basis set that one would develop for any given problem domain. It is also the believed that the computational rules for concepts and conceptual relations, defined employing the approach described in this paper, are domain independent as well. If this is actually the case, then the concepts and conceptual relations presented here are of value to other investigators dealing with a wide variety of problem domains. Furthermore, the method based on the Situation Data Model used to identify them will also be of value in identifying lower level concepts and conceptual relations.

It is also the belief of the author that the conceptual basis set presented here is complete at the upper levels of abstraction. This belief is supported by numerous attempts to identify a lexical inconsistency by trying to find words that refer to concepts or conceptual relations which at a high level of abstraction are not represented in the top-level of the conceptual basis set. Although some words have been particularly troublesome (for example philosophy, personality, and domain) it is believed that the trouble in abstraction resides in their complex semantic implications and not in the top levels of the conceptual basis set. Preliminary results of ongoing research (not presented here) indicate that additional levels of a conceptual basis set can be defined such that the concepts and conceptual relations also appear consistently across different problem domains. However, the number of problem domains examined at this point in time is not sufficient to defend these additional levels.

While it is believed that the conceptual basis set presented here, and the approach employed to derive it, are of value due to their simplicity and completeness, it is not the belief of the author that the conceptual basis set presented here is unique. There are several approaches which could be employed and each would result in the development of a significantly different conceptual basis set than the one presented here. For example, if one were to employ a different ontological model with different expectations concerning the type of computations that would be performed on a conceptual basis set it seems clear that a very different conceptual basis set would result. As an additional example, employing the grammatical categories of English as top-level concepts would result in a very different conceptual basis set. However, there are certain similarities between the concepts presented here and the conceptual implications of the grammatical categories, namely - nouns would correspond directly to objects, scenes, situations, and values; verbs would correspond directly to relations, actions, and attitudes; and to a lesser extent, adjectives would correspond to characteristics, features, attributes, and capabilities.

BIBLIOGRAPHY

Tepfenhart, W. and A. Lazzara (1988) "The Situation Data Model", Proc. of the Third Workshop on Conceptual Graphs, St. Paul, Minnesota, (pg. 3.1.10-1).

Barwise, J. and J. Perry (1983) *Situations and Attitudes*, MIT Press.

Sowa, J.F. (1984) *Conceptual Structures: Information Processing in Mind and Machine*, Addison Wesley, Reading.

Part III

Graph Compliation, Construction and Hierarchies

13

Compiled Hierarchical Retrieval

Gerard Ellis
Department of Computer Science,
University of Queensland,
Brisbane, Queensland 4072, Australia[1]

ABSTRACT

This paper addresses two major problems in conceptual graphs: subsumption and classification in a taxonomy. Conceptual graphs are stored using a directed acyclic graph data
structure based on the partial order over conceptual graphs.

We give an improved algorithm for classifying conceptual graphs into this hierarchy.
This algorithm prunes the search space in the database using the information gathered while
searching.

We show how conceptual graphs in this hierarchy can be compiled into instructions which
represent specialized cases of the canonical formation rules. This compiles subsumption of
conceptual graphs. Conceptual graphs are compiled as differences between adjacent graphs
in the hierarchy. The differences represent the rules used in deriving the graph from the
adjacent graphs.

Compilation is effected in three ways: removal of redundant data, use of simple instructions which ignore redundant checks when performing matching, and by sharing common
processing between graphs.

13.1   INTRODUCTION

The goal for the design of the conceptual graph knowledge representation is a system
of logic that can express the propositional content of sentences in natural language in
as simple and direct a manner as possible (Sowa, 1991b). First order conceptual graphs
(FOCGs) are a subset of the conceptual graph language. Atomic (or simple) conceptual
graphs are conceptual graphs containing no nested graphs, hence no logical connectives
nor quantifiers other than implicit existential quantification. We will only consider atomic
conceptual graphs here.

Semantic networks have been viewed, at best, as trivial variants of first-order logic
(FOL), at worst, confused notations with no denotation.

---

[1]Part of this work was undertaken while visiting the Department of Computer and Information Sciences,
University of California at Santa Cruz.

Conceptual graphs are an order-sorted version of Existential Graphs (EGs), a graphical system of logic developed by the nineteenth century philosopher and logician C. S. Peirce (Roberts, 1973). After making significant contributions to the linear form of logic, Peirce developed a graphical form which he called "the logic of the future".

Sowa introduced Peirce's Existential Graphs to the AI community (Sowa, 1984), adding sorts and abstraction to the language. Sowa (1984) defines an operator ϕ which maps FOCGs into first-order logic. Using this mapping Sowa gave the semantics of the language and proved the soundness and completeness of FOCG.

Conceptual graphs offers more than just another logic notation, for instance it has a standard mapping into natural language. For example the sentence *"A girl is eating pie"* could be represented by the conceptual graph;

```
[Girl]←(AGNT) ←[EAT]→(OBJ)→[PIE],
```

which could in turn be translated into FOL as

$$\exists x \, (\exists y \, (\exists z \, (\text{GIRL}(x) \wedge \text{AGNT}(y, x) \wedge \text{EAT}(y) \wedge \text{OBJ}(y, z) \wedge \text{PIE}(z))))$$

But the FOL representation contains four conjunctions, whereas the original sentence and the conceptual graph contain none. The differences in ease of mapping to natural language become even more evident for more complex examples including modal operators or plurals.

What else does FOCG offer that traditional FOL does not? Conceptual graphs could be discarded in favour of FOL with no loss of generality. However, as Shastri (1991) argues a knowledge representation should not only be judged by its representational adequacy but also by its computational effectiveness.

An important feature of conceptual graphs is its ability to structure knowledge. In conceptual graphs the representation of the sentence above would be treated as a single unit (conceptual graph). Conceptual graphs distinguish the conjunctions inside a proposition and conjunctions connecting propositions. Consider the representation of the sentence *"A girl is eating pie, and a dog is barking"* in FOCG and FOL:

```
[GIRL]←(AGNT) ←[EAT]→(OBJ)→[PIE]
```

$$\exists x \, (\exists y \, (\exists z \, (\text{GIRL}(x) \wedge \text{AGNT}(y, x) \wedge \text{EAT}(y) \wedge \text{OBJ}(y, z) \wedge \text{PIE}(z)))) \wedge$$

$$\exists u \, (\exists v \, (\text{DOG}(u) \wedge \text{AGNT}(v, u) \wedge \text{BARK}(v))).$$

A conceptual graph corresponds to a formula in FOL that is connected by variables or constants. Conjunction of conceptual graphs is represented by placing the conceptual graphs on the same page.

More dramatic is the ability to abstract complex information into single concepts or relations or individuals. This allows concepts to be deeply modelled while avoiding computation with the detail by working at a higher level of abstraction.

Semantic networks are kinds of logics, just as order-sorted logic (OSL) is a kind of logic. OSL could be considered a trivial variant of FOL. There is a simple mapping of OSL to FOL. However, the elegant formulation of problems, and computational effectiveness of OSL are remarkable. The introduction of sorts (types) into FOL can significantly reduce the number of clauses, connectives, and variables in the formulation of a knowledge base. Modified inference rules that use the sortal constraints of arguments prune the search space. The branches that are pruned are useless dead ends. Walther (1984) employed OSL to give the first mechanical solution to the theorem prover challenge problem: Schubert's Steamroller. The success was attributed to the significant reduction in the size of the problem by the OSL formulation and the reduced search space.

We argue that a parallel situation exists between FOCG and OSL. Conceptual graphs inherit the computational effectiveness of OSL through the use of sorts (concepts types). As well as sorts, FOCGs allows these sorts to be defined intensionally. This allows the sort hierarchy to be deeply modelled, which is useful for early detection of inconsistencies and in the generation of explanations. Further by abstracting information away a problem can be greatly reduced in size.

Sowa suggests the inference rules for conceptual graphs allow a proposition to be treated whole, rather than decomposed into many small formulas in clausal form in resolution theorem provers. Decomposing into clausal form increases the difficulty of finding and reassembling the pieces during the proof. Each individual step in a resolution proof is simpler than graph unification, but the number of steps is greatly increased for many small clauses.

Implementations of semantic networks differ from implementations of FOL such as Prolog in at least one major respect: a taxonomy of concepts. With the advent of languages such as LIFE (Aït-Kaci and Podelski, 1991), and TAXLOG (Hanschke, 1991), that distinction is disappearing. I would argue that what the Prolog-like implementations lack more generally is an associative memory, where assertions are not decomposed but stored whole.

Conceptual languages generally have two different languages: a terminological language (T-Box) for defining concepts intensionally; and an assertional language (A-Box) for making assertions about those concepts. The ordering between two concepts is defined by a subsumption operation. A taxonomy is a construction of the non-transitive subsumption relationship between a collection of concepts. Adding a new concept to a taxonomy is called classification.

Conceptual graphs uses the same language for both defining concepts (as well as relations and individuals) and making assertions. Thus subsumption not only defines a partial ordering over concepts in the form of a taxonomy, it takes this process one step further by defining a partial ordering over assertions. The idea of a taxonomy of concepts generalizes to a *generalization hierarchy* of assertions. The subsumption relationship for atomic conceptual graphs is defined by a subgraph relationship modulo subtyping and individuation, but for general FOCG a theorem prover must be used to compare formulas.

The generalization hierarchy is an associative memory. Consider a knowledge base as a collection of sentences. Each sentence is represented by a conceptual graph. The sentences are ordered into a generalization hierarchy which is a directed acyclic graph representing the non-transitive links in the subsumption relationship defined over conceptual graphs. A query (conceptual graph) may be made on this collection. If we regard solutions to a query as sentences that imply the query sentence, then these can be found by a two phase constrained topological search of the generalization hierarchy (classification). The search returns the virtual location of the query graph. The sub-hierarchies of the immediate successors of the query graph contain all of the solutions to the query in an ordered form.

Construction of the generalization hierarchy statically compiles many inferences. The generalization hierarchy can significantly prune search. In this paper we discuss efficient construction of the generalization hierarchy (classification) and then look at local compilation of conceptual graphs within the hierarchy.

Section 13.2 introduces a subset of the conceptual graph language, atomic conceptual graphs. Section 13.3 describes the problem of classification of conceptual graphs, and gives an improved algorithm for constructing the generalization hierarchy. Section 13.4 gives descriptions of instructions which are specialized cases of the canonical formation rules. Conceptual graphs are composed as a set of these instructions operating on their immediate generalizations, resulting in compilation. A query is then examined on a small compiled database.

13.2   WHAT ARE CONCEPTUAL GRAPHS?

Conceptual Graphs (Sowa, 1984) is a system of logic based on Charles Sanders Peirce's *Existential Graphs* (Roberts, 1973). Conceptual graphs have the full power of first-order logic, can represent modal and higher-order logic, and have simple and elegant inference rules. Conceptual graphs also have a direct translation into natural language. The following is a short introduction to the basic formalism, however the reader is advised to read Sowa (1984) for a more thorough understanding.

A *conceptual graph* is a finite, *connected*, bipartite graph. The two kinds of nodes are concepts and conceptual relations. Every conceptual relation has one or more arcs, each of which must be linked to some concept. A single concept by itself may form a conceptual graph, but every conceptual relation must be linked to some concept.

The function *type* maps concepts into a set T whose elements are type labels. The function *referent* maps concepts into a set $I = \{\#1, \#2, \#3, \ldots\}$ of *individual markers* or the *generic marker* *. An individual marker is a surrogate for some individual in the real world, a perceived world, or a hypothetical world. A concept c with $type(c) = t$ and $referent(c) = r$ may be displayed in the linear form as $[t : r]$. For example the concept [PERSON] or [PERSON: *] represents an unspecified person, and may be read *A person*. A box replaces the square brackets in the graphical form.

The partial order $\leq$ over the type labels in T, known as the *type hierarchy*, forms a lattice, called the *type lattice*. The type hierarchy makes analytic statements about types: they must be true by intension. The statement GIRL < PERSON is true, because the properties of a person are also associated with a girl.

The *minimal common supertype* of a pair of type labels s and t is written $s \cup t$. The *maximal common subtype* is written $s \cap t$. There are two primitive type labels: the *universal type* $\top$ and the *absurd type* $\bot$. For any type label t, $\bot \leq t \leq \top$. The minimal common supertype CAT $\cup$ DOG = CARNIVORE. The maximal common subtype of PET and CAT is PET-CAT. The maximal common subtype CAT $\cap$ DOG = $\bot$, means that it is logically impossible for an entity to be both a dog and a cat.

The *denotation* of type t, written δt, is the set of all entities that are instances of any concept of type t. For extensions, the union δCAT $\cup$ δDOG is the set of all cats and dogs in the world and nothing else. But for intensional type labels, CAT $\cup$ DOG is their minimal common supertype CARNIVORE, which also has subtypes BEAR, WEASEL, SKUNK, etc. The type lattice represents categories of thought, and the lattice of sets and subsets represents collections of existing things. The two lattices are not isomorphic, and the denotation operator that maps one into the other is neither one-to-one nor onto.

The function *type* also maps conceptual relations to type labels. A relation r with $type(r) = t$ may be written (t) in the linear form. A circle replaces the parenthesis in the graphical form. For two relations to have the same type they must have the same number of arcs. Concepts and conceptual relations have no type in common.

The *conformity relation* :: relates type labels to individual markers: if $t :: i$ is true, then i is said to *conform* to type t. The conformity relation obeys the following conditions:

- The referent of a concept must conform to its type label: if c is a concept, $type(c) ::$ $referent(c)$. For example the concept [INTEGER: 1] is well-formed, but *INTEGER: 3.14* is not.

- If an individual marker conforms to type s, it must also conform to all supertypes of s: if $s \leq t$ and $s :: i$, then $t :: i$. For example the number 3 conforms to the type PRIME, PRIME::3. Hence it also conforms to the supertype INTEGER, INTEGER::3.

- If an individual marker conforms to type s and t, it must also conform to their maximal common subtype: if $s :: i$ and $t :: i$, then $(s \cap t) :: i$. For example since 3 conforms to types ODD and PRIME: ODD::3; PRIME::3, then 3 also conforms to their maximal common subtype ODD-PRIME, ODD-PRIME::3.

- Every individual marker conforms to the universal type $\top$; no individual marker conforms to the absurd type $\bot$: for all i in I, $\top :: i$, but not $\bot :: i$. For example

- The generic marker * conforms to all type labels: for all type labels t, $t :: *$.

The operator ϕ maps conceptual graphs into formulas in first order predicate calculus. For the conceptual graph

$$u = [\text{GIRL}: \#3074] \leftarrow (\text{AGNT}) \leftarrow [\text{EAT}] \rightarrow (\text{OBJ}) \rightarrow [\text{PIE}]$$

the translation is

$$\phi u = \exists x \exists y (\text{GIRL}(\#3074) \wedge \text{AGNT}(x, \#3074) \wedge \text{EAT}(x) \wedge \text{OBJ}(x, y) \wedge \text{PIE}(y))$$

Generic concepts map to variables, individual concepts map to constants.

13.2.1   Canonical Graphs

To distinguish the meaningful graphs that represent real or possible situations in the external world, certain graphs are declared to be *canonical*. One source is the derivation of new canonical graphs from other canonical graphs by *formation rules*.

There are four *canonical formation rules* for deriving a conceptual graph w from conceptual graphs u and v (where u and v may be the same graph) :

- *Copy.* w is an exact copy of u.

- *Restrict.* For any concept c in u, $type(c)$ may be replaced by a subtype; if c is generic, its referent may be changed to an individual marker. These changes are permitted only if $referent(c)$ conforms to $type(c)$ before and after the change.

- *Join.* If a concept c in u is identical to a concept d in v, then let w be the graph obtained by deleting d and linking to c all arcs of conceptual relations that had been linked to d.

- *Simplify.* If conceptual relations r and s in the graph u are duplicates, then one of them may be deleted from u together with all its arcs.

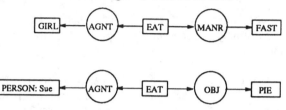

Fig. 13.1 Two canonical graphs.

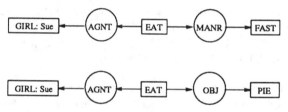

Fig. 13.2 Restriction of two graphs in Fig. 13.1.

  To illustrate the formation rules, Fig. 13.1 shows two canonical graphs. The first one may be read *A girl is eating fast;* and the second, *A person, Sue, is eating pie.* These are not formal translations of the graphs, but informal verbalizations for discussion of the graphs here.

  If the concept [GIRL] in the first graph were restricted to [GIRL: Sue] (by the rule of restriction) and the concept of type PERSON in the second graph were restricted to type GIRL (by the rule of restriction), then the graphs of Fig. 13.1 would be changed to those in Fig. 13.2. But before doing the restrictions, the conformity relation must be checked to ensure that GIRL :: Sue is true.

  The two identical pairs of concepts, [GIRL: Sue] and [EAT], can then be joined to each other. The result is Fig. 13.3.

  In the graph in Fig. 13.3, the two copies of (AGNT) are duplicates. Two conceptual relations of the same type are *duplicates* if for each i, the ith arc of one is linked to the same concept as the ith arc of the other. When one of the duplicates is deleted by simplification, the graph becomes Fig. 13.4, which may be read *A girl, Sue, is eating pie fast.* The simplification rule corresponds to the rule of logic that $R(x, y) \wedge R(x, y)$ is equivalent to just $R(x, y)$.

  The formation rules are a kind of *graph grammar* for canonical graphs. Besides defining syntax, they also enforce certain semantic constraints. The formation rules make no guarantee about truth or falsity. However, the formation rules are refutation rules. If we assert that the graph

$$[\mathrm{PERSON}] \leftarrow (\mathrm{AGNT}) \leftarrow [\mathrm{EAT}] \rightarrow (\mathrm{OBJ}) \rightarrow [\mathrm{PIE}]$$

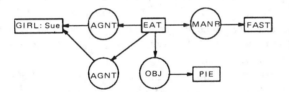

Fig. 13.3 Join of the two graphs in Fig. 13.2.

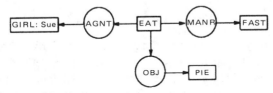

Fig. 13.4 Simplification of Fig. 13.3.

is false, then we can use the formation rules to show that

$$[\text{GIRL:Sue}] \leftarrow (\text{AGNT}) \leftarrow [\text{EAT}] \rightarrow (\text{OBJ}) \rightarrow [\text{PIE}]$$

is false. That is if a graph can be derived from a false graph, then it must in turn be false. The formation rules are falsity preserving.

The *canon* contains the information necessary for deriving a set of canonical graphs. It has four components: a type hierarchy T; a set of individual markers I; a conformity relation :: that relates labels in T to markers in I; and a finite set of conceptual graphs B, called the *canonical basis*, with all type labels in T and all referents either ∗ or markers in I. The canonical graphs are the *closure* of B under the canonical formation rules.

13.2.2 The Relationship between the Canonical Formation Rules and Subsumption of Conceptual Graphs

If a conceptual graph u is canonically derivable from a conceptual graph v (possibly with the join of other conceptual graphs $w_1, \ldots, w_n$), then u is called a *specialization* of v, written $u \leq v$, and v is called a *generalization* of u.

Generalization defines a partial ordering of conceptual graphs called the *generalization hierarchy*. The ordering is reflexive, transitive, and antisymmetric. For any conceptual graphs u, and v, the following properties are true:

- *Subgraph.* If v is a subgraph of u, then $u \leq v$.

- *Subtypes.* If u is identical to v except that one or more type labels of v are restricted to subtypes in u, then $u \leq v$.

- *Individuals.* If u is identical to v except that one or more generic concepts of v are restricted to individual concepts of the same type, then $u \leq v$.

- *Top.* The graph [T] is a generalization of all other conceptual graphs.

The graphs in Figs. 13.1, 13.2, and 13.3 are all generalizations of the graph in Fig. 13.4. We call the graphs defined so far *atomic conceptual graphs* (ACGs). They do not contain logical connectives and hence neither quantification other than the default existential quantification. A subsumption test for ACGs can be implemented as subgraph isomorphism modulo subtyping and individuation.

The generalization hierarchy is not a partial order over conceptual graphs, rather it is a partial order over equivalence classes of conceptual graphs. Consider the graphs

$$v = \texttt{[PERSON]} \leftarrow \texttt{(AGNT)} \leftarrow \texttt{[EAT]}$$

$$u = \texttt{[PERSON]} \leftarrow \texttt{(AGNT)} \leftarrow \texttt{[EAT]} \rightarrow \texttt{(AGNT)} \rightarrow \texttt{[PERSON]}$$

The graph v is a proper subgraph of u. The graph u can be derived from v by joining a copy of v on the concept $\texttt{[EAT]}$, thus $u \leq v$. However, v can be derived from u by joining the two identical concepts $\texttt{[PERSON]}$, then simplifying the duplicate $\texttt{(AGNT)}$ relations, thus $v \leq u$. Hence $u = v$ according to the generalization hierarchy. This problem has also been noted independently in Willems (1990).

If $u \leq v$, a canonical derivation of u from v corresponds to the reverse of a proof of the formula ϕv from the formula ϕu : for any conceptual graphs u and v, if $u \leq v$, then $\phi u \supset \phi v$. The result that the two graphs given in the paragraph above are equivalent should not be surprising considering their translations into predicate calculus

$$\phi v = \exists x \exists y \text{PERSON}(x)\&\text{AGNT}(y, x)\&\text{EAT}(y)$$

$$\phi u = \exists x \exists y \exists z \text{PERSON}(x)\&\text{AGNT}(y, x)\&\text{EAT}(y)\&\text{AGNT}(y, z)\&\text{PERSON}(z)$$

This is a subtle point that doesn't affect any of the subsequent theory of conceptual graphs. In practice, you can always simplify the graphs with redundant branches to derive the smallest one in each equivalence class. Conceptual graphs from now on are assumed to be the minimal element of their class.

For any conceptual graphs u and v where $u \leq v$, there must exist a mapping $\pi : v \rightarrow u$, where πv is a subgraph of u called a *projection* of v in u. The *projection operator* π has the following properties:

- For each concept c in v, πc is a concept in πv where $type(\pi c) \leq type(c)$. If c is individual, then $referent(c) = referent(\pi c)$.

- For each conceptual relation r in v, πr is a conceptual relation in πv where $type(\pi r) = type(r)$. If the ith arc of r is linked to a concept c in v, the ith arc of πr must be linked to πc in πv.

For example given

$$u = \texttt{[PERSON]} \leftarrow \texttt{(AGNT)} \leftarrow \texttt{[ACT]}$$

$$u = \texttt{[GIRL: Sue]} \leftarrow \texttt{(AGNT)} \leftarrow \texttt{[EAT]} \rightarrow \texttt{(OBJ)} \rightarrow \texttt{[PIE]}$$

then the projection from u into v would be {(([PERSON], [GIRL: Sue]), ((AGNT), (AGNT)), ([ACT], [EAT])} given PERSON > GIRL and ACT > EAT.

A graph v can be represented by the set of instances of the canonical formation rules used to construct the graph v from the graphs $w_1, \ldots, w_n$. To test if the graph v subsumes a graph u, these rule instances can be applied to the projections of u in $w_1, \ldots, w_n$. The rule instances will only succeed if v subsumes u.

We use this technique to compile conceptual graphs in a data structure representing the generalization hierarchy partial ordering.

13.2.3 Abstraction and Conceptual Graphs: Defining Taxonomies of Concepts

An n-adic abstraction, $(\lambda a_1, \ldots a_n)\ u$, consists of a canonical graph u and a list of generic concepts $a_1, \ldots, a_n$ in u, called formal parameters. Types can be defined intensionally by n-adic abstractions, and individual markers can be defined by aggregations.

A concept type s can be defined by $s = (\lambda a)\ u$. For example the type QUICK-EATER can be defined as a subtype of PERSON:

QUICK-EATER=(λx) [PERSON:*x]←(AGNT)←[EAT]→(MANR)→[FAST].

This states that a quick eater is a person who eats fast. A taxonomy refers to the partial ordering over the abstractions for concept types. The term is also used to refer to the data structure implied by the partial order.

Concept types may be expanded and contracted in a graph. For instance given the above definition, the graph

[PERSON: Sue]←(AGNT)←[EAT]→(MANR)→[FAST].

can be contracted to form the graph

[QUICK-EATER: Sue]

read *A quick eater, Sue.* It could be expanded to regain information from the definition of QUICK-EATER to get the graph

[QUICK-EATER: Sue]←(AGNT)←[EAT]→(MANR)→[FAST]

Notice that contraction of a concept type followed by expansion does not produce the original graph.

The n-ary relation type t is defined by $t = (\lambda a_1, \ldots, a_n)\ u$. For example the relation EATS may be defined

EATS $= (\lambda x, y)$ [ANIMAL:*x]←(AGNT)←[EAT]→(OBJ)→[FOOD:*y].

Similarly relation definitions may be contracted or expanded in a graph. By contracting the above definition of EATS in the graph

[GIRL]←(AGNT)←[EAT]→(OBJ)→[PIE]

results in the graph

[GIRL]→[EATS]→[PIE]

By expansion of the definition the original graph is obtained.

The individual i of type t is defined by $t(i) = u$ given $t = (\lambda a)\ v$ and $\pi : v \to u$ and $referent(\pi a) = i$. For example given a book is defined by

```
BOOK=  (λx)
       [PUBLICATION: *x]  -
       (WRITTEN-BY) → [AUTHOR]
       (ENTITLED) → [TITLE]
       (PUBLISHED-BY) → [PUBLISHER]
       (PUBLISHED-ON) → [YEAR].
```

Then the book ConceptualStructures may be defined:

```
BOOK(ConceptualStructures)=
       [PUBLICATION: ConceptualStructures]  -
       (WRITTEN-BY) → [AUTHOR: JohnSowa]
       (ENTITLED) → [TITLE: ``Conceptual Structures:
          Information Processing in Mind and Machine'']
       (PUBLISHED-BY) → [PUBLISHER: AddisonWesley]
       (PUBLISHED-ON) → [YEAR: 1984].
```

Where JohnSowa and AddisonWesley and the other individuals may also be defined by abstractions. A graph containing the concept [BOOK: ConceptualStructures] may have this individual concept expanded to access the information in the definition of ConceptualStructures.

Type labels may be replaced with their definition, further anywhere a type label can appear an unlabelled λ abstraction may appear.

Conceptual graph theory covers further topics: maximal join (the analog of unification); schema and prototypes; nested graphs and lines of identity (logical connectives and quantifiers: FOCG); elegant inference rules based on Peirce's (Roberts, 1973) *Alpha* and *Beta* rules for *Existential Graphs*; semantics of conceptual graphs; tenses and modalities; and more.

To give you a further taste of the representation consider the graph;

```
[PERSON: John] ← (AGNT) ← [THINK] → (OBJ) →
       [PROPOSITION:
       [PERSON: Sue]] ← (AGNT) ← [EAT] → (OBJ) → [PIE]
```

which may be read *John thinks Sue is eating pie*.

Now that we have the theory of *atomic* conceptual graphs we will consider how to store large sets of conceptual graphs and how to retrieve conceptual graphs once stored.

13.3 STORING AND RETRIEVING CONCEPTUAL GRAPHS

The common data structure used to store conceptual graphs is a hierarchy; a directed acyclic graph representing the non-transitive links of the partial ordering, generalization hierarchy, over conceptual graphs (Mineau, 1989), (Levinson, 1991), (Ellis, 1990a, 1990b). Levinson's earlier work used a similar data structure for organizing chemical graphs (Levinson, 1985). The taxonomy over KL-ONE concept descriptions (Schmolze and Lipkis, 1983) is a hierarchy.

13.3.1　The Generalization Hierarchy as a Data Structure for Storing Conceptual Graphs

The nodes in the generalization hierarchy are conceptual graphs and the arcs represent the non-transitive ordering between the graphs. In Fig. 13.5 the hierarchy is given for the graphs from the previous section. The canonical basis in this example would consist of the set of graphs $\{a, b, c\}$. The arc (b, d) indicates:

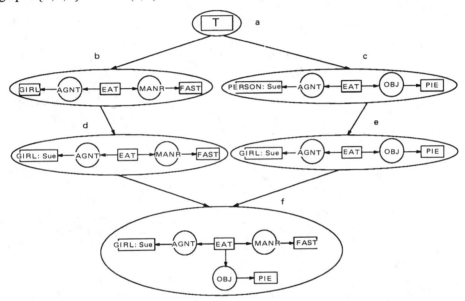

Fig. 13.5 The generalization hierarchy of the graphs in Figs. 13.1, 13.2, 13.3 and 13.4.

1. *A girl, Sue, is eating fast* is canonically derivable from *A girl is eating fast.*

2. *A girl, Sue, is eating fast* implies *A girl is eating fast.*

3. *A girl is eating fast* is a generalization of *A girl, Sue, is eating fast.*

4. *A girl, Sue, is eating fast* is a specialization of *A girl is eating fast.*

In the following sections we examine how to use the hierarchy for searching a set of conceptual graphs and how to construct the hierarchy.

13.3.2　Searching for a Conceptual Graph in the Generalization Hierarchy

The hierarchy physically stores the knowledge base. When we apply a conceptual graph query u to the knowledge base we search for u in the hierarchy. The hierarchy is a contents addressable memory.

Fig. 13.6 illustrates the search space for a query u in a hierarchy. *Primitives* are the graphs closest to the concept [T] , which are not derivable from any other graphs. *Atoms* are the leaf nodes of the knowledge base. The *generalization space* contains all the generalizations of u in the hierarchy. The *specialization* or *solution space* contains all the specializations of u in the hierarchy. *Immediate generalizations* and *immediate specializations* of u are adjacent generalizations and specializations of u respectively.

In Fig. 13.6[2] u is explicitly stored in the hierarchy. However, in many cases u will not be stored in the hierarchy explicitly. The search for u can proceed in two directions: top-down, from the graph [T] to u or bottom-up, from the atoms to u. The methods we examine here search top-down.

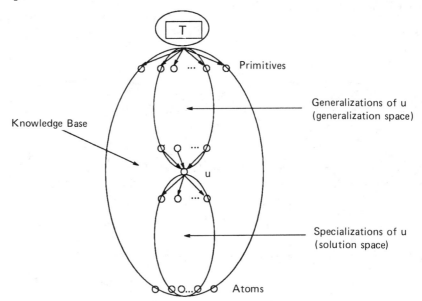

Fig. 13.6 The search space for the graph u in a generalization hierarchy.

Consider a depth-first search of the generalization space. Any path in the generalization space can be taken as they all lead to u in the hierarchy. Consider searching for the query u = *Is a girl, Sue, eating fast* in the hierarchy in Fig. 13.5. The query

$$u = [\texttt{GIRL: Sue}] \leftarrow (\texttt{AGNT}) \leftarrow [\texttt{EAT}] \rightarrow (\texttt{MANR}) \rightarrow [\texttt{FAST}]$$

matches the graph d in the hierarchy. The search starts at the graph [T] . To find the graph search from the cluster of [T] for a generalization of u. The *cluster* of v is the set of immediate specializations of v. The clusters of a, b, c, d, e, and f are $\{b, c\}$, $\{d\}$, $\{e\}$, $\{f\}$, $\{f\}$, and $\{\}$ respectively.

In a depth-first search we could select the first graph in the cluster which is a generalization of the query u as a continuation in the path to u. The conceptual graph b is a generalization in the first cluster, so we select it. The graph c is incomparable to the query u, that is it

---

[2]The search space diagram was shown to me by Fritz Lehmann.

is neither a generalization nor a specialization of u. We now search the cluster of b for a generalization. The graph d is the only graph in the cluster and it is a generalization of u. In fact d is isomorphic to u. The query graph is matched so the search terminates successfully. In this case there are two solutions $\{d, f\}$: *yes; yes, Sue is eating pie fast.*

The search does not necessarily start from the graph $[\top]$. Indexing techniques can be used to start further down the generalization space. The ultimate goal of indexing techniques is to index directly to the top of the specialization space which includes u (see (Levinson, 1991) for indexing techniques).

13.3.3 Inserting a Conceptual Graph into the Generalization Hierarchy: Classification

To insert a graph u into the hierarchy we need to compute the set of immediate generalizations and the set of immediate specializations of u in the hierarchy. This information gives us the virtual location for inserting u.

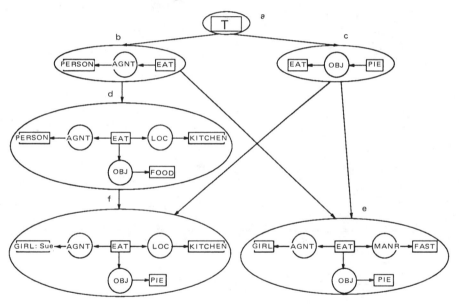

Fig. 13.7 A generalization hierarchy.

Consider inserting the graph

$$u = [\text{PERSON}] \leftarrow (\text{AGNT}) \leftarrow [\text{EAT}] \rightarrow (\text{OBJ}) \rightarrow [\text{PIE}]$$

read *A person is eating pie*, into the hierarchy in Fig. 13.7. The immediate generalizations in this case are b, *A person is eating*, and c, *A pie is being eaten*. The immediate specializations are f, *A girl, Sue, is eating pie in the kitchen*, and e, *A girl is eating pie fast*. Notice that d, *A person is eating food in the kitchen*, and u are incomparable. To insert u we remove the arcs $(b, e), (c, e)$, and (c, f), then add $(b, u), (c, u), (u, f)$ and (u, e) to get the new hierarchy in Fig. 13.8.

Searching the Generalization Space

Woods (1991) describes the standard two phase breadth-first search used for classification of KL-ONE like terms in a taxonomy. The first phase calculates the set of immediate predecessors, IP (generalizations), of the query by breadth-first search of the generalization space. The second phase breadth-first searches the subhierarchies of the immediate predecessors calculated from the first phase, the first specializations encountered in the hierarchies are the immediate successors, IS, of the query.

Woods in summarizing research on classification says "More sophisticated algorithms can and should be developed."

Levinson (1991) describes algorithms which show deeper insights into the problem. Subsumption can in general be an expensive operation. Hence methods of classification that avoid as many subsumption tests as possible are desirable. The algorithms given here for INSERTing an object into a hierarchy are extensions of Levinson's method.

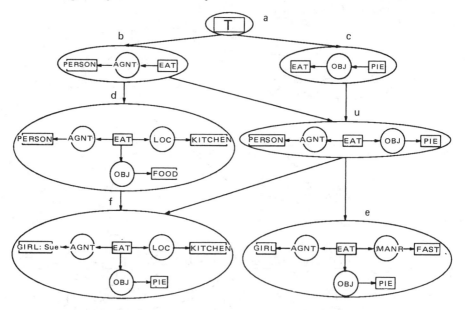

Fig. 13.8 The generalization hierarchy in Fig. 13.7 after inserting u.

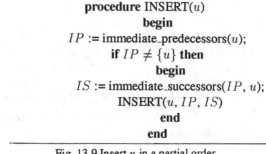

procedure INSERT(u)
begin
IP := immediate_predecessors(u);
  if $IP \neq \{u\}$ **then**
    begin
IS := immediate_successors(IP, u);
      INSERT(u, IP, IS)
    end
end

Fig. 13.9 Insert u in a partial order.

Consider the algorithm for INSERT in Fig. 13.9. The first phase of computing the imme-diate predecessors, IP, is done by the function immediate_predecessors(u) in Fig. 13.12. If u is already stored in the hierarchy, we just return it and avoid the second phase. Otherwise the subhierarchies of the members of IP are searched using immediate_successors(IP, u) in Fig. 13.14. Once the sets IP, and IS are found then the procedure INSERT(u, IP, IS) in Fig. 13.10 does the necessary housekeeping linking u to immediate predecessors and immediate successors. The procedure also maintains finishing_times of graphs in the hierarchy. This information is used to traverse the hierarchy in topological order.

---

procedure INSERT(u, IP, IS)
    begin
        for each $v \in IP$ **do for each** $w \in IS$ **do** remove (v, w) if present;
        for each $v \in IP$ **do** add (v, u);
        for each $w \in IS$ **do** add (u, w);
        u.finishing_time :=
            max($w \in IS$: w.finishing_time) + 1;
        propagate_finishing_time(IP)
    end

Fig. 13.10 Insert u in the partial order, given its neighbourhood (IP, IS).

Levinson (1991) pruned the search space using the fact that a graph is only in the generalization space (generalizations of the query u) if all of its immediate predecessors are also in the generalization space. He does this by sorting the hierarchy by size of the graphs and traversing the hierarchy in this order. Size was a necessary requirement for ordering the sorts of graphs that Levinson was sorting. However, for conceptual graphs size is not a necessary requirement.

Topological order is the level order of a hierarchy. This is reflected for each node by the distance the node is from the bottom. For example in Fig. 13.5 the graph f is on level 0, graphs d and e are on level 1, b and c are on level 2, and a is on level 3.

To see why topological order is the correct traversal method consider the hierarchy in Fig. 13.11. Nodes in the diagram represent conceptual graphs. Remember that all immediate predecessors of a graph must be compared before that graph. The immediate predecessors of the graph must be generalizations of the query if the graph is also a generalization. Assume the graphs a, b, and c in Fig. 13.11 are generalizations of the query, but d is not, and hence e also is not. A breadth-first traversal (reading left to right): a, b, c, e, d; would compare e. A topological traversal: a, c, b, d, e; would not compare e, since d is encountered beforehand and is noted as being incomparable.

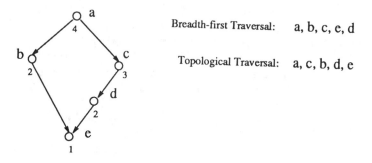

Breadth-first Traversal: a, b, c, e, d

Topological Traversal: a, c, b, d, e

Fig. 13.11 Breadth-first vs. Topological Traversal. (IP, IS).

---

function immediate_predecessors(u)
    begin
    Q.enqueue(finishing_time($\top$), $\top$)
    while not Q.empty() **do**
        begin
        $v := Q$.dequeue();
        if (**not**(seen(v)) $\wedge$ see(v) $\wedge$ all_pred_are_pred(v) $\wedge u \leq v$) **then**
            begin
            for each $w \in$ predecessors(v) **do** $IP := IP - w$;
            $IP := IP + v$;
            for each $w \in$ successors(v) **do** Q.enqueue(finishing_time(w), w);
            end
        end
    return IP
    end

Fig. 13.12 Find the immediate predecessors of u. (IP, IS).

In the algorithm in Fig. 13.12 we traverse in topological order by using the distance information (finishing_time) associated with each graph in the hierarchy. The queue used for this modified breadth-first search is a maximum priority queue. Priority is given to elements with the largest finishing_time. Using an array of FIFO queues we can enqueue and dequeue from this priority queue in constant time. Enqueuing the weighted element (i, u) involves adding u to the front of the ith queue. Dequeuing involves removing the first element on the current maximum weighted queue. Whenever the current maximum queue j becomes empty the (weight) index is decremented. Traversing the hierarchy by level order maintains the property that the $j - 1$th FIFO is necessarily non-empty at this point.

In the algorithm the call to subsumption $u \leq v$ is guarded by the test all_pred_are_pred(v). The topological traversal guarantees that we see all vs predecessors before seeing v. The predicate all_pred_are_pred(v) is true if all of vs predecessors are predecessors of the query u. Thus we use as much information we have gained so far in the search to further prune the search while avoiding subsumption tests.

The algorithm traverses the hierarchy in level order so that when we have seen all a database graphs predecessors and they were all predecessors of the query, then compare the graph to the query. If it is a predecessor, add it to the set IP, and remove all of its predecessors from IP, then search the successors of this graph for closer predecessors of the query.

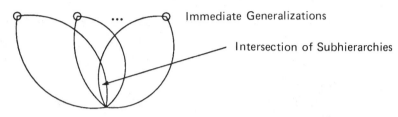

Fig. 13.13 The intersection of subhierarchies of immediate generalizations of the query u. (IP, IS).

Searching the Specialization or Solution Space

In the second phase Woods (1991) searches one of the subhierarchies of the immediate predecessors from the first phase. Only one of the hierarchies needs to be traversed, since any specialization of the query must also be a specialization of a generalization of the query. When a specialization is found it is added to the set IS and its subhierarchy is removed from consideration. However, if a graph is incomparable its subhierarchy must be traversed.

Levinson (Levinson, 1991) devised a method of avoiding many of the comparisons that are inherent in traversing a particular subhierarchy in the second phase. Notice the above method does not use any of the information about the other members of IP. Levinson (Levinson, 1991) noted that in the second phase for any database graph to be a successor of the query graph it must be in the intersection of the subhierarchies of the immediate predecessors from the first phase (see Fig. 13.13. If subsumption tests are relatively expensive compared to pointer traversal involved in walking the subhierarchy, this is particularly useful. The intersection is computed by traversing each of the hierarchies incrementing a counter for each graph. For any graph to be in the intersection it must have a count equal to the number of elements of IP. This intersection is then traversed in the breadth-first manner used by Woods above.

In the algorithm for immediate_successors in Fig. 13.14 we avoid this multiple traversal by computing the intersection incrementally in one constrained *topological* search. The algorithm uses the insight that for a graph to be in the intersection of the subhierarchies of IP the graph must have a path to each of those elements of IP. If we represent each element of the set IP with a bit we can see which of the immediate successors of elements of IP have paths to all elements by ORing the bit strings of their immediate predecessors. By propagating this information we can restrict subsumption testing of graphs that have all bits set. This algorithm also relies on the level (topological) traversal implemented by the maximum priority queue. The predicate IP_reachable(v) ORs the bit strings of vs immediate predecessors and is true if all bits are set.

```
function immediate_successors(IP, u)
    begin
    for each v ∈ IP do
        begin
        encode(v);
        for each w ∈ successors(v) do Q.enqueue(finishing_time(w), w);
        end

    while not Q.empty() do
        begin
        v := Q.dequeue();
        if not seen(v) then
            begin
            see(v);
            if (IP_reachable(v) ∧ v ≤ u) then
                begin
                see_successors(v);
                IS := IS + v
                end
            else
                for each w ∈ successors(v) do Q.enqueue(finishing_time(w), w);
            end
        end
    return IS
    end
```

Fig. 13.14 Find the immediate successors of u given the immediate predecessors.

Notice that for each INSERT the "seen" information must be reinitialised. This would mean the algorithm would perform linearly in the size of the database in every case. This can be avoided by using a token for each query. For a graph to be seen it must have the same token as the current query.

If we consider the query graph u in the classification problem as a query on the database of graphs in the hierarchy. Then solutions to the query would be everything that implied the query: the specialization space. These solutions can be listed by walking the subhierarchies of elements of IS. We would use the same algorithm for INSERT for querying.

In the worst case these algorithms perform no better than comparison of the query to each of the graphs in the database. These methods are not suited to databases where: there is little ordering information; or for total orders, where the hierarchy is a chain. The methods are suited for wide shallow hierarchies of data. We believe that many of the domains that conceptual graphs are intended to be used in do have this property. Woods (1991) argues that the typical-case complexity is logarithmic in the size of the database, and Levinson (1991) gives empirical evidence to support this argument.

Levinson (1991) also describes an indexing scheme which is a hybrid of the above method. The method is particularly useful for graphs with high degree of symmetry. Also see Levinson and Ellis (1991) for its application to conceptual graphs.

Woods (1991) states about his algorithm "No deep insights have been exploited to gain efficiency. For example, in classification, no advantage is taken of what might be learned in the course of one subsumption test that might be redundant with part of another subsumption test."

We have shown how to prune the search within the database down to the generalization and specialization space. In the following section we show how to share matching information gained from subsumption testing between related graphs.

13.4 COMPILING CONCEPTUAL GRAPHS IN GENERALIZATION HIERAR-CHY

Garner and Tsui (1987) stored graphs as the differences between adjacent graphs in the hierarchy. In their method the arcs of the hierarchy are labeled with differences. This does satisfy our aim of *removing redundant data from the database*. The differences are data used by an algorithm to reconstruct the graph, which is compared to the query using a general matcher. But this does not meet another of our aims that *the data take an active rather than passive role in matching*. This method does not meet a further aim of *sharing common computation throughout the database*.

The canonical formation rules derive a graph v from a set of more general graphs $w_1, \ldots, w_n$. The rules are breadth-first in the sense that all of immediate generalizations of a graph must be constructed before it can be constructed. This is suited to the breadth-first traversal mentioned in the previous section.

In our method conceptual graphs are represented as instructions which represent special cases of the canonical formation rules. The instructions are placed in the nodes rather than on the arcs of the hierarchy. The instructions perform the matching by using mappings of immediate generalizations into the query graph. In this way common computation can be shared through the mappings between generalizations and specializations. If we have computed projections $\pi_{w_1}, \ldots, \pi_{w_n}$ [3], we can use these mappings and the instances of the formation rules used to construct v from $w_1, \ldots, w_n$ to construct the projection π_v.

Here we will concentrate on the first phase of breadth-first search: searching the generalization space. In the first phase the aim is to find subgraph morphisms of database graphs in the query. In the second phase the aim is to find subgraph morphisms of the query in the database graphs. In the first phase the database graphs could be thought of as reading from the query graph. In the second phase the database graphs write to the query graph constructing specialized solutions.

---

[3] The notation π_v represents the projection $\pi : v \rightarrow q$, where q is the query graph.

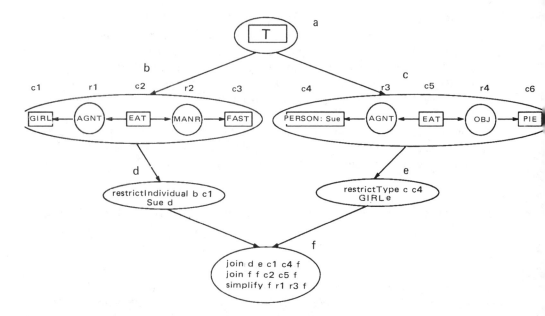

Fig. 13.15 Encoding conceptual graphs in a generalization hierarchy with canonical formation instructions. (IP, IS).

Here we give a specialized interpretation of the canonical formation rules based on the mode of operation: read or write. We examine the read mode. The graphs are reconstructed by the instructions, however here we show the operations that construct the mapping between the database graphs and the query. We examine four specialized cases of the canonical formation rules.

- *restrictType* $u\ c\ t\ w$ - if $type(\pi_u c) \le t$ then $\pi_w := \pi_u$ else fail.

  For the database graph w to be a generalization of the query graph q, q must have a subtype of t in the concept that matched the concept c in u.

- *restrictIndividual* $u\ c\ i\ w$ - if $referent(\pi_u c) = i$ then $\pi_w := \pi_u$ else fail.

  This instruction handles restriction of generic concepts to individual concepts. For $q \le u$ to be true the query q must have the same individual marker i in the concept that matched the concept c in u.

- *join* $u\ v\ c\ d\ w$ - if $\pi_u c = \pi_v d$ then $\pi_w := \pi_u + (\pi_v - (d, \pi_v d))$ else fail.

  Joining concepts c and d of database graphs u and v respectively in read mode means that c and d must map into the same concept in the query graph q.

- *simplify* $u\ r\ s\ w$ - if $\pi_u r = \pi_u s$ then $\pi_w := \pi_u - (s, \pi_u s)$ else fail.

  Simplifying two duplicate relations in a database graph in read mode means that the two relations r and s must be mapped to the same relation in the query, since the query graph cannot contain duplicates as it is a minimal graph.

In Fig. 13.15 we replace conceptual graphs with instructions. Compare this representation with the generalization hierarchy in Fig. 13.5. We have identified the concepts and relations in the conceptual graphs, so they can be referred to in the instructions. Fig. 13.16 contains the query graph u and the solution f from the generalization hierarchy in Fig. 13.15.

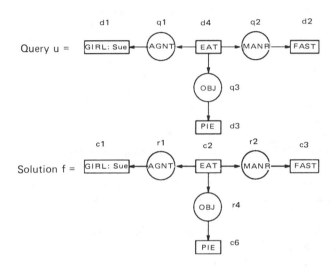

Fig. 13.16 A query u and the solution f for the generalization hierarchy in Fig. 13.15.

Let us consider what happens in each stage of the breadth-first search of the generalization hierarchy for the query u. To make matters simple we will assume there is no indexing present, so the search will start from the top of the hierarchy $[\top]$.

We first find all of the generalizations of the query graph u that are successors of the graph $[\top]$. Let us assume that we use a general matching algorithm on graphs b and c to find the subgraph isomorphisms of b and c in u, such that $\pi_b = \{(c1, d1), (r1, q1), (c2, d4), (r2, q2), (c3, d2)\}$ and $\pi_c = \{(c4, d1), (r3, q1), (c5, d4), (r4, q3), (c6, d3)\}$.

Now we look at b and c's successor graphs for generalizations of u. The successor graphs are d and e. The graph d is represented by *restrictIndividual* b c1 Sue d. This instructions translates into if *referent*$(\pi_b c1)$ = Sue then $\pi_d := \pi_b$ else fail. Since π_b c1 = d1 and *referent*(d1) = Sue, d is a generalization of u and $\pi_d := \pi_b$.

The graph e is represented by *restrictType* c c4 GIRL e. This instruction is implemented as: if *type*$(\pi_c c4) \leq$ GIRL then $\pi_e := \pi_c$ else fail. Since π_c c4 = d1 and *type*(d1) = GIRL, e is a generalization of u, and $\pi_e := \pi_c$.

Now we examine the successor graphs of d and e. The only one in this case is f. The graph f is represented by three instructions. The first instruction, *join* d e c1 c4 f, means if π_d c1 = π_e c4 then $\pi_f := \pi_d+(\pi_e-(c4, d1))$ else fail. Since π_d c1 = d1 = π_e c4, we calculate $\pi_f = \{(c1, d1), (r1, q1), (c2, d4), (r2, q2), (c3, d2), (r3, q1), (c5, d4), (r4, q3), (c6, d3)\}$.

The second instruction is *join* f f c2 c5 f. Since π_f c2 = d4 = π_f c5 we get $\pi_f = \pi_f + (\pi_f - (c5, d4))$.

The third instruction in f is *simplify* f r1 r3 f. Since π_f r1 $= \pi_f$ r3 $=$ q1 we have $\pi_f := \pi_f - (r3, q1) = \{(c1, d1), (r1, q1), (c2, d4), (r2, q2), (c3, d2), (r4, q3), (c6, d3)\}$. Thus f is a generalization of u. In fact $f = u$. Compare this result with the graphs u and f in Fig. 13.16.

In this way we remove redundant data from the database by storing the graphs as differences from their immediate generalizations. Common computation is shared throughout the database via the shared projection information placed throughout the formation rule instances. The data (graphs) take an active rather than passive role in matching, by decomposing into (efficient) instructions representing specialized instances of the canonical formation rules.

13.5 SUMMARY

Two major problems involved in processing conceptual graphs are subsumption (exponential in the size of the graph in the worst case), classification (typical case logarithmic in the number of conceptual graphs in the database). We have given an improved algorithm for pruning the search space and the number of actual subsumption tests for the classification problem.

The canonical formation rules distinguish conceptual graphs from other semantic network formalisms. They enforce semantic constraints on the canonical graphs. Algorithms to process them must be developed.

Conceptual graphs are compiled into instructions which are special cases of the canonical formation rules. In this way we compile subsumption of conceptual graphs. The instructions operate on immediate generalizations, and construct a mapping between the immediate generalizations and the graph, and hence the query graph during search. Common computation involved in matching database graphs to the query graph is shared through these mappings. Since a specialization implies a generalization, simply constructing the hierarchy compiles static inferences.

Compilation is effected in three ways: removal of redundant data, use of simple instructions which ignore redundant checks when performing matching, and by sharing common processing between graphs.

Extending this work to general first-order conceptual graphs presents many challenges. For general first-order conceptual graphs the partial ordering is implication rather than subgraph (modulo typing and individuation) for atomic conceptual graphs. The subsumption test is implemented by a theorem prover, rather than subgraph isomorphism.

Automating conceptual graphs offers many challenges, but the simple and elegant inference rules that operate over such a powerful modelling language offer more than sufficient reward.

Acknowledgements

I thank Fritz Lehmann, Robert Levinson, Peter Robinson, and John Sowa for discussions on the proceeding topics.

BIBLIOGRAPHY

Aït-Kaci, H. and Podelski, A. (1991). "Is there a meaning to LIFE", In Proc. of the 8th International Conference on Logic Programming, (ed) Koichi Furukawa, Paris, 25-28 June, MIT Press.

Ellis, G. (1990a). "Compiling Conceptual Graphs", in Proc. of the Fifth Annual workshop on Conceptual Structures, (eds) P. Eklund, and L. Gerholz, Linköping University, ISBN 91-7870-718-8.

Ellis, G. (1990b). "Sorting Conceptual Graphs", in Proc. of the Fifth Annual workshop on Conceptual Structures, (eds) P. Eklund, and L. Gerholz, Linköping University, ISBN 91-7870-718-8.

Garner, B. J. and Tsui, E. (1987). "A Self-Organizing Dictionary for Conceptual Structures", In Proc. of the Conference on Applications of Artificial Intelligence, (ed) J. F. Gilmore, pp. 356-363, SPIE Proc. 784, 18-20th May, Orlando.

Hanschke, P. (1991). "TAXLOG: A Logic Programming Language with Deeply-Modelled Type Hierarchies", draft note from DFKI, Kaiserslautern, Germany.

Levinson, R. A. (1985). A Self-Organizing Retrieval System for Graph, PhD Thesis, University of Texas.

Levinson, R. A. (1991). "Multi-Level Hierarchical Retrieval", in (ed) E. Way Proc. of the 6th Annual Conceptual Graphs Workshop, pp. 67-81, SUNY Binghamton.

Levinson, R. A. and Ellis, G. (1991). "Multi-Level Hierarchical Retrieval", To appear in Knowledge Based Systems Journal.

Mineau, G. (1989) "Induction on Conceptual Graphs: Finding Common Generalizations and Compatible Projections", In Proc. of the 4th Annual Conceptual Structures Workshop, (eds) J. A. Nagle and T. E. Nagle, Detroit.

Roberts, D. D. (1973) The Existential Graphs of Charles S. Peirce, Mouton, The Hague.

Schmolze, J. G. and Lipkis, T. A. (1983), "Classification in the KL-ONE Knowledge Representation System", In Proc. of Eighth International Joint Conference on Artificial Intelligence, (ed) Alan Bundy, William Kaufmann Inc., Los Altos, California, 8-12th August, Karlsruhe, West Germany.

Shastri, L. (1991) "Why Semantic Networks", in Principles of Semantic Networks: Explorations in the Representation of Knowledge, (ed) J.F. Sowa, Morgan Kaufmann, San Mateo, CA, pp. 109-136.

Sowa, J. F. (1984) Conceptual Structures: Information in Mind and Machine, Addison-Wesley, Reading, MA.

Sowa, J. F. (1991a) Principles of Semantic Networks: Explorations in the Representation of Knowledge, Morgan Kaufmann, San Mateo, CA.

Sowa, J. F. (1991b) "Toward the Expressive Power of Natural Language", in Principles of Semantic Networks: Explorations in the Representation of Knowledge, (ed) J.F. Sowa, Morgan Kaufmann, San Mateo, CA, pp. 157-189.

Walther, C. (1984) 'A Mechanical Solution of Schubert's Steamroller by Many-Sorted Resolution", Proc. of the 4th AAAI, Austin, Texas, pp. 330-334.

Willems, M. (1990) "Knowledge Graphs versus Conceptual Graphs", memorandum 876, University of Twente, The Netherlands.

Woods, W. A. (1991) "Understanding Subsumption and Taxonomy: A Framework for Progress", in *Principles of Semantic Networks: Explorations in the Representation of Knowledge*, (ed) J.F. Sowa, Morgan Kaufmann, San Mateo, CA, pp. 45-94.

14

Induction on Conceptual Graphs: Finding Common Generalizations and Compatible Projections

Guy W. Mineau
Département d'informatique,
Université Laval,
Ste-Foy, Québec, Canada, G1K 7P4

ABSTRACT

This chapter shows how to automatically induce a particular generalization hierarchy (Sowa, 1984) from a knowledge base whose knowledge objects are represented using first-order conceptual graphs (Sowa, 1984)[1]. This knowledge encoding structure, called *knowledge space*, is useful for different knowledge processing tasks, as it provides a generalization-based memory. Two of these tasks are presented in this paper. They concern the implementation of two useful operations on conceptual graphs: (a) finding common generalizations; (b) computing compatible projections. These are two very important operations for many conceptual graph processing systems; and they can be improved when a knowledge space representation of the knowledge base is used.

14.1 INTRODUCTION

In the conceptual graph theory of Sowa (1984), the author introduces a classification structure which induces a partial order of generality/specificity over conceptual graphs: it is called the *generalization hierarchy*. In this structure, each node represents a conceptual graph which is connected downwards to the nodes that represent more specific conceptual graphs, and upwards to the nodes representing more general conceptual graphs. A conceptual graph v is said to be more general than another conceptual graph u (written $v \geq u$), iff u is canonically derivable from v, using the COPY, RESTRICT, JOIN and SIMPLIFY canonical formation rules (Sowa, 1984). A node then represents a common generalization of its children.

Whenever knowledge, represented by conceptual graphs, can be divided into knowledge objects, a generalization hierarchy could be helpful for limiting the retrieval of knowledge

---

[1] First-order conceptual graphs are those having a corresponding first-order logic formula.

objects to those which are relevant to the problem to be solved. In effect, when a system has to solve a problem, answer a query, or search for particular knowledge objects (e.g., for certain schemata or type definitions), it often relies on *partial* knowledge. For instance, a query is usually a partial assertion that has to be confirmed or rejected by an inference engine according to the contents of *certain* knowledge objects. Naturally, it is possible to determine which knowledge objects are relevant to a particular situation by scanning them exhaustively or by using an index which will point out the knowledge objects that share some concepts with the query. Of course, an exhaustive search is prohibitive, and an index on sole concepts may not be discriminative enough, especially if the content of the knowledge base is quite homogeneous. A generalization hierarchy provides such an index on *whole* conceptual graphs, by storing directly the common generalizations of different subsets of knowledge objects. The extra memory needed is justified when the retrieval of different subsets of knowledge objects and of their common generalizations is part of a major functionality of the system.

This chapter will show how to automatically abstract a particular generalization hierarchy from the knowledge objects composing the original knowledge base (section 14.3). However, it is quite unlikely that such a structure would take a reasonable amount of memory unless some restraining conditions are imposed upon it. Hence, the generalization hierarchy presented in this paper (section 14.2), called the knowledge space, takes advantage of these restrictions in order to save space and to make the implementation of such a structure feasible. In effect, the complexity analysis of section 14.4 will demonstrate that the knowledge space has memory requirements of the same order of complexity than the original knowledge base, that is, $o(n)$ (n being the total number of knowledge objects).

Furthermore, this chapter will also show how to use the data stored in the knowledge space in order to efficiently generate *compatible projections* (Sowa, 1984), which are very useful whenever join operations are needed (section 14.5).

14.2   AN EXAMPLE

Consider three knowledge objects, each representing some knowledge on a different subject in zoology (Fig. 14.1)[2], along with the type hierarchy representing the hierarchical relationships existing between different concept types (Fig. 14.2).

---

[2]In this example, the concept type "sleg" stands for "supporting leg", that is, legs allowing mobility for a particular legged animal.

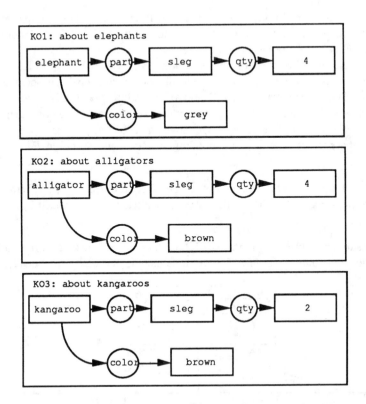

Fig. 14.1 Three knowledge objects represented as conceptual graphs.

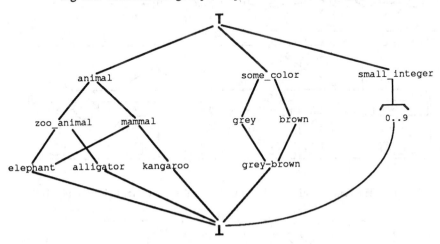

Fig. 14.2 The type hierarchy.

Fig. 14.3 shows a generalization hierarchy abstracted from these three knowledge objects, where only particular common generalizations, called *maximally specific common generalizations* (MSCG) have been kept (the type hierarchy of Fig. 14.2 had to be used in order to determine common minimal supertypes).

Let n be the number of knowledge objects. even for a small n, the number of potential MSCGs can be prohibitive, $o(2n)$: we could not store them all! Furthermore, most of these MSCGs are quite similar. In order to keep memory requirements down, we will take advantage of the inheritance property of the structure and store as little information in a node as possible. Consequently, a node will contain only the information that is not inherited from its ancestors. This intermediary data will help to reconstitute the MSCG of each descendant of the node. Here are some restrictions that make the implementation of a generalization hierarchy feasible. Let n be a node in which we want to store the corresponding MSCG, and L, the label representing the corresponding objects. then restrictions $R1$ and $R2$ are as follows;

$R1$) identical concepts and relations in all knowledge objects of L will appear in the corresponding MSCG. Those that are not identical will be replaced by the character "?".

$R2$) Any subgraph appearing in the MSCG of a node n will be deleted from all MSCGs of the descendant nodes of n. For example, here is the content of node (2,3) after $R1$ and $R2$.

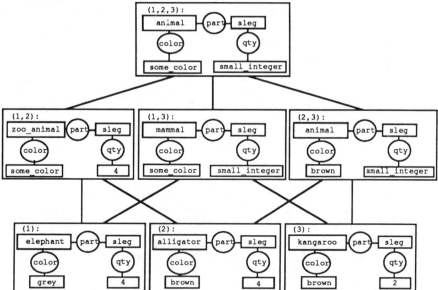

Fig. 14.3 The generalization hierarchy built over the knowledge objects of Fig. 14.1

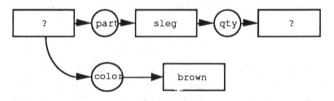

Fig. 14.4 The content of node (2,3) after R1.

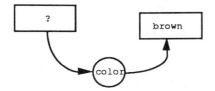

Fig. 14.5 The content of node (2,3) after R1 and R2.

Fig. 14.6 shows the entire generalization hierarchy with such intermediary forms of MSCGs as the content of each corresponding node. Because MSCGs are not kept directly in the generalization hierarchy of Fig. 14.6, some processing is needed in order to reconstitute them, and it can be summarized as follows:

1. join the different subgraphs contained in all the nodes lying between the one representing the MSCG in question and the root of the generalization hierarchy inclusively (knowing that the "?" is the neutral element of the ∩ operator (Sowa, 1984), i.e., for any type c, $c \cap ? = c$).

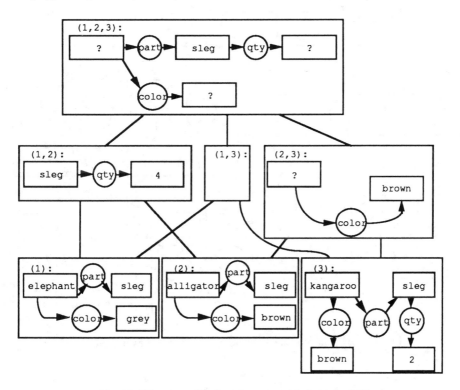

Fig. 14.6 The generalization hierarchy with *partial* MSCGs.

2. instantiate any remaining "?" by the common minimal supertype of all the concept types corresponding to this "?" in the knowledge objects appearing in L (using the type hierarchy of Fig. 14.2).

For instance, the first step of the reconstruction of the MSCG of (2,3) would be to join the graphs contained in nodes (2,3) and (1,2,3) of Fig. 14.6. The result has already been shown in Fig. 14.4. and then, node (2,3) of Fig. 3 shows the MSCG of (2,3) once the remaining "?" are instantiated according to the type hierarchy of Fig. 14.2.

In order for the join operation to produce the graph of Fig. 14.4 from nodes (2,3) and (1,2,3) of Fig. 14.6, we had to know which "?" to match together: there might have been something else (other than animal) being brown. consequently, the concepts and relations the "?" stand for in each knowledge object will accompany them. they will be placed in lists which will follow the "?" that represent them, and therefore they will appear in the appropriate nodes. Fig. 14.7 shows the generalization hierarchy of Fig. 14.5 where these lists have been added to each "?", and where empty nodes have been removed. this generalization hierarchy is equivalent to the knowledge space, which is more thoroughly introduced in the next section.

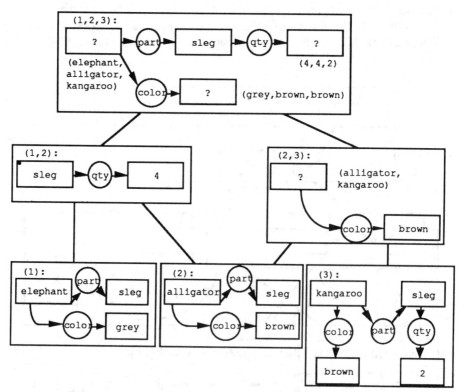

Fig. 14.7 The generalization hierarchy of Fig. 14.6 with the associated lists of concept types.

14.3   GENERATING THE KNOWLEDGE SPACE

This section presents the internal data structure chosen to represent conceptual graphs (section 14.3.1) and efficient algorithms that create the knowledge space: the node generation algorithm (section 14.3.3) and the linking algorithm (section 14.3.4). the former works in time $o(n \ log \ n)$; while the latter takes $o(n^2)$ steps to link the appropriate nodes together, where n is the total number of knowledge objects (see section 14.4). These algorithms build the knowledge space from a particular data structure, the intersection matrix, introduced in section 14.3.2.

14.3.1   Representing conceptual graphs

Most conceptual graph[3] can be decomposed without ambiguity into a set of triplets of the form $< concept1, relation, concept2 >$. therefore, knowledge objects can be seen as sets of such triplets; this is shown in Fig. 14.8.

The triplet representation permits to draw an analogy with retrieval systems where the documents are described by keywords. in effect, triplets can be used as descriptors of knowledge objects. Consequently, the classification algorithms used in these systems in order to relate documents to one another can be adapted for triplet-described knowledge objects. actually, the generalization hierarchy proposed in this paper has its origins in the work of Godin *et al.* (1986), where the authors propose a lattice of keyword subsets for classifying keyword-described documents in order to facilitate browsing.

```
KO1:  <elephant,part,sleg>
      <sleg,qty,4>
      <elephant,color,grey>
```

```
KO2:  <alligator,part,sleg>
      <sleg,qty,4>
      <alligator,color,brown>
```

```
KO3:  <kangaroo,part,sleg>
      <sleg,qty,2>
      <kangaroo,color,brown>
```

Fig. 14.8 The knowledge objects of Fig. 14.1 represented as triplets.

14.3.2   The intersection matrix

The content of any node in the knowledge space represent the similarity (common generalization) between a subset of knowledge objects. When considering the similarity between knowledge objects, one can proceed by finding the set of triplets they have in common. For example, KO1 and KO2 have in common: $< sleg, qty, 4 >$. however, KO2 and KO3 have no triplet in common, but they still are similar in the sense that they both represent brown animals. This common property may be found by first extracting the identical subparts of the two triplets (producing here $<?, color, brown >$), and then by finding the common minimal supertype for the two concepts that did not exactly match (in our example: alligator and kangaroo). Consequently, all possible subparts of all triplets (called *generalization patterns*) must be generated. a generalization pattern (GP) is obtained from a triplet by replacing some (0 or more) of its components by the wildcard character "?". there will be 8 GPs generated from each triplet (where the original triplet, called *complete triplet*,

---

[3]More precisely: those in which each concept occurs only once and in which only binary relation have been used.

is also a GP). For example, the generalization patterns of $< elephant, part, sleg >$ are: $<$ $elephant, part, sleg >, <?, part, sleg >, < elephant, ?, sleg >, < elephant, part, ? >$ $, <?, ?, sleg >, < elephant, ?, ? >, <?, part, ? >$, and $<?, ?, ? >$.

Consequently, the set of triplets describing a knowledge object will be extended as to include all GPs generated from it. with each GP is associated a list of the concepts or relation that the "?" stand for. these lists are called *element lists* (EL). Fig. 14.9 shows the previous GPs with their corresponding ELS.

$$< elephant, part, sleg > ()$$
$$<?, part, sleg > (elephant)$$
$$< elephant, ?, sleg > (part)$$
$$< elephant, part, ? > (sleg)$$
$$<?, ?, sleg > (elephant, part)$$
$$< elephant, ?, ? > (part, sleg)$$
$$<?, part, ? > (elephant, sleg)$$
$$<?, ?, ? > (elephant, part, sleg).$$

Fig. 14.9 Generalization patterns with the associated Element lists.

The intersection matrix correlates the sets of descriptors (triplets) with the knowledge objects from which they were obtained. it shows the occurance of all GPs in all knowledge objects. Fig. 14.10 shows the intersection matrix of the knowledge objects in Fig. 14.1, where the set of triplets is the union of the three sets of GPs generated from the complete triplets of Fig. 14.8. the intersection matrix is created while the sets of GPs describing each knowledge object are scanned. note that due to the commonality between the knowledge objects in the example, the number of GPs is much less (41) than it would be without overlapping knowledge objects (64).

From this intersection matrix, it is possible to directly derive the nodes of the knowledge space. examining a particular row of the intersection matrix tells exactly in which node of the knowledge space to put the corresponding GP. A GP belongs to the node identified by the x's of the corresponding row in the intersection matrix: these x's determine which knowledge objects share this GP as a descriptor. consequently, the nodes of the knowledge space will be found by scanning the rows of the intersection matrix. these nodes will not be empty.

14.3.3   The node generation algorithm

In order to present this algorithm in details, two more notions need to be introduced: the *instantiation lists* (IL) and the *most specific set* (MS set).

The instantiation lists associated with a GP tell exactly which concepts and relations have been replaced by the "?"s when the GP was generated from a complete triplet. There is one IL for each knowledge object that a GP describes. the members of each IL are the element lists (described above) which are related to this GP. So there are as many ELs in an IL as there are complete triplets in the same knowledge object from which this GP can be generated.

	KO1	KO2	KO3	
`<elephant,part,sleg>`	x			(line 1)
`<sleg,qty,4>`	x	x		
`<elephant,color,grey>`	x			
`<alligator,part,sleg>`		x		
`<alligator,color,brown>`		x		(line 5)
`<kangaroo,part,sleg>`			x	
`<sleg,qty,2>`			x	
`<kangaroo,color,brown>`			x	(line 8)
`<elephant,part,?>`	x			
`<elephant,?,sleg>`	x			
`<?,part,sleg>`	x	x	x	
`<elephant,?,?>`	x			
`<?,?,sleg>`	x	x	x	
`<?,part,?>`	x	x	x	
`<?,?,?>`	x	x	x	
`<sleg,qty,?>`	x	x	x	
`<sleg,?,4>`	x	x		
`<?,qty,4>`	x	x		
`<sleg,?,?>`	x	x	x	
`<?,?,4>`	x	x		
`<?,qty,?>`	x	x	x	
`<elephant,color,?>`	x			
`<elephant,?,grey>`	x			
`<?,color,grey>`	x			
`<?,?,grey>`	x			
`<?,color,?>`	x	x	x	
`<alligator,part,?>`		x		
`<alligator,?,slegs>`		x		
`<alligator,?,?>`		x		
`<alligator,color,?>`		x		
`<alligator,?,brown>`		x		
`<?,color,brown>`		x	x	(line 32)
`<?,?,brown>`		x	x	(line 33)
`<kangaroo,part,?>`			x	
`<kangaroo,?,sleg>`			x	
`<kangaroo,?,?>`			x	
`<sleg,?,2>`			x	
`<?,qty,2>`			x	
`<?,?,2>`			x	
`<kangaroo,color,?>`			x	
`<kangaroo,?,brown>`			x	(line 41)

Fig. 14.10 the intersection matrix associated with Fig. 14.8.

For example, let $GP_i =<?,?,brown>$ (line 33 in the intersection matrix). it would have the following two ILs (one for KO2, the other for KO3): $((alligator, color))$ and $((kangaroo, color))$. The first of these comes from KO2: $< alligator, color, brown >$ (line 5), and the second from KO3: $< kangaroo, color, brown >$ (line 8). In this example, each IL has *only one* EL, because *only one* complete triplet in each knowledge object can generate GP_i[4] If E is an arbitrary set of GPs, we will note E^+, the set obtained from E, in which the corresponding ILs have been appended to each GP. The ILs will be constructed incrementally as the knowledge objects are scanned to produce the intersection matrix.

---

[4]Note that ILs of GPs which are complete triplets are null lists and will be omitted.

Maximal transformations also need to be introduced. They are meant to avoid redundancy and to save space. When a certain position in all ELs of all ILs associated with GPi is filled with the same concept or relation, then the corresponding "?" in GPi can be instantiated (only) to that concept or relation. When a "?" in GP_i is instantiated in that manner, the ILs of GPi are updated: the corresponding concept or relation can be eliminated from all ELs of all ILs. Making any number of such instantiations on GPi generates other GPs which are said to be *transformations* of GP_i. For example, let $GP_i = <?, ?, brown>$ (line 33) and $GP_j = <?, color, brown>$ (line 32). Let their respective ILs be IL_i and IL_j. Then IL_i will be: $((alligator, color))$ and $((kangaroo, color))$, and IL_j: $((alligator))$ and $((kangaroo))$. One can see from GP_i, GP_j, IL_i and IL_j, that GP_j is a transformation of GP_i. In effect, the last element of both ELs in IL_i is equal to color: thus GP_i can be transformed into GP_j. We will say that GP' is a maximal transformation of GP_i iff it is a transformation of GP_i such that *all* "?" in GP_i which are instantiable in that manner have actually been instantiated. In the previous example, GP_j is a maximal transformation of GP_i. Also, each GP is considered to be a transformation of itself. Finally, let $MS(E^+)$ =maximal transformations of the GPs in E^+. $MS(E^+)$ is said to be the *most specific set* of E^+. It can be computed by first generating the maximal transformations of all GPs in E^+, and then by eliminating duplicates. In fact, a boolean variable is stored with each GP in the intersection matrix, telling whether the GP represents a maximal transformation of some other GP or not. This can be computed when the knowledge objects are scanned to generate the intersection matrix. Consequently, the test $(MS(GP+) = GP+)$ in the node generation algorithm below can be computed in time $O(1)$: only checking the value of the boolean variable is needed. Here follows the algorithm;

> *For each row of the intersection matrix do:*
> > *(1) the node where the GP should be placed is identified (by the x's);*
> > *(2) if (this node does not exist) then: it is created;*
> > *(3) if (the GP is a complete triplet) then: it is inserted right away;*
> > > *else if $(MS(GP+) = GP+)$ and (the node represents*
> > > *more than one knowledge object)[5]*
> > > *then: the GP is inserted with its ILs.*

14.3.4   The Linking Algorithm

The linking algorithm uses the partial order of inclusion defined over the set of labels to connect a node to its children and parents. However, by connecting the lower nodes first and working its way up to the root, only the children of the nodes to be connected have to be considered. This restrains our search to the children of a node N (the node to be connected), that is, to the nodes whose label is included in the label of N, but which do not have any parent whose label is also included in the label of N. Here is the linking algorithm.

> *For each node to be connected (called new node) do:*
> > *(1) the knowledge object numbers contained in its label are identified;*
> > *(2) for each of them do:*

---

[5]This condition states that the MSCG of a unique knowledge object is equal to this knowledge object, and needs to be described only by the complete triplets describing this knowledge object.

(2.1) identify its entry nodes[6]. {hopefully a leaf whose label is the
knowledge object number}
(3) for each entry node do:
(3.1) child ← entry node; potential child
(3.2) if (the label of the child is included
into the new node's label)
then:
findparents(child);
(4) clear all markers.

Where findparents(child) is the following recursive procedure:

if (the child has not yet been visited) then:
(1) mark it as visited;
(2) identify all its actual parents whose label is included
into the new node's label;
(3) if (this set of parents is non-empty) then:
for each of these nodes do:
(3.1) findparents(node);
else connect the new node to the child.

Fig. 14.11 shows the knowledge space built from the three knowledge objects of Fig. 14.1 using the algorithms described in this section. Note that it is equivalent to the generalization hierarchy mentioned in section 14.2 and illustrated in Fig. 14.7.

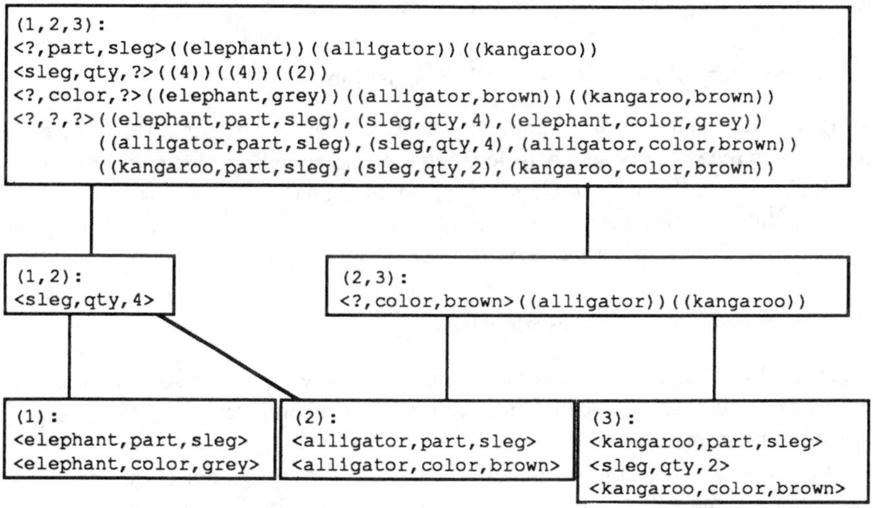

```
(1,2,3):
<?,part,sleg>((elephant))((alligator))((kangaroo))
<sleg,qty,?>((4))((4))((2))
<?,color,?>((elephant,grey))((alligator,brown))((kangaroo,brown))
<?,?,?>((elephant,part,sleg),(sleg,qty,4),(elephant,color,grey))
        ((alligator,part,sleg),(sleg,qty,4),(alligator,color,brown))
        ((kangaroo,part,sleg),(sleg,qty,2),(kangaroo,color,brown))
```

```
(1,2):
<sleg,qty,4>
```

```
(2,3):
<?,color,brown>((alligator))((kangaroo))
```

```
(1):
<elephant,part,sleg>
<elephant,color,grey>
```

```
(2):
<alligator,part,sleg>
<alligator,color,brown>
```

```
(3):
<kangaroo,part,sleg>
<sleg,qty,2>
<kangaroo,color,brown>
```

Fig. 14.11 The knowledge space generated from the knowledge objects of Fig. 14.1.

---

[6]The entry nodes of a subset of knowledge object numbers L, are those nodes whose label include L, such that they do not have any descendants which are also entry nodes of L, i.e., they are the lowest nodes whose label include L.

14.4   COMPLEXITY ANALYSIS

This section gives some important results on the complexity of the knowledge space, and on the complexity of the algorithms which generate it.

14.4.1   Memory Requirements

A fundamental question concerning the implementation of the knowledge space is the number of nodes it contains. Since there cannot be more nodes than the number of rows in the intersection matrix, obviously, the number of rows is an upper bound on the number of nodes in the worst case.

Let m be the total number of complete triplets in all knowledge objects, and p the number of nodes, then: $p \leq 8m$, since every complete triplet has 8 GPs. Setting an upper bound $kmax$ on the number of complete triplets for each knowledge object, and n being the number of knowledge objects, then: $p \leq 8\ k\ max\ n$, which is $O(n)$. However, in the average case, we could expect the number of nodes to be $O(log\ n)$, referring to Bradford's law (Brookes, 1977).

Another interesting question is the complexity of the structure as characterized by the number of links. Let q be the number of parents of a node. All ancestors of a node whose label is L, must have L contained in their labels. Any knowledge object number in L appears in at most in 8 $kmax$ labels. Thus the number of ancestors of any node is bounded by 8 $kmax$, and so is the number of parents. Then: $q \leq 8\ kmax = O(1)$. If we take the entire heterarchy, the total number of links, t, is bounded by the number of nodes multiplied by the number of parents for each node: $t \leq pq = O(n)$. For the same reason as for the number of nodes, we could expect an average case of $O(log\ n)$.

14.4.2   Complexity of the node generation algorithm

Scanning each row will take $8m$ iterations in the worst case for the main loop. If we use a balanced tree to index the node labels, locating the corresponding node and inserting it in the tree if absent, can be done in $O(log\ m)$. Computing $(MS(GP+) = GP+)$ is $O(1)$. So the generation algorithm can be done in $O(m\ log\ m)$. Since m is $O(n)$, $O(n\ log\ n)$ is the upper bound. We also expect an average case of $O((log\ n)\ log(log\ n))$.

14.4.3   Complexity of the linking algorithm

The algorithm links the nodes in the order of increasing label size. This sorting can be done while the intersection matrix is being built. Its asymptotical complexity will not change the one found in this subsection.

The treatment of line 1 implies iterating over each knowledge object number in each node's label, thus this will be the total number of iterations for the inner loop. Since each knowledge object number can appear at most in 8 $kmax$ labels, the total number of iterations is bounded by 8 $kmaxn$. In each iteration, the ancestors of the entry nodes are tested for label inclusion until the children of the node to be linked are found. The number of entry nodes is bounded by 8 $kmax$ and is thus $O(1)$. Reasoning as before, the number of ancestors of a node is $O(1)$ and so is the number of links traversed when searching for a potential child. Furthermore, because the labels can be kept sorted, the inclusion test can be done by scanning each label only once. The complexity is then bounded by the sum of the lengths of the labels. The maximum label length is n, giving a complexity of $O(n)$ for the inclusion test. Consequently the processing in line 3 of the algorithm is $O(n)$, and the whole linking algorithm is bounded by $O(n^2)$.

14.5 COMPATIBLE PROJECTIONS

The knowledge space representation of a knowledge base offers many advantages: different types of queries can be answered more efficiently (Mineau *et al.*, 1990), consistency within the knowledge base can be improved (Mineau *et al.*, 1989), a generalization hierarchy on conceptual graphs is available to the system, and compatible projections can also be efficiently computed. In effect, compatible projections are defined by (Sowa, 1984) as follows. Let π_1 and π_2 be two projections of v in u_1 and u_2, where v, u_1 and u_2 are conceptual graphs, and v is a common generalization of u_1 and u_2. Then π_1 and π_2 are said to be compatible if for each concept c in v:

1. $type(\pi_1 c) \cap type(\pi_2 c) >$ absurd concept type;

2. the referents of $\pi_1 c$ and $\pi_2 c$ conform to $type(\pi_1 c) \cap type(\pi_2 c)$;

3. if $(referent(\pi_1 c)$ is the individual marker i) then: $referent(\pi_2 c)$ is either i or *.

The knowledge space already gives common generalizations for any subset of knowledge objects. Furthermore, the intermediary forms of MSCGs as stored in the knowledge space indicate which concept types are to be checked for compatibility. In effect, compatibility needs to be tested only on concepts or relations equal to "?". This can easily be done using the type lattice of Fig. 14.2. When a common maximal subtype is found for all non-matching concept types represented by a "?", then it can replace this "?". Only the resulting complete triplets are kept: they describe the compatible projections. For example, let us find the compatible projection between KO1 and KO2. First, the GPs contained in all nodes between the entry nodes of (1,2) and the root have to be gathered. A GP is added to the resulting set of GPs only if it is still a maximal transformation when parts of its ILs relevant to (1,2) are scanned. The resulting set of triplets is shown in Fig. 14.12.

$< sleg, qty, 4 >$
$<?, part, sleg > ((elephant))((alligator))$
$<?, color, ? > ((elephant, grey))((alligator, brown))$
$<?, ?, ? > ((elephant, part, sleg), (sleg, qty, 4), (elephant, color, grey))$
$\qquad ((alligator, part, sleg), (sleg, qty, 4), (alligator, color, brown))$

Fig. 14.12 The set of triplets (and ILs) relevant to (1,2).

Then for each "?", the corresponding instantiation lists are scanned in order to find a common maximal subtype for the concept types this "?" stand for, using the type hierarchy of Fig. 14.2. The resulting triplets are shown in Fig. 14.13.

$< sleg, qty, 4 >$
$<?, part, sleg > ((elephant))((alligator))$
$<?, color, grey - brown > ((elephant))((alligator))$

$<?,?,?>$ $((elephant, part, sleg), (sleg, qty, 4), (elephant, color, grey))$
$((alligator, part, sleg), (sleg, qty, 4), (alligator, color, brown))$

Fig. 14.13 After common maximal subtypes have been found.

From these triplets, only those having no "?" are kept (that is, the first one). This GP describes the compatible projection existing between KO1 and KO2. The join can then proceed. The resulting graph is shown in Fig. 14.14.

Let us suppose that an elephant mated with an alligator, and that their offspring is both an elephant and an alligator, called elephator ($elephant \cap alligator = elephator$). Revising the triplets of Fig. 13 would produce the set of triplets of Fig. 14.15. The resulting conceptual graph is shown in Fig. 14.16. Though this example is quite particular, it demonstrates that new knowledge about common subtypes can be obtained by joining the original knowledge objects.

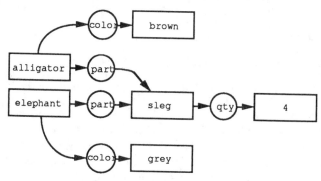

Fig. 14.14 Joining KO1 and KO2 using Fig. 14.13.

$< sleg, qty, 4 >$
$< elephator, part, sleg >$
$< elephator, color, grey-brown >$
$<?,?,?>$ $((elephant, part, sleg),$ $((alligator, part, sleg),$
                          $(sleg, qty, 4),$ $(sleg, qty, 4),$
                          $(elephant, color, grey)),$ $(alligator, color, brown))$

Fig. 14.15: Revised set of triplets.

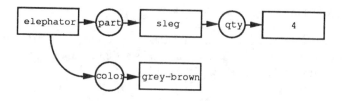

Fig. 14.16 Joining KO1 and KO2 using Fig. 15.

When using the knowledge space or the algorithms that produce it, one can compute some intermediary form of MSCG that is useful both for generating the actual MSCG of a subset of knowledge objects (which is a common generalization) and for producing their compatible projection.

Also, one can try to extend a compatible projection (or a MSCG) as computed above, by matching some of the elements of the instantiation lists accompanying $<?, ?, ? >$. In order to do this, general graph matching methods can be used, as for instance the one introduced in (McGregor, 1982). Nevertheless, the knowledge space provides a basis for finding compatible projections. When such projections often need to be computed, the intermediary data contained in the knowledge space constitute a kernel around which maximally extended compatible projections can be approximated. This information provides some already computed starting point and helps speed up the generation of compatible projections.

14.6 CONCLUSION

In this chapter, we intended to show how induction on conceptual graphs can abstract a particular generalization hierarchy, called *knowledge space*, which can improve two important operations on conceptual graphs:

 a) finding common generalizations;

 b) computing compatible projections.

These operations are vital to many conceptual graph processing systems; and unfortunately they are quite resource-consuming. The knowledge space alleviates their task by providing precomputed intermediary data from which relatively easy computation remains to be done. These advantages are available at the cost of additional memory. However, the memory requirements of the knowledge space are of the same order of complexity, $O(n)$, as those of the original knowledge base that it represents. Furthermore, it can be created in reasonable time, i.e., in $O(n^2)$ steps in the worst case.

In summary, we hope to have shown the potential usefulness of using a knowledge space for representing knowledge in any conceptual graph processing system which uses heavily the projection operator π (or its inverse: π^{-1}, in order to find compatible projections and common generalizations.

BIBLIOGRAPHY

Brookes, B.C. (1977). "Theory of the Bradford Law", Journal of Documentation 33 (3), September, 180-209.

Godin, R., Saunders, E. & Gecsei, J. (1986). "Lattice Model of Browsable Data Spaces", Information Sciences 40, 89-116.

McGregor, James J. (1982). "Backtrack Search Algorithms and the Maximal Common Subgraph Problem", Software-Practice and Experience 12, 23-34.

Mineau, G., Gecsei, J. & Godin R. (1989). "Improving consistency within knowledge bases", In)eds) Martin Schader and Wolfgang Gaul, *Knowledge, Data and Computer-Assisted Decisions.* NATO ASI Series, Springer-Verlag. 49-65.

Mineau, G., Gecsei, J. & Godin, R. (1990). "Structuring Knowledge Bases Using Automatic Learning". Proc. of the 6th International Conference on Data Engineering, Los Angeles, USA, 5-9 February, 274-280.

Sowa, J. F. (1984). *Conceptual Structures: Information Processing in Mind and Machine.* Addison-Wesley Publishing Company.

15

A Framework for Negotiating Conceptual Structures

Peter Eklund
Department of Computer Science,
The University of Adelaide,
P.O. Box 498, Adelaide,
Australia 5001

ABSTRACT

One of the long term aims of conceptual structure research is to produce knowledge engineering environments for conceptual graph acquisition. To achieve this one firstly needs to establish the consistency of the underlying inheritance hierarchy (or oracle) which describes hierarchical relationships between concepts mentioned in conceptual structures. There are two ways to treat inconsistency in inheritance hierarchies. The first is to accept the inconsistency as a reflection of a nonmonotonic characterization of the domain and the second is to skeptically treat such nonmonotonic cases as potential modeling mistakes. This chapter provides a dialog framework for inheritance hierarchy construction to ensure the network described to a system reflects operator aims. A belief set representation is used to guarantee a convergence between system inferences and operator intentions. The result of the dialog is a *situations matrix* which represents preferred specialization and generalization paths through an inheritance hierarchy.

In genuine nonmonotonic domains the dialog will lead to a network which contains mutually exclusive logical states and the situations matrix will remain inconsistent. A nonmonotonic logic is then applied to explain inconsistency. One particular nonmonotonic logic, autoepistemic logic, is used to demonstrate how a preference relation can be drawn on default inheritance links. In terms of conceptual structures, the relevance of the technique is measured by the simplification which results by the application of combination rules, RESTRICT, COPY, JOIN and SIMPLIFY, whose actions can be taken without any unnecessary recourse to nonmonotonic treatments.

15.1   INTRODUCTION

Inheritance networks represent an important class of knowledge representation devices whose primary purpose is to describe generalization/specialization relationships between concept classes and instances in the form of a taxonomy. To make proper use of inheritance hierarchies logically consistency is required and representations need to be free of ambiguous or misleading interpretations. This work provides a dialog framework for inheritance hierarchy construction which ensures that the network described reflects the intentions of the operator. In situations where the dialog leads to a network which contains mutually exclusive logical states, we apply a nonmonotonic logic (NML) to explain inconsistencies.

Since most path-based reasoners are simply variations of reachability tests and in no way attempt to analyze the semantic meaning of the arcs and labels in the network, the application of a nonmonotonic formalism ultimately depends on the logical consistency of the model presented by the operator. How then can we judge the rationality of the network without recourse to the rationality of its creator? This basic dilemma in nonmonotonic multiple inheritance cannot be overcome by any general theory for reasoning with defaults. Model construction is external to reasoning with the model. Following this line of argument the rationality of an ambiguous network topology cannot be assessed without testing the client's commitment to the network model and its implications. This is especially relevant in dynamic network construction where an inheritance hierarchy is used as a knowledge modeling aid as is the case in many of the major commercial AI shells. The main problem as Krishnaprasad (1989) puts it is, "when explicit addition of arcs to the network may destructively effect the implications supported by the initial network...". This is not only evidence that a dynamic inheritance editor is desirable but also that such interactive capabilities are being considered in more formal treatments of nonmonotonic inheritance using nonmonotonic logics.

One way to achieve this interactive capability for a dynamic inheritance editor is by using a negotiation or critiquing paradigm. Expert critiquing systems (Miller, 1984), (Rankin, 1988a) or negotiation systems are names given to a dialog paradigm where an expert user asks advice of a computer system about a tentative solution to a problem[1] The net effect of the critiquing paradigm is described by Waern (1992), "users maintain and may extend their proficiency as the system confirms correct choices and offers corrections and further information on decisions which are at variance with the systems." Inheritance hierarchy construction is used as a particular representation through which to experiment with the expert critiquing paradigm.

In order to see how negotiating dialog can be used to help resolve inconsistencies in network hierarchies we firstly examine inheritance and its inherent properties. I explain what a nonmonotonic inheritance hierarchy is, how inconsistency and ambiguity can be defined within such a hierarchy, what the rules which constitutes a legal inheritance network are, how specificity can be used as well as notions of credulous and keptical inheritance reasoners.

Section 15.3 **The Negotiation Model** provides justification for the inheritance "debugger" in terms of psychology models of human-computer dialog and the desirability of such a tool for intelligent interfaces and knowledge engineering.

---

[1] A natural language approach to expert critiquing can be found in Harrius (Harrius, 1992).

Section 15.4 **A Logic of Belief and Dialog** presents a brief survey of existing belief logics and discusses how these can be incorporated into practical dialog systems. A logic of belief and knowledge is vital to dialog management since the exchange of messages, in the form of actions taken by the user and advice given by the system, can be viewed as changing the knowledge state of the agents involved in the interaction.

In section 15.5 **Dialog Examples** illustrates how a belief set approach to dialog management for inheritance hierarchies can be used. Autoepistemic logic is introduced to resolve nonmonotonic inheritance by explaining inconsistencies.

Finally in 15.6 **Negotiating and Conceptual Graphs** I examine the results of a negotiated dialog for conceptual graphs. In particular, how the inheritance hierarchy resulting from the negotiated dialog simplifies the application of the conceptual structure inference rules SIMPLIFY, COPY, JOIN and RESTRICT.

The main contribution of this chapter to conceptual graph theory is the simplification of the canonical inference rules SIMPLIFY, COPY, JOIN and RESTRICT. This is achieved by ensuring the consistency of the user defined inheritance oracle. The net effect of this work is a framework for a knowledge engineering environment for the acquisition of conceptual graphs where the consistency of the underlying inheritance hierarchy is guaranteed by an interactive inheritance editor which scrutinizes, in terms of logical consistency, the networks that it helps to create.

15.2   INHERITANCE HIERARCHIES

Inheritance hierarchies have become almost synonymous with an efficient and convenient way of organizing knowledge in AI applications. Under the aliases of semantic networks, conceptual dependency graphs, partitioned networks and structured inheritance networks,

these hierarchical representations have their roots in the Aristotelian genus/species classification hierarchies. After initial unstructured and divergent usage in early AI efforts, the more recent approaches of Touretsky (1986), (Touretzky, 1987), (Touretzky, 1988) (Sandewall, 1986), (Etherington, 1988), (Horty *et al.*, 1990) have resulted in a general syntactic consensus of so called "bipolar nonmonotonic multiple inheritance".

15.2.1   Basic Definitions

Definition 1 An inheritance network Γ is a directed acyclic labeled graph $\Gamma = (V, E)$. The set of vertices $V = \{v_1, v_2, \ldots, v_n\}$ for $n > 0$. Any $v \in V$ has a type signature range $\mathcal{R} = \{instance, class\}$ and the set $\mathcal{I} \subseteq V$ is the set of individuals or instances with the type signature *instance*. $\mathcal{I}$ is labeled from the beginning of the alphabet, namely $a, b, c, \ldots$. $\mathcal{C}$ is a subset of vertices $\mathcal{C} \subseteq V$ which have the type signature *class*. $\mathcal{I} \cap \mathcal{C} = \emptyset$. Classes are labeled from the middle alphabet $p, q, r, s \ldots$.

Definition 2 Edges in range over the link types $\{\Rightarrow, \not\Rightarrow, \rightarrow, \not\rightarrow, \rightsquigarrow, \not\rightsquigarrow\}$ with the corresponding labels $\{is\text{-}a, is\text{-}not\text{-}a, d\text{-}is\text{-}a, d\text{-}is\text{-}not\text{-}a, ns\text{-}is\text{-}a, ns\text{-}is\text{-}not\text{-}a\}$.

In the inheritance network editor we develop there are six types of edges $\{\Rightarrow, \not\Rightarrow, \rightarrow, \not\rightarrow, \rightsquigarrow, \not\rightsquigarrow\}$. The str ict and defeasible link types correspond to the basic link types given in Touretzky (1984). The addition of the two non-specific links types $\{ns\text{-}is\text{-}a, ns\text{-}is\text{-}not\text{-}a\}$

are components used in the interactive paradigm and their intuitive semantics are explained below.

is-a *strict inheritance*: If $a \in \mathcal{I}$ and $p \in \mathcal{C}$ then $a \Rightarrow p$ is read "a is a ground instance of p". This can be interpreted by considering p as a predicate in classical logic which accepts an individual a as an argument which evaluates to true, $p(a) = \top$. Graphically we can represent this;

If $p, q \in \mathcal{C}$ then $p \Rightarrow q$ is read "p's are always q's". This can interpreted if $a \in \mathcal{I}$ and $p, q \in \mathcal{C}$ and $p(a) = \top$ then $q(a) = \top$. This is drawn;

is-not-a *strict class exclusion*: If $a \in \mathcal{I}$ then $a \not\Rightarrow p$ is read "a is not a ground instance of p". This can interpreted by considering p as a predicate which accepts a as an argument which evaluates to false, $p(a) = \bot$. This is drawn;

If $p, q \in \mathcal{C}$ then $p \not\Rightarrow q$ is read "p's are never q's". This can interpreted, if $a \in \mathcal{I}$ and $p, q \in \mathcal{C}$ and $p(a) = \top$ then $q(a) = \bot$. This is drawn;

d-is-a *default class inheritance* : $p \rightarrow q$ reads $p, q \in \mathcal{C}$ then p's are normally q's but there are exceptions, i.e. if $a \in \mathcal{I}$ then $\exists a\ p(a) = \top$ and not $q(a) = \top$. This will be drawn as;

No interpretation is given to the normative statement $p \rightarrow q$ other than "p is more specific than q".

Tourtetzky (Tourtetzky, 1986) makes the most comprehensive statement regarding the general intuitions of normative or defeasible inheritance links. Intuitively, the normative link $p \rightarrow q$ could be interpreted, typically p is a q, normally p is a q, nearly all p's are q's, p's can be assumed to be q's and the default for p, w.r.t. q, is that p is a q. What we observe is a linguistic mixture of normativity giving rise to two basic approaches to the inheritance problem which in turn have three primary interpretations for normative statements.

The first approach conforms to the argument that since normative statements have a multiplicity of intuitive interpretations, associating a formal semantic interpretation will result in a divergence from one or more of the intuitive interpretations. Therefore, no formal semantics for normative statements should be defined. Furthermore, inheritance can be characterized without any explicit discussion of normative statements by examining the general intuitive semantics of inheritance independent of such interpretations. The results are usually fairly complicated deductive definitions of preferred inheritance paths via a global analysis of the network, like those of Horty (1990).

The second approach is a local translation of normative links to a more general non-monotonic logic by reinterpreting specificity as a statement of defeasibility. The model or proof theoretic semantics of a nonmonotonic logic can be used to infer preferred paths in the network which conform to the intuitive path entailments. Thus, normative statements are either directly encoded as axioms, good examples are Pearl (1988) and Doherty (1989), or as inference rules, the most obvious example being Etherington (1988).

In the second approach, direct or local translation of normative links, opinion is divided about the formal interpretation for the normative statements between the probabilists and the rest of the community[2]. The first of these interpretations of normative links, and most vehemently argued against, is probabilistic. The idea is that a normative link $p \rightarrow q$ should have the interpretation; typically p is a q means that any randomly selected p is most likely to be a q, i.e. the conditional probability $P\left[q|p\right]$ is high.

The counter argument to a probabilistic interpretation is that the implication that em-pirical and observable statistics are needed for the likelihood of events in the particular environment is too strong. For example, few would argue that in an equatorial region $P\left[Flies(x)|Bird(x)\right]$ is $high$ but moving south to "Penguin Island" would necessitate a reduction in the probability of $P\left[Flies(x)|Bird(x)\right]$ as the frequency of encountered $penguins$ increases. The probabilities associated with normativity are thus situation de-pendent. Furthermore, the logicists argue that the intended meaning of a defeasible link $p \rightarrow q$ is: in the absence of information to the contrary about some individual a other than $a \rightarrow p$ assume that $q(a)$ is true. Such assumptions can be made irrespective of the relative likelihood of their being true, and simply reflect an adherence to convention based on information at hand. By way of this definition, conventions as default rules are themselves domain dependent but they are also adaptive in changing circumstances. Later in this chapter we examine these approaches in more detail. In summary, there are three commonly held views regarding the meaning of normative statements;

- make no formal fixed interpretation of normative statements other than that $p \rightarrow q$ indicates that p is more specific than q. Treatments conforming to this idea are often called path-based approaches to inheritance reasoning.

- normative statements as statements of fuzzily quantified or relative probabilities. Generally called probabilistic approaches to inheritance reasoning.

- normative statements as a set of axioms or inference rules in a nonmonotonic logic. These are often referred to as the model-based approaches to inheritance reasoning[3].

As a final word on normative statements, it should be mentioned that there is a significant school of thought that defeasible or default links should be kept out of any logical treatment of inheritance entirely. Proponents of this approach believe that normative reasoning should

---

[2]For want of a better label this group can be described as the logicists. This issue is not restricted to inheritance but pertains to defeasible reasoning systems in general.

[3]It is worthwhile pointing out that there is considerable inter-play between these three approaches, although the initial ideas on which they were based are different.

be incorporated into a process of belief revision. When one discovers that the original assumptions are wrong or inappropriate then the theory's assumptions are revised and one recomputes the entailment. "This is naturally slower than defaults in frame systems that you can introduce at a moment's notice; but if you want a sound system, you either have to prove consistency at each default rule, as in Reiter's (1980) logic, or you have to rethink your assumptions and restart the proof" (Sowa, 1991). While this point of view is prefectly acceptable from a practical systems aspect, it can be criticized on the basis of a lack of "cognitive adequacy" (Touretzky, 1984) since it fails to differentiate between consequences drawn from default information and those drawn from facts known to be certain in a domain. The ability to distinguish the two may be vital in domains where we need to make important decisions on the basis of reasoning with incomplete knowledge.

d-is-not-a *default class exclusion*: $p \not\rightarrow q$ reads p's are normally not q's but there are exceptions, i.e. if $a \in \mathcal{I}$ then $\exists a \ p(a) = \top$ and $q(a) = \top$. This will be drawn;

ns-is-a *non-specific class inheritance* : $p \rightsquigarrow q$ reads, either one of $p \Rightarrow q$ or $p \rightarrow q$ holds, this will be drawn;

In such cases the type of the link is uncertain and it is only known that there exists some positive inheritance relationship between p and q.

ns-is-not-a *non-specific class exclusion*: $p \not\rightsquigarrow q$ reads either $p \not\Rightarrow q$ or $p \not\rightarrow q$, this is drawn as;

This statement expresses ignorance about the link type, it is only known that there is some negative relation between p and q.

15.2.2   Nonmonotonic Multiple Inheritance

Most literature in nonmonotonic inheritance concerns either the application of path-based techniques for overcoming inconsistency in inheritance hierarchies or alternatively the translation of these networks into general nonmonotonic logics such as circumscription, default logic or autoepistemic logic.

The tendency in conceptual graph research has been to treat conceptual graphs as the primary object language, expressing logical relationships, propositions or sentences in a logical language. The individual concepts and relations are either primatively defined in a conceptual graph lexicon or part of some kind of oracle. Realistically such an oracle must take the form of a inheritance hierarchy, predefined and assumed to be logical consistent and correct. Strictly speaking any treatment of inheritance which does not include the potential for incorporating first order logic will not be generalizable to conceptual graph processing. This presents problems though because some of the significant characteristics of nonmonotonic inheritance have not been successfully translated into a recognizable logical language (Thomason, 1988). Significantly, for this treatment, these properties can easily be incorporated in software and an engineered solution, as opposed to a theoretical one, is a promising alternative.

Definition 3 Positive and negative non-specific links are written e_n^+ and e_n^- respectively. Positive and negative defeasible links are written e_d^+ and e_d^- respectively. We write e_*^* for any of the link types $\{\Rightarrow, \not\Rightarrow, \rightarrow, \not\rightarrow, \rightsquigarrow, \not\rightsquigarrow\}$. A legal path from an instance or a class p to a class q of length n is a path $\sigma = e_1, \ldots, e_{n-1}$ such that;

    (i) there is no subpath e_*^-, e of σ, $e_*^-, e \not\subseteq \sigma$
    (ii) there is no subpath e_d^+, e_s^* of σ, $e_d^+, e_s^* \not\subseteq \sigma$
    (iii) there is no subpath e_n^*, e of σ, $e_n^*, e \not\subseteq \sigma$

The definitions above state that a sequence of links is not a path if it contains a defeasible link followed by a strict link or if it contains a negative or non-specific link which is not the last link in the sequence. When the above conditions hold, a legal path between two nodes p and q can be written $\sigma_{p,q}$.

Definition 4 A legal network is a network Γ such that;

    (i) forall $p, q \in V$, $e_*^+ = \langle p, q \rangle \in \Gamma$ iff $e_*^- \notin \Gamma$
    (ii) forall $p, q \in V$, $e_*^- = \langle p, q \rangle \in \Gamma$ iff $e_*^+ \notin \Gamma$
    (iii) forall $p, q \in V$, $\sigma_{p,q}$ is a legal path.

Touretsky's specificity property is another important result in nonmonotonic inheritance. It reflects the assumption that more specific information in the network is informationally more relevant than information higher in the hierarchy.

Theorem 1 For any acyclic digraph $\Gamma = (V, E)$ with n nodes, the nodes can be labeled 1 through n such that; (i) if $p \in V$ is labeled k then all vertices that can be reached from p via a directed path are given a label which is indexically less than k.

Proof 1 The proof relies on the fact that a finite acyclic digraph always contains at least one vertex with an indegree of zero, i.e. a node with has only outgoing arcs. This is defined as the "bottom" of the inheritance hierarchy, written $\bot$. If there were no nodes with an indegree of zero then the graph contains cycles or is infinite. First time through we label all nodes with indegree zero with n and delete them and their outgoing arcs. The next nodes with indegree of zero are labeled $n - 1$ etc., and the process is repeated until there are no nodes to label.

Lemma 1 There is at least one node which is the "top" of the hierarchy having only incoming arcs. If there are n nodes with only incoming arcs they can be written $\top_1, \ldots, \top_n$.

Lemma 1 follows from proof 1 since there is always one or more nodes with outdegree zero otherwise the network contains cycles or is infinite.

Definition 5 - Link Specificity The vertices in Γ are partially ordered according to definition 4. Any edge e in Γ has a specificity corresponding to the specificity of the least specific node involved in the link. This is called the specificity class of e.

Definition 6 - On-Path Preemption in Given a path $\phi \in \Gamma$ such that $\phi = s \to p_1 \to \ldots \to p_n \to t$ and $\sigma \in \Gamma$ such that $\sigma = s \to p_1 \to \ldots \to p_n \to q_1 \to \ldots \to q_n \not\to t$ then ϕ is said to preempt σ iff there is some $p_i \in \{p_1, \ldots, p_n\}$, $q_j \in \{q_1, \ldots, q_n\}$ such that $p_i \to q_j \in \Gamma$.

Definition 7 - Off-Path Preemption in Given a path $\phi \in \Gamma$ such that $\phi = s \to r_1 \to \ldots \to r_n \not\to t$ and $\sigma \in \Gamma$ such that $\sigma = s \to p_1 \to \ldots \to p_n \to q_1 \to \ldots \to q_n \to t$, and $\forall_{i,j} r_i \neq p_j$ then, ϕ is said to off-path preempt σ iff there exists some φ such that $\varphi = s \to r_1 \to \ldots \to r_n \to q_1 \to \ldots \to q_n \to t$ and ϕ on-path preempts φ.

15.2.3 Consistency

The origin of the debate concerning the proper intuitive semantics for multiple inheritance with exceptions are so called inconsistent networks which are characterized by inconsistent states or contradictions. For example, if there is a pair $(p, q) \in \Gamma$ and two or more paths exist between p and q which have opposite polarity, Γ said to be inconsistent. Pearl (Pearl, 1987) offers a considerably more sophisticated definition of network inconsistency by considering whether a probability model exists for which all defeasible links are highly probable. If no such model exists, the network is considered to be inconsistent. For the moment, the simple minded definition will suffice to illustrate the idea.

Consider the inconsistent network Γ_1, which is a homogeneous multiple inheritance hierarchy with exceptions. Γ_1 demonstrates the fact that a is inconsistent w.r.t. q. This is because there are two paths $a \to p \not\to q$ and $a \to q$ contained in Γ_1 which are in conflict.

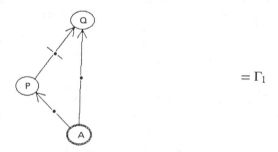

$$= \Gamma_1$$

The inconsistency is in itself no justification for ignoring Γ as a legitimate representation of the theory which Γ encodes. As it happens inconsistency amongst paths can often be resolved, as it can for Γ_1, via the preemption criteria presented above.

15.2.4 Credulous Inheritance

So far we have seen that a valid inheritance path in a network Γ is a combination of ideas. Firstly, it is an appropriate concatenation of paths using either a top-down or bottom-up reasoner. These paths should then be filtered so that paths which contradict one another and paths which are themselves preempted by other paths should be excluded. We are then faced with the question as to what to do with competing or ambiguous paths. Should they cancel one another out entirely or should an inheritance reasoner consider each competing extension as an alternative explanation for Γ?

A "credulous model" for inheritance reasoning[4] is one where we consider all paths, or propositions represented by paths, which led from an instance a to a class p as supporting belief in the inheritance of the class p by the instance a. In the case of ambiguity, credulous inheritance reasoners resolve inconsistency in a network by constructing extensions which reflect different solutions to the resolution of conflicting paths.

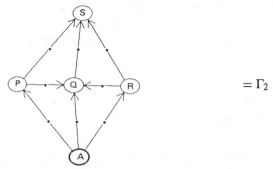 $= \Gamma_2$

In Γ_2 we see that the assertion $a \rightarrow q$ is supported by three paths $a \rightarrow q$ itself, $a \rightarrow p \rightarrow q$ and $a \rightarrow r \rightarrow q$. The idea behind the credulous strategy is so called "belief hunger" where one tries and draw as many conclusions from a network as possible. At the same time that we can conclude that a is an q, we can also conclude that a has the properties of the classes p and r as well. When networks contain mutually exclusive paths a number of consistent extensions are associated with paths through the network.

Definition 8 - Credulous Inheritance A network Γ permits the inheritance of properties in a class p from an instance a if there exists one or more non-preempted paths from a to p.

The problem with credulous inheritance is that it is computationally intractable (Selman, 1989) which leads us to consider alternative approaches which attach fewer models to inheritance hierarchies.

15.2.5 Skeptical Inheritance

The alternative to credulous models of inheritance are "skeptical" models which encapsulate the idea that conflicting paths, representing conflicting arguments, cancel or neutralize one another. Skeptical inheritance describes the notion that a proposition p may be supported by a number of different lines of reasoning but that only the facts present in all arguments for p should be used to defend it.

Blocking Ambiguity

The definition of skeptical inheritance given by Touretzky (Touretzky, 1987) is that a compound argument is neutralized by any conflicting argument which is not itself preempted. The definition allows the inheritance reasoner to rule out inconsistent compound paths like $a \rightarrow p \rightarrow r$ and $a \rightarrow q \not\rightarrow r$, but permits inconsistent direct links of the form $a \rightarrow p$

---

[4]Sometimes called opportunistic inheritance reasoning.

and $a \not\rightarrow p$[5]. The reason is the issue of deductive reasoning in the face of inconsistency. The main aim of the skeptical inheritance research is to produce an inheritance reasoner which would encapsulate the idea of the intersection of all credulous extensions, called "ideal skepticism", without generating all credulous extensions to achieve this. Touretzky's (Touretzky et al., 1987) first attempt at such a skeptical reasoner failed to give the same results as the intersection of all credulous extensions on the Nixon double diamond topology and is an example of an "ambiguity blocking" skeptical reasoner. It is called ambiguity blocking (Stein, 1989a) because as soon as it reaches an ambiguity the reasoner discontinues inheriting.

The general approach is illustrated on Γ_{3a}, if a node t is ambiguous w.r.t. a node p then all the arcs into and out of t are deleted. When the entire network has been scanned the remaining edges reveal a new network Γ_{3b} which is unambiguous w.r.t. p and represents the ambiguity blocked skeptical extension of Γ_{3c}.

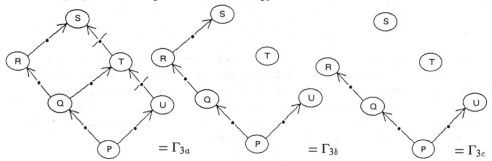

The trouble is that $q \rightarrow t$ has been eliminated which means that $\Gamma_{3b} \Vdash p \rightarrow s$, although it is not really intuitive to do so. If $q \rightarrow t$ had been considered as an "in" link then $\Gamma_{3b} \not\Vdash p \rightarrow s$. If we are to take ideal skepticism as the correct specification of a skeptical reasoning algorithm then the ambiguity blocking algorithm fails the test.

Propagating Ambiguity

The alternative is to propagate ambiguity, not by deleting all the incoming and outgoing arcs of an ambiguous node, but by marking such nodes ambiguous and continuing the network scan. Once the reasoner reaches the top of the hierarchy it backtracks over the network deleting all the arcs associated with ambiguous nodes it has marked.

The results of such processing are shown in Γ_{3c}, which represents the ambiguity propagated skeptical extension of Γ_{3a}. Although this approach appears quite promising for cascading diamond topologies, it fails for the following topology, whereas ambiguity blocking succeeds.

The argument here is that in every credulous extension that one could consider $\Gamma_4 \Vdash p \rightarrow t$[6] but ambiguity propagation rules this out. The conclusion is that there are certain network

---

[5]The intuitions behind this result come from relevance logic where inconsistent information cannot be used to derive arbitrary conclusions. In the case of direct contradiction, $a \rightarrow p$ and $a \not\rightarrow p$, the reasoner will be able to conclude $p(a)$ and $\neg p(a)$ but will not continue to draw irrelevant conclusions based on this inconsistency.

[6]Given Stein's labeling schema $p = seedless\ grape\ vine$, $q = grape\ vine$, $r = vine$, $s = arbor\ plant$, $t = plant$, $u = tree$, $v = fruit\ plant$, $w = fertile\ thing$ it seems quite obvious that regardless of the alternatives $p = seedless\ grape\ vine$ is always a $t = plant$.

topologies in which a fact will be true in every credulous extension but have no justification in the intersection of these credulous extensions. Makinson and Schlechta (1989, 1991) call such facts "floating conclusions". Subsequently, any path-based approach to generating skeptical extensions will either be unsound, in the sense that floating conclusions may be entailed with different arguments supporting each extension, or incomplete, in the sense that the floating conclusion is not entailed.

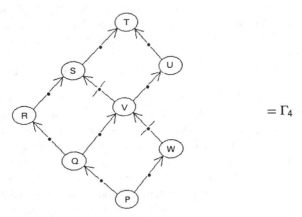

$$= \Gamma_4$$

Subsequent treatments (Geffner, 1989) introduce alternative skeptical reasoners which produce the appropriate results from the double diamond topology of Γ_2, but without any proof that it will satisfy all topologies. In a similar fashion much of the research in the area has involved the definition of a particular skeptical inheritance reasoner and subsequent papers discrediting it by showing counter examples.

Regardless of the debate between skeptical versus credulous inheritance reasoners, the main goal is to define a declarative mapping between a network and a logic representation which, given the appropriate axiomatization and model semantics, can perform both skeptical and credulous reasoning within the same logical representation. This goal has yet to be achieved.

15.3 THE NEGOTIATION MODEL

Issues concerning existing problems with intelligent interfaces are important to keep in mind when developing a system of this sort and finding ways of addressing these problems is an integral aspect to this work. Without going into too much detail these problems can be summarized as;

The role problem The advice taking role of an expert system obviously influences the degree by which the user accepts certain advice. For example, Card (1989) points out that MYCIN is committed to playing the role of the partner who actually makes decisions. Arguably, MYCIN's limited acceptance by physicians supports the conclusion that the sanctimonious tone of the systems interface did little to enhance its acceptance. In this research control of the degree of system "insistence" is controlled by the operator. System recommendations can be over-ridden anytime but only by the operator expressing explicitly a change in intention.

The automation problem Certain tasks may naturally lend themselves to automation but the consequences may not result in improved performance for the system as a whole. In such cases functions which are usually performed by the human operator are automated, possibly resulting in the alienation of the human operator from the decision making process. One solution is a mixed initiative system where the system is designed so as to maximize total efficiency and not assess efficiency by minimizing the effort of constituent elements. How then do we maximize cooperation between system and operator to their mutual benefit? Relating this to inheritance we don't want a system to draw all possible inheritance inferences without the operators knowledge. In order to establish the extent of inferences drawn by the system we first examine the nature of the communication problem in intelligent interfaces.

The Communication Problem Trying to find a framework for interacting with a user naturally leads to attempts at applying generalized linguistic discourse theories (Grice, 1975). Grice's maxims give us the idea of progressing from different states of informativity by conversation as well as a way of restricting state transitions which violate the principle of co-operation. Flouting the maxims results in indirect speech acts. Unfortunately, such linguistic discourse theories give no indication of how we should perform dynamic, communication induced changes but instead give us a general descriptive framework in which communication should take place. They tell us how we should communicate but not what content should be communicated. As Card puts it, "in order to carry on an intelligent conversation with the user, the system must be able to diagnose in an appropriate way the user's state of knowledge about the topic of conversation". This suggests the use of a belief logic for modeling such dialog.

An inheritance "debugging device" is not only desirable for knowledge engineering but can be justified in terms of psychological models of human-computer dialog.

To construct a computer system which mediates between a user acting as a knowledge source and the system as an inference device for inheritance hierarchies we need to understand what constitutes a user model. User models are commonly seen as a common set of assumptions which can influence the system output. A number of treatments with varying emphasis are described in Rich (1983), Cohen and Jones (1987), Wahlster (1988) Waern (1991).

Waern (1991) views a model of a user as a sender to a computer system as consisting of three distinct levels. The first level is where the system incorporates knowledge of human cognition characteristics. These include fallible memory, narrow attention span and proficient recognition. In a inheritance hierarchy editor these issues are addressed by a permanent sketch-pad and archive for the networks, a graphic representation which enhances the user's interest and a pictorial structure which makes even the largest networks immediately distinguishable.

The second level defined by Waern captures the idea of stereotyping users. This usually takes the form of a number of user profiles into which specific individuals, through interaction with the system, can be categorized, e.g. novice, expert and levels in between. This is usually done by either self-assessment or when accessing the system. In our case, the specialist nature of the system as a knowledge engineering interface relieves the system of this type of progressive assessment. We have a single interface and user profile, that of an operator who is either a domain expert or a knowledge engineer. In either case, such an operator has heuristic and learning competence, high motivation and interest level. According to Waern's treatment the single variable at this level of interaction is that of so called "cognitive style" which is a reflection of the conscious recognition of the potential ambiguity contained in the domain to be modeled. In other words the user makes a mindful decision about the type of model he/she intends to create. In the inheritance domain three modes of cognitive style can be identified and these are selected by the operator.

- *non-ambiguous modeling* - the model is characterized by its completeness. There are no mutually contradictory inheritance conditions. Maximal dialog takes place to prohibit the creation of ambiguous networks. Links contributing to ambiguity conditions cannot be created. Non-specific link types translate to strict inheritance.

- *no a priori assessment of domain ambiguity* - the system operates in "an alert but accept mode" where contradictory inheritance extensions are accepted with appropriate warnings. Suggestions for overcoming ambiguous situations are made. There is no enforcement of such suggestions. Non-specific link types are used and these may be refined through dialog when mutually exclusive logical states arise.

- *ambiguous model* - mutually contradictory conditions are known to be present in the domain and these may be reflected in the inheritance model. Contradictory inheritance situations are accepted with warnings. A critique takes place when the network is complete. Action to overcome ambiguity is recommended at the users request including the application of one or more nonmonotonic mechanisms. Non-specific links may never be used in this mode.

System based assessment of the user through progressive interaction is the third level of user modeling defined by Waern. This is usually done in Q&A type systems by the construction of a operator profile which reflects the user's acquired knowledge. This profile is constructed by way of the user's ability to respond correctly in certain situations.

Although no explicit tutorial mode is envisaged, a similar effect is achieved through the dialog which takes the form of questions about the specific characteristics of the inheritance network e.g. *"Are all birds descendents of dinosaurs?"*, *"Do all birds fly?"* and so on. This constant interaction keeps the user informed of the ramifications of the model under construction and, in a sense, educates the user about his own model. The system communicates its conclusions through redrawing the resulting network computed from the responses to such questions. Additionally actions which result in a violation of what constitutes an illegal network are detected and flagged and this tutors the operator in the general principles of network construction.

The three cognitive style categories discussed above, non-ambiguous modeling, no a priori assessment of domain ambiguity and ambiguous modeling will be taken up at length in **15.5 Dialog Examples**. Before these examples can be presented we take a closer look at belief logics and their potential applications in negotiation dialog.

15.4 LOGICS OF BELIEF AND DIALOG

A logic of belief and knowledge is vital to dialog management since the exchange of messages, in the form of actions taken by the user and advice given by the system, can be viewed as changing the knowledge state of the agents involved in the interaction. The process of translating "utterances"[7] into a language of knowledge and belief is somewhat simplified in the inheritance domain. The individual vocabulary of utterances possible is restricted to a series of additions or modifications to the hierarchy. A record of these utterances is maintained implicitly through a transcript of the dialog and explicitly in the network itself. This section discusses the potential for using logics of belief in dialog management for inheritance network construction.

Knowledge and Belief - Early efforts to establish a theory of communication using a belief operator by Cohen and Perrault (1979), (Cohen and Levesque, 1985) and Perrault and Allen (1980) extented a first-order axiom schema to model the intentions of utterances in natural language. Their work, belonging to speech act theory, demonstrates the feasibility of a translation of utterances in natural languages to sentences in a logical language and was subsequently extended to incorporate the "possible world" semantics by Appelt (1986) and Cohen and Levesque (1985).

The foundations for this work are Hintikka's (1962) epistemic logic where the axioms of modal logic are introduced and the possible world semantics incorporated. The idea is that in each state of the world an agent considers other worlds that are possible. An agent is said to "know" a proposition only if that proposition is true in every world thought possible by the agent. Through constraining the accessibility relation between possible worlds useful properties relevant to the notion of "belief" can be established. A major difficulty of the possible world semantics is logical omniscience where the agent must be able to deductively reason about the logical closure of any possible world. The conseqences of this are that belief in anything follows from belief in inconsistent sentences.

Syntactic Approaches - A syntactic or sentential approach has terms whose intended meaning are expressions in a well-formed formula in some object language. The basic idea is that a metalanguage is defined where propositions, as terms, can be reasoned with in the object language. However this creates problems and the notational complexity of the approach makes it difficult to work with since other primitives like negation, disjunction, truth, tests for wffs and tautologies etc, all have to be axiomatized in the metalanguage. On the other hand, it is more expressive than the possible worlds approach, for example, $\exists x$ such that $Belief(a, x)$ has no counterpart in the modal form. Its main advantage is power and formal expressibility. Semantics can be defined within the metalanguage to overcome the problem of logical omniscience.

The Deductive Approach The possible world semantics are weakened in deductive or limited inference systems which results in logics whose nonmodal part is the same as first order logic and whose modal part is weaker than the Kripke semantics. According to McArthur (McArthur, 1988) there are three approaches within this category:

The situational approach - where inconsistent beliefs are allowed. The partial worlds approach is both consistent and complete. This means that every sentence

---

[7]By "utterance" we mean an arbitrary minimal unit of communication considered meaningful.

is either believed to be true or false. A situation is like a possible world except that there is no consistency or completeness requirement and a sentence may have a truth value assigned to it or it may not. It is argued that this more closely corresponds to our intuitions since an agent may hold no particular belief about a sentence. The major disadvantages are incorporating quantifiers and nested beliefs.

Sentence semantics - is where each of the belief models includes inference rules, sentences and any other syntactic entities. To avoid logical omniscience the agents inference rules may be incomplete with respect to classical logic.

Belief sets - are independent pictures that an agent has of how the world is. Belief is identified with truth in any one particular cell and each cell is closed under deduction i.e. if an agent believes p and $p \rightarrow q$ then he also believes $p \wedge q$ and q. The belief sets approach (Gärdenfors, 1988), (Konolige, 1988) has some attractive computational properties since there is no reasoning between sets. Its major drawbacks are that computational efficiency suffers when quantifiers and nested beliefs are added.

15.4.1   Autoepistemic Logics

Autoepistemic logic (Moore, 1988) provides a formal semantics for reasoning nonmonotonically generally and for reasoning nonmonotonically in inheritance hierarchies specifically. The basic argument in favor of autoepistemic logic is that in existing nonmonotonic logics the concept of a stable expansion if not defined within the logical language but is a new metalevel property completely outside the logic. Autoepistemic logic supplements belief logic so that stable expansions are the direct results of logical consequence. The conditions under which these stable expansions occur can be directly expressed within the logic.

The essential idea behind autoepistemic logic is that a nonmonotonic axiom can be written in the form $\forall x\, Bird(x) \wedge B(Canfly(x)) \supset Canfly(x)$ which changes the traditional nonmonotonic interpretation of "typical birds fly" to "birds that are known not to fly are the only birds that can't fly". Interpreted in this fashion sentences become statements of belief rather than typicality.

The difference between say default logic and autoepistemic logic is that default logic is tentative and thus defeasible while autoepistemic logic contains context sensitive states whose evaluation may change as beliefs change. What follows from not knowing a proposition p will clearly change as soon as p has a truth value. Such a set is called a stable expansion of S. The consequences of this definition are that stable expansions contain all and only those formula supported by what is known to be true. Intuitively this corresponds to the idea that different conclusions that are drawn with incomplete information are dependent upon what someone is prepared to believe. Moore's example is that, "I believe Richard Nixon is alive simply because if he was dead I surely would have heard about it".

In the next section we see how autoepistemic logic can be used to translate a nonmonotonic inheritance hierarchy into a set T of stable expansions with appropriate explanation clauses.

15.4.2   Belief logics, dialog and nonmonotonic multiple inheritance

Having mentioned some of the formal approaches to logics of belief and given a summary of their salient features let's consider each of these in turn from an applications view. Our discussion focuses on dialog scenarios which are analogous to the belief logics I describe. A set of propositions P in the formal language would correspond to facts presented to the system by the user, in the inheritance case the various links which comprise the network, and inference rules which belong to that user model are general statements or principles of inheritance e.g. the rule corresponding to transitivity in inheritance if $a \supset b$ and $b \supset c$ then $a \supset c$. The extralogical rules of inheritance like path legality, skeptical or credulous interpretations are external to these inference rules.

The syntactic approach is considered too heavy handed for the application we have in mind, rather like trying to kill a mosquito with an M16. Its expressive capabilities may however be used to good effect in treating more complicated natural language utterances although the problem remains of distinguishing the object from the metalanguage (Appelt and Konolige, 1986), e.g. for the statement, *"Bob believes that the washing machine is broken"*, does Bob believe the utterance or the extensional fact that the utterance reports?

In the deductive approach we saw how situation models could be used to represent different, and possibly inconsistent, beliefs and the formal redefinition of the semantics enabled logical omniscience to be largely overcome.

The sentence semantics approach seems particularly appropriate for intelligent tutoring since not only the propositions representing beliefs are contained in each agents model but also the inference rules which the agent knows and can apply. For example, if a student is learning high school algebra, successfully solving the equation $5(x - 10) = 5$ for $x = 11$, would lead to a student model in which the *distributive rule* was included. In subsequent examples the system can discount distributivity as a possible cause for student error, assuming of course that the student doesn't forget what she has learned. The space of explanations based on the rules in the learning set is searched discounting the learned rules in R.

For this application the belief sets approach, where we maintain independent pictures of logical beliefs which map to relevant situations, seems the most promising. The problem of quantifiers is not relevant since inheritance hierarchies can be represented propositionally. Nested beliefs are not required since we deal with a single agent. A belief set corresponds to each human-machine interaction or negotiation round. For each of these a new belief set is constructed which reflects user specified "utterances". The system then uses its own inferences to create situations or models which are consistent with the current belief set. This process of refinement continues until the inconsistent belief set reflects a consistent set of situational models. If, after completing the negotiation, two or more inconsistent situational models remain then this is a starting point for applying a nonmonotonic logic. Autoepistemic logic can be used as a nonmonotonic logic which incorporates notions of belief into defeasible axioms in the object language.

15.5   DIALOG EXAMPLES

We now deal with several examples illustrating the dialog between system and user demonstrating the three levels of operation described in **15.3 The Negotiating Model**. Belief sets are used for controlling the dialog. The rules, legal path (Definition 2.3), specificity (Definition 2.4) and preemption (Definition 2.5) from **15.2 Inheritance Heirachies** provide criteria for preferring inheritance paths. In ambiguous domains autoepistemic logic can be applied to explain conflicting situations.

15.5.1 Non-ambiguous Modeling

In **3 The Negotiating Model** three modes representing the cognitive style of the inheritance model are defined. The first of these is non-ambiguous modeling where the domain model is characterized by its completeness. There are no mutually exclusive inheritance conditions present nor can they be created in this mode of operation. All links of the non-specific types $(\rightsquigarrow, \not\rightsquigarrow)$ correspond to strict inheritance $(\Rightarrow, \not\Rightarrow)$ within the system belief set (B_{system}). No defeasible links can be constructed in the network when operating in this mode since they have no meaning in a network incapable of supporting multiple mutually exclusive paths.

Non-ambiguous modeling means that there is no possibility of mutually exclusive states occurring in the network. For example, in Fig. 15.1, a link $c \not\rightsquigarrow sb$ could not be added to the existing network.

	n	c	m	sb
n		$n \to c$	$n \rightsquigarrow c \rightsquigarrow m$	$n \rightsquigarrow c \rightsquigarrow m \rightsquigarrow sb$
				$n \rightsquigarrow sb$
c			$c \rightsquigarrow m$	$c \rightsquigarrow m \rightsquigarrow sb$
m				$m \rightsquigarrow sb$
sb				

Fig. 15.1

$$B_{system} = \{b(n \Rightarrow c), b(n \Rightarrow sb), b(c \Rightarrow m), b(m \Rightarrow sb), b(n \Rightarrow sb),$$
$$c \supset m, m \supset sb, n \supset sb, n \supset m, c \supset sb\}$$

No situations are required in the model because the B_{system} set is deductively closed and consistent. This is verified by the reachability matrix in Fig. 15.1. Any attempt to add $c \not\rightsquigarrow sb$ would result in an inconsistent belief set and is thus forbidden in the dialog. This mode of operation is similar to existing implementations which avoid the creation of multiple extensions resulting from inconsistent networks[8].

15.5.2 No *a priori* **Domain Ambiguity**

In this mode, the user does not necessarily distinguish between defeasible and strict inheritance although he may do. The inheritance model may be constructed using so called *non-specific* (**ns-is-a** $\rightsquigarrow$ and **ns-is-not-a** $\not\rightsquigarrow$) links. If and when mutually exclusive inference can be drawn from the network, dialog is activated to type these non-specific arcs.

---

[8]For example, as reported in Horty (Horty, 1990) a knowledged based maintenance system developed by Rector (Rector, 1986) disallows networks with more than one extension. The difference here is that more than one positive path between two nodes is allowed and that the restrictions are interactively made during network creation.

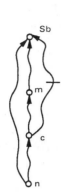

	n	c	m	sb
n		$n \rightsquigarrow c$	$n \rightsquigarrow c \rightsquigarrow m$	$n \rightsquigarrow c \rightsquigarrow m \rightsquigarrow sb$ $n \rightsquigarrow sb$ $n \rightsquigarrow c \nrightarrow sb$
c			$c \rightsquigarrow m$	$c \rightsquigarrow m \rightsquigarrow sb$ $c \nrightarrow sb$
m				$m \rightsquigarrow sb$
sb				

Fig. 15.2

The system drives the negotiating process by taking the first non-specific link (i.e. one of *ns-is-a*, *ns-is-not-a*) in the most significant matrix cell where conflict occurs. In this case $M_{n,sb}$ is chosen. Our initial belief set is $B_{user} = \{b(n \rightsquigarrow c), b(c \rightsquigarrow m), b(m \rightsquigarrow sb), b(n \rightsquigarrow sb), b(c \nrightarrow sb)\}$ corresponding directly to the links in the network. The resulting situations can be read from the reachability matrix in Fig. 15.2, $S_n = \{\{n \rightsquigarrow c \rightsquigarrow m \rightsquigarrow sb\}, \{n \rightsquigarrow sb\}, \{n \rightsquigarrow c \nrightarrow sb\}\}$. The conflict between the situations and the user and system belief sets prompts the following dialog.

```
Are there examples of n which are not sb?
```

Given a "no" response to this question the resulting user belief set is $B_{user} = \{b(n \rightsquigarrow c), b(c \rightsquigarrow m), b(m \rightsquigarrow sb), b(n \Rightarrow sb), b(c \nrightarrow sb)\}$ and the corresponding single dominant situation is $S_n = \{\{n \Rightarrow sb\}\}$ from the specificity rule Definition 5. The system belief set is constructed and concludes $B_{system} = \{n \Rightarrow sb, n \rightarrow c, c \rightarrow m, m \rightarrow sb, c \nrightarrow sb\}$. In the lack of information to the contrary the system believes that the $n \rightsquigarrow c$ link is defeasible and subsequently the links following it, namely $c \rightsquigarrow m$, $m \rightsquigarrow sb$, $c \nrightarrow sb$, are also defeasible (by Definition 4). On the other hand the user belief set knows nothing of such an assumption and the link $n \rightsquigarrow c$ remains nonspecific in B_{user}. The system assumption that $n \rightsquigarrow c$ is defeasible may later change as we shall see. Note that all belief sets and situations are now consistent with one another and no further dialog occurs at this point in time.

Fig. 15.3

$$B_{user} = \{b(n \Rightarrow c), b(n \Rightarrow sb), b(c \not\rightarrow sb), b(c \rightarrow m), b(m \rightarrow sb)\}$$

The justification for the system assumed link types in the model is that the user will be informed of these assumptions when the network is redrawn. This could be done at any arbitrary point in the dialog and when it occurs $B_{user} = B_{system}$ and the user beliefs are updated to reflect those of the system. These assumptions can then be modified. If our operator changes $n \rightarrow c$ to $n \Rightarrow c$ as illustrated in Fig. 15.3 then the assumptions about the links $c \rightarrow m$, $m \rightarrow sb$ and $c \not\rightarrow sb$ (by Definition 2.3) may not necessarily be correct. The system beliefs are revised to reflect this change;

$$B_{system} = \{b(n \Rightarrow c), b(n \Rightarrow sb), b(c \not\rightarrow sb), b(c \leadsto m), b(m \leadsto sb)\}$$

The situations resulting from B_{system} are now computed and $S_c = \{\{c \leadsto m \leadsto sb\}, \{c \not\rightarrow sb\}\}$ which reintroduces conflict and prompts the dialog.

```
Are there examples of c which are sb?
```

Given the operator replies "yes" this amounts to an admission that $c \not\rightarrow sb$ is defeasible and the resulting user belief set is $B_{user} = \{b(n \Rightarrow c), b(c \leadsto m), b(m \leadsto sb), b(n \Rightarrow sb), b(c \not\rightarrow sb)\}$. In the system belief model we have $B_{system} = \{n \Rightarrow sb, n \rightarrow c, c \not\rightarrow sb, c \leadsto m, m \leadsto sb\}$ and the following dialog results;

```
Are there examples of c which are not m? NO
```

This results in the convergent belief sets;

$$B_{user} = \{b(n \Rightarrow c), b(n \Rightarrow sb), b(c \not\rightarrow sb), b(c \Rightarrow m), b(m \rightarrow sb)\}$$
$$B_{system} = \{b(n \Rightarrow c), b(n \Rightarrow sb), b(c \not\rightarrow sb), b(c \Rightarrow m), b(m \rightarrow sb)\}$$

In summary the system assumes that given $c \Rightarrow m$ then the link $m \rightarrow sb$ is defeasible, which it must be given that $c \not\rightarrow sb$, and the resulting situation is consistent. The network corresponding to this situation is illustrated in Fig. 15.4.

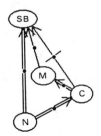

$$S = \begin{array}{c} \\ n \\ c \\ m \\ sb \end{array} \left[\begin{array}{cccc} n & c & m & sb \\ & n \Rightarrow c & n \Rightarrow c \Rightarrow m & n \Rightarrow sb \\ & & c \Rightarrow m & c \not\rightarrow sb \\ & & & m \rightarrow sb \\ \end{array} \right]$$

Fig. 15.4

15.5.3   Ambiguous Modeling

If the situations matrix still contains sets which are mutually exclusive after maximum dialog has taken place and all links in the inheritance network have been typed, then the strategy is to apply a more general theory of default reasoning. Autoepistemic logic can be applied to nonmonotonic inheritance as reported in Gelfond&Pryzmusinska (1990).

Gelfond&Pryzmusinska's notation differs somewhat to those given in section 2 however the principles remain much the same. As an illustration the idea is demonstrated without giving the formal semantics. Gelfond&Pryzmusinska introduce predicates to describe the various types of links in a nonmonotonic inheritance hierarchy Γ with the following translation;

$$c_1 \Rightarrow c_2 \equiv PS(c_1, c_2)$$
$$c_1 \nRightarrow c_2 \equiv \neg PS(c_1, c_2)$$
$$c \rightarrow p \equiv PD(c, p)$$
$$c \nrightarrow p \equiv ND(c, p)$$

In addition a number of extra predicates are required. $Holds$ states whether or not a given instance x inherits the properties of the class c.

Definition 9   the relation $Holds(x, y)$ is defined by the axioms;

$Hold(x, c)$ is true if there is a direct link between an instance x and a class c.

$$B(PS(c_1, c_2)) \wedge B(H(x, c_1)) \supset Holds(x, c_2)$$
$$B(PD(c_1, c_2)) \wedge B(H(x, c_1)) \wedge \neg B(ab(x, c_1, c_2)) \supset Holds(x, c_2)$$
$$B(ND(c_1, c_2)) \wedge B(H(x, c_1)) \wedge \neg B(ab(x, c_1, c_2)) \supset \neg Holds(x, c_2)$$

In order to incorporate Touretsky's specificity principle two auxiliary predicates are introduced. These are $MS(c_1, c_2)$, which means that c_1 is more specific than c_2, and $I(c_1, c_2, c_3)$ meaning classes c_1 and c_2 have inconsistent paths to c_3 i.e. $c_1 \rightarrow \ldots \rightarrow c_3$ and $c_2 \rightarrow \ldots \nrightarrow c_3$.

Definition 10   The I and MS predicates.

$$PS(c_1, c_2) \supset MS(c_1, c2)$$
$$MS(c_1, c) \wedge MS(c, c_2) \supset MS(c_1, c_2)$$
$$PD(c_1, c_3) \wedge ND(c_2, c_3) \supset I(c_1, c_2, c_3)$$
$$I(c_1, c_2, c_3) \supset I(c_2, c_1, c_3)$$

All the elements are now assembled to define Touretsky's specificity principle as was done in Definition 5.

Definition 11 $B(Holds(x, c)) \wedge B(Holds(x, c_1)) \wedge B(I(c_1, c_2, c_3)) \wedge B(MS(c_1, c_2)) \wedge \neg B(ab(c_1, c_3, X)) \supset ab(c_2, c_3, x)$

In words, assume that the less specific node c_2 is more likely to exhibit abnormality than the more specific node c_1.

Theorem 2   For any ground query F of the form $H(x, c)$ if;

1. $F \in E(\Gamma)$ then $H(x, c)$ is true.
2. $F \notin E(\Gamma)$ then $H(x, c)$ is false.
3. $\neg B(F) \wedge \neg B(\neg F) \in E(\Gamma)$ then $H(x, c)$ is unknown.

We are now equipped to consider an example of an ambiguous network given in Fig. 15.5.

```
\small
PS(f,e).
PS(f,d).
PD(e,c).
PD(d,b).
PD(b,a).
ND(c,a).

H(f,e).
H(f,d).

I(c,b,a).
I(d,e,a).

H(f,b) :- B(PD(d,b)), B(H(f,d)), not(B(ab(f,d,b)))
H(f,a) :- B(PD(b,a)), B(H(f,d)), not(B(ab(f,b,a)))
H(f,c) :- B(PD(e,c)), B(H(f,e)), not(B(ab(f,e,c)))
not(H(f,a)) :- B(ND(c,a)), B(H(f,c)), not(B(ab(f,e,a)))
```

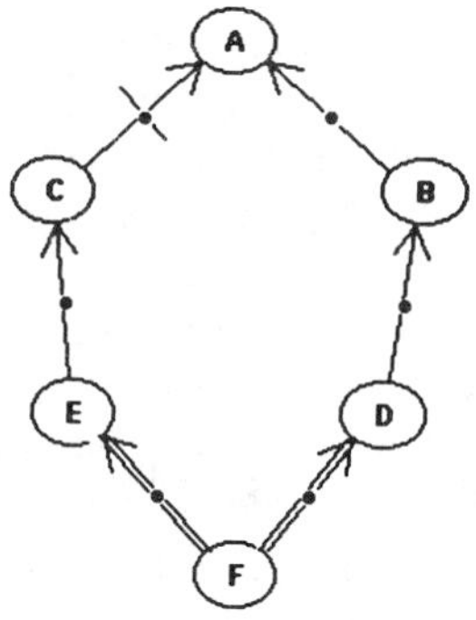

Fig. 15.5

The query $Holds(f, a)$ leads to contradiction. Object f must be atypical w.r.t. at least one of the properties b, c, d, e and therefore the expansion E of $Th(\Gamma)$ must contain at least one formula of the form $B(ab(f, c_1, c_2))$. This is impossible since the predicate ab does not appear in the conclusions of any of the axioms in $Th(\Gamma)$ since there can be no specificity assumption, asserted by definition 5.3, of c over b.

In autoepistemic logic an explanation of an AE system K is a set of sentences H such that $Th(K + H)$ has a stable expansion. After arriving at a the inheritance reasoner is faced with finding a stable expansion which diagnoses the contradiction. This can be done by assuming a non-empty subset of the predicates $\{ab(f, d, b), ab(f, b, a), ab(f, e, c), ab(f, c, a)\}$. So every subset of this set added to the initial $Th(\Gamma)$ gives rise to a consistent set of beliefs and is therefore an explanation of the inconsistencies in Γ.

Not all explanations are equally good and $H_1 = \{ab(f, b, a)\}$ and $H_2 = \{ab(f, c, a)\}$ would be the two explanations that are acceptable. To explain why consider Definition 5.3, Touretsky's specificity principle states that information about subclasses is more reliable than information about superclasses. This being so $H_3 = \{ab(f, e, c)\}$ and $H_4 = \{ab(f, d, b)\}$ are less reliable than H_1 and H_2 since $PD(d, b)$ & $PD(e, c)$ are more reliable than $PD(b, a)$ and $ND(c, a)$. In addition, combined explanations such as $H_5 = \{ab(f, d, b), ab(f, b, a)\}$ are excluded because abnormality is minimized i.e., given two equally plausible explanations select the one with the fewer exceptions.

The end result of this processing is that we get two possible explanations for inconsistency in the network. That is, the node f is abnormal with respect to the links $c \rightarrow a$ or f is abnormal with respect to $b \not\rightarrow a$. The operator can now be informed of these explanations and take action, through reorganization of the network, to overcome them.

15.5.4   Summary of Dialog Examples

Monotonic cases may not produce unique situations since there may be more than one path between any pair of nodes. These situations, however, are always consistent. The addition of links which generate inconsistent states is strictly forbidden. Consequently, the reachability matrix, and subsequently the situations, can be generated directly from the system belief set which is deductively closed under strict inheritance conditions.

When there is no *a prior* assessment of an inheritance domain belief sets can once again be put to use. The system uses the situations generated by using beliefs to drive a dialog process whose aim is to eliminate inconsistency between conflicting situations. A preference ordering is established amongst competing paths by refining the ontology of the network, in particular the link types, a process which conforms to the psychology of network construction. The convergence of user and system belief sets corresponds to agreement being reached between the two negotiating parties.

Finally, in inconsistent networks, we saw how the idea of a direct translation of the network into autoepistemic states can be supplemented with explanations to produce stable situations (more often called expansions). These explanations can then be selected optimally to rationalize inconsistencies in the network. Autoepistemic states can be used to construct a multiple belief set representation in order to express alternatives in network construction to the operator.

15.6   NEGOTIATING CONCEPTUAL GRAPHS

We have surveyed the various rules of inference for inheritance hierarchies and in particular how these rules can combine to produce ambiguous situations in an inheritance reasoner. To a large degree the belief model of system and user allows us to overcome this problem if it is caused by a modeling mistake. What this achieves for conceptual graphs is greater simplicity in automatic inference. The derivation of new conceptual graphs through the formation rules COPY, RESTRICT, JOIN and SIMPLIFY characterizes automatic inference within a conceptual graph system and represents ordered changes within the system. These rules reflect the process known as generalization and are truth preserving and monotonic.

This section examines how the negotiating process for the underlying inheritance hierarchy simplifies the application of the formation rules for conceptual graphs. In particular we discuss two examples, one in which the situation matrix for the hierarchy always represents a preferred inheritance path and another ambiguous network where autoepistemic logic augments the existing conceptual graphs with a three place relation *abnorm* in order to produce multiple versions of the final generalized conceptual graph, each of which represents a stable autoespistemic expansion of the theory entailed from the inheritance graph, the conceptual graphs and the explanations in the form of an additional abnormal relation.

In situations where no mutually exclusive paths exist within an inheritance hierarchy naturally no conflict can occur and generalization proceeds normally. By way of introduction consider the following two graphs and corresponding inheritance hierarchy;

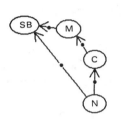

$$[PHYSOBJ] \rightarrow (ATTR) \rightarrow [SB]$$
$$[N] \rightarrow (ATTR) \rightarrow [C]$$

Fig. 15.6

By the RESTRICT rule the type label *[PHYSOBJ]* may be specialized to the subtype *[M]*.

$$[M] \rightarrow (ATTR) \rightarrow [SB]$$

Likewise *[M]* may be restricted to *[C]*;

$$[C] \rightarrow (ATTR) \rightarrow [M] \rightarrow (ATTR) \rightarrow [SB]$$

[SB] is restricted by *[N]* resulting in;

$$[C] \rightarrow (ATTR) \rightarrow [M] \rightarrow (ATTR) \rightarrow [SB] \leftarrow (ATTR) \leftarrow [N]$$

[N] $\rightarrow (ATTR) \rightarrow$ *[C]* is then joined to this graph and the result is;

$$[C] \rightarrow (ATTR) \rightarrow [M] \rightarrow (ATTR) \rightarrow [SB]$$
$$(ATTR) \longleftarrow [N] \longrightarrow (ATTR)$$

This takes care of the simple monotonic cases where the inheritance hierarchy contains no mutually exclusive conflicting paths between node pairs. Let's look at the results of generalization with the following configuration.

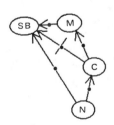

$$[PHYSOBJ] \rightarrow (ATTR) \rightarrow [SB]$$
$$[N] \rightarrow (ATTR) \rightarrow [C]$$

Fig. 15.7.

We can conclude that the results of RESTRICT and JOIN on using the inheritance hierarchy and initial conceptual graphs of Fig. 15.7 would led to the following conflicting situations;

$[N] \to (ATTR) \to [C] \to (ATTR) \to \neg[SB]$
$[N] \to (ATTR) \to [SB]$
$[N] \to (ATTR) \to [C] \to (ATTR) \to [M] \to (ATTR) \to [SB]$

If, however, the negotiation dialog has taken place then the situations matrix corresponding to the network indicates precisely what generalizations can follow from the initial graphs.

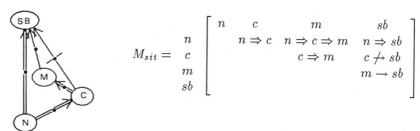

$$M_{sit} = \begin{array}{c} \\ n \\ c \\ m \\ sb \end{array} \begin{bmatrix} n & c & m & sb \\ & n \Rightarrow c & n \Rightarrow c \Rightarrow m & n \Rightarrow sb \\ & & c \Rightarrow m & c \not\Rightarrow sb \\ & & & m \to sb \\ & & & \end{bmatrix}$$

Fig. 15.8.

If our initial graphs are $[PHYSOBJ] \to (ATTR) \to [SB]$ and $[N] \to (ATTR) \to [C]$ then three restrictions can now be made;

$[N] \to (ATTR) \to [SB]$
$[C] \to (ATTR) \to \neg[SB]$
$[M] \to (ATTR) \to [SB]$

Further RESTRICT operations on these level 1 graphs results in;

$$[N] \to (\mathbf{ATTR}) \to [C] \to (\mathbf{ATTR}) \to \neg [SB]$$
$$\dotfill (a)$$
$$[C] \to (\mathbf{ATTR}) \to [M] \to (\mathbf{ATTR}) \to [SB]$$

(a) is defeated since it conflicts with a level 1 graph and the final restriction and join becomes;

$$\neg [C] \to (\mathbf{ATTR}) \to [SB] \leftarrow (\mathbf{ATTR}) \leftarrow [N]$$
$$[M] \to (ATTR)$$

Using the single element situations matrix allows us to develop a procedure for restriction in generalization which avoids nonmonotonic extensions.

As a final example let's look at the purely ambiguous case;

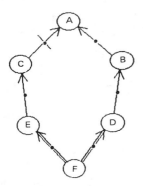

$[PHYSOBJ]\rightarrow(ATTR)\rightarrow[A]$
$[F]\rightarrow(ATTR)\rightarrow[E]$
$[F]\rightarrow(ATTR)\rightarrow[D]$

Fig. 15.9

As we have seen earlier there is no way of resolving this ambiguity beyond justifying the various extensions by way of an explanation which when added to the theory represented by the inheritance network will result in a stable autoepistemic expansion. Explanation takes the form of an abnormality which explains why one path can be preferred over another. For example, the path $f \Rightarrow e \rightarrow c \nrightarrow a$ is accepted over and above $f \Rightarrow d \rightarrow b \rightarrow a$ given that we acept the abnormality of f wrt the link $b \rightarrow a$. To model this in conceptual graphs we introduce a three place relation *abnorm* which allows the relevant conceptual graph to be constructed by restrict and join operations.

$$[F]\rightarrow(ATTR)\rightarrow[D]\rightarrow(ATTR)\rightarrow[B]\rightarrow(ATTR)\rightarrow[A]$$
$$\searrow (ABNORM)\rightarrow[C]$$
$$\searrow [A]$$

$$[F]\rightarrow(ATTR)\rightarrow[E]\rightarrow(ATTR)\rightarrow[C]\rightarrow(ATTR)\rightarrow \neg[A]$$
$$\searrow (ABNORM)\rightarrow[B]$$
$$\searrow [A]$$

The results are two independent conceptual graphs each of which is consistent with the inheritance hierarchy although not with one another.

15.7 CONCLUSION

The main contribution of this chapter to conceptual graph theory is through simplifying the canonical inference rules SIMPLIFY, COPY, JOIN and RESTRICT by ensuring the consistency of the user defined inheritance oracle. This is done by concentrating on a strategy for overcoming inconsistent or ambiguous logical extentions in inheritance hierarchies. To achieve this a number of diverse issues are unified under the heading of negotiation or critiquing systems. A psychological model for negotiation is examined. A study of belief logics gives us a means of controlling interaction and focusing the negotiation. Rules and laws of inheritance are drawn from the theoretical literature in nonmonotonic multiple inheritance as a way of defining a procedure for establishing a natural precedence ordering over competing inheritance paths. Finally nonmonotonic logic gives us a way of dealing with ambiguous cases when all else fails.

The net effect of this assembly of ideas is a framework for a knowledge engineering environment for the acquisition of conceptual graphs where the consistency of the underlying inheritance hierarchy is guaranteed by an interactive inheritance editor which scrutinizes, in terms of logical consistency, the networks that it helps to create.

Acknowledgements

This research was supported by the Swedish Board of Technical Development (STU).

BIBLIOGRAPHY

Card, S. (1989) "Intelligent Interfaces: Theory Research and Design" in (eds) P.A. Hancock, M.H. Chignell, *Human Factors and Artificial Intelligence,* North-Holland.

Doherty, P. (1989) "A Correspondence between Inheritance Hierachies and a Logics of Pref erential Entailment", International Symposium on Methodologies for Intelligent Systems.

Etherington, D. (1988) *Reasoning with incomplete information,* Research notes in AI, Morgan Kaufmann

Geffner, H. (1989) "Default Reasoning: Causal and Conditional Theories", CSL-87, Department of Computer Science, UCLA, Cognitive Systems Laboratory.

Grice, H. (1975) "Logic and Conversation", in (eds) P. Cole and J. Morgan, *Syntax and Semantics,* Academic Press.

Harrius, J. (1992) "Text Generation in Expert Critiquing Systems using Rhetorical Structure Theory" in (eds) P Eklund, T Nagle, J Nagle and L Gerholz, *Conceptual Structures: Theory and Practice,* Ellis Horwood Limited.

Horty, J. R Thomason and D Touretzky (1990) "A skeptical theory of inheritance in Nonmonotonic semantic networks", AI 42:311-348.

Krishnaprasad, D. and M Kifer and D Warren (1989) "On the Circumscriptive semantic of Inheritance Network", Methodologies for Intelligent Systems.

Pearl, J. (1988) *Probabilistic Reasoning in Intelligent Systems* Morgan Kaufman.

Touretzky, D. (1984) *The Mathematics of Inheritance Systems* Department of Computer Science, CMU-CS-84-136, CMU.

Makinson, D. and K. Schlechta (1989) "Floating Conclusions and Zombie Paths", Workshop on Nonmonotonic Reasoning, Sankt Augustin, FRG.

Makinson, D. and K. Schlechta (1991) "Floating Conclusions and Zombie Paths: Two Deep Difficulties in the directly skeptical approach to Defeasible inheritance nets", AI Journal, 48:199-209.

Miller, P.(1984) *Expert Critiquing Systems,* Springer-Verlag.

Pearl, J. (1987) "Deciding consistency in inheritance networks", Department of Computer Science, cognitive systems lab., CSD 870053: R96, UCLA.

Sandewall, E. (1986) "Nonmonotonic inference rules for multiple inheritance with exception s", Proceedings of IEEE, pages 1345-1353.

Sowa, J.F. (1984) *Conceptual Structures: Information Processing in Mind and Machine,* Addison Wesley, Reading.

Stein, L.A. (1989) "Skeptical Inheritance: Computing the Intersection of Credulous Exten sions", Workshop on Nonmonotonic Reasoning, Sankt Augustin, FRG.

Touretzky, D. (1986) *The mathematics of inheritance systems*, Research notes in Artificial Intelligence, Morgan Kaufmann.

Touretzky, D. and J. Horty and R. Thomason (1987) "A Clash of intuitions: The current state of nonmonotonic multiple inheritance systems", International Joint Conference on Artificial Intelligence.

Touretzky, D. and R. Thomason (1988) "Mixing Strict and Defeasible Inheritance" AAAI pages 427-432.

Waern, Y. and S. Hägglund, J. Löwgren, I. Rankin, T. Sokolnicki and A. Steinmann (1992) "Communication Knowledge for Knowledge Communication" to appear in the International Journal of Man-Machine Studies.

16

Normalizing Conceptual Graphs

Guy W. Mineau
Département d'informatique,
Université Laval,
Ste-Foy, Québec, Canada, G1K 7P4

ABSTRACT

One of the strengths of the conceptual graph formalism (Sowa, 1984) is its expressiveness. Because of its straightforward mapping to natural language sentences, knowledge can easily be acquired. Unfortunately, this introduces the possibility to obtain different graphs which encode similar meanings since much is left to the acquisition process. These syntactic differences introduce additional complexity when learning algorithms are to be applied onto sets of conceptual graphs, as required in Mineau (1989). Consequently, minimizing these differences is the topic of the present paper. Toward that goal, a few normalization procedures are presented. They aimed at producing more standard graphs, called normalized conceptual graphs, in a non-transparent way so that the user still benefits of the same expressiveness as mentioned before.

16.1 INTRODUCTION

The conceptual graph notation has many advantages over other knowledge representation schemes. One important advantage is that it offers ease of expression together with a neat theoretical framework which defines not only the expressiveness of the notation, but also the transformations associated with the application of certain graph operators such as π, Φ, etc (Sowa, 1984).

Whenever conceptual graphs are used to interact with the user, this ease of expression becomes even more important as the intention of the user has to be mapped as faithfully as possible onto conceptual graphs: there is often a natural mapping between conceptual graphs and natural language sentences (Sowa, 1984). However, when the conceptual graphs are intented to constitute a knowledge base on some domain, this ease of expression may introduce notation discrepancies. That is, there are no guarantees that similar meanings will be encoded using similar graphs. This is especially true when higher-level relations are used to encode these graphs, as opposed to lower-level relations (e.g., agnt, rcpt, object, source, ... (Sowa, 1984)) which lose part of their meaning when general knowledge is encoded. In effect, few knowledge domains can be efficiently described using these lower-level relations: abstractions are used to create more meaningful relations (Sowa, 1984), called *higher-level relations.* Consequently, we may end up with two different conceptual graphs which encode the same meaning.

For most knowledge processing tasks which require conceptual graph matching, like infering, generalizing, deducing and learning (Mineau *et al.*, 1990), it would be best if these notation discrepancies were minimized. Consequently this paper will introduce a method, called *normalization* of conceptual graphs, which will minimize representation alternatives for graphs encoding similar meanings: we aim at generating standardized conceptual graphs.

At the 1989 workshop on conceptual graphs, we demonstrated how learning by generalization can help structure a knowledge base (described as a set of conceptual graphs), so that common generalizations and compatible projections can efficiently be computed (Mineau, 1989). This chapter will demonstrate how learning by generalization from a set of conceptual graphs can be improved if the graphs are normalized. In effect, learning by generalization is based on similarity detection among the graphs. Thus the emphasis of this chapter is placed upon the increase in similarity when normalization takes place.

As the set of graphs (i.e., the knowledge base) grows in size, normalization becomes essential to any learning process. Learning algorithms that are applied to a vast set of conceptual graphs will work best if the graphs express explicitly the knowledge they encode. The complexity of the learning algorithms is then reduced, which makes the method applicable to large-scale knowledge bases. In general, conceptual graph matching is made easier by the normalization procedures proposed in this paper.

16.2 ACQUIRING KNOWLEDGE

In order not to restrain the expressiveness offered by the conceptual graph notation while knowledge is acquired, all normalization procedures proposed in this paper should not be visible from the user's point-of-view. That is, automatic normalization procedures are sought as much as possible. The procedures presented in this article are based on syntactic modifications of the graphs which can be automatically triggered while acquiring knowledge. They are:

1. grammar validation checks;

2. use of privileged relations;

3. symmetry completion;

4. transitivity completion;

5. use of complementing rules;

6. use of rewrite rules;

7. joining background knowledge;

8. elimination of redundancy.

These will be presented along with a brief example that will show how three conceptual graphs embedding similar knowledge may be normalized so that their similarity could be extracted more easily by a learning algorithm (such as proposed in Mineau (1989)). The above list is however in no way exhaustive. It constitutes a first proposal pleading for a complete theory of normalization for conceptual graphs.

Figs. 16.1 thru 16.3 show three conceptual graphs which embed some similar meaning which is: *"a married couple works for the same company which produces computer products"*. In order to detect this similarity, some mental processing is required. After normalization of the graphs, this similarity will become more explicitly represented, and more efficiently detectable. The normalization procedures introduced above are now applied sequentially to these graphs as explained in the following sections.

Fig. 16.1 shows a conceptual graph which states that: *"Bill is Joan's husband. Joan works as a computer scientist who works for a company (C2) employed by another company (C1) where Bill works and which produces softwares (C1)"*[1]. The second graph states that: *"IBM employs a man, Frank, and his wife, Janet"*. The third graph states that: *"Todd is married to Mary. They both work for Unisys, who manufactures computer products"*.

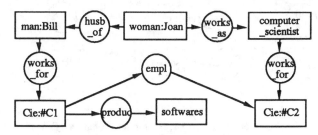

Fig. 16.1 First conceptual graph to normalize.

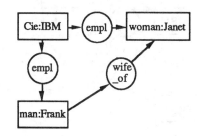

Fig. 16.2 Second conceptual graph to normalize.

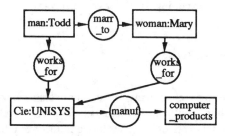

Fig. 16.3 Third conceptual graph to normalize.

---

[1]Even within a limited grammar, there may probably be other ways of encoding this information.

16.3   GRAMMAR VALIDATION CHECKS

Like with most knowledge acquisition procedures, some grammar validation checks may
take place while acquiring the knowledge. The newly acquired graphs can be validated
against the grammar of the underlying application domain. For example, let us state that the
relations husband_of and wife_of have to be replaced by married_to in the graphs (use of
synonyms from a thesaurus). Consequently, the graphs of Figs. 16.1 and 16.2 will become
those of Figs. 16.4 and 16.5.

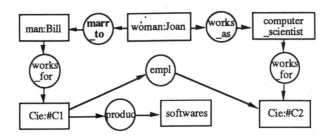

Fig. 16.4 The graph of Fig. 16.1 after grammar consistency checks.

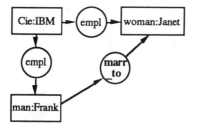

Fig. 16.5 The graph of Fig. 16.2 after grammar consistency checks.

16.4   PRIVILEGED RELATIONS

As different relations sometimes relate to inverse actions or states, it would be appropriate to
restrict the choice of relations to only one of them. For example, the relation employs (empl)
is the inverse of the relation works_for. In order to see things from the same perspective, it
would be appropriate if only one of these two would appear in all the graphs, wherever it
is needed. In our example, we chose works_for as the privileged relation. Consequently, all
employs relations will be converted to works_for. The relations of any graphs are restricted
to privileged relations. From Figs. 16.4 and 16.5 we can produce Figs. 16.6 and 16.7.

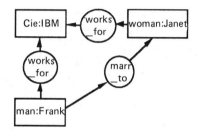

Fig. 16.6 Fig. 16.4 with only privileged relations

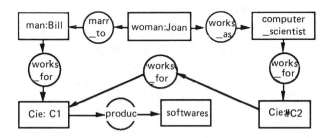

Fig. 16.7 Symmetry completion.

There are relations which are symmetrical. In that case, the inverse relation is identical to the original relation: they are both privileged and should both appear in the graph. Consequently, the graph has to be examined, and each relation which is symmetrical will trigger the creation of another relation of the same type, with source and destination concepts inverted[2]. Figs. 16.8 thru 16.10 show the graphs where *symmetry completion* has been achieved on Figs. 16.6, 16.7 and 16.3, where the only symmetrical relation was married_to.

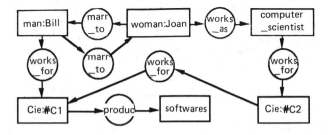

Fig. 16.8 Fig. 16.7 after symmetry completion.

---

[2]Of course, this only applies to binary relations as it would have no meaning otherwise.

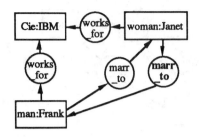

Fig. 16.9 Fig. 16.8 after symmetry completion.

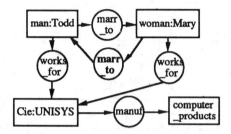

Fig. 16.10 Fig. 16.3 after symmetry completion.

16.5   TRANSITIVITY COMPLETION

Some relations are transitive. This means that a chain of such relations imply additional knowledge directly derivable from the transitivity of those relations. For example, stating that the relation works_for is transitive implies that a computer scientist (Joan) also works for Cie:#C1, as she works for Cie:#C2 and Cie:#C2 works for Cie:#C1 (see Fig. 16.8). Fig. 16.11 represents Fig. 16.8 after *transitivity completion*.

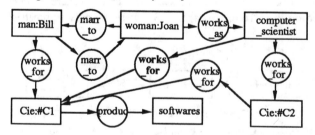

Fig. 16.11 Fig. 16.8 after transitivity completion.

16.6   COMPLEMENTING RULES

Sometimes, there are certain patterns (subgraphs of a graph), which imply other patterns. These other patterns would add information to the graph by complementing its semantics. They make explicit some knowledge that could be previously inferred from the graph. For example, let us suppose that the following rule ($pattern_1 \Rightarrow pattern_2$), called *complementing rule* is part of the system's knowledge:

```
[[person:*x]→(works_as)→
    [employed_person]→(works_for)→[Cie:*y]]⇒[[person:*x]
    →(works_for)→[Cie:*y]].
```

Under this rule (A), the graph of Fig. 16.11 can be changed to the graph of Fig. 16.12, where additional information has been added based on the firing of this rule.

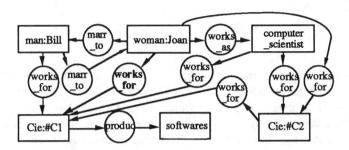

Fig. 16.12 The graph of Fig. 11 complemented under rule A.

It is obvious that pattern detection can be implemented without too many worries, maybe using some indexing mechanism[3]. What is more of a real problem is that rules can be combined and their firing sequence may be important. Also, a rule may need to be fired more than once, as newly added patterns may trigger old rules. Determining a proper sequence is a serious problem, especially if the number of rules is considerable. All sorts of rule firing policy normally applied in rule-based systems also apply here (Jackson, 1986).

16.7   REWRITE RULES

Often, patterns in a graph can be reformulated. For example, expansion and contraction operators as defined in Sowa (1984) can be viewed as rewrite rules. In a more general context, rewrite rules are used to standardize different ways of expressing the same statement. For example, let the following rule (B):

```
[[woman:*x]→(works_as)→[computer_scientist]]
               ⇒ [[computer_scientist_e:*x]]
```

be a rewrite rule[4]. Then, Fig. 16.12 can be changed to Fig. 16.13. Again, some choices must be made in order to select the appropriate rewrite rules.

---

[3] Refer to Mineau (1989), as one such indexing mechanism is proposed.
[4] Where computer_scientist_e expresses a feminine gender for the concept computer_scientist.

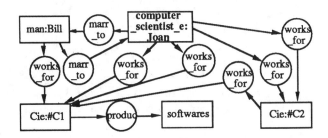

Fig. 16.13 Fig. 12 after the use of rule B.

In effect, different rewrite rules as well as background knowledge, will introduce different primitive patterns[5] which constitute the basis upon which conceptual graph matching may later on proceed. The problem of choosing which rewrite rule to fire is identical to the one cited above with complementing rules. It is up to the knowledge base designer to pinpoint which patterns should explicitly appear in the graphs when possible, i.e., which set of concepts and relations is to be considered primitive[6].

16.8   JOINING BACKGROUND KNOWLEDGE

As identical concepts appear in different graphs, one has to decide whether joining the corresponding graphs would be beneficial for the similarity detection process sought for. In our example, let us suppose that we already know the fact that IBM manufactures computer products. This constitutes background knowledge, i.e., knowledge about the application domain. Joining that information to the graph of Fig. 16.9 will increase the chances of detecting similarity among the three graphs. Consequently, we join the two graphs together, producing the one in Fig. 16.14[7].

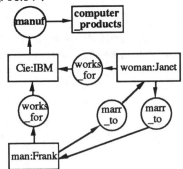

Fig. 16.14 Fig. 16.9 joined to some background knowledge.

---

[5]Primitive patterns are those which constitute a basis for comparison between graphs, and for similarity detecting.

[6]This problem remains closely related to the application domain represented by the graphs.

[7]This problem is also relevant to the choice of appropriate primitives to describe the application domain.

16.9   ELIMINATION OF REDUNDANCY

Elimination of redundancy consists of applying the simplify operator (Sowa, 1984) on the graphs processed so far in order to obtain a final normalized version of each graph. Figs. 16.15 thru 16.17 show the resulting normalized graphs.

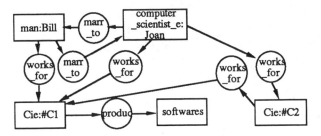

Fig. 16.15 The graph of Fig. 16.1 in normalized form.

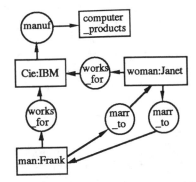

Fig. 16.16 The graph of Fig. 16.2 in normalized form.

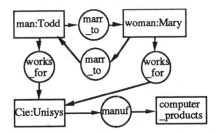

Fig. 16.17 The graph of Fig. 16.3 in normalized form.

16.10   DETECTING SIMILARITY

From the last three graphs, it is easier to detect the similarity between the graphs, that is: "A married couple works for the same company which produces computer products" as shown by Fig. 16.18. Less mental processing was required this time, since the similarity between the graphs was made more obvious (explicit) by the normalization procedures.

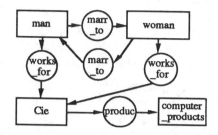

Fig. 16.18 A common generalization for the graphs of Figs. 16.15 thru 16.17.

16.11   CONCLUSION

This chapter introduced normalization procedures which constitute a first step toward a complete theory of normalization for conceptual graphs. In cases where similarity detecting is the basis for knowledge processing tasks such as inferring, generalizing, joining, or graph matching, normalization provides ways of simplifying the problem, as it gives a basis upon which similarity detection can proceed. It increases the structural similarity among graphs. That way, similarity detecting is made easier. For learning algorithms which are applied to a large set of conceptual graphs, explicit representation of primitive patterns within the graphs is helpful: when similarity between graphs is more obvious, less processing is required.

BIBLIOGRAPHY

Jackson, P. (1986). *Introduction to Expert Systems*, Addison-Wesley.

Mineau, G. (1989). "Induction on Conceptual Graphs: Finding Common Generalizations and Compatible Projections", Proc. of the 4th International Workshop on Conceptual Graphs, IJCAI-89, (eds) T. Nagle and J. Nagle, Detroit, USA, August 1989.

Mineau, G., Gecsei, J. and Godin, R. (1990). "Structuring Knowledge Bases Using Automatic Learning", Proc. of the 6th International Conference on Data Engineering, Los Angeles, USA, 5-9 February, 274-280.

Sowa, J. F. (1984). *Conceptual Structures: Information Processing in Mind and Machine*, Addison-Wesley Publishing Company.

17

An Analogical Tool: Based on Evaluations of Partial Correspondences over Conceptual Graphs

Debbie Leishman
Knowledge Science Institute,
Department of Computer Science,
University of Calgary, Canada

ABSTRACT

This chapter describes the development of an analogical tool that is based on evaluations of partial correspondences over conceptual graphs. The tool results from instantiation of a general framework for analogy that arises from analysis of previous work and characterizes analogies as "common generalizations". Using conceptual graphs (Sowa, 1984) as the knowledge representation scheme for the general framework, the tool forms analogies and performs analogical inferencing. Analogy formation in the tool derives minimal common generalizations as preferred "stronger" analogies. This formation is under the control of four formation evaluations and two ordering evaluations. Testing of the analogical tool on examples of analogy taken from significant research, shows that the tool compares well with other systems.

17.1 INTRODUCTION TO ANALOGY

17.1.1 Previous Work on Analogy

Analysis of colloquial connotations and psychological processes of analogy has generated research which can be classified as (1) abstract theories of analogy; (2) psychological models of analogy; and (3) evaluation criteria for analogy. Abstract theories view analogy as an algebraic or logical process. Comparison of works in this area reveals the common theme that analogy is the formation of a plausible partial correspondence between parts of the participating analogues. Indurkhya (1985), for example, describes a theory of analogy and metaphor called Approximate Semantic Transference which forms AT-MAPS. These maps represent an approximately coherent partial mapping of terms between source and target domains. Gaines and Shaw (1982) explicate analogy as a partial correspondence between systems represented as mathematical categories. Russell's use of determinations (Russell, 1987) also requires the formation of a plausible partial correspondence between terms.

Psychological models of analogy attempt to account for how and in what circumstances people use analogies. Comparison of works in this area reveals the common theme that a critical part of any model of analogy is the knowledge that is used and how it is represented. For instance, Gentner's Structural Mapping Theory (Gentner, 1983) is based on a principle of systematicity that attempts to maintain chains of relations when forming correspondences between domains. The choice of higher order predicate calculus as the knowledge representation scheme aids in detection of these chains.

Evaluation criteria for analogy focus on the problem of what is a plausible analogy - why one analogy is seen as more plausible than another. Comparison of works in this area reveals the need to control the formation of plausible partial correspondences through evaluation criteria which relate to psychological notions of plausibility and the applicability of analogies. For example, evaluation criteria which use generalization/specialization hierarchies are central to the CYC project being conducted at MCC (Lenat *et al.*, 1986), as well as to the work of Hofstadter and Mitchell on analogical reasoning (Hofstadter and Mitchell, 1988). Winston's (1981) early paper on analogical reasoning contains many useful criteria such as the use of case relations and matching of terms sharing the same relations between them; this latter criterion is also evident in Gentner's work.

17.1.2   A General Framework for Analogy

The above discussion based on classifying works on analogy into three categories leads to conclusions that can be seen as comprising critical functions of analogy. Any computer emulation must thus contain the following three functions:

1. Semantic schemas for representing knowledge of the domains involved in the analogies.

2. Algorithms for finding partial correspondences between abstract structures.

3. An Evaluation relation for ordering analogies by plausibility.

These functions can also be seen as arising from the description of analogy given by Polya (1954). He describes analogy as a type of plausibility reasoning showing similarity on a definite conceptual level and defines analogy in terms of forming a "common generalization" of analogues.

From this description by Polya we can describe a general framework for analogy which contains within it the three critical functions. We still need some kind of semantic schemas for representing knowledge of our domains, but we can now view the formation of partial correspondences between analogues as arising naturally from formation of a common generalization of the analogues. Those parts of the analogues which have been generalized to a common concept are also those which are put into correspondence. Also implicit in Polya's description of forming a common generalization is that often there is more than one possible common generalization which can be formed. In an effort to find these "stronger" common generalizations we need some kind of ordering relation. This points to our third critical function, the need for an evaluation relation for ordering analogies by plausibility.

The general framework for analogy in Fig. 17.1 shows two analogues and their common generalizations. Each analogue consists of parts, and each of these parts is "part-of" the analogue. The common generalization also contains parts and these parts are each a "generalization" of some part of each of the analogues. The parts of the two analogues which have a common generalization define the parts which are in correspondence with each other. Finally we need an ordering relation which determines the "stronger" analogies. In most applications of analogy, the "stronger" analogies correspond to minimal common generalizations. Fig. 17.1 shows there can be many common generalizations formed but only some are minimal. These generalizations are minimal within our ordering relation because they contain the most information; they are the most specific of the possible generalizations. There can typically be more than one of these minimal common generalizations.

Analogical inferencing can also be described in the terms used above. To perform inferencing analogically from a minimal common generalization means to look for an even more specific generalization. Usually one analogue (the source analogue) is better known than the other (the target analogue). The source analogue is often used to suggest the existence of non-evident structure in the target analogue. In this way some "part-of" the source analogue is hypothesized as existing in the target analogue.

17.2 CONCEPTUAL GRAPHS FOR ANALOGY

Conceptual graphs were chosen as the knowledge representation scheme for the analogical tool because of their linguistic and logical basis. They are a semantically rich scheme which captures much of the fullness of natural language while maintaining necessary logical connections. The choice of conceptual graphs is based on several other reasons as well:

1. They have a mapping to logic and thus are compatible with any system based on logic.

2. Their straightforward mapping to and from natural language allows for a linguistic description of analogues.

3. They are expressive enough to be able to represent examples of analogy taken from the literature.

4. They are computational in that they have well defined algorithms for manipulation of the graphs.

5. Their definition and associated operations contain elements which correspond naturally to the general framework for analogy.

The notions of "part-of", "generalization" and the "generalization ordering relation" of the general framework for analogy described above have corresponding elements in the conceptual graph model. Parts in the conceptual graph model consist of concepts, relations and the arcs between them. Generalization in the conceptual graph model can happen in two ways, by climbing the type hierarchy and by taking subgraphs of an original graph. Generalizations are also partially ordered in the conceptual graph model. These corresponding elements define how the analogical tool forms and orders analogies which are seen as minimal common generalizations, and also allows for analogical inferencing to be performed within a single framework. Thus, instantiation of the general framework using conceptual graphs results in a computational tool which can be seen to both form analogies and perform analogical inferencing. The inferencing is not an add-on to the system, rather it is an integrated extension of the existing framework.

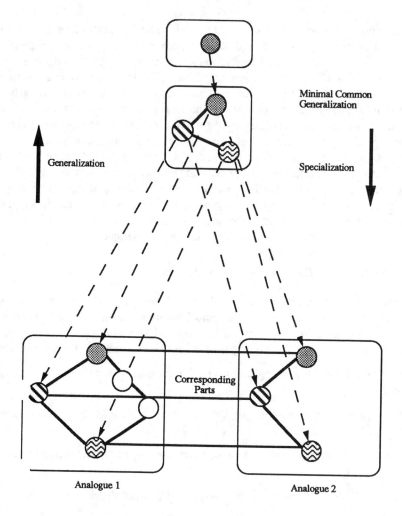

Fig. 17.1 A General Framework for Analogy

17.3   THE ANALOGICAL TOOL

17.3.1   Minimal Common Generalizations

In developing the general framework, it was noted that most applications of analogy prefer minimal common generalizations as the "stronger" analogies. The conceptual graph formalism contains a notion of minimal common generalization which directly corresponds. Fig. 17.2 gives a simple example of three ordered common generalizations that can be formed from the two analogues shown.

The lowest generalization on the page is the "stronger" minimal common generalization. It is the most specific of the three, first in concept restriction (from ANIMATE to PERSON and from ACT to EAT) and second by extent of the subgraph represented (it contains the maximum number of nodes and arcs). This minimal common generalization is the generalization as low as possible in the generalization hierarchy - such that no other is more specific. These minimal common generalizations which the analogical tool derives:

1. Are maximally extensive since the generalization chosen for each of the corresponding concepts is the lower bound of all possible common generalizations.

2. Preserve linkages in the graphs which can be seen as minimal structural criteria for plausibility.

3. Are truth preserving, a necessary logical criterion for plausibility.

4. Minimize conflicts in the type hierarchy, a minimal semantic criterion for plausibility.

In forming the minimal common generalizations, the analogical tool uses four formation evaluations to search for the generalizations, and two ordering evaluations to establish which of these are minimal. Within the conceptual graph model, graphs are generalized in two ways. First, they are generalized by choosing subgraphs of an original graph and second, by using more general concepts according to the type hierarchy. The formation evaluations and ordering evaluations presented below correspond directly to these two types of generalization.

17.3.2   Formation Evaluations

There are four formation evaluations that work together to derive the common generalizations. Three of the four can be seen as working to decide what subgraphs are chosen for the resulting common generalization. These subgraphs must be common to both analogues, and they decide what parts of the analogues are put into correspondence. Any combination of subgraphs common to both analogues will form a generalization, but specific aspects of the conceptual graph model define the more plausible subgraphs. These aspects, which are the formation evaluations, also help to cut down on the computational complexity of the search by specifying that only certain subgraphs are considered for the resulting common generalization.

Same Relation Evaluation The first evaluation requires same relations between two pairs of potentially corresponding concepts. As shown in Fig. 17.2, if [Girl] and [Person:Sue] are put into correspondence, then it is possible to put [Eat] and [Eat] into correspondence because they share the same (Agent) relation between them. If on the other hand Analogue 1 had contained [Girl] ← (Expr) ← [Think] instead, even though it would normally be possible to put [Girl] and [Person:Sue] in correspondence and also [Think] and [Eat] in correspondence (because they are both acts), using this evaluation, they cannot be put into correspondence because they no longer share the same relation between them. This evaluation is a result of the projection operator which requires that the same relation exist between connected corresponding concepts.

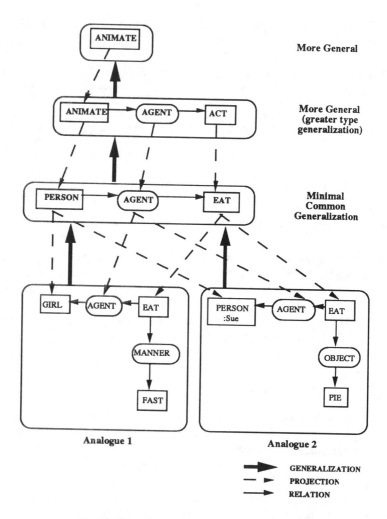

Fig. 17.2 Forming Common Generalizations

This evaluation defines one constraint on the subgraphs chosen for the common generalization. It is a very strong constraint which permits only agents to match to agents, objects
to match to objects, etc.

Co-reference Links Evaluation Co-reference links define an equality relation between
concepts. Thus, they define another structure which must be maintained when choosing subgraphs for the common generalization. If two concepts which both have
co-referents are put into correspondence, then their co-referents can only be put
into correspondence with each other - not with any other concepts. For example, if
$A = B$ and $C = D$ where A, B, C and D are concepts in a conceptual graph and $=$
represents the co-reference link, then putting A and C into correspondence requires
that B can only be put in correspondence with D or with nothing. Breaking this
evaluation means the equality relation between concepts is being invalidated. The
co-referent subgraph is a very strict evaluation that must be maintained.

Proposition Evaluation Proposition concepts which contain conceptual graphs in their referent fields define a contains relation between the proposition concept and the graphs within it. This relation defines yet another subgraph evaluation. This subgraph evaluation requires that if proposition concepts from two analogues are put into correspondence, then their respective contained graphs are candidates to be put into correspondence only with each other. The subgraph chosen here for the common generalization is the proposition concept with some or none of its contained graphs.

Comparable Concepts Evaluation This fourth evaluation conforms to the second way a graph can be generalized; that is by climbing the type hierarchy. Concepts are comparable if there exists a common generalization of them in the type hierarchy that is not the universal type. This evaluation uses the notion of type abstraction to determine if concepts are comparable and can be generalized. This evaluation works in conjunction with the part-of, subgraph evaluations by determining if specific concepts within a chosen subgraph can be generalized. Generalization using the type hierarchy also specifies particular general concepts for the resulting common generalization, as shown in Fig. 17.2. There we see [Person] as a generalization for [Girl] and [Person:Sue] for example. In this way a common generalization results in the kind of general problem solving abstraction used by researchers such as Gick and Holyoak (1983) and Greiner (1985).

17.3.3 Ordering Evaluations

The formation evaluations are a consequence of specifying an analogy as a common generalization. Specification of "stronger", more plausible analogies as minimal common generalizations has implications for ordering them. The two ordering evaluations order the generalizations and conform to the generalization criteria for conceptual graphs in much the same way the formation evaluations do. The first ordering evaluation conforms to the subgraph generalization criterion. For minimal common generalizations, the subgraphs chosen are the maximally extensive or most specific common generalizations. The second ordering evaluation conforms to generalization using the type hierarchy. Minimal common generalizations are also those which choose the lowest common supertypes for each pair of corresponding concepts as defined by the type hierarchy.

Deriving minimal common generalizations according to the first ordering evaluation amounts to ordering the common generalizations by their extent. The second ordering evaluation, semantic distance, uses the distance climbed in the type hierarchy when searching for a common supertype for corresponding pairs of concepts.

Using these ordering evaluations, as the common generalizations are formed, it can be determined if they are minimal common generalizations so far. With a complete search of all analogies, the evaluations derive the set of minimal common generalizations or "stronger" analogies.

17.3.4 Analogical Inferencing

The analogical tool described thus far forms analogies which are characterized as minimal common generalizations. These analogies are useful for many purposes such as schema abstraction (Gick and Holyoak, 1983), metaphor understanding (Indurkhya, 1985) and teaching (Murphy *et al.*, 1963). Schema abstractions allow the re-use of problem solving information when two problems are similar. Here, a generalized solution to a source problem can be used to solve a target problem. In metaphor understanding, analogies may be formed in order to explicate the similarities between otherwise unlike concepts, such as understanding what it means to say "the sky is crying". Analogies are also used to teach general principles in many subject areas such as engineering and biology. Other uses of analogy require that further reasoning take place from the analogies. This reasoning is referred to as analogical inferencing.

Performing analogical inferencing consists of extending a target analogue by hypothesizing that new concepts, relations and arcs exist in it, based on the existence of similar concepts, relations and arcs in the source analogue. These inductive hypotheses result in the formation of a new minimal common generalization which contains a generalization of these new hypothesized parts and the source parts they are inferred from.

The formation evaluations used by the analogical tool can help determine which hypotheses to make and also determine which hypotheses are valid. Although parts could be hypothesized from either of the analogues to the other, the tool only hypothesizes parts as existing in the target analogue based on their existence in the source.

17.3.5   The Extensibility Principle

When a choice must be made between two or more minimal common generalizations as to what inferencing is more plausible, the *extensibility principle* provides a resolution. If for instance one of the generalizations is not extensible at all and the other is, the extensible generalization is used because analogical inferencing can occur. If on the other hand, both are extensible, then the one which is the most extensible is preferred. Each of the extensions must still conform to the formation evaluations, but the most extensible generalization is the new minimal common generalization. We are still deriving minimal common generalizations. For example, in the use of schema abstraction for problem solving, we may already have part of a solution to a target problem and be inferencing analogically from several common generalizations and a source analogue for the rest. The *extensibility principle* will use the minimal common generalization which allows for the largest additional part of the solution to be hypothesized from the source to the target. In this way we will hypothesize as much of the solution as possible because analogies are seen as minimal common generalizations.

17.4   TESTING THE TOOL

The analogical tool has been tested on various examples of analogy from the literature. An example from the CYC (Lenat *et al.*, 1986) project shows the tool forms the same analogy as the frame based representation in CYC. Another example from Gentner and Seziorski (1986) shows the tool emulating significant scientific reasoning. An example taken from Indurkhya's PhD thesis (Indurkhya, 1985) shows the tool rationalizing processes of metaphor comprehension. Two further examples, one from Gentner (1983) and one from Russell (1987) show limitations of similarity based systems such as the analogical tool and give solutions to these limitations. The following example from Gick and Holyoak

(1983) is discussed in detail to show how analogy formation takes place in the tool and how analogical inferencing proceeds.

17.4.1   An Example from Gick and Holyoak - Schema Abstraction

In their work on schema abstraction, Gick and Holyoak studied the process of human analogical thinking. They predict that "induction of a general schema from concrete analogues will facilitate analogical transfer" . They found that if two prior analogues are given, subjects often derived a general problem solving schema as an incidental product of describing similarities of the analogues.

In Fig. 17.3, Gick and Holyoak use as an example a military problem and an analogous radiation problem. In the military problem, a commander wants to capture a fortress using a large army but cannot send the entire army down one road because they will be noticed. The solution is to send small parts of the army along many roads simultaneously. These sentences are represented in the four conceptual graphs at the top of Fig. 17.3. Co-referent links are shown by the dashed arcs connecting concepts with the same name. Context boxes representing propositions are the boxes which contain subgraphs within them.

In the analogous radiation problem, a doctor wants to use rays to destroy a tumor. The rays cannot all come from one direction without killing the patient. The analogous solution is to send low intensity rays from multiple directions simultaneously. These sentences are represented in the bottom four conceptual graphs in Fig. 17.3.

These two situations as represented are given to the analogical tool, which forms the same analogy as that presented by Gick and Holyoak. The following concept correspondences are formed by the tool:

```
(Doctor - Commander) (Rays - Army) (Destroy - Capture) (Tumor
- Fortress)
(Want - Want) (Possesses - Possesses) (Powerful - Large) (Go
- Go)
(Direction - Road) (One - One) (WeakRays - Group) (Many - Many)
(Simultaneously - Simultaneously)
```

The tool also automatically forms an abstraction similar to that described by Gick and Holyoak, by using the concept hierarchy to find common generalizations of the concepts. The general problem solving principle formed by the tool is:

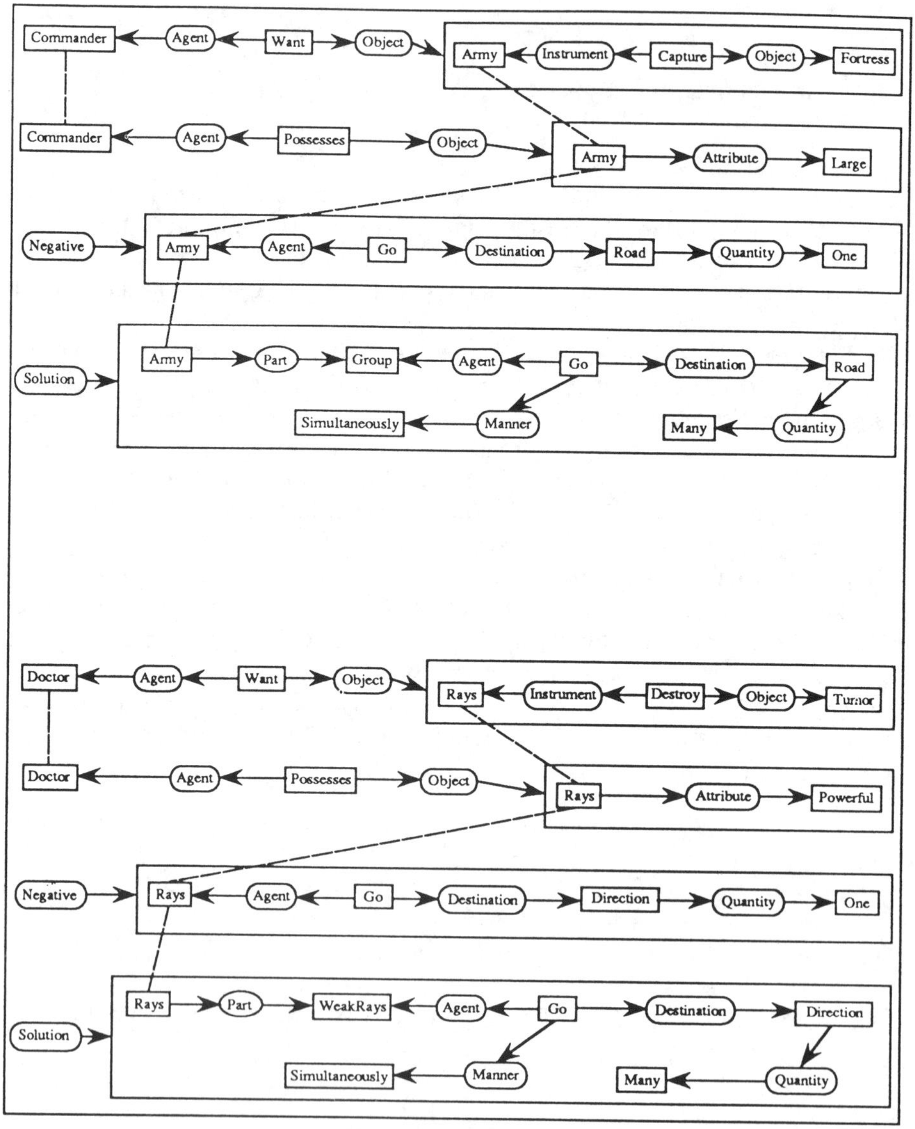

Fig. 17.3 Gick and Holyoak - Schema Abstraction

A Person wants to use a Mobile Entity to perform a Violent act on a Stationary Entity.

A Person has a Mobile Entity with an Attribute of Strength.
The Mobile Entity cannot go along one Path.
The Solution is for Parts of the Mobile Entity to Go along Many Paths
Simultaneously.

This example can also be used to show how the tool can perform simple analogical inferencing. In this case the analogues are the same with the exception that the solution to the radiation problem is not known. This is represented as an empty *Proposition* node attached to the *Solution* relation.

When the tool reports the correspondences resulting from the best analogy formed, the two Solution propositions are matched together. With substitution of corresponding terms inside the solution to the military problem, a solution to the radiation problem is realized: to have parts of the rays go in many directions simultaneously.

17.5 RELEVANCY LIMITATIONS AND SOLUTIONS

The analogical tool described thus far is a similarity based system and as such suffers from limitations due to relevancy issues. Drawing inferences from minimal analogies is an inductive process and thus potentially false. Use of the extensibility principle deals with some problems of relevancy and is similar to Gentner's (1983) use of the systematicity principle. But, analogical inferencing based on correspondence alone can be misleading if the major correspondences are not relevant to the objective of the inferencing. Russell (1987) defines one method of dealing with this problem using determinations. Determination rules are similar to dependency relations in database theories and are of the form: P determines Q. These rules are weaker than implications but serve as background knowledge which when added to the premises of an analogy, makes the conclusion follow soundly.

Current work on the analogical tool involves incorporating determination rules. The Tool uses the determination rules when t hey are available along with its evaluation criteria and uses only the evaluations when appropriate determinations are not available.

17.6 SUMMARY AND CONCLUSIONS

This chapter has described an analogical tool based on the formation of partial correspondences between knowledge structures represented as conceptual graphs. Evaluation criteria have been derived for forming and ordering analogies by plausibility that relate naturally to operations on conceptual graphs. These have been tested empirically against examples of analogical reasoning in the literature.

The use of conceptual graphs for knowledge representation has been beneficial in allowing examples of analogical reasoning in the literature expressed in natural language to be simply translated to a computational representation, and in providing a principled algebraic formulation of the essential operations of analogy formation and analogical inferencing that relates simply and naturally to the semantic constraints found in cognitive studies of analogy.

The notions of *analogy* and the relative *plausibility* of analogies are cognitively rich and it is not clear that any computational framework can capture them in full. There is certainly a very strong dependence on the underlying knowledge representation scheme that is used. The results of this study indicate that conceptual graphs naturally support the mathematical operations of forming partial correspondences and provide evaluation criteria that are strong enough to result in plausible analogies that correspond to psychological expectations.

BIBLIOGRAPHY

Gaines, B. and M. Shaw. (1982) "Analysing Analogy", (eds) Trappl, R. Ricciardi, L. and Pask, G., *Progress in Cybernetics and Systems Research vol. IX*, pp. 379-386. Washington: Hemisphere.

Gentner, D. (1983) "Structure-Mapping: a Theoretical Framework for Analogy". Cognitive Science 7, pp. 155-170.

Gentner, D. and M. Seziorski. (1986) "Historical Shifts in the Use of Analogy in Science", To appear in (eds) B. Gholson, W.R. Shadish, and A Graesser, *Psychology of Science*.

Gick, M. and K. Holyoak. (1983) "Schema Induction and Analogical Transfer". Cognitive Psychology 15, pp. 1-38.

Hofstadter, D.R. and M. Mitchell. (1988) "Concepts, Analogies and Creativity". Proc. of CSCSI'88: Seventh Biennial Conference of the Canadian Society for Computational Studies of Intelligence. pp. 94-101.

Indurkhya, B. (1985) "A Computational Theory of Metaphor Comprehension and Analogical Reasoning", PhD thesis, University of Massachusetts.

Lakoff, G. and M. Johnson. (1980) "The Metaphorical Structure of the Human Conceptual System", Cognitive Science 4, pp. 195-208.

Lenat, D., M. Prakash and M. Shepherd. (1986) "CYC: Using Common Sense Knowledge to Overcome Brittleness and Knowledge Acquisition Bottlenecks", The AI Magazine. pp. 65-85.

Murphy G., D.J. Shippy and H. L. Luo. (1963) *Engineering Analogies.* Iowa State University Press. Ames, Iowa.

Polya, G. (1954) *Induction and Analogy in Mathematics*. Volume I of Mathematics and Plausible Reasoning. Princeton University Press. Princeton.

Russell, J.S. (1987) "Analogical and Inductive Reasoning", PhD thesis. Stanford University.

Sowa, J.F. (1984) *Conceptual Structures: Information Processing in Mind and Machine*, Addison Wesley, Reading.

Winston, P. (1981) "Learning and Reasoning by Analogy", Communications of the ACM vol. 23, No. 12.

Part IV

Temporal Reasoning

18

Temporal Intervals

John W. Esch
Timothy E. Nagle
Unisys Corp, PO Box 64663, MS F2L09,
St. Paul, Mn, 55164-0525 USA

ABSTRACT

This chapter shows how to use conceptual graphs to represent and reason about temporal intervals. In the general case conceptual graphs can be used to represent relationships among intervals over any fully ordered relation. In particular, time and its temporal intervals are used for the examples. Allen's seminal work in this area, to be described shortly, is base on disjunctions of 13 fully constraining relations. This chapter defines many common disjunctions, in particular, 20 end point relations and 16 cover relations. These common disjunctions and Allen's original relations are mapped to 12 base relations which are combined through conjunction rather than disjunction. A transitivity table is given for these base relations and a rule is defined for propagating interval constraints through a conceptual graph of conjunctive interval relations. This paper also shows how the contexts of conceptual graphs can be used to help control the computational complexity common with such propagation algorithms. The material in this chapter is a refinement and extension of an earlier paper by the authors (Esch and Nagle, 1990).

18.1   BACKGROUND

In his classic paper "Maintaining Knowledge about Temporal Intervals" James Allen (1983) showed that only thirteen relations are needed to represent all possible relationships between two intervals of a fully ordered relation. These are defined in Fig. 18.1 where x and y denote temporal intervals. The first and second columns specify the full name and shorthand name given by Allen. The third column gives a pictorial definition of each relation. In these pictures, the left end of the interval indicates the start and the right end the finish of the interval. The last column gives the equivalent representation in terms of conceptual graphs as defined by Sowa (1984).

Allen also showed that these relations are closed under transitivity which consequently allows one to reason about networks of intervals connected by these interval relations. This is shown by specifying a transitivity table. The rows and columns of the table are indexed by his 13 interval relations. The intersections specify the transitive closure for that pair of relations. The value of the transitive closure for a pair of interval relations is given by a disjunction of interval relations. (See section 18.4 for more on transitivity.)

x RELATION y	KEY	PICTURE	CONCEPTUAL GRAPH
x BEFORE y	B		x → (B) → y
x MEETS y	M		x → (M) → y
x OVERLAPS y	O		x → (O) → y
x FINISHED BY y	Fi		x → (Fi) → y
x CONTAINS y	C		x → (C) → y
x STARTS y	S		x → (S) → y
x EQUALS y	E		x → (E) → y
x STARTED BY y	Si		x → (Si) → y
x DURING y	D		x → (D) → y
x FINISHES y	F		x → (F) → y
x OVERLAPPED BY y	Oi		x → (Oi) → y
x MET BY y	Mi		x → (Mi) → y
x AFTER y	A		x → (A) → y

Fig. 18.1 Allen's Relations on Intervals

In "A Common-Sense Theory of Time" (Allen, 1985) Allen provided a sounder mathematical foundation for interval relationships. He showed that all 13 relations could be expressed in terms of just the MEETS relation as illustrated in Fig. 18.2.

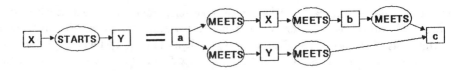

Fig. 18.2 Example Relation in terms of MEETS Relation.

Besides these definitions, six axioms about the MEETS relation were needed to provide a well-defined logic system. Fig. 18.3 illustrates one of the axioms using conceptual structures notation. (The dotted lines indicate that the sets refer to the same set of intervals.) Axiom $M1$ states that if the end points of two intervals I and J both meet an end point of a third interval k, then any interval m that one interval meets, the other also meets.

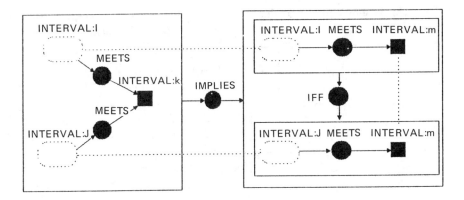

Fig. 18.3 Axiom $M1$ for Uniqueness of "Meeting Places"

Lastly, Allen extended his theories and showed that they applied to both discrete or continuous time or for that matter to any fully ordered discrete or continuous relation. This is very important because it means that the representations and software are applicable to a broad set of domains. Other example domains are distance intervals, probability intervals, and DNA intervals.

As shown in Fig. 18.1, conceptual graphs can represent intervals in a very natural way. The next few sections show how the relation definition capability of conceptual graphs can be used to define a wide variety of relations in terms of base relations or the MEETS relation, as desired. This ability, along with the ability to define axioms as illustrated in Fig. 18.3, means conceptual graphs can be used to define complete canons for temporal logic. Later sections show how to reason about networks of intervals connected by interval relations. They show how the context definition capability of conceptual graphs can be used to help control the computational complexity problems inherent in propagating transitive closure relations.

18.2   SOLVING THE DISJUNCTION PROBLEM

Each of Allen's 13 relations completely defines the relationships of both ends of two intervals with respect to each other. In many cases one does not know these relationships completely. Knowing less about the relationship between two intervals requires a disjunction of Allen's relations. Because conceptual graphs are based on conjunction and negation, disjunctions are not easily expressed by them.

Look at the pictorial column of Fig. 18.1 and note that the STARTS, EQUALS, and STARTED BY relations all restrict the two intervals to start at the same time. This situation is denoted by the SWS (starts when starts) relation. Fig. 4 show how messy a definition of SWS is when expressed as a disjunction using conceptual graph notation. (The situation is actually more complex than shown because one has to use contexts and negation to define the OR relation.)

In "Endpoint Relations on Temporal Intervals" (Matuszek *et al.*, 1988) Matuszek and his colleagues solved this problem by defining a set of twelve endpoint relations like SWS. More specific relationships between intervals are expressed as conjunctions of endpoint

relations. This is shown in Fig. 5 which gives a definition of Allen's STARTS relation in
terms of the conjunction of two endpoint relations. (FBF stands for finishes before finishes.)

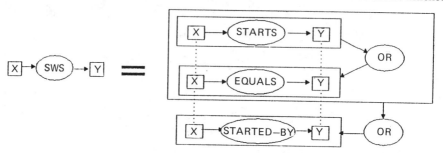

Fig. 18.4 Example Endpoint Relation as a Disjunction.

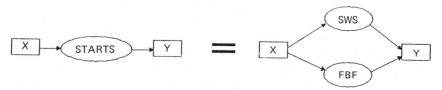

Fig. 18.5 Example Allen's Relation as a Conjunction.

Fig. 18.6 gives a more interesting example. The top part uses the pictorial notation to
define some relationships among intervals having to do with two activities, gardening and
making dinner.

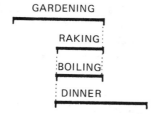

WITH ALLEN'S INTERVALS

WITH END POINT INTERVALS

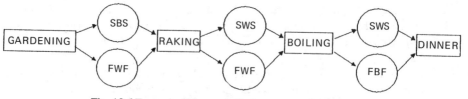

Fig. 18.6 Example of Intervals & Corresponding Networks

Since the relationships among the intervals are completely known, the conceptual graph describing some of these relationships using Allen's intervals is very natural and compact. Importantly, the equivalent graph in terms of endpoint relations is not much more complex because of the naturalness of conjunction in conceptual structure theory. (SBS stands for starts before starts and FWF stands for finishes when finishes.)

Allowing a user to express interval relations using either the endpoint or Allen's relations makes the resulting graphs very natural and intuitive. When sufficient endpoint relations are specified between two intervals, they become maximally constrained. Adding any more interval relations would result in over constraining the relationship of the two intervals with respect to each other.

When two intervals are maximally constrained by endpoint relations, there exists an equivalent Allen's relation. The conceptual graph type definition capabilities can be used to define each of Allen's relations in terms of a conjunction of endpoint relations as shown in Fig. 18.5. Consequently, the conceptual graph type contraction capabilities can be used on any maximally constrained pair of intervals to replace the conjunction of endpoint relations with a single one of Allen's relations.

The conceptual graph type expansion capabilities can be used to go the other way. It can be used to replace one of Allen's relations with a maximally constrained conjunctive set of endpoint relations. The combination of conceptual graph definition, type contraction, and type expansion capabilities effectively solves the disjunction problem. However, it turns out that there are even weaker relationships than the endpoint relations. The next section re-applies these basic ideas to a set of base relations which include these weaker relationships.

18.3 BASE RELATIONS

When trying to combine Allen's and Matuszek's work, we discovered another family of relations. We call them "cover" relations because they specify the relationship of one end of an interval to the inside of a second interval. "Inside" needs better definition as to whether the ends of the second interval, the one doing the covering, defines an open or closed interval. To include a broad range of cases and make the names of the relations more intuitive, we adopted the mathematical notation for distinguishing open and closed intervals. Thus [ ] is the closed interval and includes the end points, ( ) is the open interval and excludes the end points, [ ) is open on the right, and ( ] is open on the left.

These four basic cases are compounded by two additional degrees of freedom. One is whether the start or finish of the first interval is the point being covered by the second interval. The other is whether the first or second interval is doing the covering. The net result is 16 different cover relations.

To provide maximum flexibility, we also applied the open verses closed distinction to Matuszek's endpoint relations. For example, the starts before starts relation has a natural weaker condition of starts at or before starts. Doing this expanded the number of endpoint relations from 16 to 20. The net result provides the user with 49 (13 Allen + 20 endpoint + 16 cover) relations to chose from in specifying a relationship between two intervals. Also, conjunctions of weak relationships between two intervals are allowed as long as they don't over constrain the two intervals. And through type contraction, simplifications are possible when a particular set of conjunctions matches the definition of some other relation.

In theory a transitivity table with these 49 relations on each side is possible, but it is very difficult to work with. To solve this problem, we identified 12 base relations which are shown in Fig. 18.7. Because the base relations only specify constraints on one end of each relation, the other end is often not constrained. This is indicated by the dotted line showing a range of values still possible for the free end of the x interval. The constrained end of the x interval is shown by a vertical bar. Sometimes it may also be a range of values. In that case its range is shown by a dotted line between two vertical bars.

For example, $x S)S y$ means that the x interval starts before the y interval starts and $x F]S$ y means that the x interval finishes at or before the y interval starts.

We used these 12 base relations to define the remaining 37 relations (49-12=37) in terms of them or a conjunction of them. These definitions are given in Tab. 1. In it the columns are divided into 3 groups of 3 columns each. Each group of 3 columns defines one of the sets of relations (endpoint, cover and Allen's). Within each group, the "Rel" column identifies the relation being defined from interval x to interval y. The second and third columns give base relations which are conjoined to give the relation being defined. (Note that the base relation in the third column is from y to x.)

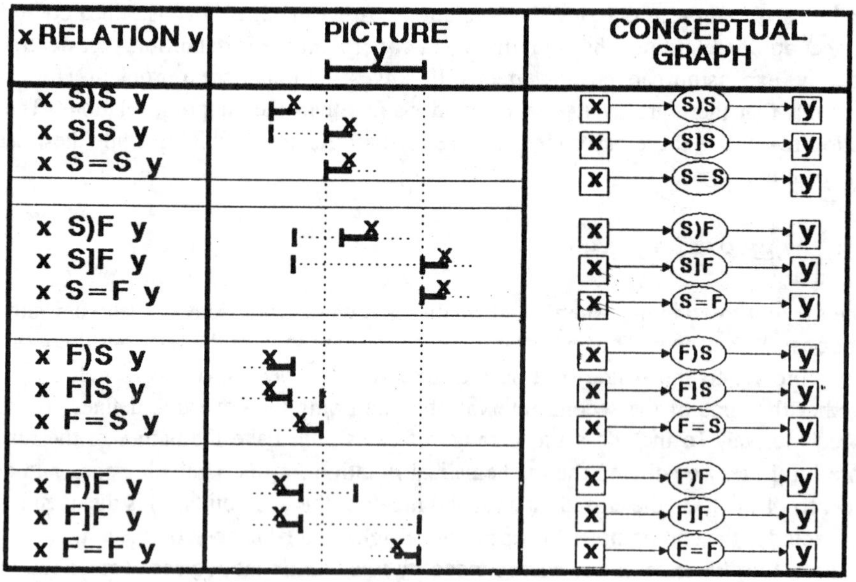

Fig. 18.7. Base Relations on Intervals

The problem of interval logic has now been divided into 4 parts,

1. expressing the relationship between two intervals in terms of a conjunction of the 12 base relations,

2. defining transitive closure over the base relations,

3. defining a rule for the case where there are

4. conjunctions of base relations, and

5. controlling the complexity of propagation.

The first part was treated in this section. The remaining parts are the subjects of the following three sections.

ENDPOINT		COVER			ALLEN'S		
Rel	xRy & yRx	Rel	xRy & yRx		Rel	xRy & yRx	
S)S =	S)S	S[] =	S]F	S]S	B =	F)S	
S]S =	S]S	[]S =	S]S	S]F	M =	F=S	
S=S =	S=S	S[) =	S)F	S]S	O =	S)S	()F
S[S =	S]S	[)S =	S]S	S)F	Fi =	S)S	F=F
S(S =	S)S	S(] =	S]F	S)S	C =	S)S	F)F
S)F =	S)F	(]S =	S)S	S]F	S =	F)F	S=S
S]F =	S]F	S() =	S)F	S)S	E =	S=S	F=F
S=F =	S=F	()S =	S)S	S)F	Si =	S=S	F)F
S[F =	F]S	F[] =	F]F	S]F	D =	F)F	S)S
S(F =	F)S	[]F =	S]F	F]F	F =	F=F	S)S
F)S =	F)S	F[) =	F)F	S]F	Oi =	S()	F)F
F]S =	F]S	[)F =	S]F	F)F	Mi =	S=F	
F=S =	F=S	F(] =	F]F	S)F	A =		F)S
F[S =	S]F	(]F =	S)F	F]F			
F(S =	S)F	F() =	F)F	S)F			
F)F =	F)F	()F =	S)F	F)F			
F]F =	F]F						
F=F =	F=F						
F[F =	F]F						
F(F =	F)F						

Tab. 1. Definition of Allen's, Endpoint & Cover Relations.

18.4   TRANSITIVE CLOSURE

First a short explanation. Look at Fig. 18.6 again and determine the relationship between GARDENING and DINNER for yourself. By looking at the pictorial diagram, you can easily see that the two intervals overlap. However, the question is, how can we get computers using conjunctions of the base relations to come to the same conclusion?

Fig. 18.8 names the nodes and gives an answer graph. For transitive closure to hold, it must be possible, given any two relations, such as R4 between I1 and I3, and R3 between I3 and I4 to infer R5, the relationship of I1 to I4. In the case of Allen's relations, the transitive closure is given by a table indexed by relations. For R4 = FINISHED BY and R3 = STARTS, the entry in the table would be OVERLAPS, labeled R5.

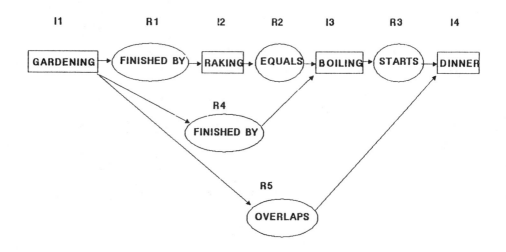

Fig. 18.8. Interval Network with Labeled Nodes.

In our approach, we want to work with the 12 base relations instead of Allen's relation because other relations can be expressed as a conjunction of them. We prefer them to Matuszek's because they include more cases. The transitive closure for them is given in tabular form in Tab. 2. A null entry means no known relationship can be implied; that is, any relation is possible.

Since one doesn't know which order one is going to encounter the relations, the inverses of the 12 base relations are also given.

One of the things that Matuszek pointed out was that the number of disjuncts in Allen's transitivity table ranged from 1 to 5 with an average of 3.8. In their endpoint transitivity table the entry is either empty or has exactly one entry with an average of 0.4. A consequence of this difference is that the data structure to store the endpoint table can be a 2-dimensional array with a simple entry while the entry for Allen's table would have to be a list. This property of simple entries also holds for the base relation transitivity table. It also has the property of either a null entry or exactly one relation and its average is 0.52.

rel	s)s	s]s	s=s	s(s	s[s	s)f	s]f	s=f	s(f	s[f	f)s	f]s	f=s	f(s	f[s	f)f	f]f	f=f	f(f	f[f
s)s	s)s	s)s	s)s	-	-	s)f	s)f	s)f	-	-	s)s	s)s	s)s	-	-	s)f	s)f	s)f	-	-
s]s	s)s	s]s	s]s	-	-	s)f	s]f	s]f	-	-	s)s	s)s	s)s	-	-	s)f	s]f	s]f	-	-
s=s	s)s	s)s	s=s	s(s	s(s	s)f	s)f	s=f	s(f	s(f	s)s	s)s	s)s	-	-	s)f	s)f	s)f	-	-
s(s	-	-	s(s	s(s	s(s	-	-	s(f	s(f	s(f	-	-	-	-	-	-	-	-	-	-
s[s	-	-	s[s	s(s	s(s	-	-	s[f	s(f	s[f	-	-	-	-	-	-	-	-	-	-
s)f	-	-	-	-	-	-	-	-	-	-	s)s	s)s	s)s	-	-	s)f	s)f	s)f	-	-
s]f	-	-	-	-	-	-	-	-	-	-	s)s	s]s	s]s	-	-	s)f	s]f	s]f	-	-
s=f	-	-	s(s	s(s	s(s	-	-	s(f	s(f	s(f	s)s	s)s	s=s	s(s	s(s	s)f	s)f	s=f	s(f	s(f
s(f	-	-	s(s	s(s	s(s	-	-	s(f	s(f	s(f	-	-	s(s	s(s	s(s	-	-	s(f	s(f	s(f
s[f	-	-	s[s	s(s	s(s	-	-	s(f	s(f	s(f	-	-	s[s	s(s	s(s	-	-	s[f	s(f	s[f
f)s	f)s	f)s	f)s	-	-	f)f	f)f	f)f	-	-	f)s	f)s	f)s	-	-	f)f	f)f	f)f	-	-
f]s	f)s	f]s	f]s	-	-	f)f	f]f	f]f	-	-	f)s	f)s	f)s	..	-	f)f	f)f	f)f	-	-
f=s	f)s	f)s	f=s	f(s	f(s	f)f	f)f	f=f	f(f	f(f	f)s	f)s	f=s	f(s	f(s	f)f	f)f	f=f	f(f	f(f
f(s	-	-	f(s	f(s	f(s	-	-	f(f	f(f	f(f	-	-	-	-	-	-	-	-	-	-
f[s	-	-	f[s	f(s	f(s	-	-	f[f	f(f	f[f	-	-	-	-	-	-	-	-	-	-
f)f	-	-	-	-	-	-	-	-	-	-	f)s	f)s	f)s	-	-	f)f	f)f	f)f	-	-
f]f	-	-	-	-	-	-	-	-	-	-	f)s	f]s	f]s	-	-	f)f	f]f	f]f	-	-
f=f	-	-	f(s	f(s	f(s	-	-	f(f	f(f	f(f	f)s	f)s	f=s	f(s	f(s	f)f	f)f	f=f	f(f	f(f
f(f	-	-	f(s	f(s	f(s	-	-	f(f	f(f	f(f	-	-	f(s	f(s	f(s	-	-	f(f	f(f	f(f
f[f	-	-	f(s	f(s	f(s	-	-	f(f	f(f	f(f	-	-	f[s	f(s	f[s	-	-	f[f	f(f	f[f

Tab. 2. Transitive Closure for Base Relations.

18.5 PROPAGATING CONJUNCTIONS

The third part of the problem is a rule for dealing with conjunctions. The FINISHED BY relation equals S)S and F=F, and the STARTS relations equals S=S and F)F. The rule for handling conjunctions is:

> form the conjunction of the transitive closures of all possible pairs of base relations.

For our example, the relation of I1 to I5 is the conjunction of the transitive closures (using Tab. 2) of all possible pairs of base relations between I1 and I4, and between I4 and I5. The set between I1 and I4 is S)S F=F and that between I4 and I5 is S=S F)F. The pairings and results of looking them up in Tab. 2 are:

PAIR		FROM	TRANSITIVE CLOSURE
I1-I4	to	I4-I5	OF EACH PAIR
S)S		S=S	S)S
S)S		F)F	S)F
F=F		S=S	F(S
F=F		F)F	F)F

Consider the first two relations in the last column to be conjoined, S)S and S)F. By definition, all intervals start before they finish. Consequently, one interval starting before another starts, S)S, is a stronger constraint than starting before it finishes, S)F. Thus, the S)S relation implies the S)F relation and the conjunction of S)S and S)F is S)S.

Now consider the last two relations to be conjoined, F(S and F)F. The inverse of x F(S y is y S)F x; that is, the inverse of x finishing after the start of y is y starting before the finish of x. Tab. 1 defines relations as the conjunction of base relations. It can be used backwards to replace a conjunction by its definition. Looking up F)F conjoined with the inverse of F(S, S)F, in Tab. 1 as a definition, we find that they define F(). Thus the conjunction of the last two entries can be replaced by F().

We have now simplified the conjunction of four relations S)S S)F F(S F)F to the conjunction of two relations S)S F(). To review how this was done, first the conjunction of S)S S)F was simplified to S)S and then the conjunction of F(S F)F was replaced by the relation it defines, F().

Continuing, we can use Tab. 1 again with S)S and F(). The inverse of F() is ()F. Looking up S)S conjoined with the inverse of F(), ()F, in Tab. 1 as a definition, we find that they define OVERLAPS, the desired result.

The process of looking up a conjunction of a pair of relations in Tab. 1 and replacing it with its definition is the same process as type contraction in the theory of conceptual graphs. As pointed out at the end of the second section, the conjunction of a number of weaker relations can often be replaced, through type contraction (using Tab. 1 backwards) by a single stronger relation. Now that a process for propagating base relations and simplifying the results has been given, the last issue is the complexity of the process.

18.6   CONTROLLING COMPUTATIONAL COMPLEXITY

The last part needed to reason about intervals is a reasonable level of computational complexity. In most cases two base relations will maximally constrain the relationship of two intervals. In a few cases three base relations are needed to maximally constrain two intervals. In all cases, four or more non-redundant base relations will over constrain the relationship between two intervals. Consequently, with base relations the relationship between two intervals can be updated at most three times before it is guaranteed to become over constrained. In most cases only two updates will suffice.

However, the effect of a successful update must be propagated to adjacent intervals. This is done using the transitivity table and propagation rule described in Sections 4 and

5 respectively. The computational complexity of the propagation is determined by the branching factor. It is the average number of other intervals to which each interval is related by a base relation or conjunction of base relations. The problem is that, as more relations are added and their constraints propagated, each interval tends to become connected to each of the other intervals. Thus, if there are n intervals, a fully connected network of intervals will have a branching factor of n-1. The total number of branches that needs to be checked becomes the number of nodes times the number of branches to other nodes divided by 2, because the branches need only be checked once, or $n(n-1)/2$.

Networks tend to become fully connected because relationships which can be inferred by the transitivity table are made explicit. The goal is to only express required relationships and deduce any derivable ones when needed. To do this Allen (Allen, 1983) adopted Kahn and Gorry's idea of reference intervals (Kahn and Gorry, 1977). This was further extended by Koomen in his TIMELOGIC system (Koomen, 1989). Koomen defines a hierarchy of intervals based of the idea of containment.

The idea of containment is strongly intuitive. A higher level interval has a greater span than the lower level intervals that are contained in it. Thus, if interval x CONTAINS, or is STARTED BY, or is FINISHED BY interval y, then x is at a higher level than y because it contains y. The disjunction of these three relations is called the downlink and is equivalent to the conjunction of S]S and F[F. The inverse of the downlink is the uplink which is the disjunction of DURING, STARTS, and FINISHES. It is equivalent to the conjunction of S[S and F]F. Note that the downlink and uplink are inverses of each other; which one is used depends on whether one is at a higher level node looking down or at a lower level node looking up.

The effect of organizing intervals into such a containment hierarchy is to simplify the number of links and amount of processing. The consequence is that the hierarchy has to be traversed (usually up and back down) to answer questions. However, because of the containment, there is a locality of reference for an interval. The result is that all reasoning (processing) can be constrained to the smallest containing interval.

Another important property of containment hierarchies is that logical assertions made about a higher level node are automatically inherited by all contained (lower level) nodes. More formally, propositional inheritance is the property that any proposition that holds over interval x necessarily holds over any subinterval (i.e. over all contained lower level intervals) and any relation between x and another, disjoint interval y, is necessarily true between any subintervals of x and y. Thus, as with objects and their inheritance hierarchies, a proposition (e.g. a value or rule) is placed as high in the hierarchy as it universally applies and is consequently inherited by all lower level objects.

The down/uplinks are only a small number of the total set of possible relations. However, they define the basic hierarchy. Sidelinks are other relations among disjoint intervals such as BEFORE or MEETS. Typically they relate siblings that are commonly contained or, less frequently, intervals in different branches of the hierarchy. Looking ahead briefly, in Fig. 18.10, the MEETS sidelink between the Dinner and Dishes intervals implies that any properly contained subinterval of Dinner will be BEFORE any similar subinterval of Dishes.

With these concepts Koomen was able to store the basic interval relationships in a containment hierarchy augmented with sidelinks is such a way as to not loose any information. The effects are rather pronounced. He tested his TIMELOGIC system with networks of 101 nodes. He randomly assigned singular relations between two intervals until all pairs of intervals had singular relations, either posted or derived, that are locally consistent. He then computed averages over these example networks. Positive results he obtained include a branching factor for the flat system of 100 and 18.3 for the hierarchical system; uplinks of 19.4 compared to 1.4, and sidelinks of 47.3 compared to 1.6. On the negative side, the reference depth (to infer a result) was 1 compared to 13.8. In effect there is a significant trade-off between size/complexity of the data structure to store the network and the traversal of that data structure. Kooman's smaller data structure required more traversal to gather all data. However, the result on total number of propagations in this one experiment was slightly more than a factor of 3 better for the hierarchical verses the flat system.

Koomen also incorporates a concept of "context" into his TIMELOGIC system (Koomen, 1989). (These are not the same as conceptual graph contexts but will be related to them shortly.) TIMELOGIC supports a tree of "contexts" of which one is the current "context". Unless a constraint (a relation between two intervals) is explicitly added to a "context," the constraint is inherited from the nearest ancestral "context", if there is one. Adding an assertion to a "context" with children is not allowed, as this may cause inconsistencies in the children.

The context mechanism of conceptual graphs combines many of the features of both the hierarchical containment and "context" mechanisms of Koomen. The semantics (denotation in logic) of both the nesting and negation of conceptual graph contexts is well-defined in the theory of conceptual graphs. Consequently, the properties of propositional inheritance and constraint inheritance of Koomen's containment hierarchies and "contexts" are obtained naturally by conceptual graph contexts. Furthermore, coreference and self reference allow a fuller, more natural range of interval representations.

When considering intervals together with contexts, there are five cases of interest. These depend on whether the interval is a leaf or context, whether the relationship is to the context of something inside it, and whether the relationship is inside a context or not. These cases are shown in Fig. 18.9.

Case 1 is the normal case of a base relation B relating two intervals I1 and I2 where I1 and I2 are both normal leaf intervals. *Case 2* depicts a sidelink relation S between an interval I3 and a context C1 which represents an interval with contained subintervals. *Case 3* depicts a sidelink relation S between an interval I4 and interval I5 that is contained inside a context. A variant of case 3 is where I4 is also coreferent with an interval in some other context. *Case 4a* depicts a down/uplink relation U between an interval I4 and its containing context C3. Note the power, inherent in the theory of conceptual graphs, of the coreference link. It is used to indicate that the context in question is the same one that contains the constraint being specified, a form of self-reference.

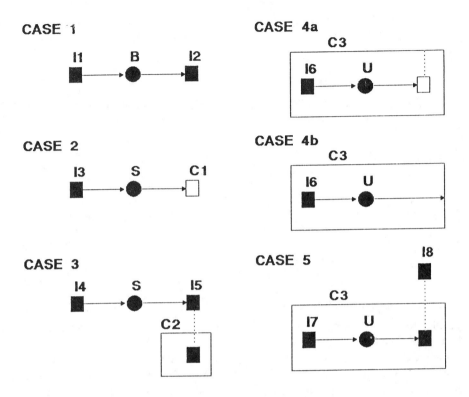

Fig. 18.9. Relations Involving Contexts

Case 4b is a notational contraction for *Case 4a* and is equivalent to it. The interpretation of an arc connected to the inside of a context is that there is an implied coreferent concept in the formal theory.

Case 5 depicts a sidelink between interval I7 and interval I8 which is coreferent with an interval outside context C4. Case 5 is actually the dual of case 3. The difference is that the perspective is from that of the interval inside a context instead of that outside the context.

The advantage that conceptual graph contexts have is the well-defined nesting structure in terms of a denotation which is logically well-defined. However, since basic conceptual graphs can not cross context boundaries they are rather limited without the concept of coreference. With it, any interval can be brought outside the context or into another context and related to other contexts or intervals as desired there. This allows for arbitrary groupings of intervals into contexts.

Koomen uses an expanded version of the Gardening and Dinner example shown in Fig. 18.6. The initial set of relations in conceptual graph notation are:

c1: [Mowing] → (STARTS) → [Gardening].
c2: [Mowing] → (BEFORE) → [Raking].
c3: [Raking] → (FINISHES) → [Gardening].
c4: [BoilWater] → (STARTS) → [Dinner].
c5: [BoilWater] → (MEETS) → [CookSpaghetti].

c6: [CookSpaghetti] → (F]S) → [EatSpagehtti].
c7: [EatSpaghetti] → (FINISHES) → [Dinner].
c8: [Dinner] → (MEETS) → [Dishes].

These were given to the TIMELOGIC system which automatically builds the containment hierarchy. He then discusses what happens when you give the system the next constraint:

c9: [Raking] → (EQUALS) → [BoilWater].

The flat system would generate, among others, the following:

c10: [Gardening] → (OVERLAPS) → [Dinner].
c11: [Mowing] → (BEFORE) → [Dinner].
c12: [Mowing] → (BEFORE) → [Dishes].

In the TIMELOGIC system a link for c9 would be included. c12 could be inferred from the hierarchy and existing links. But c10 and c11 can not be inferred and require their own links. The equivalent diagram for conceptual graphs is shown in Fig. 18.10.

The significant difference here is that the coreferent links give conceptual graphs sufficient information to infer c10-c12 and so links for them are not needed. Three additional features of the use of conceptual graph contexts are worth mentioning.

First, contexts provide firm logical boundaries for reasoning. Each provides its own temporal locality within which everything is self consistent and true. If all coreferent concepts within a context are joined, then the reasoning algorithm within a context can ignore coreferent links. In effect, there is a natural partitioning of Koomen's sidelinks into those which are within the context and those which go outside so propagation only need occur over those inside.

When the reasoning involves two intervals in different contexts, only concepts with coreferent or relation link paths between the two intervals need be considered. In this way constraints c10-c12 can be derived.

Second, when viewed abstractly, the coreferent concepts of Raking and BoilWater, that are connected by the EQUAL relation in the Today context, represent a synchronization point of two activities, Gardening and Dinner. It is also possible to put such synchronization points into their own contexts and have other, more elaborate, constraints which apply to just the synchronization.

Third, conceptual graphs contexts can be used for Koomen's "contexts" by allowing multiple contexts for the situation. For example, in the Today context, one may want to represent alternative dinners. Each could have its own context, either inside Today or inside a global Dinner context. The semantics are nearly the same as Koomen's "contexts" except that the relationship of his contexts to each other is always one of being alternatives to each other. In conceptual graphs, the relationship of the contexts can be specified by relations such as OR or XOR among the contexts. This provides additional flexibility, but any particular case, such as alternatives, requires additional relations.

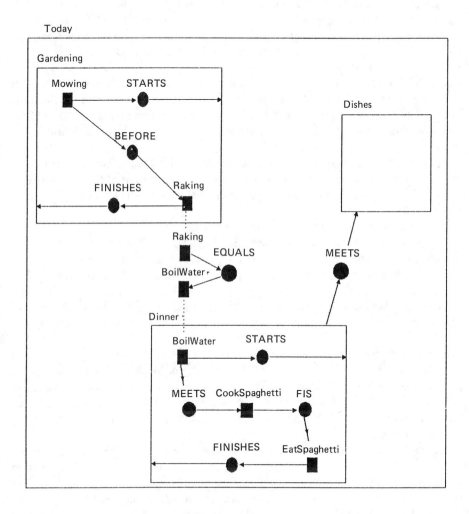

Fig. 18.10. The Gardening Example Using Contexts

18.7   APPLICATION

One of the most demanding applications of temporal intervals is representing time in natural language. There can be many different interpretations of when an event occurred. It is necessary to both separate states that describe events from intervals and allow different contexts to associate different intervals with the same state. To handle all tenses, a robust representation including locutor, event, and reference time intervals is needed. Intervals are also needed to represent aspectual properties, indicative mode, and temporal adverbs. So, not only is it necessary to separate states from intervals, but it is also necessary to provide for different kinds of intervals for each state.

Moulin (Moulin, 1990) has categorized problems of representing time in natural language. He showed how conceptual structures can be used to solve these natural language representation problems. In particular, he defines states, some tense marker relations, and interval labels. He used contexts to represent states. The graph or graphs inside the context describe the particular state.

Also, he defined MRK-S, MRK-E & MRK-R relations from these state contexts to what he calls interval labels. These relations correspond to the time of statement (the locution time), MRK_S, the time of the event, MRK-E, and a reference time, MRK-R. They relate a context containing a description of a state to important interval labels representing tense markers.

Each interval label corresponds to a temporal interval plus a unit of measurement field. Each is a concept composed of a unit, which indicates the precision of the observation, a lwr-bnd, which indicates a lower bound for the interval, and upp-bnd, which indicates an upper bound for the interval.

Lastly, he uses interval relations to specify the temporal relationships of the interval labels to each other. Since many of these are EQUAL or CONTAINS relations, the compositional hierarchies described in Section 6 can be applied to simplify his graphs. Further simplification can be obtained by using the coreference ideas also described in section 18.6.

The example Moulin uses is the statement: *"Mary called John before the storm arrived."* His graph for this example sentence, with the simplifications described above, is shown in Fig. 18.11.

Note how effective the open and closed symbols are at distinguishing things with composition from those without. (See Esch (1990) or more on graphical display techniques.) In particular, the interval labels [u1,c1,c2] and [u1,c3,c4], each correspond to a temporal context containing their respective event and reference interval labels connected by an EQUALS relation. However, for this example, it is not necessary to know the contents of these "context labels."

In Fig. 18.11, the concept on the right [u1,s1,s2] simply states, via the MKR-S relation, that it is the statement marker for the entire statement, STATE G. The BEFORE relation from the context label [u1,c3,c4] to it indicates that [u1,c3,c4] and consequently STATE 2 occurred in the past; that is, they occurred before the time of the statement, STATE G. The BEFORE relation from [u1,c1,c2] to [u1,c3,c4] indicates that STATE 1 occurred before STATE 2; that is, the instance of calling denoted by CALL occurred before the instance of arriving denoted by ARRIVE. By transitivity, it can be inferred that [u1,c1,c2] and consequently STATE 1 occurred before the time of the statement, also in the past.

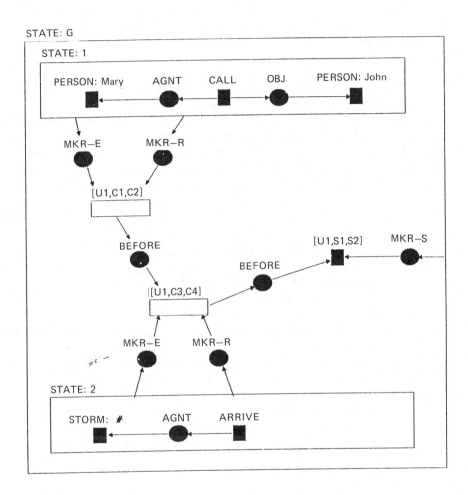

Fig. 18.11. Moulin's Example Simplified

Natural language processing of paragraphs and passages of any length would involve many statements whose interval labels would be related in an increasingly complex interval network. As that happens, the range of interval relations, transitivity table, and propagation rule described in earlier sections are needed to maintain a temporally consistent network and reason about it with acceptable computational complexity.

18.8 SUMMARY

This chapter has combined Allen's interval relations with an extended version of Matuszek's endpoint relations and a new set of relations called cover relations. Collectively, these provide a very flexible family of 49 relations for expressing relationships among temporal or other kinds of intervals.

These relations were defined in terms of 12 base relations or conjunctions of them. It was shown how these conjunctions can be represented directly in conceptual graphs as multiple relations between two intervals represented as concepts.

We illustrated how networks of intervals connected by interval relations are naturally represented in conceptual graphs. We explained how the propagation of interval constraints, as interval relations are added or deleted, is accomplished by using a transitivity table over the 12 base relations and a rule to handle conjunctive cases.

We addressed the computational complexity problem due to networks tending to become fully connected by using conceptual graph contexts to represent interval containment. We showed how the use of coreference allows very natural and effective representation of complex situations that cross context boundaries. Lastly, we gave an example application of these ideas to representing tense in natural language.

BIBLIOGRAPHY

Esch, John & Timothy E. Nagle, (1990). "Representing Temporal Intervals using Conceptual Graphs," in Proc. of the Fifth Annual workshop on Conceptual Structures, (eds) P. Eklund, and L. Gerholz, Linköping University, ISBN 91-7870-718-8.

Allen, J.F. (1983) "Maintaining Knowledge about Temporal Intervals," Comm. ACM, Vol. 26, No. 11, pp832-843.

Sowa, J.F. (1984) *Conceptual Structures: Information in Mind and Machine*, Addison-Wesley, Reading, MA.

Allen, J.F. and P. J. Hayes, (1985) "A Common Sense Theory of Time," Proc. of IJCAI-85, pp528-531.

Matuszek, D, T. Finin, R. Fritzson, & C. Overton, (1988) "Endpoint Relations on Temporal Intervals," Proc. of the Third Annual Rocky Mountain Conference on Artificial Intelligence, (pp. 182-188).

Kahn, K & G. A. Gorry, (1977) "Mechanizing Temporal Knowledge," Artificial Intelligence, 9:87-108.

Koomen, Johannes A. G. M (1989) "The TIMELOGIC Temporal Reasoning System," Univ. of Rochester, Tech. Rpt 231 (revised).

Moulin, B. and Danial Cote, (1990) "Extending the Conceptual Graph Model for Differentiating Temporal and Non-Temporal Knowledge," Proc. of the Fifth Annual Workshop on Conceptual Structures, (eds) P. Eklund, and L. Gerholz, Linköping University, ISBN 91-7870-718-8.

Esch, J.W. (1990) *"Graphical Displays for Conceptual Structures"*, in Proceedings of the Fifth Annual workshop on Conceptual Structures, (eds) P. Eklund, and L. Gerholz, Linköping University, ISBN 91-7870-718-8.

19

Extending the Conceptual Graph Model for Differentiating Temporal and Non-Temporal Knowledge

Bernard Moulin and Daniel Côté
Département d'informatique,
Universite Laval,
Ste Foy, Quebec G1K 7P4, Canada

ABSTRACT

Some difficulties are encountered when we try to represent temporal knowledge using the conceptual graph theory: the disparity of notations allowed by conceptual graph theory for expressing temporal information; the ambiguity and incompleteness of tense specification; the difficulty when trying to associate tenses with nested conceptual graphs or with conceptual graphs related by "temporal relations". We propose to distinguish non-temporal knowledge from temporal knowledge in conceptual graphs. We specify temporal knowledge by means of points in time as well as time intervals which are compatible with Allen's Model. Extending Reichenbach's three points theory for representing verb tenses, we use temporal markers in order to indicate the relative positions of the locutors time, the reference time and the event time. These markers are used to semantically specify tenses and the aspectual properties of verbs.

19.1 INTRODUCTION

Natural language generation is a research domain in which are studied the various approaches and techniques which enable a system to respond to a user using natural language utterances (Danlos, 1985) (McKeown, 1985) (McDonald, 1987a). Various types of application need a natural language generation sub-system such as question answering systems, explanation facilities in expert systems, the communication component in intelligent tutoring systems etc. (McKeown, 1986). In project GENTEXT (Generation of Text), we aim at developing a system which will be able to generate texts in the French language, starting from knowledge structures expressed in a form equivalent to Sowa's conceptual graphs (Sowa, 1984). These knowledge structures can be proposed by a user or generated by a planning system (Lizotte and Moulin, 1989a,b).

The conceptual graphs theory (Sowa 1984) provides a knowledge representation approach which is compatible with most conceptual modelling techniques used in artificial intelligence, databases design, cognitive psychology, linguistics etc. We believe that the conceptual graph approach can be used as a common representational framework for text generation. Sowa has proposed various guidelines for NL generation (Sowa, 1984), but few papers have been reporting developments in this area (Velardi *et al.*, 1988). We have encountered some difficulties when we tried to apply the conceptual graph approach for NL generation, especially when we had to express temporal knowledge. In this chapter we propose an extended conceptual graph model to overcome these difficulties.

In section 19.2 we identify some problems which arise when we try to express temporal knowledge using conceptual graphs. Most of these difficulties are encountered because of the lack of a precise model for expressing temporal knowledge within the conceptual graph theory (Côte and Moulin, 1990). We propose to extend the conceptual graph approach in order to distinguish and process separately non-temporal and temporal knowledge (section 19.3).

19.2   SOME DIFFICULTIES USING THE CONCEPTUAL GRAPH APPROACH

When we tried to apply the conceptual graph approach for NL generation, we have encountered various problems especially when modelling temporal knowledge: the disparity of notations allowed by conceptual graph theory for expressing temporal information; the ambiguity and incompleteness of tense specification; the difficulty when trying to associate tenses with nested conceptual graph or with conceptual graphs related by "temporal relations" (connectors).

19.2.1   Disparity of conceptual graphs notations for expressing temporal knowledge

In Sowa (1984) there is no specific section on temporal knowledge representation. Through the book and other papers (Sowa 1987, 1988), different indications for expressing temporal knowledge can be classified in three categories.

Monadic conceptual relations such as PAST, FUTR are used to indicate that a conceptual graph describes a situation which takes place respectively in the past and future. The relation PRST which indicates that a situation takes place in the present time is considered to be implicit and not represented in conceptual graph. As we will see in section 19.2.2 the semantics of these relations are not precise enough to express the richness of tenses in NL.

Dyadic conceptual relations such as PTIM (point in time), FREQ (frequence) or DUR (duration) are used to relate concepts to time concepts such as [TIME] and [TIME-PERIOD] within a conceptual graph. The relation SUCC is used to indicate that a time point is a successor of another. These specialized concepts and conceptual relations are useful for expressing temporal knowledge associated with points in time, but cannot be used to describe the properties of time intervals (Allen, 1983) which is necessary for NL generation.

Dyadic conceptual relations such as BFOR (before), AFTR (after) are used to express temporal information relating conceptual graphs and are called "intersentential relations" (Sowa, 1988). Indeed these relations are necessary, but as we will see in section 19.2.3, some problems arise when we have to combine intersentential relations and monadic tense relations for expressing the properties of temporal adverbs or temporal conjunctions.

19.2.2   Difficulties for specifying verb tenses within conceptual graph theory

The monadic relations PAST and FUTR (and the implicit PRST) are not precise enough and even ambiguous when we need to express verb tenses encountered in NL. The reason is that the choice of verb tenses, temporal adverbs (tomorrow, today etc.) or temporal expressions depends on the temporal properties of the described situations, which are conveyed not only by tense indications but also by aspectual characteristics (Comrie, 1985) (Dorfmüller-Karpusa, 1988). For instance using the PAST relation, we cannot differentiate the tenses of the conceptual graphs associated with the following sentences: *"John opened the door and called Mary"* (sent.1) and *"John was opening the door when he called Mary"* (sent.2). Furthermore, temporal adverbs or expressions may change the semantic interpretation of verb tenses. Consider the following sentences which express two situations taking place in the future: *"John will arrive by plane tomorrow"*and *"John arrives in a minute"*. In the second sentence using the present in conjunction with the expression *"in a minute"* corresponds to a semantic interpretation of a situation taking place in the future.

If we want to take into account aspectual properties of situations, we need to consider the time intervals during which situations take place. For instance in sent.2, the event *"John called Mary"* (sent.2.1) took place during another activity, when *"John was opening the door"* (sent 2.2). Hence the time interval associated with the situation described by sent. 2.1 is included in the time interval associated with the situation described by sent 2.2.

The present is a notion which is not easily understood and modelled. In Sowa (1984) the present is considered as a default option: when we do not attach a specific monadic tense relation to a conceptual graph, it is supposed to correspond to a situation taking place in the "present time" (usually indicated as "Now" when required). For example in (Sowa, 1984 page 113) the PAST relation is defined by the following conceptual graph:

```
Relation PAST (x) is
        [SITUATION: *x]→(PTIM)→[TIME]→(SUCC)→[TIME: Now].
```

In Sowa (1987, p. 12) "Now" is replaced by "the speech time", the time at which the sentence is uttered. This example illustrates also that in conceptual graph theory temporal knowledge is mainly expressed by points in time (see previous section). Physical time, which is usually measured with respect to periodic physical phenomena, is considered to be objective: the measurement does not depend on the measuring subject. But most NL temporal expressions cannot be expressed according to physical time. Basically "the time we speak about in our sentences" is often subjective and relative to the speaker (or locutor). Hence "Now" is not an absolute value and must be defined relatively to the "speech time" (the time when the locutor utters the sentence). It should be possible to specify the time associated with the situation relative to the speaker's time, as well as in an absolute way relatively to the "official physical time".

19.2.3   Difficulties in harmonizing tenses and intergraph temporal relations

Using the conceptual graph theory, it is difficult to associate different tenses in principal and subordinate sentences, as well as the required verb mode (infinitive, indicative, subjunctive, conditional). For instance consider the sentences: *"the dog that is barking, belongs to John"* (sent. 3.1) and *"the dog that was barking, belongs to John"* (sent. 3.2). Usually a relative clause is expressed by a l abstraction such as:

```
[(λ x)  [DOG:*x]←(AGNT)←[BARK]:#]
        ←(PAT)←[BELONG]→(RCPT)→[John].
```

To differentiate sentences 3.1 and 3.2, we should introduce a PAST relation in the conceptual graph which defines the λ-abstraction. But that is not really consistent with the fact that l abstractions are mainly used for defining concepts and that definitions should be time independent.

In order to relate two propositions, we use temporal connectives such as "when", "while", "before" etc. Sowa (1988) proposed to express in conceptual graphs such connectives by intersentential relations (BEFORE, AFTER). Sometimes, the use of a temporal connective induces a change in the tense and/or the mode of the verb of the second sentence. Such a subtlety is difficult to express, using conceptual graphs. For instance consider the following sentences and the associated conceptual graphs: *"John bought an apple and came to school"* (*"John acheta une pomme et vint à l'école"*) (sent. 4.1):

```
CG 4.1: (PAST)→[[John]←(AGNT)←[BUY]→(OBJ)→ [APPLE]]
        →(AND)→[[John]←(AGNT)← [COME]→(DEST)→[SCHOOL]]←(PAST)
```

and *"John bought an apple before coming to school"* (*"John acheta une pomme avant de venir à l'école"*)(sent. 4.2):

```
CG 4.2: (PAST)→[[John]←(AGNT)←[BUY]→(OBJ)→[APPLE]]→(BFOR)→
        [[John]←(AGNT)←[COME]→(DEST)→[SCHOOL]]←(PROG).
```

In CG 4.2 we have chosen to express the temporal relations PAST and PROGressive) to reflect the tenses required by the use of the conjunction "before". But semantically both actions of buying an apple and coming to school are occurring in the past. Hence, for expressing temporal knowledge, we need a formalism which is independent of the surface form of sentences which expresses this knowledge.

Sowa never mentioned any process which would enable us to check the coherence of temporal knowledge in conceptual graphs. Such a process is an important one for a NL generation system since it is necessary to verify that the input knowledge structures are coherent before trying to generate sentences.

19.3 FOUNDATIONS OF OUR MODEL

19.3.1 Introduction

In the preceding section we have evoked some of the problems we have encountered when we tried to express temporal knowledge, using conceptual graphs. In order to solve these problems we propose to extend the conceptual graph approach along the following guidelines.

- We need a formalism which allows us to express concepts and conceptual relations related to points in time as well as time intervals.

- This formalism must provide means to indicate time references with respect to "an absolute physical time", as well as time references relatively to the speaker's time.

- Within this formalism some constructs must enable us to express from a semantic point of view, tenses as well as aspectual properties of verbs.

- In NL some temporal structures provide intersentential relationships which support the discourse coherence. The required formalism must provide constructs which enable us to interpret combinations of verb tenses, temporal adverbs and connectives.

19.3.2 Separating temporal and non-temporal knowledge in the conceptual graph approach

In (Moulin, 1987) we suggested the idea of separating the temporal structures from non-temporal knowledge which are currently merged in Sowa's approach. In our model we use conceptual graphs for describing the non-temporal knowledge structures which are called "states". For instance

$$[\text{STATE}: \ [\text{John}] \ \leftarrow (\text{AGNT}) \leftarrow [\text{EAT}] \rightarrow (\text{OBJ}) \rightarrow [\text{APPLE}]].$$

Temporal knowledge is expressed by a temporal label which is related to a state by a conceptual relation that we will call temporarily "period" (PER). A temporal label is specified by a triplet *[unit, lwr-bnd, upp-bnd]*, where unit indicates the precision of the observations (second, minute, hour, day etc.), the lower-bound *lwr-bnd* corresponds to the point in time when the state was first observed, the upper-bound *upp-bnd* corresponds to the point in time when the state was last observed. The lower and upper bounds can be either instantiated if the speaker knows their values, or set as variables if the values are unknown. In order to specify intervals comprising a fixed duration, we can also assign to these bounds expressions in the form $(x \pm k)$, where x is variable and k a constant.

Using temporal labels we can specify information about points in time as well as time intervals. We can define relations between temporal labels similar to the relations that Allen introduced between intervals (before, equal, meets, overlaps, during, starts, finishes) (Allen, 1983).

For instance *"John buys an apple before going to school"* is expressed in our model by:

$$[\text{STATE}: [\text{John}] \leftarrow (\text{AGNT}) \leftarrow [\text{BUY}] \rightarrow (\text{OBJ}) \rightarrow [\text{APPLE}]] \rightarrow (\text{PER}) \rightarrow [\text{u1},\text{b1},\text{b2}]$$

$$[\text{STATE}: [\text{John}] \leftarrow (\text{AGNT}) \leftarrow [\text{GO}] \rightarrow (\text{DEST}) \rightarrow [\text{SCHOOL}]] \rightarrow (\text{PER}) \rightarrow [\text{u1},\text{b3},\text{b4}]$$

$$[\text{u1},\text{b1},\text{b2}] \rightarrow (\text{BFOR}) \rightarrow [\text{u1},\text{b3},\text{b4}].$$

19.3.3 Semantic interpretation of verb tenses

Let us remark that in the preceding representation we don't have any indication related to verb tenses. In order to specify verb tenses, we use an approach which was proposed by Reichenbach (1947). He localized on a time axis the point of speech (S), the point of reference (R) and the point of event (E) and gave a semantic interpretation of English tenses:

S is the time at which the statement is produced (time of locutor);
E is the time at which occurred the event represented by the statement;
R is the time of the temporal reference according to which are situated the locutor and the event.

The markers E, R, S have different relative positions on a temporal axis according to the verb tense:

```
I saw John          E,R              S
                    _____ > t

I have seen John    E                R,S
                    _____ > t

I will see John     S                E,R
                    _____ > t
```

Using the concomitance relation (noted ",") and the precedence relation (noted "_") between these markers, we have the following representations for verb tenses:

Perfect	$(E, R \_ S)$	*Je vis* (I saw)
Present perfect	$(E \_ R, S)$	*J'ai vu* (I have seen)
Pluperfect	$(E \_ R \_ S)$	*J'avais vu* (I had been seeing)
Present	(E, R, S)	*Je vois* (I see)
Future	$(S \_ R, E)$	*Je verrai* (I will see)
Future perfect	$(S \_ E \_ R)$	*J'aurai vu* (I will have seen)

This model bears some limitations. With regards to the relations introduced by Reichenbach, the markers seem to correspond to points in time. They cannot be used to describe aspectual properties of sentences such as the distinction between the perfective aspect (for instance "I saw") and the imperfective aspect (for instance "I was seeing").

Dorfmüller-Karpusa (1988) extended this approach by considering the three temporal markers as time intervals. She indicates: "The economy of language entails a large temporal indeterminacy, especially if we take in account the fact that states of affairs occupy intervals on the time axis and not points".. "The difference between the perfective and the imperfective aspects is often considered as follows: in the prefective aspect the state of affairs is felt as an inseparable whole without considering its different phases. On the other hand, a state of affairs is described in an imperfective aspect if the producer takes into account its internal structure. Temporal as well as aspectual relations are producer-dependent and, consequently, subjective, the degree of subjectivity being, however, different. Whereas the temporal relations are defined by the point of speech, the aspectual relations are defined by the point of reference, the latter being dependent upon the producer's attitude towards the state of affairs he describes".

For instance consider the following sentences and the corresponding positions of temporal markers $S, E = [ei, es]$ and $R = [ri, rs]$

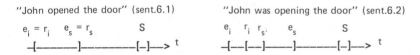

Both sentences correspond to past events (E is anterior to S). In the perfective case (sent 6.1), the event E is considered as a whole, and we can consider that the reference interval R coincides with it (according to Reichenbach's model). To represent the imperfective case, the reference interval R must be included in the event interval E.

Reichenbach's model was initially applied at the sentence level. It can also be extended to describe the temporal and aspectual structure of a text as a whole. Dorfmüller-Karpusa (1988) indicates: "In the case of a text, we have to abandon the principle of permanence of the reference point. It appears that in a text we are faced with a complex nexus of described states of affairs in such a way that the same state of affairs may represent a point of event and a point of reference for other states of affairs".

Borillo *et al.* (1988) extended Reichenbach's approach in a similar way: they represented the temporal markers as time intervals and used Allen's temporal logic to reason on their relationships. These authors demonstrated that their approach can be used to represent verb tenses at the indicative mode, as well as temporal adverbs ("yesterday", "today", "tomorrow") and temporal conjunctions ("when", "while" etc.). Algorithms can be implemented in order to check automatically the proper use of tenses, temporal adverbs and conjunctions in sentences. Hence we have a way for solving the problem of tense concordance.

19.4   DIFFERENTIATING TEMPORAL AND NON-TEMPORAL KNOWLEDGE

In our model the temporal markers S, E and R correspond to the temporal labels $[u_1, s_i, s_s]$, $[u_1, e_i, e_s]$ and $[u_1, r_i, r_s]$. The markers S, E and R are related to the non-temporal part of the conceptual graph (denoted "state") respectively by the conceptual relations MRK-S, MRK-E and MRK-R. MRK-E replaces the PER relation we introduced in section 19.3.2. We can relate the temporal markers using our relations on temporal labels, which are compatible with Borillo's approach. It is worth remarking that these markers enable us to introduce pragmatic knowledge in the model since we take into account the context in which sentences are formulated.

For instance Fig. 19.1 represents the situation associated with the sentence "*Mary called John before the storm arrived*". Note that the units and bounds of the temporal labels are undefined and represented in the graph by variables.

The global situation (STATE G) corresponds to the locutor's perspective (associated with marker $S1 = (u_1, s_1, s_2)$ which is the same marker for both situations included in the . The global situation: "*Mary called John" (STATE1)* and "*the storm arrived" (STATE 2). STATE 1* and *STATE 2* are associated respectively with markers $E1 = (u_1, e_1, e_2)$, $R1 = (u_1, r_1, r_2)$ and $E3 = (u_1, e_3, e_4)$, $R3 = (u_1, r_3, r_4)$. The relation $[E1] \rightarrow (BEFORE) \rightarrow [E3]$ expresses the precedence order existing between the two situations.

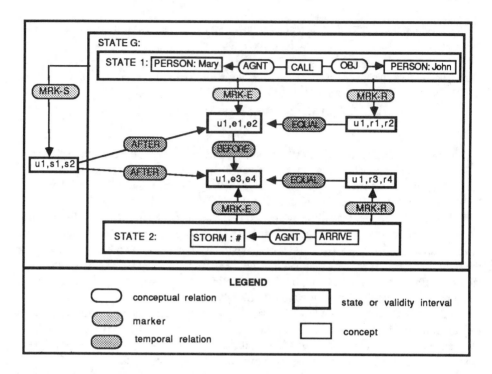

Fig.1 Representation of *"Mary called John before the storm arrived"*.

19.5   CONCLUSION

We have evoked some difficulties encountered when we represent temporal knowledge using the conceptual graph theory, mainly because of the necessity of considering time intervals as well as points in time, and because monadic relations such as PAST and FUTURE don't convey enough information for generating properly verb tenses in sentences.

We have proposed to distinguish non-temporal knowledge from temporal knowledge in conceptual graphs. We specify temporal knowledge by means of time intervals. We use temporal markers in order to indicate the relative positions of the locutor's time, reference time and the event time. These markers are used to semantically specify tenses and the aspectual properties of verbs.

Our approach may seem complex, but the proposed model can be considered as a refinement of Sowa's conceptual graphs and it can be used only when we need a precise specification of temporal knowledge for various purposes. In a forthcoming paper we will show how the constructs using temporal markers can be considered as precise definitions of temporal conceptual relations such as PTIM, DUR, PER, in conjunction with monadic tense relations PRESENT, PAST, FUTURE.

Acknowledgements

This research is supported by the Natural Sciences and Engineering Research Council of Canada, grant 5518.

BIBLIOGRAPHY

Allen J. F. (1983), "Maintaining Knowledge about Temporal Intervals", Communications of the ACM, vol 26 n 11.

Borillo A. (1988) et Borillo M., Bras M., *Une approche cognitive du raisonnement temporel*, extrait des "Actes des journés nationales en intelligence artificielle", édité par Teknea, Toulouse, mars 1988.

Comrie B. (1985), *Tense, Aspects*, 2 books published by Cambridge University Press.

Cote D. (1990) and Moulin B., "Refining Sowa's conceptual graph theory for text generation", in Proc. of the Third International Conference on Industrial and Engineering Applications of Artificial Intelligence and Expert Systems, Charleston SC, July 1990.

Danlos (1985) Danlos, L., *Un survol des recherches en génération automatique, dans la Revue québécoise de linguistique*, vol. 14, no. 2, Université du Québec à Montréal.

Dorfmüller-Karpusa K. (1988), "Temporal and aspectual relations as text-constitutive elements2, in *Text and Discourse Constitution*, J. S. Petöfi editor, Walter de Gruyter Publishers.

Fillmore C. H. (1968), "The case for case", in (eds) Bach and Harms, *Universals in linguistic Theory*, Holt, Rinehart and Winston, New York.

Lizotte M. (1989a) and Moulin B., "A Temporal Planner for Modelling Autonomous Agents", in Proc. of the European Workshop on Modeling Autonomous Agents in a Multi-Agent World, London, August 1989.

Lizotte M. (1989b) and Moulin B., "SAIRVO : A Planning System which Implements the Actem Concept", to appear in the journal Knowledge-Based Systems, vol 2 no. 4 pp. 210-218.

McDonald D.D. (1987), "Natural-language generation", in *Encyclopedia of Artificial Intelligence* (Vol. 1), Stuart C. Shapiro editor, Wiley & Sons, p.642-655.

McKeown K.R. (1985), *Text generation: Using discourse strategies and focus constraints to generate natural language text*, Cambridge University Press.

McKeown K.R. (1986), "Language Generation: Applications, Issues, and Approaches", in Proc. of the IEEE, vol. 74, no. 7, pp 961-968.

Moulin B. (1987), *Le concept d'actem pour la gestion de scénes*, dans les actes du colloque GIRICO'87, L'intelligence artificielle au service des organisations, Montréal.

Reichembach H. (1947), *Elements of Symbolic Logic*, McMillan, New-York.

Sowa, J.F. (1984) *Conceptual Structures: Information Processing in Mind and Machine*, Addison Wesley, Reading, 1984.

Sowa J.F. (1987), "There's more to logic than the predicate calculus", in Proc. of the US-Japan AI Symposium, J. Carbonell and K. Fucchi editors, Tokyo.

Sowa J.F. (1988), "Conceptual Graph Notation", in the Proc. of the third annual workshop on Conceptual Graphs, (ed) J. Esch, St. Paul Minnesota, USA.

Velardi P. (1988) and Pazienza M.T., De' Giovanetti M., "Conceptual graphs for the analysis and generation of sentences", in IBM journal for Research and Development, vol. 32 no. 2, pp 251-267.

20

Analysing Multiple Views of Software Requirements

Harry S. Delugach
Computer Science Department,
The University of Alabama in Huntsville
Huntsville, AL 35899 USA

ABSTRACT

This chapter describes an application of conceptual graphs to support software requirements development – the process of determining what software needs exist and how those needs will be filled. As a human knowledge- and experience-based activity, requirements development is an appropriate domain for applying formal models of cognitive structures. This chapter introduces the following contributions to the theory and practice in conceptual graphs:

a. the ability to represent a conceptual graph that changes over time, using a new class of node called a demon node;

b. a structure to partially manipulate informal (external) information (i.e., information not expressed in conceptual graphs), by introducing a special referent form called a private referent;

c. the ability to obtain a conceptual graph representation from a requirements specification written in one of several common notations;

d. a framework using conceptual graphs in the analysis of software requirements that effectively captures the overlap between multiple views.

20.1 INTRODUCTION

The chapter sections are organized as follows: section 20.2 discusses the general problem of software requirements, for those readers unfamiliar with this aspect of software development. Section 20.3 describes two extensions to conceptual graphs that are desirable for capturing requirements. Section 20.4 explains how conceptual graphs (as extended) are used to capture requirements. Section 20.5 outlines the framework in which multiple views are analyzed. Section 20.6 shows some partial results for an example set of requirements. Section 20.7 discusses some issues involved when using conceptual graphs in requirements.

20.2   SOFTWARE REQUIREMENTS VIEWS

Software requirements development is the process of determining what the purpose of a proposed software system is. Large-scale software development must satisfy many people and organizations, with differing viewpoints regarding a proposed software system. While many useful requirements development methods have been proposed, they are limited to a particular view, usually the view of the software developer (Alford, 1977), (Alford, 1985), (Teichroew, 1977), (Yourdon, 1979), (Ross,1977), (Ross, 1985), (Zave, 1982), who must describe all of the requirements using a single notation. Some current methods address the needs of other views, such as an end-user (Wasserman, 1982) or customer (Wartik, 1983). The latter method also introduces the idea of multiple views in that both a customer and designer's views are considered.

Since organizations and people already have a large investment in current methods (both in their monetary support for tools, and in their understanding of requirements relative to their methods), we would like to incorporate the strengths of their current methods, while at the same time overcoming their limitations.

In this chapter, we describe techniques whereby existing requirements are translated into conceptual graphs, so that several views are represented. In addition, some assumptions underlying each participant's view are expressed in graph form, so that participants' cognitive knowledge is (at least partially) captured for analysis. The resulting set of conceptual graphs can then be analyzed in several ways, such as determining a least common generalization, or performing a join such that a single set of requirements can be obtained.

20.2.1   Originating Requirements

Participants may already understand one or more current requirements paradigms. They need not abandon their understanding of the paradigms in order to benefit from using multiple views. Except for the requirements analyst, no one else needs to learn conceptual graphs; each participant starts by expressing his requirements in a language he chooses. Originating requirements are then translated into conceptual graphs for further analysis.

A participant expresses requirements for a target system in a language (notation) of his choosing. Once expressed, his set of requirements is called a requirements specification (or R-Spec). Each R-Spec is therefore identified by (1) a participant's name, (2) a notation, and (3) a target system. An R-Spec is shown in a private referent (see below) whose formal concept is given as;

$$[\_VP \; *p \; USING \; *n \; SYS \; *s \; R\text{-}Spec\_]$$

where $*p$ is the participant, $*n$ is the notation, and $*s$ is the target system. In this chapter, for illustration purposes, we will consider requirements for a patient-monitoring system where each patient is connected to sensors that record his vital signs. When a reading is out of range, an alarm sounds at the nurse's station.

Suppose a customer uses an entity-relationship-attribute diagram to express his requirements. Fig. 20.1 is an R-Spec of the patient-monitoring system requirements from a customer's point of view, using an entity-relationship diagram. Later, Fig. 20.1 will be translated into conceptual graphs.

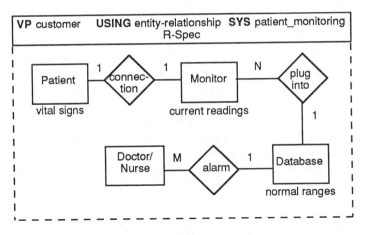

Fig. 20.1

20.2.2   Pre-Existing Assumptions

An important part of multiple-viewed analysis is the use of pre-existing assumptions. These assumptions underlie a participant's R-Spec, yet are too often left implicit during development. For example, a doctor or nurse will assume a patient's vital signs to be a particular set of measurements – temperature, pulse, respiration, and blood pressure. Since using multiple views necessarily involves information outside any one self-contained view, pre-existing assumptions contain requirements information that might not otherwise be available.

This chapter uses such assumptions (expressed as conceptual graphs) to constrain the graphs that represent requirements. Due to the nature of requirements as a people-centered activity, we must acquire these assumptions from human participants directly (i.e., manually). The requirements analyst's task is to discover these assumptions and write down their conceptual graph representations.

Each person involved in developing software requirements is called a participant. Typical participants include a customer, designer, end-user, or tester. One special participant – the requirements analyst, or simply analyst – has the task of coordinating the collection of participants' views and making some judgments about the requirements.

A view is defined as one participant's set of requirements, as well as all his underlying assumptions. Since it is impossible to capture every single assumption held by a participant, this definition tells us that our representation of a view will necessarily be incomplete. Even if we could capture a complete view, we would still not have captured all relevant requirements because there are additional participants with other views to consider, as pointed out in (Wartik, 1983), (Wood-Harper, 1985), (Finkelstein, 1989), and (Werkman, 1989).

Any single view will fail to capture the complete set of requirements. Participants have different experience and vocabulary. They need some way to judge the overlap between their views. The purpose of this methodology is to provide a framework to help people explore the consequences and implications of applying such judgments. Some human intervention is required during analysis; after all, it is human beings' requirements that are being sought.

20.3   EXTENSIONS TO CONCEPTUAL GRAPHS

Conceptual graphs have the power to express conceptual knowledge about many kinds of requirements; however, since conceptual graphs are based on first-order logic, there are well-known limitations that must be overcome before we can use them for realistic requirements.

Some cognitive structures are not adequately captured by Sowa's notation (Sowa, 1984) with only concepts, relations, and actors. Several variations have been proposed (Gardiner, 1989) that represent some structures, such as logical implication and sets, more naturally. In many cases, the variations are shorthands for equivalent (but less elegant) representations in the standard notation.

20.3.1   Demon: A Node To Represent Temporal Logic

Conceptual graphs' most important limitation with respect to requirements is the lack of explicit representation for temporal knowledge. Although first-order logic with functions is useful for capturing many requirements, there are additional requirements that reflect temporal logic. We therefore need a way to represent conceptual graphs that exist only for a limited period of time. In this chapter, a new conceptual graph node called a demon is introduced to express temporal knowledge. Further discussion of demons can be found in Delugach (1991a).

Several schemes have been proposed to handle temporal information in conceptual graphs, by identifying certain relations, such as (before), (after), (precedes), etc., whose definitions are carefully coordinated with one another. Recent work has addressed this problem (Esch, 1990), (Moulin, 1990). I would like to propose a different scheme that involves defining a new kind of node to conceptual graphs, in addition to concepts, relations and actors.

Some useful notions, such as state transition diagrams (Aho, 1972), require a dynamic structure. A new fourth class of node is needed that not only allows alteration of referents, as performed by actors, but also altering the arrangement of concepts over time as well.

The new class of node is called a *demon* in this chapter. Its syntax is similar to an actor's, except that it is enclosed in double angle brackets, as <<transition>> in the linear form, and in the display form as a double diamond.

A demon possesses the semantics of an actor node with respect to output concepts' referents, with the additional semantics that a demon actually creates its output concepts (i.e., causes them to come into existence) and then erases its input concepts (retracts them from existence). It therefore represents changes to the arrangement of concepts, etc., on the sheet of assertion.

A demon's input links must all be marked before the demon fires, just as an actor fires. By extension, the creation of a concept can mean the creation of an entire graph. Likewise destruction or retraction can involve entire graphs. What does it mean to create a concept box? Since a concept box represents an existential assertion, creating a concept box on the sheet of assertion is equivalent to asserting a new proposition. Erasure of a concept is the equivalent of retracting its asserted proposition – i.e., saying, "This fact (or context) is no longer known to be true." The added semantics allow the expression of dynamic logic, whereby prior truths may be subsequently falsified and new truths introduced. We can thereby express notions of nonmonotonic logic, such as discussed in (Turner, 1984).

Two primitive demons are proposed. An initiator demon <<T>>, possessing only output links, is presumed to fire automatically upon writing down a graph. Therefore all of its output concepts are immediately asserted. A terminator demon <<◇>> possesses only input links; its meaning is that it erases its input concepts (retracts them). As yet, it has no special semantics.

Existing conceptual graph semantics are easily extended for this purpose. A graph containing no demons is assumed to have an initiator demon whose output arcs are connected to every node in the graph. Thus the entire graph is asserted to be true at one time, in the normal sense of conceptual graphs. For example, consider the graph in Fig. 20.2 (a):

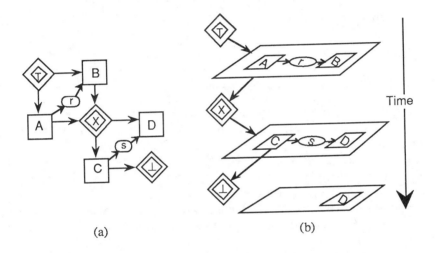

(a)   (b)

Fig. 20.2

Fig. 20.2 (a) can be envisioned as representing a series of different conceptual structures varying over time as shown in Fig. 20.2 (b), with each plane representing the arrangement at a given time.

Conceptual graphs with actors are comparable to static allocation in a conventional programming language. Adding the demon's semantics allows one to represent dynamic allocation, whereby structures may come into being and later pass from existence. Demons are used in this chapter to capture state transition semantics.

Although not considered here, some interesting issues arise regarding demons. An even more powerful demon might be able to change not only referents and arrangements, but also the type hierarchy as well. Further study is needed in these areas. This chapter employs demons primarily to simplify the identification of concepts in state transition diagrams.

20.3.2 Private Referent

As others have noted in software development (Agresti, 1987), (Zave, 1989), mental models help us identify new things that fit within our model, but at the same time, those mental models sometimes hinder us from identifying things outside our model.

Even the conceptual graph notation – our mental model for representing other mental models – falls prey to this effect. We must be able to represent some knowledge in the world that is outside of a conceptual graph. This information is shown by a structure we call a private referent – an informal referent contained in a formal concept, but considered an uninterpreted (and un-alterable) object. The concept may have one formal referent as its name.

In the display form, a private referent is shown inside a dashed bucket below a formal concept box, as in Fig. 20.3. In the linear form, only its associated type and name are shown within underline-brackets as: [_ Q: n _]; private referents may be difficult to show in linear form, since they do not have to be text.

(a)   (b)

Fig. 20.3

The meaning of Fig. 20.3 (a) is that the solid box [Q: n] is treated as a normal conceptual graph concept, with type Q and name n. The attached private referent "r" is something not represented by conceptual graphs. For example, Fig. 20.3 (b) represents the concept [PERSON: *p] with an attached private referent (the little drawing of a person). Note that *p is a formal ("public") referent, able to be changed by normal conceptual graph operations, e.g. an actor's computation.

A private referent cannot be changed, either through generalization, specialization, or the computation of an actor. It is simply carried along with the concept (and its formal referent if present).

Private referents are used in this chapter to handle requirements specifications that are not in conceptual graph form, so that we can still include them in analysis. Private referents can help us refine external information, so that informal knowledge can later be shown (at least partially) in formal conceptual graph notation.

20.4   REQUIREMENTS VIEWS IN CONCEPTUAL GRAPH FORM

Analyzing multiple views of requirements begins by translating each participant's originating requirements (R-Spec) into conceptual graph form (an R-Spec-Graph). Our purpose will be to combine the R-Spec-Graphs in order to find their common elements.

A translation scheme is an algorithm that translates a participant's requirements (R-Spec) into a conceptual graph, called a requirements specification graph (or R-Spec-Graph) which is a trial graph for validating multiple-viewed requirements. A translation scheme is specific to a particular notation.

An R-Spec-Graph will be shown as:

$[VP *p \ USING *n \ SYS *s \ R\text{-}Spec\text{-}Graph]$

VP indicates the viewer-participant's identity. $USING$ denotes the language (or notation) that is used. SYS denotes the name of the system that all participants are presumed to be

describing. These abbreviations can also be used to denote part of a graph, e.g., [VP] designer [USING] dataflow [SYS] patient-monitoring
[PATIENT] means a patient in the designer's view of a patient-monitoring system using dataflow diagrams. Later, pre-existing assumptions will be used to further constrain the R-Spec-Graph.

The following briefly summarizes how an R-Spec in each of three models is translated into conceptual graph form as an R-Spec-Graph. Algorithms, additional details and other models, are found in Delugach (1991b).

20.4.1   Translating Entity-Relationship Diagrams

Entity-relationship-attribute (ER) diagrams (Chen, 1976) consist of entities (shown by boxes), each with zero or more associated attributes, where an entity is connected to one or more other entities by a relation (shown by a diamond). Others have already studied this model (Muehlbacher, 1989, 1990), (Gray, 1991). Since this paradigm is similar to conceptual graphs, we adopt these rules for translating its structure:

- An ER entity E becomes a conceptual graph concept [ENTITY: E];

- An ER attribute A associated with entity E becomes the sub-graph
  [E] → (attribute) → [A];

- An ER relation r becomes a conceptual graph relation (r).

Additional rules determine the cardinality of each referent, based on the cardinality of the original ER relation. Using the R-Spec shown in Fig. 20.1 above, we obtain the R-Spec-Graph in Fig. 20.4:

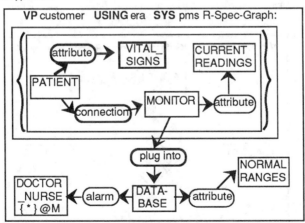

PATIENT < ENTITY.   NORMAL_RANGES < ATTRIBUTE.
MONITOR < ENTITY.   VITAL_SIGNS < ATTRIBUTE.
DATABASE < ENTITY.   CURRENT_READINGS <
DOCTOR_NURSE <ENTITY.   ATTRIBUTE.

Fig. 20.4

20.4.2   Translating Data Flow Diagrams

A data flow diagram (Yourdon, 1979) consists of process nodes connected by labeled directed arrows indicating the flow of data (Sowa, 1984). Suppose a data base designer uses data flow diagrams to express his requirements. An example data flow R-Spec is shown in Fig. 20.5.

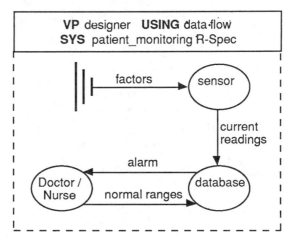

Fig. 20.5

Our structural translation rules are summarized as follows:

- A data flow process P becomes a conceptual graph actor $<P>$;

- A data flow arc from process A to B with label L becomes a conceptual graph concept of type $[L]$ linked to actor $<B>$ and from actor $<A>$.

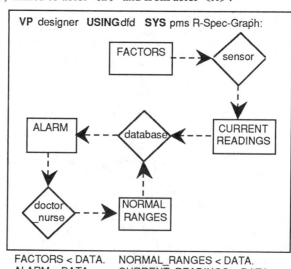

Fig. 20.6

Additional rules handle sources and sinks. Fig. 20.6 shows the translated R-Spec as an R-Spec-Graph.

Since this graph contains no relations, we will use a special dependency rule that relates actors to corresponding concepts.

20.4.3   Translating State Transition Diagrams

State transition diagrams consist of a set of states, input events, output events, a start state and a set of final states (Aho, 1972). A state transition function determines a new state and output event for every possible current state and input event. Suppose an end-user (doctor or nurse) uses state transition diagrams to express his requirements. Fig. 20.7 shows an example state transition R-Spec:

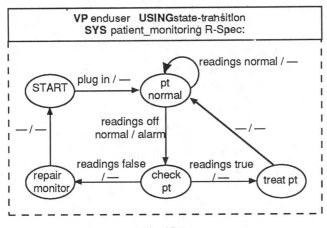

Fig. 20.7

Using our new demon node, our structural rules are as follows:

- A state S becomes a conceptual graph concept [S]. S<STATE is added to the type hierarchy;

- An input or output event J becomes a conceptual graph concept [J].J<EVENT is added to the type hierarchy;

- A final state S is denoted by attaching the monadic relation (final) as:
  (final) $\longrightarrow$ [S];

- A transition from state S with input J to state T with output K becomes a demon with links to [T] and [K], and with links from [S] and [J]. Add K < EVENT and T < STATE to the type hierarchy.

The translated R-Spec-Graph is shown in Fig. 20.8:

The transition demon's semantics (see section 20.3 above) ensure that an old state is retracted when a new state comes into existence. Once separate R-Spec-Graphs have been obtained, we will no longer refer to the originating requirements (R-Specs); instead, we use their R-Spec-Graphs.

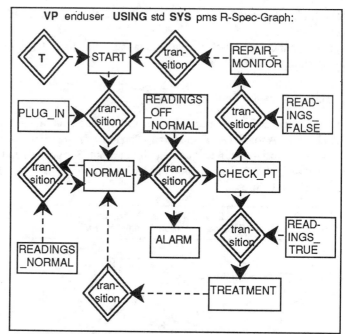

PLUG_IN < EVENT.   READINGS_NORMAL < EVENT.
ALARM < EVENT   READINGS_FALSE < EVENT.
START < STATE.   READINGS_OFF_NORMAL< EVENT.
NORMAL < STATE.   READINGS_TRUE < EVENT.
CHECK_PT < STATE.   REPAIR_MONITOR < STATE.
TREATMENT < STATE.

Fig. 20.8

20.4.4   Assumption Graphs

One problem with any specification is that there are implicit underlying assumptions which affect its meaning. Naturally we want to capture such assumptions in conceptual graph form, called an A-Graph. Some examples of underlying assumptions are:

1. Customer assumes that when an alarm sounds, doctors and nurses start treatment after a certain period of response time;

2. Designer assumes database is accessed through a query, process or response cycle;

3. Doctor/nurse assumes that current readings are either within range or out of range.

Assumption 1 is expressed the conceptual graph in Fig. 20.9. Assumption 2 is partly expressed by the conceptual graph shown in Fig. 20.10. Assumption 3 is expressed by the graph in Fig. 20.11.

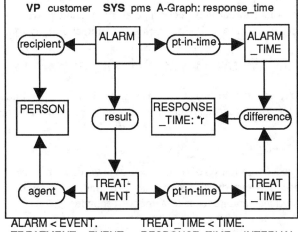

ALARM < EVENT.   TREAT_TIME < TIME.
TREATMENT < EVENT.   RESPONSE_TIME < INTERVAL.
ALARM_TIME < TIME.   PERSON < ENTITY.

Fig. 20.9

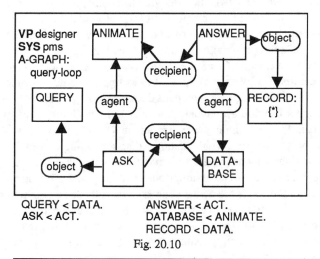

QUERY < DATA.   ANSWER < ACT.
ASK < ACT.   DATABASE < ANIMATE.
                             RECORD < DATA.

Fig. 20.10

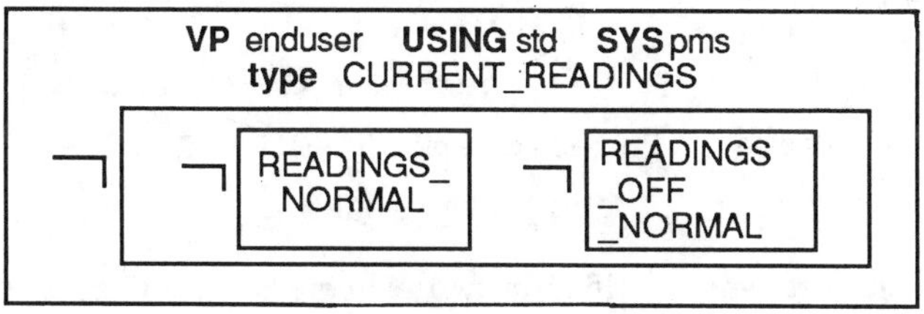

VP enduser **USING** std **SYS** pms
type CURRENT_READINGS

┐   ┐ READINGS_   ┐ READINGS
        NORMAL   _OFF
                           _NORMAL

Fig. 20.11

If these example assumptions seem simple or obvious, note that that our biggest problem with implicit assumptions is not their complexity – it is that they are hidden. Even simple assumptions, when left implicit, may not be known by all participants.

The process of applying an assumption may just mean asserting it onto the sheet of assertion. Some assumptions are thus "thrown into the pot," so to speak; once identified, they act as definitions for that view's conceptual graph context. More often, however, we wish to join an assumption to an R-Spec-Graph, or another assumption in a different view.

20.5   ANALYZING MULTIPLE VIEWS OF REQUIREMENTS

Our next step is to identify information that appears in more than one view. We use two primitive notions – counterpart and dependency – on which to base our analysis.

20.5.1   Counterparts Between Views

In order to analyze a combination of requirements views, there must be at least one common point of reference between them. We discuss two kinds of common points: concept-to-concept correspondence and concept-to-actor correspondence.

Concept-to-Concept Counterparts

A useful point of reference is to consider individuals in common between two or more R-Spec-Graphs. We call any two such individuals counterparts to each other, in that they represent the same real-world (or imagined-world) individual. In this chapter, a counterpart is restricted to being either a concept box in one or more views, or an actor-concept pair. A counterpart is a reflexive, symmetric, and transitive relation.

Counterparts are a reasonable starting point because two participants might see the same individual as members of different classes. For example a family member might see John as the concept [FATHER:John] where his doctor might see him as [PATIENT:John]. Conceptual graphs provide a convenient way of relating both concepts through a type hierarchy – their least common generalization is [PERSON:John]. A least common generalization of [T:John] would indicate that something named John exists in both views. That fact alone may not be useful in itself, but it may lead the analyst to gather more information (e.g. seek additional assumptions or refine one's originating requirements) to determine whether the Johns are actual counterparts. If the least common generalization is just [T], i.e. [T:*], however, we cannot say they are counterparts.

A generic concept stands for some arbitrary individual belonging to a certain class; in the absence of a specific referent, assume "*". For example, in the graphs above, there are three counterpart-pairs:

```
[ VP customer VP designer NORMAL_RANGES:  *  ]
[ VP customer VP designer CURRENT_READINGS:  *  ]
[ VP designer VP end-user ALARM :  *  ]
```

Once counterparts are identified in two or more R-Spec-Graphs, the graphs can be joined around the counterparts into a single graph, effectively combining multiple sets of requirements into one. The resulting combined graph can then be analyzed according to its own internal consistency, as well as having pre-existing assumptions (possibly from other multiple views) applied to it.

In Fig. 20.9, alarm is shown as an individual, whereas our counterpart is

```
[ VP designer VP end-user  ALARM ]
```

with its type defined as ALARM < EVENT.

Our definition of a counterpart allows the analyst to decide that [VP customer EVENT: alarm] is a counterpart to the already-identified counterparts, since alarm is an individual's name in VP customer. Thus we have added to the meaning of alarm by determining its counterpart in all three views:

> [VP customer VP designer VP end-user EVENT: alarm]

While some counterparts can be identified by examining results of an automatic generalization (given an appropriate type hierarchy), some counterparts cannot. Consider the case where the same individual may have different names in different views. An automated method must examine every possible concept-concept pair to determine some correspondence between them. As an example, one participant may call an analog device a "sensor", while the other calls it a "monitor". One R-Spec-Graph might contain

> [SENSOR] → (connection) → [PATIENT]

while the other might contain

> [MONITOR] → (connection) → [PATIENT]

If [PATIENT] were already identified as a counterpart, we would have evidence for establishing [SENSOR] and [MONITOR] as a counterpart, but since in this case their least common generalization is [T], only human participants can actually decide.

Two individuals, each in different views, may have the same name, but are not the same individual. An automatic method may identify an inconsistency – i.e., some fact about one that is not known to be true about the other – but human intervention must decide whether the inconsistency really exists or is simply a feature of the counterparts being in different views. For example, if the following two relations occurred in two different R-Spec-Graphs,

> [MONITOR] ⟶ (connection) ⟶ [DATABASE]
> [MONITOR] ⟶ (connection) ⟶ [PATIENT]

the two monitor definitions would be inconsistent (see below), since the minimal supertype of DATABASE and PATIENT is just "T". We discuss this situation below when we consider issues of consistency among views.

20.5.2 Dependency

A dependency between views is when there is a concept in one view whose existence is dependent upon a counterpart in another view. Dependency is intended in the sense of Schank's conceptual dependency, e.g., in Schank (1975), where the existence of one concept implies the existence of another. Dependency is thus reflexive and transitive, but it is not symmetric; i.e., if A depends on B, B will not in general depend on A.

Rules for identifying dependency among counterparts may involve information external to a participant's model, but the knowledge may be nonetheless useful in increasing understanding. Some examples of dependency rules are:

1. The output of a process depends upon its input.

2. In an ER diagram, an attribute depends upon the entity possessing it.

3. An actor C originating from a data flow diagram depends upon an entity C originating from an ER diagram, if such an entity exists.

The first rule is implemented by actors, in that an actor's output referents depend upon the result of computation using its input referents. The second rule is enforced by the links' direction in the relation (attribute). The third rule is implemented by the concept-actor rule (see section 20.4 above).

Dependency is shown by a double arrow as in $[A] \Rightarrow [B]$ meaning "B depends upon A". A relation's dependency may be kept as part of its definition; e.g., the definition of (attribute):

```
relation attribute is
          [ ENTITY: *ent ]  →  (attribute)  →  [ ATTRIBUTE:
     *att ];
                    *ent ⇒ *att.
```

20.5.3   Consistency

We can identify three kinds of consistency to be determined for multiple viewed requirements graphs, called strong consistency, weak consistency and strong inconsistency, which are explained below.

Strong Consistency A strong consistency between counterparts is where a counterpart means the same thing in both views. We consider a strong consistency as a fact about one view that is provable by facts in another view. This amounts to having a concept in one view possessing the same links and relations as its counterpart in another view.

Weak Consistency A weak consistency between views is where a counterpart means different things (i.e., has different relations and is connected to different concept types) in different views. Inconsistency is defined as where some fact about one counterpart in one view cannot be proven or disproven by facts in another view.

Weak consistency does not necessarily indicate a fault in the requirements. It may merely reflect the incompleteness or limitations of one view relative to the others. For example, if [PATIENT] is a counterpart, one view might contain:

```
     [ VP A PATIENT ]  →  (attribute)  →  [ VITAL_SIGNS ]
```

whereas another view might contain:

```
     [ VP B PATIENT ]  →  (connection)  →  [ SENSOR ]
```

These two graphs provide two orthogonal constraints on [PATIENT] : neither one is provable from the other, nor can one be disproven by the other.

Strong Inconsistency (Conflict) A conflict between views is a strong inconsistency, where a counterpart in one view is incompatible with constraints in another view. Conflict is defined as where some fact about one counterpart in one view can be proven false in another view. For example, if [VP A PERSON: p] and [VP C EVENT: p] both occur, then at least one of them must be incorrect, since their least common generalization is the type "T".

Identifying conflicts is an important part of understanding requirements. Once conflict are identified, however, participants may use that knowledge in manual or heuristic ways in order to make appropriate changes to their originating requirements.

20.5.4   Completeness

Completeness is easier to understand if we consider its inverse: incompleteness. Two forms of incompleteness may be discussed. One form of incompleteness results when existing requirements lack features than can be inferred from other existing features or pre-existing assumptions. Another form of incompleteness results from a participant failing to express one or more of his needs.

Our previous analysis addressed the first form of incompleteness. We noted that a seeming weak inconsistency may merely reflect the known fact that each view is incomplete. The second form, however, is a fundamental human limitation – although using multiple views may improve a participant's insight or judgment, completeness is more a goal to guide and inspire us than an achievable result.

Once all analysis has been performed, the overlap between two views can be characterized by the combined graph, a set of counterparts, a set of dependencies, and the results of the three kinds of consistency checks.

20.6   EXAMPLE OF MULTIPLE VIEWED REQUIREMENTS

Previous sections showed the graphs making up each view of a patient monitoring system's requirements. This section shows the summarized results of analyzing their combination. Refer to Fig. 20.13 for their display forms. The top part of the picture is the analyst's R-Spec-Graph containing the common elements from the three views.

20.6.1   Counterparts in Patient-Monitoring

Counterparts are shown in Fig. 20.13 as being connected via the (counterpart) relation. We could show the three views' graphs as being joined around the counterparts; however, the counterpart relations are retained to indicate their derivation.

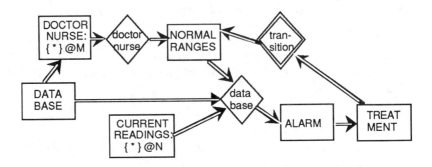

Fig. 20.12

20.6.2   Dependencies in Patient-Monitoring

The dependencies in the patient-monitoring example are shown in Fig. 20.12 above. Some of the dependencies were obtained from relation definitions not shown in this chapter, but were a part of the analyst's set of definitions for multiple viewed analysis.

20.6.3   Least Common Generalization

The least common generalization between the views is represented by the analyst's R-Spec-Graph, shown in the top portion of Fig. 20.13.

20.6.4   Joined Graphs

The combined requirements of all three participants – customer, designer, and end-user – are shown in Fig. 20.13. Note how the assumption graphs contribute to the complete set of requirements.

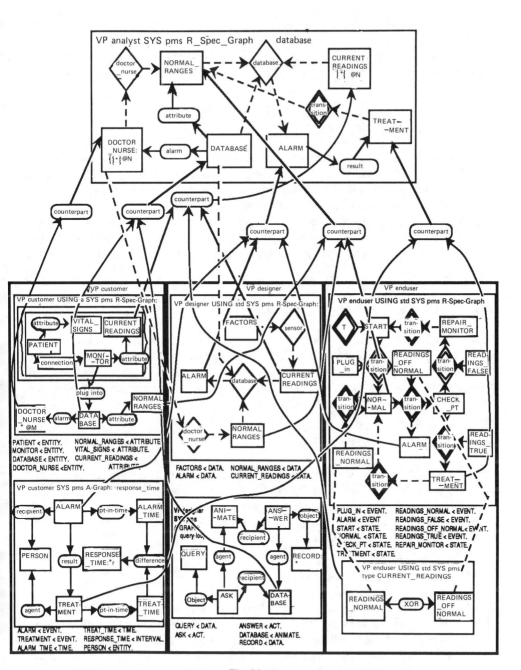

Fig. 20.13

20.7   ISSUES IN MULTIPLE VIEWED REQUIREMENTS

Many interesting issues need to be addressed in order for conceptual graphs to be a viable tool for multiple viewed requirements development. This section outlines a few of the issues involving conceptual graphs; see Delugach (1991b) for more discussion.

20.7.1 Validating Extensions To Conceptual Graphs

Like any extension, the private referent, and the demon node need to be explored more thoroughly to validate their properties with respect to our accepted meaning of conceptual graphs.

20.7.2 Presenting Results

Some results we want to present to a participant are not expressible in a participant's original view, because it was obtained from other views. Choosing a language in which to present the results is not an easy task. We can easily display a combined graph; however, unless all participants learn conceptual graphs, the combined graph will be of little use.

Since conceptual graphs can be expressed in natural language, if we capture results in conceptual graph form, we may use English paraphrases for presenting our findings to multiple participants; however, paraphrasing remains a difficult operation (see (Sowa, 1983)).

20.7.3 Acquiring Pre-Existing Assumptions

A key part of using multiple views is the acquisition of a participant's pre-existing assumptions. This task is still almost entirely heuristic, based on the requirements analyst's intuition and experience. We need automated methods to identify and formalize these assumptions. Perhaps we can involve a participant in an interactive dialogue that can automatically discover some assumptions.

20.7.4 Formal Meaning Of Overlap

Discussing multiple views is difficult because to each participant, any other view's information appears outside of his own view. Although informal knowledge of other views may be useful, we would like to know if there is some logical basis for including such external knowledge in a participant's view. How does feedback occur when knowledge of overlap results in a participant changing his original requirements?

20.7.5 Granularity and Computability

This work considers as counterparts only those concept boxes that represent the same individuals. We have made no provision for the case where a sub-graph has a counterpart. This is because to examine all sub-graphs is computationally expensive. If two views use substantially different levels of detail, then a sub-graph's counterpart might possibly be another sub-graph of any size. Without the use of constraining pre-existing assumptions, it is unlikely that differing degrees of granularity can be overcome for large sets of requirements.

A different kind of granularity involves looking at differing degrees of "counterpartness," where we have the same individual but at different times, or the same individual in different places. For example, the dependency relationship between an actor and a likenamed concept(s) is akin to a counterpart.

20.8 CONCLUSIONS

Conceptual graphs are a valuable language for capturing multiple views of software requirements. We have outlined a framework in which conceptual graphs provide a basis for analyzing multiple views, and their underlying assumptions. Overlap between views can be characterized as a set of counterparts and dependencies, along with strong and weak inconsistencies. Conceptual graphs are a promising avenue for gaining insight into the problems of multiple viewed requirements.

BIBLIOGRAPHY

Agresti, W.W. (1987) "Guidelines for Applying the Composite Specification Model," Software Engineering Laboratory, Tech. Report no. SEL-87-003, Greenbelt, MD, U.S.A.

Aho, A.V. (1972) *The Theory of Parsing*, Translation and Compiling, Prentice-Hall, Vol. I, Englewood Cliffs, NJ.

Alford, M.W. (1977) "A Requirements Engineering Methodology for Real-Time Processing Requirements," IEEE Transactions of Software Engineering, Vol. SE-3, no. 1, pp. 60-69.

Alford, M.W. (1985) "SREM at the Age of Eight: The Distributed Computing Design System," IEEE Computer, Vol. 18, no. 4, pp. 36-46.

Chen, P. Pin-Shan (1976) "The entity-relationship model – toward a unified view of data," ACM Trans. Database Sys., Vol. 1, no. 1, pp. 9-36.

Delugach, H.S. (1991a) "Dynamic Assertion and Retraction of Conceptual Graphs," Proc. 6th Annual Workshop on Conceptual Graphs, (ed) E. Way,, pp. 15-26, SUNY Binghamton, Binghamton, New York.

Delugach, H.S. (1991b) *A Multiple-Viewed Approach to Software Requirements*, Ph.D. thesis, Computer Science Department, University of Virginia, Charlottesville, Va.

Esch, J. and Timothy Nagle (1990) "Representing Temporal Intervals Using Conceptual Graphs," Proc. of the 5th Annual Workshop on Conceptual Structures, (eds) P. Eklund, and L. Gerholz, pp. 43-52, Linköping University, ISBN 91-7870-718-8.

Finkelstein, A. and Hugo Fuks (1989) "Multiparty Specification," Proc. of the 5th International Workshop, Software Specification and Design, pp. 185-195, ACM SIGSOFT.

Gardiner, D.A., Bosco Tjan, and James R. Slagle (1989) "Extended Conceptual Structures Notation," Proc. 4th Annual Workshop on Conceptual Structures, (eds) J. Nagle and T. Nagle, pp. 3.05, AAAI - IJCAI-89, Menlo Park, CA 94025.

Gray, L.C. and Ronald D. Bonnell (1991) "A Comprehensive Conceptual Analysis Using ER and Conceptual Graphs," Proc. of the 6th Annual Workshop on Conceptual Graphs, (ed) E. Way, pp. 83-96, SUNY Binghamton, Binghamton, New York.

Moulin, B. and Daniel Cote (1992) "Extending the Conceptual Graph Model for Differentiating Temporal and Non-Temporal Knowledge," in (eds) P. Eklund, T. Nagle, J. Nagle and L. Gerholz *Conceptual Structures: Research and Practice*, Ellis-Horwood.

Muehlbacher, R. (1989) "A Conceptual Graph Based Dictionary as a Source for the Generation of Entity Relationship Models," Proceedings of the 4th Annual Workshop on Conceptual Structures, (eds) J. Nagle and T. Nagle, pp. 3.8, AAAI - IJCAI-89, Menlo Park, CA 94025.

Muehlbacher, R. (1990) "Using Conceptual Graphs as a Representation Language for System Analysis Methods," Proc. of the 5th Annual Workshop on Conceptual Structures, (eds) P. Eklund, and L. Gerholz, pp. 221-232, Linköping University, ISBN 91-7870-718-8.

Ross, D.T. and Jr. Kenneth E. Schoman (1977) "Structured Analysis for Requirements Definition," IEEE Transactions on Software Engineering, Vol. SE-3, no. 1, pp. 6-15.

Ross, D. T. (1985) "Applications and Extensions of SADT," IEEE Computer, Vol. 18, no. 4, pp. 25-35.

Schank, R.C. (1975) *Conceptual Information Processing*, Elsevier Science.

Sowa, J.F. (1983) "Generating Language from Conceptual Graphs," Comp. Math. with Applications, Vol. 8.

Sowa, J.F. (1984) *Conceptual Structures: Information Processing in Mind and Machine*, Addison-Wesley, Reading, Mass. U.S.A.

Teichroew, D. and Ernest A. Hershey, III (1977) "PSL/PSA: A Computer-Aided Technique for Structured Documentation and Analysis of Information Processing Systems," IEEE Transactions of Software Engineering, Vol. SE-3, no. 1, pp. 41-48.

Turner, R. (1984) *Logics for Artificial Intelligence*, John Wiley and Sons, New York.

Wartik, Steven P. (1983) "A Multi-Level Approach to the Production of Requirements for Interactive Computer Systems," Ph.D. thesis, University of California, Santa Barbara.

Wasserman, A.I. and David T. Shewmake (1982) "Rapid Prototyping of Interactive Information Systems," ACM SIGSOFT Softw. Eng. Notes, Vol. 7, no. 5, pp. 171-180.

Werkman, K.J. and Donald K. Hillman (1989) "Designer Fabricator Interpreter System: Using Conceptual Graphs To Represent Perspectives Between Cooperating Agents," Proc. of the 4th Annual Workshop on Conceptual Structures, (ed) J Nagle, and T Nagle, pp. 4.14, AAAI - IJCAI-89, Menlo Park, CA 94025.

Wood-Harper, A. T., Lyn Antil, and D. E. Avison (1985) *Information Systems Definition: The Multiview Approach*, Blackwell, Oxford.

Yourdon, E. and Constantine L.L., (1979) *Structured Design: Fundamentals of a Discipline of Computer Program and Systems Design*, Prentice-Hall.

Zave, P., (1982) "An Operational Approach to Requirements Specification for Embedded Systems," IEEE Transactions on Software Engineering, Vol. SE-8, no. 3, pp. 250-269.

Zave, P., (1989) "A Compositional Approach to Multiparadigm Programming," IEEE Software, Vol. 6, no. 5, pp. 15-25.

Part V

Natural Language and Text Retrieval

21

Lexical Choice as Pattern Matching

Jean-Francois Nogier
Centre Scientifique IBM,
5, Place Vendôme,
75001 Paris, France

Michael Zock
LIMSI - CNRS, B.P. 133,
91403 Orsay, France

ABSTRACT

A good lexical component is a vital piece in any natural language system. We will discuss in this paper an implemented lexical component that is part of a larger system currently being developed for information retrieval. Two special features of the system are its unique knowledge representation formalism on the various levels, conceptual graphs, and a unique lexicon for the parser and generator. Lexical choices depend on various knowledge sources (pragmatic, conceptual, linguistic, etc). We will only be concerned here with the conceptual component, i.e. the words' underlying meaning or definition. We believe that word meanings and utterance meanings are isomorphic, in the sense that (a) words, sentences and texts are simply different units to convey a message, "words being shorthand labels for larger conceptual chunks," (b) the core meaning of words and texts (sentences) can be expressed by the same formalism: conceptual graphs. This view allows us to model the process of lexical choice by matching definition graphs (word-definitions) on an utterance graph (conceptual input). Furthermore, it provides a natural way for paraphrases and for explanations concerning the conceptual differences between a set of words.

21.1 THE LEXICAL COMPONENT: THE POOR COUSIN OF NATURAL LANGUAGE SYSTEMS

It is a truism to say that a good lexical component is a vital piece of any natural language system, be it for analysis[1] or synthesis (generation, abstracting, paraphrasing, or translation). Despite this fact, the most important part of the lexicon, its conceptual component (meaning), has not received the amount of attention it deserves (for an exception, see Wojcik *et al.* (1983). Compared to other aspects (syntax and morphology), it remains an

---

[1]While this seems obvious for generation, it would be wrong to believe that such a component is of little importance for parsing. True text understanding requires going beyond the information given, i.e. inferencing.

underdeveloped component. This last point is shared by many leading researchers in the field.

> *"With only few exceptions, generation researchers have so far paid little attention to the nature of words" ... "Cumming's 1985 review of generation lexicons identifies many more open problems than it does accepted solutions."* (McDonald, 1988)

> *"Most approaches simply provide engineering tools that allow their systems to make lexical choice in a reasonable, if relatively unsophisticated way"... "a truly satisfactory theoretical approach for lexical choice has yet to be developed."* (McKeown & Swartout, 1988 : 37)

> *"In some important sense, these systems have no real knowledge of lexical semantics... They use fragments of linguistic structure which eventually have words as their frontiers, but have little or no explicit knowledge of what these words mean. At best, these systems assume that each conceptual primitive corresponds to a particular unique lexical item or phrase trivializing the problem of lexical semantics to the claim that the meaning of the word can be represented by the same word in upper case." (Marcus, 1987)*

While it is true that little progress has been accomplished since Goldman's seminal work (Goldman, 1973, 1975), one must admit that things are changing.

There are several collections of papers edited by linguists (Hüllen *et al.*, 1988), psychologists (Marslen-Wilson, 1989) and computational scientists (Evens, 1988; Boguraev and Briscoe, 1989). here are two monographs by psychologists (Stemberger, 1985; Aitchinson, 1987), various empirical studies (Levelt and Maassen, 1981; Kempen and Huijbers, 1983; Levelt and Schriefers, 1985, 1987), and at least two good discussions in psycholinguistic textbooks (Clark and Clark, 1977; Levelt, 1989). Finally, there are excellent survey papers from a psychological (Butterworth, 1979; Schreuder and Flores d'Arcais, 1979) and from a computational point of view (Robin, 1990).

There was also a special issue in Computational Linguistics (see in particular the papers by Alshawi, Boguraev and Briscoe, Byrd, Hobbs, Melćuk and Polguère, Nirenburg and Raskin, Zernik and Dyer), and finally, there have been a great number of publications in proceedings or in journals, where computational linguists directly address the problem of lexical choice in natural language generation.[2]

21.2   THE FRAMEWORK

The lexical component here described has been designed in the context of a larger system, named Kalipsos (Kalipsos is an acronym standing for Knowledge Acquisition / Logical Inference Process / Symbolic Oriented Software), whose goal it is to retrieve information

---

[2]See, for example, (McDonald, 1981, 1988; Matthiessen, 1982, 1988; Steinacker and Buchberger, 1983; Talmy, 1985; Cumming, 1986; Schroeder *et al.*, 1986; Danlos, 1987; Horacek, 1987; Heid, 1987, 1989; Jacobs, 1987; Poesio, 1987; Caraceni and Stock, 1988; Hovy, 1988; Jordanskaja, 1988; Lancel, 1988; Nirenburg, 1988; Ward, 1988; Batemann and Paris, 1989; Beckwith *et al.*, 1989; Dorr, 1989a, 1989b; Pustejovsky, 1989; Reiter, 1990a, 1990b; Robin, 1990; Smadja, 1989; Sondheimer *et al.*, 1989; Sowa, 1990; Wanner and Bateman, 1990).

from financial texts. The knowledge is represented in terms of conceptual graphs (Sowa, 1984). We shall give here only a short description. For more details, see (Berard-Dugourd et al., 1988).

Kalipsos uses a single *semantic lexicon* both for analysis and for synthesis. As can be seen in the figure here below, the parser and the generator share the lexical data-base:

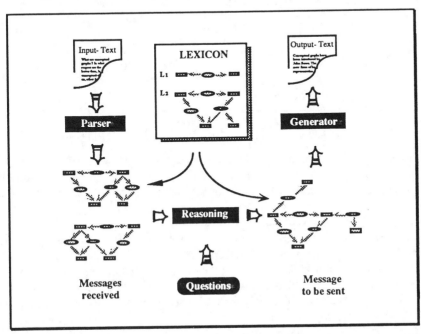

Words (lexemes) are associated with conceptual graphs which encode their underlying meaning.[3] The parser uses these graphs in order to reconstruct the underlying meaning of the sentence and its components, words.[4] Conceptual graphs represent thus not only the sentence meaning (*utterance-graph*), but also the meaning of the utterance's components, its individual words (*word definition graphs*). This has, of course, important consequences as we shall see.

If later on a user asks for information, the system's reasoning component looks at the data-base and retrieves the relevant piece of information. The result of this search and reasoning process is again a conceptual graph, representing the message to be conveyed (utterance graph). Our generator takes this message as input and produces the corresponding output (sentence). For more details on text analysis and information retrieval based on conceptual graphs, see (Berard-Dugourd et al., 1988).

---

[3] Of course, word definitions are not enough to account for meaning. In order to determine what a word really means, one needs also to know the context in which it is used.

[4] On the conceptual level there are no such units as words or sentences. One could think of an analogy of words and concepts on one hand, and sentences and propositions on the other. But, as we shall see, this kind of comparison does not lead very far.

21.3   THE CHOICE OF WORDS BASED ON CONCEPTUAL GRAPHS

Suppose that we want to express the following meaning, encoded by the utterance graph G1:

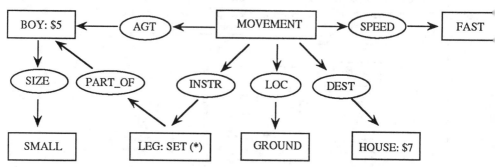

Please keep in mind, that the same formalism (conceptual graph) is used to represent the meanings on various levels (word, sentence). While G1 represents the underlying meaning of a sentence, the graphs introduced in section 3.1 (definition graphs) represent the meaning of a word.

Obviously, this graph can be verbalized in many ways. There are two extremes: (a) each concept/relation corresponds to a word (one-to- one-mapping), or (b) a single word can express the entire message, that is, all the concepts and relations encoded in the utterance graph (all-to- one-mapping). In most cases, the reality lies in between these two extremes.

An excellent example of this all-to-one-mapping is to be found in Lashley's seminal paper: "The Problem of Serial Order in Behavior", where he cites work done by Chamberlain, an ethnomethodologist:

> "The Cree Indian word "kekawewechetushekamikowanowow" is analyzed by Chamberlain (Chamberlain, 1911) into the verbal root, tusheka, "to remain", and the various particles which modify it as follows: ke(la)wow, the first and last syllables, indicating second person plural; ka, a prefix of the future tense; we, a sort of imperative mode expressing a wish; weche, indicating conjunction of subject and object; mik, a suffix bringing the verb into agreement with a third person subject and second person object; and owan, a suffix indicating that the subject is inanimate and the object animate. A literal translation: "You will I wish together remain he-you it-man you", or, freely, "May I remain with you." (Lashley, 1951)

Obviously, languages differ in their capacity to integrate conceptual chunks of variable size in single words. The example given by Lashley seemed to be an extreme case. Yet this need not be the case. Actually, there are many common words that need to be decomposed to varying degrees according to the addressee's expertise. We frequently use words like: justice, discovery, inflation, computer, etc. But on occasion each one of them is too dense or too abstract. That's why we have to decompose. Take, for example, such a common word as computer. How would you translate this idea, if you were talking to a person who comes from a culture where there are no such machines? Of course, you could use a periphrase such as "a machine that processes information". But that does not solve the problem: what is a machine ? What does it mean to process symbols or information? Each one of these defining terms may need to be decomposed in its turn. A similar problem arises in translation, where the text of the source language contains two words, while the target language requires just one. Take, for example, such frequent words as, very much, not know, etc. In each case, English requires two words where in French one needs only one: *beaucoup*, ignorer.

Besides interlingual differences, there are also differences within a given language. Consider the following pairs where two concepts are expressed by one, or by several words:

ignore	not consider
unhappy	not happy
punch	hit hard
leave	go away
	etc.

Let us now return to our topic and see how the system chooses the main verb expressing the central action (movement) of the episode encoded in G1.[5] (For more details see the sections 3.2.2 and 3.2.3) The generation of the corresponding sentence is shown in section 8.1. As the meaning of the words is defined in the same way as the meaning of the utterance, lexicalization consists in matching definition graphs (word meanings) on an utterance graph.

21.3.1 The lexicon

The words in the lexicon contain three kinds of information: their meaning (word definition graphs), their base form (lexeme, i.e. infinitive for verbs) and their possible syntactic structures (type of transitivity, voice, etc.). The following graphs (see next page), which express the underlying meaning of movement verbs, are a subset of the lexicon.[6]

---

[5]Note that: [a] sentence generation is verb-driven. [b] we will discuss here only verb choice (for lexicalization of other syntactic categories, see Nogier (1991)). [c] we assume here that a given conceptual structure is typically (by default) expressed by a specific syntactic structure. This is of course a simplification. Predicates may surface not only as verbs, but also as nouns, as adjectives, and so forth. While we do not deal in this paper with the interaction between word choice and syntactic structure, we do have a means to solve to this problem, namely, we associate to each lexeme as many syntactic structures as this particular word allows for. For instance, if a verb allows both for active and passive voice, than our lexicon must contain a graph for each one of these forms. A similar kind of approach is taken in Gross' lexicon-grammar (Gross, 1984), and in Joshi's Tree Adjoining Grammar (Joshi, 1987).

[6]It should also be noted that: (a) Even though the descriptions are given in English, they are based on the analysis of French words. (b) Even if these definitions can be challenged on various grounds [linguistic or psychological, see for example (Miller, 1972, Miller and Johnson-Laird, 1976, Schubert et al., 1979)), their changes will not affect our general point of view, namely, that lexical choice is a process of matching definition graphs on an utterance graph. (c) The reader should bear in mind, that our point is not so much to provide a fine grained knowledge representation for a specific class of words (semantic field), but rather to show a method that can account for word choice. That is, we focus on the process rather than on the data.

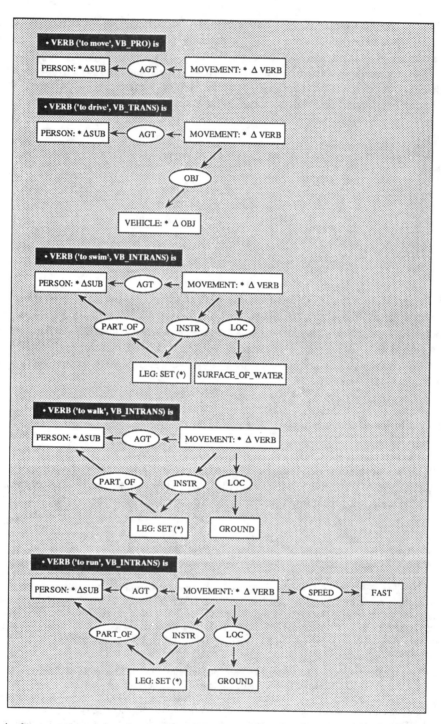

As these graphs express the word's underlying meaning, we will call them *word definition graphs*. Each lexical entry has the following structure:

NAME is CG

NAME (for instance, VERB('to walk', VB_INTRANS)') is a functional term, whose name (e.g. "VERB") is the word's syntactic category (part of speech).

- The first argument is the lexeme: 'to walk'.
- The second is the name of a generic syntactic graph (e.g. VB_INTRANS).

This syntactic graph represents the syntactic structure which is used in order to ex- press the given meaning.

CG is a generic conceptual graph which describes the underlying meaning of theword given as the first argument. It should be noted, that special signs have been added to this graph ($\Delta SUB, \Delta VERB$). These signs, which are called labels, will be used later on in the process of word choice. For example, the label $\Delta VERB$ is used to signal that this concept will surface as a verb.

As noted above, lexical items are associated not only with conceptual graphs, but also with syntactic information (the generic syntactic graph). Actually, each word contains as many conceptual graphs as there are different *syntactic structures*. In other words, we use a hybrid form of representation. The reason for this is quite simple: the same meaning can be expressed by different words, each of which may exhibit different syntactic structures.

Take, for example, the following conceptual input or utterance graph: *cause(X,Y)*, where X and Y could be expressions of arbitrary complexity (simple or complex propositions, i.e. noun phrases). In this case, we may use verbs belonging to either of the following groups:

X <causes> Y	(NP-V-NP)	Y <is due to> X	(NP-V-PP)
X <gives rise to> Y	(NP-V-NP-PP)	Y <follows from> X	(NP-V-PP)
X <brings about> Y	(NP-V-PP)	Y <is the result of> X	(NP-V-NP-PP)

According to the verb chosen (lexeme), one is committed to a specific syntactic structure: lexical and syntactic choices can not be taken independently. For a more thorough discussion concerning the interdependency between conceptual, pragmatic and linguistic choices (syntax and semantics), see Zock (1988).

21.3.2 First steps: Selection of the word

Step 1: Preselection (key word retrieval)

Because the same conceptual input can be expressed by many words, there is a great risk of combinatorial explosion. In order to avoid this problem, a first rough choice is made (key word retrieval), by trying to find a word for the most central concept of the conceptualization (typically an ACTION, STATE, or PROCESS). The task is thus to find a word which conveys the central idea of MOVEMENT as encoded in G1. As this kind of concept typically maps onto a verb, the system tries to find a verb expressing a movement, that is, the system distinguishes movement verbs from, let us say, mental states (see, hear), *transfer of possession-verbs* (buy, give, lend), etc. These verbs pertain to other semantic fields or domains.

Given what has been said above about the role of the label Δ, the word definition graphs, from which we may choose, must contain the concept [MOVEMENT: *ΔVERB]. This yields in our case the following list: *to walk, to drive, to move, to swim, to run.*

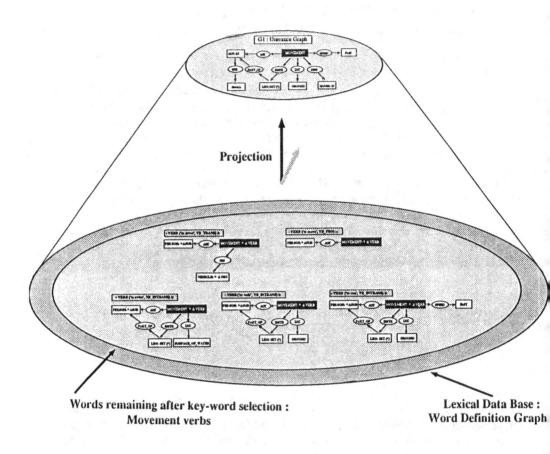

Projection

Words remaining after key-word selection :
Movement verbs

Lexical Data Base :
Word Definition Graph

Step 2: The choice of possible candidates by using pattern matching

As the resulting list contains more than one candidate, we have to eliminate all but one. In order to do so, we will rely on pattern-matching (covering, filtering), that is, we will use the projection operation as defined by Sowa (1984, p99)[7]. All the conceptual graphs previously selected are projected on the utterance graph (G1). A projection succeeds if the

---

[7] For implementation details, see (Catach, 1985, Fargues *et al.*, 1986).

word definition is a generalized subgraph of G1. The system chooses the graphs that match perfectly with G1.

The following words remain possible candidates: to move, *to walk and to run*. All other items failed the test.[8] As there is still more than one candidate, and as all them express more or less precisely the intended content, we have to reduce further the list in order to choose the best candidate.

Step 3: Selection of the best candidate on the basis of the correlation factor

The problem of word choice consists not only in selecting one item from a list of candidates, but it consists above all in determining the word that expresses most accurately the intended content (access vs. meaning). Obviously, there is more to word choice than meaning, there is also rhetorical effect. Hence, besides conceptual information, stylistic and pragmatic factors must be taken into account (Hovy, 1988).

Among the three candidates, not all words fit equally well. In our case, to run is the most adequate one, as it expresses more of the utterance graph (G1) than to walk and to move. While the former conveys the notion of a *movement*, it does not specify the *speed*. On the other hand, the latter (*to move*) does not convey any information concerning the *instrument* or the *location* (ground, water, air) of the action.

In order to determine the suitability of each word we will compute a *correlation factor*. This latter reflects the word's *appropriateness*, i.e. its *accuracy* in expressing the given conceptual structure. To compute the correlation factor, we will consider the graph resulting from the pro- jection of the definition graph VERB ('to run', VB_INTRANS) on G1. The result of this projection is called the *kernel graph*. In our example the projection results in G2:

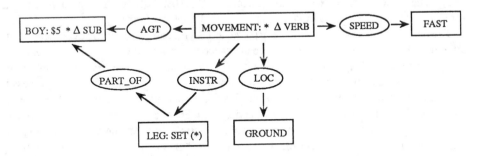

The *correlation factor* consists in the total number of concepts expressed by the kernel graph (which is, of course, identical to the number of concepts expressed by a given word, i.e. its underlying definition graph).

The correlation factor is used to select the most *accurate word*, i.e. the word whose underlying definition graph matches the greatest number of concepts contained in the

---

[8]In the case of to drive, the concept VEHICLE and the relation OBJ (object) could not be unified with LEG and INSTR; consequently this projection fails. For the verb to swim, the edge of the SURFACE_OF_ WATER could not be projected onto G1, because SURFACE_OF_WATER does not match with GROUND. Therefore, this definition is rejected too.

utterance graph: the more concepts the definition graph has, the more specific it is, hence the more accurate is the word. In consequence, the possible candidates can now be ordered in terms of *accuracy: to run* (5) being the best candidate, as it obtains the best score, followed by *to walk* (4) and *to move (2)*.

The benefits of this technique are *conceptual density* and *economy* of *linguistic resources* (number of words), hence conciseness. Instead of using one word per concept, the system tries to find a word with optimal coverage, that is to say, a word that integrates the greatest number of concepts[9] without leaving holes. By introducing criteria such as a*ppropriateness, accuracy,* etc. and by operationalizing these terms, we provide objective means for making principled choices of an item from among a set of alternatives.

21.3.3   Instantiation

Having chosen the lexical item, we still have to determine the *syntactic structure.* Remember, that we have chosen the lexical entry VERB('to run', VB_INTRANS). The *generic syntactic graph*, given as the second argument, is encoded in the following way:

• SYNTACTIC_STRUCTURE (VB_INTRANS) is

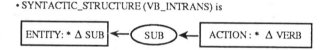

It should be noted, that from now on, the relations linking the lexical items of the future sentence are *syntactic relations* and no longer conceptual relations as in the utterance graph (G1). What used to be an AGT relation becomes SUBJECT (SUB), linking a verb to the subject of the sentence. This kind of graph is called a *syntactic graph.*

The next step consists of instantiating the generic syntactic graph with the concepts of the utterance graph. The *pending edges* of the utterance graph, whose concepts are marked syntactically in the kernel graph, - (ΔSUB, or ΔOBJ, according to the verb chosen) - are linked to the correspondingly marked concepts of the generic syntactic graph. The same process is applied to the kernel graph (G2). Once a word is found for a given concept, it will replace the corresponding variable in the generic syntactic graph. For example, the concept [ACTION: *Δ VERB] becomes ("to run") in the partial syntactic graph. As one can see, during this process we have a hybrid form of representation: [BOY] $\rightarrow$ (SIZE) $\rightarrow$ [SMALL] being purely conceptual, whereas [BOY] $\leftarrow$ (SUB) $\leftarrow$ [TO_RUN] are conceptual and syntactic.

---

[9]Of course, there are cases where maximal coverage does lead to an optimal solution. This may be the case if a word covers the entire conceptual structure. Declarative sentences require at least two words, a subject and a predicate.

The last operation consists of removing the labels (Δ...) are of no use anymore. Therefore, the generic syntactic graph becomes a partial syntactic graph named G3:

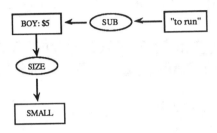

At the same time, the kernel graph (G2) is transformed into a partial conceptual graph named G4:

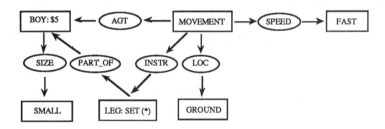

Replacement of the conceptual structure by the syntactic structure

By now, the partial syntactic graph (G3) has been instantiated with words. The partial conceptual graph (G4) underlying this syntactic construction is also complete. The final operation consists in replacing the partial conceptual graph (G4) by the partial syntactic graph (G3) in the original utterance graph (G1), and, of course, to lexicalize the remaining unexpressed concepts (HOUSE, BOY, SMALL) by performing the same kind of operations.

Since the partial conceptual graph (G4) has become an exact subgraph of the utterance graph, we are now sure that the substitution is feasible. Finally, after the process of substitution, G1 becomes:

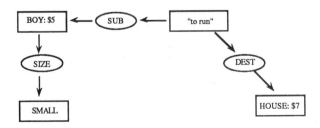

Le petit garcon court vers la maison.
(The little boy runs towards the house.)

In this way, the conceptual graph gradually becomes a syntactic graph, which is a syntactic representation of the future sentence. This graph will be interpreted by a generation automaton which will transform it into a sentence (cf. (Nogier, 1989, 1990, 1991)).

Goal	Process	Outcome
3.2.1 Find all verbs conveying the notion of [MOVEMENT].	Preselection by *key word*. Scan lexical data base and retrieve all *word-definition graphs* containing the concept [MOVEMENT: *Δ VERB]	Graph for "*to walk* " Graph for "*to drive* " Graph for "*to move* " Graph for "*to swim* " Graph for "*to run* "
3.2.2 Choice of possible candidates.	Project all previously selected word-definition graphs on the utterance graph (G1). Keep only those graphs that match perfectly with G1	*Kernel Graph* (G2) Graph for "*to move* " Graph for "*to walk* " Graph for "*to run* "
3.2.3 Choice of the most accurate word.	Compute the *correlation factor*, that is, the number of concepts shared by the word-definition graph & the utterance graph (G1). Choose the best candidate, i.e. the word that integrates the greatest number of concepts contained in the utterance graph (G1).	 *to run* (5) <— best candidate *to walk* (4) *to move* (2)
3.3 Instantiate the syntactic structure and the corresponding conceptual structure.	Retrieve the *generic syntactic graph* associated with the lexeme *to run* (VB_INTRANS), and instantiate it with the concepts of the utterance graph (G1): BOY, SMALL, and the verb "to run".	Generic syntactic graph becomes a *partial syntactic graph* (G3). [ACTION: * ΔVERB] --> ["to run"]
	Instantiate the kernel graph (G2) with the concepts of the utterance graph (G1) : BOY, SMALL	The kernel graph (G2) is transformed into a *partial conceptual graph* (G4)
3.4 Replace the conceptual structure by the syntactic structure.	Replace the partial conceptual graph (G4) by the *partial syntactic graph* (G3) in the original utterance graph (G1).	Partial syntactic graph (G3) becomes subgraph of the utterance graph (G1). Utterance graph (G1) becomes *complete syntactic graph*(G5).

The figures on following summarize and illustrate the entire process.

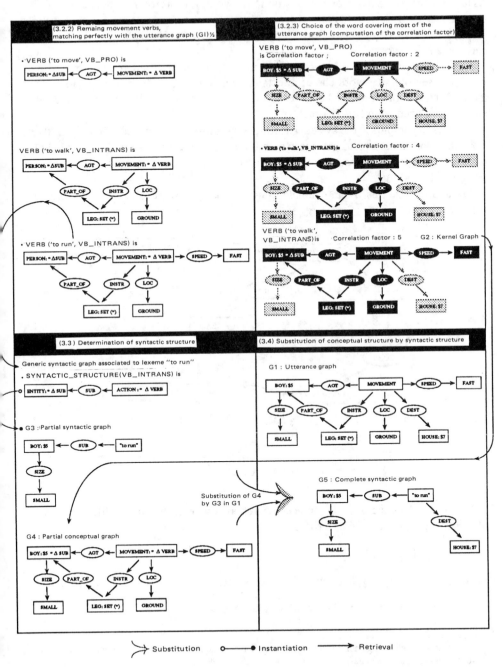

Substitution   o——•Instantiation   ——→Retrieval

Processes taking place after key-word retrieval

21.4   SEMANTIC PARAPHRASING AND EXPLANATION

As lexical choices are based on the substitution of words for parts of the utterance graph, and as words have different potentials with regards to expressing variable sizes of the utterance graph,[10] we have a natural way (a) for paraphrasing and (b) for explaining the difference between a set of words.

Paraphrases are obtained by varying the number of concepts one tries to express by a word. Please note, that word choice affects not only conceptual density per word, - hence the total number of words of the sentence,- but also the syntactic structure of the sentence and its component elements (words).

In order to paraphrase the system backtracks each time at its last decision point, moving from the most inclusive to the most specific word. More details on the use of Prolog backtracking for paraphrasing are given in Nogier (1991). For a similar approach, see (Boyer et al., 1985)[11].

Let us illustrate this by an example. Suppose that you want to express the following content:

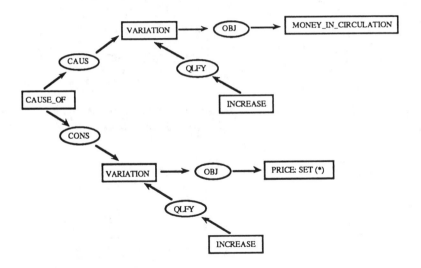

In this case the system can generate either a short version such as (a), or different versions of increasingly larger sentences (b - d):

- (a) The inflation

- (b) The increase of M1 causes a rise in prices.

- (c) Increasing money in circulation hikes prices.

---

[10]Remember, there is a large number of linguistic possibilities ranging from words expressing only one concept to words expressing a large conceptual structure, or informational chunk.

[11]Using backtracking to generate all possible coverings of the input (conceptual structure), they also build different syntactic representations of the same semantic network. However, unlike Boyer, we do not use any lexical transformation.

- (d) The increase of money in circulation gives rise to an increase in prices. etc.

Obviously, as mentioned here above (section 3), the integrative power of words (conceptual density) varies among and within a given language. In our last example, English allows for shorter versions than French (see section 8.2), as for a given conceptual chunk there are several short words in English for which there is no corresponding word in French. Hence periphrases are necessary.

(cause ((an increase) (in prize)))   ⇒ hike prizes
                                            ⇒ *provoquer la hausse des prix*

(the increase of (money in circulation)   ⇒ the increase of M1
                                            ⇒ *la hausse de la masse monétaire*

The paraphrases are thus built on the basis of the correlation factor. We start from a short version, moving to increasingly longer versions. In other words, the correlation factor can be used to adapt lexical choice to the user's expertise: dense and concise for experts, verbose and explicit for the layman.

It should be noted, however, that conceptual density, while very useful, is not the sole criteria for word choice. Besides linguistic factors, context, that is, pragmatic and stylistic factors should also be taken into account. For example, if you look at sentence (d) above, you will notice that the concept INCREASE is expressed twice by the same word (increase). This kind of repetition should, of course, be avoided. Put differently, a given concept should be expressed by different words, if it occurs twice in the same clause. One could replace the first "increase"by "rise", but this would again produce twice the same word, once for the noun (rise) and once for the verb (to give rise). If we opt for the noun "rise", than we have to change the verb "to give rise to" for something like "to cause, to bring about", etc.

It is also worth mentioning, that the principle of maximal density may be overridden on purely syntactic grounds. While unhappy may be a better choice than not happy in the context of (a) and (b), it is not a good choice in the context of (c):

(a) Hungry children are not happy.
(b) Hungry children are unhappy
(c) Not happy children cry.*
(d) Unhappy children cry.

Still another interesting point is, that pattern matching provides an easy means for explaining the difference between a set of words. For instance, if you want to know the difference between, let us say, to swim and to fly, or, to swim and to walk, it is not difficult at all for our system to tell the user that the difference lies in the type of surface or space where the travelling takes place. We walk on the ground, we swim in the water, and we fly in the sky. In order to provide this kind of explanation, it suffices to compare the words concerned, "more precisely, to match the word's underlying definition graphs" and produce an answer on the basis of the difference between the two graphs (i.e. the pending edges of the projection). For a similar approach on the discourse level, see Zock (1991).

21.5   POSSIBLE REFINEMENTS

The word definition graph here below is an attempt to show some of the problems that arise for the lexicographer trying to provide a definition:

VERB ('to walk', VB_INTRANS) is

If you compare this figure with the one given in section 3.1, you will notice two kinds of refinements:[12] (a) the object of the movement is the agent himself, (b) we added the attribute manner (MANR). The first refinement is necessary to distinguish to walk from to carry, while the second refinement is needed to distinguish to walk from to run. You will also notice, that this time SPEED is not part of the word definition graph. It is only contained in the utterance graph. Hence, we can now produce sentences like:

(a) He walked fast.

(b) He ran slowly.

both of which where impossible in the earlier version.

Obviously, the label WALKER, as opposed to RUNNER, is fairly coarse grained. It hardly can do justice to the complexity of the movement involved. Actually, the difference between to run and to walk resides probably more in the type of movement than in the speed. The feet of a runner hardly touch the ground, his arms move in a certain way, etc. The labels WALKER/ RUNNER stand for the kind of movement (manner) we have in mind (or in our mind's eye), when we think of someone walking as opposed to someone running. As gestures are hard to translate into symbolic code, - the movement of a runner or a walker would require a subgraph on their own[13] - we will just use such a coarse grained label.

---

[12]Obviously, the degree of refinement, i.e. the degree of decomposition or granularity, is a function of the number of alternatives from which an item must be distinguished within a given semantic field. If an application contains only one word for expressing movement, than there is no need to refine the definition of this word beyond that point. Since the information movement will suffice to discriminate, let us say, to walk from a mental activity verb like to think.

[13]For an interesting discussion concerning this last point, see Schubert et al. (1979, p148). According to them, most people possess at least the following knowledge about human walking, regardless of whether they can verbalize it or not. "Each foot of the walker repeatedly leaves the ground, moves freely in the walking direction for a distance comparable to the length of the walker's legs (while staying close to the ground), then is set down again, and remains in position on the ground, supporting the walker, while the other foot goes through a similar motion. The repetition rate is of the order of one repetition per second. The legs remain more or less extended. The body remains more or less erect and is carried forward at a fairly constant rate. (Further details could be added about flexing motions of feet, knees, and hips, and the slight up-and-down motion of the body, typical arm motions, and forces exerted on the ground.)"

It should also be noted, that verbs like to walk and to run have default values with regards to speed. The range of the value varies as a function of the age of the runner (child, adult, champion), the distance he is running (100 yards, marathon), status (amateur, professional) and so forth. All this information, while more cumbersome than helpful in our application, must be included in a system that accounts for sport events.

21.6   IMPLEMENTATION

The word choice algorithm is implemented in IBM Prolog (PP 5706-236, PN 5621-065) and runs under VM/370 and OS/2. Using a lexicon of about 100 graphs, the pattern matching process (i.e. search for possible word definitions and final lexical choice), when successful, takes about 400 ms. In case of failure, it takes about 20 ms. The other operations, i.e. syntactic graph instantiation and substitution, require considerably less time. The good overall performance of our system (graph-matching, in general, is intractable because it takes a long time) is due both to the efficiency of IBM Prolog and to the small size of our lexicon. Obviously, as the lexicon grows, we will have to find new methods of optimizing search.

21.7   FUTURE WORK AND CONCLUSION

We presented a method for choosing words by matching word definitions on utterance graphs. This approach has several advantages:

> it can model various linguistics, logical or psycholinguistic aspects of word choice. For example, (a) it avoids redundancies or contradictions,[14] (b) it allows for simulating observable discourse phenomena like the carrying over (to the next word or sentence) of information which could not be expressed by the word under study.[15] (c) It supports paraphrasing, and (d) it lends itself quite naturally for explaining differences between a set of words.

The proposed method can be generalized and used on other levels. In particular, it can be used in order to determine syntactic structures (Zock, 1990). The use of graph-matching as a processing strategy for word choice and for determining syntactic structure is justified both on computational and on psychological grounds. People do not process word-by-word (or concept-by-concept), rather they operate on chunks (schemata). The size of the chunks being a function of the speaker's skill and experience in this language. There are several good reasons - linguistic (Langacker, 1983, Fillmore, 1977), psychological (Miller and Johnson-Laird, 1976) and computational (Minsky, 1975, Schank and Abelson, 1977) - to believe, that the basic strategy of proficient speakers is pattern-matching, especially in a standard communicational setting. For more information, see Zock (1990).

---

[14] The following two sentences are clearly deviant from ordinary language use:
He walked on the ground. (redundancy "ground")
He swam in the sky. (contradiction)

[15] It occurs quite frequently in spontaneous discourse that we are unable to express, i.e. integrate in a single word or sentence, all the information we had planned. In this case we have three options: (a) change the initial conceptual structure by adding or deleting information; (b) look for another word or sentence structure; (c) carry the unexpressed piece of information to the next utterance cycle, i.e. try to integrate it in the next word or sentence.

There are also many problems we did not address, leave alone solve. For example: How do we control the interaction of lexical choices and syntax? How the syntactic category of the word chosen be determined? How can we avoid combinatorial explosion when choosing the words of a very complex conceptual graph?

Word choice remains a mysterious, complex problem. We do not really know how people manage to retrieve from a huge mental dictionnary the right word in such a short time. And even if we are able to simulate the process of lexical choice by machine, we are not able to do justice to the complexity and subtleties involved. For the time being one can only agree with Cumming when she writes:

> "We're a long way from having natural language generators that have the degree of control over any level of linguistic choice, grammatical or lexical, that a serious treatment of these considerations would entail; but we can design our systems so that such distinction will be able to be accommodated when we have the analyses to support them." (Cumming, 1986, p26)

In a similar vein, if our word definitions are certainly subject to change, we hope, that our method of lexical choice, -namely, matching word definition graphs on utterance graphs, - will survive.

Appendix : outputs

To allow for inputing conceptual graphs via the key board, we will use the linear form introduced by J.F. Sowa (1984, pp78-79).

Example of word choice

```
← genling(p,g14).
```

Graph : g14 is
```
['deplacement': *1]-
    (qlfy)→['rapide': *2]
    (loc.dir)→['maison': $ 7]
    (ins)→['jambe':SET(*)]→(eposs)→['garcon':$5]→
                         (chrc)→['petit':*3]
    (agt)→['garcon':$5].
```

Le petit garcon court vers la maison.
(The little boy runs towards the house.)

540ms success
← *genling(p,g14).*

Example of paraphrase generation

```
←repete genling(p,g25).
```

Graph : g25 is   ['evolution': $3]-
```
    (theme)→[augmentation:*1]
    (agt)→[prix:SET(*)]
```

```
(cons)←[cause_de:*2]→(source)→['Evolution': $1]-
    (theme)→[augmentation:*3]
    (agt)→[masse:$2]→(chrc)→['monétaire':*4].
```

L'inflation.
(The inflation.)

La hausse de la masse monétaire provoque la hausse des prix.
(The increase of money in circulation causes an increase in prices.)

La hausse de la masse monétaire provoque l'augmentation des prix.
(The increase of money in circulation causes a rise in prices.)

L'augmentation de la masse monétaire provoque la hausse des prix.
(The rise of money in circulation causes an increase in prices.)

L'augmentation de la masse monétaire provoque l'augmentation des prix.
(The rise of money in circulation causes a rise in prices.)

La hausse des prix découle de la hausse de la masse monétaire.
(The increase in prices is due to the increase of money in circulation.)

L'augmentation des prix découle de la hausse de la masse monétaire.
(The rise in prices is due to the increase of money in circulation.)

La hausse des prix découle de l'augmentation de la masse monétaire.
(The increase in prices is due to the rise of money in circulation.)

L'augmentation des prix découle de l'augmentation de la masse monétaire
(The rise in prices is due the rise of money in circulation.)

6170ms success
← repete genling (p,g25).

BIBLIOGRAPHY

Aitchinson, J. (1987) *Words in the Mind: an Introduction to the Mental Lexicon*, Oxford, Blackwell.

Alshawi, H. (1987) "Processing Dictionary Definitions with Phrasal Pattern Hierarchies", Computational Linguistics, vol.13, 3-4.

Batemann, J. and Paris, C. (1989) "Phrasing a Text in Terms the User Can Understand", IJCAI-89.

Beckwith, C. Fellbaum, D. Gross and G. Miller (1991) "WordNet: a Lexical Database Organized on Psycholinguistic Principles". In, (ed.) Zernik *Proc. First International Lexical Acquisition Workshop*, IJCAI-89., Detroit.

Berard-Dugourd, A. Fargues, J. Landau M.C. and Rogala, J.P. (1988) "Natural Language Information Retrieval from French Texts", Third International Workshop on Conceptual Graphs.

Boguraev, B. and Briscoe, T. (1987) "Large Lexicons for Natural Language Processing: Utilizing the Grammar Coding System of LDOCE", Computational Linguistics, vol.13, 3-4.

Boguraev, B. and Briscoe, T. (Eds.) (1989) *Computational Lexicography for Natural Language Processing*, Longman, London.

Boyer, M. and Lapalme, G. (1985) "Generating Paraphrases from Meaning- Text Semantic Networks", Computational Intelligence, no 1.

Byrd, R. (1987) "Tools and Methods for Computational Linguistics", Computational Linguistics, vol.13, 3-4.

Butterworth, B. (1989) "Lexical Acces in Speech Production". In, (eds.) W. Marslen-Tayler Caraceni, R. and Stock, O. (1988) Reversing a Lexically Based Parser for Generation, Applied Artificial Intelligence.

Catach, L. and Fargues, J. (1985) Déductions et Opérations pour le Modéle des Graphes Conceptuels, IBM Paris Research Report F087.

Chamberlain, A. (1911) Indians, North American. Encyclopedia Britannica 14: 452-482.

Clark, H. and Clark, E. (1977) Psychology and Language: an Introduction to Psycholinguistics, Harcourt Brace Jovanovich, New York.

Cumming, S. (1986) "The Lexicon in Text Generation", ISI Report 86-168.

Danlos, L. (1987) The Linguistic Basis of Text Generation, Cambridge University Press, Cambridge.

Dorr, B (1989a) " Lexical Conceptual Structure and Generation in Machine Translation", A.I. Memo No. 1160, MIT, AI Lab.

Dorr, B (1989b) "Conceptual Basis of the Lexicon in Machine Translation", A.I. Memo No. 1166, MIT, AI Lab.

Evens, M. (1988) Relational Models of the Lexicon. Representing Knowledge in Semantic Networks, Cambridge University Press.

Fargues, J. Berard-Dugourd, A. Landau, M.C. and Catach, L. (1986) "Conceptual Graphs for Semantics and Knowledge Processing," IBM Journal of Research and Development, vol. 30.

Fillmore, C. (1977) "Scenes and Frame Semantics in Linguistic Structures Processing." In, Zampolli, A. (Ed.), North-Holland, Amsterdam.

Goldman, N. (1973) "Sentence Paraphrasing from a Conceptual Basis," International Conference on Computational Linguistics, Pisa.

Goldman, N. (1975) "Conceptual Generation." In, Conceptual Information Processing, Schank, R.C. (Ed.), North Holland, Amsterdam.

Gross, M. (1984) "Lexicon Grammar and Syntactic Analysis of French," COLING, Stanford

Heid, U. (1987) Zur Lexikalischen Wissensquelle des Generierungssystems SEMSYN, 11th German Workshop on Artificial Intelligence, Springer-Verlag, Berlin.

Heid, U. and Raab, S. (1989) "Collocations in Multilingual Generation," European Meeting of the A.C.L, Manchester.

Hobbs, J. et al. (1987) "Common Sense Metaphysics and Lexical Semantics," Computational Linguistics, vol.13, 3-4.

Horacek, H. (1987) "Choice of Words in the Generation Process of a Natural Language Interface," Applied Artificial Intelligence, 1, Hemisphere Publishers.

Hovy, E.H. (1988) "Generating Language with a Phrasal Lexicon". In, Natural Language Generation Systems, McDonald, D.D. and Bolc, L. (Eds.), Springer Verlag, New York.

Hüllen, W. and Schulze, R. (1988) "Understanding the Lexicon. Meaning, Sense and World Knowledge in Lexical Semantics", Niemeyer Verlag, Tübingen.

Jacobs, P.S. (1986) "Knowledge Structures for Natural Language Generation", COLING.

Jacobs, P.S. (1987a) "KING: a Knowledge-Intensive Natural Language Generator". In, Kempen, G. (Ed.)

Jacobs, P.S. (1987b) "Knowledge-Intensive Natural Language Generation," Artificial Intelligence, 33, North Holland.

Jordanskaja, L. Kittredge R. and Polguere, A. (1988) "Lexical Selection and Paraphrase in a Meaning-Text Generation Model", 4th International Workshop on Natural Language Generation, Catalina Island.

Joshi, A. (1987) "The Relevance of Tree Adjoining Grammar to Generation." In, (ed.) Kempen, G., (1987) *Natural Language Generation: New Results in Artificial Intelligence, Psychology and Linguistics*, Kluwer Academic Publishers Group, Dordrecht, Netherlands.

Kempen, G. and Huijbers, P. (1983) "Lexicalization Process in Sentence Production and Naming: indirect Election of Words," Cognition, 14.

Lancel, J.M. Otani, M. Simonin, N. and Danlos, L. (1988) "Sentence Parsing and Generation with a Semantic Dictionary and a Lexicon Grammar," COLING.

Langacker, J. (1983) "Foundations of Cognitive Grammar", Indiana University Linguistics Club.

Lashley, K.S. (1951) " The Problem of Serial Order in Behavior". In, Cerebral Mechanisms in Behavior, (ed.) L.A. Jeffres, New York: John Wiley.

Levelt, W. (1989) *Speaking: from Intention to Articulation*, MIT Press, Cambridge.

Levelt, W. and Maasen, B. (1981) "Lexical Search and Order of Mention in Sentence Production". In, *Crossing the Boundaries of Linguistics*, (eds.) Klein, W. and Levelt, W., Reidel Publishing Company.

Levelt, W. and Schriefers, H. (1985) "Issues of Lexical Access in Language Production", Workshop on Language Processing, Stanford.

Levelt, W. and Schriefers, H. (1987) "Stages of Lexical Access". In, (ed.) Kempen, G. *Natural Language Generation: New Results in Artificial Intelligence,* Psychology and Linguistics, Kluwer Academic Publishers Group, Dordrecht, Netherlands.

Marcus, M. (1987) "Generation Systems Should Choose their Words", Third TINLAP.

Marslen-Taylor, W. (Ed.) (1979) *Lexical Representation and Process,* Bradford book, MIT Press, Cambridge, Mass.

Matthiessen, C. (1982) "A Grammar and a Lexicon for a Text Production System", ISI Research Report 82-102.

Matthiessen, C. (1988) "Lexico-Grammatical Choice in Text Generation", 4th International Workshop on Natural Language Generation, Catalina Island.

McDonald, D.D. (1981) "Language Production: the Source of the Dictionary", International Conference on Computational Linguistics, Stanford.

McDonald, D.D. (1988) "On the Place of Words in the Generation Process", 4th International Workshop on Natural Language Generation, Catalina Island.

McKeown, K.R. and Swartout, W.R. (1988) *"Language Generation and Explanation"* .In, (eds.) Zock, M. and Sabah, G. , vol. 1.

Mel'cuk, I.A. and Polguére, A. (1987) "A Formal Lexicon in the Meaning- Text Theory (or How to Do Lexica with Words ?)," Computational Linguistics, vol.13, 3-4.

Miller, G. (1972) "Verbs of Motion: a Case Study in Semantics and Lexical Memory." In, *Coding Processes in Human Memory*, Melton, A.W. and Martin, E (Eds.), Winston, Washington.

Miller, G. and Johnson-Laird, P. (1976) *Language and Perception*, Cambridge University Press.

Minsky, M. (1975) "A Framework for Representing Knowledge", In, *The Psychology of Computer Vision*, Winston, P. (Ed.), McGraw-Hill.

Nirenburg, S. and Raskin, V. (1987) " The Subworld Concept Lexicon and the Lexicon Management System", Computational Linguistics, vol.13.

Nirenburg, S. and Nirenburg, I. (1988a) "A Framework for Lexical Selection in Natural Language Generation", COLING.

Nirenburg, S. and Nirenburg, I. (1988b) "Lexical Selection in a Blackboard- Based Generation System", 4th International Workshop on Natural Language Generation, Catalina Island.

Nogier, J.F. (1989) "Generating Language from a Conceptual Representation", 9th International Workshop "Expert systems and their Applications", Avignon, also available as IBM Research Report F146, Scientific Center IBM, Paris.

Nogier, J.F. (1990) *Un Systme de Production de Language Fondé sur le Modéle des Graphes Conceptuels,* Ph.D dissertation, Universite de Paris VII, Jussieu.

Nogier, J.F. (1991) *Génération Automatique de Langage et Graphes Conceptuels*, Editions Hermes, Paris.

Poesio, M. (1987) "An Organization of Lexical Knowledge for Generation," 11th German Workshop on Artificial Intelligence, Springer, Berlin.

Pustejovsky, J. (1989) " Current Issues in Computational Lexical Semantics", European Meeting of the A.C.L., Manchester.

Reiter, E. (1990a) "A New Model for Lexical Choice for Open-Class Words," 5th International Workshop on Natural Language Generation, Pittsburgh.

Reiter, E. (1990b) "Generating Descriptions that Exploit a User's Domain Knowledge. In, *Current Research in Natural Language Generation*, Dale, R. Mellish, C. and Zock, M.(Eds.), Academic Press, New York.

Robin, J. (1990) "A Survey of Lexical Choice in Natural Language Generation", Technical Report CUCS 040-90, Dept. of Computer Science, University of Columbia

Rosch, E. (1978) "Principles of Categorization. In, Cognition and Categorization", Rosch, E. and Lloyd, B. (Eds.), New York Lawrence Erlbaum Associates.

Schank, R.C. and Abelson, R.P. (1977) " Scripts, Plans, Goals and Understanding", Hillsdale, Erlbaum.

Schreuder, R. and Flores d'Arcais G. (1989) "Psycholinguistic Issues in the Lexical Representation of Meaning". In, W. Marslen-Tayler (Ed.).

Schroeder, M. Imlah, B. Horacek, H. Pyka C. and Wachtel, T. (1986) "Lexical Representation", LOKI Report NLI-3.2, University of Hamburg.

Schubert, L. Goebel, R. and Cercone, N. (1979) " The Structure and Organization of a Semantic Net for Comprehension and Inference". In, *Associative Networks: Representation and Use of Knowledge by Computer*, N.Findler (Ed.), Academic Press, New York

Smadja, F. (1989) " Lexical Co-occurence; the Missing Link, Literary and Linguistic Computing", Vol. 4, No.3.

Sondheimer, N. Cumming, S. and Albano, R. (1989) "How to Realize a Concept: Lexical Selection and the Conceptual Network in Text Generation," Proc. of the Workshop on Theoretical and Computation Issues in Lexical Semantics, Brandeis University, Boston.

Sowa, J.F. (1984) *Conceptual Structures : Information Processing in Mind and Machine*, Addison Wesley, New York.

Sowa, J.F. (1990) "Lexical Structures and Conceptual Structures." In, Semantics in the Lexicon, Pustejovsky J. (Ed.) Kluwer.

Steinacker, I. and Buchberger, E. (1983) "Relating Syntax and Semantics: the Syntactico-Semantic Lexicon of the System VIE-LANG," International Conference on Computational Linguistics, Pisa.

Stemberger, N. (1985) *The Lexicon in a Model of Speech Production,* Garland, New York.

Talmy, L. (1985) "Lexicalization Patterns: Semantic Structure in Lexical Forms. In, (ed.) Shopen, T., *Language Typology and Syntactic Descriptions: Grammatical Categories and the Lexicon*, Cambridge University Press, Cambridge.

Wanner, L. and Bateman, J. (1990) "Lexical Co-occurence relations in Text Generation," 5th International Workshop on Natural Language Generation, Pittsburgh.

Ward, N. (1988) "Issues in Word Choice," COLING.

Wojcik, L. Lewicka, H. Bogacki, K. Boguslawska, G. Kreisberg, A. Lozinska, M. Thieme, M. and Zielinska, T. (1983) *Sémantique et Syntaxe des Verbes Franéais*, Panstwowe Wydawnictwo Naukowe, Warsaw.

Zernik, U. and Dyer, M. (1987) "The Self-Extending Phrasal Lexicon," Computational Linguistics, Vol.13, 3-4.

Zock, M. (1988) "Natural Languages are Flexible Tools: that's what Makes them Hard to Explain, to Learn and to Use." In, Zock, M. and Sabah, G. (Eds.), vol. 1.

Zock, M. (1990) "Sentence Generation as Pattern Matching." In, Explorations in Cognitive Linguistics, Gargov, G. and Staynov, P. (Eds.), Benjamin, Amsterdam.

Zock, M. (1991) "SWIM or SINK: The Problem of Communicating Thought. " In, The Bridge for International Communication: ITS and Foreign Language Learning, Swartz, M. and Yazdani, M. (Eds.), Springer Verlag, Berlin.

Zock M. and Sabah, G. (Eds.), (1988) *Advances in Natural Language Generation*, Ablex, New Jersey.

22

Analysis and Generation of Italian Sentences

F. Antonacci
IBM Italy,
Rome Scientific Center,
Rome, Italy

Maria Teresa Pazienza
University of Rome, *"Tor Vergata"*,
Department of Electronic Engineering,
Rome, Italy

M. Russo
IBM Italy,
Rome Scientific Center,
Rome, Italy

Paola Velardi
University of Ancona,
Istituto di Informatica,
Ancona, Italy

ABSTRACT

This paper describes a system for the analysis of short narrative texts (press agency releases on economics and finance), developed at the Rome Scientific Center. The system uses morphologic, syntactic and semantic information to build a conceptual graph representation of the input sentence. A query-answering module processes natural language queries, performs a meaning match between a query graph and the conceptual graphs stored in the analyzed texts database, and finally produces a natural language answer.

22.1 INTRODUCTION

At the IBM Rome Scientific Center a system called has been developed for processing Italian texts. The objective of this system is to:

- analyze short narrative texts (press agency releases on finance and economics);

- give a formal representation of their meaning, represented by a conceptual graph;

- consult this knowledge base in order to answer queries concerning the analyzed texts[1].

The system is implemented in VM/Prolog (IBM, 1985). According to a definition given by Ritchie (1983), the system can be classified as sentence-final: the first pass determines the morphologic features, the second builds a syntactic structure, and finally the third creates a semantic representation. As detailed in section 22.3, there is some level of interaction between syntax and semantics, but this is limited to specific conditions met during syntactic analysis. Figs. 22.1a and b illustrate the main system components. The text analyzer shown in Fig. 22.1a consists of:

1. a *morphologic analyzer*, based on a *context free* grammar and using a lexicon of 10,000 elementary lemmata (see section 22.2.1);

2. A *morphosyntactic analyzer*, also based on context free grammars, which analyzes compound verbs and numbers, dates and comparative forms of adjectives (section 22.2.2 below);

3. a *syntactic analyzer*, consisting of an attribute grammar (AG) augmented with *lookahead sets* and *semantic checks* (section 22.3.1 below);

4. a *semantic interpreter*, based on the conceptual graphs model and using a *conceptual dictionary* of word sense definitions (see section 22.3.2 and also (Pazienza and Velardi, 1992) in this volume).

The query processor (see section 22.4), shown in Fig. 22.b includes:

- a *finance query analyzer*, which produces a conceptual graph of the input natural language query, called a *Query Graph*.

- a *conceptual matcher*, retrieving the conceptual graph(s) in the knowledge base, and entailing an answer (*Answer Graph*) (section 22.4.1);

- a *answer generator*, generating a natural language answer from the answer graph (see section 22.4.2).

Due to space constraints the presentation of the above components will be schematic and only the basic system features will be highlighted. Fuller descriptions of theoretical issues and specific language phenomena (treatment of coordination, anaphoras, etc) are given in (Antonacci, 1983) (Pazienza and Velardi, 1987a) (Pazienza and Velardi, 1987b) (Russo, 1987) and (Pazienza and Velardi, 1992) in this volume. Our aim here is to provide an example of an implemented natural language system and to show how conceptual graphs can be used as an intermediate semantic notation (interlingua) for language analysis and generation.

---

[1] These examples are taken from natural corpus press agency releases

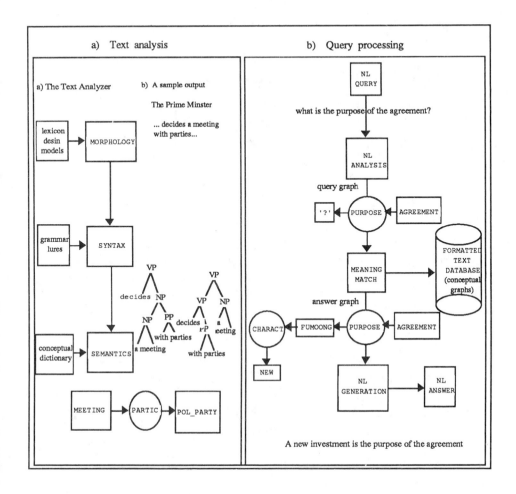

Fig. 22.1 A snapshot of DANTE.

Two problems of this project are worth mentioning. The first is that the natural language domain of application is almost unrestricted; the second is the additional complexity, compared to English, of Italian morphology and syntax. As shown in the next sections, the number of valid words which can be generated by combining stems and affixes is virtually unbound. In addition, the style of Italian texts is far more complex than English: sentences are usually very long and include nested sequences of prepositional phrases, coordinate constructions, subordinates, etc. Indeed, one purpose of this paper is to show that, in order to build a working system, linguistic theories must be flanked by pragmatic rules and tailored to the unstructured nature of the natural language problem (Newell, 1969). This is particularly true for semantics, whose problems and obscurities can hardly be categorized or even superficially attacked on a computer program. In order to resolve syntactic ambiguity and to determine the appropriate *semantic patterns* among the words of a sentence, pragmatic knowledge on word usage is to be used along with concept type definitions. This issue is addressed in detail in chapter 23 in this volume (Pazienza and Velardi, 1992).

22.2 THE MORPHOLOGIC ANALYSIS

The morphologic analyzer processes each word of a sentence, retrieving the lemma it derives from, its syntactic features (e.g. noun, adverb, etc.) and its morphologic features (e.g. plural, indicative, etc). In Italian, the creation of words is a generative process that follows several rules, as for example[2]:

> **composition:** carta (paper) → carta-moneta (paper money)
>
> **cliticization:** carta (paper) → in-car-ta-lo (to wrap it in paper)
>
> **alteration:** carta (paper) → cart-accia (waste paper)

These rules make the set of Italian words potentially unlimited and even a common dictionary might not provide sufficient information. The main issue of morphologic analysis is hence an efficient representation of the lexicon. Importantly, the *rules of word derivation* must be described, in order to derive from a limited set of lexical items all the correct Italian words. The analyzer presented hereafter has the following components:

1. a context free grammar, to describe the rules of word derivation;

2. other specific context free grammars, to recognize fixed and variable sequences of words, such as idioms, compounds, date and number expressions, comparative and superlative forms of adjectives;

3. a lexicon, structured to exploit the efficiency of the recognition process and minimize its size.

22.3 RULES OF WORD DERIVATION

Every Italian word is composed of one stem (two for compound nouns), preceded by (n)one or more *prefixes*, followed by (n)one ore more *suffixes* and *alterations*, by an ending and, if it is a verb, by (n)one or more *enclitics* (Giurescu, 1970). This structure can be described by a context free grammar, in which WORD is the axiom:

$$
\begin{aligned}
&1\ \text{WORD} \rightarrow \{\text{prefix}\}^n \langle\text{stem}\rangle\ \langle\text{REM}\rangle \\
&2\ \text{REM} \rightarrow \{\text{suffix}\}^n\ \{\text{alteration}\}^n \langle\text{TAIL}\rangle \\
&3\ \text{REM} \rightarrow \langle\text{ending}\rangle\{\text{suffix}\}^n\ \{\text{alteration}\}^n \langle\text{TAIL}\rangle \\
&4\ \text{REM} \rightarrow \langle\text{ending}\rangle\{\text{enclitic}\}^n
\end{aligned}
$$

Fig. 22.2 The grammar for WORD.

---

[2]Notice that in English the above phenomena produces more than one word, while in Italian a new single word is created where *"PORT"* is the stem of the lemma *"PORTATORE"* (to carry). *"AT"* is the ending of the past participle of the verb, *"OR"* is the stem of the deverbal suffix *"ORE"* (masculine singular) and *"I"* is the ending of the masculine plural.

The morphologic parser *recognizes* every Italian word by verifying that the word is "well-formed" in terms of the grammar in Fig. 22.2. The analyzer parses each word from left to right splitting it into elementary components and checking whether these components follow some of the above rules. For example, the word *"transportatori"* (carriers) is split into the following six parts:

prefix	prefix	stem	ending	suffix	ending
TRA	*S*	*PORT*	*AT*	*OR*	*I*

22.4 THE MORPHOSYNTACTIC ANALYZER

The analyzer also performs a morphosyntactic analysis in order to:

1. *revise* the work of morphology, by giving a single parse for compound tenses of verbs and comparative and superlative forms of adjectives, which are analyzed as separate words during the morphologic step;

2. *simplify* the work of syntax, by recognizing regular structures, such as mixed numeric forms, and by verifying the agreement in gender and number of articles and nouns, adjectives and nouns, and so on.

In order to perform the morphosyntactic analysis, four additional grammars have been written to analyze subsequences of words behaving as a unique word, as compound verbs, e.g. *"Io sono stato ieri a Roma"* ("I was in Rome yesterday"), mixed sequences of numbers and dates, e.g. *"1000 milioni di lire"* ("1000 millions of lira"), *"10 Ottebre 1987"* ("October the 10th 1987") and comparative forms of adjectives, e.g. *"il libro più interessante"* ("the most interesting book").

22.5 THE LEXICON

Two categories of lexical objects are defined: the set of lemmata and the set of word components (affixes, alterations, endings and enclitics).

The former has been structured as a relational data base under the control of SQL, (IMB, 1983): the large size and the frequent updates of the lexicon require an efficient search method (for example making use of indices) and some control strategy to avoid redundancy and inconsistency of data.

The remaining data are described by *logic predicates*; this latter set, in fact, needs not be updated, and above all its size is fixed and limited.

The lexicon is a relational database table with five attributes: the lemma, its stem, the ending class related to the stem, the syntactic feature of the lemma and an identifier specifying the type of analysis to be performed by the parser:

```
LEXICON(lemma,stem,ending_class,syntactic_feature,identifier).
```

The lemmata are called *elementary* in that they do not incorporate affixes (unlike a common dictionary). This greatly reduces the size of the lexicon. Examples of lexical entries are the following:

```
LEXICON(ancora,ancora,_,adverb,2).
LEXICON(ancora,ancor,dn_cosa,noun,2).
```

```
LEXICON(ancorare,ancor,dv_1conjug,verb,1).
LEXICON(andare,and,dvl_andare,berb,2).
LEXICON(andare,v,dv2_andare,verb,2).
LEXICON(mattino,mattin,dn_oggetto,noun,3).
LEXICON(matto,matt,da_bello,adjective,1).
LEXICON(monte,mont,dn_amore,noun,1).
LEXICON(montone,monton,dn_amore,noun,3).
```

The indentifer specifies the type of analysis to be performed: it is used to increase the efficiency of the grammar, avoiding useless or meaningless analyses as in the case, for example, of *false altered nouns*. These are words which can be analyzed as altered nouns, even if this interpretation is not used in Italian. For example, *"mattin-o"* (morning) is not a *"matt-in-o"* (little mad), just like in English "outlet" is not "a little out"! In this case the value 3 of the identifier associated to the noun *mattino* indicates that only the analysis with the longest stem is to be performed. Hence, *montone* is only to be analyzed as *"monto-e"* (mutton) and not also as *"mont-on-e"* (big mountain).

The morphologic information about a word is carried by its ending. Endings have been grouped in classes, a class of endings is the set of all the endings related to a given class of words. For example, the ending class *dv_1conjug* contains all and only the endings following the stem of every regular verb of the 1st conjugation, each one with the corresponding morphologic features. Endings are described by ternary predicates:

```
ENDING(ending_class,ending,morphologic_features).
```

Irregular verbs have been previously classified in order to detect common morphologic structures, and their endings are generally distributed in more classes. The verb *"andare"* (to go), for example, admits two different stems, *"and-"* (went) and "v-" (go-), each one related to a different subclass of endings, respectively *dv1_andare* and *dv2_andare*.

Another type of lexical object are suffixes, which change both morphologic and syntactic features of the word they apply to. Suffixes change verbs into nouns or adjectives, nouns into verbs and so on. For example, from the verb *"ancorare"* (to anchor) with the deverbal suffix *"aggio"* we obtain the noun *"ancoraggio"* (anchorage). But also from the feminine noun *"porta"* (door) with the suffix *"ale"* we obtain the masculine noun *"portale"* (door). Therefore for any suffix not only its stem must be specified, but also the ending class related to this stem (carrying the new morphologic information) and the related syntactic features (Church and Patil, 1982). Suffixes are described by quaternary predicates of the form:

```
SUFFIX(suffix,stem,ending_class,syntactic_features).
```

Other examples of morphologic data types are given in the cited papers.

22.6   STATE OF THE MORPHOLOGIC ANALYZER.

The morphologic parser presented in this section is highly flexible in the analysis of words; for example, it can be used both to *analyze* and *generate* a word, exploiting the bidirectional features of Prolog. The method required a strong initial effort in the formalization of rules (with all their exceptions) and the implementation of data structures, but enabled the full covering of all the words included in the natural corpus of derivable from them (more than 100,000 words), with a relatively small lexicon (about 10,000 elementary lemmata).

The major classes of recognized words are:

- "simple" words: directly derived from the grammar:

man-o	hand	stem-ending
man-in-a	little hand	stem-alteration-ending
man-igl-ia	hand-le	stem-suffix-ending
ri-man-egg-iare	to re-hand-le	prefix-stem-suffix-ending
man-egg-iar-lo	to-hand-le it	stem-suffix-ending-enclitic

- compond nouns: derived by applying the grammar on each of the components words and flexing them according to specific rules.

pass-a-port-o	pass-port	verb+noun.masch	*pass-a-port-i*
port-a-cener-e	ash-tray	verb+noun.fem	*port-a-cener-e*
cass-a-fort-e	stell-safe	noun+adjective	*cass-e-fort-i*

- compound tenses of verbs: recognized by means of a context free grammar whose rules are applied any time the analyzer finds a past participle of a verb in the sentence; compounds are successfully recognized even when interleaved by other words (e.g. "I have just called you").

io ho chiamato	I have called	present perfect - active
io sono chiamato	I am called	present - passive
io sono stato	I have been present	perfect - active
io sono stato chiamato	I have been called	presente perfect - passive

- comparative and superlative degree of adjectives: recognized by means of a context free grammar whose rules are applied any time the analyzer finds the adverbs *"più"* (more) or *"meno"* (less) followed by a qualifying adjective or by the past participle of a verb.

il più bello	the most beautiful	relative superlative of beautiful
più bello	more beautiful	majority comparative of beautiful
più amato	more loved majority	comparative of loved
il migliore	the best relative	superlative of good

- numeric expressions: cardinal numbers are recognized by a context free grammar which also translates string into numbers. Similarly, another grammar recognizes mixed numeric expressions.

trecentocinquanta	three hundred and fifty	350
3 milioni 500,000	three million and five hundred thousand	350,000

- date expressions: recognized by a context free grammar.

venerdi 14 aprile	friday April the 14th
25 maggio 1987	May 25th 1987

Fig. 22.3 shows a morphology analysis session. The screen shows a list of sentences, and a field which can be overwritten to introduce new text. In the single word mode, the user selects with the cursor a word; the frame appearing on the screen gives the morphologic analysis of that word.

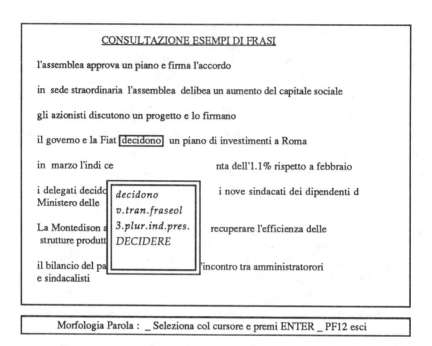

Fig. 22.3 Morphologic analysis: single word mode

The results of the morphologic and morphosyntactic analysis are input to the syntactic parser. Unlike morphology and semantics, the problem of syntactic analysis is not so much the size of the knowledge sources, but rather the risk of combinatorial explosion of the analysis process. The syntax of many languages is such that, during each step of a parsing process, several grammar rules could be applied (Charniak, 1983). As shown by the examples in this paper, Italian presents increased problems compared with English, because of the complex style of written texts. The important aspects of the syntactic analyzer are:

1. the use of an *attribute grammar* to specify rules on word sequencing and forms agreement;

2. the use of *lookahead sets* and semantic checks to further reduce syntactic ambiguity.

Hereafter, the choice of an attribute grammar to represent syntactic rules is motivated. The remainder of the section describes the adopted control strategies. The last part gives some detail on the system coverage at the current stage of implementation.

22.7   THE ATTRIBUTE GRAMMAR

Consider the following (restricted) grammar:

```
1 SENTENCE→ <PHRASE >
2 SENTENCE→ <VP >
3 PHRASE    → <NP> <VP>
4 NP        → <det>  <noun>
5 NP        → <adj>  <noun>
6 NP        → <det>  <adj>  <noun>
7 VP        → <verb>  <NP>
```

Fig. 22.4 A simple grammar.

The above grammar can analyze for example the following sentences:

1. L'importante compagnia partecipa all'accordo

2. L'important i compagnia partecipa all'accordo

3. Le importante compagnia partecipa all'accordo

   (The important company participates in the agreement)

In Italian, adjectives and determiners can be flexed; of the above sentences, only the first presents an agreement in gender and number between determiner, adjective and noun. To express in a uniform way rules of form agreement, which are more complex than in English, an attribute grammar has been adopted.

Attribute grammars were first introduced by Knuth (1971, 1968) as a method to specify the semantics of programming languages. An attribute grammar is a context free grammar augmented with *attributes* and *applicability conditions*. If S is a symbol of the grammar, an attribute associated to S is written "$S.a$". Applicability conditions are associated to the rules of the grammar (Farrow, 1982) (Lorho, 1977). Hence, for example, rules 3 and 4 of Fig. 22.4 become:

```
3' PHRASE  →  <NP> <VP>
                NP.number = VP.number
4' NP      →  <det> <noun>
                det.gender = noun.gender
                det.number = noun.number
```

In DANTE, a top-down, sequential parser based on attribute grammars has been implemented, which covers a large subset of Italian sentences (Antonacci, 1987).

In addition to the attribute conditions other control strategies have been added. A frequent phenomenon in Italian sentences is the presence of nested hypotactical structures, as for example in:

Gli azionisti in assemblea discutono la proposta di un piano per recuperare l'efficienza delle strutture produttive e di servizio.

The shareholders in a meeting discuss the proposal of a project to restore the efficiency of the productive and (of) service structures.[3]

---

[3] Recall that the following English translations are literal translations used to give the reader some insight of the sentence complexity.

The above sentence has five prepositional phrases and one conjunction. Because this represents the standard sentence complexity, an uncontrolled application of the grammar of Fig. 22.3 would be hopelessly inefficient (Church and Patil, 1982). Two strategies have been adopted to limit the number of possible inference paths to be tested at each step: *lookahead sets* and *semantic checks*.

22.8 LOOKAHEAD SETS

Lookahead sets have been introduced for the analysis of deterministic context free languages, specifically for $LL(k)$ grammars (Hopcroft and Ullman, 1979). Given a prodution p, a lookahead set is the set of all the possible *first* k terminals reachable from that production. An $LL(k)$ grammar in analyzable if the lookahead sets of all the production with the same head are disjoint. The application of lookahead sets to non deterministic grammars revealed to be a useful method to reduce the number of possible productions. In our system, to each rule the set of the *first* terminal symbols is associated; given the grammar of Fig. 22.4, the correspondent sets are:

```
    1. *DETERMINER  ADJECTIVE *
    2. *VERB*
    3. *DETERMINER, ADJECTIVE*
    4. *DETERMINER *
    5. *ADJECTIVE*
    6. *DETERMINERS*
    7. *VERB*
```

Fig. 22.5 Lookahead sets.

When more than one rule is applicable at a given step of analysis, a rule is selected such that the transitive closure of its derivations has the first terminal symbol coinciding with the current symbol under analysis. For example, given the sentence *"La Ace firma un contratto"* (The Ace company signs a contract), the backtrack over the axiom SENTENCE forces the evaluation of rule 4 of Fig. 22.4, because the first symbol of the input string is a DETERMINER (*"la"* + the). The introduction of lookahead sets reduced by a 45% the parsing time obtained with an uncontrolled top-down sequential parser.

22.9 SEMANTIC CHECKS

The use of semantic constraints in guiding syntactic analysis is not novel (Hirst and Charniak, 1982) (Oden, 1983) (Schubert, 1986); in fact most of the natural language processing systems presented in the literature perform syntactic and semantic analysis in parallel. In our system a fully interleaving between these two knowledge sources was rejected because of efficiency, as argued in what follows. Let us consider the sentence:

"La Ace richiede la quotazione del titolo Fiat presso le banche di Roma e Milano"

The Ace asks the quotation of the Fiat shares at the banks of Rome and Milan.

the following analyses are syntactically correct:

1. VP → VP(ask the quotation of the Fiat shares) PP(at the banks ...)

2. NP → Np(the quotation of the Fiat shares) PP(at the banks ...)

3. NP → NP(the Fiat shares) PP(at the banks ...)

these phrases when considered individually are also semantically correct; in fact, one can ask something at a bank, a quotation can be valid at a bank, and finally the Fiat shares could have been deposited at a bank. Only a deeper context analysis would assign a preference to the second interpretation. In other terms, during the process of syntactic analysis, semantics can only produce local interpretations, that can be rejected at a later time.

In our system, semantic checks are performed to prune implausible syntactic subparses and not to gradually build a semantic representation; the results of these tests are stored for further analysis during the semantic step. Semantic checks are introduced in the applicability conditions of the grammar rules which usually give rise to ambiguities, that is the rules including prepositional phrases, relative and parenthetic clauses.

The semantic check is performed by the predicate:

beginquote SEMANTIC_CHECK(leftnode head,functional_sign,rightnode.head)
where leftnode, and rightnode are the leftmost and rightmost symbols one the right hand side of a rule. When the symbol is not a terminal, the head is evaluated as follows:

NP.head = noun
VP.head = verb

functional_sign is a member of the list (preposition conjunction prepositional_adverb nil), where nil is the null element. For example, a semantic check over the rule b is:

SEMANTIC_CHECK(NP.quotation,AT,PP.bank).

which reads "verify whether the preposition "at" subsumes some semantically plausible conceptual relation between the words quotation and bank". The exact way this verification is performed will be discussed in the next section and in chapter 23 in this volume (Pazienza and Velardi, 1992).

The use of semantic checks, in combination with attributes and lookahead sets, dramatically reduces the number of parse trees produced by the syntactic analyzer; in most cases, no more than two parses are given even for pluri-prepositional sentences.

22.10   STATE OF THE SYNTACTIC ANALYZER

The grammar presented in this section covers a relatively large fragment of Italian; a top-down, sequential parser is automatically generated by a meta-analyzer (Antonacci, 1987), and consists of about 100 rules. Two of these rules are shown in Fig. 22.6. Note the semantic check in the attribute conditions of the second rule.

```
/* CLAUSE < - NP VP

FRASE < - GR_NOM GR_VERBALE

Attribute Conditions:
1.SOGGPRES:=NO,NOT_MEMBER(1.MODO,IMPER.GERU.PART.INF.NIL),
1.PERSONA:=TRE,NOT_MEMBER(0.NOME,SI,MI.LA.NIL)

Attribute Evaluation:
FRASE.SOGG=GR_NOM.PROVENIENZA,FRASE.OGG=1.OGG,FRASE.TIPO=1 TIPO,
FRASE.CLASSE=1.CLASSE,FRASE.ENCLIT=1.ENCLIT,FRASE.FORMA=1.FORMA,
FRASE.TIPOFRASE=0.TIPO

/* NP < - NP1 PP

GR_NOM < - GR_NOM_UNO GR_PREP

Attribute Conditions:
SEMANTIC_CHECK(FPN,0.PROVENIENZA,1.PREP,1.PROVENIENZA)0.ATTR:=NO,
0.CONGINIZ:=NO

Attribute Evaluation:
GR_NOM.GENERE=0.GENERE,GR_NOM.NUMERO=0.NUMERO,
GR_NOM.PROVENIENZA=0.PROVENIENZA,GR__NOM.PREP=1.PREP,
GR_NOM.ART=0.ARTICOLO, GR_NOM.PREPPRES:=SI,GR_NOM.SPROV:=NO,
GR_NOM.APPOS=0.APPOS, GR_NOM.TIPO=0.TIPO, GR_NOM.APP=0.APP,
GR_NOM.AGG=0.AGG, GR_NOM.AGGETTIVO=0.AGGETTIVO,GR_NOM.CONG=0.CONG,
GR_NOM.NOME=0.NOME, GR_NOM.ALTERAZIONE=0.ALTERAZIONE
```

Fig. 22.6

The meta-analyzer is provided with a user friendly interface for a "natural" insertion of grammar rules, and with a method to propose the applicability conditions on the attributes. The following is a list of syntactic structures which are successfully analyzed[4].

- Simple clauses (NP VP, VP) .

> "La regione firma un accordo"
> The local government signs an agreement

> "Inizia la costruzione di una fabbrica"
> It stats the building of a plant.

where in the second Italian sentence has no NP as subject.

- Lists of adjectives.

> "L'ultimo grande magnifico modello.."
> The last great beautiful model ...,

---

[4]The examples are taken form the natural corpus of press agency releases.

- Prepositional phrases.

    un accordo con un partner
    an agreement with a partner,

    Firmare con un partner
    To sign with a partner,

- Compounds, appositions, relative clauses.

    "Il bilancio che si è chiuso ..."
    sl The financial year which closed ...,

- Quantifiers.

    "Alcuni dei progetti"
    Some of the projects.

- Dates and numbers.

    "L'assemblea degli azionisti della Perugina (gruppo Ibp) approva il bilancio dell'esercizio che si è chiuso il 30 settembre 1981 con 660 milioni di lire di utili"
    The Perugina (an Ibp owned company) shareholder's meeting approves the budget of the financial year which closed on the 30th. of September 1981 with 660 millions lira of profits.

- Complex clauses (subordinates, conjunctions, parenthesized clauses).

    "Il progetto prevede un piano formativo che coinvolga la maggior parte dei lavoratori per recuperare l'efficienza delle strutture produttive e di servizio e rendere possibile soluzioni di mobilità interna."
    The project consists of an educational plan that involves most of the workers, to recover the efficiency of the production and to make it possible solutions of internal mobility.

    "L'assemblea nomina membri del consiglio d'amminstrazione per il triennio 1982 - 1984 Giuseppina Antonelli, Bruno Buitoni, Gianfranco Buitoni, Marco Buitoni, Silvi Pellizzoni, Vittorio Ripa di Meana"
    The council elects as members of the board of directors for the three years period 1982 - 1984 Giuseppina Antonelli, Bruno Buitoni, Gianfranco Buitoni, Marco Buitoni, Silvio Pellizzoni, Vittorio Ripa di Meana.

    "Il progetto procede velocemente e con molti risultati"
    The project proceds quickly and with many results.

- Interrogatives.

"Quale societè ha firmato un accordo ieri?"
Which company signed an agreement yesterday?,

A graphic feature has been implemented to visualize the parse trees produced for each sentence, before semantic analysis. In Fig. 22.7 it is shown the parse produced for the sentence:

"L'assemblea degli azionisti approva il bilancio con una votazione"
The shareholder's meeting approves the budget by means of a vote

Notice that, due to the semantic check, only one tree is produced; in fact the test over the subtree: NP ← NP(the budget) PP(by means of a vote) which is:

```
SEMANTIC_CHECK(NP.budget,BY_MEANS_OF,PP.vote).
```

fails, because the words vore and budget cannot be semantically related.

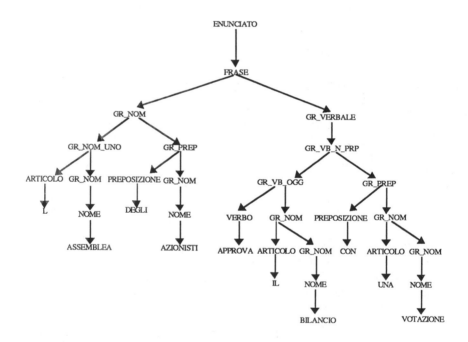

Fig. 22.7 Example of syntactic tree.

22.11 INTERFACE BETWEEN SYNTAX AND SEMANTICS

The final step is semantic analysis; at the same time, this is also the most complex component of a natural language processing system. An ontology of semantic knowledge is an onology of human knowledge; no computer system could cope with such a broad mandate. A realistic objective is to pursue some understanding of a piece of language, which ultimately makes the human-computer communication more flexible and natural than an ordinary computer language.

According to a categorization proposed by Wilks (1983), the semantic processor described in this section is a micro-semantic analyzer, that is, its objective is to produce a representation corresponding to the sentence clauses discovered during syntactic analysis.

The structure of the semantic dictionary and the algorithm for semantic interpretation are presented in chapter 23. Only the interface with syntax is discussed here.

The partial interleaving between syntax and semantics is activated on specific syntactic rules, namely prepositional phrases, parenthesized and relative clauses. The semantic check predicate is directly mapped into a *syntactic predicate*. We recall that the syntactic predicate name is the name of a syntactic node in the parse tree (e.g. np-pp = NP←NP PP) and its arguments are the left and right sons of that node. Consider for example the semantic check of the preceding session:

```
SEMANTIC _CHECK (VP.approve, BY_MEANS_OF, PP.vote).
```

This corresponds to the syntactic predicate:

$vp\_pp(approve, by\_means\_of, vote).$

which is interpreted by the semantic component as follows:

$approve(*x) \wedge MEAN(*x, *y) \wedge vote(*y)$

Only a yes/no answer is returned to the syntactic parser, which accordingly proceeds in, or rejects, the current analysis. The graph obtained by this early semantic interpretation is temporarily stored and retrieved during the semantic step to avoid repetition of identical analyses.

22.12 QUERY ANSWERING

The analysis of a sentence succeeds, provided that the words are defined in the dictionary and the syntactic component is able to parse the sentence. Obviously, the first constraint is the more selective. The results is a conceptual graph, which can be visualized through a graphic facility. Graphs are stored in form of first order logic expressions in a semantic database, and consulted by natural language queries; a query answering module retrieves graphs and procedures a natural language answer. When analyzing a text, its linguistic structure is an evidence of the problem; the objective is to explicit the conceptual model behind the text. In language generation, the problem is reversed: the *meaning* is a data, the linguistic structure is to be found (Goldman, 1975). Creating an utterance out of a purely semantic representation requires the system be able to take several decisions, as for example:

- active versus passive form, the graph:

$company : Ace \wedge AGNT(*x, Ace) \wedge sign(*x) \wedge THEME(*x, *y) \wedge contract : (*y)$

may be expressed by the utterances: "The Ace sign a contract" or "A contract is signed by the Ace".

- Synthetic versus literal. The graph:

$$delegate(*x) \land PARTICIPANT(*y, *x) \land MEETING(*y)$$

can be read: "a meeting between delegates" or "the delegates participate to a meeting". In the first case the conceptual relation is expressed by a preposition (between); in the second case, it is translated literally.

- Emphasis. The graph:

$$item(\#x) \land PART\_OF(\#x, *y \land statute(*y)$$

can be read: "the items of a statute" or "a statute with items", depending upon the focus of the sentence including this phrase.

- Ordering. The graph:

$$important(*x) \land CHRC(*y, *x) \land agreement(*y)$$

is read in English "an important agreement"; in Italian however (as all in-order languages) the adjective can also be postponed: *"un accordo importante"*.

- Synonyms. Consider the graph:

$$pol\_party(\#x) \land ORIGINATOR(\#x, *y) \land belief(*y)$$

As discussed in Velardi *et al.* (1988) semantic ambiguity of words is resolved during the analysis process: in this case, POL_PARTY indicates a political party, rather than in the good time party sense. However, a word-sense might correspond to many words (synonyms and paronyms); for example, the above graph can be read: "the belief of the party", or "the opinion of the party" or also "the view of the party".

At the current state of the project the problem of language generation has been circumscribed to query answering. Queries must concern the texts which have been previously processed by the system, and stored in form of conceptual graphs in a knowledge base. Answers to such queries, as shown in the following section, generally can be uttered by simple sentences (much simpler than the analyzed text), thus reducing generation problems. On the other hand, answering a query involves the *conceptual matching* between the query and graph stored in the knowledge base, and the entailment of an *answer graph* from which an utterance is generated.

22.13 QUERY/ANSWER MATCH

This section gives an overview of the query matching process in DANTE. When a query is formulated the system first processes it as a standard declarative sentence. The semantic interpreter however is augmented with additional features, some of which are listed below:

1. Pronouns (who, what, whom, etc.) are replaced by uninstantiated concepts (dummy concept)

2. When a pronoun is in the subject (or object) position in a syntactic predicate, two interpretations might be produced; for example, given the query:

   "Who nominates Doe?"

   the two interpretations are:

   $person(Doe) \land AGNT(*x, Doe)nominate(*x) \land PATIENT(*x, ?) \land dummy(?)$

   $dummy(?) \land AGNT(*x, ?) \land nominate(*x) \land PATIENT(*x, Doe) \land person(Doe)$

3. multiple interpretations are produced also because of the lack of semantic constraints; for example:

   What does the Ace do?

   $company(Ace) \land AGNT(?, Ace) \land dummy(?)$

   $company(Ace) \land PARTICIPANT(?, Ace) \land dummy(?)$

   The two graphs are generated because the query does not mention any specific action; in this case, the system generates all the semantically plausible graphs. In the above example, a SOCIAL_ORGANIZATION, e.g. company, can either be AGNT of, or PARTICIPANT to, an action. An example of the first case is "The Ace (AGNT) signs a contract", an example of the second is "It has been signed an agreement between (PARTICIPANT) the Ace and the Fiat";

4. pronouns, adverbs and queries making an explicit reference to a conceptual relation name, are directly mapped into that conceptual relation; examples are:

   What is the purpose of the contact?
   $contract(*x) \land PURPOSE(*x, ?) \land dummy(?)$

   Where does the meeting take place?
   $meeting(*x) \land LOC(*x, ?) \land dummy(?)$

   How long does the conference last?
   $conference(*x) \land TIME\_LENGHT(?) \land dummy(?)$

At the end of the query analysis process, one or more query graphs (QGs) are generated. The query/answer matching algorithm finds for each query graph QG_i all the graphs CG_j in the knowledge base, such that there exist a projection PQG_j of QG_j on CG_j. The projection operation[5] is here intended as in (Sowa, 1984), with the extension that for each

---

[5]Given two graphs u and v, a projection $p : v \rightarrow u$ is a graph pv such that for each concept c in v there is a concept pc in pv where $pc \Leftarrow c$ in the hierarchy, and for each relation REL in v there is a relation P_REL in pv where REL=P_REL. If the argument i of REL is c, then the argument i of P_REL is pc.

concept c of QG_i there must be a concept pc of PCG_j such that either $c = pc$ or c and pc are paronyms (for example, company and firm are paronyms).[6]

The projection operation cause the uninstantiated concepts of QG_i, $*c_1, \ldots, *c_n$ to be unified with the correspondent concepts of PCG_j. Let $x_1, \ldots, x_n$ be the instantiation in PQG_j of $*c_1, \ldots, *c_n$ in QG_i. The answer graph AG is obtained by adding to PQG_j all the modifiers of $x_1, \ldots, x_n$ which are not included in PQG_j but are included in CG_j. For example, the QG:

$$company(Ace) \wedge AGNT(?, Ace) \wedge dummy(?)$$

matches with the graph:

$$company(Ace) \wedge AGNT(\#x, Ace) \wedge sign(\#x) \wedge THEME(\#x, *y) \wedge$$

$$agreement(*y) \wedge PURPOSE(*y, *z) \wedge funding(*x) \wedge CHRC(*z, *k) \wedge new(*k)$$

the PQG is

$$company(Ace) \wedge AGNT(\#x, Ace) \wedge sign(\#x)$$

hence $x_l = sign(\#x)$; the modifier of x_l not included in PQG is

$$THEME(\#x, *y) \wedge agreement(*y)$$

and the attribute grammar will be:

$$company(Ace) \wedge AGNT(\#x, Ace) \wedge sign(\#x) \wedge THEME(\#x, *y) \wedge agreement(*y)$$

If more than one match of a QG occurs, more than one answer is produced to the initial query. Multiple answer are also generated if more than one QG of the initial query has a match in the knowledge base (the formulation of the query was ambiguous or generic).

22.14   ANSWER GENERATION

After an attribute grammar is generated, a language generation module produces an utterance in Italian. The process of utterance generation follows three basic steps:

1. starting from a conceptual relation that links a subject to the main predicate (AGNT, EXPERIENCER, PARTICIPANT etc) a nested graph is generated; for example, the graph:

    $person(Doe) \wedge AGNT(*x, Doe) \wedge nominate(*x) \wedge PATIENT(*x, Brown) \wedge person(Brown)$

    gives the nested graph:

    $AGNT(nominate(*x) \wedge PATIENT(*x, Brown) \wedge person(Brown), person(Doe))$

---

[6]Remember that the condition $c > pc$ is never met because there are not supertype relations between word-senses, as detailed in Velardi *et al.* (1988). Paronymy is a kind of "closer" brotherhood.

2. in the nested graph conceptual relation names are replaced by syntactic predicates, applying from right to left correspondence table used for semantic analysis (Velardi, 1988):

$$subj(nominate(*x) \land obj(*x, Brown) \land person(Brown), person(Doe))$$

The Attribute Grammar described in section 22.3.1 is used to produce a parse tree:

PHRASE → noun(Person(Brown)) VP
noun.number = VP.number VP → verb(nominate(*x)) noun(person(Doe))

3. the terminals at the end of step 2 are still concepts. The morphologic synthesizer replaces concepts by declined words, using the following constraints:

- gender and number of nouns are specified by the concepts referents;

- determiners are generated according to the referent type (generic or specific) and stylistic rules (e.g. names do not require a determiner);

- tenses and moods of verbs are determined by temporal and modal conceptual relations (present indicative is the default);

- adjective and verbs inherit gender and number (in Italian these can be flexed), according to the attribute conditions specified in the grammar rules.

Many important aspects are not dealt with, due to space limitations. These are for example coordinations, ordering of adjectives (Italian is an order language), emphasis, use of literal versus synthetic forms (see the beginning of this section for examples). The interested reader might refer to (Velardi et al., 1988). Some syntactic structures are not utterable at the current state of the generation module, as anaphoric references and parenthesized clauses. These however are unnecessary for answer generation, because the structure of the attribute grammars is usually simple.

22.15   STATE OF THE QUERY ANSWERING MODULE

At the current state of DANTE, in order to answer a query, the commonalities between the query formulation and the stored sentence must appear at a level which is not too general. For example, given the sentence:

> " *Ieri, nel corso di un incontro per l'acquisizione di nuovi fondi, il Presidente Doe ha nominato a Roma Mr. A, Mr. B and Mr. C membri del consiglio di amministrazione, per rafforzare la propria posizione .... "*
> During a meeting for new funding in Rome yesterday, the President Doe nominated Mr. A, Mr. B and Mr. C members of the board of directors, to enforce his team ...

The following is a list of queries the system can answer (the answer is also shown, as given by the system during a query session):

Q. *"Chi nomina il presidente Doe?"*
Who nominates the President Doe?

A. *"Il presidente Doe ha nominato membri Mr. A, Mr. B and Mr. C."*
The President Doe nominated Mr. A, Mr. B and Mr. C members

Q. *"Chi nomina Mr. B membro del consiglio di amministrazione?"*
Who nominates Mr. B members of the board of directors?

A. *"Il presidente Doe ha nominato Mr. B membro del consiglio di amministrazione."*
The President Doe nominated Mr. B member of the board of directors.

Q. *"Quando ha nominati Mr. C il presidente?"*
When did the President nominate Mr. C?

A. *"Il presidente ha nominato Mr. C ieri."*
The President nominated Mr. C yesterday.

Q. *"Dove sono stati nominati Mr. B e Mr. C?"*
Where have been Mr. B and Mr. C nominated?

A. *"Mr. B e Mr. C sono stati nominati a Roma."*
Mr. B and Mr. C were nominated at Rome.

Q. *"Che cosa ha fatto ieri il presidente?"*
What did the President do yesterday?

A. *"Il presidente ha nominato a Roma ieri in un incontro Mr. A, Mr. B and Mr. C."*
The President Doe nominated at Rome yesterday in a meeting Mr. A, Mr. B and Mr. C

Q. *"Quale è lo scopo dell'incontro?"*
What is the purpose of the meeting?

A. *"I nuovi fondi sono lo scopo dell'incontro."*
The purpose of the meeting is new funding

Whereas the following queries:

Who is now in the board of directors?
Is a nomination one of the purpose of the meeting?

require, in order to be answered, a more detailed knowledge by the system on the causes and consequences of specific situations, and the capability of mapping {indexsemantic!micro-semantic structures micro-semantic structures into deep representations. The difficulty of this mapping has been remarked in Velardi *et al.* (1988). Although the system has some important limitation, it is quite successful at answering the queries of "naive" users. In order to test system's ability to produce answers, a panel is shown to the user which lists the sentences stored in the knowledge base. The user is required to type in whatever question concerning these sentences; a correct answer is generated in the large majority of cases[7]; the screen appears as in Fig. 22.8.

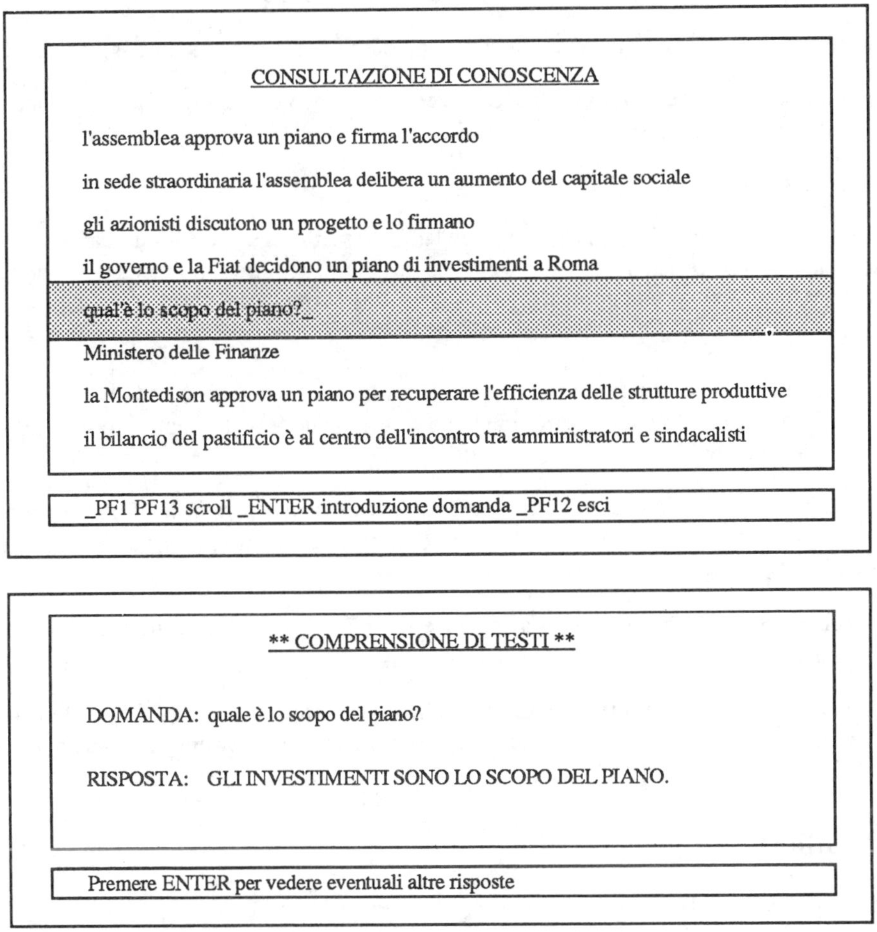

```
┌──────────────────────────────────────────────────────────────────────┐
│  ┌────────────────────────────────────────────────────────────────┐  │
│  │                  CONSULTAZIONE DI CONOSCENZA                     │  │
│  │                                                                  │  │
│  │   l'assemblea approva un piano e firma l'accordo                 │  │
│  │                                                                  │  │
│  │   in sede straordinaria l'assemblea delibera un aumento del capitale sociale │
│  │                                                                  │  │
│  │   gli azionisti discutono un progetto e lo firmano               │  │
│  │                                                                  │  │
│  │   il governo e la Fiat decidono un piano di investimenti a Roma  │  │
│  │   qual'è lo scopo del piano?_                                    │  │
│  │   Ministero delle Finanze                                       │  │
│  │                                                                  │  │
│  │   la Montedison approva un piano per recuperare l'efficienza delle strutture produttive │
│  │                                                                  │  │
│  │   il bilancio del pastificio è al centro dell'incontro tra amministratori e sindacalisti │
│  └────────────────────────────────────────────────────────────────┘  │
│                                                                        │
│  ┌────────────────────────────────────────────────────────────────┐  │
│  │  _PF1 PF13 scroll _ENTER introduzione domanda _PF12 esci        │  │
│  └────────────────────────────────────────────────────────────────┘  │
└──────────────────────────────────────────────────────────────────────┘

┌──────────────────────────────────────────────────────────────────────┐
│  ┌────────────────────────────────────────────────────────────────┐  │
│  │                  ** COMPRENSIONE DI TESTI **                    │  │
│  │                                                                  │  │
│  │   DOMANDA:  quale è lo scopo del piano?                          │  │
│  │                                                                  │  │
│  │   RISPOSTA:  GLI INVESTIMENTI SONO LO SCOPO DEL PIANO.           │  │
│  └────────────────────────────────────────────────────────────────┘  │
│                                                                        │
│  ┌────────────────────────────────────────────────────────────────┐  │
│  │  Premere ENTER per vedere eventuali altre risposte              │  │
│  └────────────────────────────────────────────────────────────────┘  │
└──────────────────────────────────────────────────────────────────────┘
```

Fig. 22.8 A snapshot of DANTE.

22.16 FINAL REMARKS

This chapter described some of the implementation issues encountered during the development of DANTE, which analyzes press agency releases on finance and economics. Space constraints did not permit to fully justify the theoretical decision taken during the design of the system; the interested reader may refer to the bibliography for extended descriptions of specific issues.

The chapter provided an example of application of the conceptual graphs model, used in the system to:

---

[7]"Large majority" is all what we can say now, given that we are dealing with a research prototype, whose features continuously change.

- represent semantic knowledge in a conceptual dictionary;

- interact with the syntactic analyzer, in order to prune implausible parses;

- build a knowledge base where the meaning of the analyzed sentences is represented;

- answer queries concerning the analyzed texts, by performing a meaning match between query and stored sentences;

- generate utterances in Italian.

The complexity and the size of the knowledge domain (press agency releases do not present any severe restriction in the sentence structure) required a considerable design effort for data structures and control algorithms. At the current state of implementation, the system is able to:

1. In addition, a pre-analyzer is used to detect idiomatic expression and proper names. derive the morphologic features of all the words included in the natural corpus (100% of coverage over some 100,000 words).

2. derive the syntactic structure of input sentences, in form of parse trees, for the majority of cases. Roughly, the estimated coverage is of about an 80% of successes over the natural corpus;

3. provide some some insight of a sentence meaning, by making word senses and the conceptual relations among them explicit;

4. store this meaning representation in a knowledge base, as a set of first order logic expressions, and consult this knowledge base in order to answer questions about the contents of the analyzed texts.

BIBLIOGRAPHY

IBM Corp. (1983) SQL/Data System, Terminal User's Reference.

IBM Corp. (1985) VM/Programming in Logic, Program Description/Operational Manual, SH20-6541-0

Antonacci, F. (1987) "Using Semantic Hints in a Syntactic Parser", IBM Technical Report no. SCR-0004.

Charniak, E., (1983) "A Parser with Something for Everyone", in (ed) M. King *Parsing Natural Language*, pp. 117-149, Academic Press.

Church, K. and R. Patil, (1982) "Coping with Syntactic Ambiguity or How to Put the Block in the Box on the Table", American Journal of Computational Linguistics, vol. 8, no. 3-4, pp. 139-149.

D'Addio, W. (1968) *Su alcune modalitè di suffissazione in Italiano*, Proc. of II Conf. of Societè Linguistica Italiana, Rome.

Davis, R. and D. Lenat, (1982) *Knowledge-based Systems in Artificial Intelligence*, McGraw Hill.

De Jong, G. (1979) "Skimming stories in real time: An experiment in integrated understanding", Yale Univ. Dept. of Computer Science, Technical Report, no. 158.

Farrow, R. (1982) LINGUIST-86 "Yet another translator writing system based on attribute grammars", Proc. of the SIGPLAN 82, Symposium on Compiler Constructions ACM, pp. 160-171.

Giurescu, A. (1970) *Problemi della formazione delle parole in Italiano*, Proc. of IV Conf. of Societé Italiana, Rome.

Goldman, N. (1975) "Conceptual generation", in Ed. R. Schank *Conceptual Information Processing*, North-Holland.

Hirst, G. and E. Charniak, (1982) "Word sense and case slot disambiguation", Proc. of AAAI, pp 95-98.

Hopcroft, J. and J. Ullman, (1979) *Introduction to automata theory, languages and computation*, pp 248-279, Addison Wesley.

Knuth, D. (1968) "Semantics of Context- free Languages", Mathematical System Theory, vol. 2, 127-145.

Knuth, D. (1971) "Semantics of Context- free Languages: Correction", Mathematica System Theory, vol. 5, 95- 96.

Lorho, B. (1977) "Semantic attribute processing in the system DELTA", in)ed) A. Ershov and C.H.A. Koster: *Methods of Algorithmic Language Implementation*, pp. 21-40, Springer-Verlag.

Moore, R. (1985) "The role of logic in knowledge representation and commonsense reasoning", in (ed) Brachman and Levesque *Readings in Knowledge Representation*, Morgan Kaufmann Publisher.

Newell, A. (1969) "Heuristic programming: ill-structured problems", in *Progress in Operations Research*, vol. 3.

Oden, C.G., (1983) "On the use of semantic constraints in guiding syntactic analysis", Int. Journal on Man-Machine Studies, no. 19, pp. 335-357, Academic Press.

Pazienza, M.T. and P. Velardi, (1987) "A structured Representation of Word Senses for Semantic Analysis", Third Conference of the European Chapter of the ACL, Copenhagen.

Pazienza, M.T. and P. Velardi, (1987) "Integrating Conceptual Graphs and Logic in a Natural Language Understanding System" in *Natural Language Understanding and Logic Programming*, North-Holland.

Ritchie, G. (1983) "Semantics in Parsing, in (ed) M. King *Parsing Natural Language*, Academic Press.

Russo, M. (1987) "A Generative Grammar Approach for the Morphologic and Morphosyntactic Analysis of Italian", Third Conference of the European Chapter of the ACL, Copenhagen.

Russo, M. (1987) "A Rule Based System for the Morphologic and Morphosyntactic Analysis of the Italian Language", in *Natural Language Understanding and Logic Programming*, North-Holland.

Schubert, L.K. (1986) "Are there preference trade-offs in attachment decisions?", Proceedings of AAAI, vol. 1.

Velardi, P. M.T. Pazienza and M. De Giovanetti, (1988) "Conceptual Graphs for the Analysis and Generation of Sentences", IBM Journal of Research and Development.

Wilks, Y. (1983) "Deep and Superficial Parsing", in (ed) M. King, *Parsing Natural Language*, Academic Press.

23

Representing Word Senses for Semantic Analysis

Maria Teresa Pazienza
University of Rome *"Tor Vergata"*
Department of Engineering Electronic,
Rome, Italy

Paola Velardi
University of Ancona,
Istituto di Informatica,
Ancona, Italy

ABSTRACT

A project for Italian text understanding is being developed at the IBM Rome Scientific Center. Morphologic, syntactic and semantic processors perform the analysis of texts fed into the system by a press-agency release database. Texts analyzed by the system components are represented in form of conceptual graphs (Sowa, 1984). This chapter deals with the definition of a Semantic Knowledge Base (SKB). Because Italian sentences have a complex structure (usually long, nested hypotactical phrases), syntactic analysis often produces a large number of parse trees. In order to fully cope with language phenomena as metonimies, ambiguity, figures of speech, etc., the semantic knowledge base stores pragmatic knowledge on word usage. Pragmatics here is knowledge about semantically valid and commonly encountered word usage (Weischedel, 1986). The knowledge representation scheme presented in this paper: (i) provides a means to solve syntactic ambiguity even for very complex sentences as encountered in the application domain; (ii) introduces criteria to solve the well known difficulties found with type hierarchies; (iii) is the basis for deriving a semantic representation of sentences.

23.1   INTRODUCTION

A Natural Language (NL) interface for text processing is being developed at the IBM Rome Scientific Center. A prototype has been implemented to analyze a database of press agency releases on finance and economics. The system analyzes each sentence and generates an internal representation of its meaning in form of Conceptual Graphs. Conceptual Graphs are stored in a database and retrieved by natural language queries (Pazienza and Velardi, 1987b).

The NL Processor (described in chapter 22), is based on four levels of analysis: i) morphologic ii) morphosyntactic iii) syntactic and iv) semantic.

The morphology (Russo, 1987) associates at least one lemma to each word; in Italian this task is particularly complex due to the presence of recursive generation mechanism, such as alternations, nominalization of verbs, etc. For example, from the lemma casa (home) it is possible to derive the words *cas-etta* (little home), *cas-ett-ina* (nice-little home), *cas-ett-in-accia* (ugly nice little home) and so on. Forms are generated using a context free grammar (Knuth, 1968) were the word is the axiom and prefixes, suffixes, alternations, endings and enclitics are the terminal elements. At present, the system performs the morphologic analysis of all the words included in the natural corpus of agency releases (about 100,000 words).

The syntactic analyzer (Antonacci, 1987) determines syntactic attachment between words by verifying grammar rules and forms agreement; the system is based on a context free grammar. Italian syntax is more complex than English. In fact sentences are usually composed by nested hypotactical phrases, rather than linked paratactical. For example, a sentence like *"John goes with his girl friend Mary to the club by the city to meet a friend for a pizza party"* might sound odd in English but is a common sentence structure in Italian.

Hence, a main problem is to determine the correct prepositional attachments between words. Syntactic relations only reveal the surface structure of a sentence; it is the task of semantics to explicit relations between words. For example, in the above sentence about John's trip the preposition "with" has the meaning of "accompaniment" ("John with Mary"), the first occurrence of the preposition to indicates the destination of the act go ("goes to the club"), the second occurrence indicates the purpose of John's trip ("to meet a friend") etc.

Conceptual Graphs seem particularly suitable for expressing semantic relations between words. Hence, they have been adopted in our system as the underlying formalism to express the meaning of a sentence and to represent semantic knowledge.

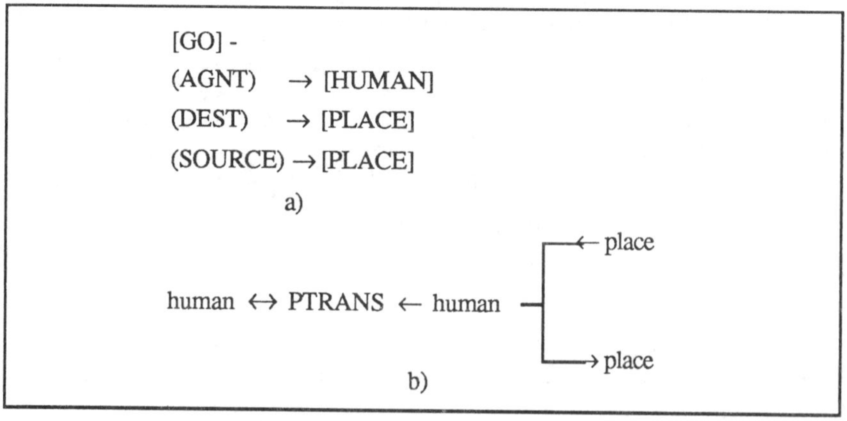

```
[GO] -
(AGNT)    → [HUMAN]
(DEST)    → [PLACE]
(SOURCE) → [PLACE]
          a)


                                           ┌─← place
                                           │
human ↔ PTRANS ← human  ─                  │
                                           └─→ place
          b)
```

Fig. 23.1 a) Conceptual Graph for GO b) Semantic Primitive for GO.

In many models semantic knowledge is prepresented by means of abstract descriptors, as semantic primitives (Schank, 1972), formulas (Wilks, 1983), semantic nets (Simmons, 1973) and canonical graphs (Sowa 1984). Abstract descriptors capture the information that strongly characterizes the conceptual model underlying a linguistic entity (e.g. word or sentence or situation). For example, the verb "go" is described in Sowa (1984) by a canonical graph associated to the concept GO, or in Schank (1972) by the semantic primitive associated the primitive act PTRANS. These two definitions are shown in Fig. 23.1.

Both definitions make explicit the *semantic expectations* of the act "go", identified by the actor of the move, and by a path (source, destination). Whether or not primitives are used, the objective of the semantic expectation approach is to eliminate syntactic and word sense ambiguity. The main limitation of this approach is that "constraints apply to what is described rather than to the expressions themselves" (Weischedel, 1986). In other words, there isn't a clear correspondence between word patterns, ruled by pragmatics, and conceptual patterns, ruled by semantic expectations.

There are several examples to show the pitfalls of semantic expectations. The first is prepositional ambiguity. Consider for example the two sentences:

"The President went to Venice for a meeting"

"The Pope went to a residence for elderly people".

In the fist sentence, the prepositional phrase beginning with "for" represents the purpose of the act "go", but in the second case, it expresses the destination of a building. In such a cases semantic expectation would not provide a guide for correct prepositional attachment; more detailed knowledge on preferential word patterns is required. The second example are figures of speech, vessels, and metonimies, as for example in:

The Fiat and the government sign an agreement

The agreement was signed at Fiat

I own a Fiat

The word "Fiat" designates a social organization, a company headquarter, and a car, respectively. Only pragmatics incorporates knowledge on these, and many other, language phenomena. In our system we adopted a pragmatic approach to express knowledge on word usage. We found this a realistic method to build a NL understanding program with a number of merits:

1. pragmatics allows one to fully cope with natural language;

2. word usage patterns are easily derived by examining existing texts (in our case a large database of press agency releases);

3. syntactic and lexical ambiguity are significantly reduced.

On the other hand, two problems remain open:

1. pragmatic knowledge is virtually unbound;

2. the semantic representation of a sentence obtained by applying word usage knowledge is micro-semantic (Wilks, 1983), i.e. close to the sentence surface structure.

As far as the first issue is concerned, the boundlessness of pragmatics and semantic knowledge is generally accepted as inherent to the nature of the NL problem. However, pragmatic knowledge is easier to acquire than semantic. On the second point, we agree that the ultimate goal of natural language understanding is to produce "deep" representations, but there are no straightforward methods of mapping superficial into deep structures. Consider for example the two sentences:

> The nomination of Brown and Doe in the board of directors took place yesterday.
>
> Brown and Doe entered yesterday in the board of directors.

Only a Conceptual Dependency representation would assign to the above sentences the same primitives. The conceptual graphs model requires the application of a generalization algorithm in order to capture the similarities between the two sentences. However, the ways of mapping surface semantic structures into a deeper semantic structure cannot be stated by some generally valid algorithm. The process of conceptual abstraction must be precisely bound to avoid meaningless generalizations. For example:

$$[\text{CONCRETE}] \leftarrow (\text{AGNT}) \leftarrow [\text{ACT}] \rightarrow (\text{OBJ}) \rightarrow [\text{CONCRETE}]$$

which would join for example the two sentences:

> John eats an apple.
>
> The wind blows the leaves.

To conclude, pragmatics is a viable choice to build a working program but do not solve the problem of creating deep semantic representations. The transition from a micro-semantic to a macro-semantic representation is a crucial research issue despite being far from understood.

The semantic knowledge scheme presented hereafter has the following objectives:

1. provide information for semantic validation of parse trees originated by non-trivial sentences;

2. solve syntactic as well as lexical ambiguity in a sentence context, provided this would have been feasible for a human reader;

3. explicit semantic links between words.

To model linguistic entities and their relations some modification and/or extension have been introduced to the conceptual graph model:

1. a catalog of conceptual relations is proposed to express the basic relations found in natural language;

2. the data structures used for semantic knowledge representation are *word usage frames*; these differ from the canonical graphs in that they express pragmatic knowledge on word usage rather than semantic expectations;

3. a hierarchy of concept types is adopted; in this hierarchy word-senses are terminal nodes; non-terminal nodes are abstract classes with no linguistic correspondent (e.g. MOVE-ACTS, HUMAN-ENTITY, etc).

The third is a consequence of the word usage approach (as argued later in this chapter), linguistic entities cannot be hierarchically ordered; some words are apparently more general than some others but their uses in a sentence context only loosely overlap.

Section 23.2 deals with conceptual relations; a correspondence is established between linguistic entities, concepts and conceptual relations. Section 23.3 and 23.4 describe in detail the structure of word-sense frames, and elaborate on type hierarchies. In order to avoid the formation of lattices, two distinct hierarchies are introduced: *natural types* and *role types*. Finally, section 23.5 presents the semantic verification algorithm. The algorithm generates a conceptual graph of a sentence (syntactically and morphologically parsed) by using knowledge of word pragmatics and *correspondence tables* between syntactic relation and conceptual relations.

23.2 CORRESPONDENCE BETWEEN LINGUISTIC ENTITIES

The problem analyzed in this section concerns the correspondence of linguistic entities with concepts and conceptual relations. Which words are concepts? Which are relations? Which, if any, are redundant for meaning representation? The task of identifying conceptual relations is rather complex. In fact, while concepts can be put in correspondence with word-senses, conceptual relations are embedded in the sentence and often have no linguistic correspondent. On the other hand, the semantic information made explicit by the conceptual graph of a sentence is entrusted to conceptual relations; concepts in most cases closely correspond to the words found in the sentence. It is hence important do define a catalog of conceptual relations to express all the basic relations found in natural language.

As pointed out by (Fillmore, 1968), semantic relationships between nouns and/or phrases in a sentence are implied by lexical surface structures, as word endings, functional signs, (prepositions, conjunctions etc.), syntactic relations (subject, object etc.). Closely analyzing these structures and the hints given in Fillmore (1968), (Wilks, 1975), (Sowa, 1984). The final set of conceptual relations (about 50) was derived, and tested for (reasonable) expressive power against a wide spectrum of sentences taken from the natural corpus of releases. This set is fully listed in Pazienza and Velardi (1987).

In the following, three correspondence rules between linguistic entities and conceptual categories (concept and relations) are given[1].

In a sentence, we distinguish three types of entities: main words, determiners and functional signs. Main words have a meaning associated with them, whereas determiners and functional signs specialize and/or link words together.

Content words are nouns, verbs, adjectives, pronouns, not-prepositional adverbs. Each word can have synonyms or multiple meanings.

Rule 1: There is a concept for each word-sense; proper names (John, Fido) are translated into the referent field of the entity type they belong to ([PERSON:John]).

---

[1]Only rule 3 is new; the other two are implicit from (Sowa 1984).

Determiners ("the", "a" and "an") indicate whether a word refers to an individual or to a generic instance.

Rule 2: Determiners are mapped into a specific or generic concept referent.

For example, "a dog" and "the dog" are translated respectively into [DOG:*] and [DOG:#], where * and # mean "a generic instance" and "a specific instance"[2].

Functional signs are prepositions, conjunctions, adverbs used as prepositions (before, under, without etc.), word endings (nic-est, fold-ing), verb ending and auxiliary verbs. Their role is to relate main words, as in "I go by bus", to strengthen a name as in "she is the nicest", to determine the tenses of verbs as in "I was going".

As for the auxiliary verbs "be" and "have", these are used as follows:

1. auxiliary verb (aux) + verb, as in "I am looking",

2. aux + adjective or adverb, as in "he was nice" and "he was late",

3. aux + noun, as in "there was a man", "he was on the chair", "he has a pen".

In the first and second case, the aux acts as a functional sign which modifies the tense of verbs or assigns some property to a noun or pronoun. In the third case "be" and "have" are synonyms of "exist", "stay" or "possess" and are hence treated as concepts.

A content words, functional signs may have more than one meaning (e.g. "by", "to" etc.).

Rule 3: A biunivocal correspondence is established between the semantic role played by functional signs and conceptual relations.

Conceptual relation occurrences which correspond to some functional sign in a phrase are said to be explicit. This does not exhaust the set of conceptual relations; there are syntactic structures which are not expressed by signs, as remarked also in Reiger (1979). For example, in the sentence "John eats" there exist a subject-verb relation between "John" and "eats", in the sentence "the nice girl", the adjective "nice" is a quality modifier of the noun "girl". Conceptual relations which correspond to those embedded links are called implicit. A conceptual relation might have both implicit or explicit occurrences. For example, the phrases "a book about history" and "a history book" both imply the argument (ARG) relation.

About 50 conceptual relations have been identified and grouped in two classes:

1. *Thematic roles.* These relations specify the role of a concept with respect to an action (e.g. John (AGNT) eats), to a function (e.g. building for (PURPOSE) residence) to an event (e.g. a meeting between (PARTY) delegates), or to some other entity (e.g. the mother of (SOCIAL-RELATION) John).

2. These relations link an entity to a description of its structure (e.g. a golden (MATTER) ring), an action to a description of it circumstance, e.g. to run (MANNER) fast, to be

---

[2]Actually, mapping determiners into specific or generic concepts is a first choice solution; the problem of concept instantiation requires a deeper context analysis.

(TIME) late, or express a mutual relation between two entities or two actions with respect to some state or circumstance, e.g. the pen into (INCL) the drawer[3].

23.3 REPRESENTATION OF WORD-SENSE

So far a correspondence has been stated between linguistic entities, concepts and conceptual relations, this section deals with word-sense representation by means of concepts and conceptual relations. In the next section we introduce the logical notation adopted in the rest of this chapter.

23.3.1 Conceptual graphs in logic

The conceptual graph formalism has been integrated in a logic programming environment; in first-order logic form, concepts are represented by predicates with one argument, and conceptual relations by predicates with two arguments. Arguments represent the concept referents and follow the same notation shown in section 23.2. for individual and generic instances, sets etc. For example, the sentence "The Ace signs a contract" is expressed by the proposition:

$$COMPANY(ACE) \land AGNT(\#x, ACE) \land SIGN(\#x) \land OBJ(\#x, y) \land AGREEMENTS(\#y).$$

corresponding to the linear form notation:

```
[COMPANY:ACE]←AGNT←[SIGN:#]←(OBJ)←[AGREEMENT:#]
```

the sentence "companies sign agreements" is expressed as follows:

$$COMPANY(\{*z\}) \land AGNT(*x, \{*z\} \land SIGN(*z) \land OBJ(*z, \{*y\}) \land AGREEMENT(\{*y\})$$

corresponding to the linear notation:

```
[COMPANY:{*}]←AGNT←[SIGN:*]←(OBJ)←[AGREEMENT:{*}]
```

The arguments of a conceptual relation are the referents of the incoming and outgoing concepts, respectively. In other words the first argument points to the concept(s) that have the relation, e.g. SIGN has an agent and an object, the second to the concept(s) that is that of the relation, e.g. COMPANY is the agent and AGREEMENT is the object of SIGN.

Let us now introduce four types of propositions used in the following to express in logic form binary relations between concepts. The proposition:

$$C_1(*x) \land REL(*x, *y) \land C_2(*y) \tag{23.39}$$

is called an abstract proposition which reads: "the relation REL is a valid semantic link between the concept class C_1 and the concept class C_2". Two examples of (23.39) are:

---

[3]This category includes spatial relations as well as those intersentential relations which describe the circumstances of an action or situation, e.g. John goes to (LOC) Roma, she drinks after (SUCC) lunch, perhaps (PSBL) I will come tomorrow. Other intersentential relations belong to thematic roles, as the one expressing conditions, cause/effect etc. e.g., If (COND) I decide to came, I will give you a call).

$$MOVE(*x) \wedge OBJ(*x, *y) \wedge CONCRETE(*y) \tag{23.40}$$

$$WATCH(*x) \wedge AGNT(*x, *y) \wedge HUMANENTITY(*y) \tag{23.41}$$

These read "concepts of type MOVE require an object (OBJ) of type CONCRETE" and "concepts of type WATCH require an agent (AGNT) of type ANIMATE". Every proposition obtained by replacing C_1 by a concept C_1', such that $C_1 > C_1'$ is called a left specialization of (1). Similarly, by replacing C_2 by $C_2' < C_2$, we obtain a right specialization. If C_1' (C_2') is a terminal node of the concept hierarchy the resulting proposition is calle specific:

$$c(*x) \wedge REL(*x, *y) \wedge c'(*y) \tag{23.42}$$

Terminal nodes are indicate with italic lower case.

23.3.2   Word-senses and Abstract Classes

Many knowledge representation formalisms for natural language order linguistic entities in a type hierarchy. This is used to deduce the properties of less general concepts from higher level concepts (property inheritance). For example, if an abstract proposition like (23.39) is true, then all the propositions obtained by replacing C_1 or/and C_2 by any of their subtypes (i.e. left and/or right specializations of (23.1) must be true. However, the application of property inheritance to word usage patterns produces frequent inconsistencies; for example the propositions:

$$GO(*x) \wedge OBJ(*x, *y) \wedge CONCRETE(*y) \tag{23.43}$$

$$WATCH(*x) \wedge AGNT(*x, *y) \wedge BLIND(*y). \tag{23.44}$$

These are obtained by left and right specialization respectively. These propositions (23.40) and (23.41), would validate sentences like "to go a pen" and "a blind watches". Let us elaborate on this crucial issue; the propositions (23.40) and (23.43) can be regarded as:

1. expressing a deep semantic constraint on the concepts types MOVE and GO; in this case, the concept GO could be described in abstract terms as a MOVE where AGNT and OBJ coincide;

2. expressing a constraint on valid surface patterns for the word senses move and go.

Once again, the problem is whether constraints apply to the conceptualization underlying a sentence or to the expression itself. Since we advocate the second strategy, we found that the pragmatics of word senses[4] like act, move and go have little in common, and most of all they are not related by supertype relations; think for example of expressions like:

John *acted* as a fool
John *moved* the chair near the wall
John *goes* to Boston by bus

---

[4]Notice that we talk about word sense usages and not about word usages. In our system, the description of move is distinct from that of move_trans ("John moved to his new apartment") and that of move_emotion ("John was moved by her sad story").

In conclusion, we found property inheritance not applicable to word sense usages.

A possible approach would be to define word usages by means of specific propositions like the (23.42). This approach has been adopted in the DTL Machine Translations System (BSO, 1987) were about 50,000 word combinations (basic units) have been listed. For an entirely automatic NL processing system this solution is however impractical; a strategy is proposed here to reduce this inconsistency of the word-sense knowledge base and at the same time taking advantage of generalizations. The hierarchy of concepts is structured as follows:

1. There are two levels of concepts: *word senses* and *abstract classes*;

2. Concepts associated to word senses (indicated by italic cases) are the leaves (terminal nodes) of the hierarchy;

3. Abstract conceptual classes, e.g. MOVE_ACTS, HUMAN_ENTITIES, SOCIAL_ACTS etc. (upper cases) are the non-terminal nodes.

In this hierarchy word-sense concepts are never linked by supertype relations to each other, but at most by brotherhood. Examples (23.41) and (23.43) show in fact that even though some word- sense may appear more general than some other ("move" and "go"), their usage in natural language only loosely overlap. In our hierarchy, "move" and "go" are both subtypes of MOVE_ACTS.

Definitions are given only for word-sense concepts, whereas abstract classes are used to generalize logical propositions on word sense usages. A definition is a list of propositions where the italic case concept is the word-sense and the other concept is some abstract class. The definition of sign for example includes:

$$sign(*x) \wedge AGNT(*x, *y) \wedge HUMAN\_ENTITY(*y)$$
$$sign(*x) \wedge OBJ(*x, *y) \wedge DOCUMENT(*y)$$
$$sign(*x) \wedge PURPOSE(*x, *y) \wedge SOCIAL\_ACT(*y)$$
$$sign(*x) \wedge LOC(*x, *y) \wedge PLACE(*y)$$
etc.

Each proposition represents:

1. a condition on a permitted word-sense usage; a concept c is the object of a sign act if its supertype is DOCUMENT agreement, contract etc. For example, the sentence "to sign a person" violates this condition.

2. A description of the concept. For example, the above definition informs us that the act sign is performed by humans, on some document, for some social purpose, in some place, etc..

The problem of inconsistency, deriving from left and right specializations, is reduced (but not eliminated) by the presence of at least one terminal node in each proposition. Consider the:

$$person(*x) \wedge AGNT(*x, *y) \wedge MOVE\_ACT(*y)$$

stating that a man is the actor of move, run, push etc. This is an obvious overgeneralization, because for example a man is not the AGNT, but rather the PARTIC of fly ("John flies from Paris to Rome"). One can easily convince oneself that it is impossible to define a hierarchy such as to eliminate these problems. The solution adopted in our system is to write strict constraints on word usages only when this is natural and easy, as for example:

$$fly(*x) \wedge PARTIC(*x,*y) \wedge person(*y)$$
$$fly(*x) \wedge AGNT(*x,*y) \wedge WINGED\_ANIMATE(*y)$$

As detailed is Section 23.43, in order to accept an expression as valid, a cross check is performed on both the word sense definitions, this eliminates residual inconsistencies. In the above example, the expression "John flies ..." would be correctly represented by a PARTIC relation. Word-sense definitions are structured in a frame data structure; the frame of a word-sense w has three fields:

1. *Type.* This field defines the supertype of w. For example:

   SUPERTYPE(SOCIAL_ACTS, agreement)
   or
   SUPERTYPE(HUMAN_ORGANIZATIONS, company)

2. *Thematic Role.* This field describes the roles of w. If w is an act, this field gives information on its subject and object types, if it is an entity, it describes its functions and roles. For example:

   agreement:
   $agreement(*x) \wedge PARTIC(*x,*y) \wedge HUMAN\_ENTITY(*y)$
   "the agreement between Ace and Fiat".
   "The agreement with the government"
   $agreement(*x) \wedge PURPOSE(*x,*y) \wedge ACT(*y)^5$
   "an agreement to obtain new funding"
   etc.

   company
   $company(*x) \wedge AGNT(*y,*x) \wedge SOCIAL\_ACTS(*y)$
   "the company signs a contract".
   "the bankruptcy of the company".
   $company(*x) \wedge POSS(*y,*x) \wedge BUILDING\{office \ headquarter \ firm\})$
   ("the headquarter of the Ace")

3. *Descriptive.* If w is an act, this field gives information on its circumstances (place, manner, time etc.): if it is an entity, gives information on its structure (parts, characteristics, matter etc.)

---

[5]Examples of SOCIAL_ACTS are to participate, to sell, to deliberate, contract etc. Fields from 2 and 3 correspond to the conceptual relation groups introduced in Section 23.40

agreement:

$agreement(*x) \wedge LOC(*x, *y) \wedge PLACE(*y)^6$
"an agreement at the Fiat Headquarters"

$agreement(*x) \wedge PTIME(*x, *y) \wedge TIME\_ENTITY(*y)^7$
"the agreement of May"

etc.

$agreement(*x) \wedge SUCC(*y, *x) \wedge COMPETITIVE\_ACTS(*y)^8$

$company(*x) \wedge PARTIC(*x, *y) \wedge HUMAN\_ENTITY(*y)$
"the employees of the company"
"John's company"

etc.

The pragmatic approach adopted for word-sense definition provides sufficient information to solve syntactic ambiguities even for complex sentences. Word-sense frames are fairly large: on the average they have about 20 Horn clauses in Prolog. However the absence of time consuming property inheritance algorithms and the simple and uniform structure of word-sense definitions simplify the semantic analysis.

2000 definitions have been manually entered during the two years of project. An automatic tool to help write definitions was prepared. This tool provides error checks, as undefined types or inconsistent definitions, editing facilities and retrieval of word occurrences from a database of 5000 press-agency news items (given a lemma, all the occurrences of this lemma and its inflections can be retrieved).

23.4 NATURAL TYPES AND ROLE TYPES.

In the previous section a distinction was proposed between word-senses and abstract concept classes. This section discusses additional problems involved with the definition of a concept hierarchy. To introduce these problems, recall the sample definition given above for the word-sense concept sign. Consider the abstract type PLACE, appearing in the definition. Where should this be located in the hierarchy? The possible subtypes of PLACE are MOBILE_ENTITY (car, bicycle etc), FURNITURE (table, chair, furniture etc.), BUILDINGS (house, office, building, etc.), NATURAL_SITES (mountain, lake etc.) and many others. A similar problem exists for the concept FOOD. All animates can be a FOOD, but considering FOOD a supertype of ANIMATE does not make much sense. On the other hand, if each animate can have more than one supertype, visiting the hierarchy for type verification may be exceedingly time-consuming and a potential source of inconsistency.

In order to avoid the formation of entangled lattices, the hierarchy of concepts have been partitioned into two distinct trees:

---

[6]Examples of PLACE are building, city, country, etc.

[7]Examples of TIME_ENTITY words are date, hour, today, yesterday.

[8]Examples   of   COMPETITIVE-ACTS   are   contention,   disagreement, fight, dispute; morover COMPETITIVE_ACTS < SOCIAL_ACTS because $role\_type(FOOD, ANIMATE) \wedge supertype(ANIMATE, lamb)$.

1. the first incudes natural types, i.e. concepts of supertype ENTITY (man, cat, fear etc.);

2. the second orders properties and roles, i.e. FUNCTIONs (food, shareholder, student, place) or CHARACTERISTICs (nice, efficiency, rough etc.).

The logic predicate: supertype (A, a) declares the supertype A of a, and the predicate role_type (P, C) declares the ENTITY or ACTION C which a given FUNCTION or CHARACTERISTIC P can be applied (for example, PLACE is a role played by MO-BILE_ENTITIES, NATURAL_SITES etc.). These two predicates are respectively used to visit a given tree and to pass from one tree to the other. To verify whether a word-sense concept w is a subtype of an abstract concept W, the following cases are checked:

1. W and w are both roles or both natural types. In this case, it is sufficient to verify in the knowledge base whether

$$supertype(W, w)$$

is true.

2. W is a role and w is a natural type. In this case, w is a subtype of W iff

$$role\_type(W, Z) \wedge supertype(Z, w)$$

3. W is a natural type and w is a role. It is necessary to verify that

$$supertype(Z, w) \wedge role\_type(Z, W)$$

For example, shareholder is a PERSON because

$$supertype(CHARGE, shareholder) \wedge role\_type(CHARGE, PERSON)$$

Consider for example the two sentences: "the shareholder sells his/her shares" and "Mr. Brown is a shareholder of the ACE company". In the first sentence, "sell" expects a PERSON as agent; in the second sentence, "is" expects a FUNCTION or CHARACTERISTIC; in this case, shareholder will be recognized as a charge. When the role concept is used as a natural type (as for example, in the sentence "the shareholder sells"), in order to verify semantic constraints the definition of the associated natural type is merged with the definition of the role type (in the above example, a shareholder-person word-sense concept is created by merging the two definitions of person and shareholder).

23.5   THE SEMANTIC INTERPRETATION ALGORITHM

This section describes the semantic interpretation algorithm. Its inputs are the results of syntactic analysis and the semantic knowledge base described in the previous sections.

23.5.1　Interfaces with the Syntactic Parser

The input to the system is provided by the syntactic parser, described in Antonacci and Russo (1987). In general a sentence has more than one syntactically valid interpretation and gives rise to several parse trees. For example the sentence "to discuss the proposal of a plan" produces the parse trees of Fig. 23.2 (determiners are omitted for brevity). In Fig. 23.2, np, vp and pp stand for noun, verb and prepositional phrase, respectively. Parse trees are internally represented by graph of syntactic predicates. A syntactic predicate is a two-place or three-place predicate:

> *syntactic_link(word_data1,word_data2)*
> *syntactic_link(word_data1 fs,,word_data2)*

where:

> *syntactic_link* = subject, object, attribute etc.
>
> *word_data* = lemma + word + morphologic_information + word_number
>
> *morphologic_information* = gender, number, tense etc.
>
> *word_number* =　position of the word in the sentence
>
> *fs* = functional sign (preposition, conjunction etc.) linking two words or clauses

For example, consider the sentence:

> *Gli azionisti in assemblea discutono la proposta di un piano per recuperare l'efficienza delle strutture produttiver*

which has the following word-by-word translation:

> *The shareholders in a meeting discuss the proposal for a plan to restore the efficiency of productive structures*

The subject-verb relation between shareholders and discuss is expressed by:

$$subject((to\_discussdiscuss(transverb)6 \\ (shareholdershareholders(nounmascplur)2))$$

For the sake of briefness only the lemma of a word will be shown

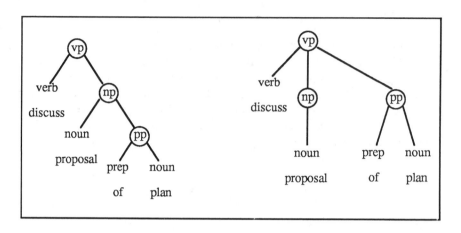

Fig. 23.2 Parse frees for the sentence "..discuss the proposal of a plan".

The above syntactic link relates couples of words; if a relation exists between clauses, e.g. as the object_verb relation between restore and the efficiency of productive structures, this is replaced by a relation between the heads of the two clauses, where:

head(np)=noun
head(vp)=verb

Hence:

head(to restore the efficiency of productive structures) = restore
head(productive structures) = structure

The conversion of syntactic links between phrases into binary relation between words is indeed a simplification. This is based on the intuitive argument that in a noun (verb) phrase it is the noun (verb) that conveys most of the semantic information. Hence, a semantic relation between phrases mostly depends upon the relation between their heads. This of course is not always true, but seems to work for the majority of cases.

Syntactic relations between words (or clauses) and prepositional phrases are expressed by three-argument syntactic predicates, as follows:

wpp(word_data1, preposition, word_data2)

where:

$$wpp = np\_pp = +pp$$

$$wpp = vp\_pp = vp + pp$$

$$pp = preposition + np$$

$$pp = preposition + vp$$

In summary, the above sentence about the shareholder's meeting is represented as follows:

sentence ←
1.*subject(discuss, shareholder)&*
2.*np_pp(shareholder,in,meeting)&*
3.*object(discuss,proposal)&*
   3.1 *vp_pp(discuss,of,plan)|4.2np_pp(proposal,of,plan,))&*
   3.2 *vp_pp(discuss,to,restore)|5.2np_pp(plan,to,restore))&*
4.*object(restore,efficiency)&*
   4.1 *vp_pp(restore,of,structure)|7.2np_pp(efficiency,of,structure))&*
5.*attribute(structure,productive).*

and gives rise to the graph of Fig. 23.3.

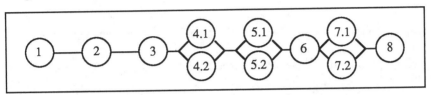

Fig. 23.3 Graph of syntactic predicates.

Each circle of Fig. 23.3 corresponds to one of the above syntactic predicates: parallel paths indicate syntactically valid alternatives; for example, as far as the syntax is concerned, the prepositional phrase *of a plan* could be attached either to the verb "discuss" or to the noun "proposal". Semantic analysis has the task of selecting the correct (or at least the more plausible) alternative.

23.5.2 Semantic Analysis

The purpose of the semantic verification is:

1. to replace words by word-sense concepts;

2. to replace syntactic relations by conceptual relations (provided that a syntact predicate corresponds to a valid semantic link);

3. to verify the existence of (at least) one path along the graph of syntactic predicates;

4. to produce a conceptual graphs of the sentence.

The semantic analysis proceeds as follows: consider for example the $np\_pp(proposal, of, plan)$. The first step is to replace lemmata by word senses. It is interesting to remark that the Italian word for "plan", *piano*, is particularly ambiguous: it means piano, project, floor and level land. When this word is first encountered in a syntactic predicate, a list of all its word-sense concepts is associated to it. Hence, the syntactic predicates give rise, after step 1, to four syntactic hypothesis where words have been replaced by word-sense concepts.

np_pp(proposal*x),of,piano(*y))
np_pp(proposal*x),of,project(*y))
np_pp(proposal*x),of,floor(*y))
np_pp(proposal*x),of,level_land(*y))

In step 2, each syntactic hypothesis is verified for semantic plausibility. The test is performed by first associating to a syntactic predicate a list of conceptual relations which could represent a semantic interpretation of a syntactic link. For example, an *np_pp* with the preposition "of" has the following interpretations:

> *np_pp(*x,of,*y)←possession(*y,*x).*
> *(e.g. "the book of Bill")*
> *np_pp(*x,of,*y)←part_of(*y,*x).*
> *(e.g. "the pages of the book")*
> *np_pp(*x,of,*y)←argument(*y,*x).*
> *(e.g. "the book of history")*
> *etc.*

The right hand sides are called semantic hypothesis. The first semantic hypothesis will be verified iff $possession(piano(*x), proposal(*y))$ is true, that is to say if "the piano possesses a proposal" is a plausible interpretation of the *np+pp* "proposal of plan", as it would be for "book of John".

A conceptual relation between two word-sense concepts is plausible iff the proposition:

$$piano(*x) \land POSS(*x, *y) \land proposal(*y)$$

is the right specialization of, or coincides with, some proposition included in the definition of proposal, and is the left specialization of, or coincides with, some proposition included in the definition of piano. The double check allows us to detect inconsistencies still contained in the word-sense definitions (see section3). For example, the definition of piano includes:

$$HUMAN(*x) \land POSS(*x, *y) \land piano(*y)$$

expressing a condition about the possessor of a piano, but this is not satisfied by proposal ($proposal < HUMAN$ is false). The symmetric proposition (where piano should appear as a possessor) is not found in the definition. Similarly, in the definition of proposal, the relation POSS is not listed as a semantically valid word-sense use (a proposal does not possess anything, neither is possessed by: it can instead be originated by). The predicate possession(piano(*x), proposal(*y)) hence fails.

The algorithm then attemps to verify a new predicate, until either a plausible relation is found, or no more rules are available for that given syntactic hypothesis. In the latter case, the syntactic hypothesis is rejected and the next one (if any) is inspected. In the example above, the syntactic hypothesis $np\_pp(proposal(*x), of, project(*y))$ is finally taken as a valid one; the underlying conceptual relation is ARG(*x, *y).

At the end of the analysis, provided that an interpretation is found for the complete sentence, the system produces either a graph, or a list of paraphrases expliciting representing the meaning of the input words (words are replaced by word-sense concepts) and the semantic relations between them. For example, $np\_pp(proposal, of, plan)$ gives the paraphrase:

> *"Project is the argument of proposal."*

A graphic facility was built to show the conceptual graphs; Fig. 23.4 shows the graph of the example.

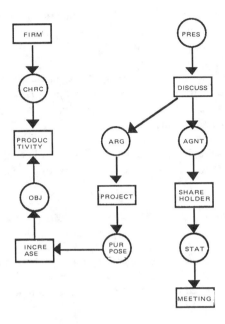

Fig. 23.4 Example of conceptual graph generated by the graphic facility.

23.6   CONCLUDING REMARKS.

In this paper a method to represent and analyze the meaning of a sentence was described based on knowledge of word usages. We found this a realistic approach to cope with such complex language phenomena as syntactic and lexical ambiguity, metonimies, figures of speech, etc. The definition of a word-sense is given as a list of first order propositions each representing a valid relation between that word and an abstract class of concepts.

Word-senses are the terminal nodes of the concept hierarchy; non terminal nodes are abstract classes like MOVE_ACTS, HUMAN entities, etc.. Concepts (word-senses and abstract classes) have been partitioned in natural types and role types. Roles are conceptual categories that do not designate an entity or an action, but rather a function or a characteristic of some entity or action. This partition makes it possible to avoid the formation of lattices when ordering concepts in a type hierarchy.

The last section of this paper presented the semantic verification algorithm; this associates to a syntactic link between words a semantic interpretation, represented by a conceptual relation between word-sense concepts. The objective of semantic verification is to represent by conceptual graphs complex, nested hypotactical sentences, as found in the application domain (press agency releases on finance and economics). The final representation is micro-semantic, in that it is still close to the sentence surface structure. In this chapter the complexities and obscurities of a superficial to deep mapping have been discussed in detail.

In summary, the features of this system are:

1. the representation is centered on expliciting semantic links, rather than on the detection of predefined semantic structures (as for scripts (Schank, 1977), conceptual cases (Schank, 1972) and formulas (Wilks, 1975);

2. word-sense definitions are given in terms of pragmatic knowledge, rather than semantic expectations (as for semantic nets (Simmons, 1973) and canonical graphs (Sowa 1984); this makes it possible to solve syntactic ambiguity even for very complex, nested hypotactical sentences;

3. word-sense definitions are fairly large but not conceptually complex data structures (the semantic interpretation algorithm performs very simple matching operations in order to verify semantic constraints);

4. word-sense usages are easily acquired by inspecting word patterns in the natural corpus of releases;

5. an approach to the well known problems found with type hierarchies is proposed;

6. semantic processing is based on pragmatic knowledge, but also takes advantage of the preceding syntactic analysis.

A first version of the system implemented in VM/PROLOG, produces the conceptual graph of sentences previously analyzed by the porphologic and syntactic components (described in the previous chapter), provided the words are included in the semantic knowledge base. The dictionary is of about 2000 word-sense, each including in the average 10 words uses in form of Prolog rules. A concept editor has been developed to facilitate the introduction of new definitions. Current work is directed towards discourse analysis, text generation and non-trivial question answering features.

APPENDIX EXERCISES

Exercise 1 Consider the following concepts: ACT, MOVE, BEHAVE, STATE, SITUATION, CHANGE. For each of them, give a "deep" definition (e.g. $[ANIMATE \wedge rbrk \leftarrow (AGNT) \rightarrow (AGNT) \leftarrow [ACT])$ and a "pragmatic" definition, i.e. the "ways of using" the above concepts in a sentence context (e.g. "Mary acted like a fool", "John acted the Amleto").

Exercise 2 Try to order the following verbs in a type hierarchy: to lower, oppose, approve, consent, satisfy, grant, increase participate, collect, make, do, behave, act, accomplish, widen, move, change, go, proceed, satisfy, open, come, approve, carry, authorize, communicate, think, cause, call, balance, close, share, begin, fight, discuss, involve, appear, accomplish, grant, appear, concern, include, reach, advise, sell, grow, produce, create, run, construct, decide, cover. Hint: each verb can be associated to more than one concept (e.g. close: OPEN_MOVE, as in "John opens the door" and OPEN_START, as in "The conference was opened yesterday"). Hint: if you are not able to accommodate all the concepts in a hierarchy, try to use abstract classes for the non-terminal nodes, e.g. MOVE_ACT > MOVE GO LOWER WIDEN GROW etc.

Exercise 3 Find the appropriate conceptual relation to represent the meaning of the preposition of in the following sentences:

> *the meaning of the preposition*
> *the roar of the lions*
> *the pages of the book*
> *the object of the tald*
> *the arm of the chair*
> *the escape of the enemy*
> *the smell of the flowers*
> *the items of the document*

BIBLIOGRAPHY

Antonacci F., Russo M. (1992) "Three Steps towards Natural Language Understanding: Morphology Morphosyntax, Syntax", in *Conceptual Structures: Current research and practice"*, (eds) P. Eklund, T. Nagle, J. Nagle and L. Gerholtz, Ellis Horwood.

Brachman P. (1979) "On the epistemological Status of Semantic networks", in *Associative Networks: Representation and use of Knowledge by Computers*, N.V Findler, Academic Press, N.Y.

"Breakthrough for BSO in DLT project in BSO nesa", Press Release Utrecht, January, 1987.

Charniak, E. Y. Wilks (1976) (eds) *Computational Semantics*, North Holland.

Fillmore, C. (1969) "The Case for Case. in Universals in Linguistic Theory", (eds) Bach and Harms Holt, Rinehart and Winston, New York.

Heidorn G.E. (1975) "Argument Phrase Structure Grammar. In Theoretical Issues", in *Natural Language Processing*, (eds) Shank and Nash-Webber, Association for Computational Linguistics.

D.E. Knuth (1968) "Semantics of context free Grammars". Mathematical Systems Theory Vol. 2, 127-145.

Pazienza M.T., Velardi A. (1987) "A Structured Representation of Word Sense for Semantical Analysis", Proc. of the 3rd Conference of the European Chapter of the ACL Copenaghen April 1-3.

Pazienza M.T., Velardi A. (1987) "Integrating Conceptual Graphs and Logic in a Natural Language Understanding System", 3rd Conference on Natural Language Processing and Logic Programming, Vancouver.

Pazienza M.T., Velardi A. (1989) "Defining a Semantic Knowledge Base for Natural Language Processing", 2nd International Conference on Knowledge Engineering Madrid, April 6-10.

Rieger C., Small S. (1979) "Word expert parsing", Proceedings of IJCAI.

Russo M. (1989) "A Generative Grammar Approach for the Morphologic and Morphosyntactic Analysis of Italian", Proc. of the 3rd Conference of the European Chapter of the ACL Copenhagen, April 1-3.

Shank R.C. (1972) "Conceptual Dependency: a theory of natural language understanding", Cognitive Psychology, Vol. 3.

Shank R., Abelson R., (1977) *Scripts, Plans, Goals and Understanding*, L. Erlbaum Associate.

Shank R. (1980) "Language and Memory". Cognitive Science, vol. 3 July-Sept.

Simmons, R.F. (1973) "Semantic networks: Their Computation and Use for Understanding English Sentences". in *Computer models for Thought and Language*, (eds) Schank and Colby, Freeman, S. Francisco.

Sowa, John F. (1984) *Conceptual structures: Information Processing in Mind and Machine*. Addison-Wesley, Reading.

Wall R. (1985) "The "New" Logic and Natural Language Processing". Computers and the Humanities.

Weischedel, R. M, (1986) "Knowledge Representation and Natural Language Processing", Proceedings of the IEEE, vol. 74 no. 7 July.

Wilks, Y. (1975) *Preference Semantics in Formal Semantics of Natural Language*, Cambridge University Press.

Wilks, Y. (1983) *Deep and Superficial Parsing in Parsing Natural Language*, (ed) Margaret King, Academic Press.

24

Conceptual Parsing: a Syntax-directed Joining Algorithm for Natural Language Understanding

Stéphane Bornerand and Gérard Sabah
LIMSI-CNRS Laboratory,
The Language and Cognition Group,
Orsay, France

ABSTRACT

Natural language processing essentially consists of encoding and decoding the meaning of sentences. The encoding is used to carry out the generation of sentences. In the reverse process, the decoding is used to understand a sentence. This chapter presents a decoding method based on a syntactic parsing to guide the coding from sentence to conceptual structure.

24.1 INTRODUCTION

The high complexity of natural languages forces a system to use other information than syntax to correctly parse sentences. The approach presented in this chapter assumes that the understanding process is a computation which is both semantic and syntactic. The semantic computation is based on the *compositional principle* where a compositional operation is defined to build a sentence meaning from the meaning of each lexical term. The syntactic computation is based on a production rule system. The set of rules gives the guidelines to inference realize compositional operations with the lexical terms of a sentence in order to build a representation. But even when using both syntax and semantics, ambiguities are not completely eliminated. An optimum search method is chosen to solve the problem of ambiguity in a general way. It defines an evaluation function depending partially on word meaning. The function may be computed from the representation of every analysis and, by selecting the best result, gives a means of choosing the correct representation. This method presupposes a non-deterministic strategy because any choice may be made during the parsing process. Thus, the method makes it possible for syntactic and semantic processes to be split into several processes.

To validate this approach, a system with a set of limited data bases has been developed. Known words are listed in a lexical dictionary. A second dictionary describes the meaning of each word in a conceptual graph formalism invented by J.F. Sowa (1984). Each entry, called a *conceptual type*, corresponds to a formal definition and to a list of selectional constraints used in the compositional operation. A file contains the matching rules between words and concepts in order to avoid mutual dependency between the dictionaries. Finally, a file contains production rules to express the syntax. A context free grammar formalism has been adapted to take the selectional constraints into account, and to supervise the semantic compositional operations.

In the first part of this chapter a conceptual graph model is presented. Section 24.3 describes a generator which produces a parser from a grammar. Section 24.4 explains the design and exploitation of a new system to demonstrate the practical aspects of the conceptual parsing approach. This chapter closes after a discussion on the results of a sample parsing process.

24.2   A CONCEPTUAL GRAPH MODEL

A conceptual graph model may be examined in many ways. Hereafter, this section begins by describing the specifications of its structures and operations, then discusses how to use the model for the natural language processing. Finally, a paragraph is devoted to the tools developed for the model.

24.2.1   Principle and Structure

The conceptual graph model defines conceptual graphs and formation rules. The principle is that all formation rules are defined from canonical formation rules and all conceptual graphs are derived from canonical graphs. The main property of the model is that a graph derived by applying canonical formation rules is canonical. A collection of canonical graphs is established to control and to avoid production of meaningless graphs that are outside the natural language modeling for instance.

A *conceptual graph* is a directed graph where each node is a concept or a relation. The concepts are linked by the relations. A concept is understood as a set of features whereas relations specify the role of concepts and relationships between various concepts. Two fields are distinguished in a concept node: a type field and a referent field. The type field tells the kind of concept while the referent field identifies an instance of that concept. The concepts and the relations may be classified according to a type hierarchy. A conceptual graph may be represented by a linear expression where the concepts appear between brackets and the relations between parenthesis. In the equivalent graphical form, the concepts are displayed with boxes and the relations with circles. The links are always represented by arrows.

The formation rules are hierarchy-based operations. They are mainly used to make *restriction* and *join* onto the nodes of a conceptual graph.

The theory of the conceptual graph has been developed by John Sowa and is presented in (Sowa, 1984). Readers not familiar with this work are urged to consult it for more details.

The next paragraphs bounds the descriptions of the conceptual graph model to the original part of the implementation whose the notions are not introduced in the reference model.

Projection is the formation rule upon which all the other formation rules are based. The join and restriction operations are always performed according to a best maximal projection. A maximal projection is defined by two maximally extended compatible projections. The best maximal projection is the maximal projection that yields the best value of an evaluation function. In the current model, the evaluation function computes the number of concepts that overlap in a maximal projection. The *score* of a best maximal projection between a conceptual graph CG_1 and a conceptual graph CG_2 is defined as follows:

$$score = max_k(E_{i=0}^n join(path_1^k(i), path_2^k(i)))$$

with

> $path_j^k$: set of concepts issue from the path of the maximally extended projection #k across CG_j.
>
> n: number of concepts in $path_1^k$ and $path_2^k$.
>
> $path_j^k(i)$: concept #i in the set $path_j^k$.

$$join(path_1^k(i), path_2^k(i)) = \begin{cases} 1 & \text{if concept join successful} \\ 0 & \text{otherwise.} \end{cases}$$

The conceptual graph model also defines a useful formation rule, the *virtual projection*. A graph can participate in several projections at a time. The virtual projection avoids duplicating structures unnecessarily. In addition, virtual projections can be composed: a graph can be projected on the result of a virtual projection although there is no computation of a global score of the virtual projection.

The join and restriction operations may be also performed according to a virtual projection.

To introduce the notions of mandatory or optional selectional constraints in the conceptual graph model, binary weights can be used in the conceptual and relational structures. In the conceptual graphs, each concept may clearly have a specific field besides the referent in order to define its binary weight. A concept with a null value in this field is an optional selectional constraints. To make certains concepts more relevant, only concepts with a non-null value can be selected in the virtual projection operation to compute the evaluation function. In a more general way, the virtual join operation can take into account continuous weights to calculate a finer evaluation of analysis representation. The evaluation function is then based on a combination of the continuous weights of the overlapped concepts. The explanation of the underlying probabilistic theory should be out of the scope of this chapter. The reader may consult (Ralescu and Baldwin, 1989) to get more details on continuous weights in the conceptual graphs.

The conformity relationships of the theory are significant at different levels in the model. A referent that has appeared in the conceptual graph of a dictionary defines a *universal conformity* with a conceptual type (i.e., the conformity relationship is true in all conditions at any time). Furthermore, the *contextual conformity* is a conformity relationship only true in a given context. A context is a concept with conceptual graphs as referent. Finally, *actual conformity* is only valid during a virtual projection operation.

24.2.2   Natural Language Modeling

A conceptual graph model provides structures to represent cognitive knowledge. The structures are language independent (Sowa, 1984). The conceptual graph model seems well-adapted to natural language processing because it incorporates the advantages of several previous models (e.g., the schema (Schank, 1972) (Fillmore, 1968) and the semantic network (Brachman, 1977)) in a unified formalism. In addition, many of the problems of these models are solved in this formalism: it deals with the quantified relationship between the referent and its type, it is equivalent to a logical formula, and it accepts functional dependencies between several referents. In particular, the underlying hierarchy makes it possible to generalize or to specify each concept and each conceptual graph simply by performing a formation rule.

Nevertheless, each theory defines its own vocabulary and the same word may not have the same meaning in each of them. Both the linguistics and the conceptual graph models use the terms "concept" and "selectional constraint". The next two paragraphs show the dissimilarity between concepts and the equivalence of the selectional constraint in these two theories.

The concept in the conceptual graph model is a structural unit, the node. It represents an occurrence of a *conceptual type* with selectional constraints. In Sowa's model, the denotation of a conceptual type is the set of all entities that are instances of any concept of this type. Here, all these instances are too the denotation of a linguistic concept considered as a cognitive unit. A conceptual type may be directly mapped to a linguistic concept.

In Sowa (1984), the author presents conceptual graphs as selectional constraints. The formation rules enforce selectional constraints by preventing certain combinations from being derived. On the other hand, linguistics theories often use the term *selectional constraints* as semantic constraints of selection between the different words of the sentence (Katz & Fodor, 1963) that avoid absurd interpretations. So, the conceptual graph can be used to represent these constraints. For instance, it is possible to attach a conceptual graph to each word and to use those graphs as conceptual constraints of selection between the different words of the sentence. In the conceptual graph model, there are many sorts of constraints. For instance, the referent verifies the conformity constraint. A referent is an entity which has a conformity relationship with a type. The concept verifies the constraint expressed by a canonical graph and a set of schema. A type verifies the constraint expressed by a partial ordering relationship and by a definition.

In the remainder of the section, a set of examples is shown to explain how the conceptual graphs can address some problems of natural language processing (NLP). Each example describes a solution implemented with conceptual graphs in order to respect a linguistic requirement. All the examples are given in the conceptual graph language defined in Sowa (1984).

In the conceptual graph model, the first difficulty is to know how to code linguistic knowledge. What is the difference between a canonical graph, a schema and a definition? The definition indicates what entity a linguistic concept refers to. The canonical graph indicates the regular use of the linguistic concept. In NLP approach, they are primarily used in parsing input sentences. The schema indicates a variation of a canonical graph. For example, let us assume you are coding the information concerning the linguistic concept ORANGE. First, you have to distinguish between the natural type corresponding to the fruit and the role type corresponding to the color. Let us assume to concern yourselves exclusively with the color ORANGE. In order to characterize it, you have to specify the relationship between ORANGE and the linguistic concept COLOR. The next conceptual graph sets up the definition of the type ORANGE as a particular color named "orange".

```
type ORANGE(x1) is
    [COLOR:x1]->(NAME)->["orange"].
```

In natural language, the term "orange" is used to assign a color to an object or a thing. Thus, a color is intended to characterize an entity. This constraint may be coded by a canonical graph that describes the context of the occurrence of an instance of the linguistic concept. The next conceptual graph is a canonical graph that expresses the selectional constraint of referents of all the concepts of type ORANGE.

```
[ORANGE] → (SOURCE) → [ENTITY].
```

In this chapter, a canonical graph of selectional constraint could be also defined by the next statement in order to be able to attach the conceptual graph as the selectional constraint of a type.

```
constraint for ORANGE is
    [ORANGE] → (SOURCE) → [ENTITY].
```

A frequent use of the linguistic concept ORANGE occurs in the French expression: "passer à l'orange" (crossing an intersection when the traffic light is orange (yellow)). The next conceptual graph is a schema whose constellation of concepts corresponds to this habitual situation.

```
schema for ORANGE(x1) is
    [TRAFFIC_LIGHT] -
        → (SIGNIFICANCE) → [SIGNALISATION:warning]
        → (SIGN) → [ORANGE:x1].
```

Such a schema describes a context with a certain variation from the canonical context (i.e., the canonical graph). In this case, the extended selectional constraints are not always verified. Most referents of the linguistic concept ORANGE are not subsumed by the extended selectional constraints.

The conceptual graph model allows the definition of selectional constraints and a set of operations to take them into account. All the operations are based on the formation rules because the formation rule services fit the NLP requirements.

The joining operation between two conceptual graphs is an overlapping of the concepts and the relations that possess hierarchical links. It only keeps the more specific concepts and relations. The next conceptual graphs show the joining operation of two constraints.

The first conceptual graph means that an animal emits a sound with the voice. The second one means that a human sings a song. The third conceptual graph means that a human sings a song with a voice. The result is more constrained than each original conceptual graph. In NLP, this increase in constraints is used to reduce the search space of the semantic solution. The NLP systems based on the conceptual graph model execute the joining operations on canonical graphs in order to apply selectional constraints on the context of the occurrence of each linguistic concept. Futhermore, the next conceptual graphs show that the joining operation allows the complementarity of selectional constraints.

```
[RUN] → (AGENT) → [ANIMAL].
[DOG] → (POSS) → [LEG].
[RUN] → (AGENT) → [DOG] → (POSS) → [LEG].
```

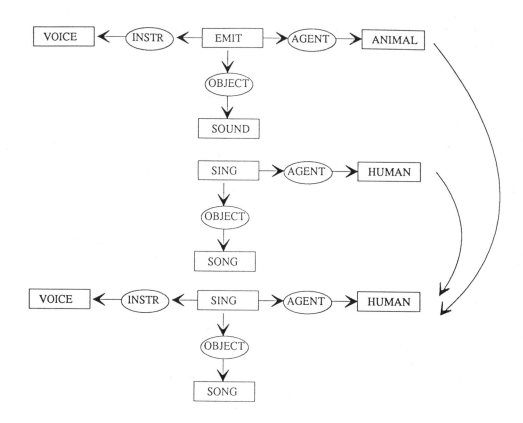

Fig. 24.1 Joining two conceptual graphs into a single conceptual graph.

There is no limit to the extension of selectional constraints.

In computational linguistics, the case structure is verb-based (Fillmore, 1968)(Tesnière, 1953). All the elements of the sentence are linked to the verb by cases. Each case defines a functional dependency between an element and the verb. A case structure defines a predestinated set of relationships between a verb and the predicted role of elements in any sentence. The NLP attempts to fit the role of each case with an element of the sentence. In the conceptual graph model, there is no privileged element. A case structure is just a canonical graph. In parsing a sentence without applying syntactic constraints, the NLP system presented in this chapter is only able to execute the joining operations between the case structure (i.e. a canonical graph) and the others elements of the sentence (i.e. canonical graphs). If the AGENT and OBJECT cases have the same type, then the join may be randomly right or wrong. For instance, let's explain the matter with the next sentence: "A man meets a girl" using the 3 following conceptual graphs in the understanding process.

```
[MAN].

[GIRL].

[MEET]-
    → (AGENT) → [HUMAN]
    → (OBJECT) → [HUMAN].
```

The join between the concept [MAN] and the conceptual graph of the verb "meet" yields two results - the join with the HUMAN as AGENT and the join with the HUMAN as OBJECT. This ambiguity occurs because there is no rule to restrict the join thanks to syntactic criteria. In this case, the semantic constraints are not strong enough to avoid a misunderstanding.

The restriction is an operation on the structural unit. This operation aims at replacing a concept or relation, in a conceptual graph by a hierarchically inferior concept or relation. The goal is to increase the selectional constraints without using canonical graphs.

```
[PLAY]-
    → (AGENT) → [HUMAN]
    → (OBJECT) → [MUSIC]
    → (INSTR) → [INSTRUMENT].

[PLAY]-
    → (AGENT) → [HUMAN]
    → (OBJECT) → [MUSIC]
    → (INSTR) → [PIANO].
```

The last conceptual graph shows the restriction of the concept from INSTRUMENT to PIANO. In NLP based on conceptual graph models, the restriction allows the introduction of local constraints. The restriction without canonical graphs replaces a joining operation with a one-concept canonical graph. Generally, the restriction is used with the natural linguistic concept (e.g. CAT, TREE and CAR). These linguistic concepts might formally have a canonical graph with one concept. In a practical system as presented here, they do not. The joining operation of the canonical graph is implicitly replaced by a restriction operation. This saves memory and increases processing efficiency.

The expansion operation is used to replace a selectional constraint by its definition. It makes it possible to increase the scope of the selectional constraints and to have several levels of selectional constraints. In computational linguistics, the theory of case grammar assumes that there is a level of conceptual representation of the meaning of the sentences where the different forms of expression with the same semantic content give an identical semantic representation. This type of representation is called the *deep structure* of the sentence. This structure is governed by the verb that defines an articulation linking the content of the words around it. The cases used with a verb are selected in a finite, specific and limited set of functions that identify the kind of conceptual relations involved. The set of cases accepted by a verb is called a case structure or case frame. The next example shows the usefulness of this *case grammar*.

(1) *John's pen is red.*
(2) *The pen which belongs to John is red.*

According to the case grammar theory, the two sentences would have the same deep structure as shown with the next conceptual graph.

```
[BELONG] –
    → (SOURCE) → [JOHN]
    → (OBJECT) → [PEN:#1] –
        ← (SOURCE) ← [RED] ; .
```

Certain NLP systems based on the case grammar theory assume that it is possible to obtain the deep structure directly from the sentence. However, these systems do not capture shades of meaning that appear with the use of the several levels of semantic representation. The availability of an expansion operation permits expression of these shades of meaning in the conceptual graph representation. All the semantic representations may be transformed into a deep structure by expansion operations. The type definition and the contraction/expansion operations produces a semantics with a variable granularity that is adjustable in terms of representation fineness with a suitable interpretative performance. The next conceptual graphs show an example of such granularity.

The first conceptual graph might be a semantic representation of the sentence (1). The second conceptual graph introduces the notion of semantics with variable granularity. The expansion of the relation POSS allows the change from any conceptual structure to the deep structure. This example shows that the granularity depends on the content of the type hierarchy that defines a static granularity and on the use of the contraction/expansion operations that defines a dynamic granularity. The static granularity is related to the number of abstract and artificial types used to compact the conceptual graphs. The dynamic granularity allows the availability of all the intermediate conceptual graphs by using subsequent contraction/expansion operations. The static granularity is fixed by the administrator of the language model whereas the dynamic granularity depends on the computation.

The hierarchy of the conceptual type in the conceptual graph theory introduces the notion of the specialization and generalization. The position of a conceptual type may be defined with necessary and sufficient conditions. The hierarchy of the relational type , while not theoretically justifiable, is actually very useful. A hierarchy of relational types may be empirically introduced but relies on no formal property. The genus and differentia notions disappear as soon as you deal with n-adic relations. In the NLP approach presented in this chapter, the hierarchy of the relational type allows a hierarchical classification of cases in the case grammar (Kettani, 1990). In fact, the accuracy of a case may vary in its use in terms of context. For instance, the locative case, LOC, collects together at least the designation of a path and a destination.

(1) *I am going to Paris.*
(2) *I am going toward Paris.*

In the case grammar, the deep structure of the two sentences come from the case structure of the verb. A common case structure is used to obtain two different deep structures. The conceptual graph model makes this possible with the instantiation of generic cases in terms of the context of the case structure. The instantiation corresponds to a restriction of the relational types and is automatically performed during the joining operations.

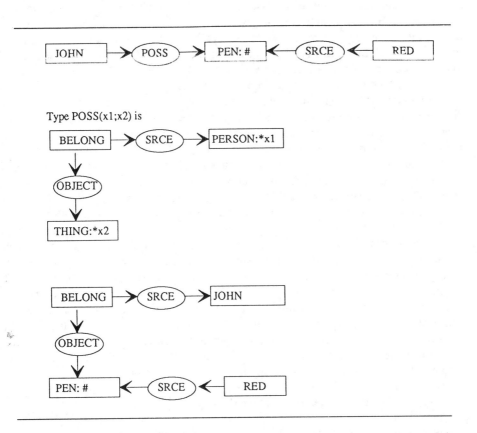

Fig. 24.2 Relational expansion.

```
[GO] -
    → (AGENT) → [PERSON]
    → (LOC) → [LOCATION] .
```

relation DEST < LOC.
relation PATH < LOC.

```
[GO] -
    → (AGENT) → [HUMAN:speaker]
    → (DEST) → [PLACE:Paris] .
```

```
[GO] -
    → (AGENT) → [HUMAN:speaker]
    → (PATH) → [PLACE:Paris] .
```

The first conceptual graph is the case structure of the verb "to go". The relation types DEST and PATH correspond to the case destination and path. The two last conceptual graphs correspond to the deep structures of sentences (1) and (2). They illustrate the restrictions of the case LOC. In Kettani (1990), an adaptive model based on this mecanism allows dynamic variation of the case structure depending on the context. The author introduces semantics with granularity in the case grammar model.

The hierarchy of the relational and conceptual type allows multiple partial ordering. A type may have several hierarchical relationships with other types. Each relationship expresses a point of view from a context or a situation. For instance, the conceptual relation DEST may be considered as a localisation relation, DEST < LOC, or as an addressee relation, DEST < RCPT. For the concepts, the multiple hierarchy allows the definition of generic constraints over the natural constraints. For instance, the verb WRITE, possesses the case INSTR, with an instrumental object requiring the natural constraint PEN. Nevertheless, this last constraint is not large enough because somebody may also write with a chalk. A chalk is also a natural constraint. To overcome this awkward situation, it is possible, if the generic term does not exist, to artificially create a conceptual type that represents all the entities used to write. This new relationship does not erase the relationship between the conceptual type PEN and the conceptual type OBJECT because a pen remains an object.

The hierarchy of the relational type may also be used to instantiate or to add a case during an attachment of a semantic structure of a prepositional group onto the case structure. This attachment is carried out during parsing and it is guided by syntactic constraints. The syntactic constraints require the semantic structure to be attached to the case of the case structure that is associated with a prepositional marker. This approach is based on the case grammar whose semantic cases are mappings of the linguistic cases.

(1) *The boy drinks a lemonade in a pub.*

The case structure of the verb "drink" does not necessarily contain the locative case.

```
[DRINK]-
    → (AGENT) → [ANIMAL]
    → (OBJT) → [LIQUID]
    → (INSTR) → [OBJECT].
```

A generic case, MARK, is added to the case structure during the prepositional group parsing.

```
[DRINK]-
    → (AGENT) → [BOY]
    → (OBJT) → [LIMONE]
    → (INSTR) → [OBJECT]
    → (MARK) → [PUB].
```

The next conceptual graph shows the definition of "preposition" by selectional constraints expressing the results of operations on the deep structure.

```
constraint for ``in'' is
    [ENTITY] ← (LOC) ← [ENTITY].
```

The applying of its prepositional constraints during the prepositional parsing triggers the instantiation of the generic case, MARK.

```
[DRINK] -
    → (AGENT) → BOY]
    → (OBJT) → [LIMONE]
    → (INSTR) → [OBJECT]
    → (LOC) → [PUB].
```

In this section, a set of examples shows that the hierarchies of relations and concepts are reasonable and interesting but they could not be universal because of the language-dependent type labels using. Meanwhile, a common background like natural types, the laws of physics and common sense, make a large common hierarchy although many variations may occur between all the languages. In the conceptual graph modeling, the common hierarchy defines the top level of concept and relation type hierarchies and the variations are represented as subtypes. According to this point of view, the adaptation of a language model will be performed by adding intralingual or interlingual extensions without any substitution or deletion. The conceptual graph modeling is then based on the reusability of language model.

This discussion closes the assumptions that constitute the foundations of the conceptual parsing approach. More details will be given in section 24.4 with a complete example of linguistics knowledge.

24.2.3 Multi-Media Modeling

The conceptual graph model presupposes that it is possible to code word meaning by leaving the word space and entering concept space. This equivalency relationship between expression and cognition may be extended to other means of communication, for instance, to video-communication. Visual perception is composed of a set of pictures or imaged icons. Let us assume it is also possible to code the meaning of pictures by leaving the picture space and entering the same previous concept space. Thus, a common modeling space allows an unified management of the multi-media issues. An example shows the power of a common formalism shared by at least two inputs. A user clicks on a window in the screen and says:"move this one". The sentence parsing gives the next conceptual graph.

```
[MOVE] -
    → (AGENT) → [SYSTEM]
    → (OBJT) → [OBJECT:active].
```

The click action generates the conceptual graph: [WINDOW:active].

The semantic network defines the hierarchical relationship: WINDOW < OBJECT. A multi-media system would have to join the two system inputs (e.g., graphic command and speech command). The next conceptual graph gives the global meaning of the user's multi-media input.

```
[MOVE] -
    → (AGENT) → [SYSTEM]
    → (OBJT) → [WINDOW:active].
```

24.2.4 Tools

A conceptual graph management tool has been developed according to the model presented in Sowa (1984). The conceptual graph model provides a knowledge representation language. An interpreter-compiler-loader tool reads all the dictionaries which are gathered in a database. The declarative knowledge of this database is entered using the syntax of language defined in Sowa (1984). The interpreter commands provide some operations that verify the integrity of the database. These tools run under MS-DOS operating system on a PC workstation and under Unix on a SUN workstation. The C++ programming language has been used to implement the conceptual graph model as an application programming interface (API). The API that is essentially a library of functions has been linked with a LISP core program to provide a conceptual graph management system in a LISP-environment.

24.3 THE SYNTAX-DIRECTED JOINING

The understanding process is based on the compositional principle, where a compositional operation is defined to build a sentence meaning from the meaning of each lexical term. The compositional operation is flexible because it is based on the joining operation that is a more powerful matching principle than a simple variable unification. Syntax-directed joining is a compositional operation based on the joining operation guided by the syntax. It sets up a partial determinism that defines rigorous compositional rules for the usual syntagmatic attachments. In the project KALIPSOS (1990), a similar approach has been adopted with the use of a directed join algorithm. However, the directed join algorithm requires the use of syntactic labels in the concepts of the conceptual graphs. In the conceptual parsing approach, no syntactic label are needed to annotate conceptual types. The concepts are linked by variables to the occurrences of the grammatical symbols in the production rules. These variables set up cross-references between the syntactic symbols and the conceptual structures.

Let us assume a set of production rules, called a *conceptual grammar*, can be used to define any valid directed joins arising during a language understanding process. Then, a driver, called the *conceptual parser*, can apply these rules in terms of the lexical-semantic input sequence. A conceptual graph can also be obtained during the parsing, and let us assume it is sufficient to capture the sentence's meaning and to evaluate the analysis performance.

24.3.1 Conceptual Grammar

In this section, a rapid overview of the attributed grammar introduces the basic foundations of the conceptual grammar. A definition presents the extensions of an attributed grammar formalism and explains how they take the conceptual graph model and the directed joins into account. Finally, the interaction between the conceptual grammar and the conceptual graph model is described in detail.

Attributed Grammar Overview

Conceptual grammar is derived from attributed grammars whose attributes are computed with both bottom-up and top-down dependency ordering.

Syntax-directed Definition A syntax-directed definition is a generalization of a context free grammar in which every grammar symbol has a set of *synthesized* and/or *inherited* attributes (Aho, 1986). The attribute value of a symbol is defined by a semantic rule associated with the production which contains the symbol. Semantic rules express the bottom-up and top-down *value passing rules* respectively for synthethized and inherited attributes. The next example shows a classical use of attributes where the $E.val$ attribute is synthethized and the $E1.type$ and $E2.type$ attributes are inherited.

Production	Semantic Rules
$E \rightarrow E1 + E2$	$E.val := E1.val + E2.val,$ $E1.type := E.type,$ $E2.type := E1.type$

Translation Scheme A translation scheme is a context free grammar in which attributes are associated with grammar symbols, and semantic actions, defined by code fragments, are embedded within the productions. Every syntax-directed definition can be mapped into an equivalent translation scheme (Aho 1986), and, every translation scheme can be implemented with a generalized LR parser (see section 24.3.2).

Formal Definition of a Conceptual Grammar

After the above summary, this section defines a conceptual grammar as a context free grammar in which the attributes of a grammar symbol are concepts, called *conceptual attributes*, and the semantic rules of a production are expressed by a conceptual graph, called *an attribute graph*. A syntax-directed definition defines functional dependencies between attributes and the semantic rule computation yields the values. A conceptual grammar defines relational dependencies between conceptual attributes and the referent values are computed by a join operation. The conceptual grammar intends to pass attribute graph among symbols at different levels in order to have the information that is needed to automatically perform the constraint-checking along the join operation. The join operation occurs whenever the parser reduces symbols into a higher-level non-terminal using a production rule. Hence, the parser performs join operations between the attribute graphs of all the symbols and the conceptual attributes of the higher-level non-terminal. Subsequent reductions along the parsing justify to make use of virtual join operations in conceptual grammars.

A syntax-directed joining is a conceptual grammar in which conceptual attributes are associated with grammar symbols, and dependency schemes, defined by code fragments, are added to the productions. The attribute graph is then called a conceptual scheme. Let's start from the example of the syntax-directed definition again and try to write it as a conceptual grammar rule. The first semantic rule becomes a code fragment of the dependency scheme and the two last semantic rules are involved in the conceptual scheme due to the conceptual

attribute sharing. Actually, the concept [TYPE] is an attribute of both the concepts [E],
[E1] and [E2].

Production	Conceptual Scheme	Dependency Scheme

$E \rightarrow E1 + E2$	[E]-
	   $\rightarrow$(ATTR)$\rightarrow$[VAL:*x1]
	   $\rightarrow$(ATTR)$\rightarrow$[TYPE]-
	   $\leftarrow$(ATTR)$\leftarrow$[E1]-
	      $\rightarrow$(ATTR)$\rightarrow$[VAL:*x2];
	   $\leftarrow$(ATTR)$\leftarrow$[E2]-
	      $\rightarrow$(ATTR)$>$[VAL:*x3];;.
		$x1 = x2 + x3$

As shown in the next example, a conceptual grammar rule is a production (1), a conceptual
scheme (2), and a dependency scheme (3).

(1) noun_group : DETERMINER NOUN
(2)

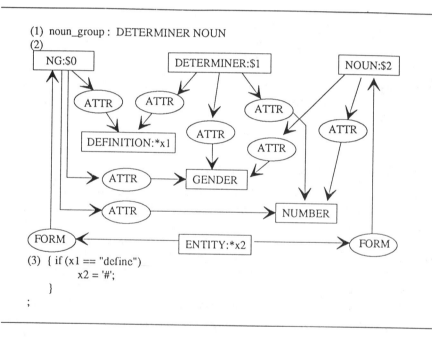

(3) { if (x1 == "define")
      x2 = '#';
  }
;

Fig. 24.3 A conceptual grammar rule.

The first part of the rule corresponds to a context free grammar production. The attribute
graph appears in the second part. The sign "$0" is used to identify the head concept of
the attribute graph and to attach it to the non-terminal symbol *noun_group* in order to
define the conceptual attributes. For a terminal symbol, as NOUN, the head concept of a
graph delivered by a lexical-semantic analysis is automatically attached to the symbol. The
sign "$n" indicates the nth symbol of the right side of the production (1) with a left-to-
right scanning. When $n is used in a reference field, the concept [$n] is linked to the

n-th symbol. During the reduction of the non-terminal symbol *noun_group* in parsing, the concept [$n] of the attribute graph is automatically joined to the head concept attached to the n-th symbol. This joining mechanism allows a one-pass computation of the conceptual attribute referent values. The variable "x_i" which appears in the reference field of a concept in (2) can be used as a C language variable in the code fragment (3). In this way, the C language statements allow a description of complex functional dependencies between referents. The dependency schemes do not come from a formal representation or notation of a theory. A dependency scheme is a kind of "escape-to-arbitrary-code" actions where the functional dependency may be included. The functional dependencies between referents are empirically determined from the study of a large amount of sentences and according to basic linguistic principles.

Finally, it is clear from these simple examples that there is a possible conversion from a conceptual grammar into a translation scheme. For more complex cases, one assumes that a conceptual grammar can be turned into an equivalent translation scheme. The fragment codes of the equivalent translation scheme rules handle all the tasks presented in the conceptual grammar compiler section (see section 24.3.2 below).

Practical Interaction with the conceptual graph Model

The rules of the conceptual grammar uses conceptual graph. However, it requires the presence of specific conceptual and relational types in the conceptual graph model to allow the interaction of the conceptual structures with the lexical data and syntactic rules . For the syntax, the declarations of the relational types, FORM and CONST, are required to link a conceptual entity to its syntagmatic form. For the lexicon, all the grammatical categories have to generate a conceptual type that is a subtype of the type, TOKEN. They are used in the cross-reference between symbols and conceptual structures. Furthermore, the relational type, NAME, distinguishes the concept from the noun used to name it. It allows the introduction of the lexical term as a conceptual type. The next conceptual graph shows an example of the lexical, syntactic and semantic interactions for a car:

```
[CAR] → (FORM) → [NOUN] → (NAME) → ["car"] .
```

The linguistic concept, CAR, has a form with a grammatical category NOUN. The grammatical category has the name of the word "car". The word is a lexical term of a linguistic concept.

24.3.2   Conceptual Parser

Based on the above discussion, the conclusion leads to assume that a generalized LR parser is sufficient to accept a conceptual grammar which describes the language that it recognises. Thus, the YACC tool has been used to implement the conceptual parser because it is an LR parser generator which provides in addition other attractive characteristics. The definition and modification of a grammar is easy because YACC supplies a language description. The time-consuming parsing is minimal because a precompilation stage optimises the grammar rules and the parsing algorithm is among the more efficient available. Most particularly, YACC allows access to the parsing algorithm, which permits easy modification of the parser code. This facility and the intensive use of the translation scheme seem to make YACC a good tool for the development of a new system.

LR Parser Overview

An LR parser is composed of four components. An input buffer contains a lexical input sequence. A stack stores the different parsing states. A parsing table indicates the operations that the parser can do on the stack and the buffer. A driver reads in the input buffer and takes the top of the stack to perform an action corresponding to a code extracted from the parsing table. A rigorous definition and operation of the LR parser can be found in Aho (1984).

The parsing table can be automatically built from a grammar. The driver is the same for all LR parsers; only the parsing table changes in terms of the grammar and the LR parsing table construction algorithm.

YACC produces a generalized LR parser (Johnson, 1975). The YACC programming language makes it possible to obtain a structured stack and to include code fragments which can be considered as actions. It is also possible to customize the parsing algorithm to take a conceptual grammar i nto account.

Asynchronous Parallel Parser

It seems adequate to use the YACC tool to program a conceptual parser. Unfortunately, YACC produces only deterministic parsers. This class of parsers does not use a backtracking parsing algorithm and hence cannot deal with an ambiguous lexical-semantic input sequence used with the conceptual grammars. A lexical ambiguity occurs when an input possesses more than one grammatical category. A semantic ambiguity occurs when an input corresponds to several concepts.

The lexical-semantic ambiguity problem has been addressed with a specific non-deterministic parsing algorithm that consists of parsing all the lexical-semantic alternative inputs by running deterministic parsers in parallel. The synchronisation task is handled by an external scheduler. So, each deterministic parser must be able to run with the capability to handle interruptions. Furthermore, an asynchronous running mode is essential to parse several sentences at the same time in spoken language processing (Bornerand, 1990).

The next part of the section consists of presenting the adaptation of the YACC driver and the YACC programming framework developed to reach this goal. The original alteration in relation to the other extensions of YACC concerns the parsing driver. In the parallel processing, the new driver emulates many deterministic parsing processes which use virtual stacks. All of them are memorized in one physical stack, called a *multiple-stack*, where the bottom is shared by all the processes until a process has been split into several ones.

The asynchronous mode forbids real actions on the stack. Only virtual actions are performed. When a deterministic parsing needs to read a lexical-semantic input, the asynchronous parallel driver interrupts the current process and it takes the directive back to a supervisor.

The YACC programming language allows the association of a conceptual graph with a production rule, to create a link between a symbol of this production and a concept of this graph, and to call the virtual join operation for each link. In addition, some fields in the stack have been defined to load the results of virtual join operations. Certains fields are treated as classical inherited attributes and others as classical synthesized attributes. The evaluation function works on these fields and it returns a score when an interrupt occurs. In this version, the score is simply the number of joined concepts.

A Conceptual Grammar Compiler

Presently, all the above descriptions are directly implemented in YACC. A modification of the conceptual grammar leads to a modification of the YACC program at the declarative and procedural level. Let us assume that a conceptual parser generator may translate a conceptual grammar file to a conceptual parser following the dataflow diagram below.

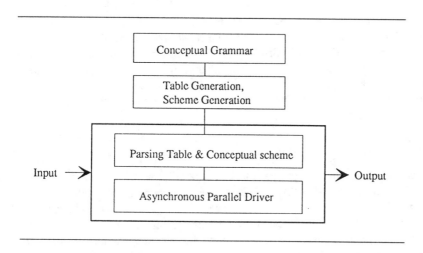

Fig. 24.4 Generating diagram of the conceptual grammar compiler.

The conceptual grammar compiler proceeds in three steps. First, a preprocessor translates an ASCII file with a conceptual grammar declaration into a YACC-format file. It also creates a file of conceptual schemes. A conceptual scheme is a conceptual graph used to do the joining operation between all the symbols of a production rule. Finally, it creates the joining operations between the underlying conceptual structures from the cross-references. The next example shows the translation of a conceptual grammar rule to a YACC-rule.

```
(1) noun_group: DETERMINER NOUN
(2) [NG:$0]-
    → (RIGHT_MEMBER) → [DETERMINER:$1]
    → (RIGHT_MEMBER) → [NOUN:$2].
(3) {$0 = '#';};
```

The YACC-rule is more procedural. Abbreviations are used to express objects and functions. A comment gives the meaning of each abbreviation.

```
(1) noun_group: DETERMINER NOUN
(2) CG = scheme (noun_group);
    /* read the CG in the conceptual scheme table */
$0.head = NG;
    /* the concept [NG] is the head concept of the CG linked
to the noun_group symbol */
join ( DETERMINER, $1.head);
    /* Joining operation between the concept [DETERMINER] and
the headconcept of the CG linked to the symbol DETERMINER */
join ( NOUN, $2.head);
    /* Joining operation between the concept [NOUN] and the headcon
of the CG linked to the symbol NOUN */
(3) NG.referent = #;
    /* the referent of the concept [NG] is individual */
```

In the second step, the compiler translates the YACC-file into a C++ source file with a YACC-derived algorithm. The parsing table construction algorithm has to deal with the ambiguous grammar (Tomita, 1985). A grammar is ambiguous when at least two differents sets of productions may apply while parsing an input string. However, this algorithm builds multiple-entry parsing tables. The parsing driver has to accept the multi-entry parsing table and to manage the asynchronous connection with the lexical-semantic analyzer. The last step is a C++ compiling.

24.3.3 Lexical-Semantic Analyzer

A lexical-semantic analysis program has been written with the LEX tool (Lesk, 1975) because it is compatible with YACC. LEX is also a generator and it supplies a programming language.

For each input string, the lexical-semantic analyzer builds a conceptual graph. The word search in a morphological-lexical dictionary accesses a conceptual graph which contains all the lexical information (gender, number, grammatical category,...). Then, the word-concept mapping file is scanned to search concepts. The concept detection triggers the search in a semantic dictionary to obtain a conceptual graph which contains semantic information. Then, the analyzer joins the two previous graphs to build a lexical-semantic graph returned to the conceptual parser.

Polymorphism and synonymy are taken into account in the same manner. For each step described above, the process can be split into several daughter processes when it encounters several candidates. A call to a lexical-semantic analyzer may also generate many lexical-semantic graphs.

In all over these search processes, a failure does not disrupt the lexical-semantic analyzer. In fact, both the failure of the word or concept searchs could lead to many results. For example, the lack of a word-concept mapping rule allows the use of functional or empty words. The analyzer only returns the conceptual graph from the lexical dictionary. In the other hand, the failure for accessing lexical dictionary may be useful if the analyzer has to provide only a semantic graph without any other kind of information. In this case, the analyzer only returns the conceptual graph from the semantic dictionary.

In a more general way, let's raise the following question: Is the analyzer able to handle unknown words? The direct answer may be that the analyzer has not been developed for this purpose. Meanwhile, it seems convenient to implement a simple procedure to deal with the unknown words. The analyzer may return a generic lexical graph when a lexical dictionary entry missing.

```
[TOKEN]-
    → (NAME) → [WORD]
    ← (FORM) ← [ENTITY].
```

The type "TOKEN" is a supertype of all the grammatical categories as the type "EN-TITY" is a supertype of all the semantic categories. The unknown word is then assigned to the referent of the concept "WORD".

A more complicated computation may be implemented in terms of the token predicted by the parser. For example, the "VERB" grammatical category implies to join an additional conceptual graph to the previous one in order to describe a generic case structure as shown below.

```
[ENTITY]-
    → (AGENT) → [ENTITY]
    → (OBJECT) → [ENTITY]
    → (INSTR) → [ENTITY]
    → (LOC) → [ENTITY]
    → (TIME) → [ENTITY].
```

The analyzer also returns a join of the generic lexical graph and the generic semantic graph as the lexical-semantic graph of an unknown word that is assumed to be a verb.

Anyhow, many other procedures have to be called in order to correctly deal with the unknown words and the purpose is then out of the scope of this chapter.

24.4   A CONCEPTUAL PARSING PROCESSOR

24.4.1   Principles

Semantics are used as soon as possible during the analysis both as a meaning construction process and as a source of further constraints for the analysis itself. In this way, semantic constraints help the resolution of ambiguity. But, there is no formal criterion to prefer one interpretation to another. The interpretation is not a categorical (yes/no) process, but is instead based on the idea of preference (Wilks, 1975). The YACC-based parser of the system has been modified to take conceptual preference into account. The conceptual preference hence reflects the grammatical agreement, the syntactic constraint and the semantic consistency. The choice is based on a complex interaction between all the conceptual constituents issue from the lexical, syntactic and semantic information of each word of the sentence. A weighting mechanism has been added to the parser so that the explanation of several solutions in parallel is possible. Each solution has a score and the best score yields the computational interpretation according to the conceptual preference principle. Nevertheless, the method is not able to deal with all the ambiguity situations. In some cases, the system may choose the wrong alternative but are humans perfect?

The basic design of such a method is based on three points:

- What alternatives must be considered?

- How much time must be devoted to each path?

- What knowledge sources contribute to the weighting and how can the weight be adjusted?

The method supports full parallelism and every alternative is examined. All the paths are pursued until the end of parsing. The *delayed decision principle* waits until the end of the parsing to select the best solution. The system uses a unified formalism to allow a simultaneous participation of all the knowledge. The evaluation function may be adjusted to compute the weights. Presently, the evaluation function computes the number of joined concepts. For instance, it may use the number of joined concepts to calculate the overlap between two conceptual graphs.

On the over hand, the compliance to the conceptual preference principle prevents partial parsing from aborting because of constraint violations. The interpretation unconsistency just increases the score of the partial parsing. A pruning may be used to delete all the bad scores.

Furthermore, this system may express preference on the basis of the context. An initial conceptual graph sets up the conceptual background on which the interpretations are going to grow. In these conditions, the conceptual preference corresponds to the maximal overlap between the initial context and an interpretation.

Finally, the non-deterministic analysis shares data to save memory space. The data sharing is performed automatically by the virtual projection operation (see section 24.2.1).

24.4.2   The Linguistic Model

A natural language processor must manage large quantities of linguistic data to understand the sentences. The language model is spread throughout many knowledge bases: morphological-lexical dictionary, semantic dictionary, conceptual grammar file, word-concept mapping file. The most of them are represented in the conceptual graph formalism because all the conceptual graph model operations use pattern-based algorithms which are meaning independent. This declarative aspect reduces the heuristic treatment to a minimum.

The determiners are introduced to the conceptual graph model with the referent. The problem of the type of determiners (e.g., define, undefine, singular and plural) can be addressed by the functional dependency issues. The prepositions may be introduced with the conceptual relations. A hundred basic relations may be sufficient to take the most of the French prepositional forms into account. The semantics of nouns, verbs and adjectives is defined by a conceptual graph whose the complexity changes in terms of the static granularity or according to the semantics context of definition. The head concept of a conceptual graph makes it possible to identify the entry point of a conceptual graph in a dictionary.

In the conceptual parsing processing, a lexical dictionary contains the words in full form where each lexical entry indicates a set of categorization features. A semantic dictionary describes the meaning of words in the conceptual graph formalism. Each entry, called a conceptual type, corresponds to a formal definition and to a list of selectional constraints used in the compositional operation. A file contains all matching rules between words and concepts in order to avoid mutual dependency inside the two above dictionaries. A concept can appear more than once to express the synonymy and a word can appear more than once to capture the polymorphism phenomena. Finally, a file contains production rules to express the syntax.

The lexical dictionary only contains conceptual graphs. Each lexical entry points out a record with a conceptual graph format. This solution allows the possibility to code all the linguistics knowledge by conceptual graphs. In any case, it is not useful to re-create a dictionary where it already exists, for instance on CD-ROM. It is better to use a generic conceptual graph along with the lexical dictionary access. A conceptual graph-instantiation procedure duplicates all information of the lexical entry in the generic conceptual graph in order to get a lexical graph.

Each lexical term is defined as a concept with the relation NAME. Each lexical concept is a subtype of the concept WORD (Sowa, 1984). At the syntactic level, the grammatical categories are defined as concepts that are subtypes of TOKEN. The phrase structures are defined as subtypes of SYNTAGM. The grammatical and syntactic relations which express the syntactic functions of the syntagms in a sentence are represented by conceptual relations. For instance, the relation, SUBJECT, links the syntagm, SENTENCE, to a nominal group, NG. Only the words, the syntagms and the sentences are handled by the system. The propositions or the situations are coded with concepts retrieving conceptual graphs as referent. The conceptual graph model accepts the embedded conceptual graphs with coreference links that link all the concepts of a same referent. Nevertheless, the joining operation is not recursive. It does not perform joining operation on the referents. In the system, a flat model is used to integrate the lexical, syntactic and semantic knowledge. All of them belong to the same level (i.e., they may be joined together). There is no proposition nor situation. In fact, the word-concept mapping file separates the cognitive level from the expression's form. For instance in natural language understanding, the access to a concept should be independent of word categorization. An opposite approach is the KALIPSOS project developed by the IBM scientific research centre in France (Landau, 1990). The following example shows that Semantic dictionary entries depend on the word's grammatical category.

```
VERB('to pass',1) is
    [MOTION: XVERB]-
        → (AGT) → [ENTITY: XSUBJ]
        → (LOC.START) → [LOCATION:]
        → (LOC.END) → [LOCATION:]
```

where "XVERB" and "XSUBJ" are grammatical category marker used in a directed join algorithm (KALIPSOS, 1988).

But for instance, a scene analysis algorithm in the image understanding system cannot use the same semantic dictionary. So, the KALIPSOS approach rejects the multi-media cognitive level because a common conceptual structure cannot be mapped with any input. The media-independent semantic dictionary defines a unique multi-media cognitive level.

24.4.3   Architecture

Parsing Process Design

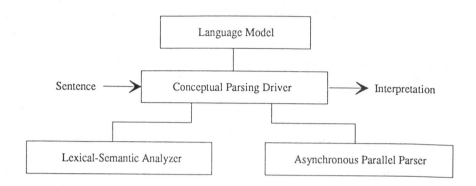

Fig. 24.5 Conceptual parsing architecture.

Computation Scheduling Description

The main goal of the conceptual parsing driver is to manage a list of interpretations which is empty at the start. The conceptual parsing driver invokes the lexical-semantic analyzer for each word of a sentence. The lexical-semantic analyzer returns a list of associations, called a *candidate list*, where the association key is a grammatical category and the association value is a lexical-semantic graph. Then, for each candidate, the driver calls the asynchronous parallel parser on all the competing interpretations. The asynchronous parallel parser continues the syntax-directed joining for each of them in terms of both the grammatical category and the lexical-semantic graph of the candidate. Each return yields a new interpretation with a score. Before scanning the next word, the list of interpretations are updated. When the sentence has been completely scanned, the best score designates the correct interpretation. The interpretation is saved by making a physical join between all the conceptual graphs used during the parsing process which has delivered this interpretation.

24.4.4   An Example

This section describes an example to show the kind of linguistic phenomena that the working system can handle. It explains how specific cases such AGENT and OBJECT are taken into account and how to introduce a direct mapping between lexical marker and semantic case for the others. An example shows the referent resolution.

The example is the following French sentence:

> *"l'ingénieur du LIMSI écrit des programmes avec un ordinateur dans un bureau."*
>
> (The LIMSI engineer writes programs with a computer in an office.)

The next part of this section presents the most of the data used in the parsing of this sentence.

The morphological-lexical dictionary indicates all the categorization features of a word in a unique conceptual graph in which a concept, named ENTITE, defines a link between the lexical and the semantic level.

```
/* Noun Declaration Area */

type "ingénieur" < WORD.
type "programmes" < WORD.
type "bureau" < WORD.
type "ordinateur" < WORD.

constraint for "ingénieur" is
[SUBSTANTIF]-
    → (NAME) → ["ingénieur"]
    → (ATTR) → [GENRE:masculin]
    → (ATTR) → [NOMBRE:singulier]
    ← (FORM) ← [ENTITE].

constraint for "programmes" is
[SUBSTANTIF]-
    → (NAME) → ["programmes"]
    → (ATTR) → [GENRE:masculin]
    → (ATTR) → [NOMBRE:pluriel]
    ← (FORM) ← [ENTITE].

constraint for "bureau" is
[SUBSTANTIF]-
    → (NAME) → ["bureau"]
    → (ATTR) → [GENRE:masculin]
    → (ATTR) → [NOMBRE:singulier]
    ← (FORM) ← [ENTITE].

constraint for "ordinateur" is
[SUBSTANTIF]-
    → (NAME) → ["ordinateur"]
    → (ATTR) → [GENRE:masculin]
    → (ATTR) → [NOMBRE:singulier]
    ← (FORM) ← [ENTITE].

/* Determiner Declaration Area */

type "l" < WORD.
type "des" < WORD.
type "un" < WORD.

constraint for "l" is
[DETERMINANT]-
    → (NAME) → ["l"]
    → (ATTR) → [ESPECE:défini]
    → (ATTR) → [NOMBRE:singulier].

constraint for "des" is
[DETERMINANT]-
    → (NAME) → ["des"]
    → (ATTR) → [ESPECE:indùfini]
    → (ATTR) → [NOMBRE:pluriel].
```

constraint for "un" is
```
[DETERMINANT]-
    → (NAME) → ["un"]
    → (ATTR) → [ESPECE:indùfini]
    → (ATTR) → [GENRE:masculin]
    → (ATTR) → [NOMBRE:singulier].
```

/* Proper Noun Declaration Area */

type "limsi" < WORD.

constraint for "limsi" is
```
[NOM_PROPRE]-
    → (NAME) → ["limsi"]
    → (ATTR) → [PERSONNE:3]
    → (ATTR) → [GENRE:masculin]
    → (ATTR) → [NOMBRE:singulier]
    ← (CONST) ← [ENTITE].
```

/* Preposition Declaration Area */

type "de" < WORD.
type "dans" < WORD.
type "avec" < WORD.

constraint for "dans" is
```
[PREPOSITION]-
    → (NAME) → ["dans"]
    0← (MARK) -
       1←[ENTITE:*x1]
       2←[ENTITE]-
          ← (LOC) ← [ENTITE:*x1];;.
```

constraint for "avec" is
```
[PREPOSITION]-
    → (NAME) → ["avec"]
    0← (MARK) -
       1←[ENTITE:*x1]
       2←[ENTITE]-
          ← (INSTR) ← [ENTITE:*x1];;.
```

/* Verb Declaration Area */

type "écrit" < WORD.

constraint for "écrit" is
```
[VRB_T_D]-
    → (NAME) → ["écrit"]
    → (ATTR) → [NOMBRE:singulier]
    → (ATTR) → [TEMPS:présent]
    → (ATTR) → [MODE:indicatif]
    → (ATTR) → [PERSONNE:3]
    → (ATTR) → [VOIX:active]
    ← (FORM) ← [ENTITE].
```

Let us explain the above graph. The word *"écrit"* (writes) is a direct transitive verb which is conjugated in the present indicative in the active voice and in the 3rd person singular.

It is the pattern of a concept. Almost all preposition declarations involve the mapping relationship between the lexical marker and the underlying semantic case. This relation, named MARK, posits a case-based relationship (see below the semantic description) between the verb and the constituent introduced by the preposition.

The semantic dictionary supplies word meanings in conceptual graph formalism.

```
/* Semantic Network Area */

type HUMAIN < ENTITE.
type OBJET < ENTITE.
type INGENIEUR < HUMAIN.
type ORDINATEUR < OBJET.
type BUREAU < LOCAL, OBJET, LIEU.
type LABORATOIRE < ENTITE.
type ECRIRE < PROCESSUS_INSTR.

constraint for ECRIRE is
ECRIRE
    —
            → (AGENT) → [ENTITE]
            → (INSTR) → [OBJET]
            → (OBJET) → [ENTITE].
```

The concept ECRIRE (to write) has a case structure in which the OBJET and AGENT case relationships, called the cases, are related to any entity. Otherwise, the type OBJET expresses a selectional constraint on the referent of the concept related by the instrumental relationship INSTR.

The remainder of the section presents some conceptual grammar rules which take place in the example parsing process.

The next rule, named *phrase (sentence)*, defines the association of the AGENT case with the subject and the association of the OBJET case with the direct/indirect object.

The attribute graph states that the predicate of the proposition is the predicate of the verbal group and that the subject fills the AGENT case.

The next rule, named *groupe_nominal (noun group)*, defines the agreement rules and shows a C language code fragment which expresses the functional dependencies of referents.

phrase: groupe_nominal_s groupe_verbal

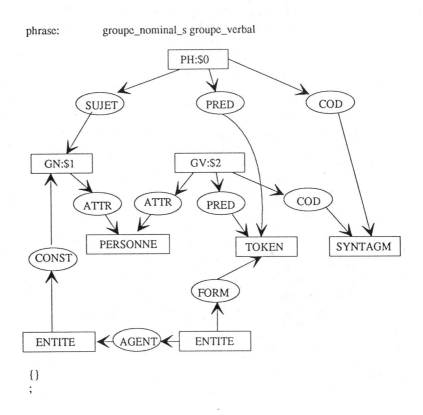

{}
;

Fig. 24.6 Rule of the case AGENT computation

The syntax-directed joining deals with the agreements thanks to the shared conceptual attributes which are connected to several concepts - remember that the concepts with a $n referent may be considered as symbols. For instance, the conceptual attribute GENRE (gender) is shared with DETERMINANT (determiner), SUBSTANTIF (noun), GN (noun group) because an ATTR relation exists with each of them. The referent computation of the concept, named [ENTITE:*x1], takes into account the gender, the number and the definition of the noun group.

The next rule, named groupe_complement (complement group), defines the marker-case mapping rule.

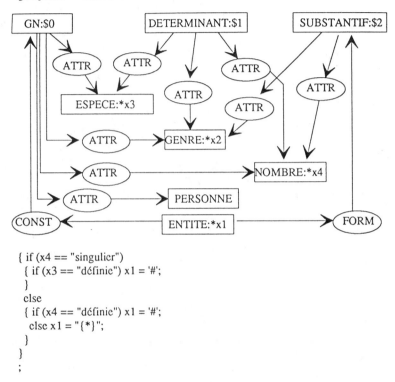

```
{ if (x4 == "singulier")
  { if (x3 == "définie") x1 = '#';
  }
  else
  { if (x4 == "définie") x1 = '#';
    else x1 = "{*}";
  }
}
;
```

Fig. 24.7 Rule handling the referent functional dependencies

The attribute graph makes it possible to project on the verb case structure the marker-case relationship, named MARK, which is involved in the lexical-semantic graph attached to the PREPOSITION symbol. If the verb is intended to receive this case, then the case is overlapped (see the previous preposition declaration area). Else, a new case is joined to the verb structure.

groupe_complement:groupe_complement PREPOSITION groupe_nominal_c

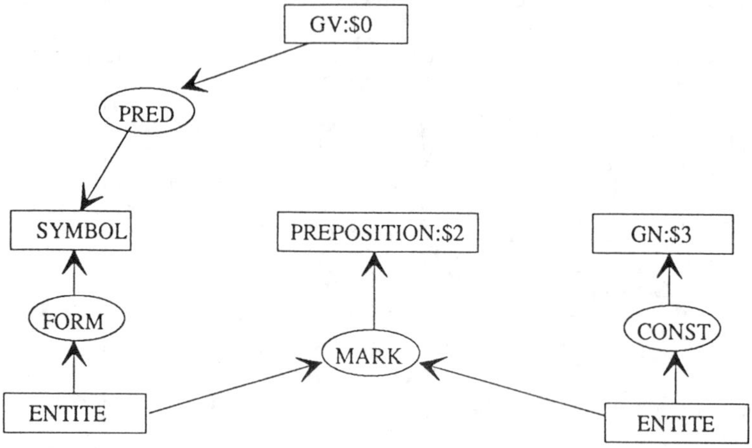

Fig. 24.8 Rule of case-marker mapping

The result of the example parsing process is a conceptual graph inserted at the end of the chapter in the appendix 24. Its analysis allows us to conclude on the following points:

- the occurrence of the non-generic referents (#, {*}) demonstrates that the system can deal with referent functional dependencies;

- the unique occurrence of the AGENT, OBJET and INSTR relations shows that the system can deal with the predestined case overlapping;

- the occurrence of the LIEU relation shows that some case relations can be added to the verb case structure;

- the occurrence of the concepts of BUREAU and ORDINATEUR show the propagation of the selectional constraints on the verb's case structure.

Otherwise, the instantiation of the case structure is only the grey part of the conceptual graph in the appendix to this chapter. The other part memorizes all the information used during the parsing process. Any observer can see they are not equal. As the evaluation function works on the entire conceptual graph, the case structure instantiation does not have the leading part. Hence, the simple criterion based on the overlapping rate of concepts loses the notion of semantic consistency. A new criterion which takes the weights of the conceptual graph into account should make it possible to preserve the relevance of case structure in the evaluation function.

24.4.5 Discussion

The reader could notice the absence of an explicit syntactic structure in the conceptual graph of the parsing example. In fact, let us assume such a structure is not required with a syntax-directed joining algorithm. The system uses a flat conceptual structure model without tree-structured syntactic representations or context-nested conceptual structures. If the syntactic structure does not appear in the example, it is not because of conceptual grammar l imitations but rather to avoid unuseful structures. Nethertheless, the syntactic representation could be necessary in a more general computation. In this case, the conceptual graph model is powerful enough to handle both the lexical, syntactic and semantic representations. For instance, the next conceptual grammar rule shows how to introduce the syntactic structures.

$$[GN] \rightarrow ("=") \rightarrow [DETERMINER] \rightarrow ("<") \rightarrow [NOUN].$$

The relation "=" means that the constituent [GN] is made of a sequence of constituents whose the constituent [DETERMINER] is the first. The relation "<" means that the constituent [DETERMINER] is followed by the constituent [NOUN]. These relations are used to define all the syntactic structures and could, if necessary, be automatically generated by the conceptual grammar compiler.

The system is based on a single model used to code both the syntax and the semantics. However, this unification effort needs not imply the waste of the ability to discriminate between one or another representation. Any information has to be extractable from the conceptual structure. The joining operation allows the conceptual aggregation to build up from a set of conceptual structures (i.e., the interpretation comes from the join of all lexical-semantic graphs of a sentence). On the other hand, the projection operations locate a selected sub-conceptual graph in a conceptual graph. First, a selectional constraint is defined by a conceptual graph. Second, the conceptual graph is projected on the conceptual aggregation. Each successful projection returns a restriction of the selectional constraint containing the desired information. The extracted information is sufficiently precise and local to allow the search of syntactic features. Moreover, a strutured chunk of information may also be extracted from a conceptual aggregation. More generally, the projection operation makes it possible to know if a conceptual graph matches with a frame and then to recognize a pattern inside of a conceptual graph. This recognition ability may be used to extract a semantic representation from the conceptual aggregation. A generic case structure is defined and projected on the conceptual aggregation to look for an instantiation of the case structure. The next example shows how the coupled projection-restriction is used in the practical systems to obtain this instantiation.

The parsing sentence is:

(1) *Paul loves marie.*

The parsing yields the following conceptual aggregation:

```
[SENTENCE] -
    → (SUBJECT) → [NOUN] -
    ← (FORM) ← [PERSON:paul] -
    ← (AGENT) ← [LOVE:*x1];;
    → (PREDICAT) → [VERB] -
```

```
← (FORM) ← [LOVE:*x1];
→ (DIRECT_OBJECT) → [NOUN] -
← (FORM) ← [PERSON:marie] -
← (OBJT) ← [LOVE:*x1];;.
```

The next conceptual graph defines a case structure model:

```
[ACT] -
    → (AGENT) → [ENTITY]
    → (OBJT) → [ENTITY].
```

The restrictions due to the projection lead to the next result:

```
[LOVE] -
    → (AGENT) → [PERSON:paul]
    → (OBJT) → [PERSON:marie].
```

The restriction of a case structure model is a semantic representation that the system is able to automatically isolate from the conceptual aggregation.

As far as the semantic representation is concerned, the conceptual graph model is involved in the process. However, the syntactic parsing algorithm is totally outside the conceptual graph model. The parsing algorithm is based on programming language compiler principles. It is derived from YACC parser as well as many other parsers. An overview of the different classes of these parsers allows the comparaison between some existing parsing algorithms with the syntax-directed joining algorithm from the perspective of the natural language processing.

LR algorithm (Aho, 1986) These algorithms are controlled by a parse table that is constructed beforehand by a table generator. The grammars are limited to the LR grammars. Most natural language grammars cannot be restricted to an LR grammar.

Pseudo-parallel LR parsing (Tomita, 1985) This is an extended LR parsing algorithm, that requires a conventional (but possibly ambiguous) parse table. The parser starts as an LR parser, but when it encounters a conflict in the parse table, it splits up into several LR parsers that work in parallel. All simple LR parsers are synchronized on their shift actions in such a way that only when all parsers have shifted on the current input symbol is the next symbol processed. The algorithm implementation uses a graph-structured stack and a tree-structured syntactic representation. The grammars are restricted to the class of finitely ambiguous context free grammars. These grammars are able to cover most common place natural language syntax without requiring semantic information.

Conceptual parser The conceptual parsing method has been developed on the basis of the parallel parsing algorithm, but incorporating the syntax-directed joining and asynchronous abilities. The syntax-directed joining algorithm uses a virtual tree-structured stack and a tree-structured conceptual aggregation. The grammars are restricted to the finitely ambiguous conceptual grammars. These grammars are able to handle the syntax and the semantics of natural language used in most applications.

24.5 CONCLUSION

This chapter presents a conceptual parsing processor for natural language understanding. It uses a modular language model in which lexical, semantic and syntactic knowledge bases are independent of the others. Also, the extension of the model is easier because the language model is built on the basis of the LEX and YACC programming tools. Hence, the linguistic phenomena may be studied faster. The conceptual grammar is defined as a formal language model where semantics and syntax are integrated in the same rules. A generator can compile a conceptual grammar to get a conceptual parser. The conceptual parser based on the syntax-directed joining algorithm are directly derived from conceptual graph theory and the LR parsing algorithm.

However, some problems which arose in the assessment of the new system reveal certain limitations in the syntax-directed joining algorithm. The conceptual grammars have some difficulties in dealing with complex linguistic phenomena because they only use local semantic rules. Furthermore, the implemented conceptual graph model does not support universal quantification.

More research is required to develop an extension of the conceptual graph model to take into account the weights in the conceptual structures and the universal quantifier with its equivalent rule-based representation. The introduction of global semantic rules in the generator implementation is also necessary. The main goal of this computational approach is to capture more and more linguistic phenomena with an extended conceptual grammar to get as close as possible to full coverage of natural language.

BIBLIOGRAPHY

Aho, A., R. Sethi, J. Ullman, (eds) (1986) *"Compilers: Principles, Techniques and Tools"*, Addison-Wesley, 1986.

Bornerand, S. (1990) "Semantic Weights derived from Syntax-directed Understanding in DTW-based Spoken Language Processing", ICSLP-90, Proc. of International Conference on Spoken Language Processing, Kobe, Japan, Nov 1990.

Brachman, R. (1977) "What's in a concept: structural foundations for semantic networks", International journal of man-machine studies, 9.

Fillmore, C. (1968) "The case for case", in *Universals in linguistic theory*, (eds) Holt, Rinehart and Winston, Bach & Harms, Chicago.

Johnson, S.C. (1975) "YACC: Yet Another Compiler Compiler", in *UNIX Programmer's Manual*, Bell Laboratories.

Kalipsos. Berard-Dugourd, J. Fargues, M.C. Landau, (1988,) "Natural Language Analysis Using Conceptual Graphs", p.265-272, Proc. of 1st International Computer Science Conference 1988, Hong Kong, Dec 1988.

Katz, J., and J. Fodor, (1963) "The structure of a semantic theory", Language, 39.

Kettani, N. (1990) *Un systéme de cas adaptatif et évolutif*, LIMSI internal report.

Landau, M.C. (1990) "Solving Ambiguities in the semantic representation of texts", p.65-70, COLING'90, Helsinki, August 20-25, 1990.

Lesk, M.E. (1975) "Lex - A Lexical Analyzer Generator", in *UNIX Programmer's Manual 2B*, Bell Laboratories.

Ralescu, A.L., J.F. Baldwin, (1989) "Concept learning from examples and counter examples", International journal of man-machine studies, 30.

Sabah, G. (1990) "CARAMEL: A flexible model for interaction between the cognitive processes underlying natural language understanding", COLING'90, Helsinski, August 20-25, 1990.

Schank, R. (1972) "Conceptual dependency: a theory of natural language understanding", Cognitive Psychology, vol. 3 (4).

Tesniére, L. (1953) *Eléments d'une syntaxe structurale*, Klincksieck, Paris.

Sowa, J.F. (1984) *Conceptual Structures: Information Processing in Mind and Machine*, Addison Wesley, Reading.

Tomita, M. (1985) "Efficient Parsing for Natural Language: A Fast Algorithm for Practical Systems", Kluwer Academic Publishers, 1986.

Wilks, Y. (1975) "Preference semantics", in *Formal semantics of natural language*, (ed) Keenan, Cambridge University Press.

APPENDIX

Example sentence (see Section 24.4.4):

> *"L'ingénieur du LIMSI écrit des programmes avec un ordinateur dans un bureau."*
>
> (The LIMSI engineer writes programs with a computer in an office)

Interpretation is a conceptual graph with 69 joined concepts:

```
[PH:x1]-
  → (SUJET) → [GN:x5]-
  ← (CONST) ← [INGENIEUR:#]-
  ← (AGENT) ← [ECRIRE:x2]-
  → (FORM) → [VRB_T_D:x6]-
  ← (PREDICAT) ← [PH:x1]
  ← (PREDICAT) ← [GV]-
  → (COD) → [GN:x3]-
  ← (COD) ← [PH:x1]
  ← (CONST) ← [PROGRAMME:*]-
  ← (OBJET) ← [ECRIRE:x2]
  → (FORM) → [SUBSTANTIF:x4]-
  → (ATTR) → [GENRE:masculin]-
  ← (ATTR) ← [GN:x3]
  ← (ATTR) ← [DETERMINANT]-
  → (ATTR) → [ESPECE:indéfini]-
  ← (ATTR) ← [GN:x3]
  → (ATTR) → [NOMBRE:pluriel]-
  ← (ATTR) ← [GN:x3]
  ← (ATTR) ← [SUBSTANTIF:x4]
  → (NAME) → ["des"]
  → (NAME) → ["programmes"]
  → (ATTR) → [PERSONNE]
  → (ATTR) → [PERSONNE:3]-
  ← (ATTR) ← [GN:x5]
  ← (ATTR) ← [VRB_T_D:x6]
  → (ATTR) → [VOIX:active]-
  ← (ATTR) ← [VRB_T_D:x6]
```

```
 → (ATTR) → [NOMBRE:singulier]-
 ← (ATTR) ← [VRB_T_D:x6]
→ (NAME) → ["écrit"]
→ (ATTR) → [TEMPS:présent]
→ (ATTR) → [MODE:indicatif]
→ (LOC) → [BUREAU:x8]-
→ (CONST) → [GN:x7]-
 → (ATTR) → [PERSONNE]
 → (ATTR) → [ESPECE:indéfini]-
 ← (ATTR) ← [DETERMINANT:x9]-
  → (ATTR) → [GENRE:masculin]-
  ← (ATTR) ← [GN:x7]
  ← (ATTR) ← [SUBSTANTIF]-
  ← (FORM) ← [BUREAU:x8]
  → (ATTR) → [NOMBRE:singulier]-
  ← (ATTR) ← [GN:x7]
  ← (ATTR) ← [DETERMINANT:x9]
  → (NAME) → ["bureau"]
  → (NAME) → ["un"]
→ (MARK)-
 1← [ECRIRE:x2]
 0→ [PREPOSITION]-
 → (NAME) → ["dans"]
→ (INSTR) → [ORDINATEUR:x11]-
→ (CONST) → [GN:x10]-
 → (ATTR) → [PERSONNE]
 → (ATTR) → [ESPECE:indéfini]-
 ← (ATTR) ← [DETERMINANT:x12]-
  → (ATTR) → [GENRE:masculin]-
  ← (ATTR) ← [GN:x10]
  ← (ATTR) ← [SUBSTANTIF]-
  ← (FORM) ← [ORDINATEUR:x11]
  → (ATTR) → [NOMBRE:singulier]-
  ← (ATTR) ← [GN:x10]
  ← (ATTR) ← [DETERMINANT:x12]
  → (NAME) → ["ordinateur"]
  → (NAME) → ["un"]
 → (MARK)-
 1← [ECRIRE:x2]
 0→ [PREPOSITION]-
 → (NAME) → ["avec"]
→ (FORM) → [SUBSTANTIF:x13]-
→ (ATTR) → [GENRE:masculin]-
← (ATTR) ← [GN:x5]
← (ATTR) ← [DETERMINANT]-
 → (ATTR) → [ESPECE:dùfini]-
 ← (ATTR) ← [GN:x5]
 → (ATTR) → [NOMBRE:singulier]-
 ← (ATTR) ← [GN:x5]
 ← (ATTR) ← [SUBSTANTIF:x13]
 → (NAME) → ["l"]
→ (NAME) → ["ingùnieur"]
 ← (POSS) ← [LABORATOIRE:"limsi"]-
 → (CONST) → [NOM_PROPRE]-
→ (NAME) → ["limsi"]
→ (ATTR) → [PERSONNE:3]
→ (ATTR) → [GENRE:masculin]
→ (ATTR) → [NOMBRE:singulier]
```

25

Text Generation in Expert Critiquing Systems using Rhetorical Structure Theory

Jonni Harrius
Department of Computer and Information Science,
Linköping University,
S-581 83 Linköping, Sweden

ABSTRACT

One main purpose for an expert critiquing systems to generate a text, which contains a critique of a proposed solution to a given problem. In order to find sound linguistic principles for such text generation, we have selected Rhetorical Structure Theory (RST) as the basis for an implementation of a system for deep generation of text in connection with expert critiquing. We discuss the role of RST in the deep generation of text. The paper demonstrates how to combine conceptual graphs with RST for knowledge representation in text planning in an expert critiquing system. A comparison between RST and conceptual graphs shows the different roles that RST and conceptual graphs have in the text generation process. It also shows that they can complement each other during the process.

25.1 INTRODUCTION

An expert critiquing system is more oriented towards supporting the user's own decision rather than directly suggesting a recommendation as a traditional expert system does. In an expert critiquing system, one of the main activities is the generatation of a critique, information in text form, about the user's proposed solution.

To produce a text, a generation system must be able to determine which information to include from all the information available in its knowledge base, and to organize it into cohesive units. This process is called the "deep generation" of text. It has often been the case previously that deep generation has been based on *ad hoc* principles. Our approach we prefer sounder linguistic grounds. Among the possible contenders Rhetorical Structure Theory (RST) has proved to be the most promising in our research. RST is a theory for text organization which can be used both as a descriptive theory for text analysis and potentially as a constructive theory for text generation. We will compare how conceptual graphs (Sowa, 1984) and the RST approach can be combined for text generation.

To use RST for text organization, we place some demands on the stored information. We need an approach that supports the storage of related chunks of information as coherent units and information about which part supports which in the knowledge base. For this purpose we are investigating the use of conceptual graphs extended with RST relations.

We have implemented a prototype for the text organization of an expert critiquing system. In our implementation the RST unit comprises two different modules. The first module, the structure builder, creates a structure from the information in the knowledge base. The second module, the structure organizer, orders and instantiates the structure. Finally, a surface generator will be used to produce the output text.

25.1.1   Expert Critiquing Systems

An expert critiquing system (Miller, 1986) differs from a traditional expert system in a number of ways. In a traditional expert system, the role of the systems is usually consultative as opposed to an expert critiquing system where the system is more oriented towards supporting the user's own decisions, rather than directly suggesting a recommendation.

In a traditional expert system, the interaction is controlled by the system. The inference mechanism controls the dialogue between the system and the user, asks for the data needed for further reasoning, and finally presents the solution of the problem. The user has a passive role and is only providing data to the system. He has no, or little, opportunity to suggest relevant information to the system if not explicitly asked. In this situation the user may become dependent upon the reliability of the expert system in such way that it can be easy to uncritically accept the system's recommendations. This may be unwise and even dangerous (Waern et al., 1988).

The user controls the interaction in an expert critiquing system. He decides on a solution to the problem, and when this is done, the system checks the solution by reviewing the user's suggestions relative to known circumstances. It then tries to evaluate the decision, to comment upon its necessary prerequisites, its risks, costs, reasonable alternatives, its merits, etc (Rankin and Hägglund, 1988). From this evaluation, the system gives a critique of the solution. The purpose of the critique can be to warn, if a solution is dangerous, confirm, if a solution is correct, and inform, if an aspect of the solution has been forgotten. The system criticizes each of the proposed decisions. As a result, the system generates a considerable amount of text and it is clearly necessary that the text be presented as correctly/coherently as possible. For this reason why we need a text generation approach relying on linguistic grounds (Rankin, 1988).

25.1.2   Rhetorical Structure Theory (RST)

RST is a theory for text organization. It is both a descriptive theory for text analysis and potentially a constructive theory for text generation. RST is based on the idea that each text of arbitrary length has a central nucleus part, which expresses the central proposition to be communicated to the user, and zero or more satellites related to the nucleus by relations (see Fig. 25.1). The function of the satellites is to support the nucleus by providing further detail.

Schemas and Schema Applications

RST consists of a set of schemas (currently 25) described in Mann (1986), each of which indicates how a unit of text structure can be composed from smaller units. A schema is defined entirely by identifying the set of relations (currently 30) which can relate a satellite to the nucleus. In a schema diagram the nucleus is positioned below the vertical line. The goal is positioned over the vertical line and the nucleus and satellite described in the schema will be merged into this goal.

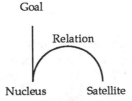

Goal

Relation

Nucleus   Satellite

Fig. 25.1

Each text unit in a text is either a nucleus or a satellite. The coherent text units in a schema instantiation will be merged into a new and larger text unit, which becomes either a nucleus or a satellite. The schemas do not constrain the order of nucleus or satellites in the text unit in which the schema is instantiated. In a schema all satellites are optional. A relation which is part of a schema may be instantiated indefinitely many times during the instantiation of the schema, reducing the corresponding text units. This instantiation process goes on recursively until there is one schema which is instantiated to describe the entire text (see Fig. 25.2).

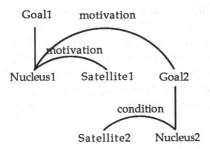

Goal1   motivation

motivation

Nucleus1   Satellite1   Goal2

condition

Satellite2   Nucleus2

Fig. 25.2

We will now give an example from Rankin (1989) that shows how RST is used recursively. For a more detailed example see Mann (1984).

1. Trimetoprim (an antibiotic) is the correct medication for this patient,

2. because she has had four urinary tract infection earlier.

3. If the patient has recently been taking Trimetoprim,

4. Selexedin should be prescribed.

The structure of the text consists of two parts, the decision (clause 1) and the justifications for the decision (clause 2 through 4).

25.2   THE AREST SYSTEM

The AREST system (Harrius, 1989) is a deep generator that uses the RST approach for text planning in an expert critiquing system that supports the treatment of urinary infections. The system uses five schemas. Each schema has a description of the included relations, a condition set describing when it is allowed to use the schema, and suggestions of connectives to put together the text units. The schemas implemented are cause, condition, elaboration, motivation and sequence.

25.2.1   The Role of the RST Model

In this implementation, the RST model is composed of two different modules. The first module, the structure builder, creates a structure from the information in the knowledge base. This structure is sent to the second module, the structure organizer. The organizer uses selected schemas to order and instantiate the structure. Finally, a surface generator is used to produce the output text.

Structure Builder

We must place some demands on the stored information in order to use RST for text organization. We need an approach that supports the storage of related chunks of information as coherent units and information about which part supports which in the knowledge base. For this purpose we are investigating the use of conceptual graphs extended with RST relations. Even if conceptual graphs extended with RST relations can represent the knowledge, there are still some open problems. We have no current approach for how to generate the knowledge base, instead we hand craft it. Does the RST structure or conceptual graphs support the retrieval of the required information from the knowledge base? This remains an open question at this preliminary stage of the research.

Structure Organizer

In this module, the order of the output text is determined. When receiving the input structure from the structure builder, the system selects a schema which matches the requirements of the text. The choice depends on the relation types of the satellites, and the number of satellites. If the selected schema does not have the number of satellites or extra elaborations needed, the schema will be expanded. The structure will then be instantiated by the schema. This process is continued recursively until the whole structure is instantiated.

Instantiation of Schemas

One main problem is how to select a schema instantiation. To solve this, it is important to first decide which relations are included and fetch the relevant schema. To get the schema with the right number of satellites, each defined schema has a default expansion behavior i.e. it can be expanded with extra satellites of the same sort. A schema of the form nucleus connective satellite can always be expanded to nucleus connective satellite satellite* and satellite. It is also possible to expand a schema with the elaboration. Rankin (1989) says, "elaboration is so common in [a critique] that each of the schema applications can be dynamically extended with an elaboration." It is possible to use the schemas recursively, i.e. the nucleus and the satellites in the schema can be merged into a nucleus or a satellite used in another schema. With this recursive behavior the text units are merged into larger and larger units until one schema is instantiated to describe the entire text.

An example which illustrates how the different steps are made from the knowledge base to the output text is shown in Fig. 25.3.

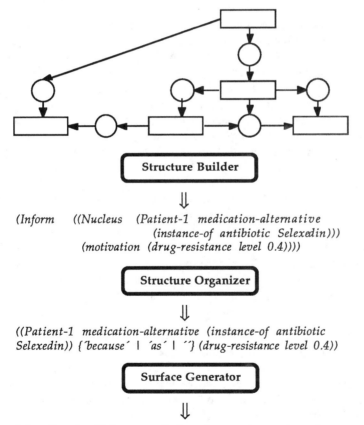

Structure Builder

⇓

(Inform   ((Nucleus   (Patient-1   medication-alternative
(instance-of antibiotic Selexedin)))
(motivation (drug-resistance level 0.4))))

Structure Organizer

⇓

((Patient-1 medication-alternative (instance-of antibiotic
Selexedin)) {'because' | 'as' | ''} (drug-resistance level 0.4))

Surface Generator

⇓

Selexedin should be prescribed as drug resistance may be suspected

Fig. 25.3

25.3   THE USE OF CONCEPTUAL GRAPHS

In this section we discuss why the natural language process of conceptual graphs is not sufficient for text generation. We will also describe how to combine conceptual graphs with RST for the knowledge representation in an expert critiquing system.

25.3.1   Conceptual Graphs and RST in Text Generation

The conceptual graph approach has a description of how to transform conceptual graphs to natural language. Sowa (1984) describes six rules for translating a conceptual graph into a sentence. These rules allow variation of the word order, i.e. a graph can be expressed with many different sentences, depending on the starting point, and the order of the traversed nodes and arcs in the graph. The rules do not permit arbitrary movement of sentence constituents. This approach, producing single sentences, is sufficient for question answering systems and other systems where the dialogue is based on short answers or paragraph-length text.

Previously the text produced by database systems and explanation systems has often been difficult to understand or oversimplified. Early efforts relied largely on technical solutions to text generation without recourse to any linguistic basis. Moreover, in order to produce multi-sentence texts, coherency between sentences also needs to be dealt with. Recent developments in text generation show that programs should express themselves like authors or speakers, rather than producing sentences strung together without any coherency. This process is not supported in the natural language part of conceptual graphs. The fields in which language generation is applicable are varied, e.g. question answering systems, systems for intelligent computer-aided instruction (ICAI) and expert systems, for more details see McKeown (1988).

Rhetorical Structure Theory (RST) is an approach for text planning. It uses discourse strategies to organize various components of the text to achieve coherency in the text. The approach is based on the observation that people generally follow standard patterns of organization when producing texts. RST is not used for the surface generation of text, i.e. lexical selection and word ordering.

If we want to use conceptual graphs to produce multi-sentence texts, we must extend it with a theory for text organization. In our work we investigate the combination of conceptual graphs and RST to generate a critique, information in text form, on the user's proposed solution in an expert critiquing system.

25.3.2   Combining Conceptual Graphs and RST

We are investigating how to combine conceptual graphs with RST when representing the knowledge in the knowledge base. We will use concepts and conceptual relations for the representation, but this is not enough. We must also know how graphs are related to other graphs. For this purpose we will use RST relations. The basic relation primitives of conceptual graphs are augmented by the relations defined in RST, e.g. in addition to rcpt, inst, obj and rate, the relations motivation, elaboration and condition are included as primitive relation types. The RST relations are defined as:

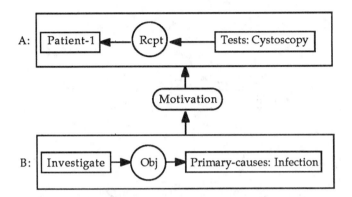

An example, describing a graph which is a motivation for another graph, is shown in Fig. 25.6.

When the knowledge is represented in this way we have to define transformation rules for the transformation from graphs to RST structures. We will use the following four rules, where the leaf can be either a graph or a transformed RST structure.

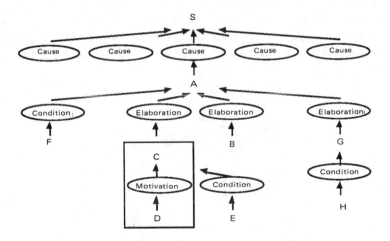

To explain the use of the transformation rules indexrule!transformation we will look at a small example.

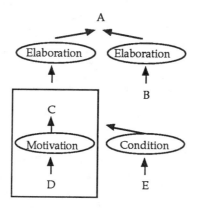

Step 1, try to transform graph A with rule Multiple satellites. This attempt fails because one child is not a leaf. Step 2, try to transform the non-leaf child. The transformation attempt of the child, [()], with the rule Nucleus recursion also fails because one child is not a leaf. Step 3, try to transform this child, graph C. This time the transformation attempt succeeds with the rule Single satellite. The result of the transformation, ((Nucleus C)(Motivation D)), forms a leaf.

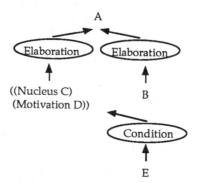

It is now time to retry step 2. This time the transformation attempt succeeds. The new transformation gives a new larger RST structure which will make the transformation of graph A successful.

Finally, retry step 1. The result of the transformation is:

```
((Nucleus A)
 (Elaboration ((Nucleus ((Nucleus C)
                          (Motivation D)))
               (Condition E)))
 (Elaboration B))
```

We have now shown the principles of how knowledge can be represented in the knowledge base. We have also given four basic transformation rules indexrule!transformation describing how to transform a conceptual graph into a RST structure. These principles are not complete and more work has to be done. One of the main problems to encounter is how to find the correct amount of knowledge to be presented to the user.

25.4 CONCLUSION

We have produced a prototype implementation, the AREST system, which shows that the RST approach has many advantages for text generation in an expert critiquing system. We have also demonstrated the general principles when using conceptual graphs in such a system, and indicated future research in the area.

BIBLIOGRAPHY

Harrius, J. (1989) "The Constructive Use of Rhetorical Structure Theory in Text Organization", Dept. of Computer and Information Science, Linköping University, LiTH-IDA-Ex-8914 MSc Thesis

Hovy, E. (1989) "Some Unsolved Problems in the Planning of Paragraphs", Proc. of the Second European Natural Language Generation Workshop, Edinburgh

Rankin, I. and Hägglund, S. (1988) "Investigating the useability of expert critiquing in knowledge-based consultation systems", ECAI.

Mann, W. (1984) "Discourse Structures for Text Generation", 10th International Conf. of Computational Linguistics

Mann, W., Sandra, and A. Thompson, A. (1986) "Discourse Structures for Text Generation", Journal of Discourse Processes, vol. 9 pages 57-90

Mann, W. (1988) "Language Generation and explanation", in *Advances in Natural Language Generation*, (eds) M. Zock and A. Sabah, Pinter

26

Generating Language from Conceptual Dependency Graphs

Afke van Rijn
Delft University of Technology,
P.O.Box 356,
2600 AJ Delft,
The Netherlands

ABSTRACT

A conceptual dependency graph is a special kind of conceptual graph and a representation of a natural language text. But it has no direct mapping to natural language, since concept nodes may contain low–level primitives. In this paper, generation of text from a conceptual dependency graph is described using a method that integrates the syntactic and semantic processing of the graph to utter. In this integration, a syntactic context free grammar is augmented with information on: firstly, the coupling between conceptual roles of concepts and syntactic roles of constituents and secondly, the way to scan the input graph in such a way that every concept node and conceptual relation is traversed at least once. The words forming an utterance are found by matching, at the lexical level of the grammar, the input conceptual dependency graph with lexical items that also contain graphs.

26.1 INTRODUCTION

An important part of many natural language processing systems is a generator with which the system can communicate with its user. Natural language generation concerns the production of sentences in a natural language. Concerning this generation an important distinction is often made between what must be said and how it must be said (McKeown, 1986). The problem to determine *what* must be said is normally handled by a text planning module. The output of this module is the representation of the text that must be uttered. The problem to determine *how* it may be said, is the linguistic part of the generation process. In this paper, we will only be dealing with this problem: how can a text be expressed that is represented by some representation, using a grammar and a lexicon.

The text that must be expressed is represented in some structured representation. There are many existing representations that may be used for generating text. The representation that will be used for the representation of a natural language text in this paper is a conceptual dependency graph.

A conceptual dependency graph is very similar to a conceptual graph. A conceptual dependency graph (CDG) as described in Rijn (1989) is different from a conceptual graph (Sowa, 1984) in two respects:

- the concept nodes in conceptual dependency graphs will often contain low-level primitives and;

- each concept node contains a label denoting the conceptual category of the concept.

These differences between the representations are based on the fact that conceptual dependency graphs will not only be used for the representation of natural language texts but also for the representation of knowledge as contained by the different modules of a flexible assembly cell. For generation, the first difference is the most important one: it implies that the word choice has still to be made when the input graph is considered. In a conceptual graph, it is also possible for a concept node to contain a low level primitive, but since this does not occur very often, the base generation method Sowa provides does not contain any possibility to handle such concept nodes. The second difference may be helpful in generating language, but is not an essential difference between conceptual dependency graphs and conceptual graphs.

This paper outlines the method that will be used for generating language from conceptual dependency graphs. A review of the theory of conceptual dependency graphs, and of some related work on generating language from conceptual graphs and networks, as constructed in conceptual dependency theory, is presented. By comparing this work with the desired results, a method for generating natural language from conceptual dependency graphs is chosen. The final section contains some concluding remarks.

26.2   CONCEPTUAL DEPENDENCY GRAPHS

Conceptual dependency graphs are very similar to conceptual graphs (Sowa, 1984), but were also based on conceptual dependency theory (Schank, 1975). The theory of conceptual dependency graphs is more general and more formal than conceptual dependency theory. Psychological concerns, as have been stated for conceptual dependency theory, were of no concern to conceptual dependency graphs. In the theory of conceptual dependency graphs a conceptual dependency graph is a high level representation independent of the concepts actually chosen. Conceptual dependency graphs are labeled, directed graphs. By using labels for both the concept nodes and the conceptual relations between those nodes, information is coded into the conceptual dependency graphs. To record what information may be contained in the labels, a concept structure is used.

In the knowledge representation, concepts are ordered in unlabeled, acyclic, directed graphs. These graphs denote the type hierarchy of the types of the concepts considered. A concept is an instantiation (subtype) of another concept, if there exists a directed path between the concepts. Concepts may have individual markers that are objects, unique in the world under consideration. Conceptual categories form a partition on the set of concepts. There is a distinct set of conceptual categories, elements of which may have an individual marker (this class of conceptual categories is called S in the remainder of the paper); this is impossible for the other conceptual categories. A conceptual category is comparable to a kind of concept type, but it is used specifically to restrict the conceptual relations that are possible between concept nodes. Thus, a restricted set of conceptual relations between conceptual categories is defined. All this is called the concept structure.

Example 1 *When TOOL is introduced as a conceptual category consisting of the concepts {normal screwdriver, Phillips screwdriver, screwdriver, hammer, fastener, gripper}, a concept ordering for this conceptual category may be:*

   {normal screwdriver, Phillips screwdriver}=screwdriver
   {screwdriver, hammer}=fastener

Thus, a normal screwdriver is an instantiation of a fastener.

The elements of the concept structure are found in the conceptual dependency graphs as labels on concept nodes, or as conceptual relations between concept nodes. Before the conceptual dependency graphs are discussed, the simple conceptual dependency graph is introduced. Simple conceptual dependency graphs are directed graphs with concept nodes that carry three labels, namely a conceptual category, a finite set of concepts belonging to this category, and an individual marker (if possible) belonging to each of these concepts, and with conceptual relations (a kind of label on arcs) that denote the relation between two or more concept nodes. Simple conceptual dependency graphs represent simple sentences.

Example 2 *To represent an assembly instruction for a specific product, the main conceptual categories are ACT, PART and TOOL. The most important ACT for assembly is 'MOUNT', representing the primitive assembly task of the robot. The conceptual categories PART and TOOL contain the different parts and tools. Tools or parts may be instantiated with an individual marker. The simple conceptual dependency graph presented below, represents the sentence "Assemble the Phillipsscrew".*

The concept nodes (in the boxes) are connected to one another with conceptual relations (in the circles). In the example, the "assemble" relation (called 'assem') and the "tool" relation (called 'tool') are used as conceptual relations. Each of the concept nodes has a label, consisting of three elements, of the form $f_1 : f_2 : f_3$, in which:

1. f_1 represents the conceptual category to which the node belongs;
2. f_2 represents a finite set of concepts;
3. f_3 represents the individual marker; it has the value "impossible" if the conceptual category given by f_1 does not allow individual markers.

In the remainder of the paper, we will use f_1, f_2 and f_3 to refer to the corresponding label elements.

Two simple conceptual dependency graphs, or a simple conceptual dependency graph and a concept node, may be related to form a conceptual dependency graph. Two conceptual dependency graphs, or a conceptual dependency graph and a concept node, may again be related to form a more complex conceptual dependency graph. Conceptual dependency graphs are labeled similarly to simple conceptual dependency graphs.

Example 3 *An example of a conceptual dependency graph representing the sentence "Assemble the egg cautiously" is*

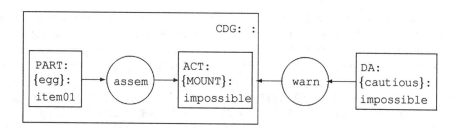

The complex node has a label, consisting of three elements similar to concept nodes of simple conceptual dependency graphs, but in this example only the first element has a value: the dummy value "CDG". DA is used as a new conceptual category, denoting a default argument.

A complex conceptual dependency graph is similar to Sowa's context, except that a complex conceptual dependency graph can get the same labels (including the individual marker) as a concept node. In this way, the possibility is created to introduce new concepts in the world by labelling conceptual dependency graphs.

To be able to distinguish between conceptual dependency graphs that may have a meaning in the world and those that have not, a subclass of conceptual dependency graphs is introduced, called: the well–formed conceptual dependency graphs. Well–formed conceptual dependency graphs are those that may be derived from the lexicon. For this purpose, besides the transformation of the word into a concept, each lexicon entry of a word contains a set of selectional constraints of the concept. These selectional constraints are specified as a (simple) conceptual dependency graph, which is a canonical graph representing the default way concepts and relations are linked together in well–formed sentences. Well–formed conceptual dependency graphs are obtained by the unification of the canonical graphs contained in lexicon entries. When the selectional constraints specified in the canonical graphs of the lexicon are well enough, it is hoped that each well–formed conceptual dependency graph is also a canonical graph.

26.3 COMPARISON WITH RELATED WORK

Conceptual dependency graphs are graphs that represent language. To generate a sentence from a conceptual dependency graph, the words forming an utterance and the syntactic relations between those words must be found.

The concept nodes of conceptual dependency graphs may contain low-level primitives. This implies that the words to form an utterance have still to be found. Since the lexicon contains for each word its mapping into some kind of conceptual graph, the input graph has to be compared with the lexical items to be able to find the words that have to be uttered. A similar problem was tackled by Goldman (1975) in his generator BABEL, and Hovy (1988) in his generator PAULINE. Both were meant for conceptual dependency theory. Goldman uses discrimination networks to make the word-choices. A discrimination network is a directed graph, in which the nodes with out–degree zero (0) represent the words, and the traversal through the graph to find the right word depends on the defining characteristics of the concept that has to be uttered. The result of the analysis of the graph using a discrimination network is a syntax network. The syntax network consists of a set of nodes containing the words to form an utterance, and a set of relations representing the syntactic relations between the words. This syntax network serves as the input for an augmented transition network to generate the sentence. Like Goldman, Hovy uses discrimination networks to determine what word to use in what context. To formulate the sentence, he does not use a grammar but what he calls "syntax specialists". The lexicon contains the information on the syntax specialist that has to be used for the generation of a certain constituent. The disadvantage of using discrimination networks is that it may require a lot of work to add a new word to the lexicon, especially when introducing additional defining characteristics. Adding defining characteristics could cause the restructuring of the whole network. For this reason discrimination networks are not used to find the word to utter when a conceptual dependency graph is analyzed, but the word is found by comparing the graph with graphs that represent words. To this end, each lexical item contains a canonical graph as a representation of the word expressed by that lexical item and its required context. The canonical graphs of the lexicon are compared with the conceptual dependency graph and, if they match, those words may be used in the text to utter. In this way, extension of the lexicon will be much less time consuming than when discrimination networks are used, since extension will only require the addition to the lexicon of a new graph representing a word.

When the graphs are processed to generate language the syntax and semantics may be separated or integrated. Velardi *et al.* (1988) separate, both for the analysis and synthesis of language, the semantic, syntactic and morphologic processing of language into conceptual graphs, and conceptual graphs into language respectively, although there is some inter-leaving between the syntactic and semantic processing. They claim that the advantage of such an approach is that it produces a cleaner and more systematic representation scheme which, they say, simplifies the analysis and synthesis algorithms. On the other hand, Sowa (1983) handles the syntactic and semantic processing of conceptual graphs into language interactively. He scans the graph and maps the concepts into words, using the kind of augmented phrase structure grammar (APSG) rules developed by Heidorn (1975). An APSG rule, as used by Heidorn, consists of an augmented context free grammar rule. The augmentation of the grammar rule consists of the addition of a list of conditions to the symbol on the left hand side of the rule (these conditions have to be true for the rule to be invoked), and of the addition of a list of actions to the non-terminals on the right hand side of the rule. There are two kinds of APSG rules, i.e. decoding rules that generate a representation of the meaning of the text when that text is parsed, and encoding rules that generate a text from a representation. In this paper, only encoding rules are considered.

When a context free grammar rule of the form "$X \longrightarrow YZw$" (with X, Y, Z non–terminal symbols and w a terminal symbol) is considered, the corresponding encoding rule in APSG is:

> X (conditions for applying this rule) $\longrightarrow$
> Y (structure building actions to be performed for this non-terminal)
> Z (structure building actions to be performed for this non-terminal)
> w

The right hand side of the rule specifies what segments the segment on the left hand side is expanded into. The list of conditions or actions may be empty. The data structure on which APSG encoding rules are applied, is a kind of semantic network consisting of records and relations between those records. The non-terminals on the right hand side of the rules represent records that may be tested or set. The APSG rules are similar to augmented transition networks.

Since the APSG rules, as Heidorn uses them, are meant for a representation different from conceptual graphs, Sowa adds specific actions and conditions to the APSG rules, meant to handle conceptual graphs. The conditions are of the general form: attribute "is" ["not"] test. The actions he uses are:

1. assignment actions, which assign a value to an attribute of a record (structure building actions);

2. move actions, which specify the direction of the movement through the conceptual graph;

3. mark actions, which indicate nodes or relations that have been visited.

In this way the semantic processing (using the conditions and actions) and the syntactic processing (using the context free grammar) of the graph into a sentence are coupled. Sowa gives a set of APSG rules for the generation of sentences from conceptual graphs. This idea of integrating syntax and semantics is very appealing. However, Sowa's set of rules cannot be directly used for conceptual dependency graphs since he assumes that concept nodes contain the words to utter, which cannot be assumed for conceptual dependency graphs. The net effect is that the APSG rules will not only be used for generating language from conceptual dependency graphs, but the actions and conditions of these rules will be changed to make the rules applicable to concept nodes containing low level primitives. The most important change that will be made is that structure building actions are to be included with terminal nodes as well; terminal nodes require graph match actions. Besides this, specific actions are required to handle the labels of the concept nodes and the conceptual relations of the conceptual dependency graph. The other actions required are the actions used by Sowa to handle conceptual graphs; these are the assignment action, the mark action and the move action.

In his article, Sowa also formulates six general rules for translating a conceptual graph into a sentence. These rules entail the way to traverse the graph. To formulate these rules, Sowa uses the notion of an utterance path. An utterance path contains the sequence of concept nodes and conceptual relations that are traversed in mapping a graph into a sentence. Since Sowa assumes in his article that the concept nodes of conceptual graphs contain the words to utter, the use of an utterance path is possible. But since concept nodes of conceptual dependency graphs may contain low–level primitives, an utterance path does not seem possible: the direct utterance of a concept when its node is traversed, might not always be the right action. For example, it might be required to use more than one node to utter one appropriate word. This implies that the use of an utterance path is not possible for conceptual dependency graphs. But some kind of path has to be chosen in such a way that every concept node and conceptual relation is traversed at least once. The utterance of a concept (or a set of concepts) or a relation with a word may be quite trivial, but it may require a match with other nodes or relations as well; it may even happen that a node is not uttered at all. For this reason, the rules Sowa uses are not directly applicable to conceptual dependency graphs, but a comparable set of rules appropriate for conceptual dependency graphs has to be constructed. This set of rules will be formulated in the next section.

26.4   METHOD FOR GENERATION

In generating language, three processes can be distinguished:

1. match lexical items with the input conceptual dependency graph to find the words to form an utterance;

2. traverse the graph in such a way that all the concept nodes and conceptual relations of the graph are visited and the corresponding words are uttered, and such that all the syntactic relations between the words are determined;

3. use a grammar to generate a sentence with the words and syntactic relations found.

The grammar used for generating the sentence, is the main process, the other two are incorporated into this process. Each of these processes will be described in sequence.

26.4.1   Matching Lexical Items with Input Graphs

A lexicon in a natural language processing system is minimally a list of words with some syntactic information. When a lexicon is used for conceptual (dependency) graphs, it also has to contain canonical conceptual (dependency) graphs that depict the default ways concepts and relations between concepts are linked together. In a lexicon for generation these canonical graphs are the entries of the lexical items, together with the required syntactic category. The output is a set of words (or expressions) one of which may be generated.

Domain specific information will be required to supplement the lexicon. This domain specific information consists of two important parts, first data on the individual markers (for example what individual markers correspond to what concept) and second information on the new concepts that were introduced to the world in the form of labels of complex conceptual dependency graphs. When a concept is introduced into the domain (during some parsing process), the name of the concept must be added to the lexicon, but information what the concept consists of is not information that ought to belong to the lexicon by nature. Both the data on the individual markers and the data on complex concepts should be kept separately from the lexicon. These domain specific data will not be considered further in this paper.

To find the necessary words to form an utterance, the canonical conceptual dependency graphs contained in the lexicon, are matched with the input conceptual dependency graph. The way the syntactic relations are determined and the order in which the lexical items are matched, is not discussed in this section. What is considered in this section is: what information is contained in lexical items for generation, in what way is an entry matched with the input graph, and is there some practical way to order the lexicon to be able to find the right word as quickly as possible.

A lexical item consists of a set of synonymous words (each of the same syntactic category), the syntactic category of each element of the set of words, and one canonical graph that represents each element of the set of words. As an entry to the lexicon, the canonical graph to match and the syntactic features of the appropriate word are used. The word to utter or a set of synonymous words one of which may be uttered, is the result of the match. In the remainder of the paper the set of words contained in the lexical item will be used as if it were one word. This is of no consequence to the generation process, since the words have to be synonyms when they are representable by an equivalent canonical graph. One of the words will be taken at random when the concept represented has to be expressed.

When the canonical graphs of the lexicon are matched with the input conceptual dependency graph, each node and relation of the input graph has to be matched at least once. To make sure that this is the case, concept nodes and conceptual relations will be marked when they have completely been dealt with. Only when all the nodes and relations of the graph are marked the generation phase may finish. But, when a concept node or conceptual relation is marked, this does not mean that it cannot be visited afterwards. To be able to specify this the graph will be augmented with marking labels on both conceptual relations and concept nodes. Both the graph of the lexical item and the graph to utter will be augmented conceptual dependency graphs.

Example 4 *An example of a graph contained in a lexical item, representing the verb "to eat" is:*

In this example the word "eat" is represented by the INGEST action of some edible object. The concept nodes representing the INGEST action and the "edible object", as well as the conceptual relation connecting these concept nodes, represent all together the word "eat". To indicate this, the marking label of these nodes and relations have the value "true". At what moment the marking labels of the corresponding elements of the input graph will also be set to true, will be discussed later in the paper.

To find the words to utter, the lexical items are matched with the input graphs. A lexical item matches with the input graph, if the graph is a specification of the canonical graph (also called the required context) contained in the lexical item. To be able to find every word that has to be uttered, the corresponding lexical items have to be found. A match function can be defined, which has a CDG, the required syntactic category and the node or relation to match as input, and a changed CDG and a matching lexical item as output. Such a match function will seem rather complex, but often the actual match is quite simple. Some common "simplifications" will be described here (in which S denotes those conceptual categories that may have an individual marker):

1. If the concept node of the input graph satisfies the constraints $f_1 \in S$ and f_3 is not unknown, then the match between the input graph and a graph from the lexicon is often a simple match, since there is a word corresponding directly to the concept (f_2); this word must always be uttered and the node is marked as being uttered;

2. If the concept node of the input graph satisfies the constraint $f_1 \in S$ but f_3 is unknown, then there exists a word corresponding with the concept; but the context has to be considered before the word corresponding to the concept (f_2) is uttered, since the concept node might be part of a conceptual dependency graph of the lexicon, consisting of more than one node corresponding to some word. This will be done in such a way that if the concept node is not marked as being uttered by any other utterance, then it will be uttered. This again is a simple match.

If the concept node of the input graph satisfies the constraint $f_1 \notin S$ then usually the match is not a simple one: a lexical item has to be found in such a way that it suits the context of that concept best. This match may give rise to the marking of more than one node or relation. A conceptual relation of the input graph will be marked "automatically", when the conceptual relation is transformed into a syntactical relation or when the conceptual relation is contained in the required context of some concept node. If a conceptual relation of the input graph is not automatically marked, the relation must be uttered with a word. This requires that a match between the input graph and a graph of the lexicon has to be found to find the word to utter depending on the context. This again is not a simple match, since it requires the matching of a graph consisting of more than one node. In these it can be seen where the f_1 label of a node comes in handy.

By supplementing each concept node and conceptual relation with a label in both the lexical item and the input graph, it can be denoted whether the concept node or conceptual relation has completely been dealt with or not. In the canonical graph of the lexical item the concept nodes or conceptual relations are indicated that are to be marked in the input graph as being dealt with. This information remains unchanged. When a lexical item is found to match with the input graph, the corresponding concept nodes and conceptual relations of the input graph have to be marked, denoting whether the node or relation has or has not completely been dealt with. But only when the node of the lexical item matches exactly with the node of the input graph, then the node in the input CDG should be labeled as being dealt with. When the nodes do not match exactly, also the relation from which the node was reached may not be marked as being visited. All this should be incorporated in the match function. Consider for example a word like 'to fasten' which will be represented in the lexicon by a graph consisting of two linked nodes; one node being the act 'MOUNT' and the second node being a tool 'FASTENER'. When the input graph contains exactly those two nodes, the word to utter is the verb 'to fasten' and both nodes may be marked (as well as the relation between the nodes). This may be indicated in the lexicon. On the other hand, when the input graph contains the nodes, but in the node containing the tool a specific fastener is named, the verb 'fasten' may still be used, but the node containing the tool must also be uttered by the specific kind of fastener and thus may not be marked before the appropriate word has been uttered.

Example 5 *To illustrate the working of the match function, some simple examples will be given. First we take as the input graph to generate, the following graph which is a representation of a sentence like "Peter eats an apple":*

When we match this graph with the graph of example 4 representing the verb "eat", we should obtain as a result of the match the following graph:

In this output graph of the match function, we see that the marking label of the concept node representing the INGEST action has indeed the value "true", but that the marking label of the concept node representing the "apple" (which is an edible object), does not have the value "true". This is caused by the fact that the concept node of the lexicon does not have exactly the same $(f_1, f_2, f_3\text{-})$labels as the corresponding concept node in the input graph. Second, we consider as an input graph the graph representing a sentence like "Peter eats":

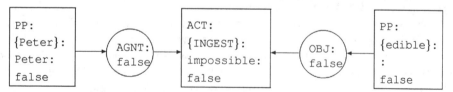

When we match the lexicon graph of example 4 with this graph, we should obtain as a result of the match function the graph:

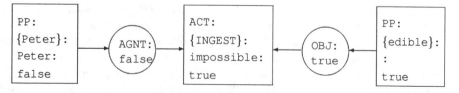

In this output graph, the concept node representing the INGEST action and the concept

node representing the "edible object", as well as the conceptual relation connecting these two nodes all obtain the value true as the new value of their marking labels. This is caused by the fact that the corresponding concept nodes and conceptual relation of the lexicon graph have exactly the same value of the concept labels and conceptual relation respectively and that they have a marking label with the value "true".

To find the right word to utter several graphs of the lexicon might fit on the input graph. This is often caused by the fact that when some specific concept fits, every more general concept fits as well. This is not really a problem, it is just something that must be considered when generating sentences. If possible, the lexicon should be ordered thus that the best fit is found as soon as possible. To this effect the lexicon is ordered in such a way that a lexical item containing a graph representing some specific word comes before a lexical item containing a graph representing a less specific word. Besides this, the lexicon is ordered according to the syntactic category of the word. These two order restrictions are caused by the fact that lexical items are matched according to their order in the lexicon and according to their syntactic category. Thus, the generation lexicon has to be an ordered lexicon.

As is implied, in this approach only the most specific lexical item is looked for. A more sophisticated approach to matching graphs of lexical items with the graph to generate, is followed in Nogier and Zock (1990). They use a correlation factor as a measure of correspondence between the lexical graphs and the graph to generate. The more concepts can be expressed with a word, the conciser the word is. Depending on the kind of user the text is to be communicated to (ranging from a novice to an expert), a certain lexical item is chosen. When it is an expert the most specific (concise) item is chosen, when it is a novice a less specific lexicon item is chosen. At this moment we have chosen a simpler approach. When we communicate with experts this approach is expected to work satisfactorily. When this is not the case, i.e. when non–experts are also expected to use the system, paraphrasing the sentence with less specific concepts, or words, might be useful.

Another important problem is that it may be possible that two or more distinct sets of lexical items fit on the same input CDG. This case is more problematic than the first one. The (rather operational) strategy that will be followed to "solve" this problem is that when a lexical item is found to fit on the input graph, the nodes of the input graph that have completely been dealt with using the lexical item, will not be considered further to find other lexical items that fit. Only when the generation process cannot finish due to the fact that no set of lexical items that fit can be found, the determined set of items will be considered again, and it will be checked if there is another set of (fitting) lexical items possible.

26.4.2 Traversing the Input Graph

To generate a sentence from the input conceptual dependency graph requires that words and syntactic relations have to be found in such a way that they exactly express the meaning of the graph. A minimal requirement to assure this, is that every concept node and conceptual relation of the graph is visited and marked as being dealt with. When this is the case, and when the graph is obtained exactly by unifying the words found, we say that the input graph has completely been dealt with. The main goal of traversing the graph is to deal completely with the graph. When the graph has completely been dealt with, every marking label should have the value 'true'. But traversing the graph does not necessarily mean that the sentence expresses the meaning of the graph, this is also dependent on the derivation of the right words and relations. In this section some general rules and principles are presented, used in the grammar rules indexgrammar!rules to steer the process of traversing the input graph. These rules and principles are meant to make a more explicit goal of finding the words and syntactic relations in such a way that they deal completely with the graph.

The main goal of the process of finding a path through the graph, can be formulated in the form of a rule:

Rule 1 *Every word to utter when generating a sentence from an input graph is found when a path through the input graph is obtained such that the input graph has completely been dealt with. The set of words that has to be uttered, consists of the words that correspond to the lexical items found in the path.*

It seems rather complex to determine if the input graph has completely been dealt with, but in practice it is expected that when the lexical items are matched correctly with the graph using the principles and rules that are formulated below, the path and lexical items found are such that they completely deal with the graph. Other problems are e.g.: when do lexical items exactly fit on a graph, and, when different sets of lexical items fit on a graph, how do you decide which set is best. But these problems are problems at the lexical level.

Lexical items are matched according to a path that is chosen through the input graph. Finding a path is steered by the syntactic processing module and is formulated here in the form of a rule supplemented by a set of principles, some of which are formulated in this paper. Besides this, also the question when concept nodes and conceptual relations in the form of the corresponding words may be uttered, will give rise to some rules.

As mentioned before, when the input graph is matched against lexical items, every concept node and every conceptual relation has to be visited at least once. To indicate that a node or relation has been dealt with, this node or relation will be marked. By combining the information from the lexical item with some matching rules, it is determined if a concept node or conceptual relation has completely been dealt with. This gives rise to the second rule of traversing the graph, which is a kind of specialization of the first rule.

Rule 2 *The path through the input graph has to visit every concept node and every conceptual relation at least once, such that every marking label is set to 'true'.*

This rule can be supplemented by several "principles" concerning the topic of how the path has to be chosen. These principles will describe the kind of algorithm that may be constructed to find a path through the graph. Some of such principles are:

Principle 1 *In matching lexical items with a simple input graph, the node with ACT as a conceptual category is always started with, since the ACT (with its context) determines which verb to utter and the verb gives the structure to the sentence. From this the concept and conceptual relation representing the subject of the sentence will be handled first.*

Principle 2 *From a concept c the path through the graph does not return to the concept from which c was reached until all relations linked to c have been dealt with (marked).*

Principle 3 *For the relations that have not yet been traversed, syntactic rules determine which relation is to follow.*

By the last principle the syntactic and semantic processing are coupled. The second principle will be used to couple for example prepositional phrases to a certain concept at the right place. To handle more complex input graphs, requires additional rules to find the right path. For example, a verb like 'to buy' gives rise to a graph consisting of two graphs with a causal relation, one representing the fact that person x gives the object bought to person y and the second, that person y, gives money to person x. The verb to utter cannot be found by just observing one ACT–node, but the whole graph has to be considered! On the other hand, a main clause with one or more subordinate clauses requires the graph representing the whole sentence to be split into several interrelated smaller graphs, processed in a certain order. A graph linked to a concept normally gives rise to a subordinate clause being a specification of the concept. A concept linked to a graph gives rise to some kind of modification of the sentence represented by that graph. More of such principles may be required, to be able to handle every graph that occurs. Thus, in matching more complex graphs, a similar process will be executed; relations between graphs, when they do not originate from the verb, give rise to subordinate clauses. When such graphs are considered, additional (inference) principles are required, which split an input graph into more than one graph.

Although the search for a path does not really involve the utterance of words, some rules will be formulated here that concern the moment when words are actually to be uttered. The first of these rules concerns the utterance of the word that satisfies the concept that has to be uttered. A word need not always be uttered when the path traverses the node containing the concept. First of all, the word may only be uttered at the moment the node is marked, when the semantic content of the node is not yet expressed by a word of another node in combination with this node. Secondly, syntactic rules may postpone the utterance of the word when this is required; for example, when constituents are moved. The second part of the first condition, being that the semantic content of the node might not yet have been expressed by a word of another node, is caused by the fact that nodes do not always contain the concept to utter, but sometimes low–level primitives. For example, the verb 'to hammer' is represented by two nodes, being the low–level primitive act 'mount' and the tool with which the mount action is performed, being a hammer. But when this graph is generated with a sentence, you want the verb 'hammer' to be uttered instead of a clause like 'mount with a hammer' or 'hammer with a hammer'. Thus, the possibility has to be created to utter more than one concept node together with the conceptual relations connecting the nodes with just one word.

Rule 3 *A word may only be uttered at the moment the concept node or conceptual relation it represents, is marked and when the syntactic rules allow the word to be uttered.*

Another rule concerns the use of anaphoric expressions. An anaphoric expression can be required by the occurrence of cyclic paths through the input graph. Cycles are paths that return to a concept node that is already marked. When a cycle occurs and a node, uttered (and marked!), is visited for a second time, it may need an anaphoric reference expression. When this happens, the relations connected to that node, do not have to be dealt with again, since they have been dealt with in the first visit of the node. But another reason for an anaphoric expression might be the occurrence of two similar nodes. If the individual markers of two different concept nodes are similar, this may require an anaphoric expression when both nodes have to be expressed by a word. To this effect, a list of the individual markers that are expressed by a word in the generated sentence, has to be kept up to date. This list is used to decide whether an anaphoric expression is required.

Rule 4 *When a graph contains cycles because a concept is reachable by two different paths through the graph, in such a way that a concept node, already marked and uttered, has to be uttered again or, when two or more concept nodes occur having the same individual markers, have all to be uttered, this gives rise to an anaphoric expression. In the case of a cycle the (already marked) conceptual relations connected to the node will not be visited again.*

Another rule is required to ascertain that no node is uttered more than once with the appropriate word.

Rule 5 *Once a concept node is marked and an appropriate word is uttered, it may not be uttered again when no cycles occur.*

Both the set of rules concerning the path and the rules concerning the utterance of words will be used in the grammar rules. They will not be mentioned explicitly in the grammar rules, but they are implicitly present.

26.4.3   Generating a Sentence

The generator uses a definite clause grammar (DCG, see Pereira and Warren (1980) to generate the sentence according to the words and relations found in the matching phase. Every rule, expressible with an APSG rule, can be expressed by a DCG rule as well. The context free grammar of DCG is augmented with conditions on the left hand side of the rule, and Prolog–goals may be included on the right hand side of the rule, which is similar to the inclusion of actions to the rule. Normally, these actions are indicated in DCG rules between braces, but, to stick to the notation as used in APSG rules, actions will be indicated between parentheses in this paper. The definite clause grammar will also be augmented with attributes to assure agreement between syntactic categories, like number–agreement between verb and subject. These attributes will not be discussed in the remainder of this paper.

The DCG consists of a set of grammar rules as required for the language and the application being described. An example of a grammar is:

$$
\begin{array}{l}
S \longrightarrow NP\ VP \\
NP \longrightarrow Det\ N \\
NP \longrightarrow Det\ N\ PP \\
VP \longrightarrow V \\
VP \longrightarrow V\ NP \\
VP \longrightarrow V\ NP\ PP \\
PP \longrightarrow P\ NP
\end{array}
$$

For illustrative purposes some of these grammar rules will be worked out. To integrate the syntactic and semantic processing, the grammar rules have to be augmented with attributes for both graph matching and traversing the graph.

Before the generation phase is started with, the input CDG has to be derived from the CDG that has to be generated. This is done by augmenting every concept node and conceptual relation of the CDG with a marking label and by giving each marking label the value 'false', which indicates that the corresponding node or relation has not been dealt with. As mentioned before, the generation is finished when a set of lexical items has been found that deal completely with the input CDG, in such a way that each marking label has the value 'true'. The correct marking of the graph, such that at the end of the generation process every marking label is set to "true", depends mainly on the correctness of the marking labels as indicated in the required context of lexical items and also on a correct working of the match function.

Before the real generation process starts, the derived input graph may first be split up into some less complex graphs. This is meant for handling graphs that are not expressible by one sentence. General rules denoting how to split a graph into smaller graphs, will not be looked at in this paper. When the input CDG to be uttered has been determined, the generation process starts with finding the verb of the main clause before applying any grammar rule. This is done to handle verbs that are represented by a complex graph, like the representation of a verb as 'to buy'. Depending on the main verb of the main clause, a certain grammar rule will be applied. This method is comparable with the method followed in the generalized phrase structure grammar (GPSG, see Gazdar (1985)).

To process conceptual dependency graphs into language, several actions are needed. The most important action that will be performed at the lexical level of the grammar is the match action that determines the right words to be uttered in the sentence. This action is required, since the nodes of conceptual dependency graphs may contain low-level primitives instead of the concepts to be uttered. Secondly, there are some actions in the grammar rules that comprise the way to traverse the graph. Since there is a distinct set of conceptual relations that are allowed between the concept nodes of the conceptual dependency graphs for a certain application, these relations can be connected to certain syntactic roles of the corresponding constituents in the sentence. To this effect, grammar rules will function according to the conceptual relations that connect the concept nodes with one another. To control this, two kinds of actions are used:

1. a move has to be made to a node: this can be done by following the direction of the relation or by going into the opposite direction; this is done by performing the actions 'move by x to node' or 'move by x from node', respectively; in these actions the clause 'by x' means that the relation with label x has to be used;

2. a node or a relation has to be marked as being visited: this is done by performing the actions 'mark node' or 'mark arc', respectively (by this action the marking labels will be set to true).

The actions 'get f_2 of node' or 'get f_3 of node' will be used as well. As a condition, attributes may be tested by conditions of the general form: attribute "is" ["not"] test.

These actions and conditions are used in formulating grammar rules. There has to be at least one syntactic rule for each conceptual relation; by the move actions the syntactic and conceptual relations are coupled (see path principles). As an example, the sentence–rule "S ⟶ NP VP" will be worked out:

> S(active) ⟶
>> NP(move by AGENT to node, cdg1, cdg2, mark AGENT, number=X),
>> VP(move by AGENT from node, cdg2, cdg3, voice=active, number=X).

As can be shown, this is not a DCG-rule, but it may be transformed into one. In this rule 'cdg1' is the input CDG of the NP clause and 'cdg2' is the output CDG (new markings!);

in the VP rule 'cdg2' is the input CDG and 'cdg3' the output CDG. In the next rules 'cdgi' will always denote the input CDG and 'cdgo' the output CDG. Or another rule the PP-rule: PP $\longrightarrow$ P NP, can be worked out as follows:

> PP $\longrightarrow$
>> P(get type of arc),
>> NP(move by type of arc to node, cdgi, cdgo, mark arc, Number)

As is shown, there is no condition on the left hand side of the rule. In this way, the rule can be applied whenever any prepositional phrase needs to be generated. This has to be possible, since prepositional phrases can occur anywhere in the sentence.

As a last part of the grammar rules: the words to utter have to be found, which means that the appropriate lexical item has to be found. By applying the grammar rules, the node (and thus also its f_1-label) to match and the syntactic category of the word to utter, is known. The match is done by an action included with the grammar rule. As an example, consider the NP-rule NP $\longrightarrow$ Det N. This rule will be augmented as follows:

> NP($(f_1, f_2$ is not proper name, $f_3)$, cdgi, cdgo, -, number=X) $\longrightarrow$
>> Det(get f_3 of node, number=X),
>> Noun((f_1, f_2,f_3), cdgi, cdgo, word, number=X)

As is shown in the condition part of the rule, this rule only applies when the current node does not represent a proper name. When this rule is applied, the lexical rules take care of the final handling of the lexicon match. Since it requires a simple match when the node represents a noun ($f_1 \in S$), the lexicon/graph match is simple in this case:

> Noun($(f_1, f_2, f_3$ is not unknown), cdgi, cdgo, word, number=sing) $\longrightarrow$
>> match(noun, (f_1, f_2,f_3), cdgi, cdgo, word)

The words to utter will mostly be found by a match, but in the case of a word like a determiner, this is different. A determiner is not a concept. For this reason, it will not be found by the match of a node on its own, but by checking the f_3-label of the input graph. If the f_3-label is unknown, no specific concept is determined and thus the determiner 'a' has to be used (if the noun is singular, otherwise the determiner will be empty); if the f_3-label is not unknown, the determiner 'the' may be used:

> Det(f_3 is unknown, number=sing) $\longrightarrow$ 'a'
> Det(f_3 is not unknown, number=X) $\longrightarrow$ 'the'
> Det(f_3 is unknown, number=pl) $\longrightarrow$

More complex matches are necessary when, for example, verbs are considered. To handle verbs, the extensions of Côté and Moulin (1990) might be useful as well.

The output of the grammar is the string of words to form an utterance. This string should be processed by a post processor to beautify the sentence. For example, a correct anaphoric expression or topicalization should be introduced by the post processor, but also the conjugation of words like verbs could be done by the post processor.

An important remaining question is whether this process can be made complete, i.e. if each graph can be handled once a grammar has been given for the application considered. Of course, this depends mainly on the grammar. Some criteria will be given here that enable one to check whether the process is complete given a grammar, a lexicon and a concept structure for a certain application. Whether the process is also correct, given a grammar, a lexicon and a concept structure for a certain application, can only be checked by giving the result of the generation process to a (native) speaker of the language generated. No criteria can be given to determine automatically whether all sentences generated are also correct sentences. But the aim of constructing a suitable generator, is to construct a generator that only generates acceptable sentences. This must be accomplished by constructing a correct grammar and a correct lexicon.

26.5 CONCLUSION

In this paper, generating language from conceptual dependency graphs is discussed. Not much attention is paid to the generation of sentences from complex conceptual dependency graphs. This will require a more advanced set of rules. As is said in Sowa (1983), this will probably need inference rules to split each graph up in more than one graph, which will give rise to the generation of more than one sentence. Also the topic of performing complex matches of lexical graphs and the graph to utter, must be considered further. It is discussed and defined here, but how it is done combining syntax and semantics, must be discussed further.

Another topic that is only mentioned but not discussed here, is the topic of what would be the best approach to lexical matches. We just take the first lexical item that fits on the graph to utter. But this might not always be the best approach. As was mentioned an approach as described in Nogier and Zock (1990), is much more sophisticated. What would be the best approach might differ from application to application. When a user friendly generator is constructed, it requires some attention. This is also required for different sets of lexicon entries that fit on the graph to utter. We just accept the first set that is found, instead of determining all sets that fit. It might be wise to look into this topic further.

A problem that remains, is the question whether cyclic graphs will actually occur or not. This is a topic that needs some attention: for example for graphs expressing some transitive relation it seems the best representation.

As can be seen, generating language from conceptual dependency graphs is a topic that still needs a lot of research. In this paper a set up was given. For the actual realisation of a generator that is extensively used, some more attention should be given to the problems mentioned above.

A small prototype of a generator of language from conceptual dependency graphs has been constructed. This prototype is implemented in Quintus Prolog on a SUN workstation. This generator uses a simplified version of the integration of the syntactic and semantic processing of a graph into a sentence, by using a kind of syntax network as output of the semantic processing and as input for the syntactic processing. The generator only produces simple sentences with one main verb and possibly one subordinate clause. The lexicon it uses is very small. It will be extended in the future.

BIBLIOGRAPHY

Côté, D. and Moulin, B. (1990) "Refining Sowa's conceptual graph theory for text generation", Proc. of Third Annual Conference on the Industrial and Engineering Applications of Artificial Intelligence and Expert Systems, vol. 1, pp. 528-537; ACM Press.

Gazdar, G., Klein, E., Pullum, G. and Sag, I. (1985) *Generalized Phrase structure grammar*, Basil Blackwell Publishers Ltd.

Goldman, N.M. (1975) "Conceptual Generation", in: (ed) R.C. Schank, *Conceptual Information Processing*, North-Holland.

Heidorn, G.E. (1975) "Augmented phrase structure grammar, in (eds) R.C. Schank and B.L. Nash-Webber; *Theoretical issues in natural language processing*, pp. 1-5.

Hovy, E.H. (1988) "Generating language with a phrasal lexicon", in (eds) D. McDonald, L. Bolc; *Natural language generation systems*, Springer Verlag.

McKeown, K.R. (1986) "Language generation: applications, issues and approaches", Proc. of the IEEE, vol. 74, no. 7, pp. 961-968.

Nogier, J.-F. and Zock, M. (1990) "Lexical choice as a process of matching word definitions on an utterance graph", Proc. of the Fifth Annual Workshop on Conceptual Structures, (eds) P. Eklund and L. Gerholz, pp. 205-220.

Pereira, F.C.N. and Warren, D.H.D. (1980) "Definite clause grammars for language analysis – A survey of the formalism and a comparison with augmented transition networks", AI, vol. 13, pp. 231-278.

Rijn, A. van (1989) "Conceptual dependency graphs", Proc. of the Fourth Annual Workshop on Conceptual Structures; (eds) by J. Nagle and T. Nagle, Available from AAAI.

Rijn, A. van (1989b) "Conceptual dependency theory and robot programming", T.U. Delft, Faculty of Techn. Mathematics and Informatics, no. 89-20.

Schank, R.C. (ed.) (1975) *Conceptual Information Processing*, North-Holland.

Sowa, J.F. (1983) "Generating language from conceptual graphs". Computers & Mathematics with Applications, Vol. 9, No. 1, pp. 29-43, 1983.

Sowa, J.F. (1984) *Conceptual Structures: Information Processing in Mind and Machine*, Addison Wesley, Reading.

Velardi, P., Pazienza, M.T. and De'Giovanetti, M. (1988) "Conceptual graphs for the analysis and generation of sentences", IBM Journal of Research and Development, vol. 32, no. 2, pp. 251-267.

27

The Dynamic Type Hierarchy Theory of Metaphor

Eileen C. Way
Department of Philosophy
State University of New York at Binghamton, USA

27.1 INTRODUCTION

The dynamic type hierarchy theory (DTH) involves a theory of metaphor that incorporates Sowa's conceptual graphs, a version of Max Black's interaction theory of metaphor, and semantic type hierarchies. Black maintains that metaphor is an *interaction* between two different "systems of commonplaces" or domains, where the subject of the metaphor (called the tenor) is seen through the "filter" of the properties of the modifier (called the vehicle).[1] An example might be "Sally is a doormat", where Sally is the subject of the metaphor and doormat is the modifier or vehicle.

One essential part of Black's theory is the rejection of the view that metaphor is reducible to a literal comparison. Instead Black holds that the interaction of ideas in metaphor involves meaning shifts and revisions of entire systems of concepts. The terms of the metaphor are not just compared; rather, the modifier "selects, emphasizes, suppresses, and organizes the features of the primary subject" (Black, 1979 p. 29). The dynamic type hierarchy theory incorporates Black's insights on metaphor by dynamically altering the internal representation of knowledge in the system in response to context and input.

The formalism of conceptual graphs is ideal for representing metaphorical processing since the graphs are so flexible: they can be partially dismantled and joined up with different graphs according to formation rules; the graphs themselves can be "turned around" for a change of emphasis with a different node as the head; there are procedures for making concepts more abstract or more restrictive by moving up or down the type hierarchy and they can inherit default information which may bring out otherwise hidden expectations.

Type hierarchies provide a rich structure for knowledge representation which lends itself to interpreting metaphor. The hierarchy used here is not a static knowledge structure, as used by Sowa in his book, but rather a dynamic one which changes and adapts over time.[2] Semantic hierarchies and their associated conceptual graphs are intended to represent the

---

[1] See Black's book *Models and Metaphors*, chapter III and Black's article "More about Metaphor" in Ortony's *Metaphor and Thought* for more information about Black's interaction view of metaphor.

[2] The details of this idea are spelled out in my book *Knowledge Representation and Metaphor*, forthcoming, Kluwer Academic Publisher, 1992.

way the speaker or hearer views the world, in other words, the hearer's metaphysical models. Thus, the nature and structure of the semantic type hierarchy and the composition of the related conceptual graphs are modeling a hearer's ontology of the world. Different beliefs and different knowledge about the world will generate a different hierarchy and a different set of conceptual graphs. Furthermore, semantic hierarchies and conceptual graphs are connected in such a way that any change in one brings about changes in the other. Thus, the view of language taken here is that language is inextricably interwoven with our knowledge and beliefs about the world, and that it is useful to represent or model this ontology using the formalisms of conceptual graphs and semantic type hierarchies.

27.2 CONTEXT MASKS

The knowledge base of the type hierarchy is context neutral, that is, it is simply an ordering of types and supertypes that reflect some kind of ontological ordering, independent of whether we believe the ordering is true, interesting, beautiful or relevant to our current situation. In other words, the type hierarchy, in itself, will not yield any illocutionary or perlocutionary acts or motivations. However, context is vital to the interpretation of both metaphor and literal speech. A given expression can often be read either literally or figuratively, depending on the context and the motivation of the speaker.

I propose that the role that context plays be represented as a set of masks which change the view of the semantic hierarchy. Whether a statement is literal, metaphoric or figurative will depend upon what mask comes into play and what connections in the hierarchy are hidden or exposed by it. For example, the metaphor *"The car is thirsty"* allows us to blur the distinction between animate and inanimate so that we can attribute animal-like properties to an object which, from a literal point of view, we know isn't an animal. How these context masks are created and selected, however, is a complex question, one which involves an empirical study of how we actually model the world. At this time we will just postulate their existence and show the role they play in accounting for the kind of mechanisms that occur in understanding metaphor.

Metaphor takes place by establishing new semantic linkages as a result of masking. The mask redescribes the subject in terms of the new hierarchy brought into play by the ontology of the modifier. And that, according to my view, is what metaphor is: the redescription of one domain in terms of the generated hierarchy and the associated conceptual graphs from another; and since these hierarchies reflect our view of the world, we are redescribing the subject in terms of a new and different view of the world.

The same thing goes on in literal speech; only here the mask is used to generate a hierarchy with the intent, not just to present a way to view the subject, but to communicate that the world or state of affairs corresponds to the resultant picture or description, i.e., that what is said is true. On this theory, metaphor cannot be a two-stage process, that is, an utterance is not first interpreted literally and then, only when the literal interpretation fails, interpreted metaphorically. On the contrary, by viewing metaphor in this way, metaphoric speech becomes just as central as literal.[3]

---

[3] There are studies which support the idea that literal and metaphoric statements may involve the same kinds of processing, and, at the very least, show that the two-stage theory is bankrupt. See Robert Hoffman & Susan

In fact, metaphoric and literal language have the same status: they are just different aspects of the hierarchy which come into play with different masks. Each mask picks out different trees and subtrees, which means that a given set of concepts may change from being connected to being disjoint, depending on what mask operation takes place. Another way to look at the masks on the hierarchy is to say that the domain of discourse changes the salience of the nodes in the type hierarchy.

27.3 METAPHOR RELATES ENTIRE CONCEPTUAL DOMAINS

Kelly and Kiel (1987) were interested in finding evidence that "comprehension of a metaphor alters one's understanding of a domain over and above the concepts explicitly stated in the metaphor." The experiment they conducted involved metaphors relating the domains of periodicals and food ("The *New Yorker* is the quiche of newspapers and magazines") and the domains of world leaders and ocean vessels ("Richard Nixon is the submarine of world leaders").

They found that comprehension of the metaphors not only increased the similarity between the subjects (The *New Yorker* and Richard Nixon) and modifiers (quiche of newspapers and submarine of world leaders) but also increased similarity between other concepts from the same domains which could have formed different appropriate metaphors if related. (For example, there was an increase in similarity between *The National Enquirer* and "rotten egg," as well as between *The New York Times* and "steak and potatoes"). Furthermore, terms from the two domains that would form inappropriate metaphors if related, tended to decrease in similarity (For example, *The New York Times* moves away from "rotten egg").

27.4 CREATION OF SUPERTYPES IN COMMON

I agree with Black that metaphor is more than just comparing features of concepts for similarity, yet similarity of some kind is involved. I hold that the "similarity" we find in common is an abstraction of some of the properties found in the subject and modifier. When we look at two aspects of a metaphor it is very difficult to say where exactly the similarity lies. For example, in the metaphor used by Kelly and Kiel above, *"Richard Nixon is the submarine of world leaders"* it is very difficult to see any similarity between Richard Nixon and a submarine. The "similarity" we find in common is an abstraction of some of the properties found in the subject and modifier. In metaphor, what is common between the modifier and subject is not features at the same level of the hierarchy. On a literal level there is nothing similar between Nixon and a submarine. Nixon does not have a steel hull nor a periscope; what is common between them is a supertype which is higher up on the semantic hierarchy and under which aspects of both the modifier and subject domains fall.

The metaphor is attributing features from the modifier domain by abstracting them to a common supertype and then using that supertype to pick out the corresponding features of the subject. Furthermore, which supertypes are chosen, assuming that there are several in common, is a function of the context and the direction of the attribution of the metaphor. In

---

Kemper's article "What Could Reaction-Time Studies Be Telling Us About Metaphor Comprehension?", *Metaphor and Symbolic Activity*, 2:3, 149-186 (1987) for a good summary of these results.

other words, the metaphor is attributing features from the modifier domain by abstracting them to a common supertype and then using that supertype to pick out only the corresponding features of the subject domain. For example, both Nixon and submarines are instances of powerful entities which use subterfuge and stealth to acheive their objectives.

In some cases, there will be no node common to both the subject and modifier which can make sense of the metaphor. In this case, a new node will have to be created. The newly created supertype will be a generalization of features and schemata from the subject and modifier nodes. This is a kind of reverse inheritance, where the background knowledge contained at a lower level becomes more general and abstract. Thus, when metaphor involves a violation of semantic constraints in the hierarchy, then these constraints are promoted upward to the new node in such a way that both the modifier and subject can fall under the new supertype. As we shall see below, the metaphor the car is thirsty, involves a violation of a constraint in that thirsty is an attribute of an animal, not a vehicle. The newly created supertype, Mobile-entities that requires liquid, however, can have both subject and modifier fall under it without violating any semantic constraints.

Furthermore, as shown by the experiments of Kelly and Keil above, once a new concept type is generated for a particular metaphor, other connections between the domains become likely. For example, other similarities between the domains of world leaders and ocean vessel may suggest themselves: Margaret Thatcher and Battleships, Pope John Paul and a Hospital Ship, etc.

Example: The car is thirsty

The metaphor, "The car is thirsty", is one of animation or personification: attributing features of living things or humans to nonliving things.

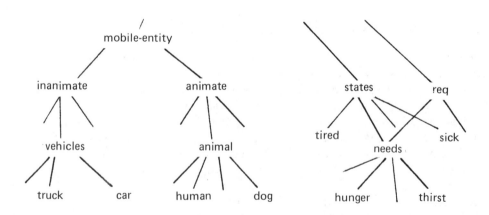

Fig. 27.1 Hierarchy before metaphor

In the above type hierarchy, a CAR is a kind of VEHICLE, and THIRSTY is a STATE. The CAR invokes the domain of INANIMATES while THIRSTY implies both the domain of STATES and the experiencers of states, ANIMATES. When we examine the conceptual graph for the concept THIRST we find that it is an attribute of an animal when it is in the state of requiring liquids. Thus, the modifier, ANIMALS, is implied by use of the term "thirst'. The conceptual graph for THIRST appears as follows:

```
[THIRSTY] -
     (ATTR) → [ANIMAL] -
          (STAT) → [REQUIRE] → (PTNT) → [LIQUID].
```

Fig. 27.2

To resolve the apparent constraint violation, the system would first compare the types
ANIMAL and CAR to find their minimal common supertype in the hierarchy: MOBILE-
ENTITY. Next, a new concept type t would be introduced as a subtype of MOBILE-
ENTITY and a supertype of both ANIMAL and CAR. We now have a place for the new
type t, but we do not have a definition of it.

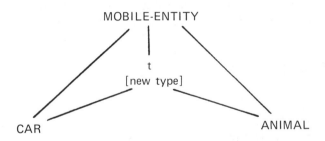

Fig. 27.3 Generation of a new type node for The car is thirsty

In order to define t, the system must search for properties of ANIMAL related to
THIRSTY. When we examine the conceptual graph for the concept THIRST we find that
thirsty is an attribute of an animal that (is in the state of) requires liquid.

Since the metaphor is attributing thirst to an object instead of an animal, the system
drops the animal and replaces it with the minimal common supertype: MOBILE-ENTITY.
The requirement of liquid can serve as the body of a lambda expression that defines t as a
mobile entity that requires liquids:

```
t= (λx) [MOBILE-ENTITY:  *x] → (STAT) → [REQUIRE]
                                       → (PTNT) → [LIQUID].
```

Thus, we make the node for MOBILE-ENTITY more specific with reference to THIRST
and get the supertype Mobile-entities which require liquids.

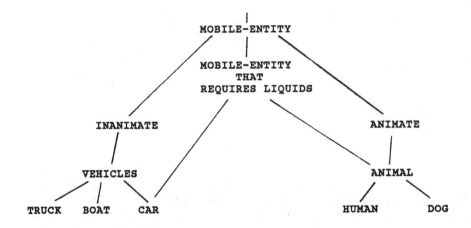

Fig. 27.4 Hierarchy after the metaphor

If we look at the schemata for cars we would find that some of the liquids it requires are water, gas and oil. The graphs might look something like the following:

```
[CAR] → (STAT) → [REQUIRE] –
       (PTNT) → [WATER]
       (PURP) → [ [COOL] → (PTNT) → [ENGINE] ] .

[CAR] → (STAT) → [REQUIRE] –
       (PTNT) → [GAS]
       (PURP) → [ [WORK] → (PTNT) → [ENGINE] ] .

[CAR] → (STAT) → [REQUIRE] –
       (PTNT) → [OIL]
       (PURP) → [ [LUBE] ← (PART) ← [ENGINE] ] .
```

Fig. 27.5

(There are other liquids a car requires, such as brake fluid, distilled water for the battery and power steering fluid etc., I have only listed the most salient needs here.) Further expansion of the schemata would provide more information about various parts of the car, how to fill it with water, oil or gas, etc., information about gas stations, how to tell when these liquids need replenishing and how often that might be and so on. In the interest of space, I will not represent all the graphs for this knowledge,here, but only point out that they are available to the system.

Since oil, gasoline and water are all liquids, they are all possible candidates for what the car needs in the sentence "The car is thirsty'. Gasoline would probably be the best choice as the needed liquid because it is needed more frequently and because it is a source of energy to the engine (a kind of fuel). However, water is also a possibility because it is a liquid that people drink. The ambiguity could be resolved by context–if someone is filling the radiator as they say "the car was thirsty" water (or antifreeze) would be the choice. If the gas gauge is being considered then gasoline would be the choice.

Once the determination of gasoline or water is made then the graph for the sentence will consist of a join between THIRSTY and CAR with MOBILE-ENTITY being restricted to CAR, and LIQUID being restricted to GAS (or WATER). The graph for the metaphor "The car is thirsty" would then appear as follows:

```
[THIRSTY]-
    (ATTR) → [CAR] →
        (STAT) → [REQUIRE] → (PTNT) → [GAS].
```

Fig. 27.6

Note, that this new supertype does not involve any kind of constraint violation or anomaly: both cars and people do require liquids, and both cars and people are mobile entities. The new concept type, t, refines the type hierarchy and allows any conceptual pattern for ANIMAL that needs LIQUID to be generalized to t. So now, for example, we could talk about the car drinking, or gulping or guzzling gas.

Furthermore, since the new type is general, any Mobile-entity which requires liquids can inherit these patterns. Thus, trucks, motorboats, and planes, for example, can all be said to drink or guzzle gas. The domains of ANIMALS and VEHICLES are now related and talk of cars being sick, limping along or a host of other human traits and characteristics can now be generated.

This does not mean that anything goes, however. There still can be nonsensical statements and metaphors that fail because the proper conceptual domains are lacking. For example, if there is no definition for the supertype created in common (for example, I cannot imagine one for the sentence "My car needs a haircut") then the metaphor is relatively meaningless for that particular knowledge base.

If these new types prove to be useful they may become entrenched in our hierarchies and may be reflected as new word senses or dead metaphors in the dictionary. If they are not frequently used then the new type will eventually disappear, and THIRSTY will revert to its original meaning of an attribute only of an ANIMAL.

According to the DTH theory, we do not differentiate between literal and figurative speech. Metaphors and idioms are so interwoven in our everyday language that we have trouble identifying the figurative from the literal. We have no problems talking about cars drinking gas or limping along or a host of other human traits and characteristics. We do not stop and check if the statement is literal at the time. If there is an intelligible way to interpret a sentence given the context and our general background knowledge, we do so. We do not balk at something that is not "literally" true as long as it is meaningful. If someone were to answer "Cars can't really drink gas" we would feel that they were being obstructionist and nitpicking. "You know what I mean" would be the typical response. The fact is that we are not always as careful with our categories as when we are concerned with truth and literal meaning. We have a different "mind set" when checking literal accuracy of statements than when trying to extract meaning. We are notorious in trying to infuse meaning even in its absence. This trait is one of the reasons early AI programs such as ELIZA succeeded; people read meaning into the empty and general replies generated by the program.[4]

---

[4]For a fuller exposition of Eliza and her effects on people, see Weizenbaum's book *Computer Power and Human Reason*, W.H. Freeman, San Francisco (1976).

27.5 PROGRAMMING THE DYNAMIC TYPE HIERARCHY

The Dynamic type hierarchy uses the same records, routines and representations as does the Cgen program, except that an implementation of the DTH requires additional features that allow the hierarchy to be flexible.[5] The extension of the Cgen program to the dynamic type hierarchy involves addition of several mechanisms to change and adapt the hierarchy. The DTH program requires the ability to create new supertypes or determinables and new links when interpreting metaphor. Another mechanism is a set of masks which operate on the hierarchy to yield different perspectives. An additional requirement for the DTH is access to the machine-readable dictionary used by the PEG parser. I will address each of these extension below.

27.6 ON-LINE DICTIONARY

The advantages of access to an on-line dictionary for an interpreter concerned with metaphor are enormous because many of the conventional metaphors and idioms common to everyday speech that can be found there. Take for example the metaphor My doctor is a butcher; the Oxford American Dictionary (1980) defines the word butcher as follows:

> butcher n. 1. a person whose trade is to slaughter animals for food, one who cuts up and sells animal flesh. 2. a person who has people killed needlessly or brutally. 3. (slang) an unskilled craftsman or artist (p. 83).

Thus, the meaning of the metaphor can be obtained simply by referring to a dictionary entry. The full power of a metaphor interpreter is not needed here since the meaning of this metaphor can be found in common usage. It has become a conventional, or as some people term it, a dead metaphor.

Language is constantly changing and evolving; unusual metaphors become a familiar part of language and new ones emerge. Because of this ongoing process we often lose track of the origins of various figures of speech. For example, the expression red herring now means "a misleading clue, something that draws attention away from the matter under consideration". But why should a red fish have this meaning? The origins of such a term, which were probably quite reasonable once, have been lost to common knowledge (although an etymologist might be able to ferret it out). But, this common background knowledge is just what is necessary in order to understand what a given metaphor is expressing.

An important part of metaphor comprehension is background knowledge. For example, if someone doesn't have the proper background to understand the role that quiche has come to play in society, they will not be able to understand the metaphor "The *New Yorker* is the quiche of magazines". Furthermore, Keil (1986) has shown that metaphor comprehension in children is dependent upon their acquisition of ontological domains, so that metaphors involving animate-inanimate distinctions were understood before those involving physical-nonphysical distinctions. Therefore, if the background knowledge or ontological distinctions necessary to understand a particular metaphor is lacking then, unless the metaphor has become a common and widely accepted part of language, the

---

[5]For more details about the Cgen interpreter, see Sowa & Way (1986) "Implementing a semantic interpreter using conceptual graphs," *IBM Journal of Research and Development*, 30:1, 57-69.

metaphor will make no sense. I would also like to add at this point that an important aspect of background knowledge for metaphors is some representation of the physical aspects of objects and how they behave. The work being done along these lines in AI is the attempt to represent a knowledge system for naive physics, that is, our intuitive notion of the physics of the world.

Thus, a metaphoric interpreter would have great difficulty in interpreting metaphors which are conventional rather than creative, because the necessary background knowledge which originally made them appropriate has been lost. This kind of metaphor is no longer generative, startling or new; rather it has become almost literal, at least to the extent that its meaning is represented in a common pool of knowledge such as a dictionary. The extent to which these common metaphors are accurately represented in a common dictionary is really quite surprising.Thus, by allowing the dynamic type hierarchy access to an on-line dictionary, many of the common idioms and metaphors can be interpreted as quickly, and in much the same way as, a literal usage.

27.7 MASKING THE HIERARCHY

As I stated earlier, the type hierarchy itself is context neutral; it is the masks which highlight and hide various nodes and connections that makes the hierarchy represent different perspectives. These masks represent different contexts, different language games, and each mask picks out different trees and subtrees of the hierarchy. For example, the concept of ATOM can change from being a subtype of SIMPLE SYSTEM to a subtype of COMPLEX SYSTEM due to the metaphor "The atom is a solar system in miniature". However, this change might only be for a scientific mask, that is, when we are genuinely interested in discussing the actual physical makeup of the world. For many everyday uses, however, we may prefer to view ATOM as a determinate of SIMPLE SYSTEMS, and forget about the details of its makeup. In this case, the mask will hide the connection of ATOM to COMPLEX SYSTEM as well as the nodes for electron and nucleus and, instead, provide a link from ATOM to SIMPLE SYSTEM. Below is a simplified version of both the scientific and everyday masks for the hierarchy.

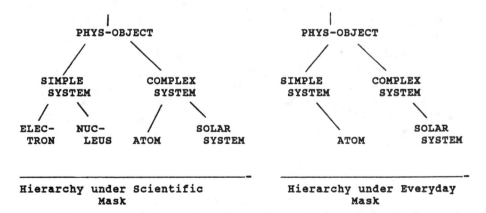

Fig. 27.7

Thus the mask on the hierarchy allows concepts to be viewed from different perspectives. In some situations it is important to view objects as complex or religious, whereas in other contexts we may be more interested in viewing them as simple or solely by their physical makeup.

The mask on the hierarchy effects the joining process of the related conceptual graphs because, whether two different concepts can be joined or not depends upon whether or not they can be restricted to the same type. Restricting a concept type to another requires that one concept type be a subtype of the other (and, of course, that the referents of the two concepts conform to each other). Thus, restriction can only occur when the two concepts are the same kind of thing, that is, when one falls under the other in a branch of the type hierarchy. For example, if a join between a statement about humans, and a statement about girls were desired, the concept type HUMAN could be restricted to its subtype GIRL because GIRL falls under the concept type for HUMAN. Therefore, if the type hierarchy has different concepts and different links between them, then the kinds of concept types that can be joined will also be different.

The questions of how these masks are obtained is a difficult one, which requires empirical and psychological research into the ways in which we actually structure our language games. I suspect that these masks are constantly changing as we learn new things and forget others. An even more difficult question is how it is known which mask is to be applied at what time. Some contexts may be easily determined, such as religious ones or scientific ones, but others are more subtle and difficult to identify. In any case, the perspective or mask used depends upon many different factors: the intentions of the speaker, his or her models of the hearer's understanding and purposes, the social framework of the discussion, as well as background knowledge and a past history of events. All I want to do here is to introduce masking as a kind of mechanism which can account for the shifting perspectives common to language and metaphor; a more detailed answer to these questions calls for another paper.

27.8   CREATION OF NEW DETERMINABLES IN COMMON

The heart of the dynamic type hierarchy, however, is the ability to generate new general categories under which the subject and modifier of a metaphor can fall. Furthermore, once the new concept has been created, it can be used to classify other phenomena. Nodes created in this way are role types; new roles that natural types can play in a language game.[6]

The creation of a new node is simply a copy of a blank concept type node. Initially, this new type node will not have a name - only some internal designation for record keeping. Eventually, however, if this type is often used it may be given a name and become a concept type like any other in the type hierarchy. Once the new type node has been created, its definition and schemata will be created by interpreting the metaphor as attributing something general from the modifier to the subject. We will turn to this procedure now.

---

[6]The distinction between natural types and role types appears to be a vital one for knowledge representation. The idea of natural types has long been familiar to philosophers, see Steven Schwartz (ed) *Naming Necessity and Natural Kinds*, Cornell University Press, Ithaca (1977), but Sowa is the first to explicate them in contrast to role types, See John Sowa's *Conceptual Structures*, Addison-Wesley Publishing Co., Reading MA.

27.9   PROCEDURE FOR INTERPRETING METAPHORS

As we saw above, the first step in interpreting a metaphor is to identify the major concept types involved; this is not always obvious. In "The car is thirsty", we saw that thirsty was not a major concept because the canonical graph for thirst has it modifying another concept, namely, animal. Thus, the implied major concept is animal. Here, the major concepts involved were discovered because of the relations in the canonical graph for thirsty: thirst does not stand alone; rather is an attribute of something, namely, an animal. Not all metaphors involve an indirect concept like thirst, however, for example, the metaphor "Bulgaria is a Russian puppet", involves just the concepts of Bulgaria and a puppet. Bulgaria is a country and a puppet is a doll on a string controlled by a hidden person or persons.

27.10   ABSTRACTING

Even though identifying the major concepts in this metaphor is straightforward, there is still information in the canonical graphs that can be useful. For example, the canonical graph for the modifier, puppet, would include the puppet as patient of being controlled, a human agent of the control, and string as the instrument of control. The case relations of AGENT, PTNT and INST provide clues for the interpretation of the metaphor and for the abstraction of concepts involved.

In applying the canonical graph for puppet to Bulgaria, certain matches are clear. Bulgaria is said to be the puppet in the metaphor, so Bulgaria would be concept related by PTNT. A Russian puppet implies that the AGNT of control is Russia, but how is the string to be applied? Because of the case relations, we already know what role the string is playing in the metaphor: the string is the instrument of controlling the country Bulgaria by Russia. We can now abstract the role that the string plays in the concept of puppet to that of some means of control. Now all that remains is to determine the appropriate means of control of one country by another, and this can be found in the background information about countries and governments.

27.11   LAMBDA DEFINITIONS

After the major concepts for the metaphor have been identified and their respective canonical graphs made available, the next step is to find the minimal common supertype for PUPPET and COUNTRY. The minimal common supertype would be ENTITY, so the definition of the new concept type node is created by specialization the definition of ENTITY using the modifier concept of a puppet. Since a puppet is a PTNT of control, the new type node could be AN ENTITY WHICH IS CONTROLLED BY ANOTHER. The new concept node is a supertype of both PUPPET and BULGARIA and a subtype of ENTITY.

The new schemata are generated in a similar way: the relations and supertypes of the concepts in the schemata for puppet provide patterns that may be applicable to Bulgaria as a controlled entity. For example, a puppet can be made to dance by pulling its string, and since dancing is a form of movement or combined actions, Bulgaria can be said to be made to act a certain way by the instrument of its control. Furthermore, once we have established a way to apply patterns from the modifier to the subject, words and relations associated with puppet and with the puppet's controller can now be applied to Bulgaria and Russia.

For example, Russia can be called the puppeteer, and Bulgaria can be said to be dancing to Russia's tune or be jerked along on its strings. In fact, dozens of relations can now be transferred from puppet to Bulgaria through the determinable created in common between them.

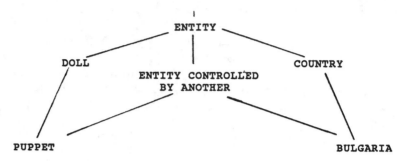

New concept type node created by the metaphor
Bulgaria is a Russian puppet.

Fig. 27.8

Thus, metaphors are generative in that they allow many patterns of associations to be abstracted and transferred from subject to modifier. In the car example, thirsty is an adjective applied to an animal; so, by generalizing the modifying role thirsty plays with respect to animal, other associated modifying patterns may be applied to car. Temperamental, energetic, sick, tired, stubborn, or loyal are all adjectives which can be applied to animals and so, might also have metaphoric application to a car.

Thus, the steps to interpret a metaphor and create determinables in common can be listed as follows:

1. Find the major concept types involved in the metaphor and copy their canonical graphs.

2. Find the minimal common supertype for these concept types.

3. Create a new concept node which is a supertype of the metaphoric concepts and a subtype of the minimal common supertype.

4. Create a Lambda abstraction for the definition of the new concept type by specializing the definition of the minimal common supertype using the modifier concept.

5. Compare the schemata and the attributes of the metaphor concepts for common facets; when the attributes clash, abstract them and try to reconcile.

6. Generate associated relations from the modifier to the subject by going through the new supertype node.

Metaphor, then, results in the creation of a new category, one which is more general and broader than either of the subject or modifier categories, and yet contains something common to each.

Once this new concept node has been created in the type hierarchy, since it has such a broad scope, it can be used to organize and classify other phenomena in new ways. The category of "Entities that are controlled by another" may be found to be applicable to certain businesses, institutions or people. Thus, metaphor creates new categories and ways to look at things which goes beyond even the original metaphor. In other words, the nodes created have surplus meaning which can then be used to classify all kinds of other experiences.

27.12   ADAPTIVE TYPE NODES

When a new type node is generated it is added to the current context mask on the hierarchy. However, to control the proliferation of nodes, each created node will be judged by two criteria: first by its range of applicability, and second by its continued use. The importance of a node in the type hierarchy can be seen by the extent to which it is interconnected with other nodes. If the range of a new determinable is only the subject and modifier of the original metaphor, then that category is neither useful nor generative. Secondly, nodes which are frequently accessed are more relevant than ones which are used very rarely. Thus, nodes which have little application to the rest of the hierarchy and those which are infrequently used should have only a temporary status in the hierarchy.

This temporary status is effected by the use of an aging factor. As soon as a new node is created, it begins to age, that is, every time the mask or masks which activate it are used the node's age variable increases. However, if the node is accessed then its age will be reduced. Thus, frequently used nodes will have a lower age and a better chance of remaining a part of the type hierarchy. If the node is never used then its increasing age will soon reach the terminal point, and the node may be deleted. Remember that we are talking about role type nodes only; the natural type nodes cannot be deleted from the hierarchy.

Before a node is deleted, however, its relation to other nodes in the type hierarchy is considered. If the node occupies a central position in the hierarchy, that is, if it is highly interconnected with other nodes, then it may get a new lease on life. Nodes which are able to classify and organize many facets of experience are obviously powerful and useful categories, and ones that we would want to keep. However, if for some reason a useful node does get deleted, it can always be reconstructed by the appropriate input. Thus, we have a mechanism of natural selection operating on the nodes in the hierarchy; only the best and most fittest will be allowed to remain.

27.13   IDENTIFYING METAPHORS

The question might now be asked, how does the system identify when a metaphor is being given? The answer is, it doesn't; or at least not always. Just as we often do not realize if we are listening to metaphors or literal statements. Now, it is true that if someone asked us "is that really true?", we would then be able to tell the difference. But, only after thinking about it. So too, if the DTH program were asked to evaluate if the metaphor was literally true, it could change to a mask which revealed only nodes and connections that are believed to be true. Then, on that mask, the metaphor would not make sense.

Thus, when a metaphor occurs within a "priming" context, then the appropriate mask is already set on the hierarchy and the input can be interpreted as if it were literal. However, for novel metaphors and metaphors that occur when a literal utterance is expected, some kind of constraint violation would be detected. A violation could also occur for literal expressions if the system is expecting metaphoric ones. In these cases, either a new mask is needed or a new supertype should be created.

The stress here is on understanding an utterance, rather than on enforcing rigid literal knowledge. The system always tries to give some kind of interpretation of the input. When the input is nonsense or a very bad metaphor then the common supertype will either fail to have a definition or have a very impoverished one. Furthermore, with these kinds of input, most or all of the schemata will fail to find any common ground.

The dynamic type hierarchy theory of metaphor is an attempt to capture some of the kinds of phenomena that are observed to take place when we use metaphor. The view that literal speech is somehow more central has not been borne out by more recent psychological studies. Rather, as Black suggested, it appears that metaphors are not reducible to literal paraphrases but involve entire domains of knowledge which shift and change, bringing new perspectives to old ideas.

BIBLIOGRAPHY

Black, Max (1962) *Models and Metaphors*, Cornell University Press, Ithaca, NY.

Black, Max (1977) "More about Metaphor," in Ortony (1979) 19-43.

Carbonell, Jaime G. (1981) "Metaphor: an inescapable phenomenon in natural-language comprehension," in Lehnert & Ringle (1982) 415-434.

Carroll, John M., & Robert L. Mack (1985) "Metaphor, Computing systems and active Learning," *International Journal of Man-Machine Studies*, 22:1, 39-57.

Davidson, Donald, (1977) "What Metaphors Mean," in Sacks, ed., 29-45.

Gentner, Dedre (1985) "Structure-Mapping: A Theoretical Framework for Analogy," *Cognitive Science*, 7, 155-170.

Gentner, Dedre (1982) "Are Scientific Analogies Metaphors?," in Miall (1982) 106-132.

Gentner, Dedre, & Donald R. Gentner, (1983), "Flowing Waters or Teeming Crowds: Mental Models of Electricty", in Gentner, D. & A. L. Stevens, eds., (1983).

Gentner, Dedre, & Albert L. Stevens, eds., (1973) *Mental Models*, Lawrence Erlbaum Associates, Publishers, Hillsdale, NJ.

Hoffman, Robert R. & Susan Kemper (1987) "What Could Reaction- Time Studies Be Telling Us About Metaphor Comprehension?" *Metaphor and Symbolic Activity*, 2:3, 149-186.

Hoffman, Robert R. (1984) "Recent Psycholinguistic Research on Figurative Language," in S. White ed., *Discourses in Reading and Linguistics*, Annals of the NY Academy of Sciences, 433, 137-166.

Jensen, K., & G.E. Heidorn (1983) "The Fitted Parse: 100Capability in a Syntactic Grammar of English," *Proceedings of the Conference on Applied Natural Language Processing*, Santa Monica, CA, Association for Computational Linguistics, 93-98.

Johnson, Mark, ed. (1981) *Philosophical Perspectives on Metaphor*, University of Minnesota Press, Minneapolis, Minn.

Johnson-Laird, P.N. (1983) *Mental Models*, Harvard University Press, Cambridge Mass.

Lakoff, George, & Mark Johnson (1980) *Metaphors We Live by*, University of Chicago Press, Chicago.

Lehnert, Wendy G., and Martin H. Ringle, eds. (1982) *Strategies for Natural Language Processing*, Lawrence Erlbaum Associates, Hillsdale, NJ.

Levin, Samuel R., (1977) *The Semantics of Metaphor*, The Johns Hopkins University Press, London.

Martin, J. & R. Harre' (1982) "Metaphor in Science," in Miall (1982) 89-105.

MacCormac, Earl R. (1985) *A Cognitive Theory of Metaphor*, MIT Press, Cambridge, MA.

Miall, David S., ed. (1982) *METAPHOR: Problems and Perspectives*, Humanities Press Inc., Atlantic Highlands, NJ.

Ortony, Andrew (1980) "Some psycholinguistic aspects of metaphor," in R. Honeck & R. Hoffman, Eds., *Cognition and Figurative Language*, Lawrence Erlbaum Associates, Inc., Hillsdale, New Jersey, 69-83.

Ortony, Andrew (1979a) "Beyond Literal Similarity," *Psychological Review*, 86:3, 161-180.

Ortony, Andrew (ed.) (1979b) *Metaphor and Thought*, Cambridge University Press, Cambridge.

Paprotte, Wolf, & Rene Driven, eds. (1985) "The Ubiquity of Metaphor", in Amsterdam Studies in the Theory of Linguistic Science, Series IV: *Current Issues in Linguistic Theory*, 29, John Benjamins Publishing Co., Amsterdam.

Reddy, Michael J. (1979) "The Conduit Metaphor - A Case of Frame Conflict in Our Language about Language," in A. Ortony, ed., 284- 324.

Sacks, Sheldon, ed. (1979) *On Metaphor*, The University of Chicago Press, Chicago.

Shibles, Warren, ed. (1972) *Essays on Metaphor*, The Language Press, Wisconsin.

Skorstad, J., B. Falkenhainer, & D. Gentner, (1978) "Analogical processing: A simulation and empirical corroboration," *Proceedings of AAAI-87*, The Sixth National Conference on Artificial Intelligence, p. 369.

Soskice, Janet Martin (1985) *Metaphor and Religious Language*, Clarendon Press, Oxford.

Sowa, John F. (1984) *Conceptual Structures: Information Processing in Mind and Machine*, Addison-Wesley Publishing Co., Inc., Reading, MA.

Sowa, John F., & E. C. Way (1986) "Implementing a semantic interpreter using conceptual graphs," *IBM Journal of Research and Development*, 30:1, 57-69.

Tourangeau, Roger & Robert J. Sternberg (1982a) "Understanding and appreciating metaphors," *Cognition*, 11, 203-244.

Tourangeau, Roger (1982b) "Metaphor and Cognitive Structure," in Miall (1982) 14-35.

Turbayne, Colin Murry (1962) *The Myth of Metaphor*, Yale University Press, New Haven.

Tversky, Amos (1977) "Features of Similarity", *Psychological Review*, 84:4, 327-352.

Weiner, Judith E. (1984) "A Knowledge Representation Approach to Understanding Metaphors", *Computational Linguistics*, 10:1, 1-14.

28

Conceptual Graphs as a Framework for Text Retrieval

Sung H. Myaeng
School of Information Studies,
Syracuse University, Syracuse,
NY 13244, USA

ABSTRACT

Text retrieval can be viewed as a process of matching common representations of user information needs and texts in a document database. While there are many intrinsically difficult problems in text retrieval which seem to explain why advances in text retrieval have been relatively slow, this chapter focuses on two intertwined problems, representation and inferencing. These, we believe, are the core of text retrieval processes. Our particular interest lies in the use of conceptual graphs as the representation language which allows us to employ informal reasoning techniques germane to text retrieval situations.

28.1 INTRODUCTION

Information retrieval (IR) is a process of identifying all and only those documents that satisfy a particular user's information needs. This process of determining how useful a piece of text would be for a given query involves many inherently difficult problems, each of which deserves a great deal of attention both individually and collectively. For instance, a seemingly simple user query is often deeply rooted to the anomalous state of user knowledge (Belkin *et al.*, 1982) and evolves from a visceral information need through a negotiation process (Taylor, 1968). The task of extracting the meaning of a document for retrieval purpose also remains a major stumbling block. A natural yet critical question in this context is how do we represent entities such as information needs and the semantics of natural language texts in a database? Answers to other questions regarding, for example, natural language processing techniques, user-system communication and cooperation, and matching techniques would depend pretty much on how rich and adequate the representation is.

As such, this chapter focuses on two intertwined issues, representation and inferencing, that seem to be the core of IR processes and often cut across other sub-areas of IR as well. In particular, discussion of our current attempt to build a non-traditional IR system will center around the conceptual structures framework (Sowa, 1984) which has been used as the representation language for our work.

28.2   CHARACTERISTICS OF INFORMATION RETRIEVAL

There are several unique characteristics that differentiate the IR process from other forms of knowledge or data processing as found in question-answering systems of various sorts or in data base systems all of which require a representation of the domain for which they are designed. Most notable characteristics of IR are:

Aboutness for IR systems, the main criterion for judging the quality of retrieved text is "aboutness," neither the truth value of a proposition in the sense of conventional logic nor the containment of a single fact as in a DB system. No proof or derivation of a proposition is sought for, and hence no variable is necessary in a query. Instead, what is important is the informational value of a text, namely, the question of whether a text contains or implies a conceptual structure of a query which is an expression of what the user wants to know more about and a manifestation of the anomalous state of the information seeker's knowledge. Because of this aboutness criterion, evaluation of IR system performance is measured based on a relatively subjective notion of "relevance" and quantified by recall and precision pair, the former measuring how many relevant documents are retrieved from among all relevant ones in the database and the latter measuring how many of the retrieved documents are relevant.

Heterogeneity unlike most AI systems, IR systems need to handle texts that are often unrestricted in scope, type, subject area, and even language. Because of the need to process and represent heterogenous databases, retrieval systems call for two seemingly conflicting requirements: an ability to handle texts independent of domains and at the same time (respond to the specifics of given text). In addition, system users are also diverse in many respects; they have their own domain of interests, they differ in their ability to articulate information needs at different abstraction levels, and they come to the system with their particular task that gives rise to the information needs. Since the user variability has a direct bearing on query formulation and subsequent relevance judgments, it must be taken into account when a retrieval technique is developed.

These characteristics are related to the types of uncertainty and ambiguity that exist in IR and have an interesting implication for representation and inferencing issues. With state-of-the-art text processing techniques, it is virtually impossible to extract and represent all the meanings underlying a text. While this difficulty in text processing is a major contributing factor for imperfect or even erroneous representations, it does not necessarily have an adverse effect on IR effectiveness. Since, due to the aboutness criterion, fine details of the semantics of some natural language utterances in a database query may not be as critical as in machine translation. For example, it can be argued that problems related to the imperfect nature of natural language processing techniques are not insurmountable when considered in a IR framework. In other words, by utilizing any utterance uncertainty or ambiguity to meet the aboutness criterion, the limitations of the domain-dependent nature of state-of-the-art natural language processing techniques can be lessened to a great extent.

Given that the document and query representations are usually imperfect, a sensible task for an IR system is to employ plausible inference (instead of strict inference) that tolerates the uncertain and fuzzy nature of IR and at the same time facilitates partial matching between the two representations. Assuming common representations of information needs and documents, an important question is how to match the two representations, in such a way that relevant documents are identified and ranked.

We take the view that the IR problem can be transformed to the problem of matching two sets of cogs. In this chapter, we address how the conceptual strcuture framework can be used to represent entities in the IR domain and how to model a form of plausible inferencing in IR (see, for example, Cohen and Kjeldsen (1987) by means of graph matching schemes. As such, we will focus on the problem of manipulating representations for "intelligent" IR, rather than transforming natural language text to a conceptual graph representation. The topic is only briefly addressed in the next section where we describe the overall configuration of our system, DR-LINK (Document retrieval with linguistic knowledge).

28.3 DESIGN PRINCIPLE AND SYSTEM ARCHITECTURE

While keyword-based representations of documents and queries, coupled with manual assignments of indexing terms or automatic statistical analyses of text, have been widely used in IR (Salton and McGill, 1983), knowledge-based approaches have gained much attention recently (Croft, 1987), where a variety of AI representation languages have been used to encode domain-specific knowledge and/or search heuristics (e.g. Smith *et al.*, 1989). However, we take the stance that for significant advances in IR to be made, it is essential to avoid not only those problems of "deep" analysis with current AI techniques as in many areas of natural language processing and knowledge-based systems, but also those incurred by keyword-based approaches (Mauldin *et al.*, 1987; Evans, 1990). In other words our design principle is to take advantage of both statistical and semantic information existing in natural language texts in such a way that these two kinds of information complement each other. The result is a more robust but shallower analysis of texts than those used in other AI systems nevertheless an analysis which seems sufficient for IR purposes. This approach of taking a "middle" ground is consistent with the theme of the new paradigm, called Text-Based Intelligent Systems (Jacobs, 1990).

As in Fig. 28.1, the general architecture of DR-LINK consists of two sub-systems: the learning sub-system responsible for the generation and maintenance of database-dependent units of feature-revealing formulae (FRF) and user-dependent units of user profiles; and the application sub-system that uses the units to perform the retrieval task. Inside the learning sub-system are two acquisition modules, one for SRF (Structure Revealing Formula) Acquisition and the other for RRF (Relation Revealing Formulae) Acquisition. With the help of a machine readable dictionary, these modules process a sample data (text) taken from the actual text database to learn various text-dependent rules (formulae) based on patterns of linguistic clues at various levels. Using the meta-knowledge obtained from linguistic theories and domain-independent heuristics from prior research (Liddy, 1988), the SRF acquisition process captures rules that would reveal overall thematic structures and their relations and help decomposing text into the corresponding components. The RRF acquisition module, on the other hand, identifies linguistically oriented formulae that determine relations among individual concepts that correspond to meaningful keywords. We contend that it is the relations that make the conceptual representations of text as opposed to keyword representations.

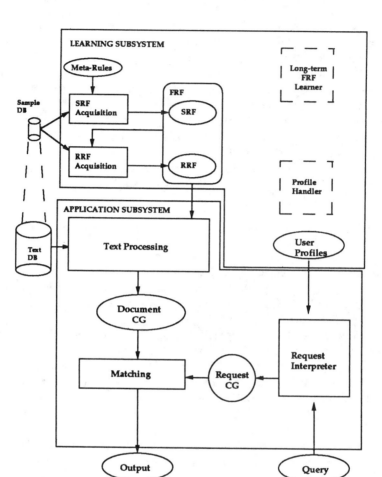

Fig. 28.1 DR-LINK Architecture

Within the application system, the text processing module takes the entire database from which the sample was drawn for the learning sub-systems and generates conceptual graphs for the documents which are available to the conceptual graph matching module at a later stage. To generate the final output, this module matches these conceptual graphs with a conceptual graph input from the request interpretation module that integrates a user query and a user profile as in Myaeng (1987).

This system is currently under development, and the least developed is the learning sub-system. Since we do not know the exact capabilities and limitations of the sub-system at this point, our discussion on the representation and matching components in the following sections is based on the assumption that important concepts and relations at various abstraction levels are extracted from texts by some processes which may have to involve some human intervention. While the overall effectiveness of the system will be determined by the capabilities of all the modules and their interactions, methods and techniques for representation and conceptual graph matching can be described and used independent of other components.

28.4 REPRESENTATION

Since Quillian proposed an associational model of human memory, called "Semantic Memory" (Quillian, 1968), where he attempted to capture the meanings of words, there have been a variety of semantic networks developed in AI but only with a few discernible common assumptions. Among them is one that they are designed to elucidate intensional relations between concepts (Jonson-Laird *et al.*, 1984). In IR, on the other hand some recent work by Wang *et al.* (1985) and Lu (1990) showed that the use of semantic relations among terms improved retrieval effectiveness. Amid these developments in both areas, a naturally emerging idea is to use a conceptual representation for IR; Although expensive, a more semantically-based representation of documents and user queries would help reduce the gap between the reality being represented (e.g. the semantics of documents) and the actual representation to be processed by an IR system and make automatic reasoning more amenable.

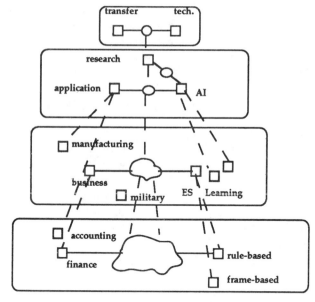

Fig. 28.2 Abstraction levels

However, as mentioned previously, we argue that the IR process is different in nature from knowledge processing for question-answering and that this difference doesn't guarantee the success of direct applications of AI techniques to IR. With this precaution in mind, we have identified a set of desirable features of a representation scheme to be used/ extended for IR. Specifically we want our representation scheme:

- to be expressive and flexible enough to encode user queries and document contents in the form of concepts and relations, which together reflect a mental model of the associational structure of human knowledge often used in cognitive activities. Since multiple sentences are often interconnected to represent the meaning of a document or a problem description, it is essential for the scheme to be able to form a coherent discourse structure out of sentences referring to each other.

- to support the need for different levels of abstraction, i.e., both coarse-grained and fine-grained concepts, in such a way that different levels of detail for information needs and document contents can be modeled and handled for efficient knowledge processing. As in Fig. 28.2, for instance, a query or a document fragment about "the use of rule-based expert systems to solve financial problems" can be abstracted to "the use of expert systems in business" and subsequently to "technology transfer". The representation scheme should be able to handle this kind of abstraction process in a systematic and principled way.

- to facilitate inexact reasoning so that the uncertainty and fuzziness of IR can be handled effectively. This is a reflection of the fact that information needs are seldom expressed precisely and completely, that there are many ambiguities in natural language texts, and that a deep analysis of natural language utterances is expensive.

- to provide an easy and natural mapping between the representations and the documents/query/output. This aspect is concerned with the user interface of DR-LINK and the ease of transforming query or document text to the target representation.

Our choice of the conceptual strcutures theory as the representation language is primarily based on the extent to which it satisfies the criteria listed above, and partially based on the fact that we have used it for other related work where we attempt to extract semantic knowledge automatically from dictionary text (Myaeng, 1989). More specifically:

- we believe that representation of "meaning" of natural language utterances is the central core of IR, and the conceptual graph framework allows nodes in a conceptual graphs to be intensional. As opposed to standard logic, for instance, where its extensionality makes the truth value of a proposition essential, conceptual graphs can be manipulated with no implication of existence of the individual being described. In addition, the type hierarchy is also intensional. While this argument has an important philosophical implication, it also has a significant impact on the linguistic and practical aspects of IR. By using the indexical referent marker, #, for example, discourse referents problems can be handled without coreferent resolution (Sowa, 1990) when more than one sentences are combined to form a single conceptual graph. This flexibility is crucial for IR situations where complete information may be unobtainable or unnecessary.

- The conceptual graphs theory supports the need for representing different levels of abstraction as illustrated in Fig. 28.2. The type lattice and the abstraction mechanism using a lambda expression not only allows for a relatively easy modeling and handling of different levels of details of information needs and document contents but also facilitate efficient knowledge processing. Considering the same topic can be expressed at different levels of abstraction, it is clear that there should be some sort of knowledge structure and well-defined operations that make the "equivalence" detectable. In the conceptual graphs framework, for example, a match between "the use of rule-based expert systems to solve financial problems" and "technology transfer in business" can be made when the two phrase are represented as;

```
[solve]-
    (object)→[problem]→(char)→[finance]
    (instrument)←[expert-system]→(char)→[rule-based]
    [technology-transfer]→(domain)→[business]
```

and there is a type definition

```
technology-transfer =
    (λx)[system]→(instrument)→[solve:*x]
                                →(object)→[problem]
```

provided that the relationships, EXPERT-SYSTEM < SYSTEM < TECHNOL-OGY and FINANCE < BUSINESS, exist in the type hierarchy. The concept node technology-transfer is expanded with the type definition, and the resulting match would consist of two conceptual graphs:

```
[solve]-
       (object)→[problem]
       (instrument)←[expert-system]
       [finance]
```

Similarly, the abstraction mechanism can be utilized to represent relations in such a way that when relation-revealing formulae are extracted from natural language utterances, they are expressed in this form and used in the same way that concept type definitions are used.

- Although conceptual graphs can be seen as a system of logic that has a model-theoretic semantics, they allow plausible reasoning with prototypes and schemata (Sowa, 1984). This duality makes the framework especially suitable for IR in that it allows us to represent concepts and relations as precisely and formally as logic and at the same time gives us freedom to employ informal, non-deductive reasoning techniques appropriate for IR situations (We share the arguments made by Israel (1983) and others that logic is distinct from reasoning). This versatility is of particular interest especially since one of our goals is to compare our representation and retrieval methods with both conventional, keyword-based approaches and other more recent AI-based approaches; it will provide us with a theoretic ground on which we can develop a unified theory for IR in the long run, as attempted in van Rijsbergen (1986).

- In general terms, the conceptual strcuture framework was originally developed with a strong interest in natural language processing in mind. It can be said, therefore, that to the extent the conceptual graphs framework is suitable for natural language processing, it lends itself to IR since IR problems cannot be dealt with properly in isolation from natural language processing. In terms of Brachman's characterization of semantic networks (Brachman, 1979), the abstraction mechanism provides a systematic facility by which conceptual level knowledge can support linguistic level knowledge, satisfying the adequacy criterion.

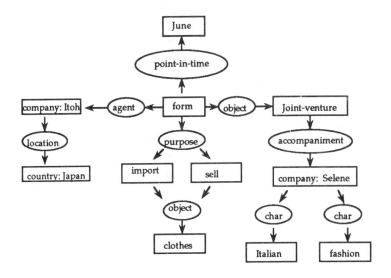

Fig. 28.3 A Document Fragment - TEXT: *"Itoh, Inc., will form a joint venture in June with the Italian firm Selebe Inc., to import and sell clothes .."*

An example of a typical document fragment and a corresponding conceptual graphs is shown in Fig. 28.3 where concept and relations nodes are almost directly mapped from the text without any abstraction. Fig. 28.4 shows two queries and corresponding conceptual graphs, each of which would match the document to a different degree, the first being a hit and the other being a mismatch.

In this section, we have argued that the flexibility and expressive power of the conceptual structure framework, together with all the operations and knowledge structures available, facilitate our effort to model IR situations in a unified way. In order to illustrate some of the points, some examples were also used. In the next section, we describe conceptual graph matching as informal reasoning techniques whicch correspond to a variety of IR processes and show how they encompass other IR models.

28.5   CONCEPTUAL GRAPH MATCHING

Uncertainty in IR situations come from a number of different sources. To name a few: A user's description of his information need is often incomplete or imprecise; The process by which NL text is transformed into a representation may not be reliable or complete; The words used in texts or information need descriptions may be ambiguous; and

Query 1: "*Cooperation between a Japanese company and an Italian Company*".

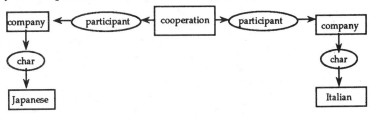

(a) The document in Fig. 28.3 should be retrieved by this query.
Query 2: "*A Japanese company selling its subsidary*".

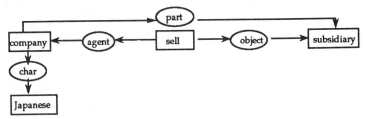

(b) The document in 3 should not be retrived by this query.

Fig. 28.4 Two queries.

The representation scheme may be limited in terms of expressiveness. Regardless of sources, however, there seem to be two places where such uncertainty can be incorporated: the representation and the retrieval or reasoning process. While it may be necessary for the current conceptual graphs framework to evolve to include uncertainty in the representation formalism, we focus on the latter in the context of conceptual graphs being used for IR.

Matching processes in IR can be classified along two dimensions as illustrated in Fig. 28.5: exact vs. partial and string vs. conceptual. While matching processes which take place as part of inferences with a knowledge representation are conceptual in nature, other matching processes without a knowledge structure as carried out in a database system are basically nothing more than string matching. In this respect, most keyword-based IR systems perform string matching whereas some recent AI-based systems employ conceptual matching.

On the other hand, the basis for determining whether a matching is exact or partial is a question of how the critical individual components of objects being matched contribute to the decision making. While matches in most database systems and conventional IR systems belong to the category of exact matching, some expert systems with certainty factors as well as the IR systems where documents and queries are represented in a vector space fall into the other category.

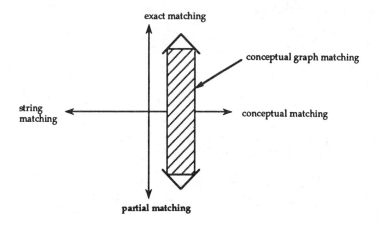

Fig. 28.5 Space of Matching.

The graph matching techniques we are developing span the first and fourth quadrants of the space as shown in Fig. 28.5. Given two conceptual graphs for a query and a document, what we need is flexible yet conceptually-oriented graph matching techniques by which a retrieval decision can be made. Unlike question-answering systems where the exact graph pattern with associated semantics of a query must exist in the database to generate an answer, the main concern of an IR system is to determine the degree to which the two graphs share the common conceptual structure. For this purpose, we begin with ordinary exact matching performed by the projection operation in the conceptual graphs framework and gradually relax various conditions imposed on the exact matching to allow for partial matching.

Finding a schematic join between a conceptual graph and schemata is often seen as a form of plausible reasoning when the join builds a plausible model for the given problem situation. Since the join process ends in itself in IR, the process of associating a query statement with a document can be seen as part of plausible reasoning in this sense. However, there is an extra level of plausibility being applied within the IR process when partial matching is allowed. In other words, the goal of relaxing constraints in conceptual graphs matching is essentially to seek plausibility of associating two conceptual graphs.

While the matching criterion can be stated generally in the context of conceptual graphs as determining the degree to which a query conceptual graphs is joinable to a document conceptual graphs, it has a number of implications for the actual matching and constraint relaxation procedures. The relevance of a document conceptual graphs with respect to a query conceptual graphs is a function of:

- structure-preserving *coverage* that measures the extent to which the document conceptual graphs contains the query conceptual graphs in the original form;

- *semantic distance* between corresponding concept types when two nodes are matched; and

- *criticality weight* of a node or subgraph, which determines how critical the node (subgraph) is in representing the natural language utterance.

For example, the document conceptual graphs in Fig. 28.3 is less relevant to the second query conceptual graphs than to the first (both in Fig. 28.4) since the semantic distance between joint-venture and sell is very large compared to the distance between joint-venture and cooperation. Assuming that the large distance prevents the two concept nodes from being joined in the former, the entire structure of the query conceptual graphs cannot be preserved even if it is joined with the document conceptual graph after constraint relaxation. The relevancy decreases even further if the concept sell is given a high importance factor.

The following is a set of more specific heuristics we are employing with the general criteria as a guiding principle:

- While projection and maximal join are the most fundamental operations for matching, other operations such as generalization and specification on type hierarchies and expansion and contraction operations based on abstractions are also useful in IR. For instance, some concept nodes in a query conceptual graphs can be expanded to form a larger conceptual graphs before a search begins. Through this process, the obvious value of using a network structure, namely precision enhancement, is complemented by these recall-enhancing operations. This aspect of matching can be greatly facilitated when we have general-purpose dictionary entries represented in conceptual graphs (Myaeng, 1989).

- The size of projection by which a maximal join can be performed must be taken into account in determining the order of matched graphs. The measure is a function of the number and the criticality of concept and relation nodes included in the projection. The criticality criterion must be based on the linguistic role of the type labels in the source natural language utterance.

- If generalization is carried out in projection, the semantic distance between graph components should be considered as a penalty as in (Garner and Tsui 1988). Since both concepts and relations can be meaningfully generalized in IR, there should be a distinction in terms of the weight of penalties between conceptual and relational distances.

- Since more than one maximal joins can exist, the number of maximal joins and the degree of overlapping between them should be considered.

- When the entire or significant portion of the query conceptual graphs has no match in the document conceptual graph, the query conceptual graphs can be split into multiple subgraphs before matching. While providing flexibility in matching, this splitting process affects the structure-preserving coverage criterion and should incur some penalty in computing the degree of match since the semantics of the query is partially lost. Nonetheless, this process responds well to IR situations in that a coherent theme reflected in a query may be described by multiple sentences in a document yet may not get combined into a single conceptual graphs by the natural language analysis task.

- Various relaxation procedures can be employed progressively to the point where the matching process is analogous to those used in other IR systems. With a relation hierarchy, for example, a projection-like operation can be applied to match two structurally equivalent graphs with different relation types or even without any relation labels at all. In the former case, it becomes a form of analogical reasoning (Gentner, 1985) whereas the matching process in the latter case is close to that used in the COP (constituent object parse) matcher (Metzler *et al.*, 1989) if the directionality is maintained. Without the directionality, the situation becomes similar to a pure network representation (Belkin and Kwasnik, 1986) whose role is limited to organizing nodes. When all the links and relations are removed for further relaxation, conceptual graphs matching degenerates to keyword matching except that the type hierarchy can be used for generalization and specification of concepts.

- In order to avoid an combinatorial explosion, only a small number of candidate conceptual graphs should be selected by means of an index and keyword-based searching and passed to the partial matching process.

28.6   CONCLUSION

The impetus of this chapter is to lay out a framework in which IR processes and situations are explained and described in the context of the conceptual graphs theory, rather than to provide a complete description of a system or algorithms. As such, much emphasis has been placed on the role of the conceptual graphs theory in IR and descriptions and justification of the approaches, with the possible exception of the last section. Details of algorithms are not included partly because of the status of the project and partly because of the nature of IR; Some of the details need to be worked out with a series of retrieval experiments. Although it is intuitively arguable that some of the conceptual graphs features and fine details are not necessary for IR, for example, any definitive conclusions can hardly be made until some experiments are done.

While the ultimate goal of this work is to build a highly effective, domain-independent text retrieval system whose power is derived from the synergy of AI-based NLP techniques and statistically oriented IR approaches, we believe that IR is a good application area for the conceptual graphs theory, and that this is an opportunity to widen the utility of the conceptual graphs framework and at the same time to strengthen the theory through possible extensions. In addition, we believe that this line of work will lead us to develop an unified theory under which many, if not all, of the IR models can be described.

BIBLIOGRAPHY

Belkin, N. J. and Kwasnik, B. (1986) "Using structural representations of anomalous states of knowledge for choosing document retrieval strategies," Proc. ACM Conference on Research and Development in Information Retrieval, pp. 11-22.

Belkin, N. J., Oddy, R. N., and Brooks, H. M. (1982) "ASK for information retrieval: Part I. Background and theory," Journal of Documentation, vol. 38, no. 2, pp. 61-71.

Brachman, R. (1979), "On the epistemological status of semantic networks," in N. V. Findler, ed., *Associative Networks: Representation and Use of Knowledge by Computers*, Academic Press: New York, pp. 3-50.

Cohen, P. R. and Kjeldsen, R. (1987) "Information retrieval by constrained spreading activation in semantic networks," Information Processing and Management, vol. 23, no. 4, pp. 255-268.

Croft, W. B. (1987) "Approaches to intelligent information retrieval," Information Processing and Management, Vol. 23, no. 4, pp. 249- 254.

Evans, D. (1990) "Concept management in text via natural-language processing: the CLARIT approach," Working Notes: Text-Based Intelligent Systems, AAAI Spring Symposium Series, Stanford University, CA, March, pp. 93-95.

Garner, B. J. and Tsui, E. (1988) "General purpose inference engine for canonical graph models," Knowledge-Based Systems, vol. 1, no. 5, pp. 266-278.

Gentner, Dedre (1985) "Structure-mapping: a theoretical framework for analogy," Cognitive Science, vol. 7, pp 157-170.

Jacobs, P. (1990) "Text power and intelligent systems," Working Notes: Text-Based Intelligent Systems, AAAI Spring Symposium Series, Stanford University, CA, March, pp. 1-4.

Israel, D. (1983) "The role of logic in knowledge representation," IEEE Computer, vol. 16, no.10, pp. 37-42.

Johnson-Laird, P. N., Herman, D. J., and Chaffin, R, (1984) "Only connections: a critique of semantic networks," Psychological Bulletin, vol. 96, no. 2, pp. 292-315.

Liddy, E. D. (1988) "The Discourse Level Structure of Natural Language Texts: An Exploratory Study of Empirical Abstracts", PhD Dissertation, School of Information Studies, Syracuse Univ., Syracuse, NY.

Lu, X. (1990) "Document retrieval: a structural approach," Information Processing and Management, vol. 26, no. 2, pp. 209-218.

Mauldin, M., Carbonell, J., and Thomason, R. (1987) "Beyond the keyword barrier: knowledge-based information retrieval," Information Services and Use, vol. 7, pp. 103-117.

Metzler, D. P., Hass, S. W., Cosic, C., and Wheeler, L. H. (1989) "Constituent object parsing for information retrieval and similar text processing problems," Journal of American Society for Information Science, vol. 40, no. 6, pp. 398-423.

Mineau, G. (1990) "Normalizing conceptual graphs," Proc. of 5th Annual Workshop on Conceptual Structures, sponsored by AAAI in conjunction with AAAI-90, Boston, MA.

Myaeng, S. H. (1987) "The Roles of User Profiles in Information Retrieval". Ph. D. Dissertation, Dept. of Computer Science and Engineering, Southern Methodist Univ., Dallas, TX.

Myaeng, S. H. (1989) "Automatic knowledge extraction from dictionary text using conceptual graphs," Proc. of 4th Annual Workshop on Conceptual Structures, sponsored by AAAI in conjunction with IJCAI-89, Detroit, MI.

Quillian, M. R. (1968) "Semantic Memory," in Minsky, ed., *Semantic Information Processing*, MIT Press: Cambridge, MA, pp. 216-270.

Salton, G. and McGill, M. (1983) *Introduction to Modern Information Retrieval*, McGraw-Hill.

Smith, P. J., Shute, S. J., and Galdes, D. (1989) "Knowledge-based search tactics for an intelligent intermediary system," ACM Transactions on Information Systems, vol. 7, no. 3, pp. 246-270.

Sowa, J. F. (1984) *Conceptual Structures: Information Processing in Mind and Machine*, Reading, MA: Addison-Wesley.

Sowa, J. F. (1990) "Towards the expressive power of natural language," Proc. of 5th Annual Workshop on Conceptual Structures, sponsored by AAAI in conjunction with AAAI-90, Boston, MA.

Taylor, Robert (1968) "Question-negotiation and information seeking in libraries," College and Research Libraries, vol. 29, no. 3, pp. 178- 194.

Wang, Y., Vanderdorpe, J., and Evans, M. (1985) "Relational thesauri in information retrieval," Journal of the American Society for Information Science, vol. 36, no. 1, pp. 15-27.

van Rijsbergen, C. J. (1986) "A non-classical logic for information retrieval," The Computer Journal, vol. 29, no. 6, pp. 481-485.

29

Conceptual Graph Information Retrieval using Linear Resolution, Generalization and Graph Splitting

Jean Fargues
IBM Paris Scientific Center,
3 et 5 Place Vendome,
75021 Paris Cedex 01, France

29.1   INTRODUCTION

The KALIPSOS prototype, which was described in Berard-Dugourd *et al.* (1988a, 1988b) is able to build a semantic representation of a text in terms of conceptual graphs, and to perform intelligent information retrieval on texts, including the application of deduction rules. The information retrieval component was mentioned very briefly in our preceding papers, but without technical details. This chapter presents these technical details.

The goal of the resolution process is more to give relevant feedback to the user than to perform a pure logical deduction on conceptual graphs. We therefore extended the deductive capacities of a pure logic resolution on conceptual graphs in order to give the user a pertinent final answer, even when the question cannot be strictly established as a logical consequence of the conceptual graphs knowledge base. This is made up of one or more sentences (i.e. conceptual graphs) found in the text and relevant to the user query. Once deductive rules have been applied, the answer contains the trace of the application of the rules (expressed in natural language). If the deduction fails, we suggest a method to explain why a sentence has been found incompatible with a rule clause or why a rule clause is too specific to be applied.

Three different techniques are used simultaneously:

1. A conceptual graphs prolog-like deduction based on the resolution of a conceptual graphs goal on a set of conceptual graph rules and facts.

2. A relaxation method of the conceptual graphs goals in the case of failure of the logic resolution, using a combination of generalization between conceptual graph and of projection on conceptual graphs.

3. A goal splitting technique, applied both in the linear resolution method and to resolve a conceptual graph query graph when the target information is partially present in distinct conceptual graphs of the text.

In fact, these three techniques were necessary for the following reasons:

- First, the deduction rule formalism is needed to code the domain knowledge. In this way the deductive power of the system for a particular application and the set of user queries on the texts that the system can handle can both be increased.

- Secondly, the end user prefers an answer expressed in terms of relevant text sentences to the simple failure of a rigorous deduction. For example, if the user ask something about the decrease of some entity, and if the text graphs only contain information about the increase of this entity, an intelligent answer must be: I cannot say anything about the decrease of X, but I found in the text this "sentence containing something about the increase of X".

  Thus, a conceptual graph goal may be relaxed by using generalization in order to give more intelligent feedback to the user. We describe the algorithm which uses both generalization and projection. Various problems are addressed, such as the reduction of the generalization search space by introducing the notion of "graph focus", and intelligent explanation when a deduction rule fails on a non-satisfiable (but relevant) text graph.

- Thirdly, the information needed to give an answer may be located in distinct sentences of a text, i.e in distinct conceptual graphs. We use a conceptual graph goal splitting technique to solve this problem. In this case, a subgraph of the current goal may be satisfied by using a first sentence graph, and the other subgraphs must be searched in the preceding sentences of the text (i.e. in the preceding conceptual graphs).

One difficulty is to check consistency during this backward search process. We must make sure, for example, that the subject remains the same in the two distinct target sentences which have been used to solve the two related goal subgraphs. Let us assume that a goal is split into two subgoals, the second one being "in France". What we must do is check that the main target sentence (for the first subgoal) belongs to a paragraph concerning France. Consistency checking detects that there is no preceding sentence contradictory to the pending subgoal "in France" before the system encounters a sentence for this subgoal. This process, which is detailed in the paper, also uses generalization and projection on conceptual graphs.

29.2   INFORMATION RETRIEVAL: THE SIMPLEST CASE

We assume here that a natural language question is translated into a conceptual graph Q. The target graphs are conceptual graphs built from a text by our KALIPSOS prototype. To simplify, we assume that each natural language sentence of the text produces only one conceptual graph. Thus, the target graphs corresponding to the text may be considered as a sequence $\{S_1, S_2, \ldots, S_n\}$ of conceptual graphs.

The information retrieval process cannot use the join operation as a basic pattern-matching function because the join does not preserve the logic truthvalue. The pattern-matching operation on conceptual graphs which does preserve the logic interpretation is projection, as presented in Sowa (1984).

Therefore, if Q is a query graph, we will say that the target graph S answers the question Q if there exists a projection of Q in S. In formal terms, if Φ is the mapping function which associates a logic formula to any conceptual graph, then:

$\Phi(S) \supset \Phi(q) \supset \Phi(Q)$ where $q = \pi(Q, S)$ is the projection of Q in S.

The Prolog predicate we implemented for the projection operation is a 4-place predicate $PROJ(Q, S, q, C)$, where q is the result of the projection of Q in S, i.e. a subgraph of S isomorphic to Q in which some concepts have been restricted. C is the remaining part of S, i.e. the set of edges in S which do not belong to q. In many cases, C is a connected set of edges and therefore is a unique conceptual graph. It may happen that C is a set of conceptual graphs corresponding to several pending parts of S, especially when the projection is done on a cyclic part of S. We will examine the way we use this C parameter in the section on graph splitting.

At this point, it can be noted that the answer graph $q = \pi(Q, S)$ is not very informative for the end user. If the query graph Q corresponds to "Is the dollar rate fluctuating in Paris?", and if the target graph corresponds to "In Paris, a 10 percent increase of the dollar occurred despite discussions between the EEC partners", the answer graph q will produce through our natural language generation system: "the dollar is going up in Paris". We therefore prefer to also give the text sentence S as an answer. Nevertheless, there is no simple way to distinguish in the pending part C of S what is informative for the user from what is not.

An example of this simple case of information retrieval is:

QUESTION: *Is the dollar rate fluctuating in Paris?*

```
Q = [EVOLUTION]-
     (AGT)→[DOLLAR]
     (THEMA)→[VARIATION]
     (LOC)→[CITY:'Paris']
```

```
S = [EVOLUTION]-
     (AGT)→[DOLLAR]
     (THEMA)→INCREASE]
     (LOC)→[CITY:'Paris']
     (CSS)→[PROPOSITION:.....]
```

SUCCESS of the projection of Q in S.

DIRECT NL ANSWER: *The dollar is going up in Paris*

FOUND SENTENCE:

In Paris, a 10 percent increase of the dollar occurred despite discussions between the EEC partners.

This first case is thus characterized by the following points:

- The answer may be generated by the selection of a single sentence S which contains sufficient information.

- The projection succeeds, i.e. the Prolog goal $PROJ(Q, S, q, C)$ succeeds.

- The typical answer may generally be prefixed by "yes" or is not contradictory to the question. The logic interpretation is such that:

$$\Phi(S) \supset \Phi(q) \supset \Phi(Q)$$

We call this first case a YES-1 strategy, YES because of the answer type, 1 because the answer may be produced from a single graph S.

29.3 QUERY RELAXATION

We assume the user question is: "Is the dollar going up in Paris?" and there is no sentence graph S in the text such that the question graph Q may be projected in S: $PROJ(Q, S, *, *)$ fails.

This case would occur if the text contained the following information, for example:

- *The dollar is going down in Paris.*

- *The dollar is going up in Tokyo.*

- *No information about the dollar, but the yen is going up in Paris.*

- *No information about the fluctuation of currencies in Paris, but some information about the mark in Frankfurt.*

An intelligent question answering system should give answers like:

> *No, it is going down in Paris.*
>
> *I don't know in Paris, but it is going up in Tokyo.*
>
> *I don't know, but the yen is going up in Paris.*
>
> *I don't know, but the mark is going down in Frankfurt.*

Each of these cases corresponds to a query relaxation process which is activated whenever there is no simple answer produced by the YES-1 strategy. Answers 3 and 4 are irrelevant and it is necessary to introduce some heuristics to avoid non pertinent relaxation.

We use the generalization algorithm on conceptual graphs. This algorithm consists in matching a graph $G1$ to a graph $G2$ to find a maximal overlap of $G1$ and $G2$ in which each concept c is the least common supertype of the two concepts $c1$ and $c2$ of $G1$ and $G2$. This operation is described in Sowa (1984) and Fargues (1886). We note $GEN(Q, S, Q')$ the 3-place Prolog predicate which computes the generalization Q' of Q and S.

The query relaxation is obtained by generalizing the question graph Q and a sentence graph S. To do this, $GEN(Q, S, Q')$ is evaluated. Several cases may occur:

- $GEN(Q, S, Q')$ fails, its result being the degenerated graph

    ENTITY

    . In this case we apply the question resolution to the next sentence graph S of the text.

- $GEN(Q, S, Q')$ succeeds, but Q is not a simple restriction of Q': the evaluation of $PROJ(Q', Q, Q1, Q2)$ produces a non-empty pending part $Q2$. This means that the question graph Q cannot be completely solved on S, because Q contains conceptual edges which cannot be matched to S. We will examine this complex case later because we apply a graph-splitting technique to solve it.

- $GEN(Q, S, Q')$ succeeds, and Q is a restriction of Q' such that $PROJ(Q', Q, Q, NIL)$ succeeds. This condition means that the generalization of the question may be answered by matching it to the current target graph S. Therefore, we evaluate $PROJ(Q', S, q, C)$. The direct natural language answer may be generated from q and the found sentence is S. The direct answer must generally be prefixed by "No, but.." or by "I don't know, but..".

We call this third case NO-BUT-1 strategy.

With the NO-BUT-1 strategy, the answers 1 to 4 we gave before as an example can be generated. We assume here that VARIATION is the least supertype of INCREASE and DECREASE in the concept lattice. If the question Q is "Is the dollar going up in Paris?", the corresponding graph is:

```
Q = [EVOLUTION]-
    (AGT) → [DOLLAR]
    (THEMA) → [INCREASE]
    (LOC) → [CITY:'Paris']
```

For answer number 1, the subgraph of sentence graph S is supposed to be:

```
[EVOLUTION]-
    (AGT) → [DOLLAR]
    (THEMA) → [DECREASE]
    (LOC) → [CITY:'Paris']
```

$PROJ(Q, S, *, *)$ fails because INCREASE is not a restriction of DECREASE, and $GEN(Q, S, Q')$ produces:

```
Q' = [EVOLUTION]-
    (AGT) → [DOLLAR]
    (THEMA) → [VARIATION]
    (LOC) → [CITY:'Paris']
```

where Q' may be projected on S to generate the final answer.

Similarly, answers 2, 3 and 4 would correspond to a generalization of:

- [CITY:'Paris'] and [CITY:'Tokyo'] for answer 2.

- [DOLLAR] generalized with [YEN] to produce [CURRENCY], for answer 3.

- [DOLLAR] generalized with [MARK], [INCREASE] with [DECREASE] and [CITY:'Paris'] with [CITY:'Frankfurt'], for answer 4.

This last answer shows that it is necessary to restrict the generalization space by applying some heuristics. We choose to affect FOCUS labels to some concepts of the question in order to forbid generalization on these concepts. Our prototype automatically puts such a FOCUS label on all the concepts which come from the syntactic subject of the natural language question. Thus, in our example, the question graph Q is in fact:

```
Q = [EVOLUTION]-
    (AGT) → [DOLLAR: * <>FOCUS]
    (THEMA) → [INCREASE]
    (LOC) → [CITY:'Paris']
```

Therefore, answers 3 and 4 are not generated because they would imply a generalization on DOLLAR, which is the subject of the question. We could imagine a more flexible system where the user could indicate the focus of the question by pointing words with a mouse. We are currently evaluating the heuristics which automatically select the subject as focus, from the ergonomic point of view.

To summarize, the NO-BUT-1 strategy is able to generate answers like "No, but..", which are pertinent to the initial question. A question is relaxed by using a controlled generalization, using the focus of the question.

29.4 MORE COMPLEX CASES INVOLVING GRAPH SPLITTING

These are other cases where $PROJ(Q, S, *, *)$ fails. We shall examine here the case where $GEN(Q, S, Q')$ succeeds but where Q is not a simple restriction of Q'. Thus, $PROJ(Q', Q, Q1, Q2)$ produces a non-empty pending graph $Q2$. Such a case occurs if the question graph Q contains a first graph which can be matched to S and a second graph which needs a resolution on a graph other than S.

For example, if the question is "Is the dollar going up in Paris?", and if the text graphs are such that:

- S_{i-k} contains "In Paris, ... event1 ...".

- $S_{i-k+1}, \ldots, S_{i-1}$ contain descriptions of facts or events located in Paris, but without reference to this implicit location.

- S_i contains the target information about the fluctuation of the dollar (without mention of Paris, which is still implicit).

Thus, $S_i - k, \ldots, S_i$ is a discourse paragraph about the situation in Paris, but this location is only mentioned in the first sentence and is implicit in the others.

In this example, $Q1$ would correspond to "Is the dollar going up" and $Q2$ to "In Paris..". Thus, $Q1$ may be solved on S_i, and $Q2$ must be searched further back in the text, i.e. on the graphs $S_{i-1}, S_{i-2}, \ldots$

More generally, after evaluating $GEN(Q, S_i, Q')$ and $PROJ(Q', Q, Q1, Q2)$, we evaluate $PROJ(Q1, S_i, q, C)$. The graphs q and S_i are used to generate the first part of the answer. The remaining part $Q2$ is matched to $S_{i-1}, \ldots, S_{i-k}$.

In our example, if Q is:

```
Q = [EVOLUTION]-
    (AGT) → [DOLLAR: * <>FOCUS]
```

```
(THEMA)→[INCREASE]
(LOC)→[CITY:'Paris']
```

then $Q1$ will be:

```
[EVOLUTION]-
    (AGT)→[DOLLAR]
    (THEMA)→[INCREASE]
```

and $Q2$ will be:

```
[EVOLUTION]→(LOC)→[CITY:'Paris']
```

$Q2$ cannot be solved as it is on the graphs S_{i-k}. The right graph to search would be:

```
[ENTITY]→(LOC)→[CITY:'Paris']
```

In fact, we attach a FOCUS label to all concepts of $Q2$ which do not occur in $Q1$. Thus, the graph $Q2$ is generalized correctly during the search process on $S_{i-1}, \ldots, S_{i-k}$.

This backward search on the text must check the consistency of the paragraph $S_{i-k}, \ldots, S_i$. For this, we make sure that there is no location other than [CITY:'Paris'] mentioned in the graphs $S_{i-1}, \ldots, S_{i-k+1}$ before matching $Q2$ to S_{i-k}. This is a heuristics to check that we are in a paragraph about Paris but not about another location. More generally, we verify that the concepts of $Q2$ which are not in $Q1$ cannot be generalized with $S_{i-1}, \ldots, S_{i-k+1}$ before matching to S_{i-k}.

Finally, the target sentence is found to be S_{i-k} and matching $Q2$ to it produces the second part of the answer.

We call this case YES-2 strategy, YES because the answer may generally be prefixed by "yes", because $PROJ(Q1, S_i, q, C)$ succeeds, and 2 because the final answer needs two graphs S_i and S_{i-k} in order to be generated.

A final more complex case occurs when $PROJ(Q1, Si, *, *)$ fails. In this case, we apply the NO-BUT-1 strategy to solve $Q1$: we evaluate $PROJ(Q', S_i, q, C)$ and we search backwards for $Q2$ in the text as in the preceding case. For example, Q is "Is the dollar going up in Paris?". S_i contains "The dollar went down" and belongs to a paragraph about the situation in Paris. S_{i-k} contains "In Paris.." and S_{i-k+j}, for $j = 1$ to $k - 1$, does not contain a reference to another city or location. So, Q' will be "Is the dollar fluctuating?" and $Q2$ will be "In Paris..". The final answer will be "No, the dollar is going down in Paris", generated from S_i and S_{i-k}. We call this ultimate case a NO-BUT-2 strategy, because the answer may generally be prefixed by "No, but.." and because it is found in two distinct graphs.

The last part of the paper concerns the application of deduction rules. When the information retrieval system does not include such rules, it successively applies the YES-1, NO-BUT-1, YES-2 and NO-BUT-2 strategies. In KALIPSOS, the YES-1 strategy is the default one. When it fails, the user may select a more powerful strategy in a window, in the same way as one may select a competence level in a computer chess game.

29.5   LINEAR RESOLUTION METHOD AND INFORMATION RETRIEVAL

We begin by recalling the principle of the linear resolution method for Horn conceptual clauses. Other details may be found in Fargues (1986).

The method is similar to the linear resolution method of Prolog but acts on conceptual graphs instead of predicate terms.

A Horn conceptual clause has the form:

$G \leftarrow G_1, G_2, \ldots, G_n$., where $G, G_1, \ldots, G_n$ are conceptual graphs.

If $n = 0, G \leftarrow$. is a simple factual assertion, as for example a graph built from a sentence in the KALIPSOS system.

A goal clause has the form:

$\rightarrow A_1, A_2, \ldots, A_n$., where $A_1, \ldots, A_n$ are conceptual graphs.

A goal clause will be interpreted as "prove A_1 and A_2 and .. A_n", and a conceptual clause as: "to prove G, try to prove G_1, then G_2, and ... G_n".

For simplicity, we assume here that the goal clause has the simple form $\leftarrow +A$., where A is a single conceptual graph. The resolution principle is as follows:

We try to find a subgraph A' of A such that there exists a most general restriction of A' and of the head G of a conceptual clause. Thus, we compute a graph R equal to $\theta 1 A'$ and to $\theta 2 G$, where:

– A' is a subgraph of the goal A.

– $\theta 1 = \left[(c_1/e_1), \ldots, (c_n/e_n) \right]$ is a substitution of the concepts c_i of A', by restriction of these concepts.

– $\theta 2 = \left[(d_1/e_1), \ldots, (d_n/e_n) \right]$ is a substitution of the concepts d_i of G, by restriction of these concepts.

– $e_1, \ldots, e_n$ are the concepts of the graph R and are the most general common restrictions of the concepts c_i and d_i.

If these conditions are satisfied, the conceptual clause whose head is G may be applied to solve the goal A. We say that there is a matching of G in A. This matching algorithm cannot be expressed in terms of projection. It corresponds to a Prolog predicate:

$MATCHING(A, G, R, \theta 1, \theta 2, A', PA)$

which computes $R, \theta 1, \theta 2$, the subgraph A' of A and the remaining part PA in A.

During the resolution process, a current goal stack and a current result stack are updated according to the recursive call of the entire procedure. Initially, the goal stack contains A and the result stack contains NIL. After selecting the conceptual clause, the current goal A is removed from the goal stack. We put in this stack the pending part PA and the instantiated subgoals $\theta 2 G_1, \theta 2 G_2, .., \theta 2 G_n$. The temporary result stack contains $\theta 1 A$. At each step, the top current goal is extracted from the goal stack in order to be solved. The recursive application produces other subgoals which are appended to the goal stack. The final resolution of a goal occurs when this current goal may be projected on a factual clause. At each step, the $\theta 1$ substitutions update the result stack such that the final result is the goal A on which all the $\theta 1$ substitutions have been applied during the resolution process. At the end, if there is no loop in the conceptual clauses and if the initial goal is satisfied, the goal stack is empty and the result stack contains the instantiated initial goal.

This resolution method uses a graph-splitting technique: the pending part PA (if it exists) of the current goal A becomes a new subgoal to be solved. This may be compared to the graph splitting technique we introduced in the preceding section on information retrieval.

From a logic point of view, if Φ associates a logic formula to a conceptual graph, then the following hold:

1. $\Phi(\theta 2 G_1)$ & ... & $\Phi(\theta 2 G_n) \supset \Phi(\theta 2 G)$, by definition of a conceptual clause.

2. $\Phi(\theta 2G) \equiv \Phi(\theta 1 A')$, by definition of the matching algorithm.

3. $\Phi(\theta 1 A') \supset \Phi(A')$

4. $\Phi(A) \equiv \Phi(A')$ & $\Phi(PA)$, because PA is the pending part. If we assume that PA have been solved or is empty, $\Phi(PA) = true$ and therefore:

5. $\Phi(\theta 1 A') \supset \Phi(A)$ holds, from 3. and 4.

Finally, using 1, 2 and 5, we obtain:

$$\Phi(\theta 2G1) \ \& \ ... \ \& \\ \Phi(\theta 2Gn) \supset \Phi(A)$$

If on the other hand PA has been solved. By recursion on the terminal case where a goal can be projected on a factual graph, and because the propagation of the substitutions preserves the logic implications, this result indicates that the resolution process is well-founded.

At this point, we want to apply the information retrieval strategies detailed in the preceding sections and this linear resolution method together. This is not easy, because the conceptual clauses are strictly interpreted as logical implications but the NO-BUT-1 and NO-BUT-2 strategies do not preserve logical truth.

The KALIPSOS system we implemented was designed to perform intelligent information retrieval on natural language texts. Therefore we choose to emphasize this aspect and we suppose that a question will need the application of conceptual clauses only in a few cases. Therefore, we place the text graphs before the conceptual clauses in the memory. Thus, a question graph will always be matched on the text graphs before being solved on the head of a conceptual clause. There is no problem in using the YES-1 and YES-2 strategies to solve a current subgoal on the text graphs, because the projection preserves the truthvalue.

Thus, a question Q may be considered as a goal clause for the ordered set of clauses made up of:

- The sequence $S_1, S_2, \ldots, S_n$ of the text graphs.

- The sequence of conceptual clauses $G \leftarrow G_1, G_2, \ldots, G_n$.

The YES-1 and YES-2 strategies are used to match Q on $S_1, \ldots, S_n$. Then the resolution method is applied to solve Q with the conceptual clauses, but each subgoal G_i is matched on the S_j graphs (with YES-1 and YES-2 strategies) before being unified with the head of other clauses. When this strategy fails we apply the NO-BUT-1 and NO-BUT-2 strategies as described below:

We solve Q on the S_i target graph with such a strategy and we generate the corresponding "No, but.." answer. Then we apply the conceptual clauses to solve Q as usual, but if the resolution of a subgoal G_i fails (with YES-1 and YES-2) we try the NO-BUT-1 and NO-BUT-2 strategies for it. If the extended matching between G_i and some text graph S succeeds, the conceptual clause which contains G_i, with a failure message indicating that G_i should be generalized for a successful match could be displayed.

This information would be especially useful, because a successful generalization may suggest that:

- Either the deduction rule may be generalized to include more cases, or

- The deduction rule cannot be applied because the sentence S is contradictory to G_i. This is more informative than if G_i fails because no relevant information has been found in the text.

In both cases, the information we get is more pertinent than a simple failure.

Finally, we think that the simultaneous use of the linear resolution method, relaxation and graph-splitting makes it possible to find correct target graphs in a more flexible and satisfying way than by a simple logic resolution method or by a simple projection.

BIBLIOGRAPHY

Berard-Dugourd, A., J. Fargues, M.C Landaun, (1988) "Natural Language Analysis Using Conceptual Graphs", Proc. of the International Computer Science Conference '88 Hong-Kong, pp 265-272.

Berard-Dugourd, A., J. Fargues, MC. Landau, JP Rogala, (1988) "Natural Language Information Retrieval from French Texts", Proc. of the Third Annual Workshop on Conceptual Graphs, St Paul, Minnesota, August 88.

Fargues, J. MC Landau, A. Dugourd, L. Catach, (1986) "Conceptual Graphs for Semantics and Information Processing", IBM Journal of Research and Development, Vol 30, No 1, pp 70-79.

Sowa, J.F. (1984) *Conceptual Structures: Information Processing in Mind and Machine*, Systems Programming Series, Addison Wesley, Reading.

Part VI

Appendix and Bibliography

30

A Notation for Conceptual Structure Graph Matchers

Timothy E. Nagle and John W. Esch
Unisys Corp,
PO Box 64663, MS F2L09,
St. Paul, Mn, 55164-0525 USA

Guy Mineau
Département d'informatique,
Université Laval,
Ste-Foy, Québec, Canada, G1K 7P4

ABSTRACT

This chapter presents a notation for describing various types of graph matchers for conceptual structures. Algorithms for determining graph isomorphism and relatedness vary from well constrained matchers to very unconstrained matchers. The notation consists of a ten (10) position vector whose values describe the salient features that a matcher might include. It is hoped that such a notation would allow researchers in the conceptual structures community to express precisely what kind of matcher they need or what their matcher does.

30.1 BACKGROUND

During the Fourth Annual Workshop on Conceptual Structures in 1989, several working groups were organized to address various topics of interest to the conceptual structures community. One such working group was devoted to studying the issues of graph matching. It was felt that resolution, rule firing, graph generalization, and mapping analogies had issues in common relating to graph matching. Determining graph isomorphism has had a long history in the graph theoretic community and is recognized by AI researchers as a central problem. Fortunately, the structures and canonical operations in Sowa's conceptual structures provide constraints which often make the isomorphism problem tractable.

Members of the working group had noticed that, in the conceptual graph chapters presented over the last few years, those of us who were faced with the matching problem have built matchers which have been based on several simplifying assumptions such as, "this matcher will check the concept type labels without looking for super/sub types and will ignore the referent field". These simplifying assumptions often are derived from particular applications and result in graph matchers with various orders of complexity. While these simplifications are helpful in reducing the computational complexity, the large variety of assumptions which could be made, makes an analysis of conceptual graph matchers a difficult task.

The goals of the working group are to:

- determine the kinds of assumptions and restrictions of conceptual structure theory which could result in particular classes of matchers;

- catalogue these classes of matchers;

- estimate orders of computational complexity for similar matchers.

We expect that the information in this chapter would be useful for:

- communicating to each other what assumptions we are making about the attributes if the graphs our matchers are designed for;

- indicating a class of complexity which we might expect for a particular matcher. While measures of complexity are not presented at this time, this chapter does provide the structure needed to form such classes;

- enabling us to more easily compare one matcher with another, and answering questions such as:

  Do two matchers make the same assumptions?
  If they are in different classes, how does their complexity compare?
  What performance could we expect from a particular matcher?
  Have we accounted for all the components in the graph while mapping the requirements from a particular domain or application onto a particular matcher? (e.g. "Are referent fields needed?" or "Should it check for supertypes?")

30.2   PREVIOUS MATCHERS

Such information would have been useful during several of the previous Conceptual Structures Workshops where several matchers were discussed. Two of these were hardware-based matchers for conceptual structures. One of these was a vector based machine by George Lendaris (1988) at Portland State University, which directly supported conceptual structures. The other was a semantic network array processor into which conceptual structures would be translated by Dan Moldovan and Wing Lee (1989) at the University of Southern California. It was difficult to characterize and compare these two since they each made different assumptions about how the conceptual graphs would be handled and which components of the graphs they would handle. George's matcher could operate with the link direction turned on or off (with an accompanying space trade-off). In Dan and Wing's design, the supertype information was not used. By each researcher describing their matcher in some standard form it would be much easier to make comparisons.

Some systems, such as the system used in Debbie Leishman's analogy work (Leishman, 1989) or Guy Mineau's work on generalization hierarchies (Mineau, 1989), use much of the structure available in Sowa's definitions. This nicely restricts the complexity. On the other hand, in the 1988 workshop, Tim and Jan Nagle proposed a suite of matchers (Nagle and Nagle, 1988), some of which use only the relations and ignore concept labels altogether[1]. Other matchers in the suite, in extreme cases, ignore all of the labels in the entire graph only matching the skeleton of the graph (a completely unconstrained search). Also in the 1988 workshop Lisa Rao (1988) proposed a two stage search consisting of a coarse matching followed by an in-depth matching. A brief review of the last several years of workshop proceedings will show various classes of matchers which range from a full implementation of Sowa's structures (and are well constrained) to matchers which operate on structures that only vaguely resemble conceptual graphs, and ignore many of the structural constraints (and are very expensive).

30.3   ANALYSIS AND NOTATION

We have broken the analysis of matchers into three related groups: *content; structure;* and *control.* Theses groups are further decomposed into related sub-components as shown in Figs. 30.1-30.3 below.

By way of notation for Figs. 30.1-30.3, if a label is between the legs of a branch point (as the word "Labels" in Fig. 30.1), it is intended that the branch be an exclusive-or branch. If the label is between a branch and an end point of a branch (as the word "Concepts" in Fig. 30.1) it is intended to indicate an inclusive-or.

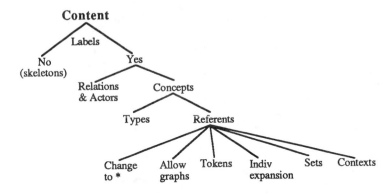

Fig. 30.1 Component Hierarchy

The nodes and leaves of these hierarchies identify possibilities for different kinds of matchers. These possibilities apply to both the components of a graph and the algorithm doing the matching. We have partitioned them according to the component or algorithm feature to which they apply. The result of this partitioning is a table with one column per feature. The entries in each column are the nodes and leaves from Figs. 30.1-30.3 that apply to it. The intent is that any particular matcher (there are several hundred of them) could be described by a ten (10) position vector. Each position in the vector usually contains a single value. In those cases where multiple values may be needed (such as specifing sets in the

---

[1] Similar to Dedre Gentner's Structure Mapping Engine (Gentner, 1986)).

referent field) the values should be contained within braces, {}. In general, the table was intended to have only one value per position. By describing the characteristics of a matcher in this way, researchers in the conceptual structures community can precisely specify the attributes of their particular matcher. Below we will describe the attributes of the component and algorithm control sections. It may be easier if we address these topics in reverse order.

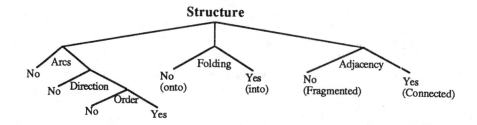

Fig. 30.2 Structure hierarchy

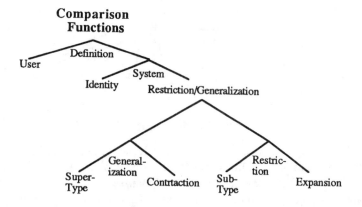

Fig. 30.3 Control hierarchy

30.3.1 Algorithm control

——————————— Components ———————————┐   ┌——————————— Algorithm Control

Concept		Referent		Relations/Actors		Arcs		Folding		Adjacency		Look Ahead		Find Count
no	None	no	None	no	None	no	None	no	None	fr	Fragments	n	n	n	nth
id	Identity	cg	Changed to *	id	Identity	nd	Non-Dir	fo	Folding	aj	Adjacency	r	Recursive	a	All
rg	Restrict/ Generalize	ag	Allow Graphs	rg	Restrict/ Generalize	dn	Direct/ non-Ordered					u	User		
gn	Generalize	ac	Allow Contexts	gn	Generalize	do	Direct/ Ordered								
sp	Super Type	at	Allow Tokens	sp	Super Type										
cn	Contraction	ix	Indiv Expansion	cn	Contraction										
rs	Restriction	{d,c,r}	Sets: {D,C,R}	rs	Restriction										
sb	Sub-Type	us	User	sb	Sub-Type										
ex	Expansion			ex	Expansion										
us	User			us	User										

———————————————┐

	Return Count		Return Function
n	n	n	None
a	All	u	User

Table 30.1 Matcher attributes and potential values.

In the Algorithm Control section of Table 30.1. there is a field headed "Folding". Folding refers to a counter-intuitive anomaly in matching. Normally, we would think of a larger graph as the more specific graph and the smaller as more general. An example might be:

G1: [Person: *] ← (agnt) ← [Likes:*]
G2: [Person: *] ← (agnt) ← [Likes:*] → (agnt) → [Person:*].

Where we would think of $G2$ as "A person likes another person." and $G2$ as more specific than $G1$. However, these two people may be the same, as "A person likes himself.". In this case, the [Person:*] concepts may be co-referent. Here the two concepts may be joined together and the agent relations simplified. This yields a contracted graph G3 which looks the same as $G1$. However $G3$ is more specific than either $G1$ or $G2$. This special case is called "Folding" and is a consideration in wether or not a matcher is designed to accommodate it.

The "Adjacency" field refers to the problem of fragmented matches. In the example below two subgraphs of $G5$, ($G5'$ and $G5''$) match subgraphs of $G4$ which are not connected (adjacent) to each other. The result is that there may be several fragments of $G4$ covered by $G5$ such that much or all of $G5$ is matched by some portion of $G4$.

G4: [Bill] –
    ← (agnt) ← [Own] → (ptnt) → [Tie]
    ← (agnt) ← [Likes] → (ptnt) → [Mary] ← (agnt) ← [Own]
                                          → (ptnt) → [Car]
G5: [Person] –
    ← (agnt) ← [Own] → (ptnt) → [Tie]

```
        ← (agnt) ← [Own] → (ptnt) → [Car]
G5':  [Person]  -
        ← (agnt) ← [Own] → (ptnt) → [Tie]
G5":  [Person]  -
        ← (agnt) ← [Own] → (ptnt) → [Car].
```

The term "look ahead" is used in Table 30.1 to indicate how many relation-concept pairs the matcher will pursue before it decides that the current concept is a match. For example, if the matcher only checked one concept at a time and the current node is [Wall], then the sub-graph $G6'$ has two possible matchings in graph $G7$. If the matcher were to look ahead one relation-concept pair, there would still be two possible matches. In this case, the matcher would have to look ahead two relation-concept pairs to find the proper binding for $G6'$.

```
G6:  [House] → (attr) → [Wall] → (matr) → [Brick]
                                        → (chrc) → [White]

G6': [Wall] → (matr) → [Brick] → (chrc) → [White]

G7:  [House]  -
        → (attr) → [Wall] → (matr) → [Brick] → (chrc) → [White]
        → (attr) → [Wall] → (matr) → [Brick] → (chrc) → [Brown]
```

There are three parameters for this field n, r, and u. The n specifies how many pairs to look ahead. The r indicates that the matcher will fully recurse through all the nodes in the sub-graph. The u specifies a user defined function to determine how far to look ahead and what to look at. It is assumed for n and r that when a relation is examined all of its arcs will be checked. However, there are cases where this may not be desirable or needed. Take for example the ternary relation in $G8$ which has a weight attached:

```
G8:  [Person]  →   (has-confidence)  -
              → [Fact: #123]
              → [Weight: @0.7].
```

We may be interested in matching the object of the relation [Fact:#123], but may not be interested in the value of the associated weight. In this case, the user specified function would treat the relation as binary rather than ternary.

It is possible that there may be several matches between graphs. The "Find Count" field specifies how many matches to attempt. For example, the graph $G9$ would have two possible matches in $G7$.

```
G9:  [House] → (attr) → [Wall] → (matr) → [Brick]
```

The "Return Count" field works in conjunction with the "Return Function" field. When several matches have been made, the value for this field specifies how many of the matches will be returned. The "Return Function" determines how the choice will be made. Some matchers may simply return the first one found. Others may use a measure of "semantic distance" similar to Foo (1989). For example, suppose that the type lattice has DWELLING > HOUSE; PARTITION > WALL; and SUBSTANCE > BRICK. A matcher may then determine that $G10$ matches $G7$. However, the semantic distance between $G10$ and $G7$ (by the type lattice) would be greater than the distance between $G9$ and $G7$.

> $G10$: [Dwelling] → (attr) → [Partition] → (matr) → [Substance]

In the future, if a standard set of functions for ranking similarity between graphs were to be developed, then they could generate the values for the Return Function field.

30.3.2 Components

When we match, it is possible to match the position of concepts in a graph and relations between them while ignoring the concepts type labels. The same is true for matching only concepts and ignoring the type of relations between them. In this case, we would use the values of "none" under the "Concepts" and "Relations/Actors" headings in the table. If we wanted to match only the relations and ignore the type of concepts, it would be similar to replacing all concept type labels with the Universal type label. In effect, we are matching the morphology of the concepts. Such a matcher is useful in finding analogies and metaphors. For example, to illustrate metaphor, Gentner (1983) quotes the poet Houseman, *"I could no more define poetry than a terrier can define a rat,"*. Here the mapping is not between the concepts of poets and terriers, and poetry and rats, but that, the relationship between a poet and poetry is like the relationship between a terrier and a rat. In this case we are not interested so much in the mapping of one concept to another, but in the relationships between them. Additionally, analogy can be characterized as a set of statements which share many relations and few attributes (ie. concepts) (Gentner, 1988). This would require a matcher which matched the relations between the concepts (Gentner's attributes) without regard to the concepts themselves.

30.4 ANNOTATED MATCHERS

If we constructed such a matcher, matching only the relation type labels, and using the concepts as place holders, we would have a matcher similar to Gentner's Structure Mapping Engine (Gentner, 1986). According to Table 30.1 we would specify "None" as the value under the "Concept" and "Referent" headings and some value other than "None" for the "Relations/Actors" heading. The descriptor for this matcher would be $\left[no, no, ex, do, x, x, x, x, x, x\right]$ (where the "x" indicates unspecified). In this case the relational structure of the graph would be matched with the relations playing the role of Gentner's propositions.

We could generalize this even further and make the relation type labels as well as the concept labels optional. In this case we would be matching an unconstrained bipartite digraph (the skeleton of a digraph) ie. just the graph morphology. This graph would be specified only by nodes (concepts) and directed unlabeled edges (the unspecified relations). Its description would be $\left[no, no, no, dn, x, x, x, x, x, x\right]$.

Besides specifing whether or not concept and relation labels are checked, we could also relax the constraints by allowing matchers which ignore the direction of the edges. This would be similar to an early specification of Lendaris's matcher (Lendaris, 1988).

Here he allowed an instance of a concept type to be connected to an instance of a relation but without the direction of the relation specified. The description of this matcher would be $[id, no, id, nd, x, x, x, x, x, x]$. His later matcher (Lendaris, 1989) would allow directions in the links as well as matching super and sub-types in the type lattice ($[rg, no, rg, dn, no, aj, 0, a, a, n]$).

The last step in relaxation is to allow the edges themselves to be optional. In this case a graph would be represented as a collection of concepts and relations with no specific relation to each other. This was used by Yim (1989) in his neural net matcher "ANNE". This would look for patterns of occurrence in sets of concepts and relations without the direction or connectivity information. It did not allow folding (as defined in the following section), graphs could be fragmented, had no look ahead, yet it would find all candidates and return the one with the highest strength. The description of ANNE would be $[id, no, id, no, no, fr, 0, a, 1, n]$.

One might wonder about the usefulness of such unconstrained matchers. One possible application of these levels of relaxation would be in a "graduated sieve" approach to matching a large set of graphs (such as in a knowledge base) to a target graph. In this case a series of "match steps" would be taken beginning with the least computationally expensive (and presumably least constrained) to the more expensive matches. At each step the potential set of graphs is narrowed until the best candidates are left for the most expensive matching. Also, when learning algorithms need to be applied to a large set of conceptual graphs (Mineau, 1990), some heuristics have to be used to make the problem more feasible. Compromising on the quality of the match is one such heuristic.

For example, one might imagine a simple counting of nodes to find a graph of approximately the right size. The graphs of the right size would then be matched by content only without regard for connectivity. That is to say, if our target graph is about cats and dogs, then our expensive matching set should be restricted to graphs with cat and dog content. Each step would become a more expensive step operating over consecutively smaller sets of match candidates until we have reached a predetermined level of specificity. That is, if our target graph contains [DOG:#123], we may only be interested in looking for graphs with generic referents ([DOG:*]) and not pay the expense of matching the referent field.

30.5   SUMMARY

This chapter specifies a set of characteristics of graph matchers appropriate to conceptual structures. A notation was developed and presented in the hopes that researchers could accurately specify requirements of a matcher needed or attributes of matchers they are proposing. Based on this notation, one could imagine a "matcher constructor" which would automatically build a matcher based on the specifications provided by this notation.

It is intended that this chapter be a living document and is expected to change as omissions are pointed out or suggestions are made. It is hoped that future revisions of this chapter would include measures of computational complexity for various classes of matchers.

BIBLIOGRAPHY

Foo, N., Garner, B., Rao, A., and Tsui, E. (1989) "Semantic Distance in Conceptual Graphs"; in Proc. of the Fourth Annual Workshop on Conceptual Structures. (eds) by J. Nagle and T. Nagle. Available from AAAI.

Gentner, D., Falkenhainer, B., and Forbus, K. (1986) "The Structure Mapping Engine"; Proc. of AAAI-86.

Gentner, D., and Clement, C.; (1988) "Evidence for Relational Selectivity in Interpreting Analogy and Metaphor" in *The Psychology of Learning and Motivation*, (ed) G. Bower, Academic Press; New York.

Gentner, D., (1983) "Structure-Mapping: A Theoretical Framework for Analogy"; Cognitive Science, vol. 7, pp. 155-170.

Lendaris, G., (1988) "Representing Conceptual Graphs for Parallel Processing"; Proc. of the Third Annual Workshop on Conceptual Graphs; AAAI-88, St. Paul, Mn.

Lendaris, G.; (1989) "Experiments on Implementing the Concept Type Lattice in a Neural Network"; in Proc. of the Fourth Annual Workshop on Conceptual Structures. (eds) J. Nagle and T. Nagle, Available from AAAI.

Leishman, D., (1989) "A Principled Analogical Tool: Based on Evaluations of Partial Correspondences Over Conceptual Graphs", Research Report No. 89/355/17; Dept. of Computer Science; University of Calgary; Calgary, Canada.

Mineau, G., (1989) "Induction on Conceptual Graphs: Finding Common Generalizations and Compatible Projections"; in Proc. of the Fourth Annual Workshop on Conceptual Structures. (eds) by J. Nagle and T. Nagle, Available from AAAI.

Mineau, G., Gecsei, J., and Godin, R.; (1990) "Structuring Knowledge Bases Using Automatic Learning"; Proc. of the 6th Int. Conference on Data Engineering; Los Angeles, Ca.

Moldovan, D., and Lee, W.; (1989) "SNAP: A Parallel Architecture for Semantic Networks"; in Proc. of the Fourth Annual Workshop on Conceptual Structures. (eds) by J. Nagle and T. Nagle, Available from AAAI.

Nagle, J., and Nagle, T.; (1988) "General Semantics and Educational Theory as a Model for Concept generalization and Exchange"; Proc. of the Third Annual Workshop on Conceptual Structures; AAAI-88, St. Paul, Mn.

Rau, L.; (1988) "Exploiting the Semantics of Conceptual Graphs for Efficient Graph Matching"; Proc. of the Third Annual Workshop on Conceptual Graphs; AAAI-88, St. Paul, Mn.

Yim, M.; (1989) "ANNE of Construct"; in Proc. of the Fourth Annual Workshop on Conceptual Structures. (eds) by J. Nagle and T. Nagle, Available from AAAI.

31

Linear Forms for Conceptual Structures

John W. Esch
Unisys Corp,
PO Box 64663, MS F2L09,
St. Paul, Mn, 55164-0525 USA

ABSTRACT

This chapter presents and discusses the syntax for the linear form (LF) of conceptual graphs (CGs). The preferred form for exchanging data is called the interchange format. The reader should be familiar with the chapter on Conceptual Graph Notation before studying this appendix. The syntax is based on papers presented at the Third and Fourth Annual Workshops on Conceptual Structures (Esch, 1989)and (Esch, 1990). It is divided into the following main sections:

1. Meta-Language Productions,

2. Low Level Productions,

3. Conceptual Graph Productions,

4. Referent Field Productions, and

5. Extended Form Productions.

The basic syntax is given explicitly in Sowa (1984) but many of the refinements and extensions are only given through examples. To help you find these definitions and examples, the notation (Sowa, 1984 p#) is used as a reference to page # of that book.

Each production is identified with a production number. The production numbers are not part of the production; they are only for identification. The first digit of each production number is the same as the section in which it is specified.

The productions in each section are followed by subsections. They describe existing, changed, or new syntax/semantics that are significant or need to be addressed. These subsections also refer back to the relevant productions.

The most significant changes from (Sowa, 1984) include the following. Syntax is given for how to handle comments in a file containing extended linear forms. In dataflow graphs, actors always need arcs to avoid ambiguity due to multiple outputs being allowed. In conceptual graphs, after a concept with multiple arcs, the continuation lines are indented and the arcs included. The syntax has been given for extended linear forms to specify canons, types, relations, actors, selecting graphs, assertions and individuals. A syntax is given to indicate a cross canon reference. Contexts are allowed to have arbitrary type labels. The syntax for referents is extended to allow a wide variety of domain specific things, like strings and literals.

31.1   META-LANGUAGE PRODUCTIONS (Sowa, 1984 p394)

100 Terminal symbols are denoted as strings, e.g. "cat". An embedded " is denoted by """" as in production 260.

110 Non-Terminal symbols are denoted by all caps, e.g. CONCEPT.

120 Alternatives are separated by a vertical bar "|", e.g. "0" | "1" means a "0" or a "1".

130 Groupings are contained in curly braces "{" and "}", e.g. {A B C} means A followed by a B followed by a C.

140 Alternatives are contained in curly braces "{" and "}" and separated by a vertical bar "|", e.g. {"←" | "→"} means either "←" or "→".

150 Options are contained in square brackets "[" and "]", e.g. [RLINK] means an optional RLINK and ["←" | "→"] means "←" or "→" or neither.

160 Repetition is denoted by "..." following a symbol, group, alternative or option, e.g. CGRAPH... means 1 or more CGRAPHs, { }... means 1 or more of the group or alternatives within a group, and [ ]... means 0 or more of the option or alternatives within the option.

170 Spaces, returns, linefeeds, tabs, etc. within a production are treated as a single space except within terminals or as otherwise explicitly noted by, e.g. a NEWLINE non-terminal. Where such a space occurs, it implies zero or more spaces, returns, linefeeds, tabs, etc. in the language being defined which are also interpreted as a single space for parsing; no space between successive terminals or non-terminals is interpreted as no space in the target language.

180 Comments in the meta and target languages are denoted by a double semicolon where the it and any other text remaining on the line are interpreted as an end of line.

31.1.1   Comments (See prods 180 & 250.)

A common practice is to store graphs in linear form in a file system. It is common to put a comment in the file describing its contents. One may also what to comment individual graphs or extended form statements. Each programming language has its own convention, so there is no standard way to specify comments. The convention of using some delimiter to indicate that the rest of the line is a comment is intuitive and easy to use and implement. The delimiter is the double semicolon, ";;", because it is not currently a delimiter used in conceptual graphs. (The previous choice of a single semicolon has been preempted by its use for annotation, a comment within a node.)

31.2 LOW LEVEL PRODUCTIONS

200	DIGIT	→ "0" | "1" | "2" | "3" | "4" | "5" | "6" | "7" | "8" | "9"
202	NUMBER	→ DIGIT...
204	LETTER	→ "A" | "B" | "C" | "D" | "E" | "F" | "G" | "H" | "I" | "J" | "K" | "L" | "M" | "N" | "O" | "P" | "Q" | "R" | "S" | "T" | "U" | "V" | "W" | "X" | "Y" | "Z"
206	PUNCTUATION	→ "[" | "]" | "(" | ")" | "{" | "}" | "<" | ">" | "@" | "#" | "*" | "," | "." | ":" | " " | " " | TAB | LAMBDA | FORALL
208	EOL	→ EOF | RETURN | NEWLINE | COMMENT
210	OTHER-CHAR	→ character-other-than-digit-letter-punctuation-or-eol
220	NAME-CHAR	→ DIGIT | LETTER | OTHER-CHAR
230	TEXT-CHAR	→ NAME-CHAR | PUNCTUATION
240	TEXT	→ {TEXT-CHAR}...
250	COMMENT	→ ";;"TEXT
260	STRING	→ """TEXT"""
270	IDENTIFIER	→ LETTER[NAME-CHAR]...
280	NAME	→ {LETTER | DIGIT}[NAME-CHAR]...
290	LONG-NAME	→ NAME{[" "]...NAME}... ;;a sequence of names

31.3 CONCEPTUAL GRAPH PRODUCTIONS (Sowa, 1984 pp 395 88 139 188)

300	CGRAPH	→ C-NODE | RELATION CONLINK | ACTOR CONLINK
310	C-NODE	→ CONCEPT [RLINK]
312	R-NODE	→ RELATION [CONLINK]
314	A-NODE	→ ACTOR [CONLINK]
320	CONCEPT	→ IND-CONCEPT | CONTEXT | EXIST-REF | STR-CONCEPT
322	IND-CONCEPT	→ "[" [TYPEFIELD] [REFFIELD] [ANNOTATION] "]"
324	TYPEFIELD	→ [NOT]TYPELABEL | LAMBDA-EXP
326	EXIST-REF	→ "[" [[TYPELABEL] ":"] "*"GENERIC-REF "]"
328	STR-CONCEPT	→ "[" STRING "]" ;;short for [WORD: STRING]
330	RELATION	→ "(" [NOT]TYPELABEL [ANNOTATION] ")"
340	ACTOR	→ "<" TYPELABEL [ANNOTATION] ">"
350	CONLINK	→ ARC C-NODE | "-" CONLIST
352	RLINK	→ {ARC R-NODE | ARC A-NODE} | "-" RLIST
354	CONLIST	→ {NEWLINE ARC C-NODE }... ","
356	RLIST	→ {NEWLINE {ARC R-NODE | ARC A-NODE} }... ","
360	TYPELABEL	→ LONG-NAME ["@"CANON-NAME]
362	CANON-NAME	→ NAME
364	ANNOTATION	→ ";" LONG-NAME
370	CONTEXT	→ [NOT] "[" {CGRAPH}... "]"
372	NEG-CONTEXT	→ NOT CONTEXT
374	NOT	→ " "
376	LAMBDA-EXP	→ LAMBDA "(" GENERIC-REF ")" CGRAPH
380	ARC	→ [NUMBER] { "←" | "→" }
390	GENERIC-REF	→ IDENTIFIER

31.3.1   Actor Arcs in Dataflow Graphs (See prod 356.)

In dataflow graphs, requiring arcs for actors is needed because an actor can have multiple outputs. The rule used for relations works because they have exactly one output. Because actors can have zero or more outputs, the same rule can not be used. There is no problem with the graph: `<A0>→[C0]→<A1>` because the arcs are explicit. However, the graph:

```
[C0]-
    <A0>
    <A1>,.
```

is ambiguous because, with either no outputs or no inputs being allowed, there are four graphs possible. With actors, the arcs must always be present which leads to:

```
[C0]-
    ←<A0>
    →<A1>,.
```

31.3.2   Continuation Arcs in Conceptual Graphs (See prod 356.)

Similar conceptual graphs can be drawn using relations instead of actors. But, because relations have exactly one output, such conceptual graphs can be interpreted unambiguously. However, they are easier to read if the arcs are given explicitly rather than implied. The syntax specified in Sowa (1984) is optional. The interchange format requires the arcs, as given in the production and shown below.

```
OPTIONAL        FORM
[C]             [JUMP]-          [C0]-
    (R1)            (NECS)           (R1)
    (R2),.          (PAST),.         (R2)-
                                      2←[C1]
                                      3→[C2],,.

INTERCHANGE     FORM
[C]             [JUMP]-          [C0]-
    ←(R1)           ←(NECS)          ←(R1)
    ←(R2),.         ←(PAST),.        1→(R2)-
                                      2←[C1]
                                      3→[C2],,.
```

The conclusion drawn from sections 31.3.1 and 31.3.2 is that the interchange format should not have any implied arcs; they should all be given explicitly.

31.3.3   Existential References (See prod 326.)

An EXIST-REF is an existential reference. It normally appears in extended form statements where negation is involved. It asserts that some referent exists. It has the form of an optional type followed by a variable, GENERIC-REF, specifying the referent. A GENERIC-REF is a name for a lambda variable that appears three places. One is in production 326 as part of the referent field of an existential reference. Another is as the variable of the genius concept of some CGRAPH. The last is in various extended form statements where the lambda variables are identified for some CGRAPH to follow. If both an existential reference and a genus concept are part of an extended form statement, they are coreferent.

31.3.4   Type Labels & Cross Canon References (See prod 360.)

In the theory of conceptual graphs the analog of a knowledge base is a canon. It differs from traditional knowledge bases in that it provides a formal mathematical definition of a knowledge base. Canons also provide modularization of knowledge with related knowledge being stored as part of the same canon. However, with modularization comes the problem of referencing one canon from another. For example, how does one distinguish my definition of CAT from your definition of CAT?

To solve this problem, cross canon references are defined. They amount to extending the definition of the TYPELABEL to allow a syntax for referencing a type in another canon. The particular syntax is not as important as the idea. Here we propose allowing a typelabel to have an optional suffix canon reference consisting of @CANON-NAME. An "@" was chosen for the delimiter because it is already used for punctuation in the referent-field but not, as yet, in the typelabel field.

For example, if there are canons representing directories for two different companies, IBM and UNISYS and if we have a working canon in which we want to reference both the directory canons, then we have a referencing pattern like the following:

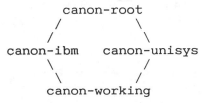

The following are statements containing example cross canon references:

```
CANON canon-root .
TYPE person(p) IS [univ:*p].

CANON canon-ibm .
TYPE john(j) IS [person@canon-root:*j] → (lastname) → [sowa].

CANON canon-unisys .
TYPE john(j) IS [person@canon-root:*j] → (lastname) → [esch].

CANON canon-working .
CANONICAL-GRAPH
    [john@canon-unisys] → (knows) → [john@canon-ibm].
```

The default is that a type without the canon qualifier is in the current canon. Thus, most graphs look the same. Its only when the type is defined by another canon that the optional qualifier is needed. With the graphical notation developed in the Display Forms and Polymorphism chapter, the cross canon referent is drawn as a type coreferent connection across canons.

31.3.5   Annotations (See prods 322, 330, 340 & 364.)

The annotation field is provided for use by the application. It does not participate in the semantic denotation of the graphs. It is, in effect, a form of comment. It differs from ordinary comments in that it is kept as part of the graph when the linear forms are parsed. The ordinary comments are lost; that is, they have no place in the internal representation. If a canon that has been parsed into some internal representation is written back out to a file in linear form format, the comments would be lost but the annotation would be retained. An example is:

```
[CAT] ← (AGNT; subj) ← [CHASE; v, active] → (PTNT; obj) → [MOUSE].
```

31.4   REFERENT FIELD PRODUCTIONS (Sowa, 1984 pp85 88 90 119 143-5 192)

The referent field has become the most complex part of the linear form notation. It is like a sublanguage unto itself. See the chapter on Conceptual Graph Notation for many other examples.

The following simplifies the syntax and generalizes the interpretation based on the principal of polymorphism as described in the chapter on Display Forms and Polymorphism and in (Esch, 1989). In effect, any referent can optionally have a name, aliases, and variable(s). The referent field consists of an ordered list of optional fields where each field is introduced by its own unique delimiter. This simplifies syntax, parsing, and semantics and allows for other extensions. For a discussion of extended referent field syntax see the chapter 3 on page 69.

31.4.1   Propositions & Typed Contests (See prods 370 & 420.)

PROPOSITIONs, as defined in Sowa (1984), are a special kind of concept, one that takes a graph or set of graphs as its referent. Sowa (1984) also allows the PROPOSITION typelabel to be optional so that `[[graph1] [graph2]]` is equivalent to `[PROPOSITION:[graph1] [graph2]]`. However, Sowa (1988) presents cases where contexts have type labels of SITUATION and GRAPH. In Esch (1989)[1] a case is made for allowing arbitrary type labels; that is, for interpreting contexts as a special kind of referent rather than a special kind of concept. In keeping with this last view, the above productions allow:

"[" [TYPELABEL":"] CONTEXT "]" as the typical linear form.

31.4.2   Literals & Lists (See prods 450 & 452.)

Concepts are about some individual which may be known or not (generic). These individuals may have names as in `[CAT:Felix]`. Concepts can be about other things such as numbers `[NUMBER:15]`. Here "15" is used to name the abstract concept of the number fifteen. The question arises, what kinds of names do we need for other things such as `[RATIO:1/3]`. The general case is `[FANCY:ffff]` were FANCY is some domain specific typelabel and

---

[1] And to a lesser extent in chapter 6 of this book.

ffff is the name of an individual of type FANCY. An example is [LIST: (a b)]. Here (a b) is the name of a particular LIST just as "15" is the name of a particular NUMBER.

The question is, how does one provide for a nearly arbitrary syntax for names? Within the framework of the Sowa (1984) syntax one can do fairly well by providing an explicit delimiter to delineate the name. The * beginning a variable, the { beginning a set, and the # beginning an individual marker indicate the parts of a name. However, in some cases the referent can be a graph which could begin with a (. This case is hard to distinguish from LIST:(.

The solution to this problem was suggested by Professor James Slagle of the University of Minnesota. His idea was to adopt the "quote" from the LISP programming language. There, a single quote mark in front of an expression indicates that it should not be evaluated but taken as is. Such a convention is adopted for referents where a single quote means to take the referent as is, not interpreted. Thus, [LIST:' (a b)] is a concept about a list whose referent was the uninterpreted value (ab). If an interpreter was given for concepts of type LIST, it might interpret this value (using the type definition in (Sowa, 1984 p121) to obtain the graph

```
[LIST: [DATA:*x] -
(HEAD) → [DATA:'a]
(TAIL) → [DATA:'b]] .
```

This graph referent can, with individualization, be simplified to [LIST: #list0521]. See Esch (1989 p9) for a little more on this idea.

31.4.3   Better Set Category Denotations (See prod 430.)

The syntax given in (Sowa, 1984) for denoting sets is confusing. As specified here, there is just one syntax inside the set and an optional keyword before the set indicates what kind of set it is. Also, the default for the option should be DIST not COLL.

31.4.4   Quantification & Quantities (See prods 420 & 440.)

Early versions in (Sowa, 1984) have given way to the form specified here from (Sowa, 1988) and the chapter on Conceptual Graph Notation. The # gives emphasis to a set; e.g. [CAT: {**}#] corresponds to "the cats." The FORALL denotes the extent of the set or, if no set is given, of the type; And @ gives a way to specify an exact number; e.g. [CAT: {**}@3] corresponds to "three cats."

31.5   EXTENDED FORM PRODUCTIONS (Sowa, 1984 pp106 114 119 129 136 146-8)

Files of conceptual graph linear forms consist of comments, linear form graphs, and extended linear forms. Extended linear forms are used for specifying the definition graphs for concept types, relation types, and actor types. They are also used for specifying schemata, canonical graphs, selecting graphs, and individuals. They are needed to build a canon.

To be able to exchange canons, an interchange format for specifying the extended liner forms as well as the canon itself is defined in this section. Three productions, 510, 524 & 528, were not given in (Sowa, 1984) but follow the same general format.

500	LF-FILE	→ {STATEMENT | COMMENT}...
502	STATEMENT	→ {CGRAPH | OTHER-STM} "."
504	OTHER-STM	→ CANON-STM | TYPE-STM
		| RELATION-STM | ACTOR-STM
		| SCHEMA-STM | PROTO-STM
		| SELECTING-STM | INDIVIDUAL-STM
		| CANONICAL-STM
510	CANON-STM	→ "CANON" CANON-NAME ["IS" CGRAPH]
512	TYPE-STM	→
	"TYPE"	[NOT]TYPELABEL ARG "IS" [EXIST-REF] CGRAPH
514	RELATION-STM	→
	"RELATION"	[NOT]TYPELABEL ARGS "IS" [EXIST-REFS] CGRAPH
516	ACTOR-STM	→
	"ACTOR"	TYPELABEL ARGS "IS" CGRAPH
520	SCHEMA-STM	→
	"SCHEMA"	TYPELABEL ARGS "IS" CGRAPH
522	PROTO-STM	→
	"PROTOTYPE"	TYPELABEL ARGS "IS" CGRAPH
524	SELECTING-STM	→
	"SELECTING-GRAPH"	TYPELABEL "IS" CGRAPH
526	INDIVIDUAL-STM	→
	"INDIVIDUAL"	TYPELABEL IND "IS" CGRAPH
528	CANONICAL-STM	→
	"CANONICAL-GRAPH"	"IS" CGRAPH
530	CANON-NAME	→ IDENTIFIER
540	ARG	→ "(" IDENTIFIER ")"
550	ARGS	→ "(" IDENTIFIER {","IDENTIFIER}... ")"
560	EXIST-REFS	→ {EXIST-REF}...
570	IND	→ "(" ["#"]IDENTIFIER ")"

31.5.1   Canon Statements (See prod 510.)

Each CANON statement establishes the named canon as the current canon. Each canon optionally contains a type lattice, individuals conforming to those types, a canonical basis, and other graphs. The type lattice, individuals, and canonical basis are established by extended linear forms. Each of the extended linear forms involves a graph. These graphs form the canonical basis[2]. The CGRAPH linear forms of production 502 establish other graphs in the canon that are not part of the canonical basis. (See Esch (1990) and the chapter in this book on Graphical Displays and Polymorphism for more on canons.)

The CGRAPH associated with a CANON statement is optional. If given, the graph specifies information about the canon. Examples of such information are the file in which it is stored and the person responsible for the canon.

31.5.2   Type, Relation, & Actor Statements (See prods 512, 514 & 516.)

These statements add the named type to the type hierarchy (lattice) of the current canon. An implementation should form separate type, relation, and actor lattices. These can be organized as part of higher order types (Sowa, 1990).

These statements establish CGRAPH as a differentia graph. It specifies necessary and sufficient conditions for a graph or a subgraph of a larger graph to be considered an instance

---

[2]Note, however, that the denotation for selecting, schemata, and prototype graphs have not been well-defined yet.

of the type being defined. Thus, it can be used for either or both creating or recognizing new individuals.

The ARGS define lambda variables which match the genus nodes in the CGRAPHs and, for negative definitions, also the existential references (EXIST-REFs) which are coreferent with their corresponding genus.

31.5.3   Schemata & Prototype Statements (See prods 520 & 522.)

These statements establish CGRAPH as information relevant to the type named. Their semantics is established by application programs. (Sowa, 1984) discusses some suggested interpretations but there are no semantics formally defined for these statements.

31.5.4   Selecting & Canonical Graph Statements (See productions 524 & 528.)

A canonical graph statement adds CGRAPH to the canonical basis of the current canon's context. It, in effect, specifies an assertion that is true in the current canon.

A selecting graph statement defines CGRAPH to be a selecting graph and establishes it as a selectional constraint for the type named. If one is specified for a type, it means that nodes of that type, in any graph in any canon, must satisfy the constraints specified for those nodes to be considered semantically well-formed.

31.5.5   Individual Statements (See prods 526 & 570.)

An IND is a name that is unique in the current context or an individual marker #IDENTI-FIER. An individual statement establishes IND to be an individual in the current canon. It establishes CGRAPH as the graph defining it. Normally, CGRAPH is a copy of the type definition graph for TYPELABEL which has been specialized.for individual IND.

However, this CGRAPH could also be a single concept of the individual's type with an un-interpreted referent. An example is `INDIVIDUAL LIST(#list0521) IS [LIST:` `'(a b)]`. (See section 31.4 above for the resulting expansion.)

31.6   SUMMARY

This appendix specifies and discusses the syntax for conceptual structures. That syntax consists of a number of changes and extensions to the syntax given in (Sowa, 1984).

The syntax specified here defines an interchange format for conceptual graphs. Such an interchange format allows communication of graphs and canons among machines, projects, and researchers.

To be complete, any software supporting conceptual graphs must also support graphical displays that are isomorphic to the linear forms. The chapter in this book on Graphical Displays and Polymorphism defines such an isomorphism.

BIBLIOGRAPHY

Esch, J. "Toward An Interchangeable Linear Form For Conceptual Graphs," Proc. Third Annual Workshop on Conceptual Graphs, Aug. 27, 1988.

Esch, J. "Conceptual Graph Linear Forms," Proc. Forth Annual Workshop on Conceptual Graphs, Aug. 20-21, 1988.

Esch, J., Timothy. E. Nagle, Morgan. L. Yim & Laurie. L. Gerholz, "Resolving Polymorphism in the Theory of Conceptual Graphs," Proc. Forth Annual Workshop on Conceptual Graphs, Aug. 20-21, 1988.

Esch, J. "Graphical Displays for Conceptual Structures," Proc. Fifth Annual Workshop on Conceptual Graphs, July 29, 1990.

Gardiner, D., Bosco Tjan, and James R. Slagle, "Extended Conceptual Structures Notation,", Proc. Fourth Annual Workshop on Conceptual Structures, (eds) J. Nagle & T. Nagle Ed., Detroit, Mich., Aug. 20-21, 1989.

Sowa, J.F. *Conceptual Structures: Information in Mind and Machine*, Addison-Wesley, Reading, MA, 1984.

Sowa, J.F. "Conceptual Graph Notation,", Proceedings Third Annual Workshop on Conceptual Graphs, (ed) J. Esch, Aug. 27, 1988.

Sowa, J.F. "Definitional Mechanisms For Restructuring Knowledge Bases," John F. Sowa, *Methodologies for Intelligent Systems 5*, (ed) Z. W. Ras, North-Holland Publishing Co., 1990.

32

Conceptual Graphs and Modalities

Jerrold L. Aronson
Philosophy and Computer and System Science,
State University of New York,
Binghamton, New York 13901, USA

Contrary-to-fact conditionals or counterfactuals, such as "If I were to release this chalk it would fall" or 'If it weren't for the fact that Mary overslept the day of the final she would have gotten an 'A' in her philosophy course', are some of the most important types of statements made in natural language. Other modal statements are just as important, e.g., 'Don't drink the wine!' says Hercule Poirot, 'It could very well kill you, *mon ami.*'

Conceptual graphs are intended to capture the meaning of all types of sentences, including those modal sentences that are to be found at the heart of everyday and scientific discourse; yet, the status of modal sentences *vis a vis* conceptual graphs is not all that clear.

What is the relationship between modal and non-modal conceptual graphs? Sowa (1984), Foo and Rao (1986) appear to think that modal operators are the key to answering this question, i.e., modalities are introduced by incorporating possible world semantics into conceptual graphs. Thus, the meaning of a modal sentence is generated by operating (possibility, necessity, etc.) on a non-modal conceptual graph. Yet, in other places, Sowa appears to maintain that laws of nature generate modalities, without the application of possible world semantics: possibility and necessity are explicated in terms of what is and what is not compatible with the laws of nature (Sowa, 1984, p.184).

In agreement with Sowa's latter position, possibility and necessity should be explicated in terms of lawlike permissibility instead of possible world semantics. For one thing, for it is not at all clear, in fact, it is highly doubtful that ordinary language users have possible worlds in mind when uttering sentences, such as 'If that ball were hit in Wrigley Field it would not have been a home run'. While a case can be made that possible worlds semantics can account for modalities in the predicate calculus, it is highly contentious that it provides a semantics of modalities for natural language. For example, if someone stated a possibility, that person would have to believe that there is a possible world in which such a possibility actually exists, for to say "'X is possible'is true.'" amounts to saying that there exists a possible world where 'X is true.'

While modal systems have the power and virtues of other formal systems, there are several criticisms in the philosophical literature of their application to everyday situations. (For example, see Bennett, Sloate.) They won't be taken up here, but when all is said and done, they should motivate us to seek an entirely different approach to characterizing modal conceptual graphs.

Instead of having an array of possible worlds, related by similarity, as our knowledge base underlying modal sentences, my view is that possible world semantics must be replaced by 'folk science', i.e., models and laws about the world which are learned and passed down from generation to generation, although not formally expressed in textbooks. Of course, many results of formal science can be and are incorporated into folk science. Thus, the problem of modalities is how to come up with a way to represent folk theories and laws.

This folk science approach is to be contrasted with P. Hayes' naive physics (1985). His approach has the virtue of replacing possible worlds with axioms and rules. Nevertheless, I still think his logicizing common sense reasoning fails to capture how folk science deals with modal reasoning. This is because Hayes works within a representational framework of the predicate calculus and, I maintain, the predicate calculus can not adequately represent the <u>models</u>, laws and counterfactuals in folk science. In fact, it was the failure of the predicate calculus to do this that made many philosophers turn to modal systems.

It is important to realize that if we are to use Hayes' system of naive physics to represent counterfactual claims, we end up with a version of modal knowledge representation known as the consequence theory: counterfactual conditionals are material conditionals that follow logically from laws – which are also conditionals – and initial conditions. For example, 'If I were to strike this match, it would light' is analyzed:

1. $D \wedge O \wedge C \wedge \neg S \neg L$

2. $(D \wedge O \wedge C \wedge S) \supset L$ 'If then' rule

3. Therefore, $S \supset L$

Where O is "The match is in the presence of oxygen", D - "The match is dry", C - "The match consists of combustible material", S - "The match is struck", L - "The match light".

If we are committed to the 'if then' rule approach about what would happen when, then add conditions until the appropriate conditional ensues. In this case, it is $S \supset L$. Unfortunately, Goodman (1955) has shown that such a program not only generates conditionals which are reasonable, the very same information yields contrary,counterintuitive conditional along side the desire ones. For example, 1 and 2 entail that if the match is struck, it will not be dry ($S \supset \neg D$) and, hence, won't light ($S \supset \neg L$). Goodman calls this the cotenability problem.

What this means is that any program based on 'If then' rules will not only generate the right conditionals but the wrong ones, as well, leaving us with an unworkable knowledge representation system for counterfactual claims. We could go about, ad hoc, ruling out the non-intuitive cases but this just dramatizes the failure of a system based on the predicate calculus, for our basis for ruling out such undesirable counterfactuals must come from another, independent source. For example, Goodman points out that ruling out $S \supset \neg D$ means that we must establish the truth of another counterfactual: If the match were struck, it would remain dry. But establishing this counterfactual has the same problems built in. In other words, establishing maintaining conditions for counterfactuals using conditions and 'If then' rules leads to a vicious regress.

There is another, related problem with the rule approach: the myriad of facts and rules appears totally undifferentiated to the computer programmed in the manner Hayes proposes.

There is no way for the computer to glean out the relevant facts and rules for a particular situation. For example, in the match example, it is not clear what conditions will determine whether the match would, in fact, light when struck. Perhaps, the population in China is a factor, perhaps not. But the point is that the above approach does not allow us to chunk initial conditions and rules in order to distinguish relevant from irrelevant information in our knowledge representation. In fact, it looks like the computer would have to carry on an indefinite search of all the conditions and laws in order to see if the totality of facts actually ends up ruling out or establishing the truth of a particular counterfactual.

Hayes is quite aware of this problem, which he calls the frame problem. Although he and others have written extensively about this problem, I don't think it can be solved by working within Hayes' framework of 'If then" rules. He believes that "the frame problem arises in attempts to formalize problem solving procedures interactions within a complex world" (1973, p.45) while I maintain the problem is a direct result of his commitment to the use of material implication to generate inferences about the world. On the contrary, I contend that material implication should be purged from any system of knowledge representation, including conceptual graphs.

So, both the modal logic approach and the 'If then' rule approach are beset with problems. The key to solving them is to come up with a proper way to represent theories, models and laws within the framework of folk science, and then see where modal propositions fit into such a scheme. What I am proposing is that if laws and theories are so properly represented, we can come up with a version of the consequence approach to counterfactuals which is readily incorporated into conceptual graphs and free of the above problems.

I have maintained elsewhere (1988, 1990) that theories, in part, are depictions of natural kinds and the way they are ordered. This means that theories are much more than sets of propositions, and that a set of 'If then' rules can not capture the content of a theory. According to the picture of theories I'm trying to present, 'If then' rules are generated by the laws of a theory and these laws are, indeed, just part of the picture. What we have is this. If theories are depictions of natural kinds, then type hierarchies provide the perfect means of representation. At the base of a theoretical hierarchy are systems of objects. They, in turn, pick out various supertypes in the hierarchy. For example, if Snoopy is a dog, Snoppy is a mammal is an animal, and so on. A rock is a collection atoms is a collection of protons and neutrons is a collection of quarks and gluons, and so on. What serves as a model for a system depends, in part, on how closely the model system resembles the real thing; I have shown elsewhere (1990) that this depends on the relative locations of the model system and the real system[1].

We can speak of the metaproperties at each node of the hierarchy. For example a metaproperty of being a mammal might be the possession of a characteristic genetic structure, a property inherited by all mammalian subtypes. Another, very important metaproperty of a given type are lawlike relations among its properties. In contrast to the traditional view, laws are not thought of as universal conditionals but instead as invariant relations among properties[2]; and, in accordance with the inheritance relation, lawlike relations are inherited by the subtypes which are linked below. For example, in the Bohr model of the atom,

---

[1] This picture of theories and models relies heavily on Eileen C. Way's work on dynamic type hierarchies (Way, 1990).

[2] The details of this characterization of laws can be found in my (1989), pp. 224-228.

the solar system and the atom are subtypes of central force fields. Now there is a general equation or law for all types of central force fields, of which the equations governing planetary motion and electron motion are instances albeit different ones.

I stated above the lawlike compatibility is the source of modalities instead of possible worlds. In order for something to be possible, it must be lawlike permissible. For example, Newton's second law tells us that is possible to accelerate a mass of one gram to any velocity while the laws of relativity say that this is not possible because such an event is incompatible with the Lorentz transformation. But there is more to possibility than compatibility with laws. The system in question

must have the "right stuff", i.e., it must have properties that allow the lawlike relation in question to hold. For example, Newton's laws do not hold for rays of light because light rays do not possess mass while Maxwell's laws of electromagnetic radiation obviously do not apply to billiard balls;however,both sets of laws would apply to magnetic billiard balls moving in an electric field. Lawlike relations, then, must be relativized to systems according to their properties.

So, there are two parts to lawlike expressions: those conditions for which the relationship between properties hold and the relationship itself. So, instead of representing a law as a universal conditional, $\forall x \ (F(x) \supset G(x))$, we say: once an object satisfies conditions, $C_1, \ldots, C_n$, the relationship among its properties, R holds for that object. Formally, this means that instead of a law being represented by a relationship between sentences or propositions, we have a mapping, $f*$, its domain being the set of ontological conditions and while its range is the set of ordered n-tuples: $C_1, \ldots, C_n \to \{< a_1, a_2, \ldots, a_n >\}$. For example, consider Newton's second law, $F = ma$, which applies to mass points. In this case, we have $f* : m \to \{< F, a >\}$, i.e., given that a body gas such and such mass various accelerations go with various forces. Its conceptual graph would look like this:

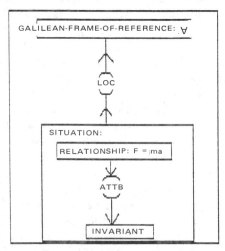

Fig. 32.1

Notice, spacetime invariance replaces possible world operators in the above graph.

Now we can explicate modalities in terms of laws. We have seen that possibility requires that the event in question is lawlike permissible for a system that satisfies the prerequisite conditions for said lawlike relationship to apply. For example, to say that the drink can possibly kill you means that it has the right stuff (chemical make-up), such that entering a biological system of a certain type would cause that system to cease to function.

> P is possible for x if and only if x satisfies $C_1, \ldots, C_n$ of a lawlike relationship, where P is the second (or more) member of one of the n-tuples of the range of $f*$.

Of course, if the drink doesn't have the right stuff, it can't possibly poison you, i.e., no lawlike relationship has death as a result of imbibing the drink.

> P is impossible for x if and only if there are no $C_1, \ldots, C_n$ that x satisfies, such that P is the second (or more) member of one of the n-tuples of the range $f*$ of a lawlike relationship.

Again, there is no mention of possible worlds in the above depictions of possibility and impossibility.

> Necessity naturally follows:

> P is necessary for x if and only if x satisfies $C_1, \ldots, C_n$ of a lawlike relationship where P is the second (or more) member of all of the n-tuples of the range of $f*$.

So, no matter what happens to x, P will occur. For example, the laws of relativity are such that no matter what we do to a material system, it will always move slower than the velocity of light.

> Now consider counterfactuals or contrary-to-fact conditionals. To say, 'If this chalk were released it would fall' means that the situation of the chalk being located in a gravitational fields has the right stuff for Newton's laws to apply; and, the laws are such that releasing the chalk is coupled with its falling. In general:'If P were the case, Q would have occurred for x if and only if $C_1, \ldots, C_n$ is true of x and there is an $f*$ with $C_1, \ldots, C_n$ as its domain while $< P, Q >$ is a member of the range of $f*$.

We thus have a characterization of counterfactuals and, I suggest, 'If then' statements where material conditionals are replaced by mappings and n-tuples. The paradoxes of material implication and many other problems associated with the logic of counterfactuals and 'If then' statements in natural language are avoided.

The above depiction of counterfactuals leaves us with this recipe for determining the truth of a counterfactual claim. What we are seeking is the relevant law for the system in question, an R where P and Q are the only variables. Since lawlike relations involve several variables, we want to factor out P and Q. In the chalk example, Newton's laws contain many more variables than net forces and falling to the earth. So, we must combine the laws until the removal of a force on the chalk and a directed motion (acceleration) variables are isolated. Then we see if removing the force that supports the chalk and acceleration of the chalk toward the ground are one of the ordered pairs of that functional relation.

What lawlike relations apply to a given system? That depends on what type of system it is. Once that is determined, we can ascertain those laws that hold for the system by seeing what supertypes it picks out. Those laws that apply are some of the metaproperties of each

supertype. We then combine the laws to factor out the antecedent and consequent variables
of the counterfactual in question, as described above.

So, by depicting laws as invariant relations of properties and placing a system in a type
hierarchy (ordering of natural kinds), we have come up with a way to incorporate modalities
into conceptual graphs, without having to add other formal systems, such as possible world
semantics. In fact, by doing so, we have adopted a version of modalities which does a
better job of capturing their use in natural language, a version that also is not open to the
cotenability problem or, as it is argued elsewhere, the frame problem.

Although some of the above cases were settled by applying physics, the exact same
strategy is used in ordinary situations, except that the laws the layperson uses – folk laws
– are not as mathematically precise as those in the natural sciences. For example, in 'If
that ball were hit in Wrigley field it would not have been a home run' is not based upon
Newton's laws but with folk laws like 'The harder the ball is hit, the further it travels' or
'The more the wind blows off Lake Michigan, the less the ball will travel.' But they'll do
for our purposes in a baseball debate because they approximate the actual physics.

We can finally answer the question of interpreting modal sentences in terms of conceptual
graphs. First, 'If P were the case, then Q would have occurred to x' amounts to attributing
the ordered pair, $< P, Q >$,to system x. So, the conceptual graph for a counterfactual has
this form:

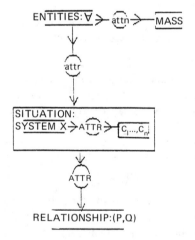

Fig. 32.2

We have seen that such a graph is generated by the type hierarchy and law combinations
where the P and Q variables have been factored out. Remember, $< P, Q >$ is just one
member among many of the range of $f*$ attributed to x.

Let us return to the above three cases of counterfactuals in order to see how the n-tuple
analysis works. The conceptual graph for 'If this match were struck, it would light' looks
like Fig. 32.3.

In other words, the match is a system possesses physical and chemical properties in such
a way that various physical and chemical laws apply to it. These laws can be combined so
that various ways of striking the match and its lighting or not lighting are isolated variables.

The resultant ordered pairs are then attributed to the match, one of them being $< S, L >$, as represented in Fig. 32.3.

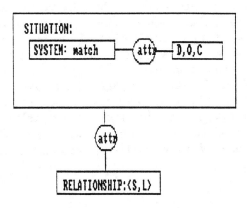

Fig. 32.3

The counterfactual, 'If this chalk were released it would fall' is treated in the same manner. In this case, we have a piece of chalk and the earth forming a Newtonian system: two masses separated by a distance. Combining the law of gravitational attraction with Newton's laws of motion, we can derive a law with only two variables: how the chalk is released and its subsequent motion. These ordered pairs are all attributed to the chalk. For example, if the chalk is thrown outward, its motion will be parabolic. On the other hand, if it is simply released, it will fall straight down.

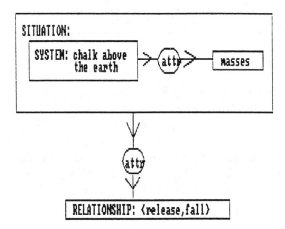

Fig. 32.4

Again, this conceptual graph represents just one ordered pair among many others that are predicated of the system.

The home run case is a bit more complicated and requires some hand waving but this example of applied folk physics utilizes the same strategy to establish a conceptual graph which has the same form as the other two. To keep things as simple as possible, suppose have a system, consisting of a bat and a ball which are located in a ball park. The ball park is Wrigley Field and has a strong wind blowing in off Lake Michigan. The ball and the bat are Newtonian masses and relative degrees of rigidity and flexibility. There are folk laws that apply to the bat and ball, for example, the harder the bat hits the ball, the further it goes, certain angles of contact make the ball go further, the more a wind blows against the path of the ball, the less it will travel, and so on.

Consider, again, 'If that ball were hit in Wrigley Field it would not have been a home run.' In the actual case, the ball just cleared the fence and there was little or no wind blowing in. Not so, Wrigley Field. So. by combining these 'folk laws', we know that if the ball barely made it over the fence in one ball park being hit, h_1, then if it were hit exactly the same way in Wrigley Field, it would have landed inside the playing field, l_1, which is represented by this conceptual graph:

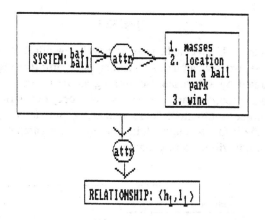

Fig. 32.5

Depending on the facts of the situation, various possibilities are attributed to it, as represented by ordered pairs in a set of conceptual graphs.

It turns out, then, that we don't get modalities by operating on conceptual graphs with possible world operators; rather, modalities or modal sentences are generated by combining certain non-modal conceptual graphs, *viz.*, those conceptual graphs that express folk science models of the actual world. So, it's the other way around. We just have to figure out what models underlie our modal assertions relative to the situation at hand.

BIBLIOGRAPHY

Aronson, J. L., (1988) "Testing for Convergent Realism," Proc. of the 1988 Biennial Meeting of the Philosophy of Science Association, (eds) A. Fine and J. Leplin, East Lansing: Philosophy of Science Association.

Aronson, J. L., (1988), "The Bayesians and the Raven Paradox," Nous, vol. 23.

Aronson, J. L., (1990), "Verisimilitude and Type Hierarchies," Philosophical Topics.

Bennett, J.., (1974), "Counterfactuals and Possible Worlds," Canadian Journal of Philosophy, Vol. IV, No. 2.

Foo, N. and Rao, A., (1986) "Modality and Truth Maintenance in a Conceptual Processor," Workshop on Conceptual Graphs, Thornwood: IBM Systems Research Institute.

Goodman, N., (1955), *Fact, Fiction and Forecast*, New York: Bobbs-Merrill.

Hayes, P., (1973), "The Frame Problem and Related Problems in Artificial Intelligence," in *Artificial and Human Thinking*, (eds) Elithorn & Jones, San Francisco:Jossey-Bass, Inc.

Hayes, P., (1975) "The Second Naive Physics Manifesto," in *Readings in Knowledge Representation*, (eds) Brachman and Levesque, Los Altos: Morgan Kaufmann, 1985.

Sloate, M., (1978), "Time in Counterfactuals," The Philosophical Review, LXXXVII, No. 1.

Sowa, J.F., (1984), *Conceptual Structures*, Reading: Addison-Wesley.

Way, E., (1990), *Knowledge Representation and Metaphor*, Dordrecht:Kluwer Academic Publishers, 1990.

33

Conceptual Structures Bibliography

Antonacci, F. (1987) Using semantic hints in a syntactic parser, Technical Report SCR-0004, IBM Rome Scientific Center, May 1987.

Antonacci, F., Russo, M. and Velardi, P. (1987) *Un Sistema per l'Analisi e la Generazione di frasi in Italiano*, Note di Informatica n.17, IBM Rome Scientific Center, December 1987.

Antonacci, F., Russo, M., Velardi, P. and Pazienza, M.T. (1988) *Metodologie di Rappresentazione e di Controllo per un Sistema di Comprensione dei Testi*, Proc. 3rd GULP Conference, Rome, May 1988.

Antonacci, F., Velardi, P. and Pazienza, M.T. (1988) A high coverage grammar for the Italian language, *Journal of the Assoc. for Literary and Linguistic Computing*.

Antonacci, F., Pazienza, M.T., Russo, M. and Velardi, P. (1988) Representation and control strategies for large knowledge domains: an application to NLP, *Applied Artificial Intelligence*, vol. 2, no. 3-4, pp. 213-249.

Antonacci, F., Russo, M., Pazienza, M. T., and Velardi, P. (1989) System for text analysis and lexical knowledge acquisition, *Data and Knowledge Engineering*, vol. 4, no. 1, p. 1-20.

Baldwin, J.F. (1985) Support Logic Programming for Expert Systems, Information Technology Research Center and the Department of Engineering Mathematics, University of Bristol.

Bell, J. (1987) A Natural Language Interface to a Conceptual Graph Environment, Technical Report, Dept. of Computer Science, James Cook University of North Queensland, October, 1987.

Berard-Dugourd, A., Fargues, J. and Landau, M.C. (1988) Natural language analysis using conceptual graphs, *Proc. International Computer Science Conference*, Hong Kong, pp. 265-272.

Berard-Dugourd, A., J. Fargues, M-C. Landau, J. P. Rogala (1989) Un systéme d'analyse de texte et de question/réponse basé sur les graphes conceptuels, in P. Degoulet, ed., *Informatique et gestion des unités de soins*, Coll. Informatique et Santé Vol. 1, Springer-Verlag.

Berg-Cross, G. and Price, M.E. (1989) Acquiring and managing knowledge using a conceptual structures approach, *IEEE Transactions on Systems, Man, and Cybernetics*, vol. 19:3, P513-27.

Billo, R.E., Henderson, M. and Rucker, R. (1989) Applying conceptual graph inferencing to feature-based engineering analysis, *Computers in Industry* :hp2.13:3:ehp2., p195-214.

Catach, L. and Fargues, J. (1985) Déduction et opérations pour le modéle des graphes conceptuels, Technical Report F.087, IBM Paris Scientific Center.

Chan, M.C., Garner, B.J. and Tsui, E. (1988) Recursive Modal Unification for Reasoning with Knowledge using a Graph Representation, *Knowledge Based Systems*, v. 1:2, March 1988, p94-104.

Cheung, B. and Chow, K.P. (1988) A three-level knowledge representation scheme for natural language processing, *Proc. International Computer Science Conference*, pp. 289-293.

Clancey, W.J. (1985) Review of *Conceptual Structures* by J. F. Sowa, *Artificial Intelligence*, v. 27, 113-128.

Coombs, M.J. and Hartley, R.T. (1987) The MGR algorithm and its application to the generation of explanations for novel events, *International Journal of Man-Machine Studies*, v. 27, pp. 679-708.

Coombs, M. J. and Hartley, R. T. (1988) Explaining novel events in process control through model based reasoning, *International Journal of Expert Systems*, v. 1:2, pp. 87-109.

Creasy, P.N. (1988) Conceptual graphs from a knowledge systems viewpoint, *Proc. Australian Joint AI Congress 88*, Adelaide.

Creasy, P.N. (1988) An information systems view of conceptual graphs, *Proc. International Computer Symposium*, Taipei.

Creasy, P.N. and Moulin, B. (1989) Refining conceptual graphs for data conceptual modelling, *Proc. AI & Creativity Workshop 89*, Melbourne.

Eklund, P. and Kellett, J. (1989) Prospects for conceptual graphs in acquisition interfaces, *Proc. 2nd Int. Conf. on Industrial and Engineering applications of AI and expert systems*, (IEA/AIE '89), Tullahoma, TN.

Eklund, P. and Kuczora, P. (1988) An implementation of conceptual graphs for knowledge base systems development, *Human and Organisational Issues of Expert Systems Conference*, Straford-on-Avon.

Ellis, G. (1989) Efficient retrieval from the generalisation hierarchy, *Proc. AI & Creativity Workshop 89*, Melbourne.

Eshner, D.P. (1989) A plan representation environment, *Proceedings of the Fourth Annual Rocky Mountain Conference on Artificial Intelligence*, Denver, 169-174.

Eshner, D.P. and Hartley, R.T. (1988) A unified approach to plan representation, *Proceedings of the Third Annual Rocky Mountain Conference on Artificial Intelligence,* Denver, 34-45.

Eskridge, T.C. and Fields, C.A. (1989) Representing strategic knowledge in continuous dynamic control, in Z.W. Ras, ed., *Methodologies for Intelligent Systems, 4,* North-Holland Publishing Co., New York, p191-198.

Fargues, J., Landau, M-C., Duguord, A. and Catach, L. (1986) Conceptual graphs for semantics and knowledge processing, *IBM Journal of Research and Development,* v. 30:1, January 1986, p70-79.

Fargues, J. (1989) Des graphes pour coder le sens des phrases, *Pour la Science,* No. 137, pp. 52-60.

Fargues, J., & A. Perrin (1990) "Synthesizing a large concept hierarchy from French hyperonyms," *COLING-90 Proceedings,* Vol 2, pp 112-117.

Fox, J.T. (1984) Search for cognitive science, *Nature,* v. 310, 437-438.

Garner, B.J. (1987a) Corporate Language Systems: Technical Issues and Their Management Implications, *Proc. 4th South Pacific Area Regional Conference,* March 1987, Brisbane.

Garner, B.J. (1987b) Expert Systems: From database to knowledge base, *Information and Software Technology,* v. 29:2, March 1987, p60-65.

Garner, B.J. and Forrester, C.L., (1986) Progress in Concepts of Decision Support for Unstructured Problem Environments, *Proc. 1st Australian AI Congress,* November 1986, Melbourne.

Garner, B.J., Larkin, K.E. and Tsui, E. (1989) Prototypical Knowledge for Case-Based Reasoning, *Proc. DARPA Workshop on Case-Based Reasoning,* Pensacola Beach, Florida.

Garner, B.J. and Lui, D. (1987) A Conceptual Graph Model for Key Management in Public Networks, *Proc. of the Congress of Cybernetics and Systems,* March 1987, New Delhi.

Garner, B.J., Lui, D. and Tsui, E. (1986) On Better Goal Type Interpretation, *Proc. 1st Australian AI Congress,* November 1986, Melbourne.

Garner, B.J., Lukose, D. and Tsui, E. (1987a) A Batch Processor for the Knowledge Base Editor, Technical Report 87/4, Xerox AI Laboratory, Division of Computing and Mathematics, Deakin University, February, 1987.

Garner, B.J., Lukose, D. and Tsui, E. (1987b) Parsing natural language through pattern correlation and modification, *Proc. of the 7th International Workshop on Expert Systems & their Applications,* Avignon 87, May 1987, France, p1285-1299.

Garner, B.J. and Kutti, S. (1987) Application of Dynamic Knowledge in Designing Distributed Operating Systems, *Proc. of Applications of AI V,* John F. Gilmore, Editor, SPIE Proc. 784, May 1987, Orlando, p391-397.

Garner, B.J. and Tsui, E. (1985a) Knowledge Representation for An Audit Office, *Australian Computer Journal,* v. 17:3, p106-112.

Garner, B.J. and Tsui, E. (1985c) First Report on the Design and Implementation of the Canonical Graph Processor, WPS-85-02, Division of Computing and Mathematics, Deakin University.

Garner, B.J. and Tsui, E. (1986b) An Extendible Graph Processor for Knowledge Engineering, *Applications of AI III,* J.F. Gilmore, Editor, SPIE Proc. 635, p415-433.

Garner, B.J. and Tsui, E. (1986d) Control Scripts for the Re-organisation of Knowledge Bases, *Proc. 1st Australian AI Congress,* November 1986, Melbourne.

Garner, B.J. and Tsui, E. (1987) A self-organising dictionary for conceptual structures, *Proc. of Applications of AI V,* J. F. Gilmore, ed., SPIE Proc. 784, May 1987, Orlando, p356-363.

Garner, B.J. and Tsui, E. (1988) General purpose inference engine for canonical graph models, *Knowledge Based Systems,* v. 1:5, p266-278.

Garner, B.J. and Tsui, E. (1989) Knowledge acquisition and reasoning with a canonical graph model in personal financial planning, in L.F. Pau, Y.H. Pao, J. Motiwala, & H.H. Teh, eds., *Expert Systems in Economics, Banking, and Management,* North-Holland, Amsterdam.

Garner, B.J., Tsui, E., Lui, D., Lukose, D. and Koh, J. (1987) Progress on an Extendible Graph Processor for Knowledge Acquisition, Planning and Reasoning, *Proc. of the 2nd Pan Pacific Computer Conference,* 26-29th August 1987, Singapore, p150-165.

Hansen, H. R., Mühlbacher, R., and Neumann, G. (1992) *Begriffsbasierte Integration von Systemanalyseverfahren,* to be published by Physica Verlag.

Hartley, R.H. (1985) Representation of Procedural Knowledge for Expert Systems, *Proc. of the IEEE Conference on Artificial Intelligence Applications,* December 1985, Miami Beach, Florida.

Hartley, R.H. (1986) The Foundations of Conceptual Programming, *Proc. 1st Annual Rocky Mountain Conference on Artificial Intelligence,* Boulder, Colarado.

Hartley, R.H. and M. J. Coombs (1991) "Reasoning with Graph Operations", in J.F. Sowa (Ed.) *Pronciples of Semantic Networks,* Morgan Kaufmann Publishers, San Mateo, CA, 1991, pp. 487-506.

Hines, T.R. and Unger, E.A. (1987) A variation of conceptual graphs: an object-oriented approach, *Proc. ACM-IEEE Fall Joint Computer Conference,* Dallas, pp. 57-64.

Hurwitz, A. and Marshall, J.B. (1987) An intelligent help system for IBM VM/SP, *SHARE 68 Proceedings,* Session G204, San Francisco.

Hurwitz, A. and Dolan, W.B. (1989) Repairing match failures in a natural language query system using logical reasoning, in Z.W. Ras, ed., *Methodologies for Intelligent Systems, 4*, North-Holland Publishing Co., New York, p110-117.

Jackman, M.K. (1988) Inference and the conceptual graph knowledge representation language, in S. Moralee, ed., *Research and development in Expert Systems IV, Proceedings of Expert Systems '87*, Cambridge University Press.

Jackman, M.K. and C. Pavelin (1988) Conceptual Graphs, in G. Ringland & D. Duce, eds., *Approaches to Knowledge Representation*, Wiley, New York, 161-174.

Joyce, R. (1987) Humor generation, Technical Report 87/2, Department of Computer Science, James Cook University of North Queensland, Australia.

Joyce, R. (1988) A knowledge representation environment for shared world knowledge, Technical Report, Department of Computer Science, James Cook University of North Queensland, Australia.

Kabbaj, K. and Moulin, B. (1987a) Structure de connaissances dans un systéme de manipulation de graphes conceptuels, Research Report DIUL-RR-8714, Université Laval, Québec.

Kabbaj, K. and Moulin, B. (1987b) Un systéme de manipulation de graphes conceptuels au coeur d'un dictionnaire conceptuel, Research Report DIUL-RR-8715, Université Laval, Québec.

Koh, J.E.K. (1986) Expert Planners/Audit Planner, Honours thesis, Division of Computing and Mathematics, Deakin University, Australia, November 1986.

Kuczora, P. and Eklund, P. (1990) A conceptual graph implementation for knowledge engineering, in *Expert systems: Human issues*, ed. by D. Berry and A. Hart, MIT Press, Cambridge, MA, pp. 169-185.

Kutti, N. and Garner, B.J. (1986) A Knowledge-based Kernel for Distributed Systems, *Proc. 1st Australian AI Congress*, November 1986, Melbourne.

Landau, M-C (1990) "Semantic representation of texts," *COLING-90 Proceedings*, Vol 2, pp 239-244.

Leishman, D. (1989) Analogy as a constrained partial correspondence over conceptual graphs, *Proc. 1st International Conference on Principles of Knowledge Representation and Reasoning*, Toronto, 223-234.

Levinson, R.A. (1992) "Pattern Associativity and the Retrieval of Semantic Networks," to appear in *Journal of Computers & Mathematics with Applications*. Special issue on Semantic Networks in Artificial Intelligence, Fritz Lehman, Guest Editor, Pergamon Press. Also to appear in the book "Semantic Networks for Artificial Inteligence". Also appears as Technical Report UCSC-CRL-90-30, University of California, Computer Research Laboratory, Santa Cruz, CA 95064.

Liquiére, M., Pingand, P. and Sallantin, J. (1990) The practical application of machine learning to the prediction of tertiary structure of proteins, Technical Report, Centre de Recherche en Informatique de Montpellier.

Liquiére, M. and Sallantin, J. (1989) INNE: A structural learning algorithm for noisy examples, *Proc. JFA*, Saint Malo.

Liquiére, M. (1989) INNE: Un algorithme d'apprentissage de structures dans le cas d'examples bruités, *Proc. RFIA 89*, Paris.

Lucena, G.J., Filho, and Prugner, N. (1988) Um editor de conhecimento baseado em grafos conceituais, *Anais do 5 Simposio Brasileiro de Inteligencia Artificial*, Universidade Federal do Rio Grande do Norte, Natal, pp. 281-298.

Lui, D. (1986) RASCS: Rule Acquisition System for Conceptual Structures, Internal Report, Division of Computing and Mathematics, Deakin University, Australia.

Lukose, D. (1986a) GPPG: General Purpose Parser Generator, Internal Report, Division of Computing and Mathematics, Deakin University, Australia.

Lukose, D. (1986b) Knowledge Representation for Discourse Understanding, Honours thesis, Division of Computing and Mathematics, Deakin University, Australia.

Magrini, Stefano (1987) Realizzazione di un sistema per la definizione semi-automatica di un dizzionario semantico per l'analisi del linguaggio naturale, Tesi di laurea in ingegneria elettronica, Universite degli Studi di Roma.

Martin, T.P., Baldwin, J.F. and Pilsworth, B.W. (1986) A Fuzzy Prolog Interpreter, Information Technology Research Center and the Department of Engineering Mathematics, University of Bristol.

Morton, S.K. and Baldwin, J.F. (1985) Conceptual Graphs and Fuzzy Qualifiers in Natural Language Interfaces, presented at the Cambridge Conference on Fuzzy sets.

Moulin, B. (1989) Refining the conceptual graph theory to model data conceptual structures, Technical Report 106, Dept. of Computer Science, University of Queensland.

Murphy, M.E. and Nagle, T.E. (1988) Automating interpretation of reconnaisance sensor imagery, *Advanced Imaging*, March-April 1988, pp. 19-26.

Nogier, J.F. (1989a) Generating language from conceptual representation, *Proc. 9th International Conference on Expert Systems and Their Applications*, Avignon, pp. 133-144.

Nogier, J.F. (1989b) A natural language production system based on conceptual graphs, Technical Report F.146, IBM Paris Scientific Center.

Nogier, J.F. (1990) *Un systéme de production de langage fondé sur le modéle des graphes conceptuels*, Thesis, University of Paris VII.

Nogier, J.F. (1990) *Génération de langage et graphes conceptuels*, Editions Hérmes, Paris.

Pau, L.F. and Nielsen, S.S. (1989) Conceptual graphs as a visual language for knowledge acquisition in architectural expert systems, *SIGART Newsletter, Special Issue on Knowledge Acquisition*, no. 108, April 1989, p. 151.

Pazienza, M.T. and P. Velardi (1986) Rappresentazione formale dei termini per l'analisi semantica dei testi, *Proc. AICA Annual Conference*, Palermo, 1986.

Pazienza, M.T. and Velardi, P. (1987) A structured representation of word senses for semantic analysis, *Proc. of the 3rd Conference of the European Chapter of the ACL*, Copenhagen, pp. 249-257.

Pazienza, M.T. and Velardi, P. (1988a) Integrating conceptual graphs and logic in a natural language understanding system, in V. Dahl & P. Saint-Dizier, eds., *Natural Language Understanding and Logic Programming II*, North-Holland Publishing Co., Amsterdam.

Pazienza, M.T. and Velardi, P. (1988b) Using a semantic knowledge base to support a natural language interface to a text database, *Proc. 7th International Conference on Entity-Relationship Approach*, Rome, North-Holland Publishing Co.

Pedersen, G.S. (1978) Conceptual graphs, Report 78/9, Institute of Datalogy, University of Copenhagen.

Poesio, M. (1987) An organization of lexical knowledge for generation, Technical report, Project WISBER, University of Hamburg.

Poesio, M. and Rullent, C. (1987) Modified caseframe parsing for speech understanding systems, *Proc. IJCAI-87*.

Ralescu, A.L. and Baldwin J.F. (1989) Concept learning from examples and counter examples, *International Journal of Man-Machine Studies*, v. 30:3, 329-354.

Rao, A.S. and Foo, N.Y. (1986) Modal horn graph resolution, *Proc. 1st Australian AI Congress*, Melbourne.

Rao, A.S. and Foo, N.Y. (1987) CONGRES: Conceptual Graph Reasoning System, *Proc. 3rd IEEE Conference on AI Applications*, Orlando, Florida.

Regoczei, S.B. and Plantinga E.P.O. (1987) Creating the domain of discourse - ontology and inventory, *International Journal of Man-Machine Studies*, v. 27:3, pp. 235-250.

Richard, G. and Berard-Dugourd, A. (1986) Le traitement des locutions dans l'analyse du langage naturel, Research Report F.101, IBM Paris Scientific Center.

Riesbeck, C. (1986) Review of *Conceptual Structures* by J. F. Sowa, *ACM Computing Reviews*, v. 27:8, 392-393.

Salveter, S., (1987) Review of *Conceptual Structures* by J. F. Sowa, *Computational Linguistics*, v. 12, pp. 218-219.

Sangal, R. and Chaitanya, V. (1987) An intermediate language for machine translation: An approach based on Sanskrit using conceptual graph notation, *Comput. Sci. Inform.* (India) v. 17:1, 1987, p9-21.

Slagle, J. R., Gardiner, D. A. and Han, K. (1990) Knowledge specification of an expert system, *IEEE Expert* :hp2.5:4:ehp2., 29-38.

Smoliar, S.W. (1987) Review of *Conceptual Structures* by J. F. Sowa, *Artificial Intelligence*, v. 33, pp. 259-266.

Sowa, J.F. (1976) Conceptual graphs for a data base interface, *IBM Journal of Research and Development*, v. 20:4, pp. 336-357.

Sowa, J.F. (1979a) Definitional mechanisms for conceptual graphs, *Graph Grammars and their Application to Computer Science and Biology*, edited by V. Claus, H. Ehrig, & G. Rozenberg, Springer Verlag, Berlin, pp. 426-439.

Sowa, J.F. (1979b) Semantics of conceptual graphs, *Proc. of the 17th Annual Meeting of the Association for Computational Linguistics*, pp. 39-44, 1979.

Sowa, J.F. (1981) A conceptual schema for knowledge based systems, *Proc. of the Workshop on Data Abstraction, Databases, and Conceptual Modeling*, ACM, pp. 193-195, 1981.

Sowa, J.F. (1983) Generating language from conceptual graphs, *Computers and Mathematics with Applications*, v. 9:1, pp. 29-43, 1983.

Sowa, J.F. (1984) *Conceptual Structures: Information Processing in Mind and Machine,* Addison-Wesley, Reading, MA.

Sowa, J.F. (1985) Una metodología para la tecnología de la informati/'an, *Programacion Informática: Sistemas Expertos*, Instituto de Ciencias del Hombre, Madrid, pp. 23-38, 1985. (Spanish translation of a talk presented in November 1984.)

Sowa, J.F. (1988a) On *Conceptual Structures*, a response to the review by S. W. Smoliar, *Artificial Intelligence*, v. 34, pp. 388-394.

Sowa, J.F. (1988b) Using a lexicon of canonical graphs in a semantic interpreter, in M. Evens, ed., *Relational Models of the Lexicon*, Cambridge University Press, pp. 113-137.

Sowa, J.F. (1988c) Lexical structures and conceptual structures, talk presented at the Lexical Semantics Workshop, Brandeis University, April 1988; paper to appear in a forthcoming volume to be edited by James Pustejovsky.

Sowa, J.F. (1989) Knowledge Acquisition by Teachable Systems, in J.P. Martins and E.M. Morgado, eds., *EPIA 89, Lecture Notes in Artificial Intelligence* :hp2.390:ehp2., Springer-Verlag, Berlin, p381-396.

Sowa, J.F. (1990) Knowledge representation in databases, expert systems, and natural language, in R.A. Meersman, Zh. Shi, & C-H. Kung, *Artificial Intelligence in Databases and Information Systems*, North-Holland Publishing Co., New York, pp. 17-50.

Sowa, J.F. (1990b) Definitional mechanisms for restructuring knowledge bases, in Z. W. Ras, M. Zemankova, & M. L. Emrich, eds., *Methodologies for Intelligent Systems, 5*, North-Holland Publishing Co., New York, pp. 194-211.

Sowa, J. F. (1991) Towards the expressive power of natural languages, in J. F. Sowa, ed., *Principles of Semantic Networks*, Morgan Kaufmann Publishers, San Mateo, CA, 1991, pp. 157-189.

Sowa, J. F. (1992) Conceptual analysis as a basis for knowledge acquisition, in R. R. Hoffman, ed., *The Cognition of Experts: Psychological Research and Empirical AI*, Springer-Verlag, Berlin.

Sowa, J.F. and Way E.C. (1986) Implementing a semantic interpreter using conceptual graphs, *IBM Journal of Research and Development,* v. 30:1, January, p57-69.

Tsui, E. (1988) Canonical Graph Models, Ph.D. thesis, Division of Computing and Mathematics, Deakin University, Australia, July 1988.

Velardi, P., Pazienza, M.T., and DeGiovanetti, M. (1988) Conceptual graphs for the analysis and generation of sentences, *IBM Journal of Research & Development*, v. 32:2, 251-267.

Velardi, P., Pazienza, M.T., and Magrini, S. (1989) Acquisition of semantic patterns from a natural corpus of texts, *SIGART Newsletter, Special Issue on Knowledge Acquisition*, no. 108, April 1989, 115-123.

Watson, I.D., M.J.R. Shave and D.S. Moralee (1989) Knowledge analysis methodology using an intermediate knowledge representation based on conceptual graphs, *Proc. 9th International Conference on Expert Systems and Their Applications*, Avignon.

Watt, M. (1988) The realization of natural language with pragmatic effects, Technical Report CSRI-215, Computer Systems Research Institute, University of Toronto.

Way, E.C. (1991) *Knowledge Representation and Metaphor*, Kluwer Academic Press, Dordrecht.

Zimbel, Roland (1991) *Graphische Spezifikationen: Ein graphik-adäquater, objektzentrierter Kalkül zur Entwicklung korrekter Programme*, PhD Dissertation, University of Karlsruhe, Forschungszentrum Informatik.

FIRST WORKSHOP ON CONCEPTUAL GRAPHS

CRIL - A Concept Relational Inference Language for Knowledge Engineering, by J. F. Baldwin & B. Crabtree.

Database Design Using Conceptual Graphs, by Gary Berg-Cross, Advanced Decision Systems, & John Hanna, United States Coast Guard Academy.

Tailoring Conceptual Graphs for Use in Natural Language Translation, by C. Brown, T. Pattabhiraman, M. Boyer, D. Massam, & V. Dahl, Simon Fraser University.

Using PLNLP in Language Processing, by George Heidorn & Karen Jensen, IBM T. J. Watson Research Center.

Knowledge Processing in KALIPSOS, by Jean Fargues, Marie-Claude Landau, Anne Dugourd, & Laurent Catach, IBM Paris Scientific Center.

Modality and Truth Maintenance in a Conceptual Processor, by Norman Foo & Anand Rao, Sydney University.

Discourse Analysis by Maximal Graph Matching, by Hiroshi Maruyama, IBM Japan Science Institute.

The Incorporation of Uncertainty into the Theory of Conceptual Graphs, by Steven Morton, Bristol University.

Conceptual Graphs in an Active Agent Paradigm, by Tim Nagle, Control Data Corporation, Minneapolis.

Pragmatic Knowledge of Word Uses for Semantic Analysis of Texts. by Maria Teresa Pazienza, Universitá la Sapienza di Roma, & Paola Velardi, IBM Rome Scientific Center.

Mental Models, Ambiguity and Metaphor, by Ed Plantinga, University of Toronto.

The Use of Facts in a Semantic Data Model, by Andrew Pletch, State University of New York at New Paltz.

A Methodology for Knowledge Acquisition, by Stephen Regoczei, Trent University.

Knowledge Representation in Conceptual Graphs, by John Sowa, IBM Systems Research Institute.

Interpreting Metaphors with Schemata, by Eileen Way, SUNY at Binghamton.

SECOND WORKSHOP ON CONCEPTUAL GRAPHS

Programming in Logic with Conceptual Graphs, by Henri Beringer, Electronique Serge Dassault.

Commonsense Knowledge as Lexical Knowledge, by Kathleen Dahlgren, IBM Los Angeles Scientific Center.

Towards Understanding French Texts Using Conceptual Graphs, by Jean Fargues, IBM Paris Scientific Center.

An Extendible Graph Processor and its Applications, by B. J. Garner & E. Tsui, Deakin University.

The Maximal Join for Conceptual Graphs, by Michael K. Jackman, Rutherford Appleton Laboratory.

Thematic Relations Hypothesis and Conceptual Graphs, by Pavel Koĉura, Herriott-Watt University.

French Natural Language Generation from Conceptual Graphs, by Jean-François Nogier, IBM Paris Scientific Center.

A Knowledge Base Management System using Conceptual Graphs, by Massimo Poesio, Hamburg University.

Nested Contexts: Stating What We Think They Mean, by Steven Regoczei, Trent University.

Context and discourse referents, by John Sowa, IBM Systems Research Institute.

Conceptual Representations for NL Dynamic and Static Situations, by Peter Stockinger, Centre National de Recherche Scientifique.

Conceptual graphs for the analysis and generation of sentences, by Paola Velardi, IBM Rome Scientific Center.

THIRD WORKSHOP ON CONCEPTUAL GRAPHS

Conceptual Graph Notation, by John F. Sowa, IBM Systems Research.

Knowledge Management using Conceptual Graphs as an Intermediate Form, by Gary Berg-Cross & Michael Price, Advanced Decision Systems.

Conceptual Programming with Constraints, by Daniel P. Eshner & Roger T. Hartley, New Mexico State University.

Natural Language Information Retrieval from French Texts, by A. Berard-Dugourd, J. Fargues, Marie-Claude Landau, & Jean-Pierre Rogala, IBM Paris Scientific Center.

Parsing into Conceptual Graphs with a Bottom-Up Chart Parser, by Jim Milstein, Digital Equipment Corporation.

An English-Like Syntax and a Smalltalk Tool for Conceptual Graphs, by Douglas Skuce, University of Ottawa.

Extensive Acquisition of a Semantic Lexicon, by Paola Velardi, University of Ancona, Maria Teresa Pazienza, Universitá Tor Vergate di Roma, & Stefano Magrini, IBM Rome Scientific Center.

An Implementation of an Intelligent Help System using Conceptual Graphs, by Hurwitz, Dolan, Ebrahimi, Hartz, Kuo, Lee, Ly, Marshall, Miecznikowski, Orel, Rothmeier, Shavit, & Wang, IBM Los Angeles Scientific Center.

Knowledge Representation and Conceptual Structures, by James R. Slagle & Jamshid A. Vayghan, University of Minnesota.

How to Realize a Concept: Lexical Selection and the Conceptual Network in Text Generation, by Norman K. Sondheimer, Susanna Cumming, & Robert Albano, USC Information Science Institute.

The Situation Data Model, by William M. Tepfenhart & Allen V. Lazzara, Knowledge Systems Concepts.

Knowledge Engineering: a Methodological Approach using Conceptual Graphs, by Awdew A. Teklemariam & James R. Slagle, University of Minnesota.

Toward an Interchangeable Linear Form for Conceptual Graphs, by John W. Esch, Unisys Defense Systems.

Reasoning with Conceptual Graphs, by David A. Gardiner, University of Minnesota.

General Semantics and Educational Theory as a Model for Concept Generalization and Exchange, by Janice A. Nagle & Timothy E. Nagle, Unisys Defense Systems.

Exploiting the Semantics of Conceptual Graphs for Efficient Graph Matching, by Lisa F. Rau, General Electric Research.

Handling Concept-Type Hierarchies through Logic Programming, by Pierre Massicotte & Veronica Dahl, Simon Fraser University.

Insights into Propositional Deduction Rules via Truth Trees, by Rob Rucker, University of Arizona.

Representing Plans and Acts, by Stuart C. Shapiro, University of Buffalo.

A Conceptual Structures Semantic Theory Based on a Semantic Game with Partial Information, by Bosco S. Tjan & James R. Slagle, University of Minnesota.

Representing Conceptual Graphs for Parallel Processing, by George G. Lendaris, Portland State University.

FOURTH WORKSHOP ON CONCEPTUAL GRAPHS

CG Information Retrieval Using Linear Resolution, Generalization, and Graph Splitting, by Jean Fargues, IBM Paris Scientific Center.

A Conceptual Graph Based Dictionary as a Source for the Generation of Entity Relationship Models, by R. Mühlbacher & G. Neumann, University of Economics and Business Administration, Vienna, Austria.

Adding Semantics to Semantic Data Models, by Peter Creasy, University of Queensland, Australia, and Bernard Moulin, Université Laval, Québec.

Integrating Structured Knowledge and Management of Uncertainty, by Anca Ralescu, University of Cincinnati, and Hamid Berenji, NASA Ames Research Center.

Truth and Semantic Networks, by Jerrold L. Aronson, Dept. of Philosophy, SUNY at Binghamton.

Induction on Conceptual Graphs, by Guy Mineau, and Départment d'Informatique, Université de Montréal.

Semantic Distance in Conceptual Graphs, by Norman Foo, Sydney University, Brian J. Garner & Eric Tsui, Deakin University, and Anand Rao, Australian AI Institute, Melbourne.

Conceptual Graphs and Open Texture, by Eileen C. Way, Dept. of Philosophy, SUNY at Binghamton.

A Principled Analogical Tool Based on Evaluations of Partial Correspondences over Conceptual Graphs, by Debbie Leishman, Dept. of Computer Science, University of Calgary.

Using Path Algebras to Encode Directed Graph Knowledge Bases, by Peter Eklund, University of Linköping, Sweden.

Designer Fabricator Interpreter System, by Keith J. Werkman & Donald J. Hillman, Dept. of Computer Science, Lehigh University.

Extended Conceptual Structures Notation; and Resolution on Conceptual Graphs with Extended Referent Field, by James A. Gardiner, Bosco S. Tjan, & James R. Slagle, Computer Science Dept., University of Minnesota.

Resolving Polymorphism in the Theory of Conceptual Graphs; ANNE of CONSTRUCT; and Message Passing in Conceptual Graphs, by John W. Esch, Timothy E. Nagle, Morgan L. Yim, & Laurie L. Gerholz, Unisys Defense Systems, St. Paul, MN.

Creating Consistent Canons for Feature Representation; Using Conceptual Structure Principles for Meta-Modeling; and Conceptual Structures in the Curriculum, by Rob Rucker, Arizona State University, Richard E. Billo, Batelle Corporation, Richland, WA, and Andrew Feller, Motorola GEG Division, Phoenix, AZ.

Representation for Communication in Distributed Systems, by Michael Hewett & M. Vaughan Johnson, Jr., Knowledge Source, Inc., Menlo Park, CA.

Experiments on Implementing the Concept-Type Lattice in a Neural Network, by George G. Lendaris, Systems Science, Portland State University.

Extended Situation Data Model Using Conceptual Graphs, by William M. Tepfenhart, Knowledge Systems Concepts, Inc., Rome, NY.

Semantic Additions to Conceptual Programming, by Heather D. Pfeiffer & Roger T. Hartley, Computing Research Laboratory, New Mexico State University.

Deterministic All-Solutions Retrieval from the Generalization Hierarchy, by Gerard Ellis, Dept. of Computer Science, University of Queensland, Australia.

CGPro, A Conceptual Graph Processor, by Lisa Amin & Pat Ryan, Computer Science Dept., University of Alabama in Huntsville.

A Multiple-Viewed Approach to Software Requirements Using Conceptual Graphs, by Harry S. Delugach, Dept. of Computer Science, University of Virginia.

Programs Guided by Conceptual Graphs, by Mario Schaffner, Boulder, Colorado.

Conceptual Dependency Graphs, by Afke van Rijn, Delft University of Technology, The Netherlands.

Simulation Results of Semantic Network Array Processor, by Dan Moldovan, Dept. of Electrical Engineering, University of Southern California.

What Does that Have to Do with the Price of Eggs? by Alan P. McDonley, Karl C. Mattson, & David W. Nichols, Martin-Marietta Information and Communication Systems.

Research Problems and Issues, by John F. Sowa, IBM Systems Research, Thornwood, NY, and Norman Y. Foo, Dept. of Computer Science, Sydney University.

FIFTH WORKSHOP ON CONCEPTUAL GRAPHS

Proc. of the Fifth Annual workshop on Conceptual Structures, (eds) P. Eklund, and L. Gerholz, Department of Computer and Information Science, Linköping University, S-581 83 Linköping, Sweden, ISBN 91-7870-718-8.

Conceptual graphs and modality, by Jerrold L. Aronson, Philosophy Department, SUNY at Binghamton.

Using conceptual graphs to analyze multiple views of software requirements, by Harry S. Delugach, Dept. of Mathematical Sciences, Memphis State University.

Compiling conceptual graphs, by Gerard Ellis, Key Centre for Software Technology, University of Queensland.

Graphical displays of conceptual structures, by John W. Esch, Unisys, St. Paul, Minnesota.

Representing temporal intervals using conceptual graphs, by John W. Esch & Timothy E. Nagle, Unisys, St. Paul, Minnesota.

Situation model creation, by David A. Gardiner & James R. Slagle, Computer Science Department, University of Minnesota.

Using conceptual structure principles in representing knowledge of Chinese Medicine, by Chia Yung Han & Yizong Cheng, Dept. of Computer Science, University of Cincinnati.

Estimating lines of code for software development efforts, by Timothy Hines & Mary Lou Hines, University of Missouri, Kansas City.

Object-oriented conceptual graphs, by Timothy Hines, Jonathan Oh, & Mary Lou Hines, University of Missouri, Kansas City.

Conceptual graphs as a vehicle for improved generalization in a neural net pattern recognition task, by George G. Lendaris, Systems Science & Electrical Engineering, Portland State University.

Normalizing conceptual graphs, by Guy Mineau, Département d'Informatique, Université de Montréal.

Extending the conceptual graph model for differentiating temporal and nontemporal knowledge, by Bernard Moulin and Daniel Coté, Département d'Informatique, Université Laval.

Conceptual graph matching as a plausible inferencing technique for text retrieval, by Sung H. Myaeng, School of Information Studies, Syracuse University.

A notation for conceptual structure graph matchers, by Timothy E. Nagle, John W. Esch, & Guy Mineau, Unisys and Université Laval.

Additions to conceptual programming for set representation and processing, by Heather D. Pfeiffer & Roger T. Hartley, Computing Research Laboratory, New Mexico State University.

The issue of semantic distance in knowledge representation with conceptual graphs, by Anca Ralescu & Adam Fadlalla, University of Cincinnati.

Direct inference rules for conceptual graphs with extended notation, by Bosco S. Tjan, David A. Gardiner, & James R. Slagle, Computer Science Department, University of Minnesota.

Development of a generalized expert system for production grinding systems using conceptual graphs, by Sridharan Venk & Rakesh Govind, University of Cincinnati.

An experimental course in knowledge base structures, by Yin-min Wei, Dept. of Computer Science, Ohio University.

Text generation in expert critiquing using rhetorical structure theory and conceptual graphs, by Jonni Harrius, Dept. of Computer and Information Science, Linköping University.

Syntax-directed joining for language understanding processing, by Stephane Bornerand & G. Sabah, LIMSI-CNRS, France.

Lexical choice as a process of matching word definitions on an utterance graph, by Jean-Francois Nogier & Michael Zock, IBM Paris Scientific Center & LIMSI-CNRS.

Using conceptual graphs as a representation language for system analysis methods, by Robert Mühlbacher, Vienna University of Economics and Business Administration.

Methods for extracting knowledge from corpora, by Maria Teresa Pazienza & Paola Velardi, II Universita di Roma and Universita di Ancona.

Towards the expressive power of natural language, by John F. Sowa, IBM Systems Research, Thornwood, NY.

Sorting conceptual graphs, by Gerard Ellis, Key Centre for Software Technology, University of Queensland.

Negotiating conceptual structures: Inheritance Hierarchies, by Peter Eklund, Computer and Information Science, Linköping University.

Deep knowledge semantics for conceptual graphs, by Pavel Koĉura, Department of Computer Studies, Loughborough University of Technology.

Generating language with conceptual dependency graphs, by Afke van Rijn, Delft University of Technology.

Conceptual representation for time reference interpretation: A focus on tense and aspect, by Patricia Zablit, IBM Paris Scientific Center.

SIXTH WORKSHOP ON CONCEPTUAL GRAPHS

Can a Large Knowledge Base be Built by Importing and Unifying Diverse Knowledge? Lessons from Scruffy Work. by Gary Berg-Cross, Advanced Decision Systems, Rosslyn, VA.

Dynamic Assertion and Retraction of Conceptual Graphs. by Harry S. Delugach, University of Alabama in Huntsville.

Generalization of Conceptual Graphs. by Mark Willems, University of Twente, The Netherlands.

Negation and Projection of Conceptual Graphs. by John E. Heaton & Pavel Koĉura, Loughborough University, U.K.

Toward Compatible Primitive Sets. by Guy Mineau, Université Laval, Québec.

Multi-Level Hierarchical Retrieval. by Robert Levinson & Gerard Ellis, UC Santa Cruz.

A Comprehensive Conceptual Analysis using ER and Conceptual Graphs. by Linda C. Gray & Ronald D. Bonnell, University of South Carolina.

Relationship Mappings: Conceptual Graphs to Object-Oriented. by Mary Lou Hines & Tim Hines, University of Missouri, Kansas City.

An Incomplete View of the Knowledge World. by Yin-min Wei, Ohio University.

Conceptual Graphs as a Framework for Case-Based Reasoning. by Vilas Wuwongse & Sookapat Niyomthai, Asian Institute of Technology, Bangkok.

A Flexible Algorithm for Matching Conceptual Graphs. by Sung H. Myaeng & Aurelio Lopez-Lopez, Syracuse University.

Current Research Issues with Conceptual Graphs. by John F. Sowa, IBM, Thornwood, NY.

On The Use of Conceptual Graphs in Representing Knowledge for Intelligent Retrieval. by Judith P. Dick, University of Toronto.

Extended Conceptual Structures for Intelligent Document Retrieval. by David A. Gardiner & James R. Slagle, University of Minnesota.

Compiled Hierarchical Retrieval. by Gerard Ellis, University of Queensland, Australia.

Building a Knowledge Base for Scientific Texts. by Sougata Mukherjea, Michael E. Cleary & Robert P. Futrelle, Northeastern University, Boston.

The Integration of Conceptual Graphs and Government-Binding Theory. by Mike L. McHale & Sung H. Myaeng, Syracuse University.

Visualizing Temporal Intervals Represented as Conceptual Graphs. by John W. Esch, Unisys, St. Paul, MN.

A Conceptual Graph Approach For Representing Temporal Information in Discourse. by Bernard Moulin, Université Laval, Québec.

An AI Model for Indexical Reference: Input from and Output to Conceptual Graphs. by John Moulton & Lawrence Roberts, Hartwick College and SUNY Binghamton.

Speech Acts in a Connected Discourse: A Computational Representation Based on Conceptual Graph Theory. by Bernard Moulin, Daniel Rousseau & Daniel Vanderveken, Université Laval, Québec.

Incremental Planning Using Conceptual Graphs. by Daniel Eshner, James Hendler & Dana Nau, University of Maryland.

Issues in Using Conceptual Graphs for Knowledge Specification. by John Yen & Jonathan Lee, Texas A&M University.

Open Systems: Toward Synergy in Conceptual Graph Processor Construction. by Jan Schmidt & Pavel Koĉura, Loughborough University, U.K.

Aspects of Conceptual Graph Processor Design. by Pavel Koĉura & Kai Kwong Ho, Loughborough University, U.K.

The Conceptual Programming Environment, CP: Time, Space and Heuristic Constraints. by Heather D. Pfeiffer & Roger T. Hartley, New Mexico State University.

Flexible Case Structure Implemented in a Deterministic Parser. by Gerard Sabah & Anne Vilnat, LIMAI-CNRS, Orsay, France.

Integrating Knowledge in Digital Systems Specifications Using Conceptual Graphs. by Walling Cyre, Virginia Polytechnic University.

Tomorrow's Spreadsheets: Conceptual Graphs as the Knowledge Based Decision Support Tool for the Management Accountant. by Simon Polovina, Loughborough University, U.K.

Approaches to Data Conceptual Modelling using Conceptual Graphs. by Peter Creasy & Bernard Moulin, University of Queensland and Université Laval.

CAMES - Expert System Administration of Money Market Services. by Bradley Smith, Loughborough University and Reuters, U.K.

Application of Conceptual Graphs to Semantic Data Fusion. by John Hanna, Vitro Corporation, New London, CT.

Model Unification With Conceptual Graphs. Sandra Perez, Concept Technology, Fairfax Station, VA.

Index